A HISTORY OF
JAPANESE LITERATURE

VOLUME TWO
The Early Middle Ages

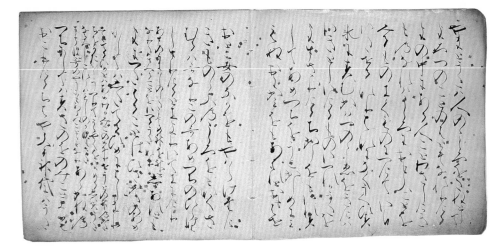

1. *Kokinshū*, copied by Shunzei, in the possession of
the Royal Household

A History of

Japanese Literature

VOLUME TWO
THE EARLY MIDDLE AGES

By Jin'ichi Konishi

TRANSLATED BY

Aileen Gatten

EDITED BY

Earl Miner

PRINCETON UNIVERSITY PRESS

Copyright © 1986 by Princeton University Press
Published by Princeton University Press, 41 William Street,
Princeton, New Jersey 08540
In the United Kingdom: Princeton University Press,
Guildford, Surrey

ISBN 0-691-06592-6 (clothbound). 10146-9 (limited paperback edition)

The publisher and author wish to thank
The Japan Foundation for its support

This book has been composed in Linotron Sabon

Printed in the United States of America by
Princeton University Press
Princeton, New Jersey

CONTENTS

LIST OF ILLUSTRATIONS
AND MAP

EDITOR'S FOREWORD

This second volume of Jin'ichi Konishi's *History of Japanese Literature* is integral with the other four volumes in offering a conception of the principles of Japanese literature as well as attention to the individual works that make up that history. There is a sense in which the conceptual elements are in advance of the current state of understanding of Japanese literature. Or at least some readers will wish to read parts by use of the table of contents or the index. There would be nothing unusual in that for a work of this kind and length. It remains true, however, that the whole work—the total argument—is necessary to the full understanding of any part. Those with knowledge of the Japanese literature of "the early middle ages" will therefore wish to devote more attention to the opening chapters than will readers with more specific or limited interests.

The translator and I have sought to meet the needs of various readers of this English version of the second volume. The Japanese version is being published more as a unit, and the author has therefore not felt it necessary to supply a preface to this volume. Given the quite separate publication of the volumes of this English version, however, there are things to be said that may be of use to readers of various kinds of interests.

The most important thing involves the long "General Introduction" to the first volume. From time to time the author, the translator, and I refer to that introduction. It is not the details but the principles of this volume that are illuminated by that introduction, and I cannot stress this enough. For example, not all specialist readers will be given to thinking that what is sometimes called "Heian literature" is that of the "Early Middle Ages." In fact, the author terms the period covered in this volume the "Chūsei Daiikki" ("The First Period of the Middle Ages"). The third volume will treat the "High Middle Ages" ("Dainiki") and the fourth the "Late Middle Ages" ("Daisanki"). For some reason, English usage for literary history seems to require the plural, "ages," after "middle." "First," "Second," and "Third Middle Age" just is not idiomatic, any more than "Early Middle Age" is appropriate for anything other than certain years of human life. If this explains our titles, the "General Introduction" in Volume One explains the principles on which the author's periodizing is based.

To provide an entry into the "Early Middle Ages," the author discusses, in Chapters 1 and 2, the legacy from the Archaic (Senkodai) and Ancient (Kodai) Ages treated in Volume One. In treating the nature of the literature of the Middle Ages in Chapters 3 and 4, he offers what amounts to an introduction to the two ensuing periods and volumes as well as to the period dealt with here.

Some readers will surely be interested to know the logic of inclusion and exclusion in this *History*, in effect what the author understands by "Japanese literature." Once again, I must refer to the "General Introduction" in the first volume. Certain lesser matters are presented in the main text of this volume without comment by the translator or myself. Those are mostly of interest to specialists, who will understand most of these matters from context. Some very small details we have left for specialists to discover, if they wish, by checking in the Japanese edition. Written Japanese and written English being what they are, however, some details emerge clearly only in translation. A few examples will show what is involved. The author follows what he believes to be the best documented pronunciations or versions of titles, names, and so forth. For example, he uses *Tannomine Shōshō* rather than *Tōnomine Shōshō*, *Utsuho Monogatari* rather than *Utsubo Monogatari*, and *Yowa no Nezame (Monogatari)* rather than *Yoru no Nezame* (or other variants). In general, his usages are those of specialists in the literature involved, and we have established them either by his specification or by my acquaintance with his preferences.

My foreword to the first volume explains our usages in capitalizing and English romanizing of Japanese names, titles, and terms. I neglected to remark there that when the author gives ages for people, we have subtracted one year to bring the count into rough approximation with English calculation.

Certain kinds of information have been added to the Japanese version. Obviously the kinds include translations of titles, terms, poems, and other excerpts. Some things have been added by me in brackets to the main text. Much more has been added to the notes. In each instance, the provenance is specified. Notes added by the translator or myself are set entirely in brackets and conclude "—Trans." or "—Ed." Sometimes the translator or I have engaged with information supplied extratextually by the author. Such notes are not bracketed but conclude with "Auth., Trans." or "Auth., Ed." in brackets.

As with the first volume, I have greatly reduced the number of cross-references sprinkled throughout. We supply detailed indexes to each volume, whereas the Japanese version will have only one briefer index in the last volume. We have not been able to fill in blanks where the author refers to an as yet unexisting page in a future volume, and our references to the first volume are often to chapters. In fact, the shortest way for a reader is to refer to the index in that volume.

For background, for information, and for much of the terminology used in this second volume, there are three books to which a reader may turn. These are Helen Craig McCullough, *Ōkagami: The Great Mirror* (Princeton, 1980), William H. and Helen Craig McCullough, *A Tale of Flower-*

ing Fortunes (a wonderfully annotated translation of the *Eiga Monogatari*; Stanford, 1980); and Earl Miner, Hiroko Odagiri, and Robert E. Morrell, *The Princeton Companion to Classical Japanese Literature* (Princeton, 1985).

The foregoing was written in December 1983. There have been delays in press, particularly before and after the manuscript entered the most capable hands of our copyeditor, Cathie Brettschneider, whom I thank with earnest appreciation.

Once again we are indebted to Shuen-fu Lin for checking matters Chinese.

I cannot omit expressions of gratitude to longtime friends at Princeton University Press. Herbert S. Bailey, Jr., who will be retired as Director when this book is published, is my oldest Princeton friend and indulgent publisher of many books, including the first, upwards of thirty years ago. Miriam Brokaw, born in Kyoto, is now retired as Editor and Associate Director. It is well known that her intelligent enthusiasm for books on Asian matters has made Princeton University Press a leader in that important area, and she is the real founder of the Princeton Library of Asian Translations. Jan Lilly, head of the design department, has again made me happy to be indebted to her artistry: this English version excels the Japanese in beauty and ease of use. Dr. Margaret Case, Asian Studies Editor, has worked successfully to gain a subsidy from the Japan Foundation. This book may not seem cheap, but it would be far more expensive without that subvention and subsidy funds generously appropriated by Princeton University Press. Her support deserves my earnest thanks.

Finally, to the scrupulous, patient author and to the skillful, painstaking translator, I express my deep gratitude. Jin'ichi Konishi has put up with letters and telephone calls. Aileen Gatten's care has awed me; her patience with my questions and retranslations arouse my gratitude, and her intelligent grasp of important issues make me wish to see her own ideas in print. I know of no other history of a national literature by a single person written on this scale. Aileen's and my responsibility as interpreters of this epic are awesome. If, as is sometimes said, Japanese take to their hearts those who fail in great enterprises, I shall personally feel more secure for work that no doubt should have been better done.

                                                                E.M.

AUTHOR'S ACKNOWLEDGMENTS

There are three reasons why I dedicate the second volume of my *History of Japanese Literature* to the late Professor Yoshikawa Kōjirō. First, his guidance enabled me, a specialist in Japanese literature, to observe my field from a Chinese literary standpoint. This volume would have been a very different creation without Professor Yoshikawa's exceptional kindness in giving me, a student unaffiliated with his own Kyoto University, nearly two years of strict training in Chinese literature. Second, the concepts of ga and zoku that form the basic framework of my *History* evolved from Professor Yoshikawa's ideas. He never systematized them as theories, but his wide-ranging interest in Chinese literature—which yielded translations of Yüan musical drama and Ming popular short stories as well as a textual revision of the *Shang Shu* and his commentary on Tu Fu's poetry—provided me with a practical application of the ga and zoku concepts. Third, Professor Yoshikawa inspired me to persist in a close reading of all texts, including historical accounts. Readers may find that my work contains an unusually large proportion of textual analysis for a history of literature. This approach gradually dominated my thought without Professor Yoshikawa's overt advocacy of the method. His emphasis on the close reading of texts was inherited from Ch'ing scholarly methodology and was put into practice long before the American New Critics broached their ideas. Although these three points apply to the entire *History*, they are particularly relevant to Volume Two, which explains why it is dedicated to Professor Yoshikawa.

This volume was written in 1982, during the first year of my appointment as a resident member of the Council of Scholars at The Library of Congress. The excellent collection of the Library and the generous assistance given me by its capable staff were surely instrumental in enabling me to complete the volume in the space of a single year. I express heartfelt thanks to Dr. Daniel J. Boorstin, the Librarian of Congress, and to Dr. Warren M. Tsuneishi, Dr. James H. Hutson, Mr. Hisao Matsumoto, and the staff of the Japanese Section. I would also like to thank Dr. Key P. Yang for his instruction in Korean linguistic matters.

The volume has been translated by Aileen Gatten and edited by Earl Miner. There are fundamental differences between Japanese and English that render translation from one language to the other difficult, and in this case the added presence of classical Chinese compounded the difficulty. We three have striven repeatedly to improve the English expression. A translation of this caliber would have been impossible without Aileen's delicate sense of language and firm grounding in the Japanese classics, and Earl's erudition and strong sense of responsibility. I cannot thank them enough for their immense labor. I am also truly grateful to Professor Shuen-fu Lin of the University of Michigan, who not only supervised the romanization of Chinese names, titles, and terms, but also pointed out errors in my reading of certain Chinese poems.

The Japanese Ministry of Education has provided the funds for the English translation of *A History of Japanese Literature* in five volumes, and my research in the United States was carried out with the assistance of the Japan–United States Friendship Commission and the Japan Foundation. Without the joint support of the Japanese and United States governments, my project would never have been realized.

J.K.

TRANSLATOR'S ACKNOWLEDGMENTS

I wish to thank two organizations at the University of Michigan whose assistance and cooperation made my task much easier: the Center for Japanese Studies, especially its director, Professor John Campbell, and Ms. Elsie Orb; and the Asia Library, most particularly Mr. Weiying Wan, Mr. Masaei Saitō, and Ms. Choo-won Suh. I am also very grateful to the senior members of the trio who produced this book. Jin'ichi Konishi's imagination, patience, and formidable command of English, and Earl Miner's collegial assistance have added immeasurably to the quality of the translation.

PART ONE

Between the Ancient Age and the Middle Ages

SOME INITIAL ISSUES

The Middle Ages are defined here as the period during which the indigenous Yamato culture was transformed by the infusion of Chinese civilization. This definition leaves unanswered one significant question: since the receipt of Chinese culture was already a striking feature of the Ancient Age, should not its later half, at the very least, be designated part of the Middle Ages? There was indeed a great influx of Chinese culture into Japan in the seventh and eighth centuries, but its effect was a largely superficial one that did not essentially transform the indigenous Yamato culture. Literature during this period was characterized by the composition of much poetry and prose in Chinese, and by the recording of national histories, also in Chinese. This, however, did not represent a Sinification of indigenous Yamato literature, composed in the Yamato tongue, but was rather a fabrication by Japanese, *using the Chinese language*, of the features of composition and reception as practiced in culturally advanced China.

This in turn might occasion a counterquestion: if we see the sudden expansion of Hitomaro's chōka (long poems) with their frequent use of alternating parallelism as the result of contact with the fu (rhapsody, rhyme prose) form, should this not be deemed evidence of the permeation of Yamato literature by Sinified expression in the Ancient Age? Yes; but such magnitude and parallelism belong to the dimension of external form. In the Ancient Age, formal features did not serve as the direct impetus moving the recipient of a work: the hearer's emotions were aroused chiefly by the action of the kotodama (word spirit). This may give rise to a further question: are we then to regard Hitomaro's creation of fictive speakers, a technique also apparently inspired by fu, as another instance of external form? This question is concerned with design, and not, of course, with the dimension of external form. But this does not mean that the technique of a fictive speaker acted as a significant emotional impetus to recipients of the work. A great many people, after all, had been moved by Hitomaro's chōka long before the presence of fictive speakers was perceived.

When a recipient is moved by a given work, the key to its effect lies in the linkage between the composer's intended content and its expression through diction, setting, plot, motif, mode, tone, and imagery, a linkage that might be called the point of contact between content and form. This point, which I shall call the conceptual focus, performs a generative function through its creation of emotive expression. In the Ancient Age, the crucial conceptual focus of literature had not yet been permeated by Sinified expression. I consider the Middle Ages to be that period when Sinified expression came to transform the conceptual focus of indigenous Yamato literature. The transformation was not sudden but developed gradually over a fairly long period. The ninth century in Japan is strongly characteristic of just such a transitional period. The ninth century, of course, is basically part of the Ancient Age; but in some respects it contains an undercurrent of phenomena that can only be seen as preparatory to movement into the Middle Ages.

CHAPTER 1

The Zenith of Poetry and Prose in Chinese

FROM THE SIX DYNASTIES STYLE TO THE T'ANG STYLE

Although in ancient Japan the composition of poetry and prose in Chinese was clearly patterned on the Six Dynasties style, we ought not overlook the fact that there was also a marked acceptance of Early T'ang poetry in Japan from the eighth century on. The Six Dynasties and Early T'ang styles scarcely differ in expressive form, however, and both might appropriately be considered Six Dynasties in the broad sense of the term. This is not to say, of course, that differences would not appear if works of the two periods were subjected to detailed stylistic analysis. But the distinctions would be largely a matter of individual differences in poetic styles, between, say, the work of a Hsü Ling or Yü Hsin contrasted with that of a Wang Po or Lo Pin-wang. That is, it is difficult to discern important stylistic differences between Late Six Dynasties poetry and that of the Early T'ang. Thus it was only natural that the Japanese of the Ancient Age found it impossible to distinguish what subtle differences existed in poetic style. The Early T'ang poetry they encountered was, in essence, Six Dynasties-style poetry that had been composed in the Early T'ang period.

During the Early T'ang (618-709) and the High T'ang (710-65) periods, the Chinese poetic style underwent a transformation into the most characteristically T'ang-style of lyric expression. Not only are Li Po (701-62) and Tu Fu (712-70) the normative poets of the High T'ang; they also occupy preeminent positions in the history of Chinese poetry. There is no indication, however, that the works of either poet were introduced into Japan during this period: the Japanese instead concentrated their efforts on importing the poetry of Po Chü-i (772-846), who flourished during the Middle T'ang period (766-835). Late T'ang (836-906) poetry received limited reception.[1] Moreover, parallel prose (p'ien-wen), the foremost prose style of the seventh century, had by the late ninth century been partially supplanted by prose (in the strict sense), san-wen.[2] Yet Han Yü (768-

---

[1] I have used Ogawa Tamaki's points of division of the T'ang into Early, High, Middle, and Late (Ogawa, 1958, 28-30).

[2] What we now call "prose" (Ch. san-wen; J. sambun) originally stood in opposition to parallel prose (p'ien-wen); prose writing that did not conform to the definition of parallel

824) and Liu Tsung-yüan (773-819), who established the plain prose style and are revered as great prose writers, were evidently not known in Japan, where Po Chü-i's prose served as the model. Today it strikes us as strange that the Japanese of this time were exposed to a T'ang literary corpus containing neither Li Po's and Tu Fu's poetry nor Han Yü's and Liu Tsung-yüan's prose. But that was indeed the case. It is our task not only to recognize the fact but to discover its significance as well.

The introduction of Po Chü-i's works into Japan was thus all the more important to Japanese literature, despite the fact that their introduction did not necessarily indicate adoption and assimilation by the Japanese. The earliest Japanese use of Po's poetry went no farther than the borrowing of diction; there were almost no Japanese able to appreciate the poet's expressive hallmarks. An even longer period would be necessary before the conceptual focus of his poetry was appreciated and given new life in Japanese compositions. It was not until their later years that Miyako Yoshika (834-79) and Sugawara Michizane (845-903) incorporated Po's conceptual focus into their poetry and prose. In their youth they had written parallel prose and shih in the Six Dynasties style. By the time Yoshika and Michizane became influenced by Po Chü-i, waka had already taken on medieval characteristics. The works written by Yoshika and Michizane during this period—in which Po's style came to pervade both their shih and their prose in Chinese—will be discussed later, in the section on the Middle Ages [ch. 6]. I would now like to consider Yoshika's and Michizane's earlier works.

Intellectual Conceptions of Shih

The three royally commissioned shih anthologies that were compiled in the first half of the ninth century were no doubt a manifestation of the confidence with which contemporary Japanese approached the composition of poetry and prose in Chinese. The numerical increase both in poems selected for inclusion and poets represented yielded collections incomparably more extensive than the *Kaifūsō* (751), compiled some sixty years earlier. The ninth-century compositions also show an appreciable rise in qualitative refinement. The proliferation of works and poets was to continue beyond this point, but the quality of the compositions hereafter tended to fall. The forty years bounded by the reigns of Saga (r. 809-23) and Nimmyō (r. 833-50) may well be called the zenith of poetry and prose composed in Chinese. In terms of the volume and quality of works com-

---

prose was considered simple prose, san-wen. Parallel prose will be seen as prose in the broad sense of the word, and simple prose as prose in the strict sense.

posed in Chinese, this half-century remains unrivaled until the flowering of Gosan literature in the High Middle Ages.

From the first of the royal shih anthologies, the *Ryōun Shinshū* (814), through the second, *Bunka Shūreishū* (818), and the third, *Keikokushū* (827), the Japanese poetic style remains largely that of the Six Dynasties. This applies, however, only to internal expression, particularly the conceptual focus. Externally, these shih sensitively reflect several new trends developed during the T'ang period. These, as already noted elsewhere (Okada, 1929b, 119-21), are as follows: (1) an increase in the number of "modern" shih (chin-t'i shih), written in seven-character lines;[3] (2) the advent of mixed-meter shih (tsa-yen shih);[4] and (3) an increased number of long poems. Although the predominance of seven-character lines over those of five characters is one of the general characteristics of T'ang shih, the seven-character quatrain is rare in Early T'ang poetry, becoming common only with the Middle T'ang period. This is reflected in the Japanese shih anthologies. The same is true for the mixed-meter shih, that is, shih combining both long and short lines. It may also be worth noting that tz'u, mixed-meter verses set to music, were composed, albeit rarely, in Japan. The tz'u, like the seven-character quatrain, was evidently first composed in the Middle T'ang.[5] Saga Tennō's "Five Mixed-Meter Songs on Fishing," together with two matching songs composed by Princess Uchiko (807-47) and five by Shigeno Sadanushi (785-852; *Keikokushū* [= KK], 14:173), have as their prototype Chang Chih-ho's tz'u, "The Fisherman's Song," composed in 774.[6] Saga's exchange with Uchiko and Sadanushi is

---

[3] [This style of poetry is characterized by the regulation of tonal patterns and strict verbal parallelism, especially between important lines.—Trans.]

[4] [A five- or seven-character shih form that occasionally contains a three- or four-character line.—Trans.]

[5] The Yüeh-fu (Music Bureau) was abolished in the T'ang period, during the reign of Hsüan-tsung, but the banquet music (yen-yüeh) gathered by the Bureau was incorporated by the Singers' Guilds (non-government-sponsored entertainment establishments) that evolved in cities in the Middle T'ang period. Banquet music was influenced by active T'ang contact with Central Asia and India, and much Hsiung-nu music was incorporated into the genre. Lyrics evolved into a complicated form of mixed meter—long and short lines used together in a single piece—to correspond to the asymmetry of the music produced by the fusion of popular and Hsiung-nu song [Kishibe, 1960, 95-103]. This form is called "tz'u," "shih-yü," or "ch'ang-tuan-chü."

[6] Few tz'u survive from the mid-T'ang; Chang Chih-ho's "The Fisherman's Song" is one member of this small corpus. The tonal pattern of "The Fisherman's Song" is as follows (L denotes a level tone, D a deflected tone, E a position where either a level or a deflected tone is permissible, and R a level-tone rhyme):

E D L L D D R / E L L D D L R
L D D D L R / L L E D D L R

The songs by Saga, Princess Uchiko, and Sadanushi all conform to this pattern in terms of rhyme but do not preserve the tonal pattern. As this was their first experience with the tz'u form, they may have been as yet unfamiliar with tonal patterns.

believed to have taken place in 823, only forty-nine years later (Kanda Kii-chirō, 1965, 7-12). We know from this that Japanese poetic circles in the early ninth century had gone beyond the poetry of the Early and High T'ang and turned their attention to Middle T'ang poetry.

The Japanese poetic circles of this time were not yet ready to concern themselves with the tonal patterns of T'ang shih. The "modern" shih form, with its regulated pattern of level and deflected tones, was established in the Early T'ang period by Shen Ch'üan-ch'i (?656-714) and Sung Chih-wen (?656-712); Japanese poets of the eighth century were incapable of assimilating the technique. The *Kaifūsō* contains a few compositions by Fujiwara Umakai (?694-737) and Isonokami Otomaro (d. 750) that conform to the tonal patterns of the "modern" shih (Okada, 1929b, 86-87), but as a rule tones are disregarded. Nearly all the poetry selected for inclusion in the three royal shih anthologies, on the other hand, either preserve the tonal patterns of the "modern" form or endeavor to do so; only a few egregious violations appear. In the space of roughly sixty years, then, the Japanese shih became significantly more Sinified.

Much the same can be said for mixed-meter shih. Its composer was not hampered by tonal pattern requirements, as with the "modern" shih, but was obliged to exercise care in the arrangement of the long and short lines and in varying the end-rhymes. This posed a set of problems different from those found in verse of more set forms. Once such formal restrictions had been rendered fairly routine by the acquisition of sufficient poetic technique, an orientation toward longer shih apparently evolved. Eighth-century Japanese poets had enough to do simply in settling upon poetic creation conforming to formal shih regulations, and as a result only rather small-scale creations were put forward. By the ninth century, however, Japanese poets were able to resolve matters of tone, rhyme, parallelism, and line arrangement without much expenditure of effort; and it is at this point that large-scale poetic creations seem to have first appeared. The terms "long" and "large-scale" are relative, of course, in the Japanese context: these shih are a part of a literature possessing as one of its principal characteristics a tendency toward brevity of form. Thus no Japanese shih can rival in length Tu Fu's "Poem Composed on an Autumn Day at the K'ui Provincial Office" (*To Shōryō Shishū* [= *TSS*], 19:1394), or Po Chü-i's "Matching Poem on a Dreamt Springtime Excursion" (*Po Hsiang-shan Shih-chi* [= *PSC*], 12:1919), both of which encompass two hundred lines. At their longest, most Japanese shih are thirty or forty lines long; Kūkai's (774-835) "Poem on an Excursion to the Mountains, Written in Envy of the Immortals" (*Seireishū* [= *SRS*], 1:159-65) is his longest at 106 lines. Kūkai's poem is written in five-character lines; "Pleasures of a Mountain Retreat" (*SRS*, 172-74), another shih by Kūkai, is in the mixed-meter form and is fifty lines long. These exceptionally lengthy poems probably resulted from Kūkai's individual need for an external form of heroic proportions with which to express his poetic conceptions.

Given this information, it might appear that ninth-century Japanese poets discarded the Six Dynasties style and skipped over the poetry of the High T'ang to absorb what was for them the newest style, that of Middle T'ang poetry. This view depends, however, on one's definition of style. If we disregard formal aspects like prosody—be it five-character, seven-character, or mixed—and rhythmic configurations based on level and deflected tones, and define style instead as characterized by the composer's grasp of concrete expression in manifesting his poetic intention—or, in other words, by the conceptual focus—then it cannot be said that ninth-century Japanese poets fully absorbed the newest poetic styles of the T'ang.

Instead, the Six Dynasties style continued to serve as the main means of poetic expression. One example of this is "A Summer's Day Visit to the South Lake of My Brother, the Crown Prince" (*Ryōun Shinshū* [= *RUSS*], 155). This shih was written by Saga Tennō (786-842), an important ninth-century poet and the driving force behind a policy of rapid acceptance of Chinese culture.[7]

Na *liang* ch'u ERH nan *ch'ih* li
Chin HSI fan *chin* pi SHUI wan
An YING chien *chih* yang LIU ch'u
T'an *hsiang* wen TE chi *he* hsien
Feng *lai* ch'ien P'U shou *yen* yüan
Niao SAN hou *lin* yü MU hsien
T'ien HSIA kung *yen* chen WAN kuo
He *lao* yü I fang *Shang* shan

By the crown prince's southern lake, I revel in the cool,
And wash off all my cares at the azure water's edge.
I discover willows in the bank's reflected image;
The fragrant depths yield a scent of caltrop, and of lotus.
A breeze comes to the pondside, taking the mists afar;
Birds scatter to the rear forest, desiring a peaceful evening.
The people all request the spread of justice to their lands:
Why fly off to Mount Shang in search of Counselor-sages?[8]

The tonal arrangement of this shih preserves the rules of alternating level

---

[7] [In the following transliteration, italics denote level-tone characters, and capitals denote deflected-tone characters. Dots under words indicate rhymes.—Trans.]

[8] That is, with you to help me in affairs of state, I need not look elsewhere for wise counselors. [Auth., Trans.]

and deflected tones in the second and fourth characters of each line, and of keeping both the second and sixth characters of each line in either a level or a deflected tone. The poet also obeys the injunction against having three consecutive level tones in the fifth, sixth, and seventh characters of a line. Only one violation of the rules occurs, in line six, where the level-tone fourth character "lin" ("forest") is isolated by the deflected-tone third and fifth characters. Nevertheless this faithful an adherence to the standards of regulated verse would probably have ensured its acceptance by a Chinese audience. The rhyming characters, though ending in a sound range between -uǎn and -ʌn, were regarded as equivalent rhymes.[9] The parallelism of lines three and four and lines five and six also follows the norms of regulated verse. In formal terms, then, this shih does not differ in the least from T'ang Chinese poems. Saga's poem differs in this respect from eighth-century Japanese shih. If its vocabulary harks back in general to Six Dynasties precedents, the poem clearly is unlike eighth-century Japanese shih in its use of words like "fan-chin" (cares), employed in poetry of the High T'ang,[10] and "te," a colloquial particle found often in T'ang shih[11] (Kojima, 1979, 1404).

Ninth-century Japanese shih must therefore be regarded as bearing a strikingly close formal relation to T'ang poetry; in the dimension of content, however, the old Six Dynasties style shows not the least sign of retreat. The central aim of Saga's shih, a regulated verse, is to achieve antitheses in the center four lines; but their conceptual focus is thoroughly rooted in the Six Dynasties style. The intent of the line, "I discover willows in the bank's reflected image," is that the speaker sees one of the banks of the lake reflected in the water, and therefore knows the location of the willows without looking directly at them. The concept takes the form of a reasoning process: "I have discovered A because of B." A corresponding example appears in these lines from a poem by Emperor Yüan of Liang (508-54) on "Viewing Spring Scenery" (*Liang Yüan-ti Chi*, 2767): "Leaves are dense: the willows' mass discovered, / Plum blossoms gone: sparse branches are revealed." The speaker knows from the dense growth pattern of the leaves that many willow branches are hanging before him, and he realizes, only after all the blossoms have fallen, how sparsely a plum tree's branches grow. The poet's intent in both cases is not framed in the usual descriptive mode, wherein a given situation is stated just as it is seen: here the intent is linked to a reasoning process involving cause and effect, to form what might be called an expository-descriptive mode. This

---

[9] Estimated T'ang pronunciation (Tōdō-Kobayashi, 1971, 66-67, 72-73).
[10] A further example appears in "Thinking of Lu Sung on a Summer Night" (*Ch'üan T'ang-shih* [= CTS], 191:1957), by Wei Ying-wu (736-?90).
[11] "Te" does not function as an indicator of potential but instead expresses a continuation of the state indicated by the preceding verb.

signifies that the composer does not state a matter outright but instead makes an indirect approach through a reasoning process involving auxiliary circumstances. This kind of expression is termed "oblique" (i-p'ang) by Wang Ch'ang-ling (698-?755) in his *Shih-ke* (*Poetics*; Konishi, 1951a, 227).

Oblique expression does not appear in the first stage of the Six Dynasties period (from Wei up to the commencement of the Western Chin). It began its development in the second stage of the Six Dynasties period (mid-Western Chin through the end of the Eastern Chin), rapidly came into use by the third stage (Liu Sung through Southern Ch'i), and was further refined in the final stage (Liang through Ch'en). If we call the first and second stages Early Six Dynasties, and the third and fourth Late Six Dynasties, then the latter period is characterized by oblique expression. Because mature Six Dynasties expression is exemplified by obliqueness, we are justified—when there is no danger of misunderstanding—in calling oblique expression the distinctive feature of the Six Dynasties style (Konishi, 1949b, 153-55). As I have observed, Early T'ang poetry was an extension of Late Six Dynasties verse; thus, when oblique expression appears in Early T'ang compositions, it may be treated as an instance of the Six Dynasties poetic style.

Consider Saga's lines, "The fragrant depths yield a scent of caltrop, and of lotus" (i.e., the speaker knows by the fragrance wafting from the depths of the lake that both caltrop and lotus are in bloom); "A breeze comes to the pondside, taking the mists afar" (i.e., a breeze disperses the mist, suddenly giving a greater view beyond the side of the large pond); and "Birds scatter to the rear forest, desiring a peaceful evening" (i.e., once the birds have flown there, the forest, at dusk, grows quiet). All share a common feature, although they display it with varying degrees of clarity: all contain, at the base of their expression, a conceptual pattern, "Because of A, I have realized B." Unless this concept is grasped, the reader cannot possibly sense the effect Saga's lines have as poetry. This pattern represents a major conceptual focus characteristic of poetic styles in the Late Six Dynasties period through the Early T'ang.

The example provided above by Emperor Yüan's couplet could be amplified indefinitely by other, similar cases (Konishi, 1949b, 156-65). Early T'ang shih perpetuate this conceptual pattern: Wang Po (647-75) writes, in "Suburban Pleasures" (*Ch'üan T'ang-shih* [= CTS], 56:676), "The rain lifts: flowers are lustrous, moist; / Winds sweep by: leaves give scanty shade." Here an expressive effect similar to that of Emperor Yüan's couplet is achieved without recourse to such explanatory terms as "discovered" and "revealed," through the exercise of greater technical refinement. Saga's three lines display an equal level of expertise. Nor was Saga the only Japanese poet to possess a Sinified conceptual focus: it was widespread among contemporary and later poets. A shih by Wake no Hiroyo (fl. ca.785-805), "Matching a Poem on 'Falling Plum Blossoms' " (*KK*, 11:158), contains these lines, for example: "Pistils are sparse: soon we shall see fruit; / Leaves are delicate, and the shade's still slight." The intent—that because the plum blossoms have fallen, fruit is forming around the stamens, and that the trees give little shade because of the relative paucity of leaves—closely resembles Emperor Yüan's couplet, quoted earlier: "Leaves are dense: the willows' mass discovered; / Plum blossoms gone: sparse branches are revealed." Hiroyo's lines, moreover, demonstrate far greater observational detail. Hsieh T'iao (464-99), in a couplet from his "On Moving to a Place of Convalescence: My Garden, a Poem Sent to My Family" (*Hsieh Hsüan-ch'eng Chi*, 3:289), employs direct expression in his choice of the expository "I see" and "I know," but his concept is otherwise identical in pattern to Hiroyo's: "Leaves hang low: I see the dew lies heavy; / The cliff is gone: I know the clouds are dense."

It is not my intent to maintain that Japanese shih poets in the ninth century regarded these Six Dynasties couplets as either authoritative or appropriate for adaptation. Heretofore, whenever scholars of Japanese literature have happened upon Chinese shih diction analogous to that in a Japanese shih, they have tended to label the Japanese shih diction a borrowing or transposition from the Chinese. Yet it is only in exceptional instances that a given expression can be shown to have been based on specific diction. Hsieh T'iao's diction finds analogous expression in a couplet from T'ao Ch'ien's (365-427) "Source of the Peach Blossoms" (*Tōshi = Tō Emmei Shishū*, 6:449): "Plants in bloom: I know the season's harmony; / Trees in decline: I see the wind's severity." A further instance is found in "A Visit to Counselor Hsieh's Villa" (*Chiang Li-ling Chi*, 2:2865), by Chiang Yen (444-505): "Clear air: I know wild geese are flying in line; / Abundant dew: I hear well the monkeys' cries." "The Heights of Mount Wu" (*Yüeh-fu Shih-chi*, 17:239), by Fan Yün (451-503), does not contain phrases like "I know" and "I hear": "Towering crags: no trace of a wild beast; / A gloomy wood: birds confused in flight." "Entertainment for the Ch'i Envoy" (*Yü K'ai-fu Chi* [= YC], 2:3775), by Yü Hsin (513-81), provides another such example: "The forest is cold: bark on trees grows thick; / The long beach curves: a flock of geese flies low." Both Saga and Hiroyo absorbed the conceptual pattern that is common to all the above examples, "Because of A, (I now know of) B." The question of whether they had recourse to specific Chinese phrasing therefore requires little consideration.

Because it provides the best illustration of Late Six Dynasties poetic style, the conceptual focus based on reasoning has been discussed here. But this does not mean that it is the sole characteristic of the Six Dynasties style. The central feature of the Six Dynasties style is its stance of intellectual appropriation, as typified by the conceptual focus based on reasoning. In describing scenery, for instance, a Six Dynasties poet will not say, "This is beautiful scenery" but will instead present a description resulting from intellectual observations of what scenery should be like. It is the recipient's task to decide whether or not the scenery is beautiful. This is the stance taken by Kuwabara Haraaka (789-825) in his "Poem on the Topic, 'Water Likened to Cloth Hung Out to Dry,' Composed at the Reizen Palace" (*Bunka Shūreishū* [= *BSS*], 3:295).

> Range on range, mountains soar steep within the grounds;
> The waterfall, a single length, spreads like hanging cloth.
> In alarm cranes fly to us, fast as scattering droplets,
> And the spray, a string of pearls, breaks in the countercurrent.
> Sun is shining near the crags, and yet rain is falling;
> Above the rocks, a cloudless sky, but always we hear thunder.
> Long have I heard of the immortals' world; now I see it here;
> Why need we then abstain from rice, and visit Mount T'ien-t'ai?[12]

In a line like "Sun is shining near the crags, and yet rain is falling," the poet seeks to introduce the irrationality of rain falling while the sun is shining, and then to have the recipient solve the problem by concluding that the "rain" is in fact the scattering spray from the waterfall. The significance of "Above the rocks, a cloudless sky, but always we hear thunder" also lies in its intent, which is to stimulate the solution that the "thunder" is actually the sound of a seething torrent. Both lines can only be termed instances of paradoxical reasoning. A plainer phrasing would turn them into similes—the scattering spray is like rain, the sound of the water is like thunder. In addition, however, the creation of a surprised sense that "this should not be" is the poet's chief aim.

When essential comparative elements are abstracted from a simile and presented in isolation, they form a conceit: this is what appears in the third and fourth lines of Haraaka's shih. Cranes fly in alarm toward the speaker: here the foaming torrent of water is compared to white cranes in full flight. Similarly, a string of white pearls caught up and dispersed in a countercurrent represents a comparison of the waterfall's spray to scattered pearls. Such conceits, together with poetic concepts based on reasoning, represent a kind of oblique expression found frequently in Late Six Dynasties shih. A couplet from Yü Hsin's "Matching a Poem on 'Dance' " (*YC*, 2:3769) compares a dancer to a phoenix and a crane: "The phoenix dances round: mirrors are all but filled; / The crane glances back: towns-

---

[12] [One was to abstain from meat, fish, and grains in preparation for visiting Mt. T'ien-t'ai in China, an abode of immortals.—Trans.]

folk are enraptured." When the dancer moves in a circle, mirrors seem able to reflect only her figure, and when she looks over her shoulder, the townspeople are fascinated indeed. A more expository conceit is found in a couplet from "On Gardenia Blossoms" (*Liang Chien-wen-ti Chi*, 2:2695), by Emperor Chien-wen of Liang (503-51): "Might they not be leaves wrapped in frost, / Or are they more like snow-covered branches?" The poet's "might they not be" ("i-wei") corresponds in feeling to the Japanese "ka to zo miru," a phrase used in waka during the *Kokinshū* period. Instances of "i" used in counterbalance with "ssu" ("resembles," "like") are more common, as in the case of this couplet from Ho Hsün's (d. 518) "Matching Professor Ssu-ma's Poem on 'Snow'" (*Ho Chi-shih Chi*, 3299): "Frozen to the steps at night, it resembles moonlight; / Swept from the trees at dawn, it might be spring blossoms."

Further examples abound, including a couplet from "An Autumn Excursion to K'un-ming Pond" (*Hsüeh Ssu-li Chi*, 3979), by Hsüeh Tao-heng (539-609): "In the depths, fish that might be carved from stone; / The sand is dark, like ashes deep submerged." Similarly, in ninth-century Japan, Kose no Shikihito (fl. ca. 823) included this couplet in his "On Falling Leaves in the Shinzen Gardens, Ninth Day of the Ninth Month" (*BSS*, 3:313): "They flutter to the grass, just like Chuang Tzu's butterfly; /[13] As they blow across the bay, they might be Kuo T'ai's boat."[14] Another shih by Shikihito, "On the Topic, 'Spring Moon,' a Poem Composed During a Royal Excursion to the Shinzen Gardens on a Spring Day" (*BSS*, 3:298), contains this couplet: "The crescent outside my window makes it seem the blinds are up; / A mirror hangs in the heavens without the aid of a stand."[15] Shikihito's concept may be based on a similar juxtaposition between "seem" and "without" ("pu-kuan," lit. "has no relationship") that is made by Yü Hsin in these lines from "Viewing the Moon From a Boat" (*YC*, 2:3779): "The mountains are bright, and seem covered with snow; / The shores are white without the presence of sand." Six Dynasties poetic diction, then, is clearly reflected in ninth-century Japanese shih.

As time went on, the technique of reasoning in verse became increasingly intellectualized. Poets tended to concentrate on the dexterity with which they grasped a subject rather than on the subject itself, with the result that their poetry inevitably imparted a sense of vacuity. The intent of

[13] [A famous episode in *Chuang Tzu* concerns one of the great philosopher's dreams. Chuang Tzu dreamt that he was a butterfly; but when he awoke he wondered whether he had indeed dreamt of being a butterfly, or whether he was actually a butterfly that was dreaming it was Chuang Tzu.—Trans.]

[14] A writer and poet of the Latter Han period, who when he left the capital of Loyang was given a grand send-off and was accompanied in his boat by the Governor of Hunan (*Hou Han Shu*, "Kuo T'ai Chuan"). [Auth., Trans.]

[15] [Ancient Japanese mirrors were first imported from China or Korea. Made of metal alloy, they were polished on one side and embossed in design on the other. Of various shapes and commonly round, they lacked handles. They were placed on stands for use, and the polished side came to be covered with a cloth.—Trans., Ed.]

Haraaka's shih, quoted above, on the artificial mountains and waterfalls constructed in the gardens of the Reizen Palace, is focused on a poorly reasoned exposition: the speaker, seeing before him so splendid a mountain landscape, no longer perceives any need to abstain from rice and other grains in preparation for a pilgrimage to see the immortals of Mt. T'ient'ai.[16] Empty logic notwithstanding, the shih was composed in situ, before a natural scene, and as such retains some descriptive elements. Yet Haraaka was also the composer of lines like the following, from his "Matching His Majesty's Poem on Landscape Frescoes in the Seiryōden" (KK, 14:171): "Black cranes fly through the clouds but do not disappear; / White gulls bathe in the water, yet remain dry." The poet presents an irrational scene of flying cranes that never recede from sight and bathing gulls that are always dry. His witty intent is to have the recipient solve the paradox by realizing that this is the normal state of things for birds in a fresco; here we have a variant of the concept discussed earlier, "Because of A, (I know) it is B." In this case, however, the poet's intent has become too far removed from nature and is now a purely conceptual matter.

Related conceptual features appear in a waka (Kokinshū [= KKS], 17:931) by Ki no Tsurayuki (?868-?945), "On Flowers Painted on a Folding Screen":

Sakisomeshi	Ever since the day
Toki yori nochi wa	That they first came into bloom,
Uchihaete	Has the world remained
Yo wa haru nare ya	Everlastingly in spring?—
Iro no tsune naru.	For their colors never fade.

Such conceptualization enjoyed great popularity among ninth-century shih poets, as is seen by the following couplet, written by Kuwabara Hirota (dates unknown) in his "Poem Composed at the Reizen Palace on the Assigned Topic, 'Reflections in the Water'" (BSS, 3:296): "I see flowers that might well have a scent; / And listen to the leaves: no sound of wind." The first line—signifying that the speaker expects fragrance to emanate from flowers reflected in the water—is, while somewhat overstated, nonetheless based more or less on the speaker's received impressions. The intent of the second line, however—that the leaves make no sound when they move, despite the speaker's efforts to hear them rustle in the wind—represents totally conceptual logic quite devoid of true feeling.

This feverish conceptualizing has parallels in waka.

---

[16] Meat was of course to be avoided. [See n. 12.—Ed.] The staples of the ascetic's diet were apparently wild plants and pine needles. The practice of eschewing grains to acquire wisdom is mentioned in the Montoku Jitsuroku for 29.VII.854 (6:63); thus this line probably reflects contemporary beliefs.

During his reign, Tamura once visited the common room used by ladies-in-waiting and viewed the paintings on some folding screens there. "That waterfall scene is charming," he said to his attendants. "Let it be your topic for a waka." Sanjō no Machi complied with the poem,

Omoiseku	Might this not be
Kokoro no uchi no	A pent-up waterfall of thoughts
Taki nare ya	Within the human heart?
Otsu to wa miredo	For we see the torrent fall
Oto no kikoenu.	And yet no sound comes to our ears.

(*KKS*, 17:930)

Tamura is another name for Montoku Tennō (r. 850-58), and Sanjō no Machi (d. 866; a sobriquet—her given name was Shizuko) was one of his concubines.

Poetic concepts involving a reasoning process were thus popular among both shih and waka poets in the mid-ninth century. A further instance is provided by Ono no Takamura (802-52) in this couplet from one of his shih: "I hate short-legged beds: the crickets sing too lustily; / I loathe hollow walls: mice chew great holes in them."[17] Here the poet's intent is that beds with short legs are hateful because the shorter they are, the closer the speaker is to the noise of chirping crickets; and that hollow walls are undesirable because they are easily gnawed into by rodents seeking shelter. The rationality of the statement is, indeed, too rational, paradoxically evoking a sense of vacuity. Since the shih treats of a visit to an ancestor's tomb, its scene would be more normally described thus: the speaker, spending an autumn night on a short-legged bed, hears the constant song of crickets; and the walls of the tomb, long left untended, contain mouseholes.

Takamura's design, which makes his shih couplet overly logical, is also characteristically present in his waka.

On Plum Blossoms in a Snowfall.
By Takamura

Hana no iro wa	Men cannot see
Yuki ni majirite	The color of the blossoms, a color
Miezu to mo	Mingled now with snow,

---

[17] The poem does not survive in its entirety. This couplet was selected for inclusion in the *Wakan Rōeishū* (*Collection of Japanese and Chinese Songs*; 1:329). The title of the shih is "A Visit to an Ancestral Tomb on an Autumn Evening."

Ka o dani nioe
Hito no shiru beku.

But only let them breathe the fragrance,
And all must know the plum trees
are in flower.[18]

(*KKS*, 6:335)

The first half of the waka is a rather more reasoned version of the concept embodied in Fan Yün's couplet, "When I left, snow fell like blossoms; / Now I return, and blossoms fall like snow" (*Gyokudai Shin'ei* [= *GDSE*], 10:649, "Pieh-shih"). The second half of the waka contains formal elements similar to those in the second line of a couplet by Emperor Yang of Sui (569-618): "Moonlight seems to still the stream's flow; / A spring breeze bears the scent of night plum" (*Sui Yang-ti Chi*, 3872, "Climbing the South Tower on the Night of the Lantern Festival"). Although not apparently based on any specific shih, Takamura's waka undoubtedly possesses the wittiness of Six Dynasties verse.

The Japanese poetic stance in the second half of the ninth century was similarly one of reveling in logic for its own sake. Shimada Tadaon (828-91) writes, in "Watching a Spider Spin a Web" (*Denshi Kashū*, 1:346): "Who wove these threads without recourse to a loom? / In the autumn cold, dewdrops are strung like rosary beads." It is a common conceit to perceive the elements of a spider's web as threads; but when the speaker asks his rhetorical question—who made the warp and woof of the threads intersect so well without using a loom?—his intent lies in anticipating a witty design. The second line is similar in concept to a waka by Fun'ya Asayasu (fl. ca. 902):

Composed at a Poetry Match
at the House of Prince Koresada

Aki no no ni
Oku shiratsuyu wa
Tama nare ya
Tsuranukikakuru
Kumo no itosuji.

Pure droplets of dew,
Settling in an autumn field,
Might very well be pearls
Strung upon and hanging from
A spider's single line of thread.

(*KKS*, 4:225)

Another of Tadaon's shih, "The Night Wind Is Cold" (*Denshi Kashū*, 1:342), contains this couplet: "Our ruler's mercy fills the land, a hearth-

---

[18] [The translation is by Brower and Miner, 1961, p. 187.—Trans. It must have been by reading waka by men adapting to it the Six Dynasties "conceptual focus" that women like Sanjō no Machi who read no Chinese also wrote in a "Chinese" vein.—Ed.]

fire burning bright: / When winter comes I shall not shrink from wearing thin robes." Not only does the speaker compare his sovereign's benevolence to a hearth-fire, he adds that his lord's warm concern will enable the speaker to wear light clothing even in winter. Tadaon probably took particular pride in these lines.

We may give the term "fabricated logic" to a poetic assertion, structured along conceptual lines, that is superficially plausible but essentially illogical or, at times, vacuous. In the second half of the ninth century, during Tadaon's lifetime, the fashion of fabricated logic in Japanese shih was at its height. One of his pupils, Michizane, also reveled in fabricated logic prior to his adoption of Po Chü-i's poetic style. "Solitary Amusement in the Twelfth Month" (*Kanke Bunsō* [= *KB*], 1:2), composed when Michizane was fourteen years old, contains the lines, "Ice covers the water: I hear no lapping of the waves; / Snow powders the forest: I look, and find the trees in bloom." The couplet was eventually included in the *Wakan Rōeishū* (1:387) and may be considered one of Michizane's representative works. The intended conceit of perceiving snow on branches as plum blossoms is found also in waka, such as Tsurayuki's poem,

Composed on the Topic "Winter"

Yuki fureba	When snowflakes fall,
Fuyugomoriseru	Each and every bush and tree
Kusa mo ki mo	Now in its winter sleep
Haru ni shirarenu	Comes abloom with flowers
Hana zo sakikeru.	Unrecognizable to Spring.

(*KKS*, 6:323)

The first line of Michizane's couplet, "Ice covers the water: I hear no lapping of the waves," is fabricated logic: a lake that is completely frozen over naturally has no waves, and the addition of "I hear no lapping of the waves" to the line goes beyond the bounds of reason into those of vacuity. Fabricated logic appears in Tsurayuki's waka when he adds his comment, "Haru ni shirarenu" ("Unrecognizable to Spring"), to the conceit of snow and blossoms.

Fabricated logic persists in Michizane's adult compositions and is particularly conspicuous in his formal pieces. Let us consider a shih believed to have been composed in 880, when Michizane was thirty-eight, "On the Topic 'Flowers in the Rain,' Given to All Who Attended the Palace Banquet in Early Spring" (*KB*, 2:85).

Blossoming faces smile, each fluttering to the ground;
How can we not speak of the plum fragrance braving the rain?

The dancers think their gauze sleeves are moist from their exertions;
Our flowered robes perchance are wetted by waves of our lord's mercy.[19]
In surprise I look for musk deer pacing the spring marsh,
And seek to comfort warblers now bereft of their night's lodging.[20]
O five-petaled flower, take no pride in the rain's blessings,
For all the realm rejoices in its abundant measure.

The sole statement relative to nature here is that plum blossoms in the rain are beautiful. Although the conceit of plum blossoms as dancing girls is not an uncommon conception, fabricated logic is clearly discernible in Michizane's invention of anthropomorphoid plum blossoms dressed in gauze, who mistakenly attribute the dampness of their costumes to perspiration from dancing. This is fabricated logic, because everyone in Michizane's audience is aware that no one is in fact making this mistaken surmise.

It is, moreover, utter fabrication to maintain that the splendid formal dress of the participants is drenched by the waves of the sovereign's benevolence and virtue: the gentlemen are presumably indoors and would not be the least bit damp. The speaker, who is only too well aware of this, notifies his audience with the word "perchance" and so informs one and all of the fabrication. The next line, "In surprise I look for musk deer pacing the spring marsh," is again a conceit, albeit one that is deliberately exaggerated. Its effect is similar to that of fabricated logic. It is assumed that both composer and recipients have temporarily forgotten their knowledge that plum blossoms have a subtle scent. No one, moreover, would actually conclude that, when rain has scattered the plum blossoms, one must comfort warblers who now have no place to nest: the idea that warblers nest in plum trees is a conventionalized poetic fiction. Behind the fabricated logic is an intent probably held jointly by composer and recipients, the wish that the plum blossoms will not let themselves be scattered by the rain. The closing lines, "O five-petaled flower, take no pride in the rain's blessings, / For all the realm rejoices in its abundant measure," is also fabricated logic. The warblers have no particular cause for pride either.

Intent based on fabricated logic is also found in works like this anonymous waka:

Kakikurashi	If rain must fall,
Koto wa furanan	Let it pour from storm-black clouds,
Harusame ni	And let spring rains

---

[19] [The sovereign's benevolence is conventionally compared to waves, as in this line, or rain, as in lines 7 and 8.—Trans.]

[20] [The warbler conventionally lodges among plum blossoms. When they fall, the warbler has nowhere to spend the night.—Trans.]

| Nureginu kisete | Be to blame in their wet clothes |
| Kimi o todomen. | That I keep you here with me.[21] |

(KKS, 8:402)

Again, the assumption is that both composer and recipient know there is
no reason for rain to wear clothing: the poet's design is to make a personified spring shower "wear wet clothes" ("nureginu kisete"), that is, be
held accountable for the speaker's own wishes. If "Harusame ni / Nureginu kisete" were replaced by the more literal "Harusame ni / Yue o owa-
sete," the waka would very nearly lose its *Kokinshū*-style effect.

Fabricated logic gradually disappeared from Michizane's compositions
as he absorbed Po Chü-i's poetic style. Even in his later years, however,
certain events and circumstances occasioned the use of fabricated logic in
his poetry. The following couplet, for example, is found in a poem probably written in 895, when Michizane was fifty-one, "On the Topic, 'Misty
Flowers Are Reflected, Winding Waters Are Crimson,' Assigned to All
Who Attended a Banquet on the Third Day of the Third Month in the
Shinzen Gardens" (*KB*, 5:383): "Trembling branches, tossing waves,
both are most distressing; / Thus in all sincerity I fear the evening wind."
When wind shakes the branches, blossoms fall, and when the wind makes
waves rise, the sake cup floating on the water comes dangerously close to
capsizing: thus states the speaker, and yet no one is likely to believe that
he seriously fears the wind. This is a deliberately assumed fear. And although not so evident as in Michizane's poem on "Flowers in the Rain,"
fabricated logic is again present. The poet in fact wishes to express his regret that evening is drawing nigh and, with it, the banquet by the winding
waters is ending. This is fabricated logic on a level, perhaps, with that of
this waka by Lady Ise (d. ca. 939):

On Plum Blossoms at the Water's Edge

Haru goto ni	Every year in spring,
Nagaruru kawa o	I fancy that the flowing stream
Hana to mite	Bursts into bloom:
Orarenu mizu ni	Shall I wet my sleeves in grasping
Sode ya nurenan.	Watery stems that will not break?

(KKS, 1:43)

It goes beyond reason to assert that plum blossoms reflected in the water
will have branches that cannot be broken off.

---

[21] [The idiom "nureginu kisete," "to shift blame onto someone else," is literally translated,
"make [the rain] wear wet clothing."—Trans.]

Another example of fabricated logic occurs in the final couplet of Michizane's "Lamenting the Falling Cherry Blossoms in Spring" (*KB*, 5:384), also thought to date from 895: "Why do I lament so bitterly the blossoms' fall? / Because this humble person occupies the post of Gleaner." This is fabricated logic on a high plane and involves the introduction of wordplay. "Gleaner" (Ch. Shih-i; J. Shūi) is the T'ang term for the Japanese court position Jijū, usually translated as "Chamberlain" or "Gentleman-in-Waiting." Michizane was awarded this post on the fifteenth of the Twelfth Month, 894. Since "gleaner"—one who gathers up things that have fallen or been dropped—is the literal meaning of his title, the speaker is upset to see the blossoms fall. Michizane's intent in this couplet resembles the wordplay that is one of the chief characteristics of the *Kokinshū* style. The following waka by the priest Sosei (fl. ca. 859-97), for example, puns on the word "kuchinashi," which means both "kerria" and "no mouth":[22]

Yamabuki no	Tell me, robe the color of
Hanairogoromo	A golden kerria rose,
Nushi ya tare	To whom do you belong?—
Toedo kotaezu	No answer did I receive,
Kuchinashi ni shite.	For there was no mouth to speak!

(*KKS*, 19:1012)

These examples demonstrate undeniably that, while evolving in the direction of T'ang verse, ninth-century Japanese poetry—shih and waka alike—retained a conceptual focus characteristic of the Six Dynasties style.

The Achievement of Kūkai: Part One

The noteworthy characteristics of ninth-century Japanese shih—which is to say the principal poetic trends—have just been described. This does not mean, however, that every composition dating from the ninth century was the product of an oblique conceptual focus. Neither does the fact that something is in the mainstream necessarily signify that it possesses great literary value. The *Genji Monogatari (The Tale of Genji)* is exceptional among Japanese prose fiction narratives, yet it possesses the highest literary value; similarly, Zeami's nō plays and Shinkei's linked verse cannot be seen as part of a contemporary mainstream. The poetry of Kūkai—or

[22] ["Kerria," by extension, signifies its fruit, which was used as a yellow dye for clothing.—Trans.]

Kōbō Daishi—definitely has no place in the stylistic mainstream of ninth-century Japanese shih, but its literary merit is nonetheless very great.

Kūkai's central concern was more with prose than with shih, and one cannot say that his shih are better than his prose. Yet Kūkai's shih, compared with those of his ninth-century countrymen, are nevertheless works of the first rank. Shinzei (800-60), Kūkai's senior disciple and the compiler of the *Seireishū*, includes this passage in his preface to the collection:

> In his "Poem on an Excursion to the Mountains, Written in Envy of the Immortals," Kūkai writes, "High in the mountains the winds easily grow strong; / The deep sea waters are difficult to gauge," and in his shih titled, "Viewing the Shinzen Gardens on an Autumn Day," he writes, "High towers of marvelous skill are not the work of man; / A mirror-lake, deep and clear, swallows the sunlight." Each couplet displays excellent metaphorical expression as well as an enormous substantial force. They excel both as works of art and as statements of thought, and should be regarded as supreme masterpieces.[23]

It is not known why Shinzei treated these two shih as normative works, although the former, "Poem on an Excursion to the Mountains, Written in Envy of the Immortals," is undeniably a masterpiece. What must next be questioned are the criteria used in determining that this poem is a masterpiece: can they be applied with similar results to the latter shih, "Viewing the Shinzen Gardens on an Autumn Day"?

The "Poem on an Excursion to the Mountains, Written in Envy of the Immortals" (*SRS*, 1:159-65) is a lengthy work, being 106 lines long; its heroic scope, so uncharacteristic of the Japanese approach, is particularly impressive. The subject of the poem, a speculative realm of unparalleled splendor, necessitates the grand scale: this, too, is rare in Japanese literature. From the beginning of the Modern Age in Japan, a cold reception has typically been given to works whose main purpose is the presentation of a philosophical outlook. This reaction is based on the idea that literature should not be a tool used to express world views or ideologies but should instead be created for its own sake. This idea evolved together with the rise of Romanticism in the West: the expression, "l'art pour l'art," with reference to literature, first appeared in 1833 (Wimsatt-Brooks, 1957, 477).

Of course, such ideas did not exist in ninth-century Japan. On the contrary, Kūkai himself considered a philosophical viewpoint a positive criterion.

> Long ago, Ho Shao and Kuo P'u spoke their minds in poems on "Wandering Immortals." Their poetry was outstanding both in structure and rhythm, their colorful phrases were lush and splendid. Yet in

---

[23] *Seireishū* (*Nihon Koten Bungaku Taikei* ed. [= NKBT], 155).

content these verses were hollow, mere trifles that did not explicate the Great Way. I perused the *Wen Hsüan*, carefully examining the works contained there; I read them several times over, only to find to my regret that they were sorely lacking in justice. Finally I took brush in hand and began to write, depicting the caves and dwellings of "immortals"—the highest of the supermundane Buddhas—and at the same time lamenting worldly delusion. The principle of impermanence is portrayed through natural and objective metaphors.

This is part of Kūkai's preface to his "Poem on an Excursion to the Mountains, Written in Envy of the Immortals" (*SRS*, 1:159). His declaration reveals that Kūkai, unlike his contemporaries in the Japanese poetic world with their fervid imitation of things Chinese, was sufficiently confident to criticize the classic poetry of the *Wen Hsüan (Selections of Refined Literature)*. This makes evident the kind of standards Kūkai used in judging his own work. His comments are based on ideological criteria supported by justice (logic); and the lack of logic in the shih on "Wandering Immortals" (*Wen Hsüan* [= *WH*], 21:459-64) by Ho Shao (d. 301) and Kuo P'u (277-324) was, in Kūkai's estimate, a serious shortcoming. Chinese poetry was termed the expression of one's intent.[24] For Kūkai, this intent was centered on a lofty ideology leading to a heightening of the truth that encompasses the cosmos; hence if logicality, which forms the impetus toward this heightening process, is absent from a work, it must be "sorely lacking in justice."

Yet Kūkai's stress on ideology and logicality as critical standards did not signify that a work need only be conspicuously ideological in order to have high literary value. It might also be noted that, in this same preface, Kūkai stresses another point, that "the principle of impermanence is portrayed through natural and objective metaphors," an indication that a work deficient in refined expressive techniques cannot qualify as art of the first order. The phrase, "portrayed through natural and objective metaphors," is reminiscent of Shinzei's "displays excellent metaphorical expression." We need not consider Kūkai's "metaphors" as limited to the narrow sense of that term: rather, the word represents figurative speech in the broad sense, expression alluding to abstract concepts by the suggestive relation of concrete objects.

The opening lines of the shih mentioned by Shinzei, "Poem on an Excursion to the Mountains, Written in Envy of the Immortals," may serve to illustrate the nature of this expressive technique.

> High in the mountains the winds easily grow strong;
> The deep sea waters are difficult to gauge.

[24] "Poetry is the expression of intent" (*Shih Ching*, 1:13).

No man can know the limits of the sky:
Only the Dharma-Body can comprehend.

The abstraction of line four—which states that only the Buddha, the embodiment of truth, can comprehend truth—is given a fairly concrete shape by line three, "No man can know the limits of the sky." Since one cannot actually see the limits of the sky, this line is not strongly concrete, whereas lines one and two are quite concrete. On the other hand, the tenor or signified of the first two lines is unclear.[25] Their implied sense may be that the wondrous and profound sphere of the Buddha is not to be distinguished in essence from the incalculably vast store of illusion and evil passion in this world. The resulting interplay between signifier and signified—ranging from the simple to the subtle and complex—and the use of various levels and categories of figurative speech may be what Kūkai meant by "portrayal through natural and objective metaphors."

Although highly refined and varied in figurative speech, the "Poem on an Excursion to the Mountains, Written in Envy of the Immortals" remains somewhat diffuse in its structural design, which was intended to sustain a 106-line work. In this respect the shih may even be inferior to the *Sangō Shiiki (Indications of the Goals of the Three Teachings)*, a product of Kūkai's youth. What may well be his most outstanding poetry in terms of structural interest is a series of five shih, all probably written after 816, beginning with "For Lord Yoshimine" (*SRS*, 1:171) and culminating in "Reply Sent in a Bark Letterbox" (*SRS*, 1:177). Kūkai, who had decided to leave the capital for Mt. Kōya, received a letter from Yoshimine Yasuyo (785-830) urging him to remain in the city. Kūkai replied with this series of shih. He sought formal diversity in the series: the first shih is in five-character lines, the second through fourth shih are in mixed meter, and the last is in seven-character lines. The principal part of the series consists of the three mixed-meter shih; this forms an extremely effective design. The lively rhythm that unfolds in the intricate pattern of long and short lines is most appropriate as an embodiment of Kūkai's bold assertion that Mt. Kōya is the best location for the practice of Buddhist austerities. Moreover, because the series is framed in a dramatic mode, it is animated by a sense of immediacy.

The second shih of the series, "Pleasures of Entering the Mountain Precincts," begins with a description of aristocrats delighting in the beautiful spring scenery of the capital:

[25] The *NKBT* edition of the *Seireishū* (p. 540) has an interpretation different from mine. [The author's mention of "illusion" in the next sentence is a tacit example of his point: the character designating "sky" also is a Buddhist term for the illusory nature of the world.—Ed.]

Do you not see? Do you not see?
In the city's great gardens peach and damson blossoms blush crimson,
Bright, bright and fragrant, fragrant, each face glows alike—
Each opened by a single shower, scattered in a single breeze:
Fluttering above, fluttering below, they fall throughout the gardens.
Maidens of spring come in a bevy, all breaking off sprays;
Warblers of spring gather, then go into the sky, beaks filled.

Later in the shih, Kūkai describes evanescence: glory passes away like a dream, like foam on the waters, and men all return to ashes and dust. He then advocates abandoning the secular world:

Do you not know? Do you not know?
Man's lot is thus: will you live forever?
Morning and night I think, think on this, my heart rent with suffering.
Your sun is halfway set behind the western mountains;
Your years are nearly spent, you are like a propped-up corpse.
Cling to this? Cling to this? A meaningless act!
Come along! Come along! You must dawdle no more.

Mt. Kōya, Kūkai declares, is an ideal refuge from the world of men: "I never tire of seeing the pines and stones of South Mountain; / I am always moved by the pure streams of South Peak."[26] His parallelism is masterly indeed.

Such shih make one feel that matters more naturally expressed in prose are here brought into poetry. Kūkai's series of poems may well be seen as an experiment to determine how far the poet's wealth of concepts could be contained within existing poetic forms. Kūkai is thus not easily compared with other shih poets of his day, poets whose chief literary concern lay in conforming to existing poetic forms. It is similarly difficult to verify Kūkai's eminence in relation to contemporary poets, since shih resembling his do not survive (and were probably never composed). One extant work, however, will enable us to evaluate Kūkai's relative position in his contemporary poetic world: the shih so highly praised by Shinzei, "Viewing the Shinzen Gardens on an Autumn Day" (*SRS*, 1:165). The nature of the composition lends itself to comparison with banquet shih, composed by courtiers in response to a royal request.

Strolling through Shinzen, I gaze at its scenery,
My mind is entranced, and I cannot turn toward home.

[26] ["South Mountain" and "South Peak" both refer to Mt. Kōya, which lies to the south of the then capital, Heiankyō.—Trans.]

> High towers of marvelous skill are not the work of man;
> A mirror-lake, deep and clear, swallows the sunlight.
> Cranes, their cries heard heavenward, favor the august gardens;
> Swans still their restless wings and make no move to fly.
> Fish play among waterplants: many bite at hooks;
> Deer bell in deep grasses: dew wets our robes.
> Fluttering here, resting there, fowl sense our lord's mercy:
> The autumn moon, autumn winds enter my door in vain.[27]
> Carrying grasses, pecking millet, birds go off in a darkling scene;
> Beasts dance and frolic, then are hidden by darkest Truth.

Kūkai observes the tonal patterns of the "modern" shih form and commits no violations.[28] Now, Shinzei comments on a couplet that "displays excellent metaphorical expression": "High towers of marvelous skill are not the work of man; / A mirror-lake, deep and clear, swallows the sunlight." Where does the "excellent metaphorical expression" appear? The *Seireishū Shiki* interprets the couplet thus: the grand towers represent the sovereign's illustrious virtues, and the lake surface that reflects a myriad images expresses the benevolence of the royal house, which is extended to all the people.[29] Similarly, lines five through eight appear at first glance to describe the birds, beasts, and fish within a great garden, but the tenor of these lines is, again, the universal extent of the sovereign's virtue. If this is the case, then these animals can all be considered symbols of an all-pervasive royal favor. When compared with the simple description of nature in Haraaka's "Poem on the Topic, 'Water Likened to Cloth Hung to Dry,'" and Michizane's expository treatment of the sovereign's virtues in "On the Topic, 'Flowers in the Rain,'" Kūkai's expression is seen to possess much greater distance between tenor and vehicle, signifier and signified.

The artistic level attained by ninth-century Japanese shih poets—including Kūkai—may be determined by comparing their compositions with continental examples. Kūkai was not the first to create expression in the descriptive mode yet suggestive of a conceptualized meaning or to create expressions that placed substantial distance between the signified and its signifier. Expression of this kind was employed in shih and fu as early

[27] [The moon and the wind in autumn conventionally bring sorrowful thoughts, but not under the auspicious circumstances described here.—Trans.]

[28] The second word in line 6, "ch'ih" ("restless"), has a deflected tone in the Sung dictionary *Kuang-yün*, which would indicate that Kūkai violated the rules of regulated verse. But the *Yü-p'ien*, another Sung dictionary, gives this character a level tone, with the result that line 6 conforms to the rules. Kūkai observes the other requirements of regulated verse.

[29] The *Seireishū Shiki* (2 fasc.) is an anonymous compilation. I have used the *Shingonshū Zensho* edition for my citation (p. 14).

as the Late Six Dynasties period. The following description, for example, appears in "A Fu on Parting" (*WH*, 16:344), by Chiang Yen:

> The wind moans and groans in sounds never heard;
> Clouds spread far and wide in colors never seen.
> The boat lingers close to the line of shore;
> The carriage makes poor progress through the mountains.
> The rowing is easy, so why do we make no headway?
> Horses whinny sadly and continuously.

The fu describes a travel scene; but the tenor of each line concerns the grief of those setting out on their journey and the misery of those left behind. The title is homologous to each situation depicted in the fu. For example, the boat and the carriage that make such poor progress symbolize the emotions of a traveler reluctant to leave.

Kūkai's shih are definitely grounded in the Six Dynasties style. It might be noted, however, that although he did absorb the poetic features described above, he made little use of the oblique expression that is one of the most striking features of the Six Dynasties style. That is not to say that oblique expression never appears in Kūkai's poetry. One example is found in his quatrain, "Hearing the Buppōsō Bird at Dawn Service" (*SRS*, 10:453):

> A silent grove: alone I sit in a grass-roofed chapel at dawn,
> And hear the cry of Three Treasures from a single bird.
> As the bird has its call, so has man his spirit:
> Call and spirit, clouds and water, all are clearly grasped.[30]

The intent of line two is that a single bird has three calls, "bup," "pō," and "sō"; this conceptual form, focused on computation, resembles Fan Yün's design in a couplet from "Gazing at the Weaver Maiden" (*GDSE*, 5:533):

> My feelings—a mere inch—are entangled a hundredfold,
> And my single heart is burdened with a myriad thoughts.[31]

A similar computational concept appears in this waka by Fujiwara Toshi-yuki (d. 907):

---

[30] [The Buppōsō bird's (*Eurystomus orientalis*) name is written with three characters signifying the Buddha, the Dharma, and the priesthood—the Three Treasures of Buddhism. The name comes from the bird's unique call, "bup-pō-sō."—Trans.]

[31] [The Weaver Maiden is the star Vega, who is the speaker of the shih. She and her lover, the Herdboy or the star Altair, were said to cross the River of Heaven (the Milky Way) for one night's union on the seventh night of the Seventh Month.—Trans., Ed.]

Composed at a Poetry Match
at the House of Prince Koresada

Shiratsuyu no	Only one color
Iro wa hitotsu o	Does the pearly dew possess:
Ika ni shite	How then, wonder I,
Aki no ko no ha o	Does it tint the autumn leaves
Chiji ni somu ran.	In a thousand thousand shades?

(*KKS*, 5:257)

Such use of oblique expression is rare with Kūkai, however, and further instances of oblique expression are not easily discovered in his poetry. Perhaps Kūkai's poetic concepts flowed too majestically to ally themselves with such techniques. Even when his work can be associated with styles of the Six Dynasties, it most resembles that of the Early Six Dynasties, which is not noted for its oblique expression.

By contrast, Kūkai's contemporary, Saga Tennō, composed shih with oblique conceptual foci, a fact that was discussed earlier. Saga's position as the leading exponent of oblique expression in Japanese shih may have accounted for the popularity enjoyed by this technique. His oblique concepts, however, remained confined to the reasoning pattern, "Because of A, (I know it is) B"; they did not reach the level of toying with fabricated logic. Another example of Saga's style is provided by a couplet from "Vernal Dawn by the River" (*BSS*, 1:197), which was apparently recited in fairly informal surroundings: "Clouds' vapors wet my robe: I know a cave is near; / A spring's babble wakens me: I find a neighboring valley."[32] The vaporous atmosphere and the sound of running water audible from the speaker's bed are perceived as reasons why he becomes aware, respectively, of the proximity of a mountain cavern and a valley spring. A corresponding degree of reasoning also appears in waka, as in the case of this anonymous poem:

Furu yuki wa	It seems the falling snow
Katsu zo kenu rashi	Melts right where it comes to rest,
Ashihiki no	For the sound of rapids
Yama no tagitsuse	Grows ever louder from the mountains
Oto masaru nari.	With their sprawling foothills.

(*KKS*, 6:319)

The fact that this conceptual pattern first enjoyed popularity during Saga's reign may well reflect the influence of Korean poetic styles. When the

---

[32] [Clouds were conventionally seen as emanating from mountain caverns.—Trans.]

sixteenth Japanese embassy to the T'ang court (in whose company Kūkai traveled) entered Ch'ang-an in the Twelfth Month of 804, the following notable Chinese poets were alive: Tu Yu, aged 71; Ling-ch'e, aged 59; Meng Chiao, aged 54; Ch'üan Te-yü, aged 46; Han Yü, aged 37; Hsüeh T'ao, aged 37; Po Chü-i, aged 33; Liu Tsung-yüan, aged 32; Yao Ho, aged 28; Yüan Chen, aged 26; Chia Tao, aged 26; and Li Ho, aged 15. All are poets of the Middle T'ang period, and yet the conceptual foci of Japanese shih from Saga's reign through that of Nimmyō (809-50) were not affected by Middle or even High T'ang poetic styles. The next or seventeenth Japanese embassy to the T'ang court went to China in 838, but expression in subsequent Japanese shih still displayed few marked changes. As long as the crossing from Japan to China was feasible, Chinese literary works could be imported, and poetic form and meter could be learned from such books without the need for instruction by foreigners. Personal contact, however, would have been a virtual necessity in order for Japanese poets to develop new expressive concepts and receive new styles of expression; and individual instruction was far more likely to have been provided by Koreans than by the Chinese.

My assertion would be a verifiable fact rather than conjecture if Korean shih survived in some quantity from the first half of the ninth century. Unfortunately, the quality and quantity of such sources as do survive are limited in scope and, for reasons that will be discussed below, are considered useless. Thus documentary evidence is unobtainable. Five poems selected for inclusion in the *Bunka Shūreishū*, however, will enable us to make an indirect appraisal of ninth-century Korean shih: they are by Wang Hsiao-lien, who served as ambassador to Japan from the country of P'o-hai.[33] One poem, "Looking at the Rain on a Spring Day" (*BSS*, 1:211-12), is believed to have been composed in 815:

> Our host has given us a banquet in the provinces;
> His guests, drunk as mud, will match any in the city.
> Perhaps the Rain God is acquainted with your sovereign's wish
> In granting us fragrant showers to soothe our travelers' hearts.[34]

The embassy left Lung-ch'üan Fu, the capital of P'o-hai, and crossed the sea to arrive, presumably, in Tsuruga, where Shigeno Sadanushi, an official envoy dispatched from the capital, received the travelers. "Our host"

---

[33] [Located in what is now southeast Manchuria and northeast Korea.—Trans.] The nation of P'o-hai was established by Ta Tsu-jung in 698 in part of Koguryŏ following the destruction of that state by T'ang forces in 668. Emperor Hsüan-tsung of T'ang granted P'o-hai a certificate of autonomy in 713. Friendly relations were maintained with Japan until P'o-hai was overrun in 926 by the Liao. The inhabitants of P'o-hai were chiefly Moho, one of the Tungusic tribes.

[34] The date is given by the *Nihon Goki*, entries for 7.I.815, 22.I, and 14.VI (24:129-33).

probably refers to Sadanushi. The intent of the poem is as follows. The embassy is gratified by the prompt welcome and by the banquet held at the provincial government buildings. The kindness of the Japanese has delighted the envoys, making them feel as if they were in the capital (Heiankyō), and they have become as "drunk as mud." This mud may well have resulted from a fragrant rain that the Rain God has showered on them in obedience to the Japanese ruler's gracious wish, made in order to solace the weary travelers. The rain of benevolence is signified by "In granting us fragrant showers"; the rain is a metaphor for the sovereign's profound solicitude, the point of the shih. The phrase may also refer to the fine sake that Sadanushi brought with him from the capital. The simultaneous expression—through the single image, "rain," of the abstract concept of benevolence and the concrete one of sake—represents the use of metaphor as a complex and advanced technique. More noteworthy still, the intent of the phrase—that we are drunk and have become like mud because of the benevolent rain of sake—contains fabricated logic. To be sure, the character for "mud" ("ni"), when used in this context, signifies a trepang, not "mud": evidently the study of Chinese in P'o-hai was not sufficiently advanced to include this knowledge.[35] When one considers, on the other hand, that up to this point the shih written during Saga's reign demonstrate no evidence of fabricated logic, the poetry of P'o-hai, with its Koguryŏ background of a received Six Dynasties poetic style, appears somewhat more advanced at this time.

Wang Hsiao-lien once again employs fabricated logic in a quatrain, probably written after his return to P'o-hai, "Composed at a Provincial Pavilion, on Receiving the Topic 'Mountain Flowers' " (BSS, 1:227). Its first couplet, "Fragrant trees are spring-colored, colored very bright; / Early blossoms open like smiles, but no voice is heard," is similar in concept to Hirota's shih verse, "And listen to the leaves: no sound of wind" and the waka lines, "No answer did I receive, / For there was no mouth to speak!"

Yet another shih by Hsiao-lien was written in reply to a poem by the royal envoy Sakanoe Imatsugu (dates unknown) and titled, "Matching Envoy Sakanoe's Poem Composed in My Honor, 'Gazing at the Moon and Longing for Home' " (BSS, 1:228). It concludes with a couplet that, while not employing fabricated logic, is in keeping with the Six Dynasties style: "Who says I am a thousand li from home? / The same light shines on men of both countries." The intent of the couplet is as follows. Imatsugu, in his poem, expresses sympathy for Hsiao-lien's wife, wondering whether she might resent being left a thousand li away in P'o-hai; but in

---

[35] "In the Southern Sea there is a mollusk, known as 'ni,' that is lively in the water but behaves drunkenly, like a lump of mud, when taken from the water" (I-mu Chih). Quoted from Morohashi, 6:1066.

Hsiao-lien's shih, the speaker notes that the moon is shining equally on both countries, implying that he does not feel as if he and his wife are separated by vast distances. The annihilation of distance through the agency of one moon shining equally on two far-off places is a conceptual mode also found in Six Dynasties poetry, as in this couplet from "On 'Parting in Spring,' Composed by Royal Request" (*GDSE*, 9:611), by Prince Hsiang-tung (later Emperor Yüan of Liang): "If the moonbeams really take no heed of near and far, / They shine upon two now apart who spend tonight in tears."

Wang Hsiao-lien was accompanied to Japan by his secretary, Shih Jen-chen, one of whose shih, "Composed at a Palace Banquet on the Seventh of the Month," also survives (*BSS*, 1:211). Its lack of notable characteristics, together with the small number of extant shih by Hsiao-lien, make it impossible to arrive at any general conclusions. On the other hand, the Late Six Dynasties poetic style was undoubtedly current in P'o-hai by the beginning of the ninth century; and since P'o-hai is unlikely to have been capable, in the first century of its existence as a nation, of forming a poetic circle on such a level without outside assistance, we may reasonably surmise that the Late Six Dynasties style was current, and practiced on a fairly high level, in contemporary Korea as well. Diplomatic exchange between Japan and Korea was more extensive than that with P'o-hai, and evidently private cultural exchange with Koreans also occurred. Thus Koreans and Japanese probably had abundant opportunity to meet individually and discuss poetic expression. Certainly the Six Dynasties mode of conceptual focus was incorporated into Japanese shih in the course of just such contacts. These conjectures, however, might require reconsideration in light of the fact that Ch'oe Ch'i-wǒn (b. 857) and a number of other ninth-century Korean poets composed in the T'ang style.

Korean shih composition increased rapidly with the founding of Koryǒ in 918, but very few shih survive from the Silla period (668-935). They are very few, that is, in comparison with the enormous number of Koryǒ compositions. Ch'oe Ch'i-wǒn, the foremost Silla literatus, has about forty extant shih. All are in five- or seven-character lines and are written either in the regulated-verse (lü-shih) or quatrain (chüeh-chü) forms.[36] There is no indication that Ch'i-wǒn, like Kūkai, experimented with various poetic modes. The nature of his writing is exemplified in "The Hollyhock" (*Samhansi Kugam*, 1:4).

> I dwell beside a lonely, desolate field,
> My frilled blossoms burdening supple stems.
> My scent, washed by summer rains, is faint;

---

[36] [These are the two most important "modern" shih forms.—Trans.]

My form, bent by wheatfield winds, is leaning.
Who will admire me from carriage or horse?
Bees and butterflies carry out inspections.
My shame is to have sprung from lowly soil:
Shall I complain that no one comes to me?

The hollyhock (Althaea rosea) is a perennial with red, purple, or white flowers that bloom during the summer rainy season. Its tall stalk bends easily. The first half of the shih describes the hollyhock's ecology, and the second half laments that the flower's beauty is wasted in desolate surroundings. Commenting on the final couplet, Ch'oe Cho-rong (1287-1340) notes that it refers to Ch'i-wŏn's "own situation": the poet may well be lamenting that his Korean origins doom him, talented though he is, to a mediocre career in the T'ang bureaucracy. The bees and butterflies of line six, that are drawn to the lovely flowers but take stock of the situation instead of drinking the nectar, allude to administrators who make no effort to find the poet a desirable post.

Ch'i-wŏn was born in Kyongju. At the age of twelve he went to study in China, and in 874, when he was eighteen, he passed the higher civil service examination. He served as Provincial Procurator in P'iao-shui and in other middle-level provincial posts until his resignation in 885, when he returned to Silla. He was twenty-nine years old at the time. During his brief career in China he also worked as a ghostwriter, composing public and private documents in enormous quantities; this indicates how highly the Chinese valued his literary abilities. Upon his return to Silla he rose to become vice-minister and was revered as the most eminent literatus of his day. Silla was, however, in decline: in its final period as a sovereign state, the country was plagued by political unrest and general chaos, and Ch'i-wŏn resigned his post. He spent the rest of his life sightseeing and visiting Buddhist temples.[37] Little is known of Ch'i-wŏn after the age of forty-seven. To judge from the record of his career, he very likely wrote "The Hollyhock" during his years in China. Let us consider another of his shih, "Stone Peak," the first of a series of ten composed at Mt. Ta-chu in 884 (*Kewŏn P'ilgyŏng*, 20:301).

Precipitous peaks strive to touch the skies;
Rising from the sea, the sun blooms, a single lotus.[38]
The mountain face is sheer: it has no use for common trees;
The lofty summit beckons only beauteous clouds and haze.
Grasses dot a wintry scene sketched with new snow;

[37] His career is described in *Samguk Sagi* (46:464-66).

[38] [I.e., the rising sun and its reflection on the sea are compared to a lotus gradually opening its petals.—Trans.]

A pleasant jingle of jewels sounds from a bubbling stream.
Quietly I muse that paradise can only be like this:
Surely when the moon is bright the immortals gather here!

Both this poem and "The Hollyhock" clearly embody the Late T'ang poetic style.

The High T'ang period, exemplified by the works of Li Po and Tu Fu, and the Middle T'ang, in which Han Yü and Po Chü-i reigned supreme, were the source of the most outstanding T'ang poetry. With the commencement of the Late T'ang, poetic expression moved toward an apparent revival of the Late Six Dynasties style. It was not simply a revival, however, for the diction of Late T'ang poetry is both freer and more subtle than that of Southern Ch'i and Liang verse (Yoshikawa, 1974, 190). Another important point is that oblique expression is either absent from or inconspicuous in Late T'ang poetry, despite the sumptuous style it shares with Late Six Dynasties verse. Ch'oe Ch'i-wŏn's shih are characteristic of the Late T'ang style, which is only natural given the years he spent in China. Three illustrious Chinese poets, Tu Mu (803-53), Li Shang-yin (812-58), and Wen T'ing-yün (812-70), were no longer alive when Ch'i-wŏn left for Korea, but the following poets were active at the time: Kao P'ien, aged 65; Kuan Hsiu, aged 54; P'i Jih-hsiu, aged 53; Lo Yin, aged 53; Wei Chuang, aged 50; Ssu-k'ung T'u, aged 49; Cheng Ku, aged 44; Han Wo, aged 42; Ts'ao Sung, aged 40; Tu Hsün-ho, aged 40; Tu Kuang-t'ing, aged 36; and Ch'i-chi, aged 25. Lo Yin, known as a man who, "having pretensions about his own talents, was not quick to praise those of others," nevertheless had a high regard for Ch'i-wŏn's shih. Similarly, Ku Yün, who passed the civil service examination in the same year as Ch'i-wŏn, was apparently his friend and sent him a poem on the occasion of the latter's return to Korea.[39]

Ch'i-wŏn's mastery of the Late T'ang poetic style was probably a natural consequence of eighteen years spent in China as a young man, and of his creative activities within Late T'ang poetic circles. It would be most inappropriate to consider such a poetic style, created by a man with a unique career, as representative of ninth-century Korean shih. A period of seventy years, moreover, separates Wang Hsiao-lien's mission to Japan from Ch'oe Ch'i-wŏn's return to Korea: thus the latter's shih are not a satisfactory basis for evaluating early ninth-century Korean shih expression. Three other shih poets of the late Silla period, Ch'oe Sŭng-u, Pak In-bŏm, and Ch'oe Kwang-yu, have left a total of eight extant poems (*Taedong Sisŏn*, 1:7-9), but all three poets, like Ch'i-wŏn, studied in China and served

[39] *Samguk Sagi* (46:466). Ku Yün's shih are not included in either the *Ch'üan T'ang-shih* or the *Zentō Shiitsu*. His poem in the *Samguk Sagi* is the sole source of the information that Ch'i-wŏn came to China at the age of 12 and passed his examination at 18.

in the Chinese bureaucracy. Furthermore, all were late ninth-century figures (Ch'oe Sŭng-u went to China in 892), and so their compositions must
be judged as having little value as data for early ninth-century Korean
shih.

If Ch'oe Ch'i-wŏn's shih were included anonymously in a collection of
Late T'ang poems, they would be nearly impossible to distinguish from
native Chinese compositions. In this respect Ch'i-wŏn's work is clearly superior to ninth-century Japanese shih, and even Kūkai's compositions
seem slightly inferior by comparison. Ch'i-wŏn's shih, on the other hand,
are no match for Kūkai's in conceptual richness. The theme of "The Hollyhock" is a lament for ill-fated genius: the poet's gifts are like beautiful
flowers, but his origins have robbed him of any hope to achieve a distinguished career. "Stone Peak" is concerned with supermundane beauty:
the very essence of the immortals' tranquil sphere is to be found in the
mountains, far away from the transient world. Yet both poems are lacking
in a grand sorrow that transcends individual grief to embrace all humanity. Nor are they concerned with the majestic pursuit of a profound and
imponderable Truth from which everything in the universe is created.
Ch'i-wŏn rivals neither Tu Fu nor Kūkai in thematic weight. The Late
T'ang period was one of decline for the "old prose" (ku-wen) style pi-
oneered by Han Yü and Liu Tsung-yüan, whereas parallel prose was re-
vived by Li Shang-yin among others. So Ch'i-wŏn also gained a thorough
knowledge of parallel prose techniques. His prose style, however, has
none of the dignity that shapes a weighty and powerful theme into forceful
expression. My criticism is not directed solely at Ch'i-wŏn: the same can
be said of most ninth-century Japanese shih poets. I wish to emphasize
that Kūkai was an exception to this rule.

FROM PARALLEL TO PLAIN PROSE

The heyday of the Six Dynasties style in shih poetry is homologous to the
triumph of parallel prose in prose literature. Parallel prose had been written in Japan as early as the compilation of the *Kaifūsō*, and it continued
to be composed, in ever more refined forms, through the ninth century and
beyond. The introduction to Japan of works by Yüan Chen (779-831) and
Po Chü-i, shortly before 838, and the composition of plain prose (san-
wen) under their influence marked the arrival of a new and different age
that corresponds to the transition to the Middle T'ang style in shih poetry.
Parallel prose was nevertheless produced in great quantities after this period and did not enter into decline until the sixteenth century: thus the title
of this section signifies the transition from a period in which parallel prose
was the sole prose style to one of its coexistence with the newly predominant plain prose style. Moreover, the Japanese reception of the new prose

style via the works of Po Chü-i (Lo-t'ien) and Yüan Chen, and not through compositions by the two great founders of the plain prose style, Han Yü and Liu Tsung-yüan, corresponds to the Japanese disregard of the shih poets Li Po and Tu Fu.

The Achievement of Kūkai: Part Two

Parallel prose was the sole prose style in terms of belletristic composition occurring in formal circumstances. Of course it was not used in letters, miscellanies, or other works of a practical nature. These informal pieces, however, cannot be considered plain prose, since they are written in what might be called a quasi-parallel prose style based on four- and six-character lines. As a coordinate concept of parallel prose, plain prose differs somewhat from the modern Japanese and Western idea of prose. The plain prose form adheres to the following conditions: (1) it is not based on rhythmed lines, unlike parallel prose with its four- or six-character lines; (2) there is no accumulated parallelism within a piece; and (3) little importance is attached to the use of diction with precedents.

In other words, a prose style based on lines of four and six characters and employing a certain amount of parallelism cannot be plain prose. As it is defined above, plain prose did not exist in the last half of the Ancient Age: the only prose styles in use were parallel prose and quasi-parallel prose. It was not until the Middle Ages were quickening into being that plain prose began to make inroads. The corresponding period in the history of Japanese shih is that during which Po Chü-i's poetic expression was adopted and absorbed.

The golden age of Japanese parallel prose, prior to the incursion of plain prose, encompasses approximately a hundred-year period between the latter half of the eighth century and the first half of the ninth. Kūkai was probably the greatest prose writer of this time. The peerless nature of his work is the result of superhuman abilities, which are also clearly perceived in the phenomenal creativity he brought to Shingon doctrine.[40] If we are to seek its source on a plane better suited to linguistic expression, however, we must cite Kūkai's total command of spoken Chinese.[41] When

---

[40] Buddhist schools customarily base their authority on the sūtras that record the teachings of Śākyamuni, the founder of Buddhism. Kūkai, by contrast, sees the true Buddha as Essential Truth that cannot be grasped intellectually; he maintains that this Essential Truth can be grasped only through symbolic experience, since Śākyamuni, in his incarnation as Prince of Magadha, preached in a human language, and all human languages are too limited to express Essential Truth (Jūjūshin Ron, 10:294-98). An equivalent approach to Christianity would state that Jesus' words, as quoted in the New Testament Gospels, do not fully transmit Truth because they are spoken in a human language. This is a good illustration of Kūkai's creativity.

[41] Saichō (767-822), who journeyed to China in the same fleet of ships as Kūkai, was ac-

prose is written in a foreign language by an adept in that language, the flow of his thoughts will conform to sentence structure rhythms to produce exceedingly natural expression.[42] Kūkai represents one such adept.

Indications of the Goals of the Three Teachings, written in the Twelfth Month of 797 when Kūkai was twenty-four, predates his period of study in China, yet its style is already that of a man proficient in spoken Chinese. The *Indications* contain three protagonists, the Confucian Master Tortoise-Hair, the Taoist recluse Nothingness, and a Buddhist mendicant monk, Nullity, as well as secondary characters like Lord Hare's-Horn, young Lord Leech's-Tusk, and "a certain man."[43] The work progresses by means of a colloquy among these characters and consists of a discussion about the relative merits of Confucianism, Taoism, and Buddhism. The *Indications* includes such literary forms as the panegyric, shih, and fu, in addition to parallel prose. The plot is as follows. Master Tortoise-Hair visits the residence of Lord Hare's-Horn and lectures the latter's profligate nephew, Leech's-Tusk, on Confucianism. The young man, having listened to the Master's logical exposition, vows to mend his ways. Hereupon the recluse Nothingness, who has been silent up to now, declares that Tortoise-Hair's discourse is no more than a mundane theory in Taoist terms, and that it is far inferior to the Way of the immortals, which seeks eternal life. Tortoise-Hair, Leech's-Tusk, and Hare's-Horn all eventually endorse this view. Then the mendicant monk, Nullity, happens by; he asserts, in a speech interspersed with shih and fu, that Buddhist enlightenment holds an unquestionable superiority over Confucianism and Taoism. The others are deeply impressed and pledge total devotion. Despite the relative length of its text, the *Indications* displays an agreeable rhythm as it progresses. This is no patchwork of language culled from the Chinese classics: the entire narrative possesses a freedom suggestive of skillful conversation.

The intensity of Kūkai's style is not solely the result of fluency in a foreign language. Its source lies far more in the sure development of the work

---

companied by an interpreter, Gishin, whereas Kūkai traveled on his own. In a little over two months, moreover, Kūkai gained a mastery of esoteric Buddhism—which was for the most part orally transmitted—sufficient to be initiated into its highest level. He probably learned much of his Chinese from continental emigrants while still living in Japan. His master Hui-kuo commented that Kūkai "comprehended faultlessly and completely all I taught, whether in Chinese or Sanskrit, as if water were being poured from one jar into another" (*Kō Fuhō Den*, 44).

[42] For example, Nitobe Inazō (1862-1933), whose English prose style was highly praised by President Theodore Roosevelt and James Bryce (1838-1922), was also known as a brilliant conversationalist during his tenure as Assistant Secretary-General of the League of Nations (Ishigami, 1979, 50-52).

[43] The characters' fictitiousness is implied by their names: tortoise hair, hare's horns, and leech's tusks are all nonexistent entities; the Taoist's name, Nothingness (Hsü-wang), is related to the Taoist concept of wu, or nonbeing; and the mendicant's name, Nullity (Chia-ming), is connected to the Buddhist ideal of k'ung, emptiness.

according to a logical structure. The author gives clear expression to his intent through this development. The *Indications* is written in a dramatic mode, whose action progresses by means of the characters' conversation, a device that was seen long ago to derive from Ssu-ma Hsiang-ju's (179-17 B.C.) "Tzu-hsü Fu" ("Master Imaginary") and "Shang-lin Fu" ("The Imperial Park") (*WH*, 7-8 [Okada, 1929b, 132]). Of course, the *Selections of Refined Literature* contains other fu written in the dramatic mode, including "Hsi-tu Fu," "Tung-tu Fu," "Hsi-ching Fu," "Tung-ching Fu," "Shu-tu Fu," "Wu-tu Fu," "Wei-tu Fu," and "Ch'ang-yang Fu," and some of the diction they employ also appears in the *Indications*. Kūkai's sources need not therefore be confined to "Master Imaginary" and "The Imperial Park" (Kojima, 1965, 1446-51).

On the other hand, the dramatic mode and certain diction are the only characteristics shared by these fu and the *Indications*, and there are marked modal differences. Although the fu mentioned above are all framed in the dramatic mode, we would do well to note that the accumulative mode also functions prominently in these poems. The accumulative mode refers to the listing of great quantities of objects; the writer anticipates that the throng of objects so named will generate a sense of mass, and so create expressive intensity. Expression in the accumulative mode is an essential characteristic of the fu. Such listing of objects is not done to express a given idea but is in itself the raison d'être of the fu.[44] Yet Kūkai does not choose to express himself in the accumulative mode, a style intrinsic to the fu.

The *Indications* is divided into three chapters titled "Master Tortoise-Hair's Argument," "The Recluse Nothingness' Argument," and "The Mendicant Nullity's Argument." It is clear from the chapter titles that the *Indications* belongs to the genre of disputations (lun); thus Kūkai would not necessarily have needed to use the accumulative mode. This leads to the conclusion that Kūkai's dramatic mode may have been inspired not by fu like "Master Imaginary" and "The Imperial Park" but was instead modeled after two compositions included in Book 26 of the *Selections of Refined Literature*, "Fei-yu Hsien-sheng Lun" ("Master Nonexistence's Argument," by Tung-fang Shuo) and "Ssu-tzu Chiang-te Lun" ("Four Gentlemen's Disputation on Human Virtue," by Wang Pao). The former work is a dialogue between Master Nonexistence and the King of Wu, and the latter is a debate among four men, Professor Vague, Grand Master Falsity, Master Float, and Mr. Ghost. Both compositions resemble the *Indications* in that they are written in the dramatic mode and their speakers are all imaginary characters.[45] The latter in particular resembles the *Indi-*

---

[44] Yüan Mei (1716-97) and others have observed that the fu possesses characteristics akin to the miscellany, the glossary, and the lexicon (Suzuki Torao, 1936, 155).

[45] The names Nonexistence, Vague, and Float all suggest either unreality or uncertainty.

cations in magnitude of scale, but a closer comparison reveals that Kūkai's work is the more impressive in its clear connection of focused theme and logical structure. Kūkai states in the preface to the *Indications* that the expression of intent should be a writer's first consideration (*Sangō Shiiki* [=*SGSK*], 84):

> For any natural phenomenon or literary work there exists a cause. The sun, the moon, and the stars appear when the sky is clear. A man writes when moved. So the Eight Trigrams of Fu Hsi, the *Tao Te Ching, The Book of Songs, The Songs of the South*, were written down by men who were inspired from within. Of course, there can be no comparison between these sages of the past and a common man of the present such as I, yet somehow I feel compelled to express my innermost feelings.[46]

Note that this assertion, which might be termed expressivist, was made during the golden age of parallel prose, when a prose stylist's foremost aim was the creation of a beautifully crafted linguistic object. The *Indications* is contemporaneous with the first stirrings of expressivism in China, a movement led by Han Yü and Liu Tsung-yüan, of which Kūkai would naturally have been unaware.[47]

Kūkai, who proclaimed and gave form to expressivism during the same period as Han Yü and Liu Tsung-yüan, stressed not only the expression of intent but the meticulous planning and organization of the artistic structure as well, so that the writer's intention might be expressed most effectively. In the first volume, I remarked that Yamanoe Okura's "Yamai ni Shizumi Mizukara Kanashimu Fumi" (following *Man'yōshū* [=*MYS*], 5:894) reads like the work of a man with a knowledge of spoken Chinese. It is nonetheless rather tedious, despite the facile, careless style, because little heed is paid to its overall structure. The intricate structure of Kūkai's composition, by contrast, even extends to one of the fu in the *Indications*, "Transiency." Fu, regardless of length, are generically obliged to consist chiefly of expression in the accumulative mode. In "Transiency," however, an orderly structure is stressed at the expense of the accumulative

---

"Wen-hsüeh" ("Professor"), the title of a government post held by preceptors of Confucianism, is in this case an honorary title. "Ch'en-ch'iu" signifies an ancient grave; here it apparently indicates a dead person ("Mr. Ghost").

[46] [The translation, with minor changes, is by Hakeda, 1972, 101-102.—Trans.]

[47] Han Yü's preface to poems composed "In Farewell to Meng Tung-yeh" (*Ch'üan T'ang-wen* [=*CTW*], 555:7125-26), written in 800, contains these lines: "Poetry originates in thoughts that, being no longer endurable, are expressed as language. Because of thoughts, songs are sung; because of emotions, tears are shed. All that escapes the human mouth and is given voice results from turbulent thoughts" (Hua, 1959, 238). The preface postdates the compostion of the *Indications* by three years, and so Kūkai could not possibly have known of it.

mode, which is sacrificed because it is not adaptable to the structure (Ko-nishi, 1973, 5-6).

One can grasp the extent of Kūkai's involvement with the structural de-sign of the *Indications* by reviewing the process that introduces the monk Nullity into the narrative. Nullity has not yet appeared when the recluse Nothingness persuades Master Tortoise-Hair, Lord Hare's-Horn, and young Lord Leech's-Tusk of the superiority of Taoism. Before Nullity is introduced into this scene, the narrator gives a lengthy description of the monk's appearance and character and of his debate with "a certain man" on the subject of loyalty and filial piety (*SGSK*, 116-24). Later, while beg-ging for alms, Nullity happens upon the house of Lord Hare's-Horn, overhears the discussion, and joins the gathering. But the ensuing debate in the house of Lord Hare's-Horn is an event chronologically separate from the debate with "a certain man," which is presented, one might say, as a flashback.[48] Four characters also appear in Wang Pao's "Four Gentle-men's Disputation on Human Virtue," but there is only one scene, one temporal dimension. The story of Nullity, on the other hand, is composite in spanning two temporalities, so yielding the dramatic features.

Kūkai's style brings to fruition through parallel prose what was actual-ized by Han Yü and Liu Tsung-yüan in their plain prose. Kūkai should be valued for his creativity. His incorporation of dramatic elements into the disputation genre was unprecedented in contemporary China. None of this, however, means that I may regard the *Indications* as the equal of the Chinese literary masterworks: evidence exists that Kūkai, prior to his de-parture for China, used a composition process that involved transforming already-conceived Japanese expression into Chinese rather than compos-ing directly from conceptions made in the Chinese language.

A variant manuscript of the *Indications* survives in Kūkai's own hand; it is titled *Rōko Shiiki (Indications of the Goals for the Deaf and Blind)*, was also written in 797, and is in the collection of the temple Kongōbuji. Its style does not differ greatly from that of the *Indications*, but the text of *Rōko Shiiki* contains interlinear notations in Japanese. The Chinese words "Shih Feng" ("Stone Peak"), for example, have the Japanese nota-tion, "Ishitsuchi no take" ("Stonehammer Peak"), and "Yün-t'ung Niang" ("Miss Yün-t'ung") has written next to it, "Suminoe no unako otome" ("a fisherman's daughter from Suminoe").[49] Such notations are evidence that Kūkai conceived the work in Japanese, and the result is a

---

[48] If these works were to be dramatized, Wang Pao's "Four Gentlemen's Disputation" would fit easily into one scene, but at least two scenes would be necessary to give proper treatment to the character of Nullity. Since the revolving stage did not exist in Kūkai's day, he would have been obliged to make use of a raised and covered "inner stage" and a lower, open-air "outer stage" (see vol. one, ch. 2).

[49] "Kamei Kotsuji Ron" (*SGSK*, 119). Ishitsuchi Peak is located in Iyo Province (present Ehime Prefecture).

2. *Rōko Shiiki*, autograph manuscript of Kūkai, in the possession of the temple Kongōbuji

text that occasionally contains unnatural Chinese expression. The following speech by the monk Nullity is among them:

> ". . . in this present kṣaṇa,[50] I lead a wraithlike existence in the south of the land from which the sun rises,[51] in a valley with bonds to the Buddha, under the rule of the Cakravarti King.[52] There I dwell on an island where jeweled seagrasses bend, by a bay where camphor trees block the sun. I have yet to attain my heart's desire, though I have passed through twenty-four springs and autumns." (*SGSK*, 128-29)

This passage would probably have been incomprehensible to a Chinese intellectual. Even if the liberal application of Buddhist terminology were to pose no problem, still the use of the Sanskrit "kṣaṇa" to denote an instant in time is unduly eccentric. Neither would it have occurred to a Chinese intellectual that "an island where jeweled seagrasses bend" ("Sanuki" in

[50] [Kūkai here uses two Chinese characters phonetically to write a Sanskrit term, which signifies an extremely short time period, an instant.—Trans.]

[51] [Kūkai's interlineation here reads "Nihon," "Japan."—Trans.]

[52] An Indian deity; but here the ruler of Japan is meant. [Auth., Trans.]

Kūkai's *Rōko Shiiki* interlineation) and "a bay where camphor trees block the sun" ("Tado" in the interlineation) signify, respectively, the province of Sanuki and Byōbu Bay, both in Japan.[53] If the *Indications* had been disseminated in China, it would certainly not have been hailed as a masterpiece.

Kūkai's style becomes very nearly free of Japanese locutions following his journey to China and his contact there with native spoken Chinese. An important instance of this style is provided by the "Epitaph for His Eminence Hui-kuo," written by Kūkai in memory of his teacher, who died on the fifteenth of the Twelfth Month, 805.[54] Although newly arrived from Japan, Kūkai was chosen from among Hui-kuo's many disciples to compose the text of the epitaph: surely he owed this honor to Chinese esteem for his literary talents. The epitaph did not betray their expectations: Kūkai gives free rein to his thoughts and feeling to produce a text that is both abundantly backed by literary precedent and seemingly unaware of the rules of parallel prose.

Once again, the orderly structure of the text is particularly impressive. This structural beauty, which also appears in a nonliterary piece, *Jūjūshin Ron (The Ten Stages of the Development of Mind)*, may be termed one of Kūkai's major characteristics. In a somewhat later period, Yoshika wrote, in an evaluation of a thesis examination, that

> a writer, in expressing his thoughts and feelings, must maintain coherence throughout and determine the function of each part of the work. If the reasoning possesses no definite order, it will be impossible to commit thoughts to paper.[55]

Such opinions surfaced otherwise only after the arrival in Japan of the T'ang plain prose style. We have every reason, therefore, to appreciate Kūkai's extraordinary ability to actualize the logical beauty of a literary structure at a time when parallel prose was the sole prose vehicle.

His interest in structural beauty, which predates Han Yü's and Liu Tsung-yüan's plain prose attempts at expressive innovation, may have been inspired by k'e-wen, Buddhist structural analyses of the sūtras (Konishi, 1983b, 56-57). The Buddhist scriptures were written in the Pali,

---

[53] The former expression was probably inspired by the pillow word "tamamo karu" ("where they gather jeweled seagrass"), and the latter is a description of an actual geographical feature. The passage has been interpreted as follows: great camphor trees grow by Byōbu Bay, in Tado County, Sanuki Province, and under those trees is a hut where Kūkai played as a child (Katō, 1935, 112).

[54] The full title is "Epitaph of Upādhyāya Hui-kuo, Anointed Master of Esoteric Buddhism, National Teacher through Three Reigns, Late of the Ch'ing-lung Temple in the Capital of China" (SRS, 2:196-207).

[55] "Criticisms and Evaluations of Sugawara Michizane's Thesis" (*Toshi Bunshū*, 5:337). Yoshika employs this criterion in pronouncing the work of Michizane, the student under examination, "generally coherent." Michizane received a grade equivalent to B +.

Prakrit, and Sanskrit languages by Indians, an Aryan race. These languages, which are related to Greek and Latin, lend themselves to the precise expression of factual matters and logic and are also conducive to the conception of orderly written structures. Although the expressive precision disappears in the Chinese translations, the basic structure has survived. Chinese scholastic monks admired the logical structure of these works—a quality missing in their own classics—and realized that, unless this structure was correctly grasped, the scriptures would not be understood. The major Buddhist scriptures were therefore subjected to structural analysis. Most of the extant analyses are of Ming and later date, but structural analyses of any date are invaluable so long as their objective is the correct interpretation of Buddhist scripture. Kūkai, accustomed to thinking in this analytical mode, evidently developed in his own writing a structure that could itself be subject to k'e-wen.

Kūkai's writing is outstanding not only in its distinct structure but also in its moving and expressive tone. His lament on Hui-kuo's death is especially vivid, as this excerpt demonstrates:

> With heavy hearts we bury a jewel,
> With stricken souls we burn a magic herb.
> We close the doors of death forever:
> What use is there to cry to heaven?
> This wretched weed sobs aloud,
> Engulfed in flames, but not consumed.
> Clouds in the skies, dark and drear, seem to share our grief;
> Wind in the pines, soft and low, makes a woeful sound.
> Green bamboo at the garden's edge: their leaves remain unchanged;
> Pines and red oaks on the burial knoll: all are new transplants.
> The orb of day speeds round and round: keen is my bitterness,
> The radiance of night circles by: my anguish is renewed.
> Alas! This torment knows no bounds!
> How shall I bear such suffering?

The diction in these lines is based almost entirely on precedent, yet Kūkai's creativity nonetheless produces fresh expression. One example is the use of the phrase, "we burn a magic herb," to denote the act of cremation. The name of the plant that is being burned is implied by association: the first line of this couplet ends with the character for "jewel," "yü," which, when read in combination with the character for "magic herb," "chih," is a synonym for the term "ling-chih," the mushroom of the immortals.[56] Here

---

[56] "Mount Chung lies beyond Pei-hai, on land annexed by Pei-hai, 19,000 li to the north of the Jo-shui River. Its height is 13,000 li, the plateau is 7,000 li in diameter, and its circumference is 30,000 li. Here grow more than forty varieties of miraculous herbs, including the

Kūkai's grief is implied by the concept that even this auspicious, life-pro-longing plant—Hui-kuo, in other words—must burn. This in turn leads to another image, based on the practice of burning weeds in a funeral pyre: the speaker, who is only a poor weed and not a magic mushroom, would like to burn in the same fire as Hui-kuo; instead the flames of mutability within himself burn endlessly. The speaker remains alive, capable only of weeping. Thus Kūkai makes his sorrow felt through the tactile image of heat. This work, though written in parallel prose, is not merely a linguistic objet d'art.

The excellence of Kūkai's writing becomes still more obvious when compared with that of an approximate contemporary, Ch'oe Ch'i-wŏn. "A Manifesto to Huang Ch'ao," composed by Ch'i-wŏn in 881 while living in China, is known as one of his major works.[57] The rebel leader to whom the work is addressed is said to have been so surprised when he read it that he fell from his chair (Kim, 1973, 101). Yet I remain quite firmly in my chair no matter how many times I read it. Ch'i-wŏn's style lacks thematic force and merely exhibits a fiery tone. He contends in the "Manifesto" that Huang Ch'ao's rebellion, raised against the all-power-ful ruling dynasty, will inevitably end in its leader's execution; Huang is therefore urged to end his resistance and submit speedily to his ruler. Such a message must be framed in the most penetrating logic if it is to win the reader's acquiescence, but Ch'i-wŏn's "Manifesto" has no logical struc-ture.

As an example will show, the rigor and clarity of Kūkai's analysis-in-spired configurations are not present in Ch'i-wŏn's work:

> You, now!
> Embodiment of evil and strife,
> Your many wrongs fill us with woe.
> You live in peril, yet feel safe;
> You err and yet will not change.
> In other words,
> Swallows that build nests on tents
> Fly away without reason into the skies;
> Fish frolicking in a cauldron
> Know not they will soon be boiled.
> Now I
> Have devised brilliant tactics,

---

yü-chih mushroom" (*Shih-chou Chi*, 62). "Attain a great age and be covered with glory in the capital" (*Pan Lan-t'ai Chi*, 363, "A Song of Mushroom [Ling-chih] Consecration at the Ancestors' Festival").

[57] *Kewŏn P'ilgyŏng*, 11 (*Houn*, 139-42).

> Mustering a great host.
> Valiant commanders speed like clouds,
> With warriors numerous as drops of rain.
> Lofty flags and banners broad
> Wave in the wind at Ch'u Fortress;
> Warships and turreted battleships
> Dam the Wu River's course.

This passage consists entirely of accumulated diction that is intended to shock its reader. If Huang persists in ignoring reality and continues his resistance, the speaker threatens,

> My forces, that unarmed kill bears and slaughter leopards,
> Will bring you crashing with one blow.
> Your band of men, undisciplined as flocks of ravens,
> Will lose heart and flee.
> Battleaxes will reduce your flesh to suet,
> And chariot wheels will grind your bones into dust.
> Your wives and children will be killed,
> Your relatives all put to death.
> Think well on this! When peril burns into your bowels,
> Then grovel though you may, it will be done too late.

Even the fiery diction is superficial: there are no elements of reason that might elicit a fearful response from the reader.

Kūkai's literary style, on the other hand, is clearly superior both in a logical structure that ensures that the reader will view Kūkai's sentiments correctly and in a design that employs elaborate turns of phrase to give fresh impressions to the writer's intent. Ch'i-wŏn, in his capacity as ghostwriter, also composed a great many more mundane pieces, among them a "Letter Accompanying the Presentation of Gold and Silver Vessels," a "Circulating Congratulatory Message to Foreign Missions," a "Letter of Resignation," and "In Thanks for the Receipt of New Tea." Ch'i-wŏn's services were much in demand by the Chinese, and his creations, not surprisingly, are lucid and flowing examples of parallel prose. They are a worthy match for such works of Kūkai as "On Presenting the Crown Prince with Writing Brushes," "An Official Statement Drafted for the Ambassador and Sent to the Inspector of Fuchou," and "On Presenting Oranges to His Majesty." Ch'i-wŏn ranks among the best prose writers of the ninth century when his work is light in intent.

The above analysis has found both Kūkai's and Ch'i-wŏn's prose excellent in terms of literary significance; this judgment, however, does not take into account the matter of euphony. The definition of the Chinese plain prose style that was given earlier also serves, when reversed, as a definition of parallel prose. If one more point, concerning euphony, is added to the definition of parallel prose, the following four characteristics emerge: (1) parallel prose is based on four- and six-character lines; (2) parallelism is employed in key passages; (3) literary precedent is emphasized in the use of key diction; and (4) specified monosyllabic words that place line units in opposition are differentiated by their level or deflected tone. In concrete terms, point (4) is characterized as follows: (a) there is alternation of tone between the second and fourth characters (of a four-character line) or the second and sixth characters (of a six-character line); (b) if the two key characters in the first line of a couplet follow the pattern "level-deflected," then their counterparts in the second line must follow the pattern "deflected-level." These characteristics are illustrated below:[58]

Shih-*wei* chiu-YÜEH	Now it is the Ninth Month;
Hsü-SHU san-*ch'iu*	The season belongs to autumn.
Ho *t'ing* fu-CHU	Cranes by the strand, mallards on the shore:
Kuei-TIEN lan-*kung*	Olive and lily perfume the palace.
Lin TI-tzu chih ch'ang-*chou*	When the sovereign comes to grace the curving shores,
Te *t'ien*-jen chih chiu-KUAN	The scene appears just vacated by heavenly beings.

(c) When a couplet begins with a line whose first half tends toward the level tone and the second half of which tends toward the deflected, then the opposing line will follow a configuration that first tends toward a deflected tone and then moves into the level; the reverse is also true (Yoshikawa, 1949, 23-31):

P'i HSIU-T'A	Open a silken door,
FU *tiao-meng*	Gaze down on carved rooftiles . . .
Lin TI-TZU chih *ch'ang-chou*	When the sovereign comes to grace the curving shores,
TE *t'ien-jen* chih CHIU-KUAN	The scene appears just vacated by heavenly beings.
Ch'iung TAO-YÜ chih *ying hui*	I look out at an island chain that forms a circle:
CHI *kang-luan* chih T'I-SHIH	It indeed resembles line on line of hills.

---

[58] [As before, italics denote level-tone characters, and capitals denote deflected-tone characters.—Trans.]

These examples are drawn from a preface by Wang Po to poems "Composed on an Autumn Day in Hung-fu, at a Farewell Banquet atop T'eng-wang Tower." We therefore know that parallel prose regulations were observed as early as the beginning of the T'ang period. Neither Kūkai nor Ch'i-wŏn can be given high marks for conformance to the rules of parallel prose. A comparison of the two writers reveals that Ch'i-wŏn's rate of conformity is slightly better than Kūkai's. But Ch'i-wŏn lived in China approximately eighteen times as long as Kūkai and arrived there over fifty years after Kūkai: clearly Ch'i-wŏn should be given a stiff handicap in any contest with Kūkai on Chinese verse or prose compositions, especially where euphony is concerned. Wang Po composed his prose preface at the age of fourteen. The claim that Kūkai's prose is first-rate requires one exception—its euphonic deficiency.

The Liberation of Plain Prose from the Chinese Model

Kūkai's lack of concern for tonal regulations in parallel prose was part of a general Japanese tendency rather than a matter of individual doctrine or taste. Kūkai merely applied this attitude to his compositions, even during his stay in China. The many parallel prose compositions written during the eighth century also reveal a general disregard for tonal regulations (Kojima, 1973, 774-80, 831-32). This is not to say that exceptions did not exist (Kojima, 1968, 247), but Japanese parallel prose conforming to tonal regulations appears only in rare instances, occasioned by special circumstances. The more common practice, evidently, was to ignore tonal regulations. This was probably also the case in contemporary Korea, although no data from there survive except the works of Ch'oe Ch'i-wŏn. Moreover, in the first half of the ninth century, after Kūkai's time, public recognition was accorded parallel prose that hardly observed the tonal regulations at all. Parallel prose compositions by able writers of this period, Sugawara Kiyotomo (?770-842), Takamura, Yoshika, and Miyoshi Kiyoyuki (847-918), all fail to observe standard T'ang tonal regulations.

This casual approach to tonal regulations—that is, the rules outlined in the previous section—nevertheless does not mean that Japanese writers were totally indifferent to them. The authors of ninth-century Japanese parallel prose were careful at least to end their couplet lines with alternating tones. Kiyotomo follows this tonal pattern in the opening lines of his "Two Examination Questions":

$$1 \begin{cases} X \ L \ X \ D \\ X \ L \ X \ L \end{cases}$$

$$2 \begin{cases} \text{X D D X X L} \\ \text{X D D X X D} \end{cases}$$

$$3 \quad \text{X X} \quad \begin{cases} \text{X D X D / X L X D} \\ \text{X D X L / X D X D}^{59} \end{cases}$$

A T'ang Chinese reader, comparing Kiyotomo's tonal patterns with those outlined in the previous section, would necessarily have criticized them as incorrect. Yet the Japanese undoubtedly believed that they were conforming to the rules of parallel prose when they ended their couplet lines in alternating tones. Both lines of the final couplet above end in a deflected tone, but this may be an error: probably the last character in the second line, "sheng" ("nature," deflected tone) was written down in place of a homonym signifying "life" (level tone). Matching-tone end syllables occur again later in this passage, which suggests that there was at this time no fixed form requiring absolute observation of the end-tone rule. Kiyotomo wrote this passage when he was a junior functionary at the university, as part of two questions composed for a qualifying examination given in the Second Month of 801. The answers, written by Michimori Miyatsugu (dates unknown), are about three times the length of the questions, but they violate the principle of alternating end-tones in only three instances. Then as now, an examiner takes more liberties than the student under examination.

Similar instances appear in Takamura's prose. Having completed his *Ryō no Gige* (*Exposition of Administrative Law*, 833), Takamura drafted a preface to appear under the name of the Minister of the Right, Kiyowara Natsuno (782-837), who was acting as the nominal editor.[60] The preface was intended to be in proper parallel prose to give an air of authority to the book, which presented an official explanation of basic national laws. Most of the couplets in the preface observe the rule of alternating end-tones, although violations do occur.

Thirty-two years earlier, a student under examination had observed the rule of alternating end-tones in a couplet, but his examiner had paid little attention to the rule in framing the examination questions: we may therefore conclude that this rule, though probably followed until the end of the eighth century, apparently did not enjoy official recognition. Observation, in other words, was desirable but not mandatory. A student writing an examination essay would have been more secure and might indeed have

---

[59] Sugawara Kiyotomo, "Two Examination Questions" (*KK*, 20:177-78). The citation is from questions written on 26.II.801.

[60] Ono no Takamura, "*Ryō no Gige* no Jo" (*Honchō Monzui* [= *HM*], 8:182-83). Compiled and presented on 15.II.833.

earned a few points if he observed the form, optional though it was. Alternating end-tones gradually evolved into a fixed form in Yoshika's and
Kiyoyuki's compositions; and exceptions had all but disappeared by the
time of Michizane and Ki no Haseo (845-912). The necessity of observing
this form is also stated plainly in "Hitsu Daitai" ("Basics of Unrhymed
Verse"), an essay that probably predates the mid-eleventh century; it appears in *Sakumon Daitai (Basics of Composition)*, compiled by Nakami-
kado Munetada (1062-1141).[61]

This form was apparently authorized upon consulting certain T'ang
parallel prose pieces written in unorthodox tonal patterns. Proper tonal
patterns, those discussed in the preceding section, were employed in China
when a writer consciously wished to create exceptionally beautiful prose;
but this does not mean that all T'ang parallel prose strictly observed the
tonal regulations. The couplets in Li Po's preface to "A Spring Night's
Banquet in the Peach- and Plum-Blossom Garden," for example, present
the following tonal pattern:

$$1 \begin{cases} \text{X D X X D X X D} \\ \text{X L X X D X X D} \end{cases}$$

$$2 \begin{cases} \text{X L X X X X D} \\ \text{X D X X X X L} \end{cases}$$

$$3 \begin{cases} \text{X L D X X L} \\ \text{X L L X X D} \end{cases}$$

$$4 \begin{cases} \text{X D X D / X L X L} \\ \text{X L X L / X L X D} \end{cases}$$

$$5 \begin{cases} \text{X D X D} \\ \text{X L X L} \end{cases}$$

$$6 \begin{cases} \text{X L L X X L} \\ \text{X D L X X D}^{62} \end{cases}$$

Even if the only stricture is that end-tones alternate in a couplet, Li Po's
preface, with its two deflected end-tones in couplet 1, must be seen as
equivalent to Kiyotomo's parallel prose piece.

By contrast, Miyatsugu's examination essay more properly conforms to
T'ang tonal patterns than does Li Po's preface; consider these couplets
from the essay:

[61] *Sakumon Daitai* is a selection, made by Munetada, of already extant essays on Chinese
prose and poetry composition, plus later additions and revisions. Ozawa Masao has proposed that "Hitsu Daitai" was written prior to the mid-eleventh century (Ozawa, 1963, 58).

[62] This is intended only as an example; it does not mean that Li Po's prose was known in
Japan at this time. The text appears in *CTW*, 349:4473.

1 $\begin{cases} \text{X L X D / X D X L} \\ \text{X D X L / X D X D} \end{cases}$

2 $\begin{cases} \text{X L X D / X D X X X L} \\ \text{X D X L / X L X X X D} \end{cases}$

3 $\begin{cases} \text{X L X D / X D X X L} \\ \text{X D X L / X L X X D} \end{cases}$

4 $\begin{cases} \text{X L X D / X D X X L} \\ \text{X D X L / X L X X D} \end{cases}$

Such conformance is more reasonably ascribed to a knowledge of proper tonal patterns than to mere chance. Despite such knowledge, however, the Japanese found it extremely difficult to use the proper tonal patterns throughout a work. It seems that the Japanese came to regard the rule of alternating end-tones in a couplet as the sole requirement of parallel prose—on the grounds that the Chinese possessed abbreviated regulations like those applied in Li Po's preface—and that this practice gradually became fixed in the course of the ninth century.

Tonal patterns were originally a secondary factor in parallel prose. Cognizance of the four tones of Chinese evolved during the time of Shen Yüeh (441-513), but the four-tone system was not applied to shih composition until the time of Shen Ch'üan-ch'i (?656-714) and Sung Chih-wen (?656-712). The tonal patterns of parallel prose were evidently inaugurated during this period: Wang Po, a contemporary writer, seems to have responded immediately.[63] Parallel prose, however, was composed prior to Shen Yüeh's time. In other words, strict tonal patterns, the last of the four requisites of parallel prose outlined above, were made obligatory at some later date. Moreover, great importance was given to tonal patterns once they became a requisite. From the T'ang period on, tonal structure and order were indispensable aesthetic elements of parallel prose. Words occupying the same position within a couplet were mutually resonant in meaning while alternating in tone, and a couplet whose first half was in the carefree level tone and whose latter half was in a more restrained deflected tone was complemented by a couplet made up first of deflected tones and then of level tones. It was reasonable that tonal patterns would become vital to literature in Chinese, a monosyllabic language; but beauty based on tonal patterns was meaningless to the Japanese and Koreans, whose languages differed strikingly from Chinese in

[63] Shen Yüeh's parallel prose employs characters in a rough tonal pattern, but it bears no comparison with Wang Po's orderly standards. Hsü Ling (507-83) was an apparent forerunner in his concern for euphony in parallel prose, to judge from his preface to the *Yü-t'ai Hsin-yung*. Tonal patterns were fixed by Wang Po's time (Liu Ling-sheng, 1936, 70-75).

terms of tone. A Japanese or Korean might truly experience this beauty only by abandoning his own language and reading or hearing the work in Chinese. Unfamiliarity with spoken Chinese, in other words, rendered one incapable of experiencing tonal beauty. In composition as well, an ignorance of Chinese pronunciation, and the concomitant obligation to look up each character in a dictionary, would surely have ruined the quality of a Japanese or Korean shih poet's concept.

The seventeenth embassy to China, which left Japan in the Sixth Month of 838, returned in the Fourth through the Sixth Months of 840. This was the last Japanese embassy to the T'ang court. Various theories have sought to explain the discontinuance of the embassies. Saeki Arikiyo's may well be correct (Saeki, 1978, 184-85). He holds that the increasingly frequent arrival of continental merchant ships at Japanese ports enabled the Japanese to acquire East Asian goods and information through Koreans and Chinese traveling in a private capacity rather than through sending embassy flotillas to China—a dangerous enterprise requiring an enormous investment of public funds. Thus the Japanese state no longer felt obliged to overstrain its resources by sending embassies to China. But lively private trade with the continent would have had little effect on furthering the Chinese-speaking abilities of Japanese intellectuals. Once these proponents of culture no longer made the journey to China and came into contact with the living language, their shih and prose works inevitably lost their proximity to spoken Chinese. Ono no Takamura, designated vice-ambassador for the seventeenth mission to China, feigned illness immediately before departure and did not board ship. This led to his dismissal from office and exile to the island of Oki (*Shoku Nihon Goki* [= *SNGK*; 15.XII.838], 81).

Sir George Sansom observed that Takamura's refusal to board ship was not based on fear, despite the extreme hardship and danger of the sea passage to China. His action was rooted instead in doubts about the embassy itself, whether such enterprises were indeed necessary to the well-being of Japan. These doubts in turn were founded on the realization that the Japanese need not depend on China for their culture or interests. Takamura's realization, according to Sansom, stemmed from a desire to combine indigenous Japanese characteristics with foreign elements, thus creating a new culture; the invention of the kana syllabaries was one concrete manifestation of this spirit (Sansom, 1958, 129-30). This is a reasonable interpretation [although it is also said that Takamura was angered by the high-handedness of Fujiwara Tsunetsugu, leader of the embassy].

It was noted above that Takamura's draft of the formal prose preface to his *Exposition of Administrative Law* does not always adhere strictly to the Japanese parallel prose form, whose sole requirement is that the final words of a couplet not have the same tone. Takamura may have consid-

ered Chinese prose composed by a Japanese for other Japanese to be satisfactory as long as its meaning was elegantly expressed, and that undue
sensitivity to tonal patterns was unnecessary in such cases.

A similar attitude dominates modern Japan. Foreign languages are
taught not in order to train interpreters but to understand and adopt elements of a foreign culture. Thus a reading knowledge of foreign works
and documents is considered sufficient, and little concern is given to pronunciation. This view may be puzzling to Westerners, but it is strongly in-
grained among both the intelligentsia and the masses in Japan. Might not
its tenaciousness be due to its deep roots in the Japanese consciousness,
roots that were put down in the ninth century? Kiyotomo and Takamura
were apparently precursors of this trend. Takamura was not merely reluctant to go to China: more likely he reasoned that leaders of society like
himself needed only to read the many books imported from China by merchants and monks traveling privately, and that the arduous journey to
China was unnecessary. Such perceptions are at the heart of the *Exposition* preface.

A Japanese approaches Chinese prose composition in one of two ways.
The first is to endeavor to honor Chinese stylistic regulations—since, after
all, the medium is Chinese prose—but to simplify them, observing the
smallest possible number purely as a matter of form. An outstanding example of this stance is the Japanese practice of relegating tonal patterns in
parallel prose to the final word of each couplet line. This pro forma treatment contrasted with the actual, more complex Chinese approach. Forms
like the five-character-line quatrain or regulated verse in seven-character
lines were borrowed from Chinese poetry, and rhyme and tonal patterns
followed Chinese practice; but Japanese literature in Chinese was cut off
from its continental model in the spoken, tonal aspects of Chinese. This
applies to almost all extant Japanese shih, from the Middle Ages up to the
present day.[64]

The second approach to Chinese prose composition is to write without
regard to form, thus producing prose in the broad sense of the word. Such
prose, however, is to be differentiated from plain prose (prose in the narrow sense), the style inaugurated by Han Yü and Liu Tsung-yüan and
standing in opposition to the parallel prose style. When the free approach
leans too far toward Japanese perceptions, the result can be a style markedly removed from native Chinese, as exemplified by the *Midō Kampaku
Ki* of Fujiwara Michinaga (966-1027) and the *Meigetsuki* of Fujiwara
Teika (1162-1241). In such cases the prose has so many indigenous locutions that it can no longer be called Chinese. On the other hand, the *Nittō*

[64] There are exceptions—Japanese who composed shih in accordance with Chinese pronunciation: Zekkai Chūshin (1336-1405), Ogyū Sorai (1666-1728), and Yoshikawa Kōjirō
(1904-80) are among them.

Guhō Junrei Kōki (Record of a Pilgrimage to China in Search of the Dharma), written by the priest Ennin (794-864), is a noteworthy example of prose that would have passed as native composition in China despite its disregard of rules for parallel prose.

Unlike Takamura, Ennin eagerly accompanied the seventeenth embassy to China. He remained there, enduring various hardships, from the Seventh Month of 838 until the Ninth Month of 847, when he returned to Japan via a Korean ship belonging to Kim Jin of Silla. The documentary value of the *Pilgrimage*, a record of Ennin's experiences in China, has become widely recognized in the West through Edwin O. Reischauer's translation.[65] Ennin's style shows little concern for the rules of Chinese prose—perhaps because his work was not intended for Chinese readers—and yet it is not the prose style of a nonspeaker of Chinese. The occasional presence in Ennin's work of T'ang period colloquialisms is evidence that he learned Chinese by ear.

If, however, the *style* of the *Pilgrimage* were evaluated by Chinese intellectuals from every period of history, their frank and unanimous response would be "Unsatisfactory." Ennin's style lacks beauty. The plain prose written by Han and Liu is elegant, and only the nature of its beauty distinguishes it from parallel prose. The plain prose style was created on the assumption that a stratum of recipients already existed who expected to read elegant prose; thus the subject matter chosen for plain prose was appropriately aesthetic, though not suited to the parallel prose style. Ennin was not obliged to take such recipients into consideration, however, since his subject matter was wholly unsuited to elegant prose. He disregarded the precedents established both by parallel prose and by plain prose in the refined style of Han and Liu and expressed reality in a new kind of prose. Established criteria dictated that his work be judged vulgar and unsatisfactory, but Ennin never considered this a problem.

Familiarity with nineteenth-century realism may enable modern Japanese to find Ennin's unadorned descriptions of reality as vivid as when they were written and possessing far more intensity than the subtle parallel prose style. When the sixteenth embassy to China set sail from Tsukushi in the Seventh Month of 804, the ships encountered a storm once they were out to sea.

> We left our native shores behind; the voyage was half done when
> A sudden storm rent our sails,
> A violent wind broke the helm.
> Monstrous waves washed the skies,
> The tiny craft spun and whirled.

[65] [Reischauer, 1955.—Trans.]

South winds blew in the morning:
In dread we contemplated Tanra's wolfish appetites;[66]
North winds rose in the evening:
In dismay we mused on the Ryukyu's tigerish ways.[67]
Grimacing at the wild tempest,
We awaited burial by tortoise-maw;
Distressed by precipitous seas,
We prepared to dwell in a whale's belly.
We rose or plunged as the waves decreed,
Went south or north as the wind desired.
Azure hues of sea and sky were all that we beheld;
Were we never again to see white mists in mountain glens?
We had drifted on the waves by then for over two months' time:
Water ran short, the men were tired;
The sea went on, land remained distant.

This description of the rigors of the sea crossing appeared in an official document sent by the Japanese ambassador, Fujiwara Kadonomaro (755-818), to the inspector of Fuchou. When he read it, the inspector marveled that the Japanese should have such a master of parallel prose among them. The document was in fact written on the ambassador's behalf by a member of his party, Kūkai (*SRS*, 5:267).

The same official would probably have concluded that the Japanese were losing their prowess at prose composition if he had lived another thirty-five years and encountered the following passage:

Then the east wind blew furiously, and the billowing waves rose high and rough. The ship sped ever faster and ran aground; in alarm, we immediately took down the sails, but our helm was broken off twice. Waves struck from both east and west, and the ship listed; the rudder seemed about to sink to the bottom of the sea and the stern was ready to collapse. We therefore cut down the mast and neglected the helm. The ship drifted at the mercy of the waves. When they struck from the east, the ship listed to the west; when they struck from the west, it listed to the east. Waves swept the deck, but what they carried off I could not tell. Everyone on board placed himself in the buddhas' hands and made vows to the gods. We were thrown into confusion. All, from the ambassador and the captain to the meanest

---

[66] "Tanra" refers to the present Chaeju Island. Ship Four of the fourteenth mission to China, carrying Unakami Mikari (dates unknown) among others, was washed ashore on Tanra; the passengers and crew were captured by the natives and never reached China (*Shoku Nihongi* [= *SNG*], *Shintei Zōho Kokushi Taikei* ed. [= *SZKT*], [10.XI.778], 444).

[67] This may refer to the wreck of Ship Three of the tenth mission to China on the island of Yakushima (*SNG* [17.I.754], 219).

sailor, stripped and made fast their loincloths. Because the ship was about to break in two, people fled either to bow or stern, each man seeking a safe place. Great waves crashed against the gunwales, separating their joints and breaking them down; then men clung to ropes they had lashed to the port and starboard railings, and struggled to save themselves. Water filled the ship, which sank to the sandy bottom. The cargo, both official and private, floated or sank as the flooding decreed.

This is Ennin's description of how his ship ran aground when it encountered a storm near the mouth of the Yangtze River, and how the shipwrecked passengers found themselves in dire straits (*Nittō Guhō Junrei Kōki* [= *NGJK*], 1:84). Ennin's account gives us a vivid picture of this frantic scene. The Japanese craft, made by men as yet unskilled in shipbuilding, breaks in two at the center, and sea water pours in with tremendous force; meanwhile the ambassador and the ship's captain strip down to their loincloths like members of the crew and cling to lifelines so as not to be washed overboard.

Nonetheless the style of this passage would certainly not be praised in China, even by proponents of Han's and Liu's plain prose style, because it is written entirely in a vernacular language with no literary antecedents and lacks any true examples of parallelism. This is only one side of the situation; the other is the inability of modern Japanese to understand why Kūkai is a great prose stylist, since they themselves cannot instantaneously recall the wealth of literary allusions Kūkai evokes. Let us not judge who is the better writer, Kūkai or Ennin. Instead we might note that Ennin is able to move twentieth-century readers with his realistic descriptions, because he writes in a living Chinese language. Ennin was also skilled in formal literary styles: the many official documents he addressed to the Governor of Teng-chou and other functionaries between the First and Third Months of 840, for example, are all written in literary language and also follow precedent in their form and structure.[68] On the other hand, when Ennin describes his journeys, he adroitly incorporates the language spoken by minor officials and villagers. Ennin's style is primarily dedicated to intelligibility. His Chinese, varying in style according to the relative formality of the piece, differs in essence from that found in Okura's facile but crude work.

Further evaluation of Ennin's prose requires that we consult a supplementary source, a memorial presented to the throne by Ōtomo Tsuguto (dates unknown), secretary of the fourteenth embassy to China. Over the course of four days in the Eleventh Month of 778, as the returning embassy was nearing Japan, a storm wrecked Ships One and Two and cast

---

[68] There are nineteen documents in all (*NGJK*, 2:99-108).

their passengers adrift. On the sixth day of their ordeal, the survivors finally reached the island of Nishi Nakajima in the district of Amakusa, Higo Province. Tsuguto describes this period as follows (*Shoku Nihongi* [=*SNG*; 13.XI.778], 445).

> At about 8 P.M. on the eighth, the wind blew hard and the waves grew rough. The lower gunwales to port and starboard were destroyed and sea water filled the ship. Then the upper gunwales were washed away and both men and cargo set adrift, with not so much as a thimbleful of rice or drinking water left us. Thirty-eight of our men, including Ambassador Ono no Iwane, and twenty-five Chinese, including Ambassador Chao Pao-ying, sank all at once beneath the waves and could not save themselves. I alone made my way out and grasped the end of the bow railing. I looked about me and concluded that there was little hope of survival. Before dawn on the eleventh, a mast fell into the ship's hold, breaking it in two. Bow and stern floated their separate ways, going we knew not where. More than forty men were crowded into the ten-foot-square bow area. As it was about to sink, we threw the hawsers and steering equipment overboard, and thus remained afloat, though only barely. We stripped and discarded our clothing, and sat naked, lashed together with ropes. It had been six days since food or water had passed our lips.

The ship broke into bow and stern sections, each of which drifted until it reached Amakusa. The writer experienced greater distress than did Ennin, and yet Tsuguto's description is not as intense. This is a reflection of the different modes used in the two passages. Tsuguto's style tends largely toward expression in the expository mode: "not so much as a thimbleful of rice or drinking water left us," "thirty-eight of our men," "twenty-five Chinese," "sank all at once beneath the waves and could not save themselves," "I alone made my way out," "concluded that there was little hope of survival," "going we knew not where," "It had been six days since food or water had passed our lips." Ennin's piece, on the other hand, is very nearly always in the descriptive mode, with only two expository expressions, "We were thrown into confusion" and "struggled to save themselves."

From the Middle Ages on, numerous works like this appear: all make a strong impression through the exclusive use of direct and factual descriptive expression. Ennin's account is a precursor of these works. His expressive strength is clearly perceptible when his phrase, "stripped and made fast their loincloths," is compared with Tsuguto's description of a similar action: "We stripped and discarded our clothing and sat naked, lashed together with ropes." Further contrasts can be made between Tsuguto's prose, which is so limited in grammatical patterns that one may surmise a poor command of spoken Chinese, and Ennin's expressive capacity, which was sufficient to shape freely into Chinese whatever he wished to describe. Ennin, who established the Tendai form of esoteric Buddhism in opposition to Kūkai's Shingon version, possessed an exceptional capacity to express himself in Chinese. Ennin surpasses Kūkai in developing expression independent of the Chinese model, a fact that becomes clearer when the differences between parallel prose and plain prose are also considered.

CHAPTER 2

Transmission and Transformation of the Japanese Style

The formation of medieval Japanese literature is not characterized by si-multaneous progression within all its genres. Prose and poetry written in Chinese were the first genres to be characterized by Sinified conceptual foci and to undergo a transformation in expressive quality. It was natural that these genres, having always been expressed in Chinese, would sensi-tively reflect Sinified expression; yet this fact alone cannot justify our con-cluding that the ninth century forms part of the Middle Ages. Indigenous Yamato literature, composed in the Yamato tongue, had not, by the ninth century, been significantly altered by Sinified expression: the ancient ex-pressive forms had been for the most part retained. By the end of the cen-tury, however, Chinese literary expression came to permeate the concep-tual focus of indigenous works, and Japanese literature embarked on a new era, that of the Middle Ages.

WAKA EMERGES FROM THE SHADOWS

Early in 759, Ōtomo Yakamochi (?718-85) recited a waka at a New Year's banquet (*MYS*, 20:4516). After this time there is a sudden decline in data that might indicate how waka were composed, received, and trans-mitted. But in all likelihood the poetic style current in the late *Man'yōshū* period was essentially continued. Certain anonymous, untitled waka in the *Kokinshū* could be read as *Man'yōshū* poetry without seeming much out of place. For example:

Kasugano wa	Today, I beg of you,
Kyō wa na yaki so	Do not burn Kasuga Plain:
Wakakusa no	Tender as young grasses
Tsuma mo komoreri	Is my wife who is hidden there,
Ware mo komoreri.	And I am also hidden there.

(*KKS*, 1:17)

Kasugano no	Come and tell us, please,
Tobu hi no nomori	Guardian to the beacon fields
Idete miyo	Of Kasuga Plain,
Ima ikuka arite	How many more days are left
Wakana tsumiten.	Till we might gather in spring herbs?[1]

(*KKS*, 1:19)

These waka were composed in the first half of the ninth century, a fact deduced by comparing them to the following poem.

A waka composed by the Ninna Monarch prior to his accession, and sent with a gift of spring herbs.

Kimi ga tame	Just for you, my dear,
Haru no no ni idete	I went into the vernal fields
Wakana tsumu	To gather springtime herbs,
Wa ga koromode ni	And all the while the snow
Yuki wa furitsutsu.	Kept falling on my sleeves.

(*KKS*, 1:21)

The years prior to the accession of the "Ninna" Monarch (Kōkō Tennō) would correspond to the interval from 876 to 883, a time during which the *Kokinshū* style matured considerably; yet this poem is very much in the style of the *Man'yōshū*. It is not clear whether Kōkō composed in this style out of personal preference or, perhaps, from a sense that an old-fashioned poem was de rigueur in such circumstances. Whichever the case, the two anonymous poems can safely be seen as predating Kōkō's.

Waka was in decline, however, by the first half of the ninth century. The rise of prose and poetry in Chinese overwhelmed the waka, particularly during the period spanned by Saga's through Nimmyō's reigns (809-50). To the regret of Tsurayuki and his circle (*KKS*, Preface, 14), the status of waka dropped commensurately. Scholars frequently call this period the Dark Age of literature in Japanese. The decline of the waka was acknowledged by the ninth-century Japanese themselves. On the twenty-sixth day of the Third Month, 849, the senior priests of Kōfukuji presented Nimmyō Tennō with their congratulatory chōka on longevity. The *Shoku Nihon Goki* records it in its entirety and then states,

---

[1] Wakana, spring herbs, were gathered in early spring as symbols of the renewed vitality of the natural world. When eaten, spring herbs were believed to impart their vitality to the eater. [Auth., Trans.]

Waka originally reigned supreme in moving men's hearts, chiefly through metaphor and other expressive devices. As time went on the art of waka entered into decline and eventually fell quite into ruin. Yet even now the ancient literary arts survive to some extent in monastic circles. Just as the precept has it, when the practices of old are no longer understood, they are to be sought among the people. That is why these events are recorded here. (*SNGK*, 19:225)

In other words, waka composition declined as an activity. Tsurayuki and his circle emphasized that waka retreated from the formal scene, but the absence of outstanding waka poets was a more basic development.

Waka were not totally excluded from formal events. They were recited in formal circumstances when the need arose, a point that will be discussed subsequently. The real problem is the absence of even one prominent poet during this period, someone who would have created and cultivated a new waka style. Generally speaking, literature is valued only when it creates a new genre or expressive form. Even a literary work of decent quality will not be deemed worthy if it does not possess something new. Chance may account for the absence of creative waka poets after Yakamochi's time. Poets of the caliber of Ariwara Narihira (825-80) or Ono no Komachi (fl. ca. 833-57) are born (or not born) largely by chance. They certainly do not come into being only under logical and comprehensible conditions. On the other hand, roughly a century separates Yakamochi from Narihira, during which time not a single talented waka poet appears: this is too long a period to attribute to chance. No doubt the zenith of poetry and prose in Chinese must be seen as a major negative factor affecting waka. Princess Uchiko (807-47), for example, wrote only shih. Their quality suggests that, had she tried her hand at waka, she would have produced compositions greater than Komachi's. The princess's world, however, was quite unlike that of the tenth century and beyond. In those later times, women who openly studied prose and poetry in Chinese were criticized as unfeminine.

There is no basis whatsoever for concluding that waka disappeared from formal events from the end of the eighth century on through the ninth. Only six waka survive by Kammu Tennō (r. 781-806), but all were recited at formal banquets. One of the poems was composed under the following circumstances. Kammu recited an old waka in the course of a banquet held on the eleventh day of the Fourth Month, 795:

Inishie no	If we could repair
Nonaka furumichi	That ancient road through the fields,
Aratameba	Built so long ago,

Aratamaran ya	Would that we could repair it soon!—
Nonaka furumichi.	That ancient road through the fields.[2]

He then commanded Princess Myŏngsin of Paekche, the principal hand-maid, to compose a reply. As she was unable to do so, Kammu composed this in her place:

Kimi koso wa	It seems my lord himself
Wasuretaru rame	Has forgotten an old road
Nikitama no	That leads to a maid
Tawayame ware wa	Mild of heart and lithe of limb:
Tsune no shiratama.	To me, this ordinary pearl!

The assembled lords applauded the poem with cries of "Splendid!" (*Ruiju Kokushi* [= *RK*], 75:388). The ancient waka asks how the government ways of old can be reformed. Myŏngsin is made to respond that old ways tend to be forgotten: His Majesty, for instance, has forgotten his old way of esteeming her, a commonplace pearl. Kammu's wit is apparent when he transforms himself into a fictive speaker, but no oblique tendencies appear in the expression itself, which might be termed an extension of the *Man'yōshū* style.

Kammu recited another waka at a banquet given on the eleventh day of the Tenth Month, 797 (ibid.):

Kono goro no	For the last few days
Shigure no ame ni	Autumn rains have fallen on
Kiku no hana	My chrysanthemums:
Chiri zo shinu beki	All the blossoms will be ruined,
Atara sono ka o.	And—alas!—what of their scent?

This poem is clearly in the *Man'yōshū* style. A third waka, composed at a banquet held on the fourth day of the First Month, 801, is rather witty (*RK*, 32:206).

Ume no hana	So impatiently
Koitsutsu oreba	Do I await the plum blossoms
Furu yuki o	That when snowflakes fall,
Hana ka mo chiru to	I tend to mistake them for
Omoitsuru ka mo.	Petals scattering everywhere!

---

[2] Kammu intends the poem as an allegory: the "ancient road" is the old system of government he has inherited, and the "repair" is government reform. [Auth., Trans.]

Snow really was falling on that day, however, so the scene described was, so to speak, before the poet's eyes. This waka may also be seen as an extension of the *Man'yōshū* style, because intent of this kind appears occasionally in works from Yakamochi's time. Other of Kammu's waka are premised on the workings of the kotodama, and in general his waka hark back to the Ancient Age.

Heizei Tennō (r. 806-809) made a royal progress to the Shinzen Gardens on the twenty-first day of the Ninth Month, 807. He and his brother, the crown prince (later Saga Tennō), sang several waka, some in praise of the chrysanthemums, to koto [zither] accompaniment. Then the crown prince recited,

Miyahito no	Gentlemen of the court
Sono ka ni mezuru	Prize the purple-trousers plant
Fujibakama	For its lovely scent:
Kimi no ōmono	I have gathered these today
Taoritaru kyō.	From the gardens of my lord.[3]

Heizei responded with,

Oru hito no	He who plucks them has
Kokoro no mama ni	A heart that is very like
Fujibakama	Purple-trousers in bloom,
Ube iro fukaku	For indeed both do glow
Nioitarikeri.	With the deepest hue of all.

(*RK*, 31:171)

These, too, are in the *Man'yōshū* style.

The following year, 808, another progress was made to the Shinzen Gardens on the nineteenth day of the Ninth Month. A waka recited there at Heizei's command by Heguri Kazemaro (dates unknown) proved to have considerably witty intent (*Nihon Goki* [= *NGK*], 17:118).

Ika ni fuku	What must it be like,
Kaze ni areba ka	The wind that blows through here?—
Ōshima no	For it has bound together
Obana no sue o	The plumes of susuki grass
Fukimusubitaru.	Growing in the royal gardens.[4]

[3] [Fujibakama (Eupatorium stoechadosmum), a member of the chrysanthemum family with lavender flowers and fragrant leaves.—Trans.]
[4] [Miscanthus sinensis, an ornamental grass with feathery, fan-shaped plumes.—Trans.]

This so moved the monarch that, then and there, he promoted the poet to the junior fifth rank, upper grade. The surface intent is a simple statement on the wind: what sort of gale could have twisted together the susuki plumes in the royal garden? Behind this lies a second meaning: the speaker wonders at the extraordinary good fortune that has given him the honor of reciting a waka in this splendid garden. The image of susuki plumes tangled in the wind represents a symbolic use of nature: susuki plumes were probably bending in the wind in the Shinzen Gardens that day. Taken as a whole, the poem has allegorical interest; and the poet seems to have been widely applauded for his technique of using the word "kaze" (wind) to suggest his given name, Kazemaro. Yet even here, no significant level of obliqueness has been reached.

On the tenth day of the Fourth Month, 813, Saga Tennō made a progress to the southern lake of an estate belonging to the crown prince (later Junna Tennō, r. 823-33) and commanded that the literati gathered there compose shih. I have already quoted the shih composed by Saga on this occasion. Fujiwara Sonohito (756-818) offered the following waka.

Kyō no hi no	On this very day,
Ike no hotori ni	As we gather by the lake,
Hototogisu	Hototogisu sing,
Taira wa chiyo to	"A peaceful rule forevermore!"—
Naku wa kikitsu ya.	Did this reach our sovereign's ear?[5]

Saga replied,

Hototogisu	The hototogisu—
Naku koe kikeba	As I listened to its song,
Utanushi to	I heard this as well:
Tomo ni chiyo ni to	"May the poet's line sustain
Ware mo kikitari.	The sovereign's rule forevermore!"

(*RK*, 31:172)

The exchange is witty, but neither waka is oblique. Instead, both reflect a

[5] [The hototogisu is the gray-headed or Asian cuckoo, cuculus poliocephalus. It arrives in Japan in early summer. It does not lay eggs in other birds' nests but takes over their nests. Instead of a two-note song, "cuck-oo," it sustains its call to "teppenkaketaka" or "honzon-kaketaka." It has more than twenty other names in Japanese, and it is sometimes confused with the larger kakkō kankodori (cuculus canorus). It differs greatly from the Western cuckoo in associations. It is the bird that never ages or dies; the bird that is repeatedly reborn; the bird that travels between this and the nether world; or the bird into which the soul of the king of Szechuan was transformed. Since these characteristics are very different from the Western cuckoo and its cultural associations with cuckoldry, we have simply called the bird "hototogisu."—Ed.]

belief in the kotodama: here auspicious elements are given voice by the speaker and are carried to the recipient by the speaker's breath, in the expectation that the auspicious event voiced will indeed come to pass. These poems, too, are reminiscent of the Ancient Age.

These poems demonstrate that waka continued to be produced and appreciated in formal circumstances, but that does not mean they are first-rate waka. Generally speaking, they definitely demonstrate expression characteristic of the Ancient Age and possess few if any oblique properties. Informal waka of this period, on the other hand, begin to show signs of oblique expression.

> *On Returning from a Lady's House at Dawn.*
> *By the Kan'in Minister of the Left*

Itsu no ma ni	How long will it last,
Koishikaru ran	This yearning in my heart for you?
Karakoromo	It will last until
Nurenishi sode no	My tear-soaked Chinese sleeves are dry,
Hiru ma bakari no.	And that will use up this whole day.

(*Gosenshū* [= GSS], 11:730)

Fujiwara Fuyutsugu (774-826) was known as the Kan'in Minister of the Left. His poem is quite witty in intent. The speaker, who is happy at night when he is with his beloved, falls prey to unbearable longing when he must leave and return home. How long will he feel this way? As long as it takes to dry his sleeves, wet from tears shed at parting; and this drying period ("hiru ma") will take all day ("hiruma"). Assuming that Fuyutsugu was twenty when he composed this waka, its date of composition would be toward the end of the eighth century. This raises the question of whether such expression existed then. Fuyutsugu hardly ever displays wit in his formal shih (*RUSS*, 117-18), and yet the appearance of so eloquent a lover's plaint in his morning-after waka does not seem particularly unnatural.

Three other waka, none of them love poems, survive by Fuyutsugu (GSS, 16, 1182, 1401), but none contains oblique expression. How then might one consider the following waka?

> *Composed at the crown prince's Villa of Fine Arts,*
> *on seeing cherry blossoms scatter and borne away*
> *by the palace stream.*[6]
> *By Sugano Takayo*

[6] The residences of royalty were surrounded by mikawamizu, shallow, narrow, stone-lined channels filled with clear running water. [Auth., Trans.]

Eda yori mo	Our wishes were in vain,
Ada ni chirinishi	For they have scattered from the bough:
Hana nareba	Such are cherry blossoms—
Ochite mo mizu no	And, once fallen, they become
Awa to koso nare.	Foam coursing down a stream.[7]

(*KKS*, 2:81)

Although Takayo's dates present problems, he was very likely an early ninth-century figure.[8] His use of a rational conception in a formal waka has long been considered anachronistic, hence the traditional view that Takayo was active in the Engi era.[9]

Similar examples, albeit few, exist from this period.

Composed on Breaking Off a Spray of Plum Blossoms. By the Minister of the Left, Tō Sanjō

Uguisu no	The warbler, it is said,
Kasa ni nuu chō	Makes himself a broad-brimmed hat
Ume no hana	From the plum blossoms:
Orite kazasan	I shall take a spray and wear it
Oikakuru ya to.	In my cap—to hide my aged face!

(*KKS*, 1:36)

Minamoto Tokiwa (812-54) was known as the Minister of the Left Tō (from East) Sanjō. Plum blossoms may well be perceived as material for a warbler's hat, but they certainly cannot hide a man's face: here fabricated logic makes an early appearance in waka. I noted earlier that oblique expression appears in Ono no Takamura's waka. He also employs fabricated logic, as in this poem.

Composed on the Death of His Sister. By Takamura

Naku namida	May the tears I shed
Ame to furanan	Fall thick and fast as pouring rain!

---

[7] In other words, cherry blossoms are elusive and oblivious to human wishes, whether they are on the branch or fallen in a stream. [Auth., Trans.]

[8] Takayo was heretofore thought to have been active in the early tenth century. An entry in the *Nihon Goki* for 4.IX.815, however, mentions that "Sugano Takayo was appointed junior vice-minister of war" (*NGK*, 24:135), and so his dates should be moved back to the early ninth century (Murase, 1971, 16).

[9] The text of the *Kokinshū* included by Kitamura Kigin (1624-1705) in his commentary, *Hachidaishū Shō*, notes that Takayo is "a man of the Engi era [901-23]" (2:39); and Keichū (1640-1701), in his *Kokin Waka Yozaishō*, identifies the "crown prince" of this waka as

Watarikawa   For if its waters rise,
Mizu masarinaba   The River of Death cannot be crossed,
Kaerikuru ga ni.   And she will be restored to me.[10]

(*KKS*, 16:829)

The poem is strongly oblique in intent: the speaker hopes that his tears
will so swell the waters of the River of Death that his sister's soul, unable
to wade beyond, will return to life. It is not clear whether this lament was
composed under formal or informal circumstances.

Takamura's contemporary, Fujiwara Sekio (805-53), composed a similar waka:

Shimo no tate   It seems a fragile fabric,
Tsuyu no nuki koso   With warp of frost and weft of dew
Yowakarashi   This brocade of the mountains:
Yama no nishiki no   For no sooner is it woven
Oreba katsu chiru.   Than it comes undone again.

(*KKS*, 5:291)

The conceit of autumn leaves as brocade is oblique, but not very strongly
so. The intent of the poem, however, definitely represents fabricated logic:
frost and dew, both fragile substances, are the components of the brocade,
and so the completed fabric—the scene of autumn leaves—is equally fragile, unraveling just when the colors are most vivid.[11] Moreover, two of
four extant waka by Yoshimine Munesada (816-?890)—who later took
holy orders and is better known as Bishop Henjō—display oblique expression.

Spring

Hana no iro wa   Though the gods may wrap
Kasumi ni komete   The flowers' hues in folds of haze
Misezu to mo   To keep them from our sight,
Ka o dani nusume   Steal at least their scent for us,

Prince Yasuakira, a son of Daigo Tennō (3:88). The Umezawa manuscript (on which the
Iwanami Bunko edition is based) notes of this waka, "Composed in Enchō 1 [923] and incorporated soon after," but its source is unknown.

[10] Once a soul crossed the River of Death, there was no hope of its returning to the land of
the living; prior to crossing, though, a soul was believed capable of returning to its body.
[Auth., Trans.]

[11] It is a convention of waka that the condensation of dew and frost turns autumn leaves
their characteristic colors.

Haru no yamakaze.   O mountain zephyr of the spring!

(*KKS*, 2:91)

Composed upon Watching the Gosechi Dancers

Amatsukaze   O winds of Heaven,
Kumo no kayoiji   Blow shut the nimbus-portals
Fukitoji yo   To the celestial road,
Otome no sugata   That we might go on awhile
Shibashi todomen.   Gazing on these fair maidens.

(*KKS*, 17:872)

The personification of the spring breeze in the first poem does not represent obliqueness of any consequence, but the speaker does employ fabricated logic when he orders the breeze to "steal at least their scent for us." The same conceptual mode again appears when the speaker asks the wind to blow the clouds together so as to prevent the Gosechi dancers—here seen as celestial maidens—from traveling back to Heaven. Munesada gave further realization to his oblique expression after he had taken his vows and assumed his religious name. Thus the single figure of Bishop Henjō (Munesada) embodies the evolution of waka toward the *Kokinshū* style. As oblique concepts gradually entered waka styles, waka rose in status and outstanding waka poets appeared. Enveloped in shadows for the hundred years since Yakamochi's time, waka was now to emerge into the light.

Song Evolves into Court Music

Japanese shih were naturally rather sensitive to stylistic changes in Chinese poetry, and yet the Six Dynasties style remained current in Japan through the first half of the ninth century. It was only after this time that the T'ang style altered Japanese shih. Still more time was apparently necessary to familiarize waka, with its characteristic form and a rhythm based on syllabic meter, to Sinified concepts. If, by the second half of the ninth century, waka expression possessed a Sinified conceptual focus, it was indicative of the Six Dynasties style. There was evidently little conscious effort made to refine Japanese song expression into more musically captivating lyrics, and there was no evidence whatsoever of Japanese attempts to implement Sinified expression in their song. The transmission of many songs, moreover, took place in connection with ceremonies, and so importance was probably attached to preserving old expression. Ancient and even archaic expression is retained in tenth-century and later song

expression. The method of preservation may well have resembled fossili-
zation, but in any case ancient and archaic expression continued to be
transmitted within song up to the High Middle Ages.

This phenomenon may in part be due to the low social status of song
transmitters. In the Archaic Age, public entertainment, including various
theatrical diversions as well as singing, was carried out by the lowest social class, or by a class corresponding to such. The same was generally true
for China and Korea: gentlefolk did not participate directly in public entertainment. During the T'ang period, for instance, slaves served as court
musicians, usually being selected from among criminals and mutineers or
the survivors of defeated foreign armies and their families. If these groups
yielded too few candidates, peasants could also be levied for service
(Kishibe, 1960, 190-93). Where T'ang professional musicians (yüeh-hu)
were slaves, however, their Japanese eighth-century counterparts (who
were called by the same T'ang term, pronounced "gakuko" in Japanese)
were free (Ogi, 1977, 220-24). On the first day of the Second Month, 675,
Temmu Tennō (r. 673-86) issued an edict to thirteen provinces, including
Yamato and Kawachi, demanding that they send as tribute "common men
and women skilled in singing" (*Nihon Shoki, Temmuki*, 336). Thus levies
of "common men and women skilled in singing" occurred in the seventh
century, and the traditional low status for musicians remained even after
the Bureau of Court Music (Uta no Tsukasa) was established in the early
eighth century.[12] Even if the status of Japanese musicians was really higher
than that of their Chinese and Korean counterparts, the plebeian origin of
those skilled in the craft of musicianship might well account for a reluctance in Japanese to develop new styles of song. Only members of a social
class capable of contact with higher cultures could be expected to create
and develop new song styles through the adoption of a foreign conceptual
focus.

By the ninth century, however, foreign music was being performed by
the Japanese nobility. Saga Tennō headed the list as an accomplished performer of the flute, as also of the seven- and the thirteen-stringed zither
(koto) and the lute (biwa; *Sandai Jitsuroku* [= *SJ*], 15:237). Nimmyō
Tennō was also an adept of the flute and zither (*SNGK*, 20:238). Moreover, the royal family and high aristocracy—including Fujiwara Tsugu-
hiko (d. 828), Yoshimine Yasuyo, Crown Princes Abo (792-842) and Ka-
doi (800-50), Prince Michino (d. 855), Fujiwara Sadatoshi (807-60),
Minamoto Hiromu (812-63), Minamoto Tadasu (815-63), and Minamoto Makoto (810-68)—were apparently familiar with the practical as-

---

[12] The performance of foreign music—music from China, Paekche, Silla, and Koguryŏ—
was assigned to emigrants and naturalized citizens from the relevant countries (*SNG*,
11:126). These musicians had low social status.

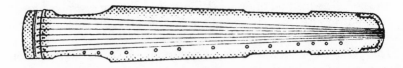

3. *Kin*, seven-stringed Chinese zither

pects of musical performance (Ogi, 1977, 195-97). This situation probably originated during Saga's through Nimmyō's reigns, when a rapidly
mounting admiration for Chinese culture arose among Japanese, together
with an increasing desire to devote themselves to the experience of anything Chinese, without adhering puritanically to their own native ideals.
The Japanese admiration of foreign music also led to an aristocratic concern for ancient native song. Yet the nobility seem not to have thought of
modernizing the ancient lyrics or composing new ones to fit the new metric regulations. Instead the songs were performed with the traditional lyrics, just as they had been transmitted. This evidently testifies to a perception that song was a genre that, by nature, should be sung just as it had
been received. The songs in the *Kinkafu (Songs for Zither Accompaniment)* are proof that seventh- and eighth-century lyrics were sung—albeit
with certain variants—in the ninth and later centuries.

How did song come to be perceived as a genre to be sung exactly as
transmitted? The reasons underlying the formation of this perception are
to be found, I believe, in the process leading up to the establishment of the
Bureau of Ancient Song (Ōutadokoro).[13] The Bureau of Court Music, inaugurated in 702, served as a training and performance center for both
foreign and Yamato music. In the latter group, however, only music transmitted from archaic times and fixed as part of important court functions—pieces like the Kume Dance, the Dance of Surrender,[14] and the Tsukushi Dance—were allotted a full administrative staff. And in later times,
the administrative staff of the foreign music section became larger than
that of the Yamato branch.

It was apparently at this juncture that the aristocracy, nostalgic for ancient Yamato song and dance, established an unofficial organization, separate from the Bureau of Court Music, for instruction in, and performance of, Yamato song and dance. This organization is presumably
mentioned in the *Man'yōshū* when it notes that "various princes and vas-

---

[13] [Ōuta (Ancient Song) is a song corpus transmitted from archaic times and performed at
yearly court functions.—Trans.]

[14] [Tatafushi no Mai, literally the Dance of Laying Down the Shields, is said to have been
first performed in celebration of Jingū Tennō's victories in Korea.—Trans.]

sals of the Bureau of Song and Dance [Utamaidokoro]" gathered in the Twelfth Month of 736 (*MYS*, 6:1011, forenote). The first documented appearance of the term "ōuta" (ancient song) occurs in 752 (*Tōdaiji Yōroku*, 2:42), but no Bureau of Ancient Song existed at that time. The "Bureau of Song and Dance" may have been in charge of Ancient Songs. The Bureau of Ancient Song was established as a governmental organ prior to the Eleventh Month of 781 (Hayashiya, 1960, 196-99). *Songs for Zither Accompaniment* is made up of one category of Ancient Song, obviously those that were performed to koto accompaniment. The process described above may have fostered the perception that such songs were to be recited exactly as they were transmitted.

The twenty-one pieces in the *Songs for Zither Accompaniment* include five that also appear in the *Chronicles* (the *Kojiki* and *Nihon Shoki*); we may thus conclude that the remaining *Zither Accompaniment* songs also date for the most part from the seventh or earlier centuries. The expressive form of the following songs, for example, demonstrates a correspondence to the more ancient of the *Chronicles* songs.

Amehito no	Once celestial folk
Tsukurishi ta no	Farmed these fields, but now
Ishida wa	They're rocky fields—
Inae	Damn 'em!
Ishida wa	When I plow
Onoo tsukureba	Those rocky fields,
Kawara to	They go a-clang,
Yura to naru	They go a-thud.
Ishida wa	Those rocky fields—
Inae	Damn 'em!
Ishida wa	Those rocky fields—
Inae.	Damn 'em!

(*Kinkafu* [= *KKF*], 7)

Soramitsu	Is the Land of Yamato,
Yamato no kuni wa	Seen against the sky,
Kamu kara ka	A perfect place to be
Ari ga hoshiki	Because it's true to the gods' ways?
Kuni kara ka	Is it a perfect place to dwell
Sumi ga hoshiki	Because it's true to the land's ways?
Ari ga hoshiki kuni wa	The land where I want to be is
Akitsushima Yamato.	The Dragonfly Islands, Yamato.

(*KKF*, 12)

Isu no kami	On Furu Mountain in
Furu no yama no	Isonokami
Kuma ga tsume mutsu	Bears have six claws,
Maro ka moshi	And I—oh my!
Ka ga tsume yatsu	Deer have eight hoofs,
Maro ka moshi	And I—oh my!
Mutsumashimi	I love him as much as that.[15]
Ware koso koko ni	There's the reason why
Idete ore	I have come here to
Sumizu.	The mountain spring.

(*KKF*, 17)

To be sure, these songs date from a time when frequent alterations were made in the course of transmission, and the extant texts cannot be regarded as identical to those that were originally composed; nor does the antiquity of their expressive form necessarily indicate a date of composition. On the other hand, these songs are more likely seventh-century or earlier transmissions rather than eighth-century compositions.

Others in the *Songs for Zither Accompaniment* demonstrate a relatively new form.

Atarashiki	As the year begins,
Toshi no hajime ni	Bright and new, then let us hold
Kaku shi koso	A pleasant banquet here,
Chitose o kanete	To offer wishes that our lord
Tanoshiki o heme.	May live for a millennium.

(*KKF*, 14)

The *Shoku Nihongi* (14:167) records that this song, with the last two lines reading "Tsukaematsurame / Yorozuyo made ni" (Faithfully to serve our lord / For a myriad generations), was recited at an official banquet on the sixteenth day of the First Month, 742.[16] The history further notes that the song was performed to koto accompaniment by members of the sixth and lower court ranks, thus confirming the fact that this is a kinka, a song accompanied by zither music. In this case it is more likely that the song is an eighth-century composition than a seventh-century song transmitted to a later age. In short, *Songs for Zither Accompaniment* enables us to surmise

[15] [I.e., excessively. The speaker's overflowing love is likened to the excessive number of bear claws and deer hoofs.—Trans.]

[16] The song also appears as a saibara (#27) and as a waka to the deity Ōnaobi (*KKS*, 20:1069). In both cases the lyrics have minor variants.

the state of seventh- and eighth-century songs as they were performed in the ninth century. We conclude that new expressive styles seem to have evolved only rarely in the sphere of song.

Japanese song may well be characterized by a resistance to the development of new styles. The nature of the courtiers, however, changed from year to year. Once members of the royal family and the upper aristocracy began to dabble in foreign music, a pastime originally forbidden them, ninth-century courtiers began to wish that they might hear the ancient Japanese songs performed in other than the traditional manner. Since song, however, originates in the zoku (popular) sphere, any attempt to develop new song expression must surely follow the dictates of the popular expressive taste. This was a difficult task for poets already exposed to the Sinified ideal of ga, polished beauty. Having mastered the art of ga expression, these poets would have resisted mightily the idea of changing to the unfamiliar zoku mode. Somewhat later, during the tenth and eleventh centuries, songs with zoku origins were rewritten to give them a sense of polished beauty. This new song genre, known as imayō ("new style"), was performed by tenth- and eleventh-century aristocrats. But such an attitude could not be expected of their ninth-century ancestors, firmly grounded as they were in the Sinified version of the ga aesthetic. Instead they contrived to make the melody and tempo of Japanese song conform to T'ang musical styles while retaining the traditional lyrics: the saibara song genre. The saibara might be said to represent the Japanese spirit combined with Chinese knowledge.

It is not clear when saibara were first sung: the most likely period is from the late eighth into the early ninth century. Princess Hiroi, who was over eighty at her death on the twenty-third day of the Tenth Month, 859, is recalled thus (SJ, 3:39):

> She was celebrated for her fine singing and was especially skilled in saibara. A great many aristocrats and their children, people with cosmopolitan tastes, came to study under her.

Common sense suggests that the princess learned to sing saibara before she reached old age. If we assume for the moment that she studied saibara between the ages of twenty and thirty, this would bring us to the beginning of the ninth century. Since this was a period of intensifying admiration for Chinese culture, saibara is surmised to have originated at approximately this time. This is not to say, of course, that the saibara texts we have today are identical to those composed in the early ninth century. These songs would have undergone various stages of revision, augmentation, and consolidation before becoming fixed, possibly in the Engi era (901-23; *Saibara* [=SBR], "Kaisetsu," 268-69).

The term "saibara" is thought to derive from "Saibaraku" ("Horse-riding Music"), the title of a T'ang-style piece composed in Japan.[17] This was evidently a folk song rearranged to conform to the melody and rhythm of T'ang music. Since, according to the theory, this was clearly the first attempt at such an amalgamation, all songs that were subsequently so adapted came to be called saibara.[18] "Saibaraku" is not the only case of correspondence to T'ang music: saibara scores are based on several other T'ang-style pieces as well (*SBR*, "Kaisetsu," 266-68). The Japanese admiration for Chinese culture clearly resulted in this attempt to sing traditional Japanese lyrics to T'ang-style melodies and tempi. That was not, however, the sole impetus: a more direct inspiration was provided by yüeh-fu (J. gafu), Chinese ballads.

The Japanese Bureau of Court Music is sometimes designated in written records by the name "Gakufu," the Sino-Japanese term for the Music Bureau of China (*Jimmu Zenki*, 119). The establishment of the Japanese bureau was probably inspired by the Chinese Music Bureau, but the functions performed by the latter—at least as concerns song—seem largely to have been performed by the Japanese Bureau of Ancient Song. The Music Bureau was established in the Former Han dynasty during the reign of Emperor Wu (r. 140-87 B.C.) and continued to operate actively through the Six Dynasties period and on into the T'ang, when it was abolished by Emperor Hsüan-tsung in the K'ai-yüan era (713-41). The ballads lost their musical characteristics after the Music Bureau was abolished, but they continued to enjoy a literary success as one of the shih forms. The ballad began to lose its preeminent position to the tz'u in the Late T'ang period.

A ballad is characterized by its fashioning of lyrics to fit a given tune. There are two general categories of ballad, the original and the imitation: the former refers to "popular folk song" by anonymous composers, and

---

[17] "Saibaraku," a piece in the Sōjō mode (corresponding roughly to the key of G minor), appears in the *Shinsen Gakufu* (*A New Selection of Music*; variant titles: *Hakuga Tekifu, Chōshūkyo Chikufu,* and *Chōchikufu*). The collection was compiled by Minamoto Hiromasa (d. 980) in 966 (Hayashi Kenzō, 1960, 89-91). The *New Selection* gives evidence that "Saibaraku," a T'ang-style piece, did exist and apparently formed the basis for the evolution of the saibara song genre (Usuda, 1938, 46-77).

[18] Doubts have surfaced about Usuda's theory, outlined in n. 17 (Hayashi Kenzō, 1959, 1-5). The reasoning behind these doubts focuses on the lack of accord between the rhythm of the T'ang-style piece "Saibaraku" and the basic rhythmic configuration of saibara. Saibara rhythms, however, did not achieve a fixed configuration until the early tenth century, about a century after the presumed emergence of saibara; Hayashi's reasoning is thus insufficient as a refutation. Another theory is posited on the many melodic and rhythmic features that saibara shares with Korean music: according to this view, the term "saibara" originated from a Japanese word for Korea, "Koma," which led by association to its homonym, signifying "pony" in Japanese. This in turn produced a composite term, "saibara," made up of "saiba" (horseriding) and "ra" (music; Yamanoi, 1966, 287-88). This theory has little to make it acceptable.

the latter to songs by literati and scholars "endeavoring to elaborate the expression" of the earlier group (Lo Ken-tse, 1931, 140-41). The imitations produced not only common motifs in the song lyrics but also, apparently, the composition of melodic motifs common to the original tunes. For example, "Ts'ai-lien Ch'ü" ("Gathering Caltrops"), originally a laborers' work song (sung particularly by those who earned their living on the water), was rearranged in the Wei dynasty. It then became a favorite song of courtiers, who performed it in formal attire while floating on a lake in dragon-prowed boats (Masuda Kiyohide, 1975, 85). Both the lyrics and the melody of the new piece retained the motifs of the original song. All subsequent ballads titled "Gathering Caltrops" would also be based on these motifs.

The Music Bureau not only provided the institutional inspiration for the Bureau of Court Music in Japan, it also served as a technical model for the instruction and performance of songs. The word "-buri" (style) that appears in connection with the *Kojiki* songs—"Hinaburi" (Country Style), for example, or "Amadaburi" (Two-Levels Style)—may have been modeled on the titles of such ballads as "Yen-ko *Hsing*," "Lo-fu *Hsing*," "Liang-fu *Yin*," "Pai-t'ou *Yin*," "Wu-ch'i *Ch'ü*," and "Yung-chou *Ch'ü*" (Kojima, 1951, 37-41).[19] If this is the case, then the fundamental technique of matching lyrics to already extant melody was very likely also inspired by Chinese ballads. Since, moreover, Japanese law stipulated that the training and performance of foreign songs was to be carried out by appointed resident aliens or naturalized citizens from the relevant countries (*SNG*, 11:126), musicians of Chinese origin could easily have taught the professional musicians at the Bureau of Court Music to match song lyrics with already extant tunes. In China, this technique involved applying Chinese lyrics to already extant Chinese melodies. The saibara, on the other hand, required that Japanese lyrics conform to foreign songs that differed from Japanese song in both tonic organization and musical scale; hence the difficulties were considerable. The conquest of these difficulties was probably accomplished during Saga's reign, a period of great eagerness to adopt as much Chinese culture as possible.

Saibara brought novelty of style solely on the musical plane, in terms of melody and rhythm. The texts were traditional, not new compositions. In most cases, then, saibara lyrics are far older than their melodies. The newest textual stratum is probably represented by one of the koto songs quoted above, "Atarashiki / Toshi no hajime ni" (As the year begins, /

[19] These song titles are mentioned as examples; they are not found in Kojima's work. Japan has only the "-furi" and "-uta" styles, by contrast with the far more numerous Chinese forms, including the "ko," "yüeh," "p'ien," "yin," and "yüan" styles. Kojima points out that the two groups nevertheless choose their terminology on the basis of common principles.

Bright and new . . .). This song evolved into a saibara titled "Atarashiki Toshi" ("As the Year Begins"; *SBR*, 27) and illustrates how saibara used traditional lyrics in a T'ang-style musical arrangement.

Another example is "Aoyagi" ("Green Willow Strands"):

(To the tune of "Ch'ang-sheng Yüeh"; 12 bars; 2 stanzas of 6 bars each.)

Aoyagi o	Green willow strands
Kataito ni yorite	One by one are twisted by—
Ya	Hey,
Oke ya	Hey now!
Uguisu no	By the warbler who—
Oke ya	Hey now!
Uguisu no	By the warbler who
Nuu to iu kasa wa	Makes himself a hat that is—
Oke ya	Hey now!
Ume no hanagasa	Is a plum-blossom hat.
Ya.	Hey!

(*SBR*, 9)

If the hayashikotoba (rhythm-marking lyrics) are omitted from this text, it takes the form of a waka; and since the conceit of plum blossoms serving as a warbler's hat is probably not a very ancient technique, the text of "Green Willow Strands" may originally have been a waka, possibly of ninth-century date, that was arranged into a saibara.[20]

Many song texts survive from earlier periods, however, including some thought to have been composed in the Nara period. The following saibara, "Sawadagawa" ("The Stream of Sawada"), for instance, sings of the Kuni Palace, residence of Shōmu Tennō (r. 724-49).

(13 bars; three stanzas, the first with 9 bars and the second and third sharing 4 bars.)[21]

Sawadagawa	The stream of Sawada
Sode tsuku bakari	Is so very shallow that—
Ya	Hey!

[20] The text appears in the *Kokinshū* (20:1081) as "an uta from the Bureau of Ancient Song." The notations that follow the title of the saibara indicate that "Green Willow Strands" conforms to the tune and tempo of "Chang-sheng Yüeh," and that the twelve bars of the song are divided equally into two stanzas, the first ending with "Uguisu no / Oke ya" and the second commencing with "Uguisu no / Nuu. . . ."

[21] The speaker is a woman; noblewomen's sleeves hung nearly to the ground. [Auth., Trans.]

Asakeredo	I barely wet my sleeves,
Hare	Ah!
Asakeredo	I barely wet my sleeves.

Kuni no miyabito	Still the Kuni gentlemen—
Ya	Hey!
Takahashi watasu	Have spanned it with a lofty bridge,
Aware	Oh my,
Soko yo shi ya	Very well indeed,
[or: Toto ya shi ya]	[or: Well it is indeed,]
Takahashi watasu.	They've spanned it with a lofty bridge.

(SBR, 2)

This song and others like it were evidently composed in the mid-eighth century.

Another saibara, "Natsuhiki" ("Summer Spinning"), provides an example of still more ancient expression.

(22 bars; two stanzas, the first with 9 bars, and the second with 13.)

Natsuhiki no	The summer spinning yielded
Shiraito	White silken thread enough
Nanahakari ari	To make seven skeins;
Sagoromo ni	These will I weave
Orite mo kisen	To make a fine robe for you,
Mashi	My love,
Me hanareyo	But you must leave your wife.

Katakuna ni	Woman, what you say
Mono iu omina kana	Is stuff and nonsense, nothing more!
Na	Eh,
Mashi	My love,
Asaginu mo	Do you think to make me
Waga me no gotoku	[or: Do you think to sew for me]
Tamoto yoku	A robe of finest linen,
Ki yoku	My love,
Kata yoku	With well-done hem
Kokubi yasura ni	Hanging straight,
Mashi	Shoulders smooth,
Kiseme ka mo	And collar tailored perfectly,
[or:	
Nuikiseme ka mo].	As my wife would do?

(SBR, 4)

This song employs a structure in the dramatic mode. The speaker of the first stanza is a woman who says she has spun seven skeins of white thread this summer, and then offers her companion to weave them into a robe for him if he will leave his wife. The man rejects her advances; he tells her she is talking nonsense and asks her if she thinks enough of herself to try making him a linen robe that is as comfortable in the shoulders and collar and as well cut in the hem as the robes his wife makes him.

Several groups of such amoebean waka appear in the *Man'yōshū* (3305-22); "Summer Spinning" is more in the folk song style than are they. It seems to have been arranged for saibara at a relatively late date, but the lyrics are in an ancient style.[22] "Kazuraki" (*SBR*, 34) is thought to have been arranged for saibara at much the same time as "Summer Spinning."

Kazuraki

(22 bars; three stanzas, the first with 6 bars, the second with 7, and the third with 9.)

Kazuraki no	Right in front of
Tera no mae naru ya	The temple of Kazuraki,
Toyora no tera no	Off to the west of
Nishi naru ya	Toyora Temple,
Enohai ni	Stands Hackberryleaf Well,
Shiratama shizuku ya	Where white jewels lie submerged,
Mashiratama shizuku ya	Pure white jewels submerged—
Ōshitodo	Ōshitodo,
Oshitodo	Oshitodo!
Shikashiteba	If this be true,
Kuni zo sakaen ya	The land will surely flourish,
Waiera zo	And my family too
Tomisen ya	Will indeed grow rich.
Ōshitodo	Ōshitodo,
Toshitondo	Toshitondo,
Ōshitondo	Ōshitondo,
Toshitondo.	Toshitondo!

These lyrics are nearly identical to the text of a wazauta (spell song) sung

---

[22] The music is identical, both in melody and tempo, to the prelude to the T'ang-style piece "Kainraku" ("Summer Spinning Music"). "Summer Spinning," however, is easily set to music, notwithstanding the usual problem of arranging the lyrics to correspond to bars. The lyrics probably predate the music for "Kainraku," which was composed expressly for them (Hayashi Kenzō, 1960, 100). "Kainraku" is attributed to Nimmyō Tennō.

prior to Kōnin Tennō's (r. 770-81) accession to the throne and subsequently recorded (SNG, 31:383). The song would thus have been current just before 770, but its saibara arrangement is probably of much later date.[23]

The character compound for "wazauta" can also be read "dōyō" (children's song), but the two words have very different meanings: wazauta are songs that originated spontaneously among the people, either to announce portents of auspicious or inauspicious events, or to satirize current affairs. Spontaneous though they were, wazauta were composed by individuals. A wazauta need not be a new composition: many were apparently adaptations or reworkings of already extant songs. "Kazuraki," as recorded in the Shoku Nihongi, is a folk song embodying the popular belief that good things will come to anyone who sees a white object lying at the bottom of a bubbling spring. As these examples demonstrate, saibara attained a polished beauty (ga) in its music but remained close to the popular (zoku) sphere in its lyrics.

The Bureau of Ancient Song was in a better position than the Bureau of Court Song to carry out functions characteristic of the Chinese Music Bureau, particularly as concerned ancient Japanese song. The number and variety of songs taught and performed at the Music Bureau in China became quite large, and the active repertoire fluctuated with each succeeding age. There was therefore no logical classification of songs in China. The systems most generally used followed the twelve categories outlined in the Sung period Yüeh-fu Shih-chi (Collected Ballads, ed. Kuo Mao-ch'ien), or the ten categories postulated by Lo Ken-tse in his revision of the Sung work (Lo, 1931, 24-25). The oldest and most venerated such category concerns songs recited at the Solstice Ceremony.[24] This corpus contains several subcategories of song: celebrations of the gods of heaven and earth, prayers to ancestral spirits, and supplications for bountiful grain harvests. The ceremonial procedures are equally varied. A characteristic example may be the songs performed at the Winter Solstice Festival during the Sui dynasty (Sui Shu, 15:360-62).[25] Primary emphasis is given to structure, and lyrics appear only in part.

[23] This song was apparently also sung during Shōmu's reign (Nihon Ryōiki [= NRK], 3:434). A New Selection of Music states that it is sung to the tune of "Kayōsei" ("Hackberryleaf Well"). "Kayōsei," a title meaningless in Chinese, may be a T'ang-style piece composed in Japan. Musical arrangements matching T'ang-style melodies and tempi with Japanese lyrics were evidently a later phenomenon occurring at a somewhat more mature stage.

[24] Chiao-miao, held outdoors at the summer and winter solstices. The emperor was the chief officiant. [Auth., Trans.]

[25] The music and lyrics were written in 601, during the Sui dynasty, by a large committee. The songs do not differ greatly from earlier versions. The Music Bureau reached its largest size during the Sui, when it administered approximately 30,000 musicians. Hence the Sui version has been chosen as the best. It also appears in Yüeh-fu Shih-chi (4:51-53), with a few textual variants.

To invoke the deities, "Chao-hsia" is sung to musical accompaniment.

> We perform solemn rites
> On this auspicious day:
> Marvelous dishes are prepared
> As we wait for the gods.
> Ceremonies all accomplished,
> Varied music is performed,
> So to move their august hearts
> To turn their thoughts toward earth. . . .
> All-pervasive bliss
> Extends everywhere.

As the emperor mounts the steps to the high altar, "Huang-hsia" is sung to musical accompaniment.

> Oh! Our august sovereign!
> His brilliant virtue fills the land:
> His guidance extends to the very borders,
> His influence reaches up to Heaven. . . .
> He formulates wise policy,
> And loves the people as himself.
> Therefore the state will long endure,
> Felicitous eras will be everlasting.

Hereupon "Teng-ko" is sung.

> The Emperor's virtue is grand and splendid;
> Many are the fruits of his benevolence.
> Now on the throne, His Majesty humbly
> And solemnly prays for his ancestors' rest. . . .[26]
> That the gods might hear his earnest plea,
> Recorders and priests relate his true deeds;
> Respectfully accepting divine revelation,
> We are favored with bountiful blessings.

As the Emperor makes the first offering of wine, "Ch'eng-hsia" is sung to musical accompaniment.

> As the celebration begins,
> We raise our voices to the august Spirits,
> Tendering them our greatest respect
> And proffering them the truest of hearts. . . .

---

[26] That is, that now departed emperors be allocated proper dwellings in Heaven. [Auth., Trans.]

The millet we offer is wholly clean,
The wine we present is exceedingly pure.
O ye great gods, look down upon this
And shower us with myriad blessings.

After the Emperor has made his offerings of wine and grain, civil officials perform a dance and sing,

Oh most august Emperor,
Recipient of the Heavenly Mandate:
Your governance is the very best,
Your civilizing words spread afar. . . .
Auspicious signs are manifested,
Order is established far and wide.
A sovereign's acts are regulated
Like frost in fall and rain in spring.

While the Emperor is drinking the celebratory wine, "Hsü-hsia" is sung to musical accompaniment.

Respectfully we attend our lord,
And in due time we offer repast:
Namely, wine both white and dark,
And choice grains, well prepared. . . .
The Ten Moralities are all observed;
Bliss by the hundredfold fills the land.
The imperial virtue grows ever greater
To form the base for a nation eternal.

Military officials perform a dance and sing,

He reigns in the most apposite of times,
As the manifestation of Trigram Ch'ien.[27]
Great is his prowess in crushing rebellion;
He governs in step with the laws of nature. . . .
Abundant indeed are the people's blessings:
Our sovereign embodies Peace itself!
May he be pleased to share with us
Life long as Heaven, eternal as Earth.

As the gods withdraw, a reprise of "Chao-hsia" is sung to musical accompaniment.

---

[27] Ch'ien, one of the eight basic Trigrams described in the *I Ching (Book of Changes)*, symbolizes such concepts as the Creative Principle, Heaven, Grandeur, Activity, and Government. [Auth., Trans.]

> Order rules the earth,
> And regulates our worship:
> Your divine chariots
> Have been well equipped
> To carry you through the skies.
> Your glory will linger:
> View our earnest hearts
> As sacrificial smoke. . . .
> Grant your people's hearts
> Everlasting blessings.

The structure is as follows: "Chao-hsia" is performed to invite the gods to descend to earth; "Huang-hsia" is performed as the emperor mounts the steps to the high altar; appropriate offertories are sung as the emperor presents offerings to the gods; the civil officials' dance is performed; the sovereign partakes of celebratory wine as "Hsü-hsia" is sung; the military officials' dance is performed; and finally, "Chao-hsia" (with different lyrics) is sung to honor departure. This structure, significantly, is basically identical to a kagura configuration. At its most complete stage, kagura presents the following structure (*Kagura* [= *KR*], "Kaisetsu," 260-63).[28]

I. Wand[29] (Invocation of the God)
   A. Traditional Wand Pieces ("Sakaki Bough," "Sacred Festoons," "The Staff," "Bamboo Grasses," "The Bow," "The Sword," "The Halberd," "The Ladle," "Vines")
   B. Invocations for Foreign Gods (Korean Gods)
II. Opening Songs (Entertainment of the God)
   A. Major Opening Songs ("Gentlemen of the Court," "Mulberry-bark Festoons," "Naniwa Bay," "Grebes," "Inano," "My Girl")
   B. Lesser Opening Songs ("Pillow of Sheaves," "Sedge by the Cottage," "Isora Point," "Rippling Waves," "Spreading Elms," "Trefoil Knots," "The Palace," "Minato Field," "Crickets")
   C. Auxiliary Opening Songs ("Rite of the Chiliad," "A Light Song")
III. Star (The God Departs)
   A. Songs of Farewell to the Deity ("Morning Star," "The Palace Lady," "Making Mulberry-bark Festoons," "Song to the Sun Goddess," "Song of Boiling Water," "The God Ascends")

---

[28] The structure is that of court kagura as it probably existed in the early tenth century (*KR*, "Kaisetsu," 259-60).

[29] [Torimono, the object that the lead dancer holds in his hand. The god to be invoked is believed to dwell, during his visitation, in the Wand, which can be any of the objects listed under "Traditional Wand Pieces."—Trans.]

B. Auxiliary Songs of Farewell to the Deity ("Asakura," "That Pony," "Music for the Hearth Hall," "The Brewing Hall Song")

This structure is indisputably identical to that of the Chinese Winter Solstice Festival program. Now, a ceremonial form that begins by inviting a deity to descend from the skies, continues with offerings of wine and the presentation of song and dance, and concludes with farewells to the departing deity, is probably of archaic date. On this ground, the idea of its being patterned on Chinese ballad forms seems superfluous. The preservation of the form (Invocation → Entertainment → Departure) within present-day provincial Shinto ceremonies enables us to acknowledge an archaic prototype. The problem, however, concerns a structural process: at some point, a large number of disparate songs were synthesized by means of an orderly classification system—such as that provided by the above list—and were converted for use in official court functions. Such a process cannot be considered to have developed naturally from archaic times. The Winter Solstice songs were definitely known to administrators in the Bureau of Ancient Song.

The most primitive kagura is "Achime no Waza" ("The Rite of Achime"). Its singers, divided into Left (Motokata) and Right (Suekata), exchange four rounds of meaningless, apparently incantatory lyrics. The first round is as follows:

LEFT: Achime!
           Oh, oh, oh, oh!
RIGHT: *Oke.*
           Achime!
           Oh, oh, oh, oh!
LEFT: *Oke.*
BOTH: Oh, oh, oh!
RIGHT: *Oke.*

This song shares certain features with the meaningless, incantatory-like utterances of primitive tribes treated in Volume One. The archaic kotodama survives, in this respect, in kagura.

With the exception of "The Rite of Achime," the oldest stratum of expressive song form probably appears in the Lesser Opening Songs (Kosaibari). "Sasanami" ("Rippling Waves") is one such example.[30]

LEFT:
Sasanami ya   Oh, the rippling waves

---

[30] Repeated lines and hayashikotoba are omitted.

Shiga no Karasaki	By Kara Cape in Shiga,
Ya	Oh!
Mishine tsuku	You pretty girl
Omina no yosa	A-hulling of your rice—
Saya	Yes indeed!
Sore mo gana	You're the one I want,
Kore mo gana	You're the one I need.
Itokose ni	Will you take me,
Ma	Well,
Itokose ni sen ya	Take me for your loving man?

RIGHT:

Ashiharada no	Oh,
Inatsukigani no	Can it be that you—
Ya	You rice-hulling crab from
Onore sae	A reed-choked paddy—
Yome o ezu tote ya	Cannot get a bride
Sasagete wa oroshi	Though you lift your claws and drop 'em,
Ya	Oh,
Oroshite wa sasage	And drop your claws and lift 'em,
Ya	Oh,
Kainage o suru ya.	And beg with outstretched arms?

(*KR*, 49-50)

The Left, singing the man's part, asks a beautiful woman hulling rice if she will have him for her loving husband. The Right, taking the part of the woman, replies by addressing a nearby crab: "Rice-hulling crab, you raise and lower your claws again and again, but even you can't find a bride!" A certain kind of crab, when on a beach, waves both its claws at once: "rice-hulling crab" probably refers to this type of crab. The female speaker compares the man's supplicating motions to a crab waving its claws and mocks him by asking if even one such as he would like a bride. When "Rippling Waves" was composed, entreaty seems to have been expressed through raising and lowering one's arms.

Similar mocking exchanges survive in great number in modern Japanese folk celebrations. Paradoxically, this convention enhances feelings of affection and intimacy through raillery. The Major Opening Songs (Ōsai-bari), on the other hand, are also rearranged from ancient song, and yet their form strongly reflects ga, polished beauty. This may account for the traditional division of Opening Songs into "Major" and "Lesser" categories. Certain of the Major Opening Songs, such as "Shinagadori" ("Grebes"), are reminiscent of folk song:

LEFT:

Shingadoru[31]	Grebes at their play,
Ya	Oh,
Ina no minato ni	By the mouth of Ina River,
Aiso	My yes,
Iru fune no	Where a ship draws nigh:
Kaji yoku makase	Helmsman, do your work well,
Fune katabuku na	And do not let the ship list,
Fune katabuku na.	And do not let the ship list!

RIGHT:

Wakakusa no	Tender as young grasses,
Ya	Oh,
Imo mo nosetari	Is the girl I have on board,
Aiso	My yes,
Ware mo noritari	And I too am on board,
Ya	Oh,
Fune katabuku na	So do not let the ship list,
Fune katabuku na.	Oh do not let the ship list!

(*KR*, 39)

The part taken by the Right is cast in the same conceptual mode as the waka "Kasugano wa" (*KKS*, 1:17), suggesting again that ancient folk melodies had common prototypes.

Another Major Opening Song, "Miyabito" ("Gentlemen of the Court"), is by contrast based on the waka form. The tendency of this song to favor the ga style over the folk song manner is characteristic of Major Opening Songs in general.

LEFT:

Miyabito no	Gentlemen of the court
Ōyosogoromo	Wear a simple robe that falls
Hiza tōshi	Far below the knee,

RIGHT:

Hiza tōshi	Far below the knee,
Ki no yoroshi mo yo	And is quite comfortable to wear,
Ōyosogoromo.	The gentlemen's simple robe.

(*KR*, 35)

[31] The original meaning of "shinagadoru" (a pillow-word for the place names Ina and Awa) is unknown and may represent a faulty transmission of "shinagadori," "little grebe."

The problem presented by this bias in favor of the ga style is one of expressive form and need not necessarily concern composition dates. The *Kogo Shūi* (comp. 807) contains what is acknowledged to be the original text of "Gentlemen of the Court."[32] Many eighth-century songs were thus undeniably arranged at some later date into kagura. "Yūshide" ("Mulberry-bark Festoons"; *KR*, 36) and "Naniwagata" ("Naniwa Bay"; *KR*, 37) also appear, in what are evidently their original forms, in *Songs for Zither Accompaniment (Kinkafu)*, and similar waka are to be found in the *Man'yōshū*. The kagura versions of the two pieces, then, were very likely arranged from eighth-century songs. "Naniwa Bay" probably represents the conversion, through oral transmission, of waka by Kurohito or Akahito into folk song.

One of the formative principles of kagura is that it follows a pattern of humble origins and upward mobility: kagura were originally folk songs that were later selected for refinement by courtiers. Prior to this process, however, an earlier phenomenon probably existed: compositions by *Man'yōshū* period poets were disseminated and transmitted orally among the common people to produce a pattern of lofty origin and downward mobility. The Wand songs probably belong to a newer stratum. Place names mentioned in such Wand pieces as "Tsurugi" ("The Sword") suggest an eighth-century composition date.

LEFT:

Shirogane no	At his side a sword
Menuki no tachi o	With ornate silver hilt-studs,
Sagehakite	He goes on promenade
Nara no miyako o	Through Nara, our capital:
Neru wa ta ga ko zo	Whose is this strolling lad?
Neru wa ta ga ko zo.	Whose is this strolling lad?

RIGHT:

Isonokami	Oh, if I could have
Furu ya otoko no	The sword worn by the lad from Furu
Tachi mo ga na	In Isonokami:
Kumi no o shidete	With its braided trappings trailing,
Miyaji kayowan	I'd traverse the avenues,
Miyaji kayowan.	I'd traverse the avenues.[33]

(*KR*, 21-22)

---

[32] The *Kogo Shūi* (200) also quotes a variant of this song.

[33] ["Miyaji" (here translated "avenues") signifies the major thoroughfares of the capital city.—Trans.]

The expressive form of several other kagura may indicate a ninth-century date. "Kazura" ("Vines") is one such song.

LEFT:

Wagimoko ga	My beloved,
Anashi no yama no	That you dwell in the Anashi hills,
Yamabito to	A mountain maid,
Hito mo shiru beku	Is something all should know:
Yamakazura se yo	Wear in your hair a wreath of vines,
Yamakazura se yo.	Wear in your hair a wreath of vines.

RIGHT:

Miyama ni wa	Hail must be falling
Arare furu rashi	Deep within the mountains, for
Toyama naru	On the nearby hills
Masaki no kazura	The vine-like spindle trees
Irozukinikeri	Have taken on their autumn hues,
Irozukinikeri.	Have taken on their autumn hues.[34]

(*KR*, 29-30)

The concepts of both stanzas are based on a reasoning process, however faint, and are cast in the ninth-century style.

The songs quoted above illustrate that kagura of both strata are alike in that their song styles predate the late ninth century, the apparent period of their arrangement. Another point of resemblance is the absence of Chinese poetic influence on kagura lyrics, despite the court-style musical arrangements to which they were set. Since the purpose of kagura is to effect contact of gods and mortals, the ancient Japanese kotodama played an active role in many songs, and this also necessitated preserving the old lyric styles. Some bizarre exceptions do exist. One of these is "Senzai no Hō" ("Rite of the Chiliad"), one of the songs that follows the Lesser Opening Songs. (Refrains are omitted.)

LEFT:

Senzai	Everlasting as
Senzai	A chiliad,

---

[34] ["Masaki" refers to the Euonymus (Spindle Tree) family of trees and shrubs, many of which have brilliant red fall foliage. Strictly speaking, a masaki is not a vine, though its characteristic spindly shape does suggest climbing vines. In an emotional episode of the *Izumi Shikibu Nikki* the prince breaks off bright spindle tree foliage for the lady. Such an association of plants with love is very old. It and the recurrent mountain imagery suggest the "reasoning process" the author speaks of.—Trans., Ed.]

Senzai ya	A chiliad!
Chitose no	Everlasting as
Senzai ya.	A thousand years!

RIGHT:

Manzai	Everlasting as
Manzai	Ten chiliads,
Manzai ya	Ten chiliads!
Yorozuyo no	Everlasting as
Manzai ya.	Ten thousand years!

(*KR*, 57)

"Senzai" and "manzai" are Chinese compounds, but Chinese vocabulary is not commonly used either in song or waka. I have attempted to interpret "Rite of the Chiliad" as the equivalent in significance of the T'ang non-melodic recitative (ten) (*KR*, forenote, 332). If "Rite of the Chiliad" is seen as an incantation composed of Chinese vocabulary—words that correspond to the Yamato language in "The Rite of Achime"—then neither piece can be considered song or waka, and my explanation becomes tentatively valid. But how then shall we interpret these lyrics from "Akaboshi" ("Morning Star"), a song bidding farewell to the god? (Refrains are omitted.)

Kichiri kichiri	Auspicious, auspicious,
Senzai yō	A chiliad of prosperity!
Hakishūtō	"I say unto the people,
Teisetsu shinchō	'Hearken at morning to the hymns
Seiseikei	I chant to purify your hearts.' "
Ya	Ah—
Akaboshi wa	The Morning Star,
Myōjō wa	Phosphoros—
Kuhaya	Well now!
Koko nari ya	There it is!
Nani shi kamo	But why, oh why
Koyoi no tsuki no	Does the nighttime moon
Tada koko ni masu ya	Graciously remain here,
Tada koko ni masu ya.	Graciously remain here?[35]

(*KR*, 70)

"Kichiri kichiri / Senzai yō" is thought to be a Chinese congratulatory for-

[35] The Morning Star (Venus) and the moon here symbolize the most eminent members of the kagura audience. [Auth., Trans.]

mula.[36] And the lines that follow, "Hakishūtō / Teisetsu shinchō / Seisei-kei," is the Morning Hymn from the Hokke Sembō, a Buddhist ceremony.[37]

Why was non-Yamato language incorporated into this song? Here again, my tentative explanation will be valid if we read the first part of "Morning Star" in the same way as "Rite of the Chiliad." In both cases the lyrics were not originally intended for song but were instead incantations in the Chinese style. Another feature of "Morning Star" cannot be overlooked: no sooner is the Yamato word "akaboshi" (morning star) uttered in the song proper than the sense of the word is repeated by the Chinese compound "myōjō" (Phosphoros). This may seem a small matter; yet the infiltration of non-Yamato vocabulary into kagura—a genre that ought to preserve the purest Yamato idiom—is a reflection, albeit faint, of the transition from the Ancient Age into the Middle Ages.

The function of the Bureau of Ancient Song, to transfer the properties of the Chinese ballad to Japanese song, is also manifested in the Bureau's teaching and performance of fuzoku songs.[38] Royal commands for court compilations of folk songs and dances from all parts of Japan date back to Temmu's reign, but systematic instruction in, and performance of, these pieces probably postdates the establishment of the Bureau of Ancient Song. Book 20 of the *Kokinshū* (*KKS*, 20:1069-1100) is made up of "Songs from the Bureau of Ancient Song," among which are the Azumauta (Songs from the Eastern Provinces), which originated to the east of the province of Ise. So it is evident that fuzoku songs were also administered by the Bureau of Ancient Song. Needless to say, fuzoku were not sung in the manner of provincial folk song but were probably arranged to accord with the court style. The lyrics, however, retain their original folk elements.

Fuzoku are never concerned with the many and varied phenomena occurring in society, differing greatly in this respect from Chinese ballads. A subcategory of Chinese ballad, the amoebean song (hsiang-ho ko), may correspond to fuzoku, although the two groups are very different in their respective abundance of subject matter. The amoebean or dialogue songs, like fuzoku, are based on folk melodies but are arranged in a court style. Regional Japanese songs were probably taught and performed by the staff

---

[36] The characters transliterated as "kichiri kichiri" have heretofore been read "kirikiri" and interpreted as an incantation in the Yamato tongue. Chinese sources, however, state that the words "chi-li chi-li" (J. "kichiri kichiri," lit. "felicity and fortune") were conventionally chanted at weddings (*Liang Shu*, "Chu-i Chuan"). Clearly, therefore, the phrase was used idiomatically in China to signify "auspicious, auspicious" (Miura, 1975, 42-43).

[37] [The *Hokke Sembō*, literally the Lotus Confession, includes readings from the *Lotus Sūtra* and a confession of transgressions.—Trans.]

[38] ["Fuzoku uta" is the author's clear pronunciation, based on various evidence. The main dictionary entries are usually under "fūzoku uta."—Ed.]

of the Bureau of Ancient Song out of a conviction that Japan should establish a song category corresponding to the Chinese amoebean songs, one of the vital components of the Chinese ballad corpus. Fuzoku nevertheless retained their ties to lyrical folk song, as "Koyorogi" demonstrates (*Fuzoku* [= FZ], 2).

Koyorogi no	At Koyorogi
Iso tachinarashi	There is a beach she always goes,
Iso narashi	A beach she always goes,
Na tsumu mezashi	This girl gathering seaweed.
Nurasu na	Don't get her wet,
Nurasu na	Don't get her wet!
Oki ni ore	Stay back in the offing,
Ore	Stay back,
Nami ya.	You waves!
Nuronuro mo	I may be dripping wet,
Kimi ga mesu beki	But I'll gather seaweed for you,
Mesu beki na o shi tsumi	Seaweed for your table:
Tsumitebaya.	I want to gather it!

These songs are not the least concerned with urban topics like those found in "Yen-ko Hsing" ("A Song of Love"), "T'ung-ch'üeh Chi" ("The Singing Girl at the T'ung-ch'üeh Terrace"), "Chih-chiu Kao-t'ang Shang" ("Banquet in the Great Hall"), "Che Yang-liu Hsing" ("Breaking Off a Willow Branch"),[39] "Ch'ang-an Yu Hsia-hsieh Hsing" ("In Ch'ang-an There Are Pleasure Quarters"), "Tung Hsi Men Hsing" ("The Eastern and the Western Gates"), or "Men Yu Chü-ma K'o Hsing" ("Before the Gates Are Carriages and Horsemen"). This is due to the reluctance of Japanese court literati to engage in song composition, and it contrasts sharply with the energetic composition of amoebean songs by renowned Chinese poets. The song genres under the control of the Bureau of Ancient Song share another characteristic in their disregard for a major ballad category, that of martial music (ku-ch'ui ch'ü). The considerations mentioned present the principal reasons why Japanese song retained traits from the Ancient Age over a relatively long period.

[39] Since the willow symbolizes amorous pursuits, this title suggests the winning of a beauty's love. This song, like "Yen-ko Hsing," is concerned with the pleasures of city life. Note that the Chinese songs deal in general with the delights of love, whereas waka approach love as an individual, actual event fraught with suffering and melancholy. [Auth., Trans.]

PART TWO

The Middle Ages:
The Age of Fūryū

CHAPTER 3

The Nature of the Middle Ages

As I noted in the General Introduction (vol. one), the Middle Ages are a period of transformation: the acceptance of Chinese culture fundamentally altered the Japanese expressive consciousness toward their principal genres. The Middle Ages are divided here into Early, High, and Late, in accordance with the nature of the received Chinese culture. The central idea of each period, respectively, is fūryū (Ch. feng-liu), the elegance characteristic of the Six Dynasties period; michi (Ch. tao), or artistic vocation, a T'ang ideal; and jōri (Ch. ch'ing-li), the Sung period conflict between reason and feeling. Before these periods are considered individually, I would like to look at the Middle Ages as a whole so as to determine which aspects of Chinese culture contributed to their formation.

COMPOSER AND AUDIENCE: CRITICAL CONSCIOUSNESS BASED ON A SHARED CIRCLE

The Middle Ages—which commence in the latter half of the ninth century and end in the first half of the nineteenth—possess two principal genres, waka and monogatari (narrative fiction). Renga (linked poetry) and nō may be added to these genres with the advent of the High Middle Ages; and haikai (unconventional poetry), ukiyozōshi (stories of middling classes), and jōruri (Edo-period urban theatre) with the Late Middle Ages. Being tantamount to commonplaces, these observations are unlikely to elicit any disagreement. I should nevertheless note that the word "principal" here signifies those genres made remarkable by having reached their zeniths. It is *not* meant to imply that the acceptance given a genre by society was commensurately warm.

If the generic succession represented by waka, renga, and haikai is compared with that by monogatari, nō, ukiyozōshi, and jōruri, the two groups will display a clearly perceptible difference in their social acceptance. The works in the former group are accompanied by their composers' names— "Ariwara Motokata," for example, or "the work of Gosaga In," or "Bashō"—whereas the names of composers do not appear in the latter group. A passage in the *Murasaki Shikibu Nikki* depicts Fujiwara Kintō (966-1041) peeping into space occupied by the author and saying, "I do beg your pardon, but is little Murasaki about?"[1] It was common knowledge at the time, as this passage reveals, that Murasaki Shikibu (?978-?1031) was writing *The Tale of Genji*; yet the author's name is not recorded at either the beginning or the end of any surviving *Genji* text. Ukiyozōshi present a somewhat different situation. Rakugetsuan Saigin, in his postscript to *Kōshoku Ichidai Otoko (One Man Who Devoted His Life to Love)* attests that the work was written by "Master Saikaku"; similarly, the author signs himself "Saikaku" in the preface to *Seken Munezan'yo (Worldly Reckonings)*. Prefaces and postscripts, however, are explanatory pieces prepared at the time of publication, and writing them is not the same as putting one's name at the beginning of a work to declare it as one's own composition. Thus *Kōshoku Gonin Onna (Five Women Who Devoted Their Lives to Love)* and *Nippon Eitaikura (The Japanese Family Storehouse)*, neither of which has a preface or postscript, provide no textual information concerning their author's identity.

The practice of publishing a work in an anonymous format manifests a perception of that work as one not worthy of a recorded author and acknowledges the work as belonging to a very lowly genre of literature. Within the highly valued genre, compositions may record the composer's name—for example, " 'A Memorial to the Throne Requesting Extraordinary Funding for Four Ascetic Monks,' by Ōe no Asatsuna."[2] Or the author's name or sobriquet may be incorporated in the title of the work, as in *Kanke Bunsō (The Writings of Lord Sugawara* [Michizane]) or *Hosshōji Kampaku Goshū (The Waka Collection of the Hosshōji Chancellor* [Fujiwara Tadamichi, 1097-1164]).

Matters are rather more complicated in the case of nō. This theatre possessed a low social status in the fifteenth century, and so the texts of plays copied by Kanze Motokiyo Zeami (1363-1443) do not bear the playwrights' names. Several kinds of "sakusha zuke," notations identifying the writer of a given play, were produced in the sixteenth century, but the playwright's name was not given in the nō text itself. In the eighteenth century, however, the head of the Kanze school of nō presented the Bakufu with a list enumerating the writer of each play. And Motoakira, the fifteenth Kanze head, compiled a "List of Two Hundred and Ten Plays" ("Nihyakujūban Utai Mokuroku") that gave the playwright's name for every nō collected in the Meiwa (1764-72) revised edition of nō texts (Nose, 1938, 1347-48).[3] As the acknowledged formal entertainment of

[1] *Murasaki Shikibu Nikki* [= MSN], 470.

[2] *HM*, 120. The author's name is also given at the end of the text: "Submitted by Consultant Ōe no Asatsuna, Senior Fourth Rank, Lower Grade."

[3] The earliest date recorded in extant lists is 1721, but the content is identical regardless of the year (Nose, 1938, 1347). The first list may have been made at the end of the seventeenth century.

samurai families, nō rose in status during the Edo period, and this rise may have obliged the Kanze head to designate a playwright's name for each play. The poet's name is also customarily given in the case of haikai composition; this practice may reflect a point in its history, during the life of Matsunaga Teitoku (1571-1653), when haikai began to be treated on a level with renga. The oldest extant collection of haikai, *Chikuba Kyōginshū*, has a preface dated 1499: the contributors' names are not given.[4] The same is true for the next oldest collection, *Haikai Rengashō* (commonly known as *Inu Tsukuba Shū*).[5]

One can only conclude from these examples that the medieval Japanese differentiated between worthy genres and unworthy ones. Or, if that is too overstated, Kuwabara Takeo's well-known terminology might be employed instead, and the conclusion rephrased: waka, renga, and haikai were perceived as premier arts, while monogatari, ukiyozōshi, and jōruri were secondary arts.[6] The distinction was made in other arts besides literature: calligraphy, gagaku (court music), and painting were evidently premier arts. Their status, however, depended on certain stipulations. They were considered to be premier arts because they could be mastered by courtiers busy with affairs of state, scholastic monks dedicated to study and prayer, and high-ranking intellectuals. Mastery of these arts did not demand great effort at the expense of official duties. Arts requiring technical training by professionals, on the other hand, were perceived as secondary, if they were thought of as art at all. Unkei (d. 1223) and Tankei (1173-1256) were indeed famed as masters of their craft, but sculpture was never acknowledged as a premier art. Similarly, Meikū (mid-thirteenth–early fourteenth centuries) and Ryūdatsu (d. 1611) enjoyed much social success, but that did not mean their sōga ("fast-songs," light in tone) and kouta (miscellaneous songs) were considered premier arts. In other words, premier arts were the sphere of the amateur, and the professional arts were given secondary or even lower status.

An amateur could not become a creator of expression—a writer or performer—in the professional arts. He was thus obliged to appreciate the professional arts solely from the standpoint of recipient. The creators of expression formed one circle, and the recipients another. Contact took place, in special circumstances, between the creators' circle and the recipients' circle, but in general the two circles were mutually isolated. This was the situation for medieval secondary arts. By contrast, professionals were excluded from creative expression in the premier arts, a sphere made up

[4] The original manuscript is in the Tenri Library collection. Kimura Miyogo's edition of *Chikuba Kyōginshū* includes photographic reproductions, a transcription of the text, and a variorum section.

[5] Fukui, 1948.

[6] Kuwabara Takeo, 1946, 55, 63.

exclusively of amateurs. Creators could also participate as recipients in this sphere, and recipients became creators. At a moment's notice, then, a waka recipient could become a poet: this is exemplified by the utaawase (waka matches). Since participants in renga and haikai gatherings have always carried out simultaneous composition and reception, their composers are not easily distinguished from recipients.

Moreover, when nō was elevated to a premier art in the Late Middle Ages, the military aristocracy stopped being mere recipients. Instead they began studying recitation and dance and put on amateur performances. Nō consequently has now become an art that cannot be fully appreciated without preliminary training in its recitation, dance, and performance. On the other hand, the composer is distinguished from the recipient in monogatari and its successors, the ukiyozōshi and ninjōbon (sentimental fiction), and so these genres were deemed secondary arts. This was not connected to a composer's social status. Murasaki Shikibu appears by name as a waka poet in the *Goshūishū*, but that did not make her *Tale of Genji* a premier work of art. The monogatari competition—in which any court member could compose a monogatari and present it to the assembled company for evaluation—did not exist in Murasaki Shikibu's day, and monogatari were therefore given secondary status. In 1055 the Kamo High Priestess of Rokujō held a gathering that, although called a "monogatari competition," was in fact a match between poets of waka culled from various monogatari. It was not a competition involving the monogatari themselves.[7] Here again, the writers of monogatari were perceived as either professionals or their equivalent.

To my mind, the perception of the premier arts as being essentially based on a circle shared by composer and recipient is definitely not an indigenous Yamato idea but rather a Chinese accretion. The premier arts of China were the shih, fu, and formal prose genres; and dabbling in calligraphy or the zither was considered an equally worthy activity. Prose fiction (hsiao-shuo; J. shōsetsu) and comic drama (tsa-chü), on the other hand, were treated as secondary arts at best. Virtuosity in shih, fu, and parallel prose composition was a means of enhancing one's worth in China, and so, not surprisingly, these literary forms figured in the Chinese civil service examination for nearly a millennium. The opposite was true for prose fiction and comic drama, which lowered the worth of anyone who so much as read or heard them, much less composed them. Chang Cho (?660-?740) certainly did not write "Yu Hsien-k'u" ("The Visit to the Immortals' Dwelling") to enhance his literary fame: he probably

---

[7] *Utaawase Shū* [= *UAS*], 171-74. It is called a "monogatari competition" in the *Eiga Monogatari* ("Keburi no Ato") and in the *Goshūishū* (15:876). Evidently the reciter of a given waka was also the author of the monogatari from which it was taken (Horibe, 1943, 259).

wished to wallow in self-recrimination by deliberately writing in a socially disparaged genre.

The dearth of commentaries in China on prose fiction and comic drama also reveals that these genres were not recognized as premier arts. Works having an acknowledged value were customarily accompanied by commentaries in China. If a commentary came to be regarded as valuable in itself, commentaries on the commentary (shu) were then composed for further elucidation. A work that had both primary commentaries and shu was recognized as supremely authoritative and was known as a "classic" (ching or tien). Prose fiction and comic drama texts, however, did not usually have commentaries. There are critiques (p'ing; J. hyō) of such masterpieces of prose fiction as *Shui Hu Chuan (The Water Margin)*, but their texts were not annotated. Only two commentaries on fiction existed by the late Ch'ing dynasty, and both (the one written by Lü Chan-en in 1825 and the other by Ho Yin in 1839) dealt with the *Liao-chai Chih-i*.[8] Genres recognized as premier art were also the subject of treatises (lun), which elucidated the aesthetic characteristics of the genre, examined its expressive techniques, and criticized compositions in that genre. Well over one hundred shih treatises survive from the T'ang and Sung periods alone, and if one added to this the writings collected in the *Chung-kuo Wen-hsüeh P'i-p'ing Tzü-liao Hui-pien (Compendium of Documents on Literary Criticism in China)*, the total volume would be immense. Treatises on prose fiction techniques, on the other hand, are virtually nonexistent: a few appear here and there among the many scholarly works of Chin Sheng-t'an and Mao Sheng-shan.

This striking discrepancy in the treatment accorded to genres must reflect the relation between the creator of expression and his recipient in a given genre. In other words, the distinction is based on whether or not they were members of the same circle. Members of a shih or fu audience were simultaneously composers, or were at least capable of composing. By contrast, the qualifications demanded of a prose fiction or comic drama audience did not include an ability to compose in those genres. Calligraphy, which one could both appreciate and create by taking brush in hand, was revered as a premier art, but painting and sculpture, which lacked this dual aspect, were considered mere crafts (kung) produced by artisans. Of course, from the Late T'ang period on, certain kinds of painting were considered the aesthetic equals of calligraphy, but this was because the artists were members of a class—the literati—that had heretofore served solely as recipient. Performance on musical instruments like the zither, which recipients could play as well as appreciate, was probably treated as a pre-

[8] A collection of mystery stories written in the early Ch'ing dynasty by P'u Sung-ling. [Auth., Trans.]

mier artistic activity.[9] But music that could not be performed except by professional musicians, and that required too much technical training to permit participation by the amateurs making up the audience, would of course be deemed a task for technicians. In the *Li Chi (Book of Rites)*, Tzu Kung, remarking to Master I, a musician, that everyone is supposed to have an aptitude for song, asks the master what kind of song is suitable to Tzu Kung's own abilities. Master I replies,

> "I am only a humble technician, not the sort of man you should ask for advice. Permit me, though, to tell you what I have heard. Kindly accept or reject it as you please."[10]

Note that the musician, I, refers to himself as a "humble technician" in speaking to Tzu Kung, a literatus. Members of the literati class gave song performances, hence Tzu Kung's question. The technical aspects of song, however, would not benefit an amateur and literatus; and the kind of music that could be performed only by highly skilled professionals was no longer a premier art but rather a task for "humble technicians."

The Chinese government system distinguished between two kinds of officials: the kuan, who determined the general features of government policy along Confucian doctrinal lines, and the li, who served the kuan and were in charge of government administration. The difference between kuan and li was more than a matter of high versus minor bureaucrat: a great gulf existed between the two. No matter how distinguished a li might become, he was fated to advance only within the ranks of li and could never become a kuan. From the T'ang period on, kuan were chosen by means of the higher civil service examination. The examination subjects remained virtually unchanged for nearly a millennium, in accordance with a basic policy: the questions were to be directed only toward cultivated upper class intellectuals and were to discount aptitude in practical administration and law (Murakami, 1980, 124-27). Consequently, literati destined to become kuan kept away from artistic spheres corresponding to practical administration. Calligraphy was indeed a premier art, but calligraphic work displaying technique alone—and devoid of the freedom that reflects noble spirit—was scorned as a "li hand," the brushwork of a clerk. The "noble spirit" was thought to originate in an education applying classical doctrine to life in society and was apparently limited to the ranks of the literati, who were well educated in the subjects that appeared in the civil service examination. Techniques that did not draw on the classics were never accorded significant value.

---

[9] Ever since the Six Dynasties period, literati have favored the zither, which Po Chü-i included among his "three friends"—the other two being poetry and wine (see vol. one, ch. 3).
[10] *Li Chi*, 39:701.

To become a literatus, it was mandatory that one receive strict individual training in the classics from boyhood on, acquiring an astonishing breadth of knowledge. These requirements resulted in a homogenized literati education. The classics were made up of works officially recognized by society to be objects of reverence and faith for all intellectual gentlemen; and though the classics were vast in number, they were limited in variety. Those who zealously studied these many works of limited scope took identical stances both in composition and reception. The shared mental stance, coupled with a common intellectual and educational background, facilitated composition and reception among fellow literati, since a composer could, by the merest suggestion, anticipate making either a subtle or a resounding effect on his audience. Composition and reception rooted in common experience were possible—and valued—only within the self-contained society made up by members of the circle. Chinese literati society held that valued expressive activity results from composition and reception carried out within a social class by a homogeneous group. This perception, I believe, came to dominate Japanese social thinking as well.

CENTRAL IDEAS AND KEYNOTES OF EXPRESSION

The Affective-Expressive Mode and Literary Stance

When the artist and the audience are all members of the same circle, literary activity within that circle tends to take a specific course. Sharing a mental approach and educational level, the members of the circle serve both as creators of expression and as audience. As a result, creators within the circle need not be motivated to strong measures to move their audience, so differing from other creators uncertain how their audience will receive them. Even restrained expression will evoke a full and uniform emotional response within the shared circle. This circumstance is the base from which an important Japanese literary characteristic evolved: affective-expressive literature. A creator who assumes there will be a shared emotional response with the audience will take an expressive stance different from that necessary before an unpredictable audience. The former, closed-circle stance may be divided into four components: retrospectivity, subtlety, fragmentation, and profundity. The first two qualities are applicable to the Middle Ages as a whole, whereas the latter two only become marked in the High Middle Ages. All four characteristics are of the greatest importance in viewing Japanese literature in a world context. The closed-circle stance is further manifested by implicitness of tone, another important characteristic of Japanese literature. These points will be considered in the following pages.

   Literary actions premised on a shared response between creator and audience require above all a standard corresponding to the means of response. In the sphere of waka, for instance, the standard is exemplified by
sama (style), a term that appears in the Japanese Preface to the *Kokinshū*.
Waka led a lively existence in the mid-ninth century, when it acted as an
"ambassador of love." Those who employed poetry for amorous ends
were indeed members of the same circle; but sama was not a requisite for
waka whose primary purpose was to bring about a mutual understanding
of amorous intentions. Such utilitarian waka, on the other hand, could
not attain the status of a premier art. Six Dynasties shih set the sama for
Chinese poetry; as long as waka lacked a similar sama, it would remain a
secondary art. Tsurayuki and his circle display great concern for the presence of sama in waka. They criticize the great poets of the past: "His sama
is coarse," or "His sama does not match the content of his poetry."[11] Early
waka poets are collectively denounced as "thinking only of the poem
while remaining ignorant of its sama." Tsurayuki and his circle made
waka into a premier art equivalent to the shih by adopting a waka style
inspired by Six Dynasties poetry. We may say that with the imbuing by
sama of that most native of Japanese genres, waka, the Middle Ages had
begun.
   Style, in the sense just discussed, was stressed in daily life as well as in
the realm of art. The Heian aristocracy may impress modern observers as
having been wholly absorbed in scandalous love affairs; but that is not to
say that Heian morals were corrupt. Love had an inviolable code. A young
nobleman visiting his lady in secret was, if discovered by her parents,
obliged to scramble from the precincts without even stopping to put on his
shoes.[12] Immorality was criticized for what it was, but love affairs of this
nature are described in tolerant terms, because they had sama. A backdrop of refined sensuality represented the proper sama of love: the lovers'
exchange of waka brimming with grace and wit; the combination produced by the poetic subject (a natural phenomenon), the note paper, and
the object to which the note was affixed;[13] the exchange of ingenious gifts;
and—once the lovers finally reached the stage of the nocturnal rendezvous—the clothing and accessories appropriate to season and circumstance, and the aroma incensed into robes and fans. An affair lacking this
sama was no better than the lowest debauchery. Yoshida Kenkō's (1282-
1350) use of the word "amorous" (iro), in his dictum that a man with no

---

   [11] [Criticisms, respectively, of the waka of Ōtomo Kuronushi and Fun'ya Yasuhide in Tsurayuki's Japanese preface to the *Kokinshū*, whence the phrase "ambassador of love" (kachō
no tsukai) is also taken.—Trans., Ed.]
   [12] *Heichū Monogatari* (dan [episode] 27), 85-87.
   [13] For example, if snow is the subject of a waka, the poem would be written on white note
paper and might be attached to a silver pine branch for delivery.

taste for amorous pursuits is like a fine winecup without a bottom, doubt-less refers to properly stylish romantic liaisons.[14] The concept of sama is also reflected in Shinkei's (1406-75) choice of words when he calls Nijō Yoshimoto (1320-88) and his fellow fourteenth-century renga masters "amorous men par excellence."[15]

To medieval Japanese proper style consisted essentially of already ex-tant expression. Harmonizing with already extant expression therefore yielded literature that was favorably received. The technique of allusive variation (honkadori) is a normative example of this view, but it is by no means the only one: beautiful expression was possible whenever diction and concepts rested completely on literary precedent. Perusal of the many waka treatises written by twelfth-century poets, beginning with Fujiwara Kiyosuke (1104-77), may utterly amaze modern readers unaccustomed to the practice then of memorizing a vast body of literary precedents. We are amazed because we live in the present age. Medieval readers and poets thought little of amassing so many precedents. Composer and audience shared an enormous store of literary precedents, and drawing on this com-mon asset enabled waka expression to take on its characteristic form.

Circumstances were similar in China. The Chinese perception that beautiful expression is based on precedent remained essentially un-changed for over two millennia. This perception was rooted in the basic nature of the Han people, who held that perfection was to be found in the past. If "retrospective" accurately describes the stance that beautiful expression is linked to literary precedent, then the spirit of the Han peo-ple, the bearers of Chinese culture, may be termed a model of retrospective orientation. A mere recitation of past literary exemplars, however, is not the major factor in bringing forth beautiful expression. Reliance on liter-ary precedent begins after one effective precedent out of many becomes validated through accumulated experience. In other words, selectivity must be practiced over a long period of years. Criteria are formed, during the selective process, determining why A is acceptable while Z must be dis-carded; these criteria, when put to practical use, were called "fa" (J. hō, method). The purpose of calligraphic techniques, for example, is to write characters, but the art of calligraphy is more than the ability to write a good hand: if calligraphy is to attain the eminence of a premier art, it must have its own special method of expression. The Chinese called this method "shu-fa," "the calligraphy method," and the copybooks from which the calligraphy method was learned were called "fa-t'ieh," "method books." "Fa," translated into waka parlance, is "sama."

When composer and audience belong to the same circle, and the criteria

---

[14] *Tsurezuregusa* (dan 3), 89.
[15] *Sasamegoto* (*Rengaron Shū*, 122): "kashikoki irogonomi."

of composition and reception are based on the method or sama embodied
by centuries of accumulated literary precedents, original expression naturally becomes difficult to create. For those outside the circle, and even for
those insiders with rather weak retrospective orientations, sama was condemned to being insipid expression, no more than the repetition ad infi-
nitum of banal diction and concepts. Well-adjusted members of the circle,
on the other hand, perceived composition conforming to accumulated
past precedents as a means of grasping true originality.

Fujiwara Teika, the founder of medieval poetics, declares in his *Eika no
Taigai (Principles of Waka Composition)* that a poem should be old in diction and new in spirit.[16] The significance of "old diction" is made perfectly
clear by Teika himself in a notation stating that poetic diction must not
leave the bounds established by the first three royal waka anthologies.[17]
Teika's "new spirit," however, was later interpreted one way by the Nijō
school of waka and another way by the Kyōgoku-Reizei school. The Nijō
view, essentially the standard medieval interpretation, found that "new
spirit" does not mean devising a completely new idea but instead refers to
manipulating existing poetic concepts to evoke new sensations (*Nomori
no Kagami*, 1).[18] Zeami took this approach one step further in his principle of hana, "the flower." According to Zeami, hana (expressive effect)
arises from a sense of the marvelous; the marvelous, however, is evoked
not by an extraordinary acting style but is instead grasped by an actor who
performs commonplace actions at the most appropriate moment.[19] Although based on the Nijō interpretation, Zeami's assertion also fully utilizes the more liberal, original Kyōgoku-Reizei position (Konishi, 1961,
44-63).

The excellent properties of inconspicuously original expression are not
easily grasped. A recipient seeking the wealth of emotion hidden in well-
worn diction and ordinary concepts must first be aware that a given work
has a subtle individuality despite its reliance on preexisting expression.
This perception often depends on keen receptive powers; and if that keen-
ness is to function, a recipient must be trained as much as possible to discriminate accurately between the degree to which the work under examination follows preexisting expression and the degree to which it is
original. As originality of expression becomes more subtle, the recipient
will grow increasingly incapable of sensing the difference between original
components and preexisting expression—unless possessed of a thorough

---

[16] *Karon Shū*, 114.
[17] [The *Kokinshū* (905-20), the *Gosenshū* (951), and the *Shūishū* (ca. 985)—although, as
the author observes in Volume One, Teika softens the restriction with a "they say"
(iwaku).—Trans., Ed.]
[18] *Kagaku Taikei*, 4:76-77. This approach also came to dominate renga.
[19] *Zeami Shū* 55, 56. (Konishi, 1961, 44-63.)

knowledge of the old. If, however, a composer knows that the audience is made up entirely of people fully acquainted with preexisting expression, it is possible to create in confidence with the very subtlest originality. No matter how understated this originality may be, the audience will be fully cognizant of it and might even be annoyed at the presence of too much originality. A construction site is so noisy that one must shout to be understood, but the faint babble of a stream can be clearly heard in the solitude of the mountains. The mountain scene describes the situation of a recipient who, being able to distinguish accurately the subtleties presented by a work based on accumulated literary precedent, dislikes too much novelty.

As we have seen, Chinese customarily appended commentary to any written work perceived as valuable. A glance at the "Liu Ch'en" (Six Scholars) commentary on the *Selections of Refined Literature* clearly reveals that most of the enormous amount of labor put into the task of compilation was taken up by the search for literary precedents, that is, already extant diction. Because this vast assemblage of preexisting diction is not always useful in understanding the linguistic aspects of the *Selections* it strikes us today as both taxing and peculiar. Such an assemblage will prove extremely significant, however, if we observe in it the compilers' concern that their audience appreciate the subtlest aspect of shih, fu, and prose in the context of preexisting expression.

Concepts as well as diction are distinctly connected to preexisting expression, although in the case of concepts related, valued ideas take the place of verbal precedent. A composer's own feelings become secondary when a conceptual method, level with preexisting expression, is set for a certain subject. Permissible ways of thinking and feeling become restricted and stereotyped. The composer's individual feelings are therefore not easily discerned. This tendency appears most typically in Six Dynasties poetry and prose. It is as difficult—for me, at least—to distinguish among the expressive characteristics of Hsieh Ling-yün (385-433), Pao Chao (?412-66), Hsieh T'iao (464-99), and Yü Hsin (512-76) as it is to recognize the stylistic differences in waka by Ki no Tomonori (d. ca. 905), Tsurayuki (?868-?945), Ōshikōchi Mitsune (dates uncertain; contemporary with the others named), and Mibu no Tadamine (d. ca. 920).[20] Six Dynasties poets did not deprecate similarity of conception. To the contrary, like the waka poets of the *Kokinshū* (905-20) period, they would have thought, "because it is similar it is good."

The retrospective, subtle stance was augmented in the twelfth century

---

[20] "Yü Hsin's style is clear and fresh; / And Pao Chao's elegant and free" (*T'ang-Sung Ch'uan-ch'i Chi* [= *TSCC*], 1:1102): as these lines demonstrate, allusions were occasionally made to these poets' stylistic hallmarks (see vol. one). Critics were able to discriminate among their styles because both critics and poets were members of the same circle; a critic outside the circle would encounter more difficulty.

by two more approaches, fragmentation and profundity: these amplified the nature of medieval literature. The latter two elements were, apparently, also a result of a deepening entry of Japanese culture by Sinified ideas.

One of the basic properties of indigenous Yamato literature is the lack of opposition between natural and human. Waka expression after the twelfth century, however, began to place a distance between nature as a poetic topic and the poet who composed on that topic. More generally speaking, the active mind seeking an appropriate means of expression (the expressive mind), as well as the thoughts and feelings forming the essence of that expression (expressed affect), came to be very keenly perceived by the twelfth century. Poetic distance in waka was an attendant phenomenon. Here the subject who expresses and the object expressed are mutually separated in a certain sense. This separation is also manifested on the expressive plane. In twelfth-century and later waka expression, a word flow that should be expressed in a single breath instead tends to break into fragments, and by the thirteenth century definite breaks make conspicuous and frequent appearances in waka expression. Teika and his circle provide the most marked examples of such waka. (This will be treated in Volume Three.) The rise of linked poetry after the thirteenth century, moreover, may not be unrelated to the increasing number of breaks within waka.

An agglutinative language, Japanese is by nature strongly inclined toward linkage between succeeding verbal elements. Therefore an absence of breaks in expression in Japanese shih and waka communicates the greatest possible sense of ease and stability. Waka poets of this time were no doubt following other dictates in producing breaks in expression that ran counter to the original characteristics of the Japanese language. Nevertheless the sensation communicated by this means of expression seems quite un-Japanese.

Fragmentation is far more noticeable in Chinese poetry. Chinese poetry was originally conceived as a means of giving voice to one's thoughts and feelings.[21] Yet by the middle of the Six Dynasties period (or, in terms of poets, the time of Hsieh Ling-yün), emphasis began to shift from the composer's own feelings to the nature of the design to be expressed. This stance clearly distinguished the mind that expresses from the intent expressed. Waka poets of the *Kokinshū* (905-20) period absorbed this expressive consciousness and adapted it to suit Japanese needs. It was not until after the *Kin'yōshū* (1124-27) period, however, that poets gradually became aware that an impetus, called perhaps "distance" or "detachment," was present in this awareness. The detachment, notably in the re-

---

[21] "Poetry is the expression of intent" (*Shih Ching*, 1:13).

lation of the human and natural, is more striking in Chinese literature. The Han spirit has always tended to alienate itself from nature, and poetry centered on nature itself did not exist in ancient China. Poems on nature began to appear in the mid–Six Dynasties period, but they did not display a closeness between the human spirit and nature; much less was there a recognizable sense of "communion with nature" (sympathetische Natur-gefühl), as one aesthetician has phrased it.[22] It is not until the poetry of Tu Fu that the human mingles with the natural, and even then, this synthesis cannot be seen as a common feature of shih. The distance placed between expressive mind and expressed intent in Japanese literature cannot be proved positively to result from the absorption of a similar Chinese distancing phenomenon. Considering, however, that the phenomenon of distance between the human and nature never existed among the Japanese, their distancing phenomenon was very likely effected through contact with Sinified expressive stances.

Furthermore, Chinese methods clearly include fragmentation. The monosyllabic, isolated nature of the Chinese language spontaneously fosters a discrete linguistic expression and results in breaks within shih expression. Breaks become most noticeable in poetry involving parallelism. This normative characteristic of Chinese literature is in fact the expression of corresponding elements through the medium of fragmentation. If the break is not clean, the effect made by the correspondence will be poor. Parallel expression was already part of Japanese literature by the *Man'yōshū* period, but only in a formal dimension. Fragmentation in parallelism did not penetrate the deepest strata of expressive awareness in waka until the *Kin'yōshū* period, although we might note that concern and interest in parallel expression began to grow somewhat earlier, in the *Shūishū* (1005-1009) period. It would hardly be exaggeration to say, for instance, that the *Wakan Rōeishū* (*Collection of Japanese and Chinese Song*, 1013) was compiled to facilitate the appreciation of parallelism. The fragmentation involved in these phenomena was distinctly the result of the Japanese reception of Chinese literature.

Expression through fragmentation, however, would have seemed extraneous to the Japanese. The aim to transcend fragmentation and synthesize discrete or detached expression at a profound level of awareness—a tendency that appeared in Fujiwara Shunzei's (1114-1204) time—may well have developed naturally from the earlier aesthetic. Shunzei conceived of synthesis as rooted in the Tendai (Ch. T'ien-t'ai) Buddhist practice of contemplation (shikan), a practice not limited, however, to Japan. Shunzei not only united two separate twelfth-century entities, the expressive mind

---

[22] The expression is taken from Alfred Biese, *Die Entwicklung des Naturgefühl bei den Griechen und Römern*, as cited by Ōnishi Yoshinori (Ōnishi, 1943, 101-12).

and expressed intent. He also synthesized the aim for detachment at another profound level of awareness even while allowing for that aim in itself.

Unlike the *Man'yōshū* poets, who found no separation between themselves and the subjects of their poems, Shunzei belonged to an age in which the poetic subject and the poet's own received impressions did not always conform to the same ideal. Suppose, for example, that autumn drizzle is to be the subject of a waka.[23] Shunzei's personal feelings toward a drizzly occasion would probably vary according to time and circumstance. But the twelfth-century waka circle had determined how a poet would write on autumn rain. Drizzle in its truest form, called "the spirit [kokoro] of drizzle," was acknowledged by waka poets, although there was no reason for it to accord with the composer's mind. Shunzei nevertheless did not alter the topic of drizzle, as it was conventionally recognized, to suit his own feelings, nor did he shelve his feelings and conform his poetic style to the conventional associations of autumn rain. Instead he attempted to consolidate both aspects by immersing himself in the very essence of autumn rain.

Abandoning routine feelings, the Shunzei-like poet is struck by the supreme ideal of drizzle—its essence, one might say. Previous individual preconceptions about drizzle dissolve in this essence, while the standard view of what makes drizzle to be drizzle also dissolves within an essence received at an even more profound stratum. In other words, the subject, the drizzle, fuses with the spirit of its poet. The fusion is carried out at an extremely profound level of awareness, while on the surface level the spirit of drizzle may remain, as before, detached and opposed to the poet's spirit. Buddhist contemplation is achieved by deeply penetrating the essence of a given subject. The object is to obtain a complete conviction and realization that distinctions and oppositions essentially do not exist, despite their recognized presence on the phenomenal plane. This practice is in accord with Shunzei's method of shikan meditation.

Distancing and opposition between the expressive mind and expressed intent, or between man and nature, also appear in China from the Six Dynasties period into the Early T'ang; the two elements are intermingled, however, in Tu Fu's shih, as was already noted. Tu Fu achieved this fusion in his mature work, although he did not propose it as a theory. Wang

---

[23] [Drizzle (shigure) is an intermittent light, cold rain taken to fall in autumn and winter. In waka, the spirit of drizzle (shigure no kokoro), referred to shortly, is taken to be an experience arousing sad, suffering thoughts. Drizzle is also taken, like dew and frost, to be an agent tinting leaves in autumn: "Unable to withstand the drizzle, / The leaves have now changed their color" (Shigure ni aezu / Momijitarikeri). In renga, the first drizzle (hatsushigure) is taken to be a winter term, although "shigure" refers either to autumn or to winter. Presumptions like these, familiar to students of classical poetry, underlie the author's argument and will aid the nonspecialist reader in following the argument.—Ed.]

Ch'ang-ling (698-?755) and Chiao-jan (730-99) did propose theories along these lines.[24] Both sought a perfect expressive stance in which the poet's expressive spirit (called "i," "intention," by Ch'ang-ling) deeply penetrated the image of the expressed subject (called "ching," "world," by Ch'ang-ling). "Intention," in this theory, corresponds to "chih" (wisdom) in T'ien-t'ai contemplative terms: "ching" is also employed in a similar sense. The practical act of orientation toward unity between world and wisdom is also identical in T'ien-t'ai contemplation, and so this theory may be seen as very much in the T'ien-t'ai spirit. To judge from his shih, Chiao-jan seems to have been either a T'ien-t'ai or San-lun priest, and Wang Ch'ang-ling was probably also well versed in T'ien-t'ai theology. We can easily grasp the qualitative correspondence of Shunzei's expressive consciousness to that of Wang Ch'ang-ling and Chiao-jan if we keep in mind that both Shunzei and the Chinese poets shared an assumption about conceptual depth, that of T'ien-t'ai contemplation.

T'ien-t'ai contemplation was to form part of the heritage of Zen devotional practice, although Zen evolved special expressive methods not present in T'ien-t'ai. When these latter methods were absorbed into artistic expression, they produced distinctive art that might be termed radical innovation. I shall discuss this matter in the volume on the High Middle Ages.

From Ga to Zoku

The orientations examined in the preceding section became vital to the principal genres of medieval Japan, but this does not mean that the Middle Ages are entirely represented by these orientations. Other medieval orientations may in fact have guided a greater number of compositions. If I have nonetheless attempted to characterize the Middle Ages through the points discussed above, it is because, in classifying periods of literary history, no index exists that can rationally classify every genre and literary phenomenon. When dividing literary history into chronological periods, one is obliged to employ as classifying indices those orientations and ideas that become central to the principal genres, and to situate other genres each according to its relation to the principal ones. Not that the group of writers practicing the principal genres always maintained the same orientations. It was certainly not rare for a waka poet whose style was retrospective and subtle suddenly to compose, under certain circumstances, poetry that was free and innovative. On the other hand, that poet was unlikely to forget that waka was a valued art precisely because its stylistic

[24] Wang Ch'ang-ling's theory appears in *Shih-ke*, and Chiao-jan's in *Shih-i*. Neither work survives, although both are quoted extensively by Kūkai in his *Bunkyō Hifuron*. (See Konishi, 1948-51a-53d.)

ideal was retrospective and subtle. Such ideas were dominant in the Middle Ages.

It is in this sense that the Middle Ages represent a period when both composer and audience were members of the same circle, and in which the keynote was a retrospective, subtle, fragmented, and profound expression. These characteristics have already been noted to be distinctly Sinified in nature. Thus I have defined the Middle Ages in Japanese literary history as the period in which literature was transformed by the adoption of Chinese culture. Resemblances between Japanese and Chinese literary phenomena have been seen by some as manifestations of separate entities developed independently and spontaneously rather than as cultural interchange of any kind. This view is totally untenable unless medieval Japan could be demonstrated to have felt nothing but indifference for Chinese culture.

"Chinese culture," on the other hand, signifies considerably different things depending on the historical period. For example, a comparative study of Japanese literature that drew on an amalgam of cultural characteristics from the Six Dynasties, T'ang, and Sung periods could not possibly yield any valid results. The Japanese acceptance of Chinese literature frequently consisted of such simple perceptions as "a famous Chinese poet" or "an important Chinese shih collection." Evidently the Japanese did not consider it awkward, for instance, to appreciate Po Chü-i's shih according to critical patterns characteristic of the earlier Six Dynasties period.[25] This explains how a relatively homogeneous perception of ga was shaped and maintained throughout the Japanese Middle Ages. The special characteristics displayed by Chinese works in the Six Dynasties, T'ang, and particularly the Sung periods nevertheless have considerable bearing on the evolution of Japanese literature.

Through the eleventh century, ga in waka was perceived as an expressive realm ruled by wit in the Six Dynasties style. In the twelfth century a T'ang-style orientation developed that emphasized the composer's subjectivity, an orientation concentrated by Shunzei and Teika into contemplative expression.[26] In addition, the poetic style called yōen (ethereal beauty), with its similarities to Late T'ang poetry styles, joined the ranks of ga. The dominant ideal in Japan by the fourteenth century was a Sung-inspired aesthetic outlook that esteemed what can only be called an ele-

---

[25] Several theories heretofore seem to assume that Six Dynasties shih styles were discarded by the Japanese as soon as they encountered and absorbed T'ang poetic styles; but this runs counter to fact, as has been mentioned earlier.

[26] "T'ang-style" refers to the modality of the High and Middle T'ang periods. The Early T'ang carried on the Six Dynasties poetic style, and poetic idiosyncrasies are too pronounced in Late T'ang poetry.

gant simplicity deemphasizing the sensuous beauty in which it was rooted. These developments had occurred, respectively, approximately three hundred and fifty years earlier in their country of origin, China. It should be noted that the period of delay is more or less a fixed-year figure regardless of the historical period (see the General Introduction in vol. one).

The problem is one of expressive standards in literature and art, but similar observations apply to the broader ideas on which standards are based. The Middle Ages consist of three subdivisions, each of which has a governing principle: fūryū (elegance) for the Early Middle Ages, michi (artistic vocation) for the High Middle Ages, and jōri (reason and feeling) for the Late Middle Ages (again see the General Introduction in vol. one). The Taoist world of immortals forms the central ideal of fūryū; and, because Taoism evolved into an established philosophy between Ko Hung's (?260-340) time and the Late Six Dynasties period (Shimode, 1975, 28-31), fūryū may be considered a Six Dynasties principle. Taoism reached its apogee in the T'ang period and continued to flourish long after that, but the ideal image of the immortals' realm was a legacy inherited from the Late Six Dynasties period. Fūryū is therefore correctly regarded as the Six Dynasties manner. The core concept of michi, the guiding principle of the High Middle Ages, was apparently shaped by the Tendai doctrine of the Perfect and Immediate Precept (J. endonkai; Konishi, 1956, 21-22). Michi may be regarded therefore as a T'ang principle. Michi also owes much to Zen, an inheritor of the Tendai legacy, for its establishment and consolidation, but it remains a T'ang-style principle because its philosophical approach is characteristic of Tendai. We are speaking here of Buddhism, not of a religion peculiar to China (e.g., T'ien-t'ai); nevertheless Tendai and Zen both originated in China and are very Sinified in comparison with Indian Buddhism. They should thus be seen as aspects of Chinese culture in the broad sense of the term. The principle of reason that forms the core of jōri, the keynote of the Late Middle Ages, is certainly at the heart of Sung period culture. Each of the three stages of medieval culture undeniably reflects a specific period in Chinese history.

The preceding discussion makes clear that the three stages of Japanese medieval literature each evolved in correspondence with its own specific kind of Chinese culture. The three stages, though differing from one another, have a further facet that must not be overlooked, that of the features they share. Waka and renga, for example, are opposites in various ways, but a single keynote sounds throughout both. The normative waka and renga poets of the High Middle Ages are generally agreed to be, in chronological order, Shunzei—Teika—Tamekane—Ryōshun—Shōtetsu—Shinkei. The connecting lines indicate either a direct or chronologically distant master-disciple relationship. Since all these men were noted in their day for expressive technique and depth of insight, the names joined above into master-pupil relationships might well appear to represent the poetic mainstream of the High Middle Ages. This is not unreasonable from a modern standpoint.

The waka produced by the Kyōgoku-Reizei school, as well as its poetic treatises—which are reminiscent in certain ways of treatises by Wang Ch'ang-ling and Chiao-jan—have an essence that remains appealing today.[27] And yet those poets whose names appear after Tamekane's are all men of remarkable talent who appeared quite by chance in the High Middle Ages. An alternate poetic line for this period seems to have many proponents: Teika—Tameie—Tameyo—Tsuneyori—Sōgi—Sōseki—Jōha.[28] This line created a tranquil wittiness that, although based on the *Kokinshū* style (with Six Dynasties shih as its prototype), also incorporated the reverence for elegant simplicity that was advocated by Sung poetic treatises.

Although works of this line are unlikely to elicit much response from readers today, it must be considered the principal poetic line of the High Middle Ages. The Kyōgoku-Reizei school violently condemned the expression produced by this line, and yet waka throughout the Middle Ages remained rooted in the *Kokinshū* style. In the fifteenth century the Kyōgoku-Reizei school apparently entered into gradual decline, despite a new coexistence established with the mainstream, *Kokinshū*-style school. Fierce though it was, the dispute between the Nijō and Kyōgoku-Reizei schools was nothing but a fight within a Six Dynasties-style framework—insofar as medieval waka is wholly rooted in the *Kokinshū* style, itself modeled on Six Dynasties shih styles. My assertion is founded on the assumption that T'ang and Sung poetic treatises, despite their distinctive characteristics, are revealed in rough overview to perpetuate Six Dynasties and later expressive prototypes rather than breaking completely with them.

Therefore ga, as recognized in medieval Japan, belongs to the same general framework as the expressive consciousness common to the Six Dynasties through the Sung periods in China. Here we must note that, rare though such occurrences were, extremely talented composers did attempt to break out of this framework. Tsurayuki was one such man. In his youth Tsurayuki led a group dedicated to establishing a Six Dynasties style of

[27] Citations from *Bumpitsu Ganshinshō* indicate that Tamekane had come in contact with the *Shih-ke* and *Shih-i* (*Hanazono Tennō Shinki* [28.XII.1325], 2). Unaware that these theories were posited by Wang Ch'ang-ling and Chiao-jan, Tamekane probably assumed the treatises were Kūkai's.

[28] The complex master-disciple relationships between Sōseki and Jōha have been abridged for convenience and condensed into a single line.

elegance in the sphere of waka; yet in his last years he became skeptical of the ga style, apparently believing that true waka were composed in language drawn from the common expressive consciousness of his day—language, paradoxically, that could only be perceived as clumsy—for these were waka charged with true human feeling. A similar phenomenon occurred with Teika. His group was the flower of the *Shinkokinshū* (1201-1206ff.) period, and their work—fittingly described as ethereal beauty (yōen)—possesses the beauty of Late T'ang poetry transferred to waka. But in his old age Teika also moved toward plain, frank, and tranquil expression.

The pattern reappears in Zeami's nō treatises. There Zeami describes, in his own words, only those conclusions he himself has thoroughly absorbed, with the result that direct relationships to Sinified artistic ideas are not easily discerned. Zeami's earlier expression was undeniably oriented toward a ga principle qualitatively similar to that advocated by the young Teika and his circle. Yet in old age Zeami turned his attention to a new artistic area called kyakuraika, "the flower of the return." Zeami does not always elucidate the significance of this term, but the treatises of Komparu Zenchiku (1405-68) suggest that kyakuraika refers to an art directed toward attaining fresh, primitive expression through a childlike simplicity (Konishi, 1961, 232-36). Bashō's concept of karumi (lightness) is probably not unrelated.

Why did these men abandon, as if by prearrangement, the expressive realm of ga in their last years? Note that in all cases this event occurred during the composer's old age. To secure the prestige of their respective arts, they were obliged to direct them toward expression based on the Sinified ga principle. They did so out of an enforced awareness that only one criterion, ga, determined whether one produced art or nonart, and whether one's art was premier or merely secondary. Perhaps ga, an expressive concept rooted in a foreign culture, was harbored by the Japanese but was somehow never made their own. Somewhere in the Yamato consciousness lies a latent resistance to ga. This resistance might be temporarily suppressed in devoting youthful passions and talents to ga, but old age seems to bring the sudden realization that the resistance, heretofore unnoticed, has not in fact been completely conquered. This is when a composer wishes to return to expression that evokes no feelings of resistance. Kyakuraika must refer to just such a return.[29] One's destination on this return, of course, is a realm of expression that transcends ga.

Up to this time, a composer in pursuit of art has pushed aside, without regret, pure, open, free, true beauty: this is the beauty of zoku, the popu-

[29] See Konishi, 1961, 216-17, and Volume Three.

lar, in the most profound sense of the word. To be sure, it represents the commonplace, the slipshod, and the bland in the eyes of art. But an old composer, having had more than enough of refinement, does not decline into dullness and rigidity but displays on the contrary receptive powers far more subtle and flexible than those he had in youth. Through these powers he discovers and savors a profound goodness hidden in expression that appears merely mediocre and slipshod. Those who strive to create elegant expression in the Sinified realm of ga return to the zoku sphere when, after long years of diligence, they are seized with sudden nostalgia for Yamato.

CHAPTER 4

Remnants of the Archaic and Ancient Ages

As discussed in the preceding chapter, zoku signifies the commonplace or ordinary sphere to which a composer returns once he has reached the heights of ga, and as such zoku possesses a specific range of meaning. There is also a wider meaning of zoku that includes the more specific use of the term. This wider meaning is of special importance to the Middle Ages. Since the nature of zoku is not greatly influenced by time, the Middle Ages inherited a zoku principle identical to that which functioned in the Archaic and Ancient Ages. Conceived solely in terms of time factors, this indicates that both the Archaic and the Ancient Ages survived within the Middle Ages. Zoku, then, is essentially not a function of time periods, although this or that of its features changes with the times. The zoku of the return did not exist in either the Archaic or the Ancient Age. Both the immutable nature of medieval zoku and its constantly changing sides are explored below.

KOTODAMA WITHIN ACTION

Zoku expression in the Archaic and Ancient Ages is liveliest when linked to the kotodama. To be sure, the kotodama declined after the second half of the Ancient Age, moving closer to the principle of ga; but this is true only in comparison with the archaic and early ancient kotodama. From the second half of the Ancient Age and throughout the Middle Ages the kotodama was transformed on certain fronts, but on the whole it remained fairly vigorous.

Let us consider this point in terms of waka. On the twenty-ninth day of the Third Month, 803, after completion of the final decisions on personnel for the sixteenth embassy to China, a farewell banquet was held for the ambassador, Fujiwara Kadonomaro, and his vice-ambassador, Ishikawa Michiyasu (dates unknown). Care was taken at this banquet that "all be done in the Chinese fashion," but after several cups of sake had been downed, Kammu Tennō summoned Kadonomaro to his side and presented him with a waka:

Kono sake wa	This is sake
Obo ni wa arazu	Far from ordinary brew,
Tairaka ni	For with this drink
Kaerikomase to	We have performed the vow—
Iwaitaru sake.	"Come safely back to us."

Kadonomaro's tears are said to have fallen like rain, and not one among the assembled noblemen could keep from weeping.[1]

When Tajihi Hironari (d. 739), ambassador of the ninth embassy to China, left for the continent in 733, Yamanoe Okura composed a waka sequence, "Kōkyo Kōrai no Uta" ("A Fine Journey, a Fine Return"; *MYS*, 5:894-96), to wish Hironari a safe journey. In it Okura sings of Yamato, the "land where the kotodama / Brings us good fortune." His words demonstrate that, in the middle of the Ancient Age, belief remained strong in the kotodama's power to effect good events upon the pronouncement of auspicious words.

The same is true for the later Ancient Age: Kammu and his courtiers seem to have had no doubts on the subject. A few years before Kadonomaro's banquet, on the thirteenth of the Eighth Month, 798, Kammu went on a hunting trip to Kitano. On the return journey, he and his party had an informal meal, and Kammu, seeing that it was growing dark, recited,

Kesa no asake	This morning we were told
Naku chō shika no	The stags here would bell at dawn:
Sono koe o	Now we shall not leave
Kikazu wa ikaji	Until we finally hear their cry—
Yo wa fukenu to mo.	No matter how late night grows!

No sooner had he finished his recitation than a stag cried. Kammu was delighted: he had his suite recite the waka in unison and returned forthwith to the palace despite the late hour.[2] The stag cried out because the action of the kotodama had reached the animal; and Kammu's reason for returning to his palace regardless of the hour lay in his kotodama-filled words, "Now we shall not leave / Until we finally hear their cry— / No matter how late night grows!" Once he had heard the cry of the stag, he must immediately return to his palace or risk incurring bad luck.

On the twenty-sixth of the Third Month, 849, the senior priests of Kōfukuji presented Nimmyō Tennō with a chōka in honor of his fortieth birthday. It is recorded in its entirety in the *Shoku Nihon Goki* (Book 19).[3]

[1] *Nihon Kiryaku* [= NKR], 13:279.   [2] *RK*, 32:194-95.
[3] *SNGK*, 19:223-25; *RK*, 28:159-61.

As literature it is clumsy, being in effect an enumeration of auspicious manifestations of longevity. But little concern need be taken with the relative skill displayed by this kind of poem. The priests composed it in the belief that speaking a great many longevity-related phrases would propel the kotodama in their utterances toward their sovereign and grant him long life. The passage that follows occurs near the end of the chōka.

Ōmiyo o	That your august reign
Yorozuyo inori	May continue evermore,
Hotoke ni mo	Humbly we beseech
Kami ni mo mōshi	The Buddha and all the gods
Tatematsuru	To hear this our prayer.
Koto no kotoba wa	The words that form our poem
Kono kuni no	Are drawn wholly from
Mototsu kotoba ni	The language used of old
Oiyorite	In this our land:
Morokoshi no	We do not need
Kotoba o karazu	Chinese vocabulary,
Fumi shirusu	And seek no help from
Hakase yatowazu	Professors who write Chinese prose.
Kono kuni no	As generations past
Iitsutauraku	Have long said of this our land:
Hinomoto no	The land of Yamato,
Yamato no kuni wa	Country of the rising sun,
Kotodama no	Is a land of blessings
Sakiwau kuni to zo	Granted by the kotodama.
Furugoto ni	Thus have we believed
Nagarekitareru	Ever since the days of old;
Kamugoto ni	Thus has it been told
Tsutaekitareru	As it was spoken by the gods.
Tsutaekoshi	And as we follow
Koto no manimani	Faithfully our ancient ways,
Mototsu yo no	And deeply contemplating
Koto tazunureba	Things that are now long past,
Utagoto ni	We used these words
Utaikaeshite	To compose poem after poem,
Kamuwaza ni	And the poems served
Mochiikitareri	To praise and glorify the gods;
Kimigoto ni	Also they became
Tsukaikitareri	Offerings to our sovereign lord.
Moto no yo ni	Thus we call upon
Yorishitagaite	Both the Buddha and the gods,
Hotoke ni mo	Following the path

Kami ni mo mōshi	Of venerable tradition
Kotoage shite	And utter a kotoage:
Inorishi makoto wa	May the words of our prayer,
Nemogoro to	Sprung from sincere hearts,
Kikoshimeshiten . . .	Be made pleasing to their ears . . .

The priests were aware that their chōka, a virtual list of auspicious things, was recited in anticipation that the kotodama would function. The composers state, moreover, that Chinese vocabulary is to be eschewed, since the kotodama lodges only within Yamato words. I consider the latter point particularly important (see vol. one, 394-95). The priests were probably also in agreement that the kotodama would not function if the gist of their chōka were stated in prose. The kotoage that activated the kotodama was necessarily to be uttered in a tone unlike that of ordinary speech, and waka was useful in supplying a form for this purpose.

The waka form, of course, was not the only medium employed to activate the kotodama: verse-prose was also useful. The murohoki, a subgenre of verse-prose, is made up of a series of auspicious phrases concerning a given building; their utterance anticipates that the kotodama within the words will bring about propitious events. Prince Woke's murohoki, quoted in the previous volume, is a characteristic example.

The semmyō, ancient and medieval royal proclamations framed in the Yamato language, was another expressive form that endeavored to activate the kotodama through verse-prose. The semmyō is by nature a state document, not literature; but unlike later state documents, semmyō were imbued with the kotodama. The annals compiled by the Japanese government, from the *Shoku Nihongi* (793) to the *Sandai Jitsuroku* (901), are all written in Chinese. When semmyō appear in these annals, they are treated like song and waka; instead of being transcribed in Chinese, they are recorded in their original Japanese form and are accompanied by pronunciation and intonation guides to facilitate oral recitation.[4]

Tone and pronunciation were apparently important factors in activating the kotodama. Let us consider, as an example of a semmyō, one issued on the eleventh day of the Seventh Month, 850, which promoted the enshrined deities of the Tatsuta and Hirose Shrines to the junior fifth court rank, upper grade.

---

[4] "The prince so excelled in the performance of yogoto [a congratulatory recitation wishing the sovereign a long and happy reign] and semmyō that he became a paragon of recitation and composition. Because few among the royal house and the nobility knew the proper methods of performing these works, his majesty commanded Fujiwara Mototsune and Ōe no Otondo to visit the prince at his Rokujō residence and to learn recitation from him, with emphasis on the subtler points" (*SJ*, 14:209). The prince mentioned here is Kammu's son Prince Nakano (792-867), who learned the art from Fujiwara Otsugu (773-843).

I speak his majesty's words in the presence of deities he has proclaimed the Pillars of Heaven and the Pillars of Earth: "Many months
and years have passed since you were last granted court rank for
keeping the country at peace. I have therefore sent Lord Ōnakatomi
Hisayo, senior sixth rank, upper grade and junior vice-minister of the
Bureau of Shrines, to raise your rank and to honor your names. From
this time forth, I humbly beseech you, may the winds and the rains
arrive in due season; may the five grains ripen in all abundance; may
the world be at peace; and may you aid and sustain the sovereign's
government, making it a steady rock, an everlasting rock."[5]

Yamato vocabulary is used throughout, with the exception of "senior
sixth rank, upper grade, and junior vice-minister of the Bureau of
Shrines," the official rank and title of the messenger. "A steady rock, an
everlasting rock" (kakiwa ni tokiwa), a formula from ancient times, was
also probably intended to activate the kotodama. Semmyō were issued on
various occasions: accession to the throne, the change of an era name, the
commendation of a subject or a foreign visitor, the celebration of a solemn
ceremony, the issuing of an exhortation, and the announcement of punishment. The *Shoku Nihongi* and ensuing official histories faithfully record a great many semmyō, which must manifest their compilers' concern
to transmit the original texts to verse-prose imbued with the kotodama.

The kotodama very likely functioned most vigorously in kagura. Kagura is essentially performed to effect, through song and dance, amicable
relations between gods and human beings. It thus requires a medium that
will enable each party to comprehend the other's thoughts and feelings.
Only the kotodama could have served as an effective medium between
them. Kagura structure has been discussed. One of its song groups, the
Wand (Torimono) corpus, probably relies the most on the functioning of
the kotodama. (The Wand is the object held in the lead dancer's hand.)
There are nine kinds of Wand, each with its own song. These objects serve
as the divine locus upon which the god descends.

The first Wand song, "Sakaki" ("Sakaki Bough"), provides an example.[6]

Sakakiba no	Leaves of the sakaki
Ka o kaguwashimi	Have a scent whose loveliness

---

[5] *Montoku Jitsuroku*, 2:15. Unlike their Western counterparts, Japanese gods are extremely numerous and, for the most part, rather low in status. The rank bestowed at this time
on the two deities of the Tatsuta and the deity of Hirose Shrines corresponded to that held
by a junior vice-minister in the Central Affairs Ministry, a department head in the Court
School, or a second in command of the Gate Guards.

[6] [The sakaki (Cleyera ochnacea), is an evergreen member of the camellia family; it is often
translated "sacred tree."—Trans.]

Tomekureba	Brought me after it,
Yaso ujibito zo	And here found men from every clan
Matoiserikeru	Seated in a circle round it,
Matoiserikeru.	Seated in a circle round it.

Kamigaki no	A sacred fence surrounds
Mimuro no yama no	The mountain where the gods descend:
Sakakiba wa	There sakaki leaves,
Kami no mimae ni	Full in the divine presence,
Shigeriainikeri	Have grown most vigorously,
Shigeriainikeri.	Have grown most vigorously.

(*KR*, 2-3)

Here the sakaki leaves are praised both for smell and sight. A recitation of the tree's splendid attributes activates the kotodama within the singers' voices to reach and affect the god; the god then becomes inclined to visit the site of the kagura ceremony. Both Yamato and Ryukyuan Japanese still believe that gods and spirits lodge in trees.[7] The sakaki was perceived as the gods' favorite arboreal dwelling; the Chinese character for "sakaki" (a character indigenous to Japan) is a synthesis of the characters for "tree" and "god" (Tsugita, 1938, 1-4). The "Sakaki Bough" songs can be interpreted as invitations to the god, requesting that it come to dwell within the sakaki branch held by the leading dancer. The song is not a direct invitation: rather an evocation of the splendor of the tree. This stance is probably rooted in the belief that the kotodama will effect beneficent situations if auspicious things are uttered according to proper form. The Opening Songs (Saibari) and Star (Hoshi) songs already examined may be similarly interpreted.

Kotodama linked to song and dance reappears in the High Middle Ages in nō. The best example is *Okina (Old Man)*, a play that did not originate as nō. The play now known as *Okina* was originally performed by shushi actors.[8] When their number began to decline in the fourteenth century, the shushi repertoire was taken over by sarugaku, the predecessor of nō, and transmitted within the nō corpus (Nose, 1938, 176-84). *Okina* opens with the following unintelligible lines:

Tōtō tarari tararira

---

[7] Ryukyuan villages are usually located near an utaki, a holy forest where gods and spirits are enshrined (McCune, 1975, 67-68). Most utaki are on high ground, though some are located in plains and rice paddies. In all cases a dense grove of trees is the requisite element of an utaki. [Cf. Latin "lucus."—Ed.]

[8] Shushi actors used magic ritual to invoke peace and abundant harvest. By the twelfth century, shushi actors were beginning to display their magic as entertainment, and this element gradually took precedence over the religious aspects. [Auth., Trans.]

Tarari agari rararitō

Chiriya tarari tararira
Tarari agari rararitō.

These meaningless lines have been related to Tibetan incantation, but that view is no longer accorded scholarly credence. Their significance is unknown, but their incantatory nature, invoking peace on earth and abundant harvest, is nevertheless immediately apparent. The underlying perception in these lines is also common to kotodama belief: the breath accompanying specially uttered words is anticipated to come in contact with land, people, and plant life, and to effect auspicious results. The difference lies in the unknown significance of "Tōtō tarari. . . ." The kotodama functions when intelligible Yamato language is uttered.

The dhāraṇī of esoteric Buddhism are probably the origin of the perception that magical effects can also be obtained from words of unknown meaning. Esoteric Buddhism also considers such meaningless monosyllables as "a," "i," "un," and "ka" to possess magic properties. My intention is not to assert that "Tōtō tarari . . ." is a dhāraṇī but to propose that esoteric Buddhism fostered a perception among the people that meaningless sounds might also possess magical powers. And because popular belief in the kotodama—a power activated by meaningful sounds—already existed, it served as the foundation on which the new perception was built.

It is well worth noting that the indigenous Yamato belief in the kotodama had intermingled with a foreign esoteric consciousness by the High Middle Ages. This consciousness not only was current among the common people but apparently penetrated the ranks of the intelligentsia as well. Mujū's (1226-1312) dictum, "Waka is dhāraṇī," clearly manifests this. Dhāraṇī are meaningless to anyone unfamiliar with Sanskrit; Mujū notes, however, that in India dhāraṇī are meaningful words, and he discusses how waka—which also possess meaning—can be dhāraṇī as well.[9] Thus the indigenous Yamato faith in the kotodama, though somewhat altered by esoteric Buddhism, nevertheless retained its essential property beyond the High Middle Ages, that is, its ability to produce auspicious results when meaningful sounds are expressed in a given form.

Faith in the kotodama also appears in renga. This is not the case for all renga, but several sequences were dedicated to the gods in prayer for re-

[9] "In India dhāraṇī is ordinary language, yet, when recited for religious purposes, its effect is to erase sin and obliterate suffering. Similarly, the vocabulary of waka does not differ from everyday language, but if a man expresses his thoughts and feelings through waka, they are moving indeed. Waka imbued with the Buddhist spirit are more moving still: these are undoubtedly dhāraṇī" (*Shasekishū*, 5:223). Mujū's concept set the precedent for incorporating a hymn from the *Hokke Sembō* into a kagura song that otherwise would have had only Yamato expression.

covery from illness or for victory in battle. An example of the latter is Sō-chō's (1445-1532) thousand-stanza sequence, composed on the occasion of Imagawa Ujichika's (1470-1526) departure for battle on the twenty-fifth of the Tenth Month, 1504. An example of the former is a hokku by Sōgi (1421-1502), composed in the First Month of 1471, that beseeches the god of Mishima Shrine to cure the illness of Takeichimaru, the son of Tō no Tsuneyori (1401-94). Sōgi's subsequent thousand-stanza sequence in thanks for the boy's recovery is a further instance. This practice survived up to the Edo Period (Yamada, 1937, 149-51). These facts reveal that the kotodama, despite a gradual debilitation and alteration, remained a living entity in the Middle Ages.

Kotodama Within Expression

The preceding discussion has concerned expression in the broad sense of the term, or rather the idea that kotodama could be made to function through the act of expression and that it was thought the act brought about a propitious event. Expression in the strict sense, by contrast, itself contains the kotodama, although in it the functioning of the kotodama is obscure: sometimes neither composer nor recipient is immediately aware that the kotodama is functioning. By "expression in the strict sense" is meant a unified statement, or some part of it, that is shaped according to a given design. Waka concerned with nature are examples of this.

Natural scenes often appear in Japanese song and waka and represent a major characteristic of Japanese literature. These points have been made repeatedly, and not erroneously. To state, however, that nature waka, whether by Man'yōshū poets or modern writers of tanka, are in all cases descriptions of scenery, and that these descriptions can be seen en masse as a characteristic of Japanese literature, is to take a position greatly in need of modification. Nature waka from the Ancient Age are place-panegyrics invigorated by an inherited archaic kotodama. In the latter half of the Ancient Age, orientation toward the kotodama weakened and scenery for its own sake gradually became aesthetically appealing. These waka nevertheless retain their essential character as place-panegyrics and so remain unaffected by modern concepts like objective portrayal. Masaoka Shiki's (1867-1902) school endeavored to read the poetry of the Man'yōshū according to the concept of objective portrayal, and in so doing they misapplied the concept of objectivity. This misconception led to results that were nearly the exact opposite of those aimed for, a point I shall clarify by referring to aesthetic studies on human communion with nature.

Emotion inspired by nature (Naturgefühl) is the direct response of human emotion to features of the natural world. There are both objective and subjective emotions inspired by nature. In the former case, a distance exists between the self as subject and nature as object; intellectual interest, utilitarian concerns, and related elements are sometimes interposed between the human and the natural. Here the mental approach is one of objectivity. In the latter category, the heart is deeply stirred by a keen emotional response to, and sympathy with, nature. Separation and opposition between the human and the natural have been part of Western culture since its inception in ancient Greece. Thus, as Schiller first indicated, the West manifests little emotional concern (Herzensanteil) for nature; its feelings toward nature are instead chiefly composed of analytical interest. On the other hand, subjective emotions toward nature—typified by a communion with nature (sympathetische Naturgefühl) introducing subjective emotions into nature as object and achieving complete fusion between observation and feeling—appeared in the West only in recent times, with Goethe as its best [German] proponent. Communion with nature is to be found in abundance in Japan, however, in the *Chronicles* songs and the poetry of the *Man'yōshū*: this represents a major difference from the West. Because Japan and the West cannot be said to experience an identical communion with nature, it is best to distinguish between them by calling the former a naive communion with nature, and the latter a romantic communion (Ōnishi, 1948, 1-12).

The Japanese naive communion with nature, though subdivided into several related components, refers in general to the original emotional fusing of life and nature by the Yamato people, who retained a way of life in accordance with nature. The source of the Yamato consciousness may have been linked in some respects to animism or to what Lucien Lévy-Bruhl calls "participation mystique." Exchange between nature and humanity was therefore effected directly and virtually unconsciously through the dynamic functioning of all senses on both the physical and the spiritual plane. In the West there had always been distance between the natural and the human, so that even the romantic communion with nature perfected by writers like Goethe demanded deep if externally imperceptible powers of spiritual concentration to bind the human with the natural (Ōnishi, 1948, 66-69). Psychological distance between the two was an impossibility in archaic and ancient Japan, and so the objective contemplation of nature could not exist. An objective response to nature first appears in medieval waka. Here, however, the situation is the opposite of that encountered by Western poets, whose spiritual powers were of necessity concentrated on binding together the human and natural worlds: the spiritual concentration demanded of waka poets was directed toward maintaining a distance from nature sufficient to make it an object for contemplation.

According to Ōnishi, waka written in the *Kokinshū* style should demonstrate an objective response to nature. From the standpoint of cultural consciousness, naive communion with nature pertains to an extremely simple intellectual level; as cultural and artistic consciousness evolves, human intelligence is liberated from the emotions and begins to take pleasure in intellectual activity for its own sake (Ōnishi, 1948, 89-93). The deep, ancient bond between the human and the natural in Japan, however, rendered infeasible the spontaneous development of contemplative distance. The diffusion of Chinese shih into their culture provided the Japanese with the literary force for contemplating nature at a distance. Distance between the human and the natural existed in China as well as the West. For up to the middle of the Six Dynasties period, nature appeared only exceptionally as a poetic subject and figured elsewhere in poetry as a mere metaphorical vehicle for human affairs.[10] Composition of shih on objects and natural scenes increased around the time of the Eastern Chin dynasty (Aoki, 1935a, 574-81). The attitude taken toward nature in these poems, however, is strictly descriptive. Only in the High T'ang period did Wang Wei (?699-761) and Tu Fu create expression in which the composer's feelings mingled with natural scenes and objects. The extreme rationality of the Han people suggests that the Chinese passed beyond the stage of naive communion with nature several centuries before the birth of Christ.

Waka poets, ignorant of High T'ang poetic expression, shaped their first "artistic waka" to conform to the intellectual style of Late Six Dynasties shih; and because intellectuality is incompatible with a naive communion with nature, the kotodama—which had only barely survived, in formal waka, into the late ninth century—quickly vanished from formal poetry with the commencement of the tenth century. The kotodama did not become extinct, although waka that openly manifested the kotodama indeed disappeared. This was a superficial disappearance: the kotodama lived on, only in a more obscure manner. Once the *Kokinshū* style had been authorized as standard for waka, its extreme tenacity resulted in the kotodama's never recapturing a role it had played in waka since at least the Ancient Age. The increasingly marked emergence of nature waka, beginning with the late eleventh century, was nevertheless inspired by kotodama reverberations. The numerical increase of nature waka might be dismissed as reflecting the popularity of nature as a poetic topic: but why did topics on nature increase in number? There must have been present a latent, profound perception of solidarity with nature that harked back to a time when Japanese thought the plant world capable of speech (see vol. one, 107).

[10] Nature is the subject of such poems as "Tung-shan" and "Chien-chia" in the *Shih Ching (The Book of Songs)*. Descriptions of nature are also found, for example, in "Chü-sung" in the *Ch'u-tz'u (The Songs of the South)*.

If waka on nature were only objective portrayals of natural scenes, they would not be seen as significant art. In fact, they would be severely criticized for transgressing aesthetic boundaries. An objective portrayal of nature might be considered valuable in a geomorphological treatise. Poetry being what it is, a nature-related topic must be given substance by emotion. In Western poetry emotion is usually expressed by joining portrayals of natural scenes with a certain amount of treatment in the expository or declarative mode. There are hardly any instances of poetry in a pure descriptive mode throughout.[11] With the end of the eleventh century, however, purely descriptive waka began appearing in some quantity, together with a strong tendency to evaluate these waka favorably. Their favorable reception was due to the audience's expectation that the nature depicted in the poem would speak in its own words, without the need for explanation from the composer. The premise inherent in their expectation is that the audience and nature have established, in the poem, a dialogue that does not rely on human language. Many twentieth-century Japanese who have been deeply moved by tanka or haiku in a pure descriptive mode would have great difficulty explaining the substance of their emotion to a foreigner. Even an adequate explanation must necessarily leave some elements unexplained, including the most important ones. The unexplained portion is what we are told in a voiceless, formless language, harking back to a time when not only the plant world but the very stones could speak. In general, neither poet nor audience is aware of this: the sole impression is of being indefinably moved.

Mutual involvement between the natural and the human appears not only in waka composition but in natural images frequently found within waka, particularly cherry blossoms and the moon. A Japanese feels more than aesthetic admiration in looking at cherry blossoms: a special emotion is experienced on coming into contact with the spirit of the cherry blossoms. The spiritual nature of cherry blossoms is evident in festivals like the Chinkasai, which celebrates the evil-averting powers of the blossoms. This festival already existed by the eighth century, was celebrated throughout the Middle Ages, and persists to this day.[12] The annual Japanese practice of viewing cherry blossoms should be seen in terms transcending the usual reports of tens of thousands of people crowding the

---

[11] Occasional instances occur in Western poetry, but insofar as they are incidental, they do not pose a threat to this theory. Imagist poetry makes much use of an intentionally pure descriptive mode, but this is due to the influence of haiku (Miner, 1958, 157-201).

[12] The Chinkasai is first mentioned in extant documents in the *Ryō no Gige* (2:77), compiled in 833. The festival was administered by the Department of Shrines, but it probably originated as a folk festival. In the Third Month of 1156, people are recorded to have chanted a waka, "Yasuraibana ya," and worshipped the gods at Murasakino (*Ryōjin Hishō* [= *RH*], "Kudenshū," 14:170-73); the same lyrics are still sung at the Chinkasai celebration at Imamiya Shrine in Murasakino, now part of Kyoto (Asano, 1953, 119-37).

parks when the cherries are in bloom. Consider, in addition, that the acts of drinking sake together and singing under the canopy of blossoms are performed to achieve communion with the spirit of the blossoms.

Modern Japanese are not aware of this. In the Middle Ages, the masses gathered under blossoming trees, drank and made merry, and composed linked verse, a practice that came to be known as "renga under the blossoms" (hana no moto no renga). The spirit of the blossoms was available to people because their gatherings took place beneath the flowering trees. Conversely, communion with the blossoms was impossible if they were viewed from a distance. The modern practice of viewing cherry blossoms has inherited this attitude: unless one has been directly under the blossoming branches, one cannot claim to have been viewing cherry blossoms. Another familiar Japanese event occurs on the night of the harvest moon, the fifteenth night of the Eighth Month according to the lunar calendar, when offerings of rice dumplings and susuki grasses are made to the moon. This is no mere custom: being in the moonlight evokes special emotions in the Japanese and is therefore an experience not easily understood by other nationalities.[13]

Cherry blossoms, the moon, and other natural objects are frequently employed as central images in nō. The central image appears repeatedly within a given nō and symbolizes its theme, a fact first noted by Ezra Pound (Miner, 1958, 135-55). Unifying images are often used in plays by Zeami and the group of playwrights associated with him. Those of cherry blossoms and the moon, however, are by far the most frequently used (Konishi, 1962b, 372-73). This point was discussed in Volume One in connection with moon imagery in the nō play *Izutsu*. Now I shall employ the imagery of cherry blossoms for the same purpose. The shite (protagonist) of Zeami's play *Tadanori* is a commander of the Heike forces. Tadanori, a soldier who is also a dedicated waka poet, entrusts the following poem to Shunzei before leaving for battle:

Sasanami ya   The capital at Shiga,
Shiga no miyako wa   Where rippling wavelets wash,
Arenishi o   Has fallen into ruin,

[13] I once heard this story about a Japanese medical student studying in Germany. On the night of the harvest moon, he went to a park and gazed at the moon to his heart's content. When he returned to his lodgings, the landlady questioned him closely about where he had been and what had kept him out so late. His reply—that he had been in the park looking at the moon—elicited no understanding from the landlady, who retorted that no one went to the park just to see the moon, and that her lodger must have been at some disreputable place. He could not communicate to the landlady, despite his excellent German, the feeling that moon-viewing could not be properly done from a window: one must be bathed in moonlight and view the moon from a place where there is vegetation. [Note curtailed.—Ed.]

| Mukashi nagara no | And yet its mountain cherry trees |
| Yamazakura kana. | Bloom as they did in days of yore![14] |

Shunzei subsequently selected Tadanori's poem for inclusion in the royal waka collection he compiled, the *Senzaishū* (1:66). But because the Heike were considered enemies of the crown, the poem was entered anonymously.

Tadanori fights bravely against the Genji forces and dies a heroic death, but he cannot achieve buddhahood while his treasured poem remains ostensibly anonymous. Tadanori's ghost, appearing before the waki (deuteragonist), a priest, asks him to contrive that Tadanori be given recognition for his waka. The ghost then relates how he died in a gallant battle long in the past. The play is filled with cherry blossom imagery: it begins with the waki singing "Even cherry blossoms displease / One turned from the world" (Hana o mo ushi to / Sutsuru mi no), and concludes with the words ". . . cherry blossoms / Are now to be my hosts!" (. . . hana koso / Aruji narikere). The play also incorporates Tandanori's death poem:

Yukikurete	It darkens as I go,
Konoshitakage o	And if I make my lodging place
Yado to seba	Under cover of the tree,
Hana ya koyoi no	Then I can claim that tonight
Aruji naramashi.	The cherry blossoms are my hosts.

It should not be difficult for Westerners to understand that these cherry blossoms represent certain things—that they symbolize waka, that essential feature of Heian culture, and that they symbolize in the fall of their petals the resolute death of a valiant commander. This interpretation is certainly not incorrect, and yet I sense that something more than this emanates from the stage during the play. When I watch a master actor perform *Tadanori*, his slightest movement seems to fill the stage with cherry trees in full bloom, and their energy advances toward me in the form of an emotion transcending meaning. This is not an explicable dimension like symbolizing a theme through imagery. It is a dialogue with the plant world, conducted in a voiceless, formless animatistic language that has survived within the Japanese people since archaic times. It is in this dialogue that the most nō-like expression is to be found.

The kind of emotion evoked in such a work may be characterized as emanating from a single concentrated image of expression inspired by waka

---

[14] "Shiga no miyako" is the capital established by Tenji Tennō (r. 662-72) on the shore of Lake Biwa; here the cherry blossoms symbolize its bygone glory. [Auth., Trans.]

in the pure descriptive mode. A closely related concept, that of seasonal diction (kigo) in haikai, should also be mentioned. Seasonal diction originally appeared in renga; its sole use was in the hokku (the first seventeen syllables of a renga sequence), where its only importance was to designate the seasonal circumstances of the time of composition. Seasonal diction was inherited by haikai but continued to be used only as a convention for hokku (opening stanzas). Matsuo Bashō's (1644-94) establishment of the "Bashō style" (Shōfū) altered the situation (as will be treated at large in Volume Four). The Bashō style first appeared in hokku written in a purely descriptive mode. The style is essentially identical to that of waka on nature in the pure descriptive mode: we readers, gradually savoring its expression, experience a welling-up of inexplicable emotion from the depths of our being. This emotion is evoked when the recipient is addressed in an animatistic language by nature itself, a nature lying concealed deep in the landscape. If the recipient is separated from nature by the spiritual barrier of objectivity, he will not experience this kind of emotion. The *Hototogisu* school and its offshoots regarded Bashō's purely descriptive hokku merely as objective portrayal, and the extent of their misreading needs no further description. When the properties inherent in Bashō's purely descriptive style are concentrated into a single image, they become seasonal diction. Bashō's seasonal diction is no mere convention but a medium through which the recipient converses directly with nature. This represents the survival of perceptions identical to those felt by the Yamato people of the Archaic Age. In this sense, even the Bashō seasonal style is myth.

The nature poetry in the *Man'yōshū*, some medieval nature waka, and hokku in the pure descriptive mode of Bashō-style haikai all share certain features. As central imagery, these features are also common to some nō and to haikai seasonal diction in the Bashō style (but not other styles). Archaic myth has survived into the Late Middle Ages. When it occasionally leaves the zoku world to permeate the Sinified sphere of ga, it shares an impetus to create not only novel but superb expression. This does not mean, however, that all nature waka are rooted in myth as it is conceived above: mythless descriptions of nature are in fact greater in quantity. What must be noted here is that the Middle Ages, though defined as the age of ga, are inhabited at their deepest stratum by zoku, a Yamato style of expression; and that the zoku aesthetic retained enough vitality to infuse ga occasionally with new life.

PART THREE

The Early Middle Ages:
The Age of Fūryū

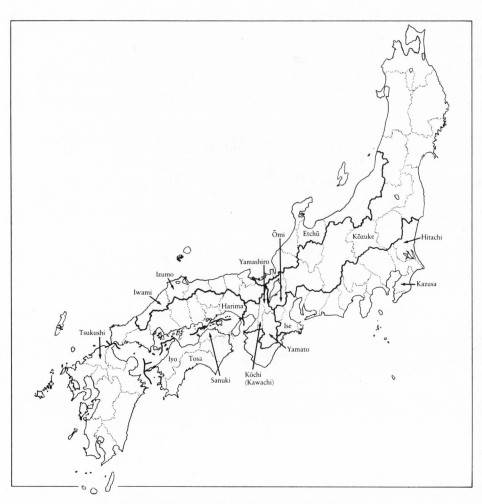

Selected Provinces for Early and Medieval Japan

CHAPTER 5

The Nature of
the Early Middle Ages

Following my criteria, if Japanese literature were perceived solely in terms of its poetry and prose in Chinese, their absorption of the Sinified ga aesthetic in the early ninth century would mark the beginning of the Middle Ages at that time. If, on the other hand, we consider that waka, the normative literary form conceived and expressed in the Japanese language by Japanese, had not yet been fully adapted to Chinese perceptions of the central focus creating expression from concepts, any point earlier than the mid-ninth century becomes unlikely. A Sinified conceptual focus had permeated waka by the late ninth century, and the tenth century saw the establishment of a ga style expressed in pure Yamato vocabulary. The symbolic point of ga establishment in waka is 905, the year a royal command was issued to compile the *Kokinshū*.[1] Japanese ga attained the ranks of the premier arts in this general period.

The sphere of ga expressed in the pure Yamato language not only gave birth to many masterpieces: these works definitely surpassed in quality Japanese efforts at composition in Chinese prose and poetry. The tenth and eleventh centuries thus truly represent the first high point of the Middle Ages as well as its most ideal period, its golden age, one might say. Later generations perceived these centuries as the locus of ga at its best; and their attempts at literary innovation were all based on tenth- and eleventh-century concepts of ga.[2] Westerners may find this a trait special to Japan. Hesiod's references to a golden age are to a period in the distant past, one followed by the silver and bronze ages.[3] The Japanese sought their golden age in the more recent past: their perception is linked not to a nostalgia for pastoral origins but rather to the view that ultimately good

---

[1] Periods of literary history cannot be divided by month or year. It is commonplace for literary phenomena belonging to an earlier age to survive into a later one, and for literary phenomena of a later age to show their first signs in an earlier age. A "symbolic point" represents a specific point in time established for the purpose of making conceptual demarcations. (See the General Introduction, vol. one.)

[2] This attitude has survived in the modern Japanese mind. The classical grammar courses taught in Japanese junior and senior high schools, for example, are organized around tenth- and eleventh-century waka and prose, which form the comparative base whereby modes of writing from other periods are explained.

[3] Hesiod's *Works and Days* contains a section on the "Five Ages of the World" (lines 106-201); the section on the golden age is found in lines 109-26 (Hirokawa, 1975, 404-407).

and beauty are to be found in a culture at its height, "glorious as flowers in bloom" (*MYS*, 3:328). The Japanese saw that they had reached "a goodly time" in their history when their level of cultural development equaled that of their advanced neighbor, China. The culture of Japan, however, was not to be a borrowed culture but one subjected to thorough Japanification. This idea was actualized in the tenth and eleventh centuries through the Japanese ga style characteristically found in waka.

Japanese literature could not be represented indefinitely by ga in the pure Yamato language. The *Shinkokinshū*, a royal anthology encompassing the most beautiful of all waka achievements, was created in the thirteenth century. Renga inherited this beauty and perpetuated it until the seventeenth century. Elsewhere, however, a new style of writing, a mixed form (wakan konkōbun) consisting of pure Japanese mingled with Chinese loanwords, led to the creation of works rivaling the waka and renga masterpieces.

The fate of literature is influenced above all by the presence of masterworks. The creation of superb Japanese literature written in the mixed style—works like the *Heike Monogatari (The Tale of the Heike)*, *Tsurezuregusa (Essays in Idleness)*, and nō by Zeami and his followers—was a literary phenomenon differing significantly in nature from works of the tenth and eleventh centuries. A distinction must therefore be made between the period in which masterpieces were written only in the pure Yamato idiom and that in which literature was written in the mixed linguistic style. The distinction is made here in my division of the Early Middle Ages (pure Yamato idiom) from the High Middle Ages (mixed style). Compositions in the mixed style most definitely did not arise out of an opposition to, or criticism of, early medieval ga. On the contrary, mixed-style literature idolizes the ga of bygone days and wishes to recreate its sublime beauty. High medieval compositions differ from their predecessors—despite an identical orientation toward ga—in their focus on fresh expression to move the high medieval audience. The same is true for high medieval genres that express ga in the pure Yamato language. One reflection of this is the high medieval response to the *Kokinshū*, the emblematic work of early medieval ga. Poets revered it as a source of vast authority, and yet they dared compile a waka collection titled the *New Kokinshū (Shinkokinshū)*.

Compositions in the mixed style appeared in considerable quantity in the twelfth century, but this corpus did not contain any masterworks great enough to change the course of Japanese literature. The year 1205 is perhaps an appropriate symbolic point at which to divide the Early from the High Middle Ages, since it marks the compilation of the *Shinkokinshū*, a collection that demonstrates high esteem for early medieval ga yet whose title manifests an intention to set the work apart from earlier waka collections. This point occurs precisely three hundred years after that which marks the commencement of the Early Middle Ages. This portion of my history will discuss the stages preceding the maturation of neoclassical compositions. Before concerning myself with actual compositions and literary phenomena, however, I should like to consider the spiritual basis that shaped early medieval ga: the principle of fūryū.

FŪRYŪ AND THE BEAUTY OF EN

The principle of fūryū was familiar to the Japanese as early as the second half of the Ancient Age: its function as a coordinate concept to orthodox Confucianism, and the role it played in a courtier's ideal life—Confucianism as his public philosophy and fūryū for his private life—were discussed in the first volume. This concept was further amplified and refined in the Early Middle Ages. Most important, the assimilation and normalization of fūryū within aristocratic life resulted in an increasing unawareness among the nobility that their lives were rooted in the fūryū principle. To be sure, "fūryū" was a word much used in the Middle Ages, but its meaning had been altered by then to suggest elaborate splendor.[4] Not only had the original Chinese sense been forgotten. But as time passed, fewer people remembered how "fūryū" had been used in the context of the later Ancient Age. "Miyabi," the Japanese reading of the Chinese characters for "feng-liu" (J. fūryū), barely retained a portion of the original Chinese meaning. The incorporation of fūryū into aristocratic life—a process so subtle it was unnoticed by the participants—and the nobility's practical application of fūryū in its full original Chinese senses, can only indicate how thoroughly aristocratic society absorbed the principle. These points, which are the reason for designating the Early Middle Ages as the age of fūryū, also furnish the basis for differentiating between fūryū and ga as it is manifested in the High Middle Ages.

As noted earlier, Chinese feng-liu (fūryū) signified an idealized sphere of worldly pleasures and was symbolized by four components: zither, poetry, wine, and singing-girls. These may be rephrased as music, literature, merrymaking, and the company of women. All four, as practiced in the world of men, are inevitably accompanied to some degree by feelings of want or dissatisfaction. The removal of want and dissatisfaction from their practice, and the addition of pleasure, as provided by the four components, equivalent to that enjoyed by the Taoist immortals, can only describe a state of fūryū (Konishi, 1962a, 271-78). The following discussion summarizes how such an interpretation is possible. To generalize from in-

---

[4] For example, the comment, "Kazan In was indeed a man of fūryū" (Ōkagami [= OK], 3:151), is made in reference to his innovative architectural plans, suggestive of Thomas Jefferson's, and to his elaborately beautiful designs for household furnishings.

stances in Chinese poetry, the term "feng-liu" (translated below as "elegant") appears very frequently in connection with the words "zither,"
"poetry," "wine," and "singing-girls," or with a composite of the four.
Examples follow.[5]

> Long ago in the Ch'en Palace, I wrote the finest *poem*,
> And when the banquet ended all the *elegant* people left.
>
> (Lo Yin, "At the House of Mr. Chiang, Governor of
> Ch'ing-hsi")
>
> Gathered here are *elegant* people, all respected *poets*
> Who praise the *wine* and entertainment and forget affairs of state.
>
> (Hsü Chen, "At the Lei Embankment")
>
> Hsieh An-shih is the most *elegant* of men:
> He willingly retired to Mount Tung with his *girl*.
>
> (Po Chü-i, "Written on a Sliding Door at
> Mr. Hsieh's Mt. Tung Villa")
>
> *Elegant*, the snow by the Lo River;
> Dawn and dusk, clouds trail across Yang-t'ai.[6]
> I hear a *zither*, but cannot listen to it,
> And must not seem to gaze on Lady Cho.[7]
>
> (Li Po, "On Seeing a Beauty and Hearing Her
> Zither Without Listening")

These lines provide definite corroboration that the material essence of
feng-liu was a life of poetry composition and reception, the enjoyment of
music and drinking parties, and delight in the company of women. "Feng-
liu," in the sense used here, appears in the Late Six Dynasties, T'ang, and
Sung periods. Significantly, the fourth component of feng-liu—the enjoyment of female society—became the focus of intense consciousness with
the T'ang period. The association between feng-liu and beautiful women
dates back to the Late Six Dynasties period, as is demonstrated by a couplet from "Jesting with His Ladylove," by the wife of Fan Ching: "*Elegant*

---

[5] Sources are as follows: Lo (*CTS*, 656:7544), Hsü (*CTS*, 774:8775), Po (*Haku Kōzan Shishū* [= *HKS*], sequel 15:2346), and Li (*CTS*, 773:8769).

[6] Since the Lo River and Yang-t'ai are both sites of trysts, with a king (in the former instance), and a nobleman (the latter case), their "elegance" has erotic associations. [Auth.,
Trans.]

[7] Cho Wen-chün was a gifted beauty of the Han period, made famous by her liaison with
the fu poet, Ssu-ma Hsiang-ju. The speaker here compares his ladylove to Lady Cho. [Auth.,
Trans.]

creature, I'm in love with you: / Can such a *passion* as this be concealed?" (*GDSE*, 5:529).[8] The association is most frequently found in informal T'ang compositions. The protagonist of "The Visit to the Immortals' Dwelling," introducing himself to two beautiful women named Five-Ma-trons and Ten-Maidens, employs "feng-liu" in a sense closer to "passion" than "elegance": "Ever since my youth I've been fond of affairs with sing-ing-girls. Longing for the right woman, I've roamed the wide world in search of feng-liu" (*Yu Hsien-k'u*; *Yūsenkutsu*, 116). A similar instance appears in a couplet by Yang Chü-yüan, quoted in "The Story of Ying-ying" ("Ying-ying Chuan") by Yüan Chen: "This *elegant* and noble youth has passionate thoughts aplenty: / He's pierced to the quick by his lady-love's letter." Here feng-liu is characterized by the young man's intense yet refined emotional involvement. The story begins with a friend asking the young man why he, a twenty-three-year-old, still has no ladylove. The youth replies, " 'I am in point of fact an amorous man, but I have yet to find the right girl' " (ibid., 299). Since this speech corresponds to the ear-lier couplet, "amorous" (hao-se) must have the same significance as "ele-gant" (feng-liu).

Although amorousness was a major component of feng-liu as inherited by the Japanese Early Middle Ages, the term "feng-liu" itself was soon transposed into the Yamato language as "miyabi" or "suki" (amorous-ness), and the relation to the Chinese term was forgotten. "Amorousness" meant more than "sexual pleasure" to Japanese courtiers. By itself, sexual pleasure would not lend a sense of miyabi or amorousness to relations with the opposite sex: exchanges of sophisticated, witty waka and highly polished conversation were also essential. Before Chang, the hero of "The Visit to the Immortals' Dwelling," consummates his love with Ten-Maid-ens, they exchange poems in a scene so leisurely that the modern reader is either dazed or driven to desperation, and yet without the exchange the scene would have no feng-liu. Sexual relations acquire feng-liu only when accompanied by a lover's dialogue that is liberally adorned with lofty, re-fined, witty poetry. Actions lacking this feature are to be condemned as (in the words of the young man in "The Story of Ying-ying") "Not at all an amorous act, but rather a barbarian's!" (*T'ang-Sung Ch'uan-ch'i Chi* [= *TSCC*], 4:299). Similarly, a Japanese youth just come of age is capti-vated by the sight of two charming sisters; he tears a strip from the hem of his everyday robe, writes the following love poem on it, and sends it to them.

---

[8] "Hsiao-niang," here translated "ladylove," literally means "Dame Hsiao" and refers to the fictional character Nung-yü, wife of the Ch'in Dynasty syrinx virtuoso Hsiao Shih (*Lieh-hsien Chuan*, 1:29-30). "Hsiao-niang" subsequently evolved into a common noun denoting a man's sweetheart or wife. The corresponding term used by a woman to denote her lover or husband is "hsiao-lang."

Kasugano no	Tender purple roots
Wakamurasaki no	From the fields of Kasuga
Surigoromo	Color my print robe
Shinobu no midare	With a fern-pattern wild
Kagiri shirarezu.	As my maddening, boundless love.

The narrator of the story judges that the waka displays "quick-witted mi-yabi" (*Ise Monogatari* [= *IM*], dan 1:111). "Miyabi" is here used in the same sense as it was in the second half of the Ancient Age, when the term served as the Japanese equivalent of "feng-liu." This waka episode, though very brief, portrays a world of amorous passion underscored by witty, poetic refinement; and, if amplified in complexity and density and adjusted for differences of tone between purity and decadent splendor, it is the very world depicted in "The Visit to the Immortals' Dwelling."

To the Heian aristocracy, a life filled with pleasures equivalent to those of the Chinese zither, shih, wine, and singing-girls was life at its most routine. They played wind instruments and strings; sang saibara, fuzoku, and poetry set to music; and composed extemporaneous shih and waka at gatherings they called "amusements" (asobi); needless to say, drinking also played a role in these events. The presence of women would make the "amusement" still more pleasant: court ladies probably served in this capacity at the royal palace. Noblewomen did not usually let themselves be seen by men other than close family members, but a kind of work mentality seems to have sanctioned the unusual act of ladies attending palace banquets. Their attendance led at times to liaisons, conduct also approved (or openly tolerated) under special circumstances. Sexual morality was strict in contemporary aristocratic society, and violators were condemned to severe punishment; only court ladies who served as banqueting companions were accorded special treatment. It is doubtful whether these court ladies can be compared with Chinese singing-girls. Of course the Japanese group's social status quite transcended that of Po Chü-i's singing-girl mistresses, Fan-su and Hsiao-man.

The degree of freedom permitted noblemen in their relations with court ladies is amply and easily illustrated by works like the *Makura no Sōshi (The Pillow Book)*. One might wonder whether such works describe only unusual events involving extroverted women like Sei Shōnagon (fl. ca. 1000). Yet circumstances were in fact little different for Murasaki Shikibu (?978–?1031). Fujiwara Michinaga once addressed her with the following waka and came knocking on the door of her bedroom that same night (*MSN*, 504):

| Sukimono to | Rumor has it that |
| Na ni shi tatereba | You are a most alluring flower: |

Miru hito no	Therefore any man
Orade suguru wa	Who sees you will be loath to pass
Araji to zo omou.	Unless he pluck you for himself.

Murasaki Shikibu, a more circumspect woman than her colleague Sei Shōnagon, leaves no clue in her nikki as to whether Michinaga's assertion—that she is a well-known "sukimono," or amorous woman—was false or somewhat accurate. Michinaga, on the other hand, would not have addressed her with such a waka if, in Murasaki Shikibu's and Sei Shōnagon's day, certain court ladies had not been worthy of the epithet "amorous"; nor would Murasaki Shikibu have included in her nikki the story of Michinaga's nocturnal visit if such trips to court ladies' bedrooms were regarded as acts of madness for eminent noblemen. Michinaga's behavior, amplified and translated into a fictional world, is precisely that of the Radiant Genji.

Such conduct toward a woman, whether performed by Michinaga or Genji, would be branded an abominable crime by modern women's-rights advocates. Yet this and similar passages in Heian nikki and monogatari seem to portray the men involved as thinking their behavior virtuous. Their perception evolved, I believe, from the Chinese concept of feng-liu/fūryū known to their forebears. By the Early Middle Ages, fūryū had become fixed, made routine within aristocratic life under the rubrics of "miyabi" and "amorousness." A man living in the second half of the Ancient Age ideally divided his stance toward life into a Confucian approach—for formal situations—and a Taoist or Buddhist approach for his private life.

This modus vivendi, however, had only recently been introduced into Japan, and considerable time was necessary before it became a fixed practice of daily life. The idea of following Confucian and Buddhist precepts may not have been greatly resisted by the Japanese, but the Taoist style of fūryū, especially putting into daily practice the more erotic aspects, was no easy accomplishment. As was perhaps natural, given the circumstances, more than a century elapsed before the Japanese could bring themselves to perceive these aspects as virtues. By the second half of the Ancient Age, the amorous features of fūryū had become intellectually acceptable and worthy of incorporation as poetic concepts in both shih and waka; but the normalization of these aspects, beginning with their being perceived as virtues, demanded not only the passage of time but the considerable influence exerted by a widening Japanese knowledge of the fūryū life as it was led in China.

The role of Po Lo-t'ien in modeling the feng-liu life has been discussed in Volume One. His governing principle was to lead his public life as Po Chü-i, according to orthodox Confucianism, and as the private citizen Lo-t'ien, to live according to the rules of feng-liu. This principle was apparently familiar to Japanese aristocratic society by the tenth century. Their knowledge came not only from *Po's Anthology (Po-shih Wen-chi*; J. *Hakushi Monjū)*, but also undoubtedly from reports made by continental emigrants. Lo-t'ien had two singing-girls, Fan-su and Hsiao-man, as mistresses. During his tenure as governor of Hangchow (822-24), moreover, he formed a liaison with the most famous singing-girl in the region, Su Hsiao-hsiao, and even appears to have brought her back to the capital for a while. Po wrote "Twenty Poems in Reply to 'Late Spring' " (*HKS*, sequel 9:2237) in 829, when he was fifty-eight; the final poem contains memories of Hangchow. [The question posed in the first line is answered in what follows.]

> Where does late spring appear finest?
> Spring is stunning in singing-girls' houses.
> Their eyebrows might well pass for willow leaves;
> Their crimson skirts shame the pomegranate blossoms.
> Orchids and musk perfume their going-out clothes;
> Gold and copper decorate their carriages.
> And they say that Su Hsiao-hsiao of Hangchow
> Is the most bewitching girl of all.

The themes of drinking and singing-girls appear most often in shih describing Po's stay in Hangchow, an indication of his way of life there. When reports of Po's life in Hangchow reached the capital, his friend Liu Yü-hsi (772-819) sent Po a shih informing him of the growing rumors that linked him with Hsiao-hsiao (*CTS*, 360:4060).

Another of Liu's poems, "Reply to Lo-t'ien's Verse Recollecting Times Once Spent Together" (*CTS*, 356:4003), notes that "people are still talking about" Po's drinking parties in Chiang-chou. Now that time has passed, Liu continues, and the two friends live far apart, "What has become of Su Hsiao-hsiao of Ch'ien-t'ang? / She longs for you, her tears falling on a pomegranate skirt." Liu adds further elucidation in a note to his poem: "The singing-girl kept by Po has recently left the capital and gone back to Ch'ien-t'ang." The poem immediately preceding this in the *Ch'üan T'ang-shih (Complete T'ang Poems)*, also the work of Liu, is titled, "Thinking of Ch'un-ts'ao"; it, too, is accompanied by a notation, "Ch'un-ts'ao is the name of Lo-t'ien's singing-girl." This woman was apparently under Po's protection in Loyang. Lo-t'ien is here very much in his element. His private penchant for parties graced by pretty women was nevertheless perceived as a virtue and did not pose the least contradiction to his equally virtuous conduct as a public figure dedicated to improving the commoners' lot. Former Japanese Prime Minister Katayama Tetsu has praised Po's shih solely in terms of their social criticism (Katayama,

1956), a view that can only be called narrow. No matter how great a man's ability to execute useful national policy, he would not have been considered an ideal figure by his contemporaries unless his abilities had been further refined by the experience of drunkenly pillowing his head in a beautiful woman's lap.

Once Po Chü-i's work had become known in Japan, no one else's compositions rivaled it in popularity. Li Po, Tu Fu, and Han Yü all gained wide respect in Japan, but not until the seventeenth century. The practice of orthodox Confucianism in public life and fūryū in private life is found in Japan beginning with the eighth century, a point that has been made repeatedly. And its evolution into a fixed, daily element of life was given considerable impetus by the recognition that Po Chü-i, the normative cultivated Chinese, had indeed practiced this modus vivendi. This conception was, of course, based on a dual image of Po, in which orthodox Confucianism coexisted with feng-liu or, in Yamato parlance, the serious (mame) coexisted with the amorous. Thus Michinaga, Murasaki Shikibu's nocturnal visitor, was by day a diligent senior official (Sansom, 1958, 173-74). Genji, who is thought to be modeled after Michinaga, does not, however, appear particularly conscientious in affairs of state. He is a master of the zither; his waka exchanges and conversational style are so elegant and witty that his ladies are deeply impressed and wonder " 'wherever he comes up with' " such skillful language.[9] Although sake is not much emphasized in *The Tale of Genji*, the hero's wideranging love affairs make him the personification of fūryū. For this reason, the reader has only a vague impression of the time Genji spends performing court duties. The *Genji*, written by a woman for other women and concerned with these women's own world, selects for its subject matter only private facets of Genji's life, his miyabi and amorousness. If Genji had actually existed, he would also undoubtedly have directed government affairs as a diligent and capable senior bureaucrat.

The leading principles of the Early Middle Ages, miyabi and amorousness, are both equivalent to the Chinese principle of feng-liu. This is the basis from which to grasp the significance of a further fact, that the highest aesthetic ideal for contemporary Japanese was "en" (refined beauty). The expression "en nari" (refined) is frequently employed in the *Genji* to underscore the beauty of a scene. The manuscript line descended from Teika's Aobyōshi recension of the *Genji* contains fifty-two instances of "en nari," to which may be added the ten times that related expressions occur (i.e., "en ari," "en garu," "en ge nari," "en datsu"), a total of sixty-two appearances of "en" in the *Genji*. "En nari" is often found in contemporary compositions, and it is particularly noteworthy that judgments

[9] *Genji Monogatari* [= GM], "Hahakigi," 96.

handed down at waka matches frequently deem a poem that is "en" the winner because it is "superior" (yū nari). Now, why would these various texts, all written in the Yamato language, contain so many instances of the Chinese loanword "en nari"? This is of course the adjectival form of "en" (Ch. yen). The expression "en nari," derived from the Chinese, was deliberately employed in Japanese texts because the Yamato language could not express what Japanese writers sensed and wished to verbalize. What, then, was the sensation communicated by the Chinese word "yen"? This term will be considered within the larger sphere of feng-liu/fūryū, especially as concerns its connection to one of the components of feng-liu, singing-girls.

"Yen" is often used in Chinese sources to describe beautiful women or brightly colored flowers like peonies and azaleas. The term also came to be employed in literary criticism to signify an ornate formal beauty—rather than beauty of content—in a work of prose or poetry (Umeno, 1979, 7-62). A beautiful woman described as "yen" is no ordinary beauty but a prototypical female immortal from the Taoist paradise. The composer was obliged to evoke associations of a female immortal sparkling with eternal youth if she is to be depicted as "yen."

> Both had *yen* features, and their gifts were splendid,
> But my willful nature rendered me ungrateful.
> (*WH*, 15:312, "Ssu-hsüan Fu")

> "Hey you, do you see that girl?
> Who in the world is she?
> How can any creature be so *yen*?"
> (*WH*, 19:402, "Goddess of the Lo")

The former example is taken from a monologue in which the speaker describes the splendid gifts he received from Princess Fu, goddess of the River Lo, and from a female immortal of Mt. T'ai-hua. These supernatural women are depicted thus: "Their scarlet lips parted in a smile, / And their faces glowed with radiant beauty." In the latter example, the speaker asks his driver about a beautiful woman he has just glimpsed near the River Lo. She proves to be Princess Fu and is subsequently described at length. The following section, drawn from the description of the goddess, sets forth concretely the essence of yen.

> Her shoulders were finely carved,
> Her hips supple as gathered silk;
> A graceful neck, a delicate nape,
> An alabaster skin were seen.

Perfumed hair oil had no place,
Nor had she use for paints and powders;
Her lofty chignon rose in splendor,
Her long eyebrows curved gently.
Outside, her ruby lips dazzled;
Inside, pearly teeth shone.
Her bright eyes were fine and charming,
And her cheeks were round and dimpled;
Her jewellike person, infinitely *yen*,
Was quiet in demeanor, graceful of form.

Mortal women, if depicted as immortals, also vividly illustrate the meaning of yen. One example appears in these lines from the second of Liu Ling-hsien's (sixth century A.D.) "Two Poems in Reply to My Husband" (*GDSE*, 6:547):

She is the evening moon, goddesslike,
Yielding as Princess Fu, as morning mist;
And when I look again into my mirror,
I know I cannot rival her in *yen*.

The speaker laments that the woman next door is as beautiful as the moon and the mist and so lovely that she resembles a goddess, particularly Princess Fu of the River Lo. As for herself, she needs but a glance at her mirror to realize her inferiority in terms of yen. This aptly demonstrates the associative relationship between yen and a female immortal. Another example, from "Peonies" (*CTS*, 643:7377) by Li Shan-fu (b. 820), treats of flora: "Clusters of immortals' *yen* emerge from the flames; / A moment of extraordinary scent descends from the heavens." Here scarlet peonies are compared to female immortals.

The association between yen/en and female immortals seems to have faded gradually from the Japanese consciousness. This occurred as the bonds weakened between the immortals' world and the principle of fūryū, leaving in its wake only a vague sense of things Chinese. En became the normative aesthetic principle of the Early Middle Ages, during which the new concept, ga, was being created from the fusion of Chinese and Yamato elements. The Japanese principle of en differs somewhat from the Chinese word.[10] Where the Chinese gives a sense of vividness and activity, the Japanese tends more toward the subdued and passive. An example of the Japanese version occurs in *The Tale of Genji*, in "Sakaki" ("The Sa-

---

[10] ["Yen" is usually translated as "voluptuous" or "gorgeous" and can convey a sense of overblown beauty.—Trans.]

cred Tree"): Genji is traveling to Sagano one autumn day to pay a visit to the Rokujō lady, who will soon be leaving for Ise with her daughter, newly designated to be High Priestess (*Genji Monogatari* [= GM], "Sakaki," 368).

> It was over a reed plain of melancholy beauty that he made his way to the shrine. The autumn flowers were gone and insects hummed in the wintry tangles. A wind whistling through the pines brought snatches of music, though so distant that he could not tell what was being played. The setting was most refined.[11]

This scene, which takes place on the seventh day of the ninth lunar month, is pronounced "most refined" (ito en nari) by the narrator of the *Genji*. Her use of "en" would not be easily understood by the Chinese poet who conceived of "yen" in terms of peonies ablaze with color. Of course, the *Genji* passage provides rather an extreme example of Japanese en: more positive instances appear in other Heian works. On the whole, however, the beauty of en undeniably possesses more passive connotations than the original Chinese term; the same is true for fūryū as contrasted with feng-liu. Implicitness, one of the characteristic features of Japanese literature (as discussed in the General Introduction), is one of the most striking properties acquired by things Chinese in the process of adaptation by the Japanese.

The early medieval perception of en as the leading aesthetic principle influenced subsequent ages considerably. A fixed conception emerged in the High Middle Ages of feminine beauty as the supreme aesthetic element. En has always denoted a feminine beauty. When Chinese works describe people as "yen," the subjects are exclusively women, never men (Umeno, 1979, 7-15). En, originally rooted in the image of the immortals' realm, evolved into a leading aesthetic principle as fūryū became a dominant way of life. The principle of en was further strengthened in Japan by the perception that kana literature was written chiefly by women, and that this literature included *The Tale of Genji*, the supreme prose masterwork.

Feminine beauty therefore deserved to occupy an aesthetic place of honor. This is why *The Tale of the Heike*, whose chief concern, properly speaking, should be with "the movement of bristling muscles" and "the gleam of the sun and the sweat of men and horses," has among its most highly prized episodes "Giō," "Kogō," "Kosaishō," and "Yokobue," all tragic stories of elegant and refined women. What is more, the peculiar phenomenon of the *Heike*—its unification through "that opening statement of pathos in the imayō style" (see vol. one, General Introduction)—

---

[11] [The translation is taken, with minor changes, from Murasaki Shikibu, *The Tale of Genji*, Seidensticker, 1976, 1:186.—Trans.]

does not seem unnatural if it is interpreted as the result of fixing the feminine aesthetic, en, within the reader's consciousness. In nō as well, the most highly valued pieces are those whose shite is a refined woman, and nō actors over the centuries have been delighted and honored to perform these plays. A revealing feature of the Middle Ages is the nō actor's perception that the plays most worth performing have a refined woman, not a valiant soldier or menacing demon, for the protagonist. The foundations for this perception were laid in the Early Middle Ages with the establishment of en as an expressive principle.

TRANSCRIPTION AND TEXTUAL FORM

Fūryū as a way of life, the expressive principle en, and the expressive technique of the oblique conceptual focus all elicited response from a great many composers and recipients. Their response gave rise to the literary activity that was to shape the Middle Ages. The Middle Ages might therefore be defined as a period that was shaped by the absorption of Chinese culture by Japan. The impetus behind the formation of the Middle Ages, however, came not only from an adopted Chinese culture. There was in addition an opposing force advocating the conservation of Yamato elements. The energy that resulted from the two forces may well be termed a fusion of Chinese and Yamato cultural strengths. The influence of the latter appears most conspicuously in the transcription and textual form of literature.

The Hiragana Syllabary and Prose in Japanese

Transcribing the Japanese language in Chinese characters entailed extreme difficulty. Ō no Yasumaro (d. 723) and his collaborators, laboring mightily to compile the Kojiki, carried out an important experiment in employing Chinese characters phonetically while abstracting their semantic meaning. Their idea was probably inspired by similar Korean experiments. The phonetic use of Chinese characters is particularly marked in song and waka, and characters so employed are often called "Man'-yōgana" (Man'yōshū kana). Phonetic use of Chinese characters is not limited to the Man'yōshū, however, and so I shall substitute the term "magana" in the following discussion.[12] The Chinese characters first employed as syllabic symbols were both numerous and varied, but by the early ninth century a given Japanese syllable was being expressed by an increasingly limited variety of characters. It gradually became common

---

[12] [The author is stressing the fact that "magana" or "Man'yōgana" in fact antedates the Man'yōshū, having been used in the first extant Japanese work, the Kojiki.—Ed.]

practice for this relatively restricted group to be transcribed, for purposes of speed and facility, in a curvilinear abbreviated style called sōsho. Characters written in sōsho were further simplified into shapes differing markedly from their original Chinese character forms, to produce the syllabic graphs of the hiragana syllabary. Another practice, developed contemporaneously, involved taking one part of a phonetically used Chinese character and employing it symbolically in place of the phonetically used character itself. These symbols, which were probably fixed as standard graphic forms prior to the mid-tenth century, came to be called the katakana syllabary.

The hiragana syllabary was more influential than the katakana system in the evolution of medieval literature. The two were employed in different situations. Katakana was chiefly used for lecture notes about works written in Chinese (i.e., the Chinese classics and Buddhist scriptures) and may thus be seen as a graphic form lending itself to bookish expression. Hiragana, by contrast, was employed in the most informal of circumstances. Shortly before the beginning of the tenth century, the Chinese classics and Buddhist scriptures began to be perceived as works to be avoided by well-bred women. This perception was accompanied by a general feeling that women were more suited to hiragana than to katakana, and the hiragana syllabary consequently came to be called the "woman's hand" (onna no te, or onnade).[13] This does not mean that hiragana was used exclusively by women, since men also employed this syllabary, if only in informal situations. The significance of the term is that women were permitted to use hiragana in formal as well as informal circumstances. This accords with the masculine practice of writing Chinese prose at formal events, whereas women used Japanese prose on both formal and informal occasions.

At some point in the early tenth century, however, an event occurred that ran contrary to contemporary common wisdom. The *Kokinshū*, a waka anthology compiled by royal command, was transcribed in hiragana. The oldest extant copy of the *Kokinshū*, the Sekido manuscript, is of early eleventh-century date, and the original text is unknown.[14] Nevertheless, the physical appearance of all extant *Kokinshū* manuscripts, corroborated by the fact that every subsequent royal waka anthology was recorded in hiragana, leads to the conclusion that the original *Kokinshū* text was also undoubtedly recorded in hiragana. I say it was recorded in hiragana, although a few words, including proper nouns and official titles,

---

[13] Hiragana is called "onna no te" ("Kurabiraki," Pt. 2:275) or "onnade" ("Kuniyuzuri," Pt. 1:319) in the tenth-century *Utsuho Monogatari*.

[14] A letter by Fujiwara Sadayori, now in the Hokuni Bunko collection, provides the basis for the surmise that the Sekido manuscript was begun in the winter of 1020 and completed the following year (Kyūsojin, 1961, 62-65).

were necessarily written in Chinese characters. In principle, however, the *Kokinshū* strictly observes a policy of using only hiragana; the policy is in fact so strict that modern Japanese are baffled when confronted with a *Kokinshū* text that has not been recast with an appropriate proportion of Chinese characters. The compilers acted most resolutely in their choice of transcriptive style: the hiragana syllabic system had barely reached the level of a fixed form by the time the *Kokinshū* was compiled.

The oldest extant source materials written in hiragana are a memorandum, dated 867, from a census conducted in Sanuki province,[15] and the priest Enchin's (814-91) holograph of "Byōchū Gonjōshō" ("A Letter Written from My Sickbed"), which belongs to the same period. Both documents are extremely brief, and the characters in them are not significantly different from sōsho, remaining instead on the borderline between recognizable hiragana and magana. We know, however, that abbreviated characters worthy of the name hiragana did exist at this time: characters extremely similar to hiragana are used in an ink inscription on a cypress fan that was discovered inside a statue of the thousand-armed Kannon (Avalokiteśvara) at the temple of Tōji in Kyoto. The *Kokinshū* was compiled at the beginning of the tenth century; the waka documents that served as its source material—Narihira's compositions, for example—were very likely written in abbreviated characters closely resembling modern hiragana (Tsukishima, 1981, 99-104). The hiragana syllabary was, however, not widely used until perhaps the end of the ninth century; thus the royal command of 905, directing that a waka anthology be compiled in hiragana, might very well be described as a great event, a resolute act.

The Preface to the *Kokinshū* clearly states that Tsurayuki and his colleagues were commanded to compile the anthology in order to demonstrate that waka was a premier art equivalent to shih. Tsurayuki writes in the Preface that waka, an art dating back to the creation of Heaven and Earth, was accorded great importance by past rulers of Japan and reaped incalculable honors when recited in formal settings. Some time ago, Tsurayuki continues, waka retreated to the informal sphere, where its sole raison d'être was to serve as go-between in love affairs.[16] He refers to a period of roughly four decades (809-50), during the reigns of Saga, Junna, and Nimmyō, when waka was overwhelmed by the ascendant genres of Chinese poetry and prose and very nearly abdicated its place as a premier art. In the ninth century, waka were no longer composed on glorious public occasions. This was not the case in previous centuries: Jitō Tennō (r. 690-97), during a progress to Yoshino, commanded that Kakinomoto Hi-

---

[15] [The document is called "Sanuki no Kuni Kosekichō Hashigaki," a descriptive title the gist of which is translated above.—Trans.]

[16] *KKS*, Preface, 10-11, 14-16. Tsurayuki is exaggerating somewhat: as we have seen, even in the ninth century waka was not completely absent from palace banquets.

tomaro (fl. ca. 680-700) "present a waka," and the poet's extemporaneous response began,

—Yasumishishi—	She who holds sway,
Waga Ōkimi no	Our Sovereign Lady,
Kikoshiosu	Is pleased to rule
Ame no shita ni . . .	The many provinces . . .

It is not clear who served as the guiding force behind the movement to restore waka to its former glory. From our modern vantage point it is extremely difficult to surmise, much less substantiate, that the movement was led by, say, the cloistered sovereign Uda (r. 887-97) or by Daigo Tennō (r. 897-930). Nevertheless there can be no doubt that the *Kokinshū* was born from a passionate wish to place waka on an equal footing with shih as a premier art. Two practical steps were taken to achieve this goal: transcribing waka in the hiragana syllabary, and limiting waka expression to Japanese vocabulary.

Another syllabary, magana, was employed as early as the compilation period of the *Chronicles* to transcribe songs and waka; magana was used for similar purposes in later periods, in the *Nihon Goki* and the *Ruiju Kokushi*. Transcription by means of hiragana is in principle identical to transcription by magana in that both systems use Chinese characters phonetically; but because hiragana represents a marked Japanification of the character forms, the act of writing waka in hiragana, corresponding to the transcription of shih in Chinese characters, had the emotional effect of sanctioning an independent waka sphere. The established perception that waka should be expressed only in the Yamato language, moreover, had not only an emotional effect but a momentous impact on the internal aspects of poetic diction. The Yamato language has never been capable of clearly expressing abstract concepts and logic, and so Chinese loanwords—Chinese characters used both phonetically and semantically—were necessarily employed to express these concepts.[17] If Chinese loanwords were excluded from the realm of waka, the expressed essence of waka would tend inevitably toward lyricism, and advanced concepts like those found in Kūkai's shih could be incorporated only with difficulty. Of course, waka cannot be labeled simply lyric poetry. But it is true that the evolution of waka within a specific, lyrically oriented scope was given decisive impetus by the royal order to compile the *Kokinshū*.

This scope allowed for a new kind of ga, expressed solely in the Yamato language and transcribed in hiragana. Its strong emphasis on Japanese

---

[17] I have defined the term "Chinese loanwords" (kango) thus because many of their number were coined in Japan and were not current in China itself.

characteristics suggests an aesthetic wholly different from the earlier form of ga, with its marked predisposition toward things Chinese. The "new" ga, however, was in fact one produced straightforwardly in an attempt to create a Japanese ga corresponding to the Chinese ideal that was its prototype. The creation of a new Japanese ga would have been impossible without the prior incorporation of the Chinese ideal. The penetration of the Chinese ga aesthetic into Japanese culture, and the later transformation of that aesthetic into something so Japanese that the Chinese prototype became indistinguishable, represents an adoption of Chinese culture at the most advanced level. The many examples of Chinese poetic diction incorporated into waka—accomplished by "transforming the bones and discarding the womb"[18]—in turn represent the adoption of Chinese culture on a lower level. One might even say that the most thorough Japanese adoption of Chinese culture is to be found in waka, which, through Yamato diction and hiragana, gave shape to a ga aesthetic equivalent to that possessed by shih. The equation defining this transformation, moreover, is found in the conceptual focus made through fabricated logic. All this clearly displays the elaborate course taken from China to Japan.

The building of a closed sphere, limited to Yamato diction, within Japanese literature is a matter holding great significance for subsequent literary development. In principle, waka were to have only Yamato diction, but that did not mean exceptions did not occur. Some exceptions to the rule, albeit very few, even appear in the royal waka anthologies:

Ryōzen no	Upon *Vulture Peak*
Shaka no mimae ni	In Śākya's august presence
Chigiriteshi	We made our vows,
Shinnyo kuchisezu	Fulfilled for our devotion to the *Truth*
Aimitsuru kana.	And so we met each other in this life.[19]

(*Shūishū* [= SIS], 20:1348)

Such works, however, are exceedingly rare. Any waka thought worthy of criticism was expected to be entirely free of Chinese loanwords or other

---

[18] [A Chinese expression signifying the use of ancient poetry and prose as material inspiration for one's own compositions.—Trans.]

[19] "Ryōzen" (Vulture Peak) is the mountain from which Śākya expounded the *Lotus Sūtra*; "Shaka" (Śākya) is the family name of the holy man Gautama, who later became the Buddha; and "shinnyo" (Truth) is a translation of the Sanskrit tathatā, which signifies the elemental reality that gives life to universal existence. All three terms are vocabulary drawn from Chinese translations of the Buddhist scriptures. The speaker of this waka sees himself, in his previous incarnation, as a disciple of Śākya, and the vows to which he refers were taken together with another disciple in that life. He now implies they have vowed to propagate the Buddhist concept of Truth in Japan during their next incarnation, and to meet each other again in the life to come.

words of foreign provenance. Japanese colloquialisms were also excluded. The only vocabulary acceptable for shih was contained in the Chinese classics.[20] Thus Japanese colloquialisms had to be eschewed in waka if it was to achieve a ga equivalent to that enjoyed by shih poetry. This tradition was perpetuated in renga. As long as renga was considered a mere diversion far lower than waka in status, Chinese loanwords and Japanese colloquialisms were acceptable. But once it had been elevated to a ga art on a level with waka, only Yamato diction was permissible. From that time forth, renga containing colloquialisms and Chinese loanwords evolved into a different genre called "haikai renga," informal linked verse. Its literary status was one step lower than that held by proper renga, and the relationship of haikai renga to the formal version was much like that between early renga and waka.

Other literature that was written entirely in Yamato diction and transcribed by syllabary includes works of prose in the broad sense of the term: nikki and monogatari.[21] The earliest work in Japanese vernacular prose bearing a definite date of composition is the *Tosa Nikki (The Tosa Diary)*, but the extant texts of *Taketori Monogatari (The Bamboo Cutter)* and *Ise Monogatari (Tales of Ise)* probably date from much the same period.[22] Unlike waka, proclaimed as a premier art rivaling the shih, these compositions were written for more humdrum purposes, for diversion, or for preserving transmitted legend, and were not perceived as works of art. Since in consequence ga was not as necessary an element to them as it was to waka, their texts included not only official titles and proper nouns but some commonly used Chinese loanwords that had lost most of their Sinified connotations. What seem colloquialisms also appear in their characters' speeches. A far larger proportion of their texts, however, employs Yamato diction. Written with a definite audience in mind, these compositions cannot be relegated to a realm completely removed from that of waka. Because vernacular prose compositions and waka apparently shared the same audience, or social class, some degree of literary status would have been accorded the prose works. These vernacular prose compositions belong, if you will, to a ga-zoku genre, a further product generated by the ga aesthetic of pure Yamato diction in waka.

[20] Colloquialisms appear occasionally in Po Chü-i's shih (Hanabusa, 1971, 430-43). Since, however, the Japanese lost contact with spoken Chinese after 838, the year of the last embassy to the T'ang court, a tenth-century courtier would not have been able to distinguish colloquialisms from written diction.

[21] To the Chinese, all prose compositions that do not fit into the category of parallel prose are deemed san-wen; I have called this view "prose in the narrow sense of the term." That concept corresponding to the English word "prose" will be termed "prose in the broad sense" (see ch. 1).

[22] This because their style is basically congruent with that of the *Tosa Nikki*, as will be discussed subsequently.

Literature in the Mixed Style

If the term "vernacular prose" is used to denote prose (in the broad sense) that consists principally of Yamato diction and contains very few colloquialisms and Chinese loanwords, then it may be said without exaggeration that waka and vernacular prose are the normative genres of early medieval literature. This is true because, as was discussed earlier, the zenith of a given genre is signaled by the appearance of composers who lead in creating new genres or expressive forms. Therefore the ninth century represents a period of decline for waka and, conversely, the zenith of prose and poetry in Chinese. The core section of the Early Middle Ages is defined as beginning in the tenth century, with the entry into and assimilation by waka of a Sinified conceptual focus, and ending in the eleventh century, with the refining and perfection of that process. The zenith of prose and poetry in Chinese thus occurred at an earlier stage, one that is characteristic of a transitional period between the Ancient Age and the Middle Ages. Kūkai and Princess Uchiko were active over a period of four decades, a very short time in comparison with the years encompassed by the tenth and eleventh centuries. Waka and vernacular prose compositions are undeniably the major genres of the Early Middle Ages. The shih of this period are no match for the achievement in waka and vernacular prose, whether it be in outstanding composers or in the number of compositions.

At the beginning of the thirteenth century, prose works began to be written in a style other than that of vernacular prose, the mixed style (wakan konkōbun). Prose compositions in the mixed style not only make ample use of Chinese loanwords but are written in a manner suggestive of Chinese prose. The *Hōjōki (An Account of My Hut)* is an exemplary work of this period. The mixed style uses both Chinese characters and a syllabary in its transcription. This method is extremely ancient, and its evolutionary course is quite complex. Modern scholarship has found three origins of the method (Tsukishima, 1981, 282-313).

1. A system using both Chinese characters and a syllabary, created to indicate the Japanese readings for Buddhist scriptures and Chinese classics.

2. The substitution of katakana or hiragana in place of the more cumbersome magana syllabary in the semmyō form of transcription.

3. A system using both Chinese characters and a syllabary, created by appending katakana or hiragana to Chinese prose adapted for reading in Japanese.

The oldest antecedent, in terms of documentary data, is the semmyō form. It is transcribed in a combination of Chinese characters and magana; the latter component, written in smaller characters, designates inflections and particles in the text.[23] This method is used not only in sem-myō but in norito and waka as well.[24] Since its normative usage is in semmyō, however, it is usually called the semmyō form. The oldest extant examples are two semmyō drafts, dated the twenty-fifth of the Third Month, 757, and the Eighth Month of 758 respectively.[25] The semmyō form of transcription was therefore devised prior to the late eighth cen-tury. If katakana are substituted for the magana that indicate inflection and particles in the semmyō text, the transcriptive method will resemble that of the *Konjaku Monogatari Shū (Tales of Times Now Past*, ca. 1120).[26] The oldest extant example of a Buddhist text using a combina-tion of Chinese characters and syllabary, and written to indicate Japanese readings, is a copy of the *Konkōmyō Saishōōkyō (Suvarṇa-prabhāsa Sū-tra)* owned by the temple Saidaiji in Nara. The notations are presumed to date from about 828 (Kasuga, 1943, 17-20).[27]

Another document dating from much the same period, a draft of pray-ers recited at the temple Tōdaiji in Nara, is written not in Chinese with appended notations but as an independent text in the mixed style.[28] Prose in Chinese that has been adapted for Japanese reading (waka kambun, also called hentai kambun) remains essentially Chinese prose, although the peculiarly Japanese nature of its syntax would make portions incom-prehensible to native Chinese. The texts of the *Kojiki* and the *Izumo no Kuni Fudoki (Izumo Topography)* are among the precursors of this form. Both, however, try wherever possible to observe Chinese syntax and to use Japanese locutions only when absolutely necessary. On the other hand, the diaries kept by Japanese rulers and court literati from the end of the ninth century on do not faithfully reproduce Chinese vocabulary and syn-tax but should instead be seen as another form of Japanese prose. These diaries, though principally transcribed in Chinese characters, occasionally

[23] For an example of this transcriptive method, see ch. 4.

[24] For instance, the congratulatory chōka presented to the throne by the chief priests of Kōfukuji, quoted above. The original text (*SNGK*, 19:223-25) is written in the semmyō form.

[25] The oldest known semmyō was issued by Mommu Tennō (r. 697-707) on the occasion of his accession to the throne, and it was recorded in the *Shoku Nihongi*. His proclamation, however, was very likely rewritten in an already established semmyō form in 793, the year the *Shoku Nihongi* was compiled; thus it is of limited value as a primary source (Tsukishima, 1981, 292-93).

[26] See ch. 8 for examples of this method of transcription.

[27] The sutra was copied in 762, but kunten (marks facilitating the reading of a Chinese text according to Japanese syntax) were added on two separate occasions, in about 828 and again in 1097. The notations, a combination of Chinese characters and kana, were written by the same scribe who added the first set of kunten.

[28] [The document is known as the *Tōdaiji Fūjumonkō*, a descriptive title.—Trans.] This draft, formerly in the possession of Satō Tatsujirō, burned during an air raid in the Second World War. Fortunately a collotype copy, made in 1939, exists and can be utilized as re-search material.

contain passages where a syllabary is used together with the Chinese characters (Tsukishima, 1981, 308-309).

Texts like these represent nothing more than a combining of Chinese characters with a syllabary as a means of transcription and are not to be considered examples of the mixed style of prose. The first work written in the mixed style may or may not be *Tales of Times Now Past*, which occupies a borderline position. The present scholarly community is strongly inclined to view it as a work in the mixed style. Its text, however, presents abundant evidence that it was written in a variant of the semmyō form, wherein magana sections are replaced by katakana. Originally belonging to the corpus of prose compositions in Chinese, *Tales of Times Now Past* is not easily considered an example of the mixed style. The mixed style is best defined as the result of vernacular prose expression combined with expression from that sector of prose in Chinese that was intended to be read along the lines of Japanese grammar and with some Yamato vocabulary. *Tales of Times Now Past* is totally unconnected to vernacular prose and therefore cannot be termed a mixed-style composition. Similarly, the *Uchigiki Shū*, which is also transcribed in the katakana variant of the semmyō form, is not an example of the mixed style. Generally speaking, setsuwa collections transcribed by means of Chinese characters combined with katakana are not mixed-style compositions. The hiragana syllabary, it will be recalled, was known as the "woman's hand": women used hiragana for formal prose.[29] Katakana was used chiefly for lecture notes on Buddhist scriptures or Chinese classics and so tended to be associated with "masculine" prose styles. The mixed style may best be approached not as a problem of transcription so much as a problem posed by a new style created by combining feminine, Japanese elements with masculine, Chinese ones.

The first step was made toward creating the mixed style when Chinese compositions were incorporated into vernacular prose. One example appears in a passage from the *Eiga Monogatari* (*A Tale of Flowering Fortunes*, ca. 1045; Kasuga, 1936, 320), in which the narrator prefaces her praise of Fujiwara Michinaga with impressions of his piety. Italics indicate Chinese loanwords in the original.

> There is a difference between fact and aspiration for people in this world, regardless of their status. Though a tree may wish to remain motionless, winds never cease to blow; though a son may intend to be *filial*, parents do not live forever. *Whoever lives* upon *this earth* must *perish*. A *life span* may be *immeasurably long*, but there is always a *limit*. Those who prosper must decline; where there is meet-

---

[29] Waka represents a separate case, in which both men and women were required to use hiragana exclusively.

ing, *parting* will follow. All is *cause* and *effect*; nothing is eternal. Fortunes that prospered yesterday may decline today. Even spring blossoms and autumn leaves are spoiled and lose their beauty when they
are enshrouded by spring haze and autumn mist. And after a gust of
wind scatters them, they are nothing but debris in a garden or froth
on the water. (*Eiga Monogatari* [= EM], "Utagai," 457)[30]

The first half of this passage is thought to have been taken directly from
the *Ōjō Yōshū* (*Essentials of Deliverance*, 984).[31] The latter half is apparently not based on any source, nor does it employ Chinese loanwords. But
its intricate parallelism is nonetheless well worth noting, although that is
probably not indigenous to vernacular prose.[32]

haru no hana ⎫
aki no momiji ⎭   to iedomo

haru no kasumi   tanabiki ⎫
aki no kiri   tachikome ⎭   tsureba

koborete nioi mo miezu   tada hitowatari no kaze ni chirinureba

niwa no chiri ⎫
mizu no awa ⎭   to koso wa narumere

Even { spring blossoms and
      { autumn leaves

are { spoiled and
    { lose their beauty

when they are enshrouded by { spring haze and
                             { autumn mist.

And after a gust of wind scatters them,

they are nothing but { debris in a garden or
                      { froth on the water.

The mixed style is not created simply by mixing Yamato diction with
Chinese loanwords. It must also make full use, within a vernacular prose
framework, of parallelism and other characteristically beautiful techniques of Chinese poetry and prose. *Flowering Fortunes*, however, is
based on various source materials and cannot generally be termed a precursor of the mixed style because this style does not appear in sections that

[30] [The translation is taken, with minor changes, from McCullough and McCullough,
1980, 2:515-16.—Trans.]

[31] Similar passages appear in the *Han-shih Wai-chuan* and *K'ung-tzu Chia-yü*, but the *Eiga*
passage probably drew on these sources only as quoted in the *Ōjō Yōshū* [by the Tendai
bishop, Genshin (942-1017)].

[32] Parallelism appears in Hitomaro's chōka, but prose should be distinguished as a separate matter. The Japanese Preface to the *Kokinshū* frequently uses parallelism, but this characteristic must be seen as patterned on styles in the *Wen Hsüan* and the *Yü-t'ai Hsin-yung*.

are thought to draw on court ladies' nikki. The first composition that clearly demonstrates the mixed style is *An Account of My Hut*, by Kamo no Chōmei (?1153-1216). Chōmei skillfully exploits the expressive potential of Chinese loanwords and fully calculates the literary effects of parallelism. These features fuse admirably with the lyrical aspects of vernacular prose to create a harmonious style.

An Account of My Hut, the first work written in the mixed style, was composed in 1212. Its composition date, as well as its perception of the tenth and eleventh centuries as a golden age, suggest that it is most appropriately considered a work of the High Middle Ages. It is not implied that the mixed style appeared suddenly: before the *Account* was written, Japanese writers produced such examples of the mixed style as the passage in *Flowering Fortunes*.

The vanguard of the High Middle Ages reaches into the twelfth century. This same century, moreover, shaped a conception of the tenth and eleventh centuries as a golden age.[33] And it perfected the early medieval aesthetic of ga. The twelfth century therefore represents a transitional period between the Early and High Middle Ages. The Early Middle Ages not only are a core section formed by the tenth and eleventh centuries but encompass the ninth and twelfth as well. It must be remembered, however, that the Ancient Age casts its shadow forward into the ninth century, as the High Middle Ages casts its own backward into the twelfth.

[33] Many twelfth-century collections of documents, including the *Ruiju Utaawase Maki*, the *Konjaku Monogatari Shū*, and the *Gōke Shidai*, reflect a conscious distinction between past and present and a desire to acknowledge the value of things past.

CHAPTER 6

Poetry and Prose in Chinese

THE INTRODUCTION AND DIFFUSION OF PO CHÜ-I'S POETRY IN JAPAN

Scholarly opinion differs on the question of how best to approach the evolution of early medieval literature in Chinese. If the principal object is literary expression, the most useful view may be Kojima Noriyuki's division of literature in Chinese into two periods, that preceding the introduction of Po Chü-i's poetry into Japan, and that following. We would attach still more importance to the literary aspects, however, if we focus our attention on the period when Po's characteristic poetic expression dominated Japanese shih expression, rather than on the date of the introduction of his work into Japan. The introduction of Po's poetry had no immediate effect on Japanese shih, which continued to be written in the Six Dynasties style. Not until forty years after the introduction of his poetry into the country were attempts made in Japan to compose in Po's style.

The importation of Po Chü-i's poetry to Japan is confirmed in one of the official Japanese annals: in 838, Fujiwara Takemori (808-51), deputy viceroy of Dazaifu, found the works of Yüan Chen and Po Chü-i among the goods imported by a Chinese merchant and presented them to Nimmyō Tennō. For this meritorious act, Takemori was promoted to the junior fifth rank, upper grade (*Montoku Jitsuroku*, 3:31). This event is well known (Okada, 1929b, 173). Po Chü-i was still alive in 838, and the first collection of his works, *Po-shih Ch'ang-ch'ing Chi* (50 fascs.; comp. 824), together with Yüan Chen's *Yüan-shih Ch'ang-ch'ing Chi* (comp. 823), were already extant. It is not clear, however, if these collections were among the works introduced to Japan at this time.[1] The imported works

---

[1] Po Chü-i's collected works appeared in fascicle groups of 50, 60, 65, 67, and 75. All were compiled by the author. In addition, the following collections, their titles and number of fascicles each recorded by the author, were transmitted separately: *Yüan Po Ch'ang-ho Chi* and *Yin-chi Chi*, 17 fascs. combined; *Liu Po Ch'ang-ho Chi*, 5 fascs.; and *Lo-hsia Yu-shang-yen Chi*, 10 fascs. (Hanabusa, 1960, 312-55). One of the texts brought to Japan was a copy made in 844 by the priest Egaku in China: it was acquired by the Sugawara family, and a copy of the copy is now in the collection of the Kanazawa Bunko (Suzuki Torao, 1936, 156-62). Another priest, Ennin, sent 6 fascs. of Po's poetry collection, titled *Po-chia Shih-chi*, to Japan. This information is found in *Jikaku Daishi Zaitō Sōshinroku* (entry for 19.I.840) and *Nittō Shingu Shōgyō Mokuroku* (1078-84). [Note curtailed.—Ed.]

may well have been the *Yüan Po Ch'ang-ho Chi* (17 fascs.), a series of poems exchanged between Yüan Chen and Po Chü-i; another possibility is that they were shorter works like *Po-chia Shih-chi* (6 fascs.), Po's small poetry collection, or the single-fascicle "Jen-shih Yüan-ko Hsing." Vocabulary thought to have been taken from Po's shih appears occasionally in compositions by Ono no Takamura and Koreyoshi Harumichi (dates unknown), which raises the possibility that some of Po's oeuvre was transmitted to Japan before 838. Depending on the vocabulary involved, the likely periods of transmission occur between 824 and 833, or between 810 and 824; but any work brought to Japan before the compilation of the fifty-fascicle *Po-shih Ch'ang-ch'ing Chi* is thought to have been transmitted orally (Kojima, 1973, 618-97). Research carried out by my senior colleagues thus establishes virtually beyond a doubt that the poetry of Po Chü-i was introduced to Japan before the middle of the ninth century. After this time, diction drawn from Po's poetry indeed appears with increasing frequency in Japanese shih, so much so that the idea of dividing Japanese literature in Chinese into pre- and post- Po Chü-i periods appears most reasonable. One question that demands reconsideration, however, is, what significance did the acceptance of Po's poetry hold for ninth-century Japan?

Let us first consider why Po's poetry met with so enthusiastic a reception from the ninth-century Japanese. The only possible reasons are the very high esteem Po's poetry enjoyed in China and its subsequent renown in other East Asian countries. During his lifetime, his poetry circulated widely among courtiers, intellectuals, and commoners alike. Yüan Chen describes the popularity of Po's poetry in his introduction to *Po-shih Ch'ang-ch'ing Chi.*[2]

> Over the last twenty years, these poems have appeared everywhere—at court and in government offices, in Taoist and Buddhist temples, at relay stations and on fences and walls; and everyone has recited them—princes and nobles, wives and concubines, cowherds and packhorse drivers. Some even wrote them down or made tracings and sold them in the market. Others here and there exchanged them for wine and tea.

By the time Po had reached his thirties, his poetry had become beloved by people from every social class. The poet himself corroborates this in part of a long letter to Yüan Chen ("Yü Yüan Chiu Shu").[3]

---

[2] Ssu-pu Ts'ung-k'an (ts'e 724), *Po-shih Ch'ang-ch'ing Chi* (Preface, 2); or *CTW*, 653:8424.
[3] Ssu-pu Ts'ung-k'an (ts'e 7), *Po-shih Ch'ang-ch'ing Chi*, 45:1094-104; or *CTW*, 675:8737-41.

Here is something else I've heard. A civilian inspector of military affairs named Kao Hsia-yü tried to procure a certain singing-girl; but she drew herself up and said, "*I* can recite Academician Po's 'Song of Everlasting Sorrow'! I'm not like the rest of these girls." I was told she'd used this accomplishment to raise her price.

In a postscript to his collected works, moreover, Po states that copies of his collection have been taken to Japan and Korea.[4] Yüan Chen refers to this in his introduction to *Po-shih Ch'ang-ch'ing Chi* when he reports,

Korean merchants search the markets eagerly for Po's compositions. One man told me, "Our chief minister pays one hundred gold pieces for every poem written by Po Chü-i, and he can always tell which are out-and-out forgeries."

This suggests that his poems were sold individually on occasion. Those of Po's works that came to Japan before 838 were very likely not oral transmissions but individually produced poems that made their way to Japan via Korea. The presence of forgeries on the market may reflect the great demand for Po's works in Korea; and the minister's ability to distinguish forgeries probably indicates that his reading of Po's poetry was on a level high enough to enable him to make fairly analytical observations of the poet's expressive style. Furthermore, Li Shang-yin (813-58) states in his "Inscription for Lord Po's Tombstone" (*CTW*, 780:10286) that "his name crossed the seas and spread to Korea, Vietnam, and other literate lands." A declaration that Po's "name" was known abroad need not signify that his literary collection had been circulated in foreign countries. On the other hand, it is difficult for a poet's fame to grow in the absence of his works. It is therefore probable that individual compositions also made their way to the area around Vietnam.

Okada Masayuki gives three reasons why the poetry of Po Chü-i received an enthusiastic reception in ninth-century Japan: (1) Po was famed in China for his poetry, (2) his poetic expression is clear and simple, and (3) his poetry is well disposed toward Buddhism (Okada, 1929b, 176-78). Kaneko Hikojirō adds four more reasons (Kaneko, 1943, 97-101). Okada's first reason is precisely to the point, and the preceding discussion has merely complemented or commented upon his theory. But the other points, including those made by Kaneko, are only mediate reasons that lack the power to explain why Po's poetry was so successful in Japan. If a fondness for Buddhism was the only requisite for achieving success in medieval Japan, Wang Wei would have been as famous there as Po Chü-i. Certainly the Buddhist features of Po's poetry further improved its recep-

---

[4] *Ssu-pu Ts'ung-k'an* (ts'e 747), *Po-shih Ch'ang-ch'ing Chi*, 71, postscript, dated 1.V.845. This was noted and translated by Arthur Waley (Waley, 1949, 212).

tion in Japan, but it was not the cause of the enthusiastic reception. The matter of Po's clear, simple expression is more problematic. Wang Wei's poetry is expressed with equal clarity and simplicity: the problem rests in the nature of Po's simplicity. An anecdote is often quoted to explain Po's simplicity of style (*Ling-chai Yüeh-hua*, 1:6, "An Old Woman Explicates Poetry").

> Every time Po Lo-t'ien composed a poem, he would request that a certain old woman explain it to him. "Well, do you understand it?" he would ask. If the old woman replied, "Yes," he would consider the poem to be finished, but if she replied, "No," he would redo it. This is why Late T'ang poetry is so vulgar.

The story is probably apocryphal and therefore unreliable. It is not at all odd that such stories were fabricated, however, since their chief stimulus is clearly evident in Po's poetry: much of its diction is conventional language used in T'ang daily life (Hanabusa, 1971, 430-44), and its topics as well often draw on everyday experiences (ibid., 461-74). Po's poetry was therefore easily understood—but only by the Chinese. Readers of other nationalities probably found certain features of Po's poetry incomprehensible.[5] The Chinese language studied by Japanese intellectuals was a literary or classical language, not ordinary spoken Chinese. There was virtually no spoken contact with mainland Chinese, and people like the priest Egaku (ninth century), who made four trips to China, were extremely unusual. Wang Wei's poetry is not only as clear, simple, and easily understood as Po's; it is also written in the literary language. The fact that his poetry was not read in early medieval Japan necessitates that certain revisions be made in the theory attributing the popularity of Po's poetry in Japan to its comprehensibility.

Another significant problem arises when Po's success in Japan is ascribed chiefly to his fame on the continent. Ninth-century Japanese intellectuals had probably not reached a cultural level high enough to enable them to understand why Po was highly regarded as a poet in China or, consequently, to comprehend the substance of his poetry. T'ang poetry reached its apogee with the works of such High T'ang poets as Li Po, Tu Fu, Wang Ch'ang-ling, and Wang Wei. Tu Fu in particular is unrivaled in his admirable fusion of a sublime topic and subtle diction with intensity of tone. His rate of success was so high that later poets probably labored long and hard to carve out for themselves artistic ground not already claimed by Tu Fu. This gave rise to two trends during the Middle T'ang

---

[5] I can understand Po's poetry when it is written in the literary language, but my lack of expertise in the Chinese language means I am at a loss when confronted with poems that contain colloquial T'ang Chinese (a frequent occurrence in Po's regulated verse). This is more than a matter of missing the linguistic sense: I simply do not understand the meaning.

period. The first was an attempt to depart from the High T'ang style—the culmination of a poetic style polished since the Six Dynasties period and perfected by Tu Fu (ga expression, if you will)—in order to evoke a sense of freshness through a revival of older poetic expression. The expression employed dated back to the Chou, Ch'in, Han, and Wei Dynasties. The result was a new kind of ga poetry comparable to that composed in the Meiji period by the *Araragi* waka poets, who used *Man'yōshū* diction to give vivid expression to the new feelings of the age. This trend is typified by the poetry of Han Yü. A second trend, arising in reaction to the subtle, strained expression of High T'ang poetry, aimed to create a new poetic sphere through mundane subject matter, colloquial expressions, and a simple tone. Po Chü-i's poetry is characteristic of this trend (Toyota, 1944, 159-83).

If considered only in this light, Po's poetry appears banal, vapid, and lacking in elegance. Yet the intimacy and easy accessibility of his poems, their natural tone and delicate emotional design, give the reader a sense of tremendous freshness. The grand pathos evoked by Tu Fu is strongly moving because it transcends the poet's individual dimension to become the elemental sorrow all of us must confront. The more intense the emotion evoked, however, the more likely the poem is to lack delicacy. Po's poetry, by contrast, may appear to be banal expression, but closer acquaintance will yield the truth hidden beneath its commonplace surface. The very lack of intensity within his poetry results, paradoxically, in more vivid impressions. The plainness of Po's poetry is the product of constant, repeated revisions of expression or, in Po's own words, "frequent revisions of my old verses" (*HKS*, sequel 5:2168, "On Poetry"). His actions were motivated by a desire to surpass High T'ang poetry. To ignore this point and imitate only the external aspects of Po's style is to risk lapsing into almost hopeless superficiality. Early medieval Japanese readers, however, skipped over the High T'ang period, leaping instead from Six Dynasties and Early T'ang poetry to that of Po Chü-i (Waley, 1949, 213). Not only were the ninth-century Japanese ignorant of Li Po and Tu Fu; they also knew nothing of Han Yü, whose works exemplify half of the Middle T'ang poetic corpus. Why did their acceptance of Chinese poetry follow this curious fashion? Because, I believe, the Japanese poetic world had not then become advanced enough to discriminate among Chinese poetic styles and appreciate them critically. Thus the Japanese chose Chinese poets solely on the basis of continental reputations.

One more important problem remains. When I stated earlier that Po's poetry seems to lack elegance if it is considered only in terms of the trend toward mundane poetic topics, my reference to "Po's poetry" was to that corpus we modern readers find most characteristic of Po Chü-i's poetry, not to his complete poetic works. What we perceive as typical of Po is expression that evokes a deep response despite its plainness and simplicity. But this is not true for all his poetry. Po Chü-i was a many-sided man who did not always adhere to a single approach. Just as he adapted his approaches toward life in accordance with the many things presented by public and private events, so did he employ various expressive techniques in his poetry in response to various settings. He sometimes tried his hand at oblique expression in the Six Dynasties style, and his oblique verse was quoted in Japan. More important, Japanese responded lukewarmly to the political aspects of Po's poetry, and this despite the poet's own conviction that social and political criticism was his proper province.[6] Of all the Japanese shih poets, only Sugawara Michizane incorporates a political consciousness in his work, and even here it is meager in quantity. Of course the *Ch'in-chung Yin (Songs of Ch'in)* and the *Hsin Yüeh-fu (New Ballads)* were read in Japan, but only as sources for poetic diction. Several problems are raised by the Japanese avoidance of the sharp criticism in Po's poetry.

This discussion has dealt with poetry, but a similar phenomenon also appears in prose. Parallel prose, a Six Dynasties style, was the dominant prose form in ninth-century Japan; plain prose began making gradual inroads as the tenth century approached. These inroads, however, were the result of Japanese writers imitating Po's and Yüan's plain prose and were not the product of exposure to plain prose written by the great stylists Han Yü and Liu Tsung-yüan. Han's poetry is interesting, but it has never impressed me as superb. This may not be a fair judgment, since my poetic criteria tend to be based on those appropriate to renga. On the other hand, I cannot help but marvel at Han's plain prose style. And despite my taste founded on renga, I am struck by the true excellence of Liu's plain prose expression. Neither Po's nor Yüan's plain prose (excepting the latter's "Story of Ying-ying"), however, has moved me very much. The received impression of plainness, lackluster, and inelegance seems far more appositely applied to their plain prose than to their poetry.

THE ACHIEVEMENT OF MICHIZANE

The poetic style of Japanese shih changed dramatically in the late ninth and early tenth centuries. This change, the result of the impact of Po Chü-i on Japanese shih, was principally carried out by Sugawara Michizane. Japanese shih poets did not, of course, immediately abandon the Six

---

[6] In his long letter to Yüan Chen, telling the story of the singing-girl who raises her fee because she knows his "Song of Everlasting Sorrow," Po goes on to state that his poetry is recited everywhere, although in fact "the world values most those pieces I value least." Po adds that he himself feels that "people may see my poetry and understand my principles" if they read his admonitory verses and his poems on tranquillity ("Yü Yüan Chiu Shu").

Dynasties style and its extension, the Early T'ang style, for that of Po Chü-i. Even Michizane employed both styles throughout his life. His work gives little indication of a sudden, distinct shift to the Po style, and he maintained a witty and oblique poetic stance to the end, as was noted earlier. The Ancient Age, when shih poetry was written in the Six Dynasties style, thus deeply influenced the sphere of Japanese shih up to the end of Michizane's life, and in this respect he serves as rearguard commander for the Ancient Age. Yet Michizane was also responsible for the rapid dissemination of the Po style in Japan, and so he can also be perceived as moving in the vanguard of the Middle Ages. The late ninth and early tenth centuries are in effect transitional years for the Japanese shih as it moves from the Ancient Age to the Middle Ages, and Michizane's poetic style is often seen to correspond to fluctuations in his personal environment. Four periods are normally distinguished:

> First period of success (845-84): residing in the capital.
> First period of despair (885-90): governor of Sanuki.
> Second period of success (891-900): residing in the capital.
> Second period of despair (901-903): exiled to Dazaifu.

Michizane's style, however, cannot always be divided neatly into periods. Since his shih style is on the whole duofaceted, ranging between the Six Dynasties and the Po styles, circumstance likely determined which style would appear at a specific time.

In Michizane's day, shih were composed to correspond to a given situation. Shih intended for recitation at a formal court banquet were expected to employ the ornate (Ch. ch'i-li; J. kirei) expression characteristic of the Six Dynasties style. More modern expression, such as that produced by two poets branded "frivolous Yüan [Chen] and vulgar Po [Chü-i]," was best avoided in formal circumstances. Michizane was probably the premier poet of his time in composing beautiful shih for formal banquet settings. He very likely retained this talent throughout his life, although some phases of his career—his rustication as provincial governor and his exile at Dazaifu—offered little opportunity to compose banquet poems. Michizane's shih, "On the Topic, 'Flowers in the Rain,' " was quoted and discussed above as an illustration of his capacity to create lovely poetry in the Six Dynasties style. Let us consider another example.

> "Is your silky skin too fine to bear the weight of clothes?"
> Her quick reply: "The heavy air of spring wraps around my waist!"
> Ruined makeup?—She's too bored to open her jeweled case;
> A little stroll?—She's loath to step beyond her dressing room.
> Bewitching glances, wave on wave, raise tempests in my heart;
> Her dancing figure, swirling snow, flies on when skies have cleared.

In flowering boughs, the sun sets, and flutes cease their song:
Seen from afar, a little cloud returns to her cave.[7]

The shih is titled, "On the Topic, 'In Spring a Beauty Quite Lacks Energy,'
Given by His Majesty to All Who Attended an Informal Banquet in Early
Spring at the Jijūden" (*KB*, 2:148). It was composed on the twenty-first of
the First Month, 885, when Michizane was forty-one years old. This
poem also has a fine prose preface that will be discussed later. Female musicians customarily played at informal court banquets, and this particular
occasion also included performances by singers and dancers from the Female Dancers' and Musicians' Office.[8] The dancers become the subject
matter of Michizane's poem. He and other courtiers were composing
poems developing the selected topic, "In spring a beauty quite lacks energy," a line from a poem by Po Chü-i ("Composed on a Spring Excursion
in Loyang and Sent to My Friends," *HKS*, sequel 12:2284). The shih were
to center on the circumstances suggested by Po's line of poetry. Freed from
the problem of what to write about, the poets directed their concern solely
to how the subject should be expressed. It consequently became routine
for poets to emphasize verbal technique in shih composed on an assigned
Chinese verse-topic. Such shih can be splendid examples of linguistic tech-
nology. "Beauty" (wa) in Po's line of poetry suggests a soft, slender figure
that in turn evokes the image of willow branches swaying languidly in the
breeze: hence his expression "quite lacks energy" (wu ch'i-li). In Michizane's poem, the speaker asks the dancer if her costume is not too heavy
for her fair, silky skin and delicate frame. The dancer gives an unexpected
response: the costume is weighed down by the air of spring that rises to
envelop her legs and torso. Fūryū is manifested here in the speaker's and
the lovely dancer's shared delight in fabricated logic, represented in this
couplet by the conceit that the atmosphere of spring possesses a physical
weight. The lines that follow are also rich in ornate beauty. In its high col-
oration, the linguistic sense of the poem is certainly closer to the *Yü-t'ai
Hsin-yung (New Songs from the Jade Terrace)* than to the *Wen Hsüan (Selections of Refined Literature)*.

   The Six Dynasties style of beauty in Michizane's shih surpasses that
found in earlier ninth-century Japanese achievements in Chinese prose
and poetry—the products of the "golden age" of prose and poetry in
Chinese. Compare, for example, Michizane's poem with Princess Uchi-

---

   [7] In Chinese poetry, clouds conventionally originate in caves. Here Michizane reverses the
convention to have the "cloud" (the dancer) return to her "cave" (her dressing room) once
the performance is over. [Auth., Trans.]

   [8] "On 21.I. [885], during the reign of Kōkō Tennō, an informal banquet for royal attendants was held in the Jijūden. The Musicians' Office had charge of performances by female
musicians and dancers. In addition to the attendants, five or six literary gentlemen were present and recited their shih" (*RK*, 72:341).

ko's "Matching the Former Sovereign's Poem on 'New Year's Eve' " (*KK*, 13:167).

The recluse shuns festivities, borne along with time
And heedless that the disappointing year is soon to pass.
At dawn the lamps are half empty, yet the starlight fades;
With only winter flowers in bloom, the snow is much too bright.
A sunlit grove: the haze seems warm, and birdsong issues forth;
A hidden brook: its ice is gone, but the water makes no sound.
Old chests packed with spring clothes—all night, looking through them,
She wonders if tomorrow she'll see sprouts on willow branches.

Uchiko's shih, matching Saga's poem on "New Year's Eve," surpasses his in descriptive beauty. Similarly, Shigeno Sadanushi's and Koreyoshi Harumichi's shih, composed on the same occasion and subject, are inferior to the princess's poem in every respect. Since Uchiko's poem differs in subject matter from Michizane's, their respective beauty must also be substantively different. Still, the princess's shih is probably the finest composed in Japan in the first half of the ninth century. Michizane's poem is nevertheless more beautiful, in the Six Dynasties sense, than is Uchiko's. It is by no means easy to determine which is superior in beauty, Uchiko's composition—rather reminiscent of poetry in *Selections of Refined Literature*—or Michizane's shih, written much in the poetic style of *New Songs from the Jade Terrace*. Where the third through sixth lines of Uchiko's poem are expressed in a simple descriptive mode, however, Michizane's displays unique virtuosity in the treatment of symbolic imagery. The opening words of line six of his poem, "Her dancing figure, swirling snow," signifies that the girl's dancing style resembles falling snow. This is only a metaphor; the second half of the line, "flies on when skies have cleared," on the other hand, is not a depiction of a natural scene. Its significance is that the sight of snow dancing in the sky remains as an afterimage in the speaker's mind long after the snow has stopped. And the tenor or signified of the phrase is that the speaker retains an indelible impression of the pretty girl's dance. "Flutes cease their song," in line seven, clearly marks the end of the dance; and in line eight, the image of a cloud—a small one glimpsed through flowering trees at dusk, as it quietly returns to the mountains—is employed symbolically to express the dancer's leaving the stage. The signified of "a little cloud" is the dancer, and that of "flowering boughs" in line seven is both a natural scene and an afterimage of the lovely dance. Ornate expression of this kind did not exist in Japan in the first half of the ninth century.

The appearance, in Michizane's shih, of expression in the Po style did not result from the poet's criticizing and rejecting the Six Dynasties aesthetic that characterizes his banquet poetry. On the contrary, Michizane experimented with the Po style long before he abandoned the Six Dynasties style. His stylistic proximity to Po can be seen in a composition thought to date from Michizane's twenty-third or twenty-sixth year, "Matching Professor Abe's Poem, 'Composed on Behalf of Master Anonymous, and Addressed to Little Lord Pride' " (KB, 1:15). The subjects of the poem are the young scion of a powerful house, a man given to haughtiness despite his lack of ability, and a Confucian scholar who admonishes him. It seems Michizane based his poem on contemporary people and events.[9]

Various characters and events are depicted in earlier ninth-century Japanese shih, but in all cases they represent types rather than individuals. Princess Uchiko obviously intends to refer to herself in her "New Year's Eve" poem, but the terms of reference are such that they can easily refer to others. The "recluse" of the poem could be anyone who leads an inconspicuous, quiet life, or it could denote a prototypical character representative of such a person, someone, so to speak, known by a common rather than a proper noun. By contrast, the man known as Master Anonymous requires the name "Anonymous," paradoxically, because he really existed. He is said to represent Michizane's father Koreyoshi (812-80; KB, supp. notes:640). Michizane was the first Japanese shih poet to depict characters whose sole artistic purpose is their strong resemblance to actual people, and this practice was probably inspired by Po's poetry.[10]

It is very easy to find shih in the Po style written by Michizane in his thirties. He had already mastered the Po style when he composed, " 'In Spring a Beauty Quite Lacks Energy,' " a supreme representation of the Six Dynasties aesthetic. An embassy from P'o-hai arrived in Japan in the Eleventh Month of 882 and entered the capital on the twenty-eighth of the Fourth Month, 883 (SJ, 42:535). On the latter occasion nine shih were exchanged between Michizane and P'ei T'ing, the P'o-hai ambassador (KB, 2:104-12). P'ei's impression of the exchange is quoted in a letter from Sugano Korenori (fl. ca. 885-88) to Michizane: " 'The Vice Minister of Civil Affairs [Michizane] has mastered Po Chü-i's style' " (KB, 2:119, Michizane's notation). Michizane comments that the ambassador flattered him; but flattery cannot emerge from pure fabrication, and so P'ei's impression was very likely based largely on fact. It is equally undeniable to the mod-

---

[9] "Professor Abe" is Abe no Okiyuki, who became professor of letters at the Court School in 888. "Master Anonymous" and "Little Lord Pride" are fictional characters modeled on actual people, along the lines of Kūkai's "Recluse Nothingness" and "Young Lord Leech's Tusk."

[10] For example, in the first line of Po's "Song of Everlasting Sorrow"—"The Han Emperor, amorous, longed for a devastating beauty" (HKS, 12:1911)—"the Han Emperor" clearly stands for Emperor Hsüan-tsung of the T'ang Dynasty. Failure to recognize this results in an incomplete appreciation of the poem.

ern reader that, by the time of his thirties, Michizane had acquired a considerable understanding of Po Chü-i's style. On the sixteenth of the Eighth
Month, 900, eighteen years after the visit of the P'o-hai embassy, Michizane presented a collection of his shih in twenty-eight fascicles to Daigo
Tennō (*NKR*, pt. 2, 1:6). Daigo responded with a shih in praise of Michizane, titled "On Reading the Shih Collection Presented by the Minister of
the Right" (*Kanke Kōshū* [= *KKKS*], 471-72). The shih concludes with
the couplet, "Sugawara's style surpasses even that of Po; / Lo-t'ien's
works I now consign to chests to gather dust." This praise is unmistakably
exaggerated. Nevertheless the couplet indicates that Michizane's shih
were widely acknowledged to be modeled on the Po style. Yet despite
Michizane's longstanding orientation toward the Po style, he continued
beyond his forties to compose ornate shih in the Six Dynasties style. How
are we to view this?

"The Po style" has been used here to indicate that expressive form most
characteristic of Po Chü-i's poetry; but this is not to say that Po composed
only that kind of poetry. His public persona of the diligent worker, and its
private counterpart, the lover of the feng-liu life, was noted earlier. Po's
poetry is similarly duofaceted. He would certainly not have composed political poetry, along the lines of the *Songs of Ch'in*, while immersed in elegant revels at a singing-girl's establishment. Such women's clientele was
made up chiefly of literati, with a smattering of wealthy merchants, and
entertainment took place in a cultivated social setting. Singing-girls were
thus required to have some knowledge of literature; some were erudite
enough to exchange shih with chuang-yüan, those men who had scored
highest in the civil service examination (Kishibe, 1960, 105). Such women
probably favored ornate poetry. Po's "Twenty Poems in Reply to 'Late
Spring' " is an example of this style. Having patterned his poetic style on
Po's entire corpus, and not just on the "Po style" in the narrow sense,
Michizane would not have considered the ornate poetry incompatible
with Po's style. Most of Michizane's fellow shih poets very likely shared
his attitude.

Nevertheless the "Po style," that perceived as most typical of Po's poetry, did in fact gradually and profoundly dominate the Japanese shih circle, and in due course it was thought to be solely representative of Po's
work. This process may be better understood if we first grasp what it is
that makes up Po's characteristic poetic style. Many scholars have directed their attention to this question; a summary, based particularly on
Hanabusa Hideki's apposite and detailed exposition, follows (Hanabusa,
1971, 430-87).

1. Po's vocabulary generally adheres closely to that found in T'ang life,
with few unusual words appearing.

2. Natural qualities are prized in poetic structure: Po does not care for marked breaks or thematic leaps in couplets, or for abrupt transitions.

3. Subject matter is generally based on the poet's experiences, including miscellaneous personal matters and topics current in society. Historical personages sometimes appear in Po's poetry.

4. His themes involve respect for humanity and are rooted in Confucian ethics.

A few more elements will be added to this list when Michizane's shih are discussed, but the analysis will be based largely on the four stylistic characteristics.

The major characteristics of Michizane's shih are unlike those of earlier ninth-century poetry. To begin with matters of form, the difference is manifested in Michizane's development of long shih. I say "long shih," although the genre is intrinsically limited by the characteristic Japanese tendency toward brevity in literature, and therefore his poetry does not reach any great length. Michizane's longest composition is the two-hundred-line "Reminiscences, a Poem in One Hundred Rhymed Couplets" (KKKS, 484). He also has a hundred-line poem, "Five Events Seen from a Boat" (KB, 3:236), as well as several compositions greater than twenty lines long.[11] "Late Chrysanthemums" (KB, 1:3), a twenty-line shih composed by Michizane when he was sixteen years old, indicates an early tendency toward long poems. It is difficult, given the early appearance of such poems, to ascribe their length to Po's influence. The longer Michizane's shih grow, the greater is the content the poet wishes to express. Japanese shih composed in the first half of the ninth century (Kūkai's excepted) did no more than repeat long-established Chinese stances, subjects, and conventional responses. By contrast, a poet who attempted to express his own feelings in his own persona inevitably tended to compose long works. We should also note Michizane's adoption of the dramatic mode as a technique for emphasizing his message. Not that use of the dramatic mode was in itself a novel technique. As we have seen, Kūkai had already experimented with it. What I would like to stress, however, is that Michizane's decision to adopt this mode was inspired by Po's poetry. Specific instances will be discussed below.

Increasing the number of lines and experimenting with the dramatic mode—the latter an anomaly in Japanese shih—were, for Michizane, phenomena resulting from the content he wished to express. But why did he wish to express that content? The answer must be sought in events actually experienced by Michizane. "Dreaming of Amaro" (KB 2:117), a

---

[11] Shih twenty lines or longer are as follows (numbering is according to the NKBT ed.): numbers 3, 4, 5, 75, 87, 98, 117, 118, 193, 219, 236, 254, 262, 269, 279, 292, 354, 357, 360, 373, 449, 477, 483, 484, 486, 490, 500.

twenty-eight-line shih, is a lament for his favorite son Amaro, who died at the age of five. Regulated verse, one of the most frequently used shih forms, was not only too brief to allow Michizane full and satisfactory expression of his emotions; its orderly nature was also inappropriate for the content the poet wished to express.

> . . . Only ten days gone since drugs first quelled your agony;
> Your wandering soul, zephyr-led, reached the Underworld.
> Thereafter I reproached the gods, reproached the buddhas too,
> For a time perceiving neither earth nor heaven above.
> Gazing at my knees, I am filled with self-contempt,
> And grieve that your little brother followed you in death. . . .

Amaro died ten days after the onset of his illness, having suffered severe pain, and his infant brother also died of illness. The speaker, gazing at knees once clung to by playful children and deriding his wretched fate, is Michizane himself. There is no aesthetic distance between poet and speaker. A description of keepsakes left behind by Amaro suggests that Michizane's experience is expressed exactly as it happened:

> . . . On the door, a bow of mulberry wood and mugwort arrows;[12]
> Near the fence, your bamboo hobbyhorse and vine-stalk whip.
> Seeds you playfully sowed now flower in the garden;
> Chinese characters on the wall still bear your kana gloss.[13]
> Whenever I recall your laughing speech, you seem alive;
> I wait to see you move—and my distraction is complete. . . .

The mulberry-wood bow and mugwort arrows invoking health at a baby's birth, the bamboo hobbyhorse and vine whip Amaro frolicked with, the corner of the garden where he planted seeds the previous year, seeds that are now flourishing plants—everything before the speaker's eyes reminds him of the past. One senses an especial depth in the scholar Michizane's grief-stricken recollections of Chinese characters left written on the wall. In ordinary households, a five-year-old boy would probably not have advanced far enough in his education to be able to write Chinese characters on a wall, much less add the katakana gloss necessary for reading the characters in Japanese. It was, however, to be expected in the scholarly Sugawara family.

[12] [Both were hung to ward off evil.—Trans.]

[13] [As part of his reading lessons, Amaro would have been required to "translate" simple Chinese sentences into Japanese by reordering the characters and adding particles and inflected endings where necessary. Here the speaker describes the remains of Amaro's last lesson.—Trans.]

Michizane's shih deal not only with personal events but with topics current in society. When he went into exile at Dazaifu, Michizane was allowed to take with him only his youngest son and daughter. In a shih titled "To Comfort My Little Son and Daughter" (*KKKS*, 483), Michizane depicts truly pitiable people in order to persuade his children of their own good fortune: their only hardship is to go into exile with their father.

> . . . Some years back I saw a wretched child
> Who roamed the city streets and had no home.
> A naked pauper with a love for gambling
> Was known on the street as Nansuke;
> And a barefoot woman who played the zither—
> All the townsfolk called her Lady Ben.
> Both their fathers had been high court nobles:
> How luxurious and grand their lives once were! . . .

Nansuke, according to Michizane's interlinear note, was "the Minamibuchi Major Counselor's son: assistant director of the Palace Storehouse Bureau, and a gambler. He is still known as Nansuke."[14] Minamibuchi Yoshiomi (dates unknown), son of Toshina (808-877), a major counselor, went bankrupt after his father's death and became a professional gambler. He seems to have been called Nansuke by his friends at court, and it remained his name even after his ruin. Michizane notes of "Lady Ben": "The Fujiwara Consultant also served as major controller [ben], and that is why his daughter is called Lady Ben." The identity of the "Fujiwara Consultant" is not known, but his position as consultant and major controller confirms that he was a high court official. Michizane was probably told by an acquaintance that the consultant's daughter had been reduced to begging a living, barefoot, by playing the zither. The use of this kind of factual material in shih is unprecedented before Michizane's time.

Michizane's shih are concerned with more than private events and miscellaneous social topics. They also characteristically record the feelings he experiences in connection with such events. In the Sixth Month of 882, the Fujiwara Major Counselor (either Fujiwara Yoshiyo [823-900] or Fujiwara Fuyuo [808-90]) was slandered in an anonymous shih composed with such mastery that it was rumored to be the work of Michizane. Indignant, Michizane responded with a shih called "Impressions" (*KB*, 2:98). In it he describes his state of mind on first hearing the rumor.

> . . . A man came and told me of it; I did not believe him.

---

[14] ["Nansuke" was the man's court sobriquet, made by combining the Sino-Japanese reading of "Minami," the first character of his surname, and "suke" (assistant director), part of his official title.—Trans.]

A second came and told me, but still I refused to listen.
By the time a third arrived, my mind had grown uneasy,
And the fourth and fifth men's words deepened my distress. . . .

Nothing in this passage is worthy of the term poetic diction, and the structure, built around a numbered succession of visitors, is reminiscent of orally composed and aurally received song. What is more noteworthy, however, is the fact that the "I" of this poem is none other than Sugawara Michizane, Professor of Letters. It is, in other words, a completely personal shih. Nor is the poet's indignation mere private emotion: it is rooted in a sense of social justice.

The stance of personal expression grounded in social justice appears again, with striking effect, in his "Winter Morning: Ten Poems" (*KB*, 3:200-209), written in 886. The "ten poems" of the title actually form a sequence and might best be read as a single long work made up of ten eight-line stanzas. "Winter Morning" portrays several of the lowliest members of society struggling to survive an unusually early onset of cold weather: a vagrant couple, the man carrying their child, beg for food; a worker in a medicinal herb garden cannot afford medicine for his own illness; packhorse drivers dressed only in singlets are driven as hard as their scrawny horses; and a salt peddler with barely enough custom to pay his taxes is exploited by powerful merchants and throws himself on the mercy of officials. It is important to note that Michizane's subject is an aspect of society never before dealt with in Japanese shih. But it is even more worthy of serious consideration that the poet's social awareness leads him to question a society condoning the suffering of such people. A similar awareness strongly pervades his "Five Events Seen from a Boat," composed in 887. Again, the form is sequential: the speaker, making his rounds by boat, describes among others an old fisherman distraught at the loss of his only fishhook; a fawn separated from its mother and pursued by a hunter; an old man whose entire fortune, a cargo of salt, has been lost in a shipwreck; and a monk on the verge of starvation, trying to eat enough to stay alive while telling the world he is practicing a religious fast. These are not simply intended as descriptions of situations: the speaker's opinions appear here and there in the poem, although they themselves are not particularly moving.

Both works mentioned are surpassed in excellence of expression by Michizane's "On the Road I Met an Old, Old Man" (*KB*, 3:221), also written in 887. The content of the shih is as follows. While traveling, the speaker encounters a ninety-eight-year-old man who, despite his lonely and impoverished state, has a face ruddy with health. When the speaker asks him how this can be, the old man replies at length: in 876 and 877, he says, the provincial administration was harsh, and over forty thousand families were reduced to the most abject poverty; then, happily, Lord Abe no Okiyuki (fl. ca. 880-90) was appointed governor, and he was succeeded by Lord Fujiwara Yasunori (825-95). Thenceforth life in the region was greatly improved (the old man continues), not just in terms of economic progress but in the people's heightened moral standards and their enjoyment of every peaceful day. Though poor, he has a healthy complexion, the result, he surmises, of inner tranquillity. The speaker, having listened to the old man, concludes that his own term as governor may not be as successful as those of his predecessors, but he vows to do his best with the talents he has. We know from "Winter Morning" that the arduous lives of the lower classes were not bettered by Michizane's predecessors. He probably invented the old man as a face-saving device for his friends Okiyuki and Yasunori. One more feature of this shih deserves attention: its emphasis of the Confucian ideal that an administrator blessed with such a man will see the people's morality rise along with their standard of living. Michizane probably borrowed this concept from Po Chü-i. His "Old Man of Hsin-feng with a Broken Arm," from the New Ballads (HKS, 3:1775), resembles Michizane's poem in its topic—a dialogue with a humble old man—and in its discourse on government. Michizane's poem begins:

On the road I met an old, old man.
His hair was white as snow but his face still glowed with health.
He began to speak: "I am ninety-eight years old.
With neither wife nor child, I lead a lonely, wretched life.
My humble house, eighteen feet wide, lies near the Southern Hills;
With no land to farm, no trade, I'm wrapped in clouds and mist.
Inside the house, my prize possession is an oaken chest;
Within the chest there is a bamboo basket, nothing more."
Thus spoke the white-haired man; I asked him in reply,
"How is it that, despite your years, your face glows with health?
You have no wife, no children, nor are you a wealthy man:
Tell me in detail about your thoughts, your way of life. . . ."

The old man's response then unfolds.

Po's poem begins, "An aged man from Hsin-feng is eighty-eight years old; / Head and sidelocks, beard and eyebrows, all are white as snow." Like Michizane, Po introduces the main character by remarking on his age and white hair. The speaker notices that the man's right arm shows signs of an old break, asking him how many years ago and under what circumstances it was broken. The old man replies as follows. His youth was prosperous and the country was at peace, until the T'ien-pao era (742-56), when an order was issued to muster an army for a foreign campaign. One out of every three young men was taken for military service. The war, he heard, was in Yunnan, where the weather was most intemperate and two or three men out of ten died en route. The old man was twenty-four years old at the time. One night he secretly broke his arm with a large stone and was then exempted from military service. The arm still hurts on cold days, the old man says, but that is as nothing when he thinks how it has enabled him to live a long life.

The two shih have a common structure. The speaker of Po's poem, having listened to the old man's response, addresses the reader: he notes that Sung Ching, prime minister during the prosperous K'ai-yüan era (713-42), avoided futile military expeditions, whereas Yang Kuo-chung, prime minister during the T'ien-pao era, began a border war and incurred the people's enmity. The poem concludes with the speaker advising the reader to ask this old man how it all happened. Here again Po's poem resembles Michizane's in the speaker's expressing the poet's personal opinion at the end of the work. Another similarity is the technique of using the names of actual eras and officials. More important, though, is the topic of both poems, political criticism—and criticism rooted in a Confucian spirit. Michizane undoubtedly modeled "On the Road I Met an Old, Old Man" on Po's "The Old Man of Hsin-feng with a Broken Arm."

The dearth of political topics in Japanese shih and waka is a curious phenomenon in world literature. Michizane's compositions are the sole Japanese exceptions. Their exceptional quality is, I believe, the result of Michizane's borrowing political topics from Po's poetry. Japan never had the proper soil in which to nurture political poetry. When Michizane, using Po's work, forcibly incorporated political elements into Japanese shih, they failed to take root. The most beloved of Po's shih in Japan were those the poet himself called poems of "heartache" (kan-shang); his next most popular category was poems on "tranquillity" (hsien-shih). On the other hand, Po's political poetry, which he termed "admonishments" (feng-yü) and valued over all his other works, served only as a source of diction in Japan; their political character never entered Japanese shih. Here we can perceive the limitations of the Japanese acceptance of Chinese poetry.

Several problems, related to these limitations, occur in connection with Michizane's poor command of spoken Chinese. Colloquial language, a principal feature of Po's shih, was probably not comprehended accurately by Michizane. As a result, Japanese locutions inevitably appear in his shih.[15] Only seventeen years passed between the virtual discontinuance of embassies to China and the eleven-year-old Michizane's first shih com-

---

[15] For instance, Michizane's expression "chiu nuan," signifying "becomes warmer" (KB, 2:79, Preface), has been shown to be unnatural Chinese diction (Sugano, 1978, 13-24). This was probably the result of Michizane's lack of proficiency in spoken Chinese rather than conformity to contemporary use of Japanese locutions in shih.

position in 855, and yet great changes had taken place. Chinese studies (kangaku) were now conducted almost completely by books, and these books—the Chinese classics—were increasingly taught and studied according to the Japanese reading of their texts. At the time of his death, Michizane's little son Amaro was already learning from his father how to convert a Chinese text into the Japanese reading order.

The Decline and Fall of Shih

During the latter half of the ninth century, Po Chü-i's poetry had a numerically impressive Japanese audience. Except for Michizane, however, poets benefited little from Po's work. Because Po was the most famous Chinese poet of his day, his work was chosen to furnish the Japanese with the right poetic diction. Only Michizane adopted the "Po style," the expression most characteristic of Po's shih. All other ninth-century Japanese shih poets can, without undue exaggeration, be called mere borrowers of diction. Since, as we have just seen, Michizane's shih corpus embraced both the Six Dynasties and the Po styles, it embodies the period of transition from the Ancient Age to the Middle Ages.

The Po style affected tenth- and eleventh-century Japanese shih in two ways. First, it diluted the existing ornate Six Dynasties style with simplicity in the Po style. Yet, instead of moving toward ever more understated beauty, shih came increasingly to lack emotional effect. Second, the plainness of Po's style (in the narrow sense), a characteristic criticized as typical of "frivolous Yüan and vulgar Po," resulted in a loss of poetic tension. Poets moved toward cruder expression rather than freer versification. Compositions reflecting Po's style in the wider sense, such as Minamoto Shitagō's (911-83) "Song of a Tailless Ox" (*Honchō Monzui* [= *HM*], 1:21) and Prince Kaneakira's (914-87) "Fu on T'u-ch'iu" (ibid., 12), are rescued by their acuity of subject matter and are appealing in their own way. Most shih of this period, however, are composed on more commonplace topics, and consequently few of their number inspire admiration. This is the process by which the tenth- and eleventh-century shih circle began its decline.

The situation was mainly brought about by the shih circle's neglect of High T'ang poetry and its consequent abrupt leap from Six Dynasties and Early T'ang shih to the poetry of Po Chü-i. I noted earlier that the Po style (in the narrow sense) inherited the advanced achievements of the High T'ang poets, particularly Li Po and Tu Fu, and that it is the result of an attempt to produce new expression rivaling that of the High T'ang. Thus only a full awareness of the grandeur of Li's and Tu's poetry will truly convince a reader of the freshness and subtlety of Po's shih. The tenth- and eleventh-century Japanese shih circle valued Po's poetry alone, ignoring other Middle T'ang poets like Han Yü. This attitude would have made it nearly impossible for the Japanese to comprehend the effectiveness of the expressive modes in Po's poetry.

A further complication was the fact that Japanese shih poets had no contact with spoken Chinese. This can be recognized as early as Michizane's time, in the substantial influence exercised on Chinese studies (kangaku) by the virtual discontinuance of embassies to China. By the tenth century it was even more striking. During this time people seem to have come to believe that the Chinese classics provided the only proper approach to kangaku. Little attention was therefore paid to the vast extent of literary possibilities inherent in Chinese but not yet expressed in writing. The presence of vernacular language in Po's poetry should not delude the reader into imagining that Po writes entirely in the vernacular. A composition cannot be a shih unless it is expressed in the literary language. Po's shih do occasionally contain seemingly colloquial expressions. An audience whose daily life revolved around the T'ang Chinese language would have firmly grasped the larger, unspoken meanings behind such apparent colloquialisms, but a similar feat would have been impossible for a Japanese audience whose only contact with the Chinese language was in its written form.

When a Japanese poet, unable to perceive how fresh and rich Po's seemingly colloquial expression is, imitates only the superficial aspects of Po's poetry, what is the result? The tenth-century Japanese shih themselves provide the answer. Put simply, the result is lax delineation and a tendency toward the prosaic. Only the first part of Minamoto Fusaakira's (d. 940) "On Discovering Gray Hair" (*HM*, 1:17) need be quoted to illustrate the marked prosiness of such poetry.

> My age is thirty-five: I am as yet
> An innocent to physical decline.
> This morning, gazing into a bright mirror,
> I saw reflected there a graying self.
> Suspicious of the mirror, I would not trust it;
> I rubbed my eyes and scrutinized my beard.
> Woe is me! With my silver tweezers,
> I extracted several grizzled strands.
> The onset of autumn brings much sorrow;
> This can only double my distress. . . .

The content of the poem—a youngish man's despondency at discovering a few gray hairs—is set forth in great detail. As recorded literature, shih has never valued exhaustive description. On the contrary, the presence of the inexpressible makes a work normatively a shih. Shih expression is focused precisely on the problem of filling the gap made by this inexpressible element. In Six Dynasties poetry the gap is filled by oblique reasoning that elicits the recipient's understanding and approval; in Tu Fu's shih the gap seems bridged by symbolic impression. Fusaakira's poem, however, has no gap in the flow of meaning. The poet strives to tell everything. In the latter part of the poem, the speaker, Fusaakira himself, states that he received the fourth princely rank at the age of fifteen, at sixteen was made court chamberlain, and has progressed with equal smoothness through the rest of his career. The resulting sense of security, Fusaakira continues, accounts for the relatively late appearance of gray hair, particularly in comparison with Yen Hui or P'an Yüeh.[16] This conclusion is preceded by an explanatory couplet: "Abandoning gloom, I think on why I've grayed; / The following reasons should help me understand." Having told us of his initial dejection, his reconsideration of the matter, and his conviction that the problem must logically be considered as he will explain, the speaker proceeds with his exposition in the second half of the shih. The effect is of textbook prose organized into pentameter. The poet has explored his subject so thoroughly that nothing more can be added. The filling in of narrative gaps is a prose practice, and Fusaakira's shih style unquestionably lacks poetic focus. Unfocused poetic expression naturally lacks intensity, degenerating into vague, slack language.

"On Discovering Gray Hair" is patterned after Po's "Looking in the Mirror and Rejoicing in Old Age" (HKS, sequel 4:2130). The works share a topic, subject matter, structure, and diction. Michizane's "On the Road I Met an Old, Old Man" is also patterned after one of Po's poems, "The Old Man of Hsin-feng with a Broken Arm," but it never loses its expressive tension. "On Discovering Gray Hair" is inferior in all respects to Michizane's poem. A single misstep by a follower of the Po style will result in irredeemably banal and weak poetry. An adept at the ornate style of poetry composition, Po must have been well aware that the "Yüan-Po style"—as it was called in his day—could in certain circumstances be irrevocably linked to unpoetic qualities. He also acknowledged that "Li Po and Tu Fu are known everywhere as particularly fine poets. Their works display a marvelous talent that no other poet can hope to match."[17] Po was therefore taking a considerable risk in daring to attempt surpassing these two poetic giants with his "Po style" (in the narrow sense). Unaware

[16] Yen Hui (513-482 B.C.) was Confucius's most outstanding disciple; his hair turned white before he was thirty (Shih Chi, "Chung-ni Ti-tzu Lieh-chuan"). P'an Yüeh (d. A.D. 300), a literatus famous for his good looks, states in his "Ch'iu-hsing Fu" ("Rhapsody on Autumnal Emotions," WH, 13) that he began to grow gray at an early age. [Auth., Trans.]

[17] The passage appears in his "Letter to Yüan Chen" (see earlier in this chapter, and n. 6). Po recalls how certain experiences added maturity to his poetic compositions, and he criticizes idealistic views of poetry from a historical standpoint; the passage thus gives further meaning to Po's own poetic style.

of the hazards, Japanese shih poets from the tenth century on erroneously perceived that Po's special poetic nature lay in a clarity easily accessible even to foreigners. The shih produced under this misapprehension, with their obligatory exhaustive, clear expression, inevitably tend toward decadence.

Another Japanese shih provides an example of the depths of mediocrity reached in the tenth through twelfth centuries, solely from misreading Po's poetry. It is a quatrain in seven-character lines by Sugawara Sukemasa (925-1009), Michizane's great-grandson. Its title is "Composed, at His Majesty's Command, on the Occasion of the First Lecture on *The Classic of Filial Piety*, which Was Delivered to the Eldest Prince in the Hikyōsha on a Winter's Day" (*Honchō Reisō* [= HR], 2:220). The shih was composed on the thirteenth of the Eleventh Month, 1005.

> Though I have reached the great old age of over eighty years,
> I have yet to see sagacity to match our lord's.
> Your highness, memorize this dotard's inapt utterance:
> Do not forget a single *Classic*, even for a moment!

This formal occasion was graced by many other officials, including Fujiwara Michinaga, minister of the left, and the prose preface to Sukemasa's poem was composed by Ōe no Yukitoki (955-1010). The shih itself must nonetheless be characterized as pedestrian in both content and diction. The poet gets by with the plainest possible expression, an indication that the traditional Po style employed by the Sugawara family had reached its nadir.

Michinaga's own poem, composed on the same occasion and topic, is far more compact in tone than Sukemasa's effort. Michinaga's merits as a shih poet, however, are better perceived in another work. When he invited the minister of state, Fujiwara Korechika (984-1010), and nine other nobles to his residence in Tō Sanjō, shih were composed on the topic, "Falling Blossoms Dance across the Waters."[18] This was Michinaga's contribution:

> Blossoms fall in spring breezes on a clear lake surface,
> And come to dance on garden streams, joined by singing warblers.
> Like hairpin-flowers in disarray, petals drift downstream:
> Their hue as they near the bank suggests the finest gauze.
> Costumed dancers stray toward the lake as evening deepens;

---

[18] The preface to Michinaga's shih states that Tō Sanjō became a temporary palace (sato dairi) for the Tennō. This dates Michinaga's gathering, and the poems composed then, no earlier than 1006; Korechika's presence at the gathering indicates that it took place before 1010, the year of his death.

Musicians find it hard to see, and amble through the waves.
Happily this place possesses charms both old and new:
May our lord graciously progress again to P'ei![19]

The array of beautiful diction in the Six Dynasties style is appropriate to the setting and bears no comparison with Sukemasa's poem. Michinaga's shih also follows the correct tonal pattern. But if it is compared with Michizane's " 'Flowers in the Rain' " or Princess Uchiko's "Matching the Former Sovereign's Poem on 'New Year's Eve,' " Michinaga's shih is revealed to lack creativity and to be somewhat formulaic in its descriptive method and choice of diction. It is also excessively simple and consequently rather unimpressive. The simplicity is probably the result of Po Chü-i's influence. The last two lines in particular reduce the topic to quotidian dimensions: the speaker gratefully notes the abundance of both antique and novel features at his residence and therefore requests that his majesty make a progress, as Kao-tsu did in the past, to "P'ei." This, too, may be attributed to a misreading of Po's poetry. Not that such faults are Michinaga's alone: tenth- and eleventh-century Japanese shih generally display much the same tendency, and the received impression is of the lovely wine of the Six Dynasties style adulterated by the water of the Po style.

These were the circumstances in which courtiers composed great quantities of shih suggestive of watered vintage wine, and many of these compositions are extant. To the modern eye they are hardly more than repetitions of subtle techniques within the same expressive framework. I find such poetry tedious. But it is tedious because it is being read by a twentieth-century person conscious of the excellence of Tu Fu's and Li Po's poetry. The members of the Japanese shih circle in the tenth and eleventh centuries, on the other hand, undoubtedly found it greatly moving to discern a minute quantity of freshness within repetitions of similar expression. Otherwise the Japanese would not have spent three centuries composing exclusively large quantities of the same kind of shih.

This is no mere conjecture. Fujiwara Sanesuke (957-1046) notes in his diary: "The Civil Affairs Counselor [Minamoto Toshikata] sent me a letter; he writes, 'at our shih gathering yesterday, every line of the Provincial Deputy's [Korechika's] shih was moving, and all present wiped away a tear' " (Shōyūki [=SYK; 1.IV.1005], 106). In 996, Korechika was forced

[19] HR, 1:207. Emperor Kao-tsu (255-194 B.C.), having founded the Han Dynasty, paid a visit to P'ei, his home town. There he hosted ten days of freewheeling banqueting for the local populace, exempted them from taxation, and bestowed other benefits on them (Shih Chi, 8:389-90). Ichijō Tennō, whose palace was destroyed by fire in 1005, resided for a short time at Michinaga's Tsuchimikado mansion. Here Michinaga compares Kao-tsu's town of P'ei to Tō Sanjō and requests that Ichijō make a progress there as well.

to resign the post of palace minister and go into exile as provisional vice-roy of Dazaifu for his part in an attack on the former sovereign Kazan (r. 984-86; OK, 4:182).[20] He was recalled to the capital the following year and by 1001 had been restored to his former rank, the senior third. On the twenty-fifth day of the Second Month, 1005, Korechika was given the title honorary minister (gidōsanshi), a post created especially for him.[21] The shih he composed at Toshikata's house on the thirtieth of the Third Month, 1005, may have concerned his exile in Dazaifu, and his gratitude at his recent appointment to honorary minister may have made his com-position rather emotional. Yet the fifteen shih by Korechika that appear in the extant *Honchō Reisō (Outstanding Literature of Japan)* are all cast in the expressive form typical of his time, and none is especially moving. The subject of Korechika's shih may have been his life in Dazaifu or his impres-sions of that life, but that need not mean that the poet was capable of im-mediately employing the requisite expressive techniques. Unless Kore-chika were blessed with the genius of a Michizane, his style could not possibly have altered in accordance with circumstance. The shih Kore-chika composed at Toshikata's house was probably not much different in style from his fifteen extant shih. On the other hand, it may have diverged from conventional expression in some phrases. His contemporaries, who responded as one to a given shih, would have reacted sensitively to the slightest departure from the usual.[22] Korechika's handful of departures re-sulted, I believe, in "every line of [his] poem" being "moving, and all pres-ent wiped away a tear." Would not the emotion expressed have had more to do with the audience than with the poet?

Readers felt considerable interest in a work, despite its lack of fresh sub-ject matter or diction, because of their uniform education. This enabled them to find great interest in minute, ordinarily imperceptible differences. There is another, more concrete reason: the reader's shifting focus from

[20] [One of the great scandals of the Heian period. Korechika had been visiting a certain lady, a great beauty, at her house in Takatsuka. When Kazan began courting this lady's less attractive sister, Korechika concluded that Kazan was really interested in the more beautiful woman. Korechika consulted his brother Takaie on how best to rid himself of his rival. Ta-kaie suggested that they frighten Kazan as he rode his horse home from his usual tryst one night. In carrying out the plan, Takaie and his friends shot some arrows at Kazan, and one ripped his sleeve. Attacks on the royal family (even in jest, as this presumably was) were of course regarded as lèse-majesté. The scandal was compounded by the personalities of its em-inent principals—the powerful, controversial, and brash young Korechika and a former sov-ereign who, several years earlier, had taken Buddhist orders, including a vow of celibacy. The anecdote also appears in *Eiga Monogatari*, on which account this summary is based.—Trans.]

[21] The position ranked between minister of state and major counselor (*Midō Kampaku Ki* [25.II.1005], 135).

[22] The tenth- and eleventh-century shih contained in the *Honchō Reisō* and *Honchō Mu-daishi* are very nearly identical in expressive form: there is no apparent difference between poets, nor is any other individuality displayed.

the entire poem to the parallel couplet unit. In regulated verse, the standard eight-line "modern shih" form, the third and fourth lines are required to use parallel ordering, as are lines five and six. This naturally led to an increasing preoccupation with parallel couplets that culminated in the reception of couplets freed from their poetic context. The topic of a regulated verse frequently appears in the last two lines, and an exclusive devotion to parallel couplets must represent the poet's disregard for the poetic topic and the reader's focus on fragmented expressive techniques. Although this is an abnormal practice, it was in fact popular in Japan from the tenth through the twelfth centuries. Fujiwara Kintō's *Wakan Rōeishū* (*Collection of Japanese and Chinese Songs*) and Fujiwara Mototoshi's (1056-1142) *Shinsen Rōeishū* (*New Collection of Songs*) form, to put it somewhat grandiloquently, the main text and sequel of a "Compendium of Selected Parallel Couplets."

"Rōei" refers to the recitation or singing of waka and lines from prose and poetry in Chinese. It is not limited to parallel couplets in the case of works in Chinese, although couplets do in effect make up most of the works in this category. This reflects the contemporary Japanese readers' great fondness for parallel couplets. Was it not natural for the Japanese to make antithesis one of their main foci as they searched for interest within short literary works? Furthermore, the partial recitation of an illustrious poem or prose work in Chinese probably called to mind the entire piece, so that the parallel couplets were appreciated within their proper context. For example, the lines "There were days when peach and plum blossomed in spring breezes, / And times when Chinese-parasol leaves fell with the autumn dews" (*Wakan Rōeishū* [= WRS], 2:781) were well known to both the reciter of the couplet and his audience as part of a scene from the "Song of Everlasting Sorrow" (*HKS*, 12:1912).

Less familiar couplets were probably appreciated as independent units. When the reader focuses on parallelism, even mediocre poetry, if read in couplet units, often becomes interesting. The lines "Middle of the fifteenth night: the moon, new-risen, glows; / Two thousand li away, I sense an old friend's thoughts" (*WRS*, 1:242) are extremely commonplace when considered individually, and they can hardly be thought poetry when translated into English. The Chinese found, however, a secondary interest independent of the stated meaning of the lines, an interest stemming from the antitheses formed by the words "fifteenth" (lit. "three fives") and "two thousand," "middle" and "away," and "new" and "old."[23] Much the same can be said for medieval Japan. This couplet was admired solely for its interesting antitheses; it did not matter whether its reciter or audi-

[23] [The appeal of this couplet lies in its inexorable parallelism: each character in line 1 is balanced by an antithetical counterpart in line 2. This cannot properly be carried out in

ence knew the provenance of the couplet, Po Chü-i's "On Night Duty at the Palace, on the Fifteenth of the Eighth Month: Looking at the Moon and Thinking of Yüan Chen" (*HKS*, 14:1945).

An expressive technique found throughout Chinese literature, parallelism is not of course characteristic of Po's poetry alone. Although Six Dynasties poets thought of parallelism as an important technical element, they also relied on various other elements that maximize technique: ornate diction, abundant classical allusions, and skillfully wrought oblique design. Parallelism, then, is not a conspicuous feature of Six Dynasties poetry, whereas the reader of poetry written in the plain Po style is impressed solely by the appeal of its parallel couplets. Parallel couplet expression in the Po style, moreover, does not leave the recipient with strong impressions: the effect is rather one of quiet contrasts. A reader wishing to perceive these subtle contrasts must approach Po's poetry with considerable care. Parallelism is a technique that, when motivated by contrast, shifts from one line to the next. In Po's shih the calm, quiet transition from one line to the next contains a definite yet inconspicuous break. Such breaks appear definite only to the most receptive readers. Breaks are also present in Po's line-to-line transitions when contrast is not a motivating force. Their detection requires even greater and subtler attention than does Po's parallelism, which is transitive expression with a contrastive impetus. The technique of subtle transition from one line to the next came to dominate waka expression and gave rise to changes within it.

Po's poetry made up much of the corpus of parallel couplet units appreciated by the medieval Japanese. Out of a total of 195 T'ang poetry excerpts in the *Collection of Japanese and Chinese Songs*, 135 are by Po, and the remaining sixty are divided among twenty-six other poets. This is indicative of Po's overwhelming popularity. The phenomenon did not, however, originate suddenly at the time of the *Collection*. A preference for Po's work is already apparent in the *Senzai Kaku (A Millennium of Superlative Couplets)*, said to have been compiled by Ōe no Koretoki (888-963). This work classifies by topic 1,078 two-line units selected from the T'ang poetry corpus. Of that number, 512 are by Po, and the other 566 are divided among 148 named and anonymous poets (five units that appear more than once are counted only once). The reception of shih, particularly Po's,

---

translation without losing much of the meaning of the lines. The following literal translation may give the reader an idea of the original word distribution.

| three fives | night | middle | new moon's | glow |
| two thousand | li | away | old friend's | thoughts |

"Three fives" is an elegant way of saying "fifteen"; the fifteenth night of the lunar month is the night of the full moon. Thus "new moon" is not intended by the poet to signify the moon in its first phase but rather a moon that has just come into view, presumably from behind the rim of a mountain.—Trans.]

in couplet units thus considerably predates Kintō. The heyday of the preference was, however, from the end of the tenth century through the early years of the eleventh.[24] The significance of reading shih in couplet units is indicated by the vital role it played in the domination of waka by T'ang (and especially Po's) poetic expression. It undeniably narrowed, however, the range of shih topics.

It must be emphasized that when the object of reading is a couplet drawn from a given shih, the result is a disregard for the original subject of the entire shih. Naturally the subject affects every line in the poem, but this does not mean that its weight is divided equally among the lines. A couplet that can be admired on its own, independent of its poetic context, is unlikely to express the general topic clearly. Thus, when a single couplet is the object of attention, the reader can easily conceive a new subject appropriate to that couplet. There is nothing wrong with this practice in itself. The topics that can be sustained by a single couplet, however, are not likely to be grand or profound but tend to occupy a narrow range. Short shih with grand or profound topics were first perfected in Japan in Bashō's time. They could never have been accomplished with the literary skills available to tenth- and eleventh-century poets. This accounts for the gradual lack of concern felt by Japanese shih poets of the time for the narrowness of their topics. Political criticism and related topics were increasingly driven from the poetic scene.

An accompanying phenomenon is the popularity of verse-topic (kudai) shih. This refers to the practice of composing a shih on a topic taken from an existing line of shih poetry. Verse-topics were quite popular in China in the Late Six Dynasties period and were composed in Japan as early as the ninth century. The first documented instance of a Japanese verse-topic shih is by Saga Tennō, who composed his poem for the Chrysanthemum Festival on the ninth day of the Ninth Month on the verse-topic, " 'Autumn Has Yielded a Most Bountiful Harvest' " (*RUSS*, 115).[25] By Michizane's time the popularity of verse-topic shih had grown considerably. One example is that poem on the verse-topic, " 'In Spring a Beauty Quite Lacks Energy.' " Michizane's practice does not mark the zenith of verse-topic shih. Their number increases suddenly during Ōe no Masahira's

[24] *Senzai Kaku* is apparently a collection of exemplary verses compiled for reference in shih composition and therefore provides no evidence that the reception of Po's poetry was carried out in couplet units at this time. *Senzai Kaku* is mentioned only three times, all in the Gōdanshō of Ōe no Masafusa (1041-1111). This suggests that the work was used as an Ōe family handbook. There is no evidence that it had a wider readership.

[25] A line from a shih by Wang Wei, "Composed to Match His Majesty's August Composition, in Response to an Imperial Request for Poems on the Topic, 'At the Chrysanthemum Festival, Ministers and Senior Officials Wish His Majesty Long Life' " (*Ō I*, 11:1544). Verse-topic shih are rarely encountered at this early time in Japan.

(952-1012) lifetime, and the eleventh century was their heyday.[26] Since the topic was already given in a verse-topic shih and did not reflect the poet's own concepts or emotions, it is perhaps natural that such single-line topics should become narrower in scope. The rise of verse-topic shih seems to have limited the already narrow range of shih topics available from the tenth century onward.

There was also a tendency toward limitations in subject matter. The Chinese ballad style was known in ninth-century Japan, as is made clear by such examples of the form as Saga's "Reproach in the Tall Gate Palace" ("Chōmon'en"; BSS, 2:247).[27] Very few ballad topics were current in Japan, and in fact the Japanese virtually ignored the great variety of subjects found in Chinese ballad poetry. In China, the range of subject matter for ballads grew enormously from the Six Dynasties period on in response to various social phenomena. Ballad topics reflecting contemporary social realities include "Chieh-k'o Shao-nien-ch'ang Hsing" (Yüeh-fu Shih-chi, 66:948-52), a ballad about drunken, sword-happy slum youths, and works like "Yu-hsia P'ien" and "Hsia-k'o Hsing" (ibid., 966-69) that depict homicidal myrmidons ready to risk anything to accomplish their mission. One ballad in particular, Chang Hua's (232-300) "Po-ling-wang-kung Hsia-ch'ü" (ibid., 969), has an intense scene in the descriptive mode in which righteous young desperadoes avenge a friend by cutting down several people in the street. Violence was equally common in Heiankyō. A gang of thieves once broke into the residence of the general of the right, Fujiwara Akimitsu (944-1021), took several articles from the rooms of Tachibana Uchinari (dates unknown)—who was living in part of the mansion—and wounded his son, and fled after shooting arrows into the stables to kill the horses. Uchinari was out at the time and so escaped danger; an investigation later revealed that the attack was in revenge for wrongs he supposedly inflicted (SYK [14.VI.966], 15). Such events appear time and again in courtiers' diaries, and yet social realities do not provide subject matter for Japanese shih. This was probably because shih were perceived as belonging essentially to the fūryū world. A further reason should not be overlooked. Japanese shih poets had become accustomed to a range of topics narrow enough to be comprehended in one or two lines of Chinese poetry. There may also have been external

[26] Two sources confirm this dating: Masahira's personal shih collection, Gō Rihō Shū; and the Honchō Reisō, which is chiefly made up of tenth- and eleventh-century shih. One shih collection, probably compiled in the mid-twelfth century (1162-64), is called Honchō Mudaishi (Japanese Shih without Topics; Yamagishi, 1935, 83). Despite the title of the work, its shih do indeed have topics. They are called "shih without topics" because they are not composed on verse-topics. The triumph of verse-topic shih is reflected in this practice.

[27] [The subject treated in Saga's poem, the resentment of the neglected Empress Ch'en, first appears in the "Ch'ang-men Fu" ("Tall Gate Palace Rhapsody") by the Han poet Ssu-ma Hsiang-ju. It became a ballad topic in the Six Dynasties period.—Trans.]

causes, such as the inability to procure appropriate books for the study of Chinese ballad poetry.[28]

ORNATE BEAUTY AND PLAINNESS
OF PROSE IN CHINESE

The evolution of Japanese prose in Chinese resembles what we have just seen in Japanese shih. The Japanese began by composing ornate parallel prose in the Six Dynasties and Early T'ang styles and after that devised a plain prose. Japanese plain prose was patterned on compositions by Po Chü-i and Yüan Chen while works by those two luminaries of plain prose, Han Yü and Liu Tsung-yüan, were evidently not read. This was due to circumstances similar to those in which Japanese shih poets disregarded Li Po's and Tu Fu's poetry. The limitations of the Japanese approach to prose were apparent also in terms of result: many of their prose compositions represent a miniaturization of the Po style.

Parallel prose advanced considerably during this period. Adroit antithetical expression and beautiful diction, replete with classical allusions, were mastered without the intrusion of Japanese locutions; but of course all this is true of only one man, Michizane. A characteristic example of his parallel prose style is the preface to his shih, "On the Topic, 'In Spring a Beauty Quite Lacks Energy,' Given by His Majesty to All Who Attended an Informal Banquet in Early Spring at the Jijūden" (*KB*, 2:148).[29]

An
Informal banquet held in early spring
Is not a practice found in the *Annual Events of Ch'u*,[30]
Nor does it transmit Chou and Han festivities:
Established by a sovereign, it was handed down to our Sage Majesty.[31]
The palace garden enchants us more than
Mount Sung, where a man became immortal astride a crane;[32]
The scene before us is far too splendid
To suffer from the warbler's lack of voice, the fading blossoms by the
    stream.

[28] The most complete collection of ballad-style poetry, the Sung period *Yüeh-fu Shih-chi* (100 fascs.) edited by Kuo Mao-ch'ien, was probably not yet available in Japan.

[29] The prose preface and shih also appear in *HM*, 9:211.

[30] *Ching Ch'u Sui-shih Chi*, compiled by Tsung Lin in the Liang Dynasty.

[31] The "sovereign" to whom Michizane refers is Heizei Tennō, who instituted the informal banquet in 809 (*RK*, 72:337). "Our Sage Majesty" is Kōkō Tennō (r. 884-87).

[32] Wang-tzu Ch'iao, who lived in the Chou period, is said to have been transported by a white crane to Mt. Sung, where he lived evermore in seclusion (*Lieh-hsien Chuan*, 1:23-24). Michizane's meaning is that the gardens of the Jijūden are more splendid than the scenery of Mt. Sung.

The New Year has indeed arrived: our sovereign welcomes it with joy;
Quickly does time pass, but His Majesty's life span knows no bounds.
Here, then,
Virtuosi perform in a grand hall
While costumed dancers mount the stage.
Their delicate arms and slender legs were bequeathed by father and
    mother;
Their hair is fine and soft as clouds, their skin as white as damson
    blossoms.[33]
Truly,
The fine weather intoxicates them;
They gaze at the splendid staircase, quite out of breath.
Brilliant sunlight soaks their frames:
They will grow fatigued, fluttering those scarlet sleeves.
They,
Finding that their robes of gauze are far too heavy,
Blame the weaving-woman for her heartlessness;[34]
And, feeling that the music goes on far too long,
Are vexed that the musicians will not stop performing.
Their captivating, varied dance enchants us and enchants us yet again;
Their singing, fresh and lively, makes us wonder if we do not dream.[35]
This vassal,
Admitted through the myriad gates,
Stumbled when he climbed the stairs of rainbow mist;
For half a day I became immortal;
The bluebird has taught me celestial songs.[36]
The performance so enthralls me that I cannot voice my praise:
Then let me be the border guard who wished long life to Emperor Yao![37]
With this my Preface is concluded.

The beauty of this preface cannot be fully appreciated in translation. In choosing his phrasing, Michizane knew that his audience would be aware of its classical provenance. An audience unfamiliar with the antecedent lit-

---

[33] "Our bodies, our hair and skin, are bequeathed us by father and mother. The first act of filial piety is to avoid harming these gifts" (*Hsiao Ching*, 1:11).

[34] This couplet was selected for inclusion in the *Wakan Rōeishū* (2:466) and was well known.

[35] This couplet is quoted in the nagauta "Aki no Irokusa" and has been well known since the Edo period.

[36] The bluebird is the messenger of the Queen Mother of the West (Ch. Hsi Wang-mu; J. Seiōbo). In *Han Wu Ku-shih*, the bluebird flies from the immortals' realm on Mt. K'un-lun to the dwelling of Emperor Wu of the Han Dynasty.

[37] "Yao made an imperial progress to Hua. There a border guard said, 'Your Majesty! Let me offer my humble prayer to Your Sage Majesty, that you enjoy long life'" (*Chuang Tzu*, "T'ien-ti," 187-89). Michizane's application to himself and his sovereign needs no stress.

erature would, however, find his diction burdensome. Consider, for example, Michizane's line, "Their hair is fine and soft as clouds, their skin as white as damson blossoms" (lit., "Soft clouds, clustered damson blossoms"). An audience familiar with passages like the following would know that "cloud" is a metaphor for "hair."

> The mirror reflects her rouged and powdered face;
> She puts a flower in her coiffed *cloud-hair*.
>> (*GDSE*, 4:515, "The Mirror Stand")
>
> Her sleeveless gauze dress is woven with gold;
> Her *cloud-hair* is dressed with flowery pins.
>> (*GDSE*, 5:520, "A Poem for Newlyweds")
>
> At morning her *cloud-hair* leaves the pillow;
> At night her moth-eyebrows touch it again.
>> (*GDSE*, 10:628, "The Camphorwood Pillow")

But that audience might not understand that "soft" expresses the fluffiness of beautiful hair unless it can connect the word to instances like "Her brows and eyes first captivated my heart; / Her lovely *softness* strokes her waist and legs" (*GDSE*, 7:563, "On Seeing a Beauty from My Carriage"). An audience that is aware of passages likening a woman's rouge and powder toilette to peach and white damson blossoms—as in the lines "Crimson as peach blossoms, white as damson, such is my morning toilette; / Still my wasted face is put to shame by the young poplars" (*GDSE*, 9:610, "Matching Hsiao Tzü-hsien's 'Farewell to Spring' ")—will be impressed by Michizane's innovative analogy of white damson blossoms not to face powder but to the dancing-girls' skin. They will also understand that Michizane has included a line from the *Classic of Filial Piety* as a precedent in order to emphasize his design.[38]

Again, a couplet like "Some are like luxuriant *damson blossoms*; / Others, like lotuses shining in the water" (*GDSE*, 8:572, "Based on Ts'ao Chih's 'Beautiful Women' ") will inform an audience that the whiteness depicted by the image of damson blossoms suggests voluptuous beauty rather than purity, since the damson blossom, a metaphor for a beautiful woman, is linked to the word "luxuriant" (nung). This does not refer, in other words, to a single blossom but to the whiteness produced by several clusters. "Delicate arms and slender legs" indicates that the dancers in Michizane's preface are slender—the preferred feminine figure during the Six Dynasties period.[39] It may seem too much of an exaggeration to depict

---

[38] [See n. 33.—Ed.]

[39] From the Han period through the Early T'ang, an ideally beautiful woman was slender. This is known from contemporary literature as well as from Ku K'ai-chih's (?347-?408)

these girls as so slender as to be weighed down by silk gauze, and to have them resent the weaver who has made such heavy costumes. The concept, however, is not uncommon. For example, the couplet "Her slender hips, so very delicate, / Felt weighted down by her winter clothes" (*GDSE*, 8:579, "The Winter Boudoir") follows Michizane's design precisely if "robes of gauze" is substituted for "winter clothes."[40] There are further instances of the expression "robes of gauze," such as "*Robes of gauze* I make for my beloved, / To send to him, ten thousand li away" (*GDSE*, 5:519, "Matching Minister Chang's Poem on 'Sadness at Parting'"). With these poetic phrases in mind, Michizane's audience would also recall the Chinese poetic sources of phrases in the preface and the lovely scenes depicted there. An ornately beautiful world, in the style of the Six Dynasties, extends beyond the scene described in Michizane's preface, and only those thoroughly acquainted with that world can truly appreciate the beauty of the preface.

Expression of this kind may strike some modern readers as excessively ornate, and its content might be criticized as philosophically shallow. We would do well to recognize that Michizane's preface and the shih that follows it were presented at a public banquet. There the New Year was celebrated with song and dance, prose and poetry were composed in Chinese, and the tennō and his courtiers enjoyed themselves thoroughly. Ornate beauty was highly appropriate to such a setting. Today the words ambassadors and cabinet officers exchange at banquets given by heads of state are expected to be beautiful, even if the nature of that beauty differs from that familiar to the ninth-century Japanese court. On the other hand, if a courtier had wished to speak his mind under informal circumstances, he would indeed have had trouble expressing himself satisfactorily in parallel prose. The importation of plain prose to Japan at the end of the ninth century was greatly beneficial in this respect. The tenth century marks the beginning of a period of decline and fall for Japanese shih. This was not necessarily the case for prose in Chinese, which was invigorated by the

---

"Picture of a Lady at Her Sewing" (extant in a T'ang copy). In Hsüan-tsung's reign (713-56), full figures began to set the standard for feminine beauty. This has been attributed, although without evidence, to the influence of his well-endowed consort, Yang Kuei-fei. The Japanese preference for plump women is first found in the eighth-century painting of the divinity Kichijō (Skt. Srīmakādevī), owned by the temple of Yakushiji, and in its contemporary, the "Torige Tachi Onna" (picture of a standing woman, her robe decorated with feathers), preserved in the Shōsōin. [See the frontispiece to vol. one.] Plumpness continued to be a feminine ideal in Japan through the twelfth century, as can be told from the women depicted in the *Genji Monogatari Emaki* (Fujii, 1966, 136-43). Michizane's preface and shih, then, express preferences from the Six Dynasties and early T'ang rather than later.

[40] Michizane follows his preface with a shih (ch. 1) that contains the phrase "too fine to bear the weight of clothes." From this we may conclude that he knew "The Winter Boudoir" and used it as a source in composing his preface. His depiction of such frail beauties is therefore a conception inspired by Six Dynasties poetry.

conceptual and expressive freedom of plain prose. Not all its influences, however, were positive.

The greatest difficulty inherent in Japanese plain prose in Chinese has been stated repeatedly: the Japanese were not exposed to the plain prose styles of Han Yü and Liu Tsung-yüan. Even if their plain prose works had been introduced into Japan, they would very likely not have been properly appreciated, particularly in their rhythms. When Han's plain prose is read in modern Chinese pronunciation its superb rhythms are startling. Of course there are great differences between T'ang and modern Chinese pronunciation, but their common features are much greater. Considerable variation exists between the rhythms I find in Han's plain prose and those found by a T'ang audience, but the differences are outweighed by what is perceived in common.[41] Then again, a native Chinese would surely find Han's prose rhythms far more splendid than I understand them. Such appreciation would have been extremely difficult for a tenth- or eleventh-century Japanese audience, because the beauty of Han's prose rhythms is linked to the meaning of the prose. If a native Chinese reads Six Dynasties parallel prose to me, my limitations in the language guarantee that I will not understand quite a few passages. All the same, the rhythms remain truly beautiful. This is not the case for Han's prose. Unless its meaning is grasped its rhythmic beauty cannot be fully perceived. Perhaps I appear too much taken up with Han's prose, but much the same assessment applies to Liu Tsung-yüan's prose. Po Chü-i's and Yüan Chen's plain prose, when measured by Han's and Liu's standards, is loose rhythmically and lacks intensity. I may not be entirely fair in grounding my plain prose criteria in Han's and Liu's prose works. But was the Japanese literary world in the tenth through twelfth centuries more just than I when it chose to adopt only Po's and Yüan's prose styles?

Plain prose was not, however, the predominant Chinese prose form in Japan during the tenth and eleventh centuries. Parallel prose continued to predominate, particularly in the genres of formal Buddhist prayers (gammon) and sponsor's statements (hyōbyaku), where parallel prose held a monopoly until the sixteenth century.[42] Plain prose is nonetheless well

---

[41] T'ang Chinese had four tones (sheng): level (p'ing), rising (shang), falling (ch'ü), and entering (ju). Characters pronounced in the level tone were considered unaccented, and characters in the other three tones were perceived as accented syllables. The "entering" tone has disappeared from modern standard Chinese, but the distinction between accented and unaccented syllables is still very much present. Syllables that were unaccented in T'ang times remain so today, and the same is true for accented syllables. Tone values may differ, but the rhythms produced by tonal patterns survive. Since Chinese is a monosyllabic language, moreover, the number of word-syllables making up a line constitutes the elements of rhythmic form. T'ang Chinese and modern Chinese do not differ in this respect.

[42] A hyōbyaku (also kaibyaku, keihaku), or sponsor's statement, was presented by a petitioner to his temple when he sponsored a Buddhist service; the document stated the reasons for his sponsorship. Neither gammon nor hyōbyaku could be written by anyone of average

represented in noteworthy compositions. Pioneering experiments include Miyako Yoshika's "Fujisan no Ki" ("Account of Mount Fuji") and "Dōjō Hōshi Den" ("Sketch of the Priest Dōjō"), followed chronologically by Michizane's "Shosaiki" ("Account of My Study").[43] The "account" (Ch. chi, J. ki), a kind originating in the T'ang period, is a description of factual events, a work of reportage, one might say. Such works being short, their style must be highly polished to attract an audience. Let us examine one example, Liu's "Account of the New Hall Constructed by Mr. Wei, Governor of Yung."[44]

The content of the essay is simple: the governor of Yung clears some wasteland and builds a splendid hall on a picturesque spot. Liu begins by presenting the absurd engineering practices common in his time; he then describes how different Governor Wei's ideas, plans, and means of execution are from the norm; and he concludes the account with a politically based investigation of why Wei succeeds at his project. Liu's style is unique in its divergence from the usual Chinese preference for parallel couplets. Instead he attempts a structure based on tripartite units: valley, ravine, and lake, for example, or sky, earth, and man; mountain range, high plain, and forested mountain base; or plants, stones, and waterheads. His lines generally form groups of three, five, seven, and nine characters or are in mixed meter, with an occasional four-character group interposed. This is somewhat reminiscent of parallel prose. But Liu carefully avoids making his an ordinary parallel prose composition by omitting six-character lines. He employs compound parallelism as well as the simple, couplet-unit variety. Their use in combination forms a pattern like the following (each letter represents a character, and the numerals 1 and 2 indicate parallel elements):

$$
\left.\begin{array}{l} A\ B_1 \\ A\ B_2 \end{array}\right\} \quad C\ D\ E\ F \quad \left\{\begin{array}{llll} G_1 & G_2 & I_1 & J_1 \\ H_1 & H_2 & I_2 & J_2 \end{array}\right\}
$$

$$
\left\{\begin{array}{llllllll} K & L & M_1 & N & O_1 & P_1 & Q_1 & R_1 \\ K & L & M_2 & N & O_2 & P_2 & Q_2 & R_2 \end{array}\right\} \quad S\ T\ U\ V\ W\ X\ Y\ Z
$$

Liu alters the number of characters in his groups from two to four to three and finally to five; he also interposes single lines like C D E F and

---

literacy, since the rules of parallel prose composition are complex. Usually lay scholars of Chinese literature or scholastic monks composed these prayers and statements for interested parties. [Auth., Trans.]

[43] "Fujisan no Ki" and "Shosaiki" appear in HM, 12:295-96, and "Dōjō Hōshi Den" in HM, 12:300-301.

[44] CTW, 580:7447. Since Liu's essay is long, the CTW does not quote the entire text. The complete work can easily be found in another collection, T'ang Sung Pa-chia-wen (fasc. 8).

S T U V to protect his style from the monotony engendered by exclusive parallelism, as well as to aid in accelerating the progress of his narrative. Another noteworthy device appears in the parallel elements represented by the symbols R_1 and R_2, which form a rhyme. Liu's plain prose, then, has expanded the overly formulaic Six Dynasties parallel prose style to include more varied rhythms and has thus created a new kind of elegant prose. The new rhythms in Liu's prose, moreover, are not isolated from its content. Consider, for example, a structure made up of a group of parallel five-character lines with abstract content, followed by parallel seven-character lines with concrete content: the rhythm is created by the different kinds of *meaning* in the parallel groups. A further technique is demonstrated in one of the parallel groups above, where an arrangement of important words symbolized as

$$\left. \begin{array}{cc} G_1 & G_2 \\ H_1 & H_2 \end{array} \right\}$$

is disassembled later in the essay and its opposing parts reversed to produce this pattern:

$$\left. \begin{array}{l} H_2 \ldots H_1 \ldots \ldots \\ G_2 \ldots G_1 \ldots \ldots \end{array} \right\}$$

An awareness of this technique, by which the same words reappear in loci of opposition, will lead to another discovery: tripartite parallelism used early in the essay, that is,

$$\left. \begin{array}{cc} A_1 & A_2 \\ B_1 & B_2 \\ C_1 & C_2 \end{array} \right\} \quad D \ E \ F \ G \ \ldots.$$

will reappear later, but with words slightly different in meaning:

$$\left. \begin{array}{cc} A'_1 & A'_2 \\ B'_1 & B'_2 \\ C'_1 & C'_2 \end{array} \right\} \quad H \ I \ J \ K \ \ldots.$$

$A_1\ A_2$ might represent "valleys and ravines," and $A'_1\ A'_2$, "plants and trees"; $B_1\ B_2$ as set against $B'_1\ B'_2$ could be "minerals and rocks" versus "earth and stone"; $C_1\ C_2$, "pools and ponds," is contrasted with $C'_1\ C'_2$, "waters and springs." Related words are expressed in each case. Tripartite parallelism, such as is expressed in the group

$$\left. \begin{array}{l} \text{mountain range} \\ \text{high plain} \\ \text{forested [mountain] base,} \end{array} \right\}$$

may also reappear later in a slightly abbreviated form, thus:

mountain
plain
forested [mountain] base. }

Tripartite parallelism is one of Liu's characteristic techniques and is easily recognized in his work.

Liu's prose is therefore elegant and meticulously planned. It differs from the Six Dynasties parallel prose style only in the nature of its aesthetic appeal. Where Six Dynasties parallel prose tends to employ diction too elaborate for the meaning expressed, Liu's prose diction is chosen to accord with the actual significance of the content, and so it gives the reader a sense of simplicity. The stronger this sense, however, the more effective Liu's antithetical structure and unprecedented rhythms become, and the greater the tension within the work as a whole. The same is generally true for Han's prose. His practice of achieving freshness through archaic diction results in stronger effects than are found in Liu's work, moreover, and the acuity of Han's theoretically based topics makes his prose more lucid and persuasive. "Plain prose" inadvertently calls to mind a free, plain style. But the single characteristic that Han's and Liu's prose shares is strictness of expression.

Only a complete awareness of Han's and Liu's formal strictness will enable a reader to perceive that Yüan's and Po's prose, with its simple yet subtly rich style, is indeed worthy expression. Japanese plain prose writers, lacking this comprehensive view, sought to imitate only Yüan's and Po's prose styles. The result was lax expression and a gradual lowering of aesthetic expectations. Yoshika's "Account of Mount Fuji" is a product of the earliest period of Japanese plain [Chinese] prose, and so it would not be right to criticize its workmanship. Even Michizane's "Account of My Study" lacks a tight structure, and it is no more than a detailed description of the author's daily life. Several lines may be deleted without significantly affecting the coherence of the whole. Lax expression is more or less unavoidable in Japanese plain prose written during the tenth and eleventh centuries. These works can only escape criticism if we accord little importance to expression and focus exclusively on the appeal of the subject matter. Such an evaluative method would find Michizane's "Account of My Study" an interesting description of one part of his scholarly life. Two other essays are noteworthy as early expressions of the philosophy of seclusion: Prince Kaneakira's "Chitei no Ki" ("Account of My Lakeside Arbor"), the first Japanese work to express the concept of fleeing the miseries of the corrupt world by delighting in the beauties of a lake and garden viewed from a small arbor; and an essay with the same title by Yoshishige Yasutane (?934-97).[45] Both are clearly inferior in expression,

[45] The relationship between the content of both the "Chitei no Ki" essays and the philos-

however, compared with the works on which they are modeled, Po Chü-i's "Around My Lake: A Poem and Preface" and "An Account of My Thatch-roofed Arbor."[46] Japan seemed to be acquiring a critical view that momentarily suspended judgment on stylistic grounds and evaluated a literary work only in terms of the appeal of its subject matter.

The biographical sketch (Ch. chuan; J. den), a description of a given individual's personality and acts, is a genre whose subject matter is strongly appealing, since the subjects of these sketches are people possessing qualities that attract especial interest. Yoshika's "Sketch of the Priest Dōjō" is the first biographical sketch written by a Japanese in plain Chinese prose, and so its stylistic quality is of little concern. It should be noted, however, that its subject matter takes the form of a miraculous tale: a man and his wife, having aided a fallen thunder god, are rewarded with the birth of a son who has unparalleled superhuman strength. When the son is grown, he wrestles with a demon in the bell tower of the Gangōji Temple and pulls out the demon's hair. The story continues in similar fashion. When the author's chief aim is an interesting subject, his concern for expression tends to become subordinate. The result is that the writer will not try to attract an audience by virtue of his Chinese prose style. For those who thought the Po style simple and exhaustive expression, the growing appeal of subject matter apparently meant a commensurately dwindling concern for style. This was also the case in other genres, a fact well illustrated by Fujiwara Akihira's (989-1066) "Shin Sarugaku no Ki" ("Account of the New Sarugaku"). It cannot be criticized as a formal composition because it is not included in the *Honchō Monzui* (which Akihira edited). The very composition of such prose nonetheless indicates the Japanese writers' weakening resolve in maintaining a proper Chinese prose style.

Akihira's "New Sarugaku" is a humorous piece concerning a junior assistant commander of the Right Gate Guards and his family. They have come from the west side of town to see the new sarugaku, a form of entertainment that became popular during the eleventh century.[47] Each character's introduction is also a lively reflection of contemporary life. It is made more vivid by elements never seen before in Chinese prose, the nat-

---

ophy of seclusion expressed in the *Hōjōki* has been known for some time; Kaneko's discussion is one of the most lucid of many on the subject (Kaneko, 1942, 29-93).

[46] Kaneko believes that the Japanese works are modeled solely on Po's "Around My Lake" ("Ch'ih-shang P'ien"; *Po-shih Ch'ang-ch'ing Chi*, 68:1699-1700). But his "Thatched-roof Arbor" ("Ts'ao-t'ang Chi"; ibid., 43:1063-65) may also have provided sources for the Japanese authors.

[47] Originally, "sarugaku" was the name given to the mostly comic entertainment imported from China and performed at the Japanese court. Around the eleventh century sarugaku evolved into a new art form that included mime (J. monomane): this "new sarugaku" was performed before commoners as well as courtiers (Nose, 1938, 72-81). The "new sarugaku" may have resembled the kyōgen drama of later times.

ural result of emphasizing subject matter over style. A single Chinese word often has several meanings in Japanese. A similar phenomenon occurs between English and Japanese: the English "too," for example, can be translated as either "mata" (also) or "amari" (excessively). Now, "mata" can signify, in addition to "also," the English words "again," "and," and "fork [in a road or tree]." If a Japanese writing in English intends to signify "again" but puts down "too" in its place (i.e., "I hope to see you too" instead of "I hope to see you again"), his English-speaking reader will misunderstand the intended meaning. Conversely, if a Japanese were to signify "fork" with the word "too" (i.e., "I will meet you at the too in the road"), his prose would be incomprehensible. Akihira sometimes makes errors of the same nature as this last example in his "New Sarugaku." It is questionable whether we should call a prose unintelligible to native Chinese "prose in Chinese." It certainly cannot be evaluated in the same way as a prose composition written in correct Chinese. Akihira also wrote the "Unshū Shōsoku" ("Izumo Correspondence," also known as "Meikō Ōrai," "Akihira's Letters"), a collection of exemplary letters. Again, his style abounds in Japanese locutions and demonstrates such degeneration that it cannot be compared with the letters in Kūkai's collected prose works, *Kōya Zappitsu Shū*.[48]

Akihira was far from the first Japanese to write compositions that resemble Chinese prose but are incomprehensible to native Chinese. The subject of the *Shōmon Ki (An Account of Masakado)*, probably a mid-tenth-century work, is the insurrection led by Taira Masakado (d. 940) between 935 and 940.[49] Its author attempts a style reminiscent of parallel prose, but he seems not to have been rigorously trained in writing correct Chinese prose. As a result he frequently violates Chinese grammatical rules and uses Chinese character compounds that are intelligible only to a Japanese audience. The *Account of Masakado* was probably written by a low-level bureaucrat who had served in the eastern provinces, the scene of Masakado's rebellion.

The appearance at this time of anomalous Chinese prose compositions may indicate a tolerance for Japanese locutions so widespread as to elicit scant opposition. Otherwise a scholar of Chinese literature like Akihira would never have circulated his "New Sarugaku," a humorous piece filled with Japanese locutions. The tolerance for Japanese expressions in Chinese prose grew ever greater after Akihira's time.

Of course, "New Sarugaku" is an extreme example. When properly instructed in Chinese prose composition, Akihira's contemporaries rarely

---

[48] Many of Kūkai's letters are included in *Kōya Zappitsu Shū* (*ZGRJ*, vol. 319).

[49] The *Shōmon Ki* has a probably spurious postscript that states, "Composed in the middle of the Sixth Month, [940]." The style, however, can be dated no later than the tenth century. ["Shōmon" is simply the Sinified pronunciation of the characters for "Masakado."—Ed.]

use Japanese locutions even when their pieces concern mundane events. Yasutane's *Nihon Ōjō Gokuraku Ki (Accounts of Japanese Reborn in Paradise)* contains much description of auspicious signs and marvelous stories connected with rebirth, but it manages to observe the rules of Chinese prose composition and maintain clear, plain diction and sentence structure. To my mind, however, the plainness and clarity of the work seem to be due to Yasutane's conceptual method: he probably conceived it in Japanese and then wrote it to conform with standard Chinese sentence structure, using whatever vocabulary came to mind. Seemingly plain, clear prose written by native Chinese will, when analyzed for underlying concepts, yield passages that only a native Chinese could express and that few but native Chinese can understand. At least many such passages are beyond my grasp of Chinese. Yasutane's prose, on the other hand, is easily read even by someone like myself. Yasutane's conceptual method may be perceived in a passage describing a certain priest's death (*Nihon Ōjō Gokuraku Ki*, 503). Two Chinese characters that are intended to signify "breathed his last" instead form an anomalous compound that would be read by a native Chinese as an unnatural expression meaning something like "his breath stopped." Yasutane's literal translations have no grammatical oddities, but some of his expressions would never be used by native Chinese. The compound here translated as "his breath stopped" is probably a literal translation of the Japanese "iki taenu."

Genshin's (942-1017) *Ōjō Yōshū (Essentials of Deliverance)* is valued by some as Buddhist literature, but it will not be discussed here as a prose composition. Frequently called the *Divine Comedy* of Japan, it has certainly moved many readers with its descriptions of the Buddhist Hell of Torture (Jigoku) and Amitābha's Paradise (Gokuraku Jōdo). These descriptions, however, are direct quotations from the sutras, not Genshin's own prose. It is the style of the sutras, translated from Sanskrit into Chinese, that so intensely impresses readers, and Genshin's role is an intermediary one.

CHAPTER 7

Waka

COMPOSITION, RECEPTION, AND TRANSMISSION

To pick a symbolic date, in 905 waka took on its distinct medieval character, the year the royal command was issued to compile the *Kokinshū*. Needless to say, medieval expression was not completely—or first—manifested in 905. Informal waka was already tending toward a medieval style of obliqueness by the first half of the ninth century. But the medieval waka style is not characterized by oblique expression alone. Several other noteworthy poetic phenomena arose at the end of the ninth century. Their synthesis with oblique expression signals the formation of the medieval waka style. Oblique expression did not in fact become a fixed feature of formal waka until the dawn of the tenth century.

Composition and Reception Based on Waka Topics

From the latter half of the ninth century there is a significantly increased incidence of waka composed on assigned topics (daiei). Waka in the Ancient Age were composed on the basis of a given situation: they describe matters directly experienced by the poet or personal thoughts or feelings about an experience. The commencement of the Middle Ages marked a growing preference for composition on an assigned topic, a practice in which someone other than the poet designates the concern of a waka. The composition of shih on assigned topics, which first became popular in China during the Six Dynasties period, evolved from the practice of composing poems about animate or inanimate objects. As was noted earlier, the ancient Chinese rarely composed nature poetry. By the Eastern Chin Dynasty, however, poems on nature and specific objects—birds, flowers, the moon—had greatly increased in number. Those poems composed about specific objects and those composed on assigned topics share common features, but they are not identical. A poem on a specific object is composed when a poet has freely selected that object for treatment. By contrast, if a poet is requested to compose a poem on a given object, the result is a poem composed on an assigned topic.

In Chinese literature, assigned topics are most evident in ballad poetry, poets being provided in advance with the topic to be expressed in verse. For example, the topic "Reproach in the Tall Gate Palace" ("Ch'ang-men Yüan") requires that a poet depict the grief of Empress Ch'en of the Former Han Dynasty, whose jealousy for a rival concubine brought about the empress's confinement in the Tall Gate Palace and her estrangement from Emperor Wu, her husband. Similarly, the topic "The Orphan" ("Ku-erh Hsing") obliges a poet to describe the trials of an orphan boy tormented by his older brother's wife. Shih on assigned topics first appear in Japanese literature in the early ninth century. They are not included in the *Kaifūsō*, although shih about specific objects are. Examples of early Japanese shih on assigned topics include Saga's "Baikaraku" ("Plum Blossoms Are Falling"; *BSS*, 2:67) and four poems from his *Kayō Jūei* (*Ten Poems on Hoyang; BSS*, 3:96-99): "Kayōka" ("Blossoms of Hoyang"), "Kōjōsen" ("Boats on the River"), "Kōhensō" ("Grasses by the River"), and "Sanjishō" ("The Mountain Temple Bell").[1] We should also note that the literature of this time contains a few verse-topic shih (kudaishi), a special kind of poetry on an assigned topic [in that the topic is a line of verse]. Saga and Ono no Minemori (778-830) composed shih on the verse-topic "Near Mount Lung the Autumn Moon Is Bright" (*BSS*, 3:134-35), which is in turn the opening line of a Chinese shih, "The River near Lung," by Ch'en Shih-tao (1059-1101). The incidence of shih composed on assigned topics—including verse-topic shih—gradually increased toward the close of the ninth century.

These circumstances led to the appearance of assigned topics in waka. The first documented instances of waka composed on topics occurred on the twenty-ninth day of the Eighth Month, 882, at the royal banquet following the end of a series of lectures on the *Nihon Shoki*.[2] The topics in this case—all drawn from divine and human characters depicted in the *Nihon Shoki*—resemble certain shih topics, as this shih title illustrates: "On the Topic, 'Chang Tzu-fang' [a name] Assigned at the Royal Banquet Following the Concluding Lecture on the *Shih Chi*" (*BSS*, 2:42). These waka may therefore be seen as something of a special case, given their topics. The first instances of what were to become common waka topics appear in a series of waka competitions held at the house of the Minister for Civil Affairs between 885 and 887: the assigned topics are "The Hototogisu" and "Thwarted Love."[3] Since waka topics did in fact exist prior to this

[1] Hoyang is the name of a region in China, in present Hunan Province. Saga, of course, composed his shih in Japan, but he likens the area described in the poems—the northern reaches of the Yodo River, near the town of Yamazaki—to this part of China. [Auth., Trans.]

[2] The series of *Nihon Shoki* lectures, a formal court event, was concluded with a banquet; before 882, shih were customarily composed on this occasion, and thereafter waka were composed in place of shih. Waka topics in 882 included "The God Kuni no Tokotachi," "The God Kotoshironushi," "Princess Shitateru," "Ōsasagi [Nintoku] Tennō," and "Takeuchi Sukune." ["Waka" in the medieval context of course designates almost solely the five-line tanka, although the lengthier chōka were still sometimes written.—Ed.]

[3] [Known in Japanese by the descriptive title, *Zai Mimbukyō Ke Utaawase*.—Trans.] The "Minister for Civil Affairs" is Ariwara Yukihira (818-93). The competition has also been thought to have been held in 887 (*HCUT*, 1:7).

time, the two given above were probably selected from a larger corpus. This series was occasionally convened in the summer, and so "The Hototogisu" was very likely chosen as appropriate to the season. The topic "Thwarted Love" naturally presupposes the existence of another, "Consummated Love," and it in turn indicates that still more subcategories of "Love" possibly existed at the time: "Beginning Love," for example, or "Hidden Love," "Pledged Love," "Resentful Love," or "Love Broken Off."[4] This granted, we may reasonably conclude that "The Hototogisu," a topic pertaining to the natural features of a given season, was one among several kinds of acknowledged topics. The *Kambyō no Ōntoki Kisai no Miya Utaawase (Her Majesty's Kambyō Era Waka Match)*, held only on paper and apparently compiled before 893, consists of twenty rounds (forty poems) on the topics "Spring," "Summer," "Autumn," "Winter," and "Love."[5] Ten of the "Summer" poems are devoted to the hototogisu, an indication of its contemporary popularity as a poetic subject. Topics were not assigned at this waka competition, but the tendency to fashion popular natural subjects into fixed topics is nonetheless present.

Assigned topics for waka composition apparently began gaining in popularity between the end of the ninth century and the beginning of the tenth. The sequence composed at Ki no Tsurayuki's stream banquet, in which Tsurayuki plays a central role, is thought to date from between 898 and 901.[6] The topics assigned for the waka were "Flowers Drift on Vernal Waters," "Hanging Lanterns Light the Water's Edge," and "The Moon Sets, and Blossom-rapids Darken." The last two are verse-topics taken from Chinese shih. In 894, somewhat before Tsurayuki's stream banquet, the *Ōe no Chisato Shū (Collected Waka of Ōe no Chisato*; also called *Kudai Waka, Verse-topic Waka)* was compiled.[7] The collection was an experiment in composing waka along the lines of verse-topic shih, using topics provided by individual lines from Chinese poems. Chisato (fl. 897-903)

---

[4] "Love" has forty-two subcategories in the list of topics for the twelfth-century *Horikawa Hyakushu*. Similarly, the topic "Love" would have had several subdivisions in the late ninth century. [As for the hototogisu, for the reason given in ch. 2, n. 5, the bird is classified as a summer poetic topic and is in fact the most important topic of the season. In *Kokinshū*, 3, there are thirty-four summer poems (135-68), twenty-five of which feature the hototogisu as topic (140-64).—Ed.]

[5] The *Shinsen Man'yōshū*, a waka collection drawing heavily on the poetry produced at this competition, has a preface dated 893, and so the results of the match are assumed to have been compiled prior to this year. The terminus a quo is probably 889.

[6] [The banquet is known in Japanese by the descriptive title, *Ki no Shishō Kyokusuien no Waka*.—Trans.] Probably held during the Shōtai era (898-901; Yamada, 1948, 18-20). A "stream banquet" (kyokusuien) always included a game involving poetry composition: a sake cup was floated down the curving garden stream, and the participant in question had to compose a waka or shih before the cup reached him. If he failed to do so, the cup was filled with sake and he was obliged to drink it down—a not unpleasant penalty. [Auth., Trans.]

[7] One manuscript tradition has the year as 894, and another has 897. I follow the former (Kaneko, 1943, 233).

also participated in Tsurayuki's stream banquet. Revered by Chisato as a master of waka, Tsurayuki was of course familiar with the verse-topic waka making up Chisato's *Collected Waka*, and he probably made use of the idea in his stream banquet. The popular practice of composing waka with assigned topics (including verse-topics) dominated waka from the eleventh century on and attained such heights by the thirteenth century that the then modern waka not composed on topics were rarely selected for inclusion in formal anthologies. The period of greatest popularity for verse-topic shih roughly parallels that for waka composed on assigned topics. The composition of verse-topic shih became predominant in the eleventh century, a period when the word "shih" was understood to signify verse-topic shih, and other shih were especially labeled "shih without topics." There can be no doubt that the practice of composing waka on assigned topics owed its popularity to the influence of shih.

On the other hand, the influence exerted by shih was probably indirect. Because shih had assigned topics, poets concluded they had best set some topics for waka as well. Assigned waka topics (as they appear from the tenth century on) are thought to have been directly shaped by the subgenre of screen waka (byōbuuta). Screen waka appear together with a painting or paintings on one or more decorative screens. Waka were first so employed for the Great Thanksgiving Service held at the palace (Daijōe), and the more eminent nobility later developed the practice of commissioning decorative screens for congratulatory banquets. Japanese screens were originally decorated with paintings in the Chinese style, and so the accompanying poetry was naturally written in Chinese. Yamatoe, the Japanese style of painting, developed in the latter half of the ninth century and soon thereafter came to be employed for screen decoration. Waka first appeared at this time, on Yamatoe screens. The early period of screen waka is represented in compositions by Taira Sadafum' (fl. ca. 870; *SIS*, 17:1091) and Ōnakatomi Yorimoto (884-958; *SIS*, 19:1247), which date from the reign of Kōkō Tennō (r. 884-87). The number of screen waka increased rapidly in the tenth century. Tsurayuki in particular was requested to write a very great many.[8] It has long been known that screen waka contributed to the development of assigned topics in waka (Koyama, 1928, 89-93), but the vital significance of this fact may have become clear only in connection with the question of Lady Ise's screen waka (Tamagami, 1953, 198-202). When the royal consort Onshi was as yet a junior consort to the crown prince (later Uda Tennō), possibly in the year 887, she assigned Lady Ise (d. ca. 939) several topics for some screen waka. The corpus of eighteen poems Ise produced is included in her *Ise*

---

[8] Out of 864 waka in the *Tsurayuki Shū* (Nishi Honganji manuscript) 539 are screen poems.

Shū (*Collected Waka of Lady Ise*; poems 34-51), and begins in this fashion.

At a time when our sovereign's consort was still known by the title of junior consort to the crown prince, she issued several poetic topics for waka to decorate a screen. One picture showed a man speaking to a lady he has happened to meet on the road. He had once courted and won her with a poem on plum blossoms; now, with the trees again in bloom, and with hopes of his former success, he addresses her on the same subject.

Mishi hito ni	She I saw and loved—
Mata mo ya au to	With hopes to meet with her again
Ume no hana	I never pass a day
Sakishi atari ni	Without a visit to this place
Yukanu hi zo naki.	Where once the plum tree bloomed.

Her reply:

Hitotabi ni	Enjoyed but once,
Korinishi ume no	The plum tree that I knew too well
Hana nareba	Was shorn of blossoms;
Chirinu to kikedo	People tell me they have fallen,
Mata mo minaku ni.	But I desired no second view.[9]

The scene then changes, successively, to depictions of cherry blossoms, wisteria, orange blossoms, the hototogisu, Shinto purification rites in the Sixth Month, the Seventh Night (Tanabata), autumn fields, and cold drizzle. The sequence concludes with a snow scene.

Kaerusa no	I do not believe
Michi yuku beku mo	That I can return upon the road
Omōezu	I should take to home;
Kōrite yuki no	Because on its icy surface
Furishimasareba.	The snow keeps piling higher.

Day was dawning as he spoke. Then he said,

---

[9] ["Korinishi" (shorn) also means "left the wiser through bitter experience." The plum blossoms are a metaphor for the love once shared by the man and woman. The blossoms (the delights of love) are glorious but disappointingly short-lived: the tree, though in full bloom, is pruned, just as the speaker's love is destroyed by a single disillusioning rendezvous. This unpleasant experience has left her with no wish ever to see the "blossoms" again. She feels no regret for the past affair, even when she hears that her former lover's affections have faded.—Trans.]

Au koto no	It is true we talked,
Awanu yo nagara	But you granted no fulfillment,
Akenureba	And as dawn now breaks,
Ware koso kaere	Although the rest of me goes home,
Kokoro ya wa yuku.	How can my heart depart from here?

The matter of debate is whether the man and woman depicted in the screen paintings are the same throughout. There is no definitive evidence, but if we consider that "the *same* man" (36) and "*that* man" (39) are mentioned in forenotes to poems, we may well interpret the sequence as depicting the progress of one love affair. The couple seem close to consummating their union when the woman's parents learn of the affair and forbid a marriage. The woman has no alternative but to ask her lover, in a waka, to return home. He replies with the poems "I do not believe" and "It is true we talked" and then leaves, but his heart remains with her. This is very likely the end of the affair. In other words, the progression of events, from the lovers' first meeting until they go their separate ways, is integrated into a single sequence. The lovers' progress, moreover, is accompanied by seasonal progression. The sequence is so unified that, with a bit more explanatory prose, it might have become an utamonogatari (a brief narrative centered around one or more waka [see Chapter 8]). The waka in the sequence are discrete units, but they are also linked together; their seasonal order is also very significant in terms of reading. These points will be discussed further in another context.

Screen waka may well have influenced waka composition in another notable way, in effecting a separation between poet and speaker. Lady Ise is undoubtedly the composer of the screen waka quoted above, but the characters in the sequence are different from the poet, Lady Ise. The waka must be read as exchanges between the man and woman in the paintings. The composer of a screen waka characteristically takes the part of a person in the painting; conversely, waka that merely describe the scenes depicted in screen paintings cannot be considered screen waka. A waka quoted earlier, "Omoiseku / Kokoro no uchi no / Taki nare ya . . ." (Might this not be / A pent-up waterfall of thoughts / Within the human heart? . . .), was composed on the topic of a waterfall painted on a screen. The poem is composed from the poet's viewpoint, as she views a waterfall scene. But since she does not put herself in the position of a person in the painting, her poem is not a screen waka. The distinction is also clearly made in the Nishi Honganji manuscript of the *Tsurayuki Shū (Collected Waka of Tsurayuki)* and in other manuscript copies that reserve separate sections for Tsurayuki's screen waka: all the manuscripts place his poem "Sakisomeshi" (Ever since the day . . .)—composed on a screen painting—not in a screen waka section but in a section given over to miscellaneous poems (Tamagami, 1953, 193-94). Composition in which the poet's standpoint is distinct from that of the character in the poem was practiced as early as the *Man'yōshū* period, and ancient poets even went so far as to experiment in creating provisional speakers. So it is not entirely misdirected to conclude that the late-ninth-century proliferation of waka with speakers distinct from composers was not an aberration but the result of natural evolution. The phenomenon was given further vigor by external factors that accelerated the natural process. The popularity of screen waka was evidently one such factor.

In Chinese poetry there is frequently a distance between the poet and the poetic speaker. There are several instances in the *New Songs from the Jade Terrace*, and by the beginning of the ninth century they also appear in Japanese shih. Asano Katori (774-843), for example, begins his long shih "Matching His Majesty's Poem on 'Melancholy in a Spring Boudoir' " (*BSS*, 2:52) with a couplet whose speaker is obviously not himself but a woman: "In Ch'ang-an I once led a life of utter luxury: / My dresses, perfumes, complexion were all akin to flowers!" This shih technique undoubtedly affected waka composition. The distance between poet and speaker was further defined by screen waka, in which the speaker's identity as a figure in a painting was visually delineated. Screen waka suddenly reached new heights of popularity in the tenth century as (1) screen paintings and their accompanying waka increased in number; (2) it became a practice to make a set of several decorated screens; and (3) a fixed, sequential poetic form, treating the yearly succession of natural scenes and human events, gradually took shape (Ozawa, 1961, 253-59). A rapid increase both in the number of compositions possessing distance between speaker and poet and in the appreciation of such compositions must result from the influence of screen waka.

A sequential poetic form, linking the natural scenes and human events of a year, was fixed by the early tenth century. Evidence of this is provided by the waka sequence composed by Tsurayuki for a consort's screens in the Fifth Month of 902 (*Tsurayuki Shū* [= *TYS*], 2:139-60), and in another of Tsurayuki's sequences, composed in 906 for screens depicting the twelve months (ibid., 1:3-22). These sequences, incidentally, date from much the same time as the compilation period of the *Kokinshū*.

Because the same natural scenes and human events are repeated in the same succession every year, their poetic treatment is also easily fixed so that the same events are always described in the same manner. If, for example, a waka was concerned with the outings to gather pine seedlings, made every year on the Day of the Rat [auspicious as being the first sign of the zodiac] in the First and Second Months, the poet was expected to compose a work linking pine trees to the auspicious properties of spring. The evolution toward a fixed poetic treatment of a given subject may also be connected to the composition of a sequence of screen waka. The sponsor of a sequence rarely showed his screen paintings to the poet before commissioning him to compose the requisite poems. Yet the more usual process seems to have been to give a poet the topics and, once he had completed his commission, to select those waka most appropriate to the paintings (Shimizu, 1976, 239-54). Apparently such commissions were ordinarily given to two or more poets, although a master of screen waka like Tsurayuki would have been commissioned to work without competition. Even Tsurayuki collaborated on a sequence, however, working with Ki no Tomonori (?850-?904), Ōshikōchi Mitsune (fl. 898-922), Mibu no Tadamine (fl. 898-920), Sakanoe Korenori (fl. ca. 898-930), and the priest Sosei (fl. ca. 859-97) to produce the screen waka commemorating the fortieth-year celebration for Fujiwara Sadakuni (fl. ca. 901-15) on the twenty-first of the Second Month, 905 (*TYS*, 1:1-2).

Occasionally fairly detailed instructions seem to have accompanied the topics assigned when a sequence was commissioned. Consider, for example, these lengthy forenotes to some of the screen waka in Tsurayuki's *Collected Waka*.

> Women emerge from a house into the garden. They look at the plum blossoms, and gaze at the mountains, still capped with snow. (1:60)

> It is a morning during the services of the Buddhas' Names.[10] As the officiant leaves, priests and laymen withdraw to a palace garden. Carrying sprays of plum blossom, they amuse themselves, while someone breaks off a spray on which snow has fallen. (2:126)

> Women who live near the mountains have gone on an excursion to distant plains, whence they gaze in the direction of home. (3:220)

> Men and women are gathered beneath a tree, as a man passes before them in a boat. He is pointing at something, and seems to be speaking. He may be telling them to listen for the hototogisu. (4:460)

The forenotes probably reproduce directions given by sponsors of sequences. There are also short forenotes in Tsurayuki's *Collected Waka*, such as "Fulling cloth" (1:18) and "Snow is falling" (2:138), as well as simple headings like "Spring" (3:280-87) and "Autumn" (3:288-94), and the slightly more limited topics "New Year's Day" (4:410) and "The fifth day of the Fifth Month" (4:478).[11] Much was left to the poet's discretion

[10] Butsumyōe, Buddhist services held from the nineteenth through the twenty-first of the Twelfth Month at the royal palace and at great temples. The *Butsumyōkyō (Sūtra on the Buddhas' Names)* was read, the names of buddhas and bodhisattvas were intoned, and confession was made of wrongdoings committed during the past year.

[11] ["Fulling cloth" ("Koromo utsu") is an autumn topic.—Trans.]

in the majority of commissions. Detailed instructions may have enabled a poet to keep from straying too far from the subjects of the paintings, but when given virtual carte blanche, there were no doubt difficulties in co-ordinating the poetry with the paintings. There would have been few embarrassments, however, since the scenes depicted in screen paintings were evidently confined to more or less fixed categories. Thus, a poet might have a vague topic like "Spring," but as long as he knew the number of poems required—six, for instance, or ten—one of his poems was sure to match the painting: the spring scenes depicted in that many waka would not have varied greatly.

The problem lay, rather, in the poet's stance. How was one to treat the scene assigned? On the twentieth day of the Ninth Month, 917, Mitsune received a letter from the Governor of Ōmi, informing him that the cloistered sovereign Uda was to pay a visit to the temple Ishiyamadera the following day, and the poet was requested to come to Ōmi immediately. Upon his arrival, Mitsune was shown several folding and sliding screens and was asked to compose waka appropriate to the scenes depicted on each. That night, having finished composing the poems, he was requested to inscribe them on the screens. Unable to refuse, Mitsune took on the additional task of calligrapher. The waka he wrote on this occasion appear in his *Mitsune Shū* (*Collected Waka of Mitsune*; 2:271-80), with the proud comment, "The poems I wrote for the folding and sliding screens were each adapted to fit a separate topic" (Nishi Honganji manuscript). The *Kasenkashū* version has ". . . adapted to fit the import of a separate topic" (dai no omomuki ni shitagaeri) rather than "adapted to fit a separate topic" (dai ni shitagau). But in either case the text may be interpreted as a statement that the waka were well coordinated with the central ideas displayed in the paintings. In other words, when a given scene was to be the subject of a waka, the criteria governing its composition seem to have been generally the same for all poets of the waka circle.

The criteria took on still more definite form by the mid-tenth century. In *The Hollow Tree (Utsuho Monogatari)* Masayori and his family make a pilgrimage to the Kasuga Shrine in Nara. When the time comes to compose some waka, Masayori asks Nakayori to "choose us a few likely subjects for waka topics." Nakayori writes down the following.

> We are now indeed in the midst of the three months of spring, and last night we awaited the late-rising moon.[12] We anticipate the warbler's song that tempts blossoms to open. Wild geese, all in a line, em-

---

[12] An elaborate way of saying, "Today is the twentieth day of the Second Month." The "three months of Spring" are the first three months of the lunar calendar, and the night of the "late-rising moon" (nemachi) occurs on the nineteenth day of the lunar month. [Auth., Trans.]

bark on their spring journey, and mallards gather by the riverbanks. Buds swell and spring into life as my lord travels to Kasuga, the Shrine of Vernal Day.[13]

Then it is that warblers come to rest on blossoming plum branches, and cicadas [find] lodgings in the pine trees.[14] [Plants, sensing the arrival of spring,] are startled [when people walk among them]; the time draws near for mountain cherries to bloom. Wisteria in spring is but faintly tinted; it intertwines with slender willow boughs. [Spring rain is set off by a background of color; and although the breeze blows gently, the plum blossoms by the fence have faded.]

Morning mist clothes the greenery, and evening clouds become golden brocade. In the mountains winter is still young, while on the plains spring is growing old. Seeing you today, the nearby plains envy your flowers; distant mountains hear of your splendor, while their peaks are brilliant still with snow.[15] Grasses grow beneath the snow, and young shoots flourish atop the hoarfrost. Pale green are the buds on trees, while plum blossoms grow ever more crimson. Spring ferns emerge as the snow disappears; stones, warmed by the sun's fire, quickly melt the ice.

Evergreens oblivious to the changing season; blossoms that return each spring; a hermit dwelling quietly on the plain; deer belling lustily in the hills; boughs yielding to a breeze; plants brought into bud by the rain; plants lamenting the passing of spring; insects inviting the advent of summer; leaves that await the autumn; birds that rue the winter; [delighting in a moon not quite full; admiring a moon just past full]. ("Kasuga Mōde," 68[262-63])

The members of the pilgrimage party use this as a basis for composing waka on thirty-eight individual topics, including "The Late-rising Moon," "Tempting the Blossoms," "Anticipating the Warbler," "Wild Geese All in a Line," "Mallards by the Riverbanks," and "Buds Swell and Spring into Life." *The Hollow Tree* is of course a fictional narrative, but the events it depicts were not intended to impress its audience as unnatural. We may fairly conclude that, by the mid-tenth century, waka topics— that is, subjects frequently treated in waka—were becoming qualitatively

[13] The descriptions of the wild geese and mallards allude to Masayori's impressive procession and his flocks of attendants. "Kasuga" is written with characters that signify "spring day." [Auth., Trans.]

[14] The Maeda manuscript copy of the *Utsuho*, from which this translation is made, is supplemented with the Hamada manuscript in the possession of the Seikadō Bunko. In this and the next two paragraphs, translations from the latter manuscript are given [by the author] in brackets.

[15] "Nearby plains" and "distant mountains" are metaphors, respectively, for the onlookers at Masayori's procession to the Kasuga Shrine and those who will hear of it later. [Auth., Trans.]

fixed while tending toward diversity of categories.[16] The first steps toward fixed quality and categorical diversity were therefore probably made in the early tenth century.

Set waka topics were also an important means of composition and judgment in waka matches (utaawase). Although "waka match" signifies a variety of events, in all cases they were based on striving for superiority over a rival. A critical judgment was more easily made in a competition if the two competing poems possessed some feature in common. It was probably impossible for a judge to find a comparative focus between two waka sharing nothing whatsoever. Waka topics were exceedingly useful in this sense, since they provided matched poems with a common feature. The subjects used, and even the poets' treatment of these subjects, tended increasingly to assume something of a fixed form. Thus a judge had a valuable criterion in hand once he had determined whether a poet "adapted" his treatment "to fit the import of" the topic. The use of assigned topics in the oldest extant waka match, the *Zai Mimbukyō Ke Utaawase*, held from 885 to 887 at the house of Ariwara Yukihira (?818-?93), Minister for Civil Affairs, can only reflect the circumstances described above. Other late ninth-century waka matches include a palace competition, in which the competing entries were units consisting of a waka and a chrysanthemum (known as the *Dairi Kikuawase*); a match held at Prince Koresada's residence (*Koresada no Miko Ke Utaawase*); another held at the residence of the consort Inshi (*Kisai no Miya Inshi Ke Utaawase*); and a waka-and-ladyflower match held at the Suzaku Palace (*Suzakuin Ominaeshiawase*).[17] Not all had assigned topics, although the waka-chrysanthemum and waka-ladyflower competitions each had what would correspond to a topic—"Chrysanthemums" and "Ladyflowers," respectively. Further, Prince Koresada's competition, devoted to poems on autumn, very likely corresponds to a competition with assigned topics, since topics like "Spring" and "Autumn" appear in connection with screen waka. When, however, the range of topics embraces love as well as the four seasons, as in *Her Majesty's Kambyō Era Waka Match* and the competition held at Inshi's residence, "Spring" and "Autumn" must be seen more characteristically to represent classifications rather than topics (Ozawa, 1961, 262-63). This extensive awareness of waka topics and classifications presages

---

[16] The *Makura no Sōshi* of Sei Shōnagon mentions the *Utsuho Monogatari* in dan 212; the *Utsuho* was thus probably composed in the mid-tenth century.

[17] [Ominaeshi, here translated "ladyflower," is a member of the valerian family, Patrinia scabiosaefolia.—Trans.] The years in which the four waka competitions were held are as follows. *Dairi Kikuawase* (topic: Chrysanthemums): 888-91; *Koresada no Miko Ke Utaawase* (no topics): prior to the Ninth Month of 893; *Kisai no Miya Inshi Ke Utaawase* (topics: "Spring," "Summer," "Autumn," "Winter," "Love"): prior to the Sixth Month of 896; *Suzakuin Ominaeshiawase* (no topics): year not known. Dating follows that in *HCUT* (1:13-111).

the creation, shortly after this period, of the sequential structure so characteristic of the *Kokinshū*.

Waka Matches and Their Influence

The rise of waka matches at the end of the ninth century, and the popularity they enjoyed thereafter, had vital significance. To begin with, the waka match was the origin of a characteristic Japanese literary feature, the za (group composition); second, it spurred the development of waka poetics and its offshoot, literary criticism; and third, it gave rise to a concept of reading or hearing by sequence and category rather than by individual works.

Various hypotheses have sought to explain the origin of waka matches, but all are in effect suppositions, since none has ever been conclusively proved. Everything from Chinese folk pastimes—wildflower contests, cockfights, song contests—to the Japanese sports of sumō, archery meets, and horse racing has been suggested as the progenitor.[18] In all these events, victory or defeat is decided when one of two teams, the [senior] Left and the [junior] Right, accumulates the larger total from its members' individual scores. The only conclusion that can be drawn is that all such matches possess a similar form, and the waka version cannot be proved to have been modeled on any of them. The origins of the waka match must remain a mystery.

To judge from the *Teiji In Utaawase (Teiji In Waka Match)* of the third of the Third Month, 913, we observe that a formal competition progressed as follows at its highest developmental stage.

1. Assembly of all participants. (Formal dress for both men and women.)

2. Presentation of the compositions to His Majesty (Daigo Tennō). (The Left and Right each present a written record of topics, waka, and participants in the competition. An elaborate centerpiece [suhama] is submitted by each side. Saibara are performed.)

3. Recitation and judging. (Lectors recite each round—one waka each from the Left and the Right—and a judge or judges determine the winner.)

4. Concert. (A performance, possibly of saibara, by both the Left and the Right.)

5. Bestowal of gifts. (His Majesty makes gifts of clothing to the poets' designated proxies [katōdo].)

A suhama is a tray with short curved legs that has constructed on it an exquisite miniature landscape, often of a seacoast. In the *Teiji In Waka Match*, waka written on poem cards were added to the landscape for fur-

[18] *HCUT*, 10:2903-12, 2934-38. *UAS* ("Kaisetsu" [Kodaihen]), 9-19.

ther ornamentation: waka on "Mist" were attached to a miniature mountain, waka on "The Warbler" were attached to artificial blossoming boughs (perhaps a plum tree's), waka on "The Hototogisu" were attached to artificial blossoming deutzia branches, and the rest of the poems were put into little iron braziers hanging from miniature cormorant-fishing boats.

Forty-seven years later, at the *Tentoku Waka Match* (held at the royal palace in 960), the suhama were made of gold, silver, and aloeswood: the mountains were aloeswood, water was represented by mirrors, branches of kerria were constructed with gold for the blossoms and silver for the leaves, and figures of human beings, birds, and beasts were also included in the landscapes. The concert making up the latter part of the competition had T'ang-style music ("In Spring the Warblers Twitter" and "The Willow-blossom Lament") as well as saibara. Each time a round took place and a winner was determined, the sake cup was passed round, so that the group became utterly blissful: "The assembled courtiers grew merry and drunk, and could not restrain themselves from various diversions" (*Tentoku Utaawase* [= *TTU*], 92). The competition was a model fūryū gathering: it certainly had three of the requisite elements—poetry, music, and wine—and probably also the fourth, beautiful women.

Now, in order to state that za (group) literature originates in the poetry match, a definition of za literature is first required. Za literature, typified by renga (linked poetry), has three essential factors: (1) everyone present at the session participates as both composer and recipient; (2) the session includes periods set aside for criticism; and (3) an intimate atmosphere prevails among the participants. The first requisite is partially fulfilled by the waka match: several poets present compositions, and many people make up their audience. Certain features of a royal waka match, like that described above, however, do not always meet this requisite. Those invited to participate tended to be famous poets who were, for the most part, low-ranking officials. By established practice, they would not attend waka competitions held in the royal presence.[19] Instead, a poet would entrust compositions to a proxy of suitably high rank, who attended the competition in place of the poet. The proxy was responsible for defending "his" poems from criticism and issuing rebuttals. Since criticism of the other side's poems is surely a form of reception, the proxy may be considered equivalent to the composer-recipients present at the competition. At informal or small waka matches, the participants were of course all composers who doubled as recipients.

[19] The records of the Teiji In Utaawase have "Poets [in a certain round]: Fujiwara Okikaze, Ōshikōchi Mitsune" and "Poets: Korenori, Tsurayuki" (*UAS*, 53). After this there is no instance of low-ranking composers attending a competition. Early waka competitions had probably not yet fixed the usages that later prevailed during royal waka competitions.

The second requisite is easily fulfilled by the waka match, since judgments (han) were given on competing waka. Judgments were not made in some waka matches, but that is so rare as to be safely disregarded. In renga, there is no judgment to determine a victor, but the quality of each link is evaluated on a point system. No difference exists, however, between the two forms in audience response: in both cases it results from criticism of the compositions.

The third requisite presents certain difficulties: the absence of recorded informal waka matches means that we cannot know whether an intimate atmosphere prevailed. We may nevertheless assume that these events included a convivial banquet, even if it did not attain the scale of a palace-sponsored match. Banquets were also extremely important features of renga sessions.[20] In very informal circumstances the banquet might be omitted, but the gathering was still expected to maintain a spirit and form fostering thorough enjoyment by host and guests alike.

The waka match is based essentially on the contest form, a fact that is certainly connected to the development of criticism in Japan. Participants in early waka matches were interested in the game, and the dominant mood was light. As a result, the competitive element was not taken very seriously. Instead, the primary object was the third requisite given above, that host and guests enjoy themselves thoroughly. This was particularly true with royal waka matches. Their luxurious appointments occasioned much pleasure and admiration. Criticism was not carried out in earnest under such circumstances. Quite the contrary: overly apposite criticism might keep host and guests from enjoying themselves to the full. Consider, for example, a passage from the *Teiji In Waka Match* (21-22).

Judgment: Draw

The Left: [Fujiwara] Okikaze (fl. ca. 900-15)

Mite kaeru	I cannot look and leave
Kokoro akeneba	Before my heart is satisfied—
Sakurabana	The flowering cherry trees—
Sakeru atari ni	Oh, would that there were lodgings
Yado ya karamashi.	In this area where they bloom!

The Right: [Fujiwara] Yorimoto (fl. ca. 901-15)

Shinonome ni	As dawn breaks
Okite mitsureba	I arise and look at them again—
Sakurabana	The flowering cherry trees—

[20] The kyōgen play *Chigiriki*, concerning a sixteenth-century renga competition, gives a good depiction of a drinking party that follows a poetry session (*Kyōgen, Torahiro Manuscript*, 2:338-47). The same custom apparently prevailed in the provinces: several extant

| Mada yo o komete | Blossoms have been falling all the while |
| Chirinikeru kana. | The night kept us in darkness. |

His Majesty remarked of the Right's poem: "He seems to be rubbing the sleep from his eyes as he looks at the blossoms—charming, I'm sure."

Lord Sadakata replied, "It reminds me of Lord Noboru arriving at court."

His timing was perfect. "Oh, very well," said His Majesty, declaring the match a draw.

The judge—the cloistered sovereign Uda—is speaking ironically when he calls "charming" the lines "As dawn breaks / I arise and look at them again." A beautiful woman sleepily gazing at cherry blossoms conjures up a fine picture, but a male speaker in similar circumstances was thought to lessen the beauty of the blossoms. So Yorimoto's poem merited mild criticism. It was deflected, however, and the match declared a draw, by an opportune comment made by Yorimoto's proxy Sadakata. Minamoto Noboru (890-918) held at this time the joint posts of Middle Counselor and Minister for Civil Affairs and probably had a reputation for conscientiousness. Sadakata's interpretation—that the speaker of the poem is not implausible if he is seen to be an industrious official like Noboru—won Uda's approval. Sadakata's wit also very likely drew smiles from the assembled company, since Noboru was apparently present on this occasion. Certain of the audience may have smiled in admiration, too, if they happened to remember a Chinese verse, "Cocks are crowing as loyal officials await the dawn."[21] In any case, the criticism offered in this round might be termed rather casual.

Criticism centering on problems of conception and style was not totally absent, of course. The following instance also occurs in the *Teiji In Waka Match* (7-8).

The Left: [Minamoto] Suekata (fl. ca. 901-15)

Isonokami	Are the cherry trees
Furu no yamabe no	Round the hills of Old Furu
Sakurabana	In Isonokami
Kozo mishi hana no	Blooming in the very hue
Iro ya nokoreru.	That we beheld last year?

---

contemporary diaries record the programs of renga sessions held by priests at the Grand Shrine of Ise (Okuno, 1975, 446-47).

[21] *WRS*, 1:63. The line is taken from "Feng Wei Wang Fu" (not included in *CTW*).

The Right: Lady Ise (Winner)

Hodo mo naku	In no time at all
Chirinan mono o	They flutter from the bough to earth—
Sakurabana	The blossoms of the cherry—
Kokora hisa ni mo	And yet what a long while they made
Matasetsuru kana.	Our hearts wait to enjoy them!

The Left loses because its poem "is taken up with last year alone; no intent is directed toward the present year."[22]

The topic of the round is "The Second Month of Spring," and so the waka are expected to be written as if composed just at that time. The Left loses the round because the idea expressed in its waka—that last year's beauty lingers into this year—fails to address a topic whose chief concern is the present year. Just as the "adapting" of waka "to fit the import of a topic" became an important criterion in screen waka, so, similarly, does the judge's comment in this round reflect a position that poets must keep within the compositional sphere the assigned topic implies. This position fostered the doctrine of the hon'i (essential nature) of waka referred to in Chapter 3.

Other comments in the records of the *Teiji In Match* also indicate critical standards: a poet is criticized for using the suffix "-ran" twice in his poem (*Teiji In Utaawase* [= *TJI*], 3), and another for using outmoded expression (*TJI*, 26). Most of the rounds in this match, however, are not evaluated—an indication that criticism may not have been thought to be the most vital element of a waka competition. By the time of the *Tentoku Waka Match*, however, all waka were given comments that go beyond judging by set standards as well as critical evaluations. The most noteworthy refer to distinctions in tone ("The poetry of this waka is *beautiful*" [*TTU*, 17]; "It lacks *strength*, but is nonetheless acceptable" [*TTU*, 31]) and to judgments leading to the development of two important poetic doctrines, kokoro ari [or ushin, propriety of feeling] and hon'i ("Although the poem seems to have *proper feeling*, one has no sense of the kerria rose's *essential nature*, only that of the double-flowering variety" [*TTU*, 16]). The former group of standards reveals that recognized distinctions in tone had evolved before 960.

The dictinctions made by Tadamine in his preface to *Wakatei Jusshu (Ten Kinds of Waka Styles)*, recorded as compiled in the Tenth Month of 945, may have resulted from similar criteria.[23]

---

[22] The translation is made from the Jukkan manuscript of *Ruiju Utaawase Maki*, 1:3 ("Hommonhen"), with emendations taken from the Nijukkan manuscript ("Hommonhen," 55).

[23] One theory sees *Wakatei Jusshu* as a *Shūishū* period (985-1015) work that was written

1. Antique style (kokatei)	6. Lofty style (kōseitei)
2. Marvelous style (shimmyōtei)	7. Moral style (kiryōtei)
3. Direct style (jikitei)	8. Metaphorical style (hikyōtei)
4. Evocative style (yoseitei)	9. Gorgeous style (kaentei)
5. Contemplative style (shashitei)	10. Twofold style (ryōhōtei)

Kintō's *Shinsen Zuinō (New Essentials of Waka)* makes several distinctions of tone in its general criteria.

> A waka may in effect be deemed outstanding when it is strongly *appealing, pleasing* in form [sugata], and possesses something *evocative* in its design [kokoro]. A clumsy poem appears as nothing but a string of metaphors. One should compose in a simple yet *confident* [sukuyaka ni] manner. If it proves difficult to express both concept [kokoro] and form [sugata] in a harmonious way, then it is best to concentrate only on the concept for the time being. If the concept nevertheless remains *shallow* [fukakarazu], one would do well to polish the form. The waka will then take this configuration: it will sound *pleasing* to the ear [kikikiyoge ni], will be expressed tastefully and perceived as true poetry, and may employ *fresh* [mezurashiku] metaphors. (*Shinsen Zuinō*, 26)

Such distinctions probably resulted from the influence of early T'ang poetic treatises like the *Wen-pi Shih* and the *T'ang-ch'ao Hsin-ting Shih-ke*, which were known among waka poets (Konishi, 1951a, 261-70). The treatises were read because poets needed a command of various literary concepts, including the classification of poetic tones, in order to make criticisms at waka matches. ("Ushin" and "hon'i" will be discussed at length in the third volume of this work.)

The drive to appreciate waka matches in terms of sequences or categories may be taken as a second element. The essence of a waka match is not necessarily made up of sequences or categories. The bond between the waka match and assigned topics evolved from the circumstance of evaluating two competing poems per round: poems were more easily compared when they had a common topic. Once assigned topics became standard usage, poets developed an awareness of the interrelationships among topics. A few topics presented no particular difficulties, but some design was

---

under the name of Tadamine (Hazama, 1962, 110-13). Minamoto Michinari's (d. 1019) *Waka Juttei* is based on *Wakatei Jusshu*, however, suggesting that the latter was written no later than the end of the tenth century. [The appearance of "kokoro ari" in the *Tentoku Utaawase* appears to be the first usage extant. Although the term—or its Sinified version, "ushin"—came to designate conviction of feeling, at this early stage its meaning is that of a response proper to the stimulus and guided by fūryū.—Ed.]

required in dealing with a larger number. Again, if the assigned topics were seasonal ("Spring" and "Autumn," for example), "Spring" would naturally come first. Here, too, we find a natural drive to rank waka topics in a certain order. *Her Majesty's Kambyō Era Waka Match* is one reflection of this.[24] The competition had the topics "Spring," "Summer," "Autumn," "Winter," and "Love," each of which was apparently subdivided into more detailed topic groups. The "Spring" topic begins with poems on the warbler in a blossoming plum tree and then moves on to poems on the warbler singing among cherry blossoms; these are followed by waka on spring showers, mist, and "falling blossoms." After a summation of the passing spring, the topic shifts to "Summer." The configuration, in other words, is one of an early spring sequence followed by a sequence on spring at its height, and another on late spring. In this, two things are worth noting: sequences, or waka topic groups, have become units of audience expectation; and the sequences develop a structure in terms of poetic progression.

Topics are necessary to the construction of a waka sequence. A sequence on "Early Spring," for instance, would immediately call to mind such appropriate topics as "Snow," "The Warbler," "Plum Blossoms," "Trees in Bud," "Thawing Ice," and "Young Grasses." An "Early Spring" group thus consists of such topics; and if progression is then made from "Early Spring" to "The Height of Spring" and on to "Late Spring," the resulting composition will resemble *Her Majesty's Kambyō Era Waka Match* and, even more, the *Kokinshū*.

A somewhat later editorial attitude was not much given to progression, concentrating instead on the waka topics themselves. This is the attitude evident in the *Kokin Rokujō (The Six-Book Anthology of Old and New Waka)*, which was probably compiled at the end of the tenth century.[25] There, waka topics are arranged in groups, and the poetry is classified accordingly. Progression does appear in the section on "The Year," as in these spring topics:

The First Day of Spring[26]	Festival of the Blue Horses[27]
The First Month	The Height of Spring

[24] The competition probably existed only on paper (*HCUT*, 10:2918). This does not affect the value of the work as data demonstrating the link between waka competitions and an awareness of poetic sequences, since the work is indeed organized in the format of a waka match.

[25] The *Kokin Waka Rokujō (Kokin Rokujō, Rokujō)*, compiled in the late tenth century, is the oldest extant waka anthology arranged by topic.

[26] The first day of spring could occur before New Year's Day, according to the lunar calendar; hence the placement of this topic before "The First Month" and "New Year's Day" below. [See *KKS*, 1:1.—Ed.]

[27] [Held on the seventh day of the First Month. The festival centered on a parade of twenty-one pale "blue" horses (probably light grays or roans), symbols of the yang (male)

New Year's Day	The Third Month
Patches of Snow	The Double Third[28]
The Day of the Rat	The Last Day of Spring
Young Herbs	

In general, however, the topics do not follow a progression, as the section on "Dwellings" illustrates.

Houses	The Gate
Neighbors	A Door
The Well	Hanging Blinds
Hedges	A Bed
A Garden	Straw Mats
Chickens	

Even the section on "Love" has no progression, differing in this respect from the corresponding sections in the *Kokinshū*. The *Six-Book Anthology* section-topics on "Love" are as follows:

Love	Resentment
Unrequited Love	Without Resentment
Visions of the Beloved	Treated Shabbily
Napping[29]	Other Kinds of Longing
A River of Tears	

The collection of shih couplets by Ōe no Koretoki (888-963), *A Millennium of Superlative Couplets*, and Kintō's *Collection of Japanese and Chinese Songs*, both of which apparently predate the *Six-Book Anthology* by a few years, are also arranged according to topic classification. Scholars of Chinese literature may therefore have introduced the format to waka collections. The *I-wen Lei-chü*, compiled by Ou-yang Hsün (557-641) and evidently current in Japan by the eighth century, also follows the classified-topic format. The transmission of waka in compound units—whether sequential (accompanied by progression) or categorized (unaccompanied by progression)—reached a peak by the tenth century. As we shall see further, this is an important literary phenomenon.

---

principle. The horses were viewed by the Tennō and his court so as to ward off illness in the coming year. For further details on this festival, see McCullough and McCullough, 1980, 1:382-83.—Trans. As this and other examples show, the progression the author speaks of involves not only natural phenomena but the order of occurrence of events in the court's *Annual Observances (Nenjūgyōji)*.—Ed.]

[28] The third day of the Third Month, one of five "double" fête-days. The others are New Year's Day, the Double Fifth, the Seventh Night (Tanabata), and the Double Ninth. [Auth., Trans.]

[29] In waka, napping (utatane) conventionally signifies dreaming of the beloved.

The Thesis of Classical Waka

The Formation of the Kokinshū *Style*

The "*Kokinshū* style" is the style that modern readers find most typical of that waka anthology. The title of the collection informs the reader that the *Kokinshū* contains waka both old (ko) and new (kin), and the point is proudly restated in the Japanese (Kana) Preface: "Will not our readers revere the poetry of the past while admiring that of the present?" (*KKS*, Preface, 22). The style of the "present" poetry corpus is what I have called the *Kokinshū* style. The style employed by the "poetry of the past"—composed between the late eighth and the mid-ninth centuries—also appears in the *Kokinshū*, but it is not the "*Kokinshū* style."

The Japanese Preface further envisions a "recent time" that preceded the "present" and gives the names of six poets belonging to this "recent" period: Bishop Henjō (816-?90), Ariwara Narihira (825-80), Fun'ya Yasuhide (fl. ca. 858-83), the priest Kisen (fl. ca. 810-24), Ono no Komachi (fl. 833-57), and Ōtomo Kuronushi (fl. 885-97; *KKS*, Preface, 18-20). Since they are known collectively as the Six Celebrated Poets (rokkasen), the "recent time" to which they belong will be called the Six Poets period in the discussion that follows. The style of this age differs little from that of the "present," which is to say the compilation period of the *Kokinshū* (ca. 885-ca. 914). In a broader range of meaning, therefore, the Six Poets style may justifiably be included within the "present" style. Yet in the Japanese Preface, Tsurayuki finds varying degrees of fault with the six poets, indicating that their poetry was thought somehow unsatisfactory by the compiling poets of the "present." Differentiation between the Six Poets period and the Compilation period, therefore, is hardly meaningless. The waka in the "old" group essentially represent an extension of the *Man'yōshū* style and can thus be termed the products of a quasi-*Man'yōshū* period. This being so, the *Kokinshū* period may be thought to comprehend the "present" style of poetry as it is embodied in compositions of the Six Poets and Compilation periods.

To summarize:

Junnin (r. 758-64) Shōtoku (r. 764-70) Kōnin (r. 770-81) Kammu (r. 781-806) Heizei (r. 806-809)	Quasi-*Man'yōshū* period ("old" waka)
Saga (r. 809-23) Junna (r. 823-33) Nimmyō (r. 833-50)	Period of decline for waka; the apogee of shih poetry

Montoku (r. 850-58)
Seiwa (r. 858-76)   Six Poets
Yōzei (r. 876-84)   Period   Kokinshū period
Kōkō (r. 884-87)

Uda (r. 887-97)   Compilation   ("present" waka)
Daigo (r. 897-930)   Period

The list begins with Junnin because it was during his reign, in 759, that the *Man'yōshū* poem with the latest known composition date was written (20:4516). Although 930, the year of Daigo's abdication, is given above as the end of the Compilation period, I would in fact prefer to conceive the *Kokinshū* period as ending around 914, the approximate year in which the collection assumed its present form.[30] Of course, waka in the *Kokinshū* style continued to enjoy great success after 914: this period will be treated separately, as that of the *Kokinshū* style. These divisions reflect only mainstream trends. I have noted earlier that the first half of the ninth century yields a few waka written in a style similar to that of the *Kokinshū*.

Only a few waka survive from the first half of the ninth century, so it cannot be stated positively whether the phenomenon of oblique expression in waka was mere accident. Waka was generally in an inactive state, with no prominent waka poet to set the tone for the period. A single style was therefore unlikely to have won enough support to be developed as a new poetic movement. The vanguard of the *Kokinshū* style was set forth in the early ninth century, then, but the motion was probably accidental. The *Kokinshū* style evolved into a movement only at the beginning of the Six Poets period, its evolution accelerated by waka matches and screen waka. The movement rapidly reached its zenith: probably by Daigo's reign, the new style had won so much confidence that its proponents dared to criticize the leading composers of the Six Poets period. Just before, by Uda's reign, the movement had already showed signs of reaching its peak. This was the direct result of a close, if tangential, relation between waka and shih, a point that is supported by several facts.

---

[30] There is still no generally accepted view as to whether 18.IV.905 is the date Daigo was presented with the completed *Kokinshū*, or whether it is the day the royal command was issued for the compilation of the *Kokinshū*. My view in the past has been that the first royal command was issued at some point between 899 and 904, and a second on 18.IV.905 (Konishi, 1949a, 25-27), but this is not correct: instead, the first royal command for compilation was issued on 18.IV.905 (Okumura, 1971, 121-35). The compilers' government posts, recorded in the Japanese and Chinese Prefaces, indicate that the prefaces were written between II.906 and I.907 (Kyūsojin, 1961, 376-77); therefore the manuscript presented to Daigo would also have been completed during this period. Additions were later made to the text: waka from the *Teiji In Utaawase* of 913 are included in the *Kokinshū*. Thus the formation date of the text as we have it is set at 914 or somewhat later. [The latest date usually mentioned in recent years is 920.—Ed.]

The first symbolic contact between waka and shih is represented by the compilation of the *Shinsen Man'yōshū*. The anthology principally consists of waka from *Her Majesty's Kambyō Era Waka Match*. The poems, however, are transcribed not in hiragana but in magana, the orthographic style of the *Man'yōshū*, in which Chinese characters are used both phonetically and logographically; each waka is then "translated" into a shih quatrain.[31] The translations contain a larger volume of poetry than do the original waka, a natural result considering the shih form. The shortest form of shih is the quatrain, and so a shih must necessarily have more content than a waka. The briefest shih line form is the five-character line. A Chinese word is generally one or two syllables long, whereas a waka may include perhaps ten conceptual words within its thirty-one syllables. Thus a shih couplet in five-character lines corresonds roughly to an entire waka, as discussed in Volume One. It follows that a shih "translation" would inevitably be more prolix than the original waka. Well aware of the differences between the two poetic forms, the translators leaned strongly toward free translation by padding their shih compositions with content not present in the original and by other means. The thoughts and feelings expressed by a waka were nonetheless effectively transmitted in its shih translation.

The experiment of translating waka into shih was based on an assumption that the two forms shared certain traits. If this assumption had not existed, the differences described above would have discouraged the idea of shih translations. An awareness of features shared by both waka and shih contributed in no small way to the emerging conviction that waka and shih had equal literary merit. The idea may seem obvious, once conceived, that waka is to Japan what the shih is to China. But such a conviction was not easily reached in ninth-century Japan, when shih composition was the dominant literary activity. In this respect the compilation of the *Shinsen Man'yōshū*—a work recognizing, if only vaguely, the features shared by waka and shih—is significant as a guide toward a work realized twelve years later, the *Kokinshū*. One ideal held by Tsurayuki and his circle was that waka was the literary equal of shih.

A belief in the equality of waka to shih is also manifested in the consummation of individual poets' waka collections. When Tsurayuki and his fellow poets received the royal command to compile the *Kokinshū*, the first task of each was apparently to perfect his own waka collection for presentation. This is suggested by the Chinese (Mana) Preface to the *Kokinshū*:

---

[31] The First Compilation manuscript line of the *Shinsen Man'yōshū* has shih "translations" only for the waka in its first fascicle (Preface dated 893), but the Augmented manuscript line also has shih "translations" for the second fascicle (Preface dated 913). Because the shih contained in the second fascicle are very clumsy indeed, they cannot be considered the work of Michizane.

Thereupon His Majesty commanded that Ki no Tomonori, Senior Private Secretary at the Central Affairs Ministry, Ki no Tsurayuki, Acting Royal Librarian, Ōshikōchi Mitsune, former Junior Vice-Governor of Kai, and Mibu no Tadamine, Junior Lieutenant in the Right Gate Guards, each present his own collected poems along with those handed down from the past. (*KKS*, Preface, 269)

Since paper was a valuable commodity at the time, the *Kokinshū* compilers—among whom Tomonori, a Private Secretary, held the highest rank—were unlikely to have had personal poetry collections in a form readily presentable to their sovereign. They may have been given paper from the royal stores for the purpose. Yet if the poets had not customarily kept some kind of drafts of their poems, they could not immediately have produced clean copies. The four compilers had probably preserved their poems in some form. Nor were they the only poets commanded by the Tennō to submit poetic material: the forenote to one of Lady Ise's waka (*KKS*, 18:1000) reads, "Composed upon receipt of His Majesty's order to submit her poems, and written on the last page of the submitted manuscript."[32] Notable waka poets other than compilers, then, were also apparently commanded to submit material for inclusion in the *Kokinshū*. It is unlikely that these texts were in the form of personal waka collections; possibly they were rough drafts that had not yet been organized.[33] Compositions that had not yet been compiled into personal waka collections probably also existed at this time. By the Tenryaku era (947-57), the practice of compiling personal waka collections seems universal.

During the Tenryaku era, His Majesty commanded that Nakatsukasa submit Ise's personal waka collection.[34] On doing so, she recited,

Shiguretsutsu	The wintry drizzle
Furinishi yado no	Keeps on falling, turning old a house
Koto no ha wa	Whose leaves of poetry

---

[32] Ise was a favorite of Uda Tennō and bore him a son. *Ise Shū*, her personal waka collection, has certain noteworthy characteristics [involving screen paintings and poems] mentioned above.

[33] "Tatematsuru tote yomite," in Ise's forenote, probably signifies a new composition written on receipt of the royal command. It is difficult to accept the view that Ise submitted a finished waka collection (Murase, 1971, 100-101). She may have submitted several waka in addition to the one recorded in the *Kokinshū*. [The author is distinguishing between finished, polished poems and orderly personal collections. The latter were just coming into being under the stimulus of Uda and Daigo.—Ed.]

[34] ["His Majesty" is Murakami Tennō (r. 946-67). Nakatsukasa (ca. 920-80) was Ise's daughter.—Trans.]

Kakiatsumuredo   Have been gathered up for you—
Tomarazarikeri.   But how sad it is they are so scarce.

(*SIS*, 17:1141)

The poem indicates that personal waka collections were often compiled in response to some sort of request, and that these collections were not necessarily definitive texts. Nevertheless the concept of a personal waka collection, evident as early as 905 (and notwithstanding the fact that most such collections seem actually to have been disorganized rough drafts), undoubtedly reflects an awareness that a poet's waka corpus, like his shih, should be preserved in collections. *Nihonkoku Genzaisho Mokuroku (An Inventory of Written Works Extant in Japan)*, compiled in the Kambyō era (889-98), lists the personal shih collections of 133 Six Dynasties and T'ang poets (39:*Besshūka*). These works, prized possessions of the royal family, were probably only perused by a few favored individuals. It was common knowledge, however, that the Chinese had a great many personal shih collections (besshū). The opportunity granted waka poets to present their personal collections to the throne apparently enhanced considerably the belief that waka is a literary equal of shih.

If waka was to be on an equal footing with shih, the two genres had to share certain characteristics. A simple assertion of ideological equality would have elicited no support. Tsurayuki and his circle sought these shared characteristics in the sama, or desirable stylistic techniques, of waka. The Japanese Preface to the *Kokinshū* stresses the importance of sama. Henjō's poetry is found "to possess sama but to lack sincerity"; Yasuhide's has "skillful diction but ill-fitting sama"; and Kuronushi writes poems that have "a coarse sama." Other poets are dismissed as "thinking only of the poem while remaining ignorant of its sama" (*KKS*, Preface, 18-20). Tsurayuki employs "sama" to signify the witty expressive techniques found in the Six Dynasties style of shih. I noted earlier that these techniques were being used in waka on a limited basis by the first half of the ninth century. It was probably not until the turn of the tenth century, however, that the techniques were perceived as features shared by shih and waka, and that they were vital to making waka the literary equivalent of the shih. One important factor in effecting this conviction was evidently the carrying out of direct, individual comparisons between the techniques of waka and shih.

The *Shinsen Man'yōshū* was one such experiment. Because its waka are "translated" as Chinese quatrains in seven-character lines, the shih "translations" accommodate more materials than the waka originals. The correspondence between waka and shih is not particularly strict. Chisato's *Verse-Topic Waka*, compiled not long after the *Shinsen Man'yōshū*, attempts to effect correspondence in meaning between one line of a shih and an entire thirty-one-syllable waka. The results prove to be extremely useful in elucidating the nature of sama as a common feature of waka and shih expression. (This is discussed in Volume One.) In verse-topic waka a poet attempts to adapt the topic (a shih verse) to waka by "translating" a line of Chinese poetry into a thirty-one-syllable waka. Since the significance of the verse-topic is to be rephrased in the waka, both forms must express a common meaning. If possible, the waka should also employ techniques similar to those used in the shih line, so that it might best evoke the effect of the verse-topic. If, for example, the verse-topic centers on a metaphor, the waka should employ a similar metaphor.

The use of a shih technique in waka is linked to an awareness of the equality of waka and shih. This in turn creates another conviction: by using techniques in common with shih, waka is for that reason a literary form equivalent to it. It should be noted in this case that the technique in question is oblique expression as employed in the Six Dynasties style of shih poetry. For Tsurayuki and his circle, sama *was* oblique expression. Unless waka possessed sama, it could not become a premier art like the shih. This assumption may well have been at the root of Tsurayuki's radical declaration, that many contemporary waka poets are "thinking only of the poem while remaining ignorant of its sama" (*KKS*, Preface, 20). The *Kokinshū* style, then, was formed by recasting a Six Dynasties style into a Japanese context.

This becomes even more evident upon examining the expression in the shih verses used as waka topics. Most contemporary verse-topics were taken from shih by Po Chü-i. Of the 116 verse-topics in Chisato's *Collected Waka*, seventy-four come from the works of Po and ten from those of Yüan Chen (779-831; Kaneko, 1943, 184-213). Their provenance, however, does not immediately identify them as T'ang-style verse. Commonplace, simple concepts and diction characterize much of Po's canon. But it also contains much that is adroitly beautiful in the Six Dynasties style. The latter feature was the one chiefly emulated in Japan. In Chisato's *Collected Waka*, verse-topics taken from Po's and Yüan's poetry focus principally on witty concepts that run directly opposite to simple, natural orientations:

Often I return late because of flower-viewing. (*Ōe no Chisato Shū* [= OCS], 6)

Under the blossoms, return is forgotten: the cause is the fine scenery. (OCS, 14)

How can we not bid Spring a fond farewell? (OCS, 15)

The spring scenery in both places departs on the same day. (*OCS,* 17)³⁵

It is the winter solstice, when a night is long indeed. (*OCS,* 59)

Choked by mists, perhaps, the mountain warbler sings but rarely. (*OCS,* 1)

Once parted, we'll not easily meet, no matter what the distance. (*OCS,* 94)

(The last two verses are by Yüan Chen.) The collection also has instances of poetic conceit.

The moon illumines smooth sand—frost on a summer's night. (*OCS,* 33)

Wind-blown whitecaps become flower petals by the thousand. (*OCS,* 69)

Moonlight on a wave reveals a single jewel inside. (*OCS,* 70)

These shih lines are "translated" into waka, and the results are typical of the *Kokinshū.* Not that the *Kokinshū* style is represented solely by witty waka. But it is significant that when shih lines are converted into waka, they acquire greater wittiness. For example:

"*Birds nest among the autumn leaves.*"

Aki sugiba	When autumn has gone by,
Chirinan mono o	Leaves are bound to fall in earnest:
Naku tori no	Why do songbirds, then,
Nado momijiba no	Choose to make their homes among
Eda ni shi mo sumu.	The branches bright in foliage?

(*OCS,* 53)

The verse-topic "Birds nest among the autumn leaves" simply describes an autumn scene, whereas the waka introduces fabricated logic. Chisato's inclinations toward wittiness, in other words, move him to introduce fabricated logic into a shih line that is devoid of wittiness. Chisato also adds causation to some of his waka (italics indicate causative vocabulary):

³⁵ The speaker of the shih and the object of his thoughts are in separate locations. The speaker seeks to draw closer to the distant beloved by stressing that the spring sun shines equally on both locations, and that spring ends for both on the same day—the last day of the Third Month, when this shih was written. [Auth., Trans.]

"Autumn's advent brings a growing sense of my decline."

Ōkata no   It visits everyone,
Aki kuru *kara ni*   And *because* it visits me
   Waga mi koso   Now I understand
Kanashiki mono to   That throughout my being
Omoishirinure.   I have become a melancholy thing.

(OCS, 38)

"The beauties of nature belong to people of leisure."

Sadamenaku   One never knows
Fukikuru kaze o   Where the wind will choose to blow:
   Sashiwakete   *Why then* does it go
Nado ka shizukeki   Paying calls particularly
Hito ni tsuku ran.   On those who live in quiet?

(OCS, 77)

"I see a distant house: if trees bloom there I'll go to it."

Yoso nite mo   *Because* the blossoms
Hana o aware to   Quite take the heart even when
   Miru *kara ni*   Viewed from far away,
Shiranu yado ni zo   I shall not hesitate to enter
Mazu irinikeru.   A strange house for better view.

(OCS, 84)

"I know that, like a drifting cloud, I have no fixed abode."

Waga mi o ba   *Because* I liken
Ukaberu kumo ni   Myself to a drifting cloud,
   Nasere*ba zo*   That self has become
Tsuku kata mo naku   Something with no fixed abode,
Hakanakarikeru.   Ephemerality itself!

(OCS, 111)

Not only is the wittiness in a line of Chinese poetry incorporated into its waka "translation"; another kind of wit already established in waka is introduced into the shih to yield a new interpretation. Chisato was probably not the only waka poet to display this much command of the Six Dynasties style. We know from the preface to his *Collected Waka* that the work was written at Uda's behest. An interpenetration of waka and shih techniques, focusing on the Six Dynasties style of wit found in verse-topic

waka, had probably become sufficiently advanced by the end of the ninth
century to have received royal support.

The Achievement of Tsurayuki and His Circle

One senses a certain overemphasis in the efforts by Tsurayuki and his circle to raise waka to a literary level equivalent with the shih, and to define
worthy waka through a Six Dynasties style of sama. All waka that did not
clearly display wit were judged to lack sama. As we have seen, even the
great poets of the late ninth century were criticized on this point, and the
Six Dynasties style of witty expression was current in the Japanese shih
circle as early as the beginning of the ninth century. Such expression,
though not differing significantly from the *Kokinshū* style, had yet to
achieve equal currency in waka. Tsurayuki and his fellow *Kokinshū* compilers were doubtless aware of this lag, and so they put particular emphasis on the idea of equality between shih and waka.

In the Japanese Preface, Tsurayuki gives the following reasons for
stressing, if not exaggerating, the importance of sama (*KKS*, Preface, 14-
20):

1. In the past, tennō frequently summoned their courtiers, on various
occasions, to compose waka. The summons was made partly in order to
test the courtier's poetic abilities.

2. People's hearts are now given over to frivolity, and present waka
expression accords with this poetic climate. Thus waka functions only in
the world of love and is never employed on formal occasions.

3. This situation has resulted from waka poets' ignorance of sama, an
ignorance so pervasive that even the great poets of recent times have failed
to master sama in their waka.

The "past" (inishie) mentioned in the Japanese Preface probably refers
to the late eighth through the early ninth centuries. Waka were indeed recited at formal banquets during this period, as we have observed. The decline of waka in the mid-ninth century very likely followed the course described by the *Shoku Nihongi* in an entry for the year 849: "As time went
on the art of waka entered into decline and eventually fell quite into ruin."
The Japanese Preface states that the waka form declined because it had
become no more than "frivolous poems shallowly expressed." The Preface thus reverses the causation, asserting that waka expression became
frivolous because the art retreated to an informal sphere.

The art of waka declined because it was overwhelmed by the rising popularity of shih composition in Japan (Yoshizawa, 1923, 396). The fortunes of the Japanese shih reached their apogee during the roughly four
decades spanned by the reigns of Saga, Junna, and Nimmyō (809-50). We
may recall the innumerable contemporary records of shih recited at for-

mal banquets. Waka, thus superseded, began to disappear from formal occasions. Yoshizawa Yoshinori calls this period the "dark age of Japanese literature" (kokufū ankoku jidai). Tsurayuki and his circle were aware of this fact. But they would not have found it easy, as partisans of a genre relegated to second place since the early ninth century, to declare that the shih had ejected waka from the formal scene. Instead they became self-effacing and stated that no one composed waka at formal banquets because waka expression had become frivolous.

When applied to historical fact, the assertions in the Japanese Preface yield the following results:

> The quasi-*Man'yōshū* period ("the past"): waka are composed at formal functions.
> The period of waka decline: superseded by shih, waka retreats from formal functions to the informal sphere.
> The *Kokinshū* period ("the present"): signs of a waka revival appear, and it is fervently hoped that waka will return to the formal scene.

Tsurayuki's wish was more than realized. Not only did waka enter the ranks of the premier arts, but it has remained there for the last millennium.

When waka finally returned to the formal scene, it no longer employed the quasi-*Man'yōshū* style of expression. It had been transformed by the witty *Kokinshū* style. This pronounced transformation occurred within a mere five decades, a phenomenon made possible by two facts: the period of waka decline coincided with the most active period for shih composition; and the Six Dynasties style of expression dominated contemporary Japanese shih (Konishi, 1949a, 19-22). In a matter of fifty years, Japanese courtiers, deprived of the opportunity to compose formal waka, grew distant from, and eventually forgot, the old, quasi-*Man'yōshū* style. Their literary awareness was radically altered during this period by shih written in the witty Six Dynasties style.

Waka had withdrawn from the formal scene, but it lived on for informal matters. This, in effect, was the sphere of love, which the Japanese Preface terms "the habitations of the amorous." A woman of rank did not customarily meet an unknown man face to face, and so a prospective lover was obliged to rely on letters to make himself known to the lady and to communicate his sentiments. Waka were the focus of such letters, it is conjectured, and a poor waka poet would meet with little success. Even when the affair progressed from correspondence to conversation, its focus remained waka. The prospects of an affair were dismal indeed if one of the principals was not able to give a quick, clever reply to the other's poems. The witty Six Dynasties style probably proved quite effective in such circumstances. Thus waka tended increasingly toward witty expression during its sojourn in the informal sphere. A man had charge of half of a love affair, and men considered shih an essential part of their culture. It seems that from male experience with shih certain turns of phrase, refractions of the Six Dynasties style, crept into the language of love in waka.

Witty expression in the Six Dynasties style was certainly at the height of its authority as poets attempted to restore waka to its place in the formal sphere. It was not enough, however, for waka to employ the kind of intricate wit found in love letters and courtship. Michizane was a master of the (narrow) Po style, and yet his response to a royal command for a preface and shih, to be recited at a formal banquet, was a splendid parallel prose preface in the Six Dynasties style accompanied by an ornate shih. As we have also seen, in his old age Michizane employed oblique expression based on fabricated logic in a work composed at a royal banquet in the Shinzen Gardens. In formal situations, waka needed enough Six Dynasties-inspired sama to rival the equally formal compositions in Chinese. This is why sama is emphasized in the Japanese Preface.

The emphasis is more than rhetorical: it is also reflected in the tasks of editing and compilation that Tsurayuki's circle performed. Eight poets—Mitsune, Fujiwara Korehira (886-946), Tomonori, Okikaze, Chisato, Korenori, Tadamine, and Tsurayuki—contributed waka at Tsurayuki's stream banquet, which probably dates from between 898 and 901. With the exception of Korehira, who was somewhat younger than the others, these poets all served as editors of the *Kokinshū* or were represented in that collection. Yet not a single waka from the stream banquet appears in the *Kokinshū*.[36] The stream banquet poems are not casual compositions dashed off for the amusement of those present. A proud statement in Mitsune's preface informs us that the poets were, on the contrary, pleased with their work: "Those not present at this evening's gathering will wander ignorant of the path of waka, yet continue to assume learned airs in society" (*Ki no Shishō Kyokusuien Waka* [= *KSKW*], 211).

The only possible reason why none of these poems was selected is their perceived lack of sama, which rendered them inappropriate as contributions to a royal anthology. More concretely stated, the poems did not have sufficient wit. Even Tsurayuki, a revered master of waka, produced poems like this at his stream banquet.

"The Moon Sets, and Blossom-rapids Darken"

| Haru nareba | With spring's coming |
| Ume ni sakura o | Cherry blossoms fall with plum |

---

[36] Korehira has two waka in the *Gosenshū* and five in the *Shūishū*. At the time of the stream banquet he was in his early or mid-twenties and was Provisional Lieutenant in the Left Military Guards.

Kokimazete   By Minase River
Nagasu Minase no   As it pours into the distance,
Kawa no ka zo suru. Having brought the sweet scent here.

Kagaribi no   On a night in spring
Ueshita wakanu   So dark fishing flares cannot be told
  Haru no yo wa   From their reflections,
Mizu naranu mi mo   Even I, who am not the stream,
Sayakekarikeri.   Can be seen most vividly.

Irinureba   Once it has set
Ogura no yama no   Far away beyond the darkness
  Ochi ni koso   Of Ogura Hills,
Tsuki naki hana no   The moon deserts the blossoms
Se to mo narinure.   That fall in fragrant rapids.

(*KSKW*, 211)

The expression in these poems is certainly not oblique. Nor, on the other hand, are the poems particularly clumsy. Quite the contrary: they apparently represent the standard poetic style of their day. If one were to take all the *Kokinshū*-period waka from the *Kokin Rokujō* or *Six-Book Anthology*, and then consider only those poems that do not also appear in the *Kokinshū*, one would find that the remaining waka are about as witty as the three poems given above. The *Kokinshū*, then, is the product of a compilation process that allotted, for its time, exceptional importance to the characteristic of wittiness. The results are particularly conspicuous in the first ten books of the anthology. Further consideration will be given to the significance of this feature later.

The emphasis on wit in the *Kokinshū* editors' criteria of selection is related in many respects to the expressive techniques employed by the waka selected for inclusion. One striking example is a decrease in, or transmutation of, pillow words and prefaces in the *Kokinshū* poems. The guide phrase originally provided a lodging place for the kotodama; by the second half of the Ancient Age, the kotodama had lost its vitality, and guide phrases gradually became decorative prefixes influencing a subsequent word. Thus the term "guide phrase" no longer applies after the second half of the Ancient Age, and I shall employ hereafter the traditional terms: "pillow word" (makurakotoba) for the five-syllable, single-line "guide phrase," and "preface" (jokotoba) for those consisting of multiple lines.[37] The transition occurred at the same time as the state of Yamato began to evolve into something more appropriately called Japan.

---

[37] [The distinction between the kotodama-evoking guide phrase (the author's coinage) and pillow words and prefaces is made at length in Volume One.—Ed.]

The change that occurred in pillow words and prefaces during the *Kokinshū* period is manifested, first of all, in a sharp quantitative decline. Pillow words and prefaces began to decline numerically as early as the second half of the Ancient Age; Yakamochi nonetheless uses ninety pillow words a total of 237 times. By contrast, the extant *Kokinshū* (Teika manuscript) has nineteen pillow words used forty-two times in the first half (ten books) of the anthology, and seventy used 119 times in the second half (ten books).[38] These figures reflect separate investigations of each half of the *Kokinshū*: fourteen pillow words overlap between the two parts, and so there are a total of seventy-five pillow words used in all twenty books of the collection. The degree of decline in the number of pillow words can be appreciated when Yakamochi's output of 479 waka is compared with the 1,100 waka in the *Kokinshū*. If, moreover, the poets surveyed are limited to those belonging to the *Kokinshū* period as I have defined it, the first half of the *Kokinshū* is found to contain sixteen pillow words used twenty-eight times, and the second half, thirty-seven used fifty-seven times.[39] This is a dramatic decrease indeed, especially in the case of the first half of the *Kokinshū*. The pillow words used in the first half, and the number of times they are employed by poets of the *Kokinshū* period, are given below (the expressions italicized).

1. *ashihiki no* (meaning unknown; now glossed by characters meaning "straining one's legs"; modifies "mountains," "hills"): 3.
2. *azusayumi* ("catalpa bow"; modifies "strain," "pull," "shoot"): 2.
3. *aratama no* ("as a new-cut gem"; modifies "year," "month"): 1.
4. *Isonokami* ("in Isonokami"; Isonokami is the name of an area lying within a larger region called Furu, and so "Isonokami" modifies "Furu" and its homonyms, which signify "old" and "to shake"): 1.
5. *unohana no* ("as with deutzia blossoms"; modifies "u" homonyms like "hare" and "misery"): 1.
6. *karakoromo* ("clothes of Chinese cut"; modifies "wear," "cut," "cord"): 1.
7. *Shirayama no* ("as on White Mountain"; modifies "snow"): 1.
8. *shirakumo no* ("as a white cloud"; modifies "to break off," "to leave"): 2.

[38] In some cases, pillow words cannot be precisely identified. Another reading finds ninety-six pillow words in the *Kokinshū* (Shimada, 1969, 282-92). I have followed Saeki Umetomo in the Iwanami Bunko edition of the *Kokinshū*, with a few revisions.

[39] I have omitted anonymous waka, since most are thought to have been composed in the quasi-*Man'yōshū* period. Anonymous waka from the *Kokinshū* period do exist, but as they contain few pillow words, they may safely be ignored.

9. *shirotae no* ("white as mulberry-cloth"; modifies "robe," "sleeve," "cord," "sash"): 2.

10. *tamakushige* ("as a fine comb-box"; modifies "lid," "open," "cover"): 1.

11. *tarachine no* ("she with withered breasts"; modifies "mother," "parent"): 1.

12. *chihayaburu* ("mighty they are"; modifies "gods," "god." The meaning of "chihayaburu" was apparently lost by the High Middle Ages): 3.

13. *harugasumi* ("spring haze"; modifies "to rise," "to veil"): 2.

14. *hisakata no* ("far-distant"; modifies "heaven," "sky," "light"): 4.

15. *mubatama no* ("black as lily seeds"; modifies "night," "dream"): 2.

16. *yūzukuyo* ("evening moon"; modifies "Ogura" [a place name and homonym for "dusky"], "to set"): 1.

All are indisputably pillow words of very limited scope that continued in common use for the next several centuries.

Seven waka in the first half of the *Kokinshū* employ prefaces, and seventy-nine in the second half. The latter section contains chōka (long poems), one of which uses four prefaces (18:1003); thus the incidence of preface use in the first half is seven times versus eighty-two times in the second. Prefaces in the *Kokinshū* are characteristically "meaningful" (ushin): a meaningful preface contributes to the meaning of the modified word. In the first half of the *Kokinshū*, five waka with prefaces are by *Kokinshū* period poets, and three of the five are by Tsurayuki. Instances of poems with meaningful prefaces include:

Composed on the Seventh Night.[40]
By Mitsune

Tanabata ni	*Like the silken threads*
Kashitsuru ito no	*Offered to the Weaver Maid*
Uchihaete	By her beloved,
Toshi no o nagaku	Surely her love for him will stretch
Koi ya wataran.	Over the long cord of the year.

(4:180)

[40] [The celebration of the conjunction of stars, Vega and Altair, on the seventh day of the Seventh Month. They were personified as the Weaver Maid and the Herdboy, lovers who could meet only once a year, on this night by crossing the River of Heaven (the Milky Way).—Trans.]

While crossing the Shiga mountains he came upon a spring
girded by rocks, and there formed an attachment with a lady.
He composed this when they parted.
By Tsurayuki

Musubu te no	*As the cupped hands*
Shizuku ni nigoru	*Soil with their spilling drops*
Yama no i no	*The mountain spring,*
Akade mo hito ni	So, my thirst as yet unquenched,
Wakarenuru kana.	The moment of our parting comes.

(8:404)

The preface "Like the silken threads / Offered to the Weaver Maid" refers to a custom carried out during Kikkōden, on the seventh day of the Seventh Month, in which women made offerings to the Weaver Maid of needles threaded with five colors of silk, and prayed to her to make them proficient needlewomen. The thread suggests length, which in turn invokes the tenor of the poem, "Uchihaete . . ." (the last three lines). Similarly, the preface of the second poem, "As the cupped hands / Soil with their spilling drops / The mountain spring," signifies that water clouded by spilling or leaking drops from a drinker's hands cannot immediately be drunk, and the speaker is left with his thirst still unquenched; this invokes the tenor "Akade mo . . ." (the last two lines) in reference to the speaker's love for the lady. In both cases the prefaces have background facts given in their forenotes. In addition to invoking the signified of each poem, the signifying prefaces make full use of the setting, within the import of the poems. Such prefaces differ in function from the archaic guide phrase, which existed independently of the poetic import, and whose sole purpose was to guide the kotodama to the signified of a poem.

The differentiation and transmutation of the pillow word and the preface from their common origin, the guide phrase, are noteworthy phenomena. By the Middle Ages the pillow word had become a decorative prefix: it was essentially devoid of function because the kotodama had become inactive. Conceiving of pillow words as entities to be used according to customs inherited from the Ancient Age, medieval waka poets affixed "straining one's legs" to "mountains," "mighty they are" to "gods," and "far-distant" to celestial phenomena. They did not find it necessary to inquire into the meanings of each as they used them. In that case, why would a waka poet use up five of only thirty-one syllables with a meaningless pillow word? In his *Mumyōshō (Untitled Writings)*, Kamo no Chōmei records a poem by Henjō:

Tarachine wa	Did not my parents
Kakare tote shi mo	Anticipate what was to be
Mubatama no	In my present state
Waga kurokami o	When they stroked my dark hair,
Nadezu ya ariken.	*As black as lily seeds?*[41]

(*GSS*, 17:1241)

When his waka master, Shun'e (b. 1113; fl. 1160-80), asks Chōmei which lines of the waka he finds outstanding, he answers that he thinks "Mubatama no" ("As black as lily seeds") is very good. Shun'e praises him for having understood the heart of the poem and comments that the placement of the pillow word in the third line [of the Japanese] has the effect of creating a pause in the expression, thus improving the structural tone of the waka. Chōmei then records his teacher's explanation of a line consisting of a pillow word: it resembles a hampi, a short sleeveless garment worn under a courtier's formal outer robe.[42]

"In ancient times it was called a hampi line. A hampi serves no practical purpose, but it does add ornament to formal court dress. When all one's poetic concepts must be expressed within the confines of a thirty-one-syllable waka, one is reluctant to include a single meaningless syllable; yet a hampi line will always add refinement and beauty to a poem. A poem that is exceedingly beautiful will also spontaneously communicate inexpressible feelings. One who has grasped these points may be said to have reached the essence."[43] (*MMS*, 61-62)

Shun'e's thesis is that the effect of a pillow word—as long as it forms the third line of a waka—lies not in its statement but in the pause it creates. This is a clear perception of the properties inherent in the medieval pillow word.[44] Thus the pillow word grew increasingly devoid of meaning while the preface—despite its identical origin in the guide phrase—gained significance. The older style of preface, comprising several lines yet re-

---

[41] Composed when Henjō took monastic vows and the tonsure. This is the text of the waka as it appears in the *Mumyōshō* ([= *MMS*], 61). Minor variants exist between this text and that in the Teika manuscript of the *Gosenshū*.

[42] The hampi, an article of formal court dress, was worn, rather like a vest, between a courtier's under-robes (equivalent to a shirt) and his court robe (equivalent to a formal suit). The hampi might be glimpsed, around the collar area, when a courtier was fully dressed. It did not provide much decoration, and yet formal court dress without a hampi would have been considered odd.

[43] That is, to have attained the most profound level of understanding of waka. [Auth., Trans.]

[44] This was a generally accepted view during the High Middle Ages. Shinkei's views are much the same as Shun'e's (Konishi, 1978, 79-81).

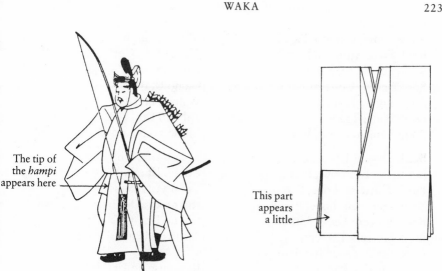

The tip of
the *hampi*
appears here

This part
appears
a little

4. *Hampi*, courtier's short, sleeveless mid-garment

maining essentially unconnected to the import of the poem, gradually lost
the medieval poet's understanding and sympathy. Despite the opposite
courses taken by the pillow word and the preface, then, their transmutation into entities separate from the original guide phrase evidently indicates the precipitate decline of the kotodama in medieval waka. The gradual enervation of the kotodama in the second half of the Ancient Age
resulted from the domination of Japanese aesthetics by a spirit strongly
imbued with the Chinese principle of li, reason. By the Early Middle Ages,
a Sinified artistic awareness had influenced the conceptual focus of waka
poets. Having functioned since the Archaic Age, the Yamato artistic
awareness now passed into oblivion, at least as concerned formal waka.

On the other hand, the ancient style of expressive awareness did not
necessarily vanish from informal waka. Earlier in this section, in the discussion of the decrease in number of pillow words and prefaces, data were
presented in two groups: the first ten books and the second ten books of
the *Kokinshū*. A striking numerical decrease is immediately noticeable in
the first ten books, whereas the second ten display the tendency much less
conspicuously. This reflects the nature of the two groups: the first ten
books contain formal waka, and the second ten, informal waka. As is well
known, the *Kokinshū* consists of twenty parts.

Book One: Spring, Part 1   [Haru no Uta, Jō]
Book Two: Spring, Part 2   [Haru no Uta, Ge]
Book Three: Summer   [Natsu no Uta]

Book Four: Autumn, Part 1	[Aki no Uta, Jō]
Book Five: Autumn, Part 2	[Aki no Uta, Ge]
Book Six: Winter	[Fuyu no Uta]
Book Seven: Congratulatory Waka	[Ga no Uta]
Book Eight: Parting	[Wakare no Uta]
Book Nine: Travel	[Tabi no Uta]
Book Ten: Acrostic Waka	[Mono no Na no Uta]
Book Eleven: Love, Part 1	[Koi no Uta, Ichi]
Book Twelve: Love, Part 2	[Koi no Uta, Ni]
Book Thirteen: Love, Part 3	[Koi no Uta, San]
Book Fourteen: Love, Part 4	[Koi no Uta, Shi]
Book Fifteen: Love, Part 5	[Koi no Uta, Go]
Book Sixteen: Laments	[Aishō no Uta]
Book Seventeen: Miscellaneous Waka, Part 1	[Kusagusa no Uta, Jō]
Book Eighteen: Miscellaneous Waka, Part 2	[Kusagusa no Uta, Ge]
Book Nineteen: Chōka, Sedōka, and Indecorous Waka	[Zattei no Uta]
Book Twenty: Waka from the Bureau of Ancient Song	[Ōutadokoro no Ōn'uta][45]

The seasonal and love poetry form the nucleus of the collection, and the rest belong to subsidiary categories. *Her Majesty's Kambyō Era Waka Match* and the *Shinsen Man'yōshū*, compiled at much the same time as the *Kokinshū*, both arrange their waka sequences in this order:

Spring
Summer
Autumn
Winter
Love

This indicates the importance of these categories as poetic material.

---

[45] [The Japanese readings of the characters used for several categories or scrolls are given so inconsistently by various scholars and dictionaries that I asked the author to specify and explain. The results are those given in brackets in the text. The principle he uses is employment of a Japanese reading (kundoku) if it exists, since waka uses such readings. The result is that we read "Wakare no Uta" rather than "Ribetsuka" and "Tabi no Uta" rather than "Kiryoka." Where kundoku equivalents are lacking, ondoku (Sinified readings) must perforce be used: "Aishō no Uta" and "Zattei no Uta." And given the veneration of songs of the Ōutadokoro, "ōn'uta" is more suitable than the lesser honorifics, "miuta," "outa," or even "on'uta." The author also specifies that the "Indecorous Waka" should be read "Hikai no Uta" rather than "Haikai no Uta." To many readers, this will be mumbo-jumbo. But having wandered blankly over this terrain for many years, I thought some others might also find a rational account useful.—Ed.]

In other words, the *Kokinshū* is evidently composed of two parts: Part One centers on seasonal waka, with the rest of the first ten books, including congratulatory waka, playing a secondary role; and Part Two centers on love poetry, with the remaining five books, including laments, as subsidiary poetry (Konishi, 1949a, 30-32). Acrostic waka (mono no na) may have been placed at the end of Part One because the word game they represent—in which a homonym of a given topic is imbedded within a waka text—was deemed a less refined pastime than the composition of waka in other categories.[46] Such word games are found quite frequently in Chinese poetry; acrostic waka were probably experiments inspired by the Chinese model (Konishi, 1949b, 162-63). Since a Chinese acrostic precedent existed, the not very formal category of acrostic waka could not be relegated to Part Two of the *Kokinshū* and was instead put at the very end of Part One.

The Japanese Preface describes the love poems of the past as "frivolous poems shallowly expressed . . . hidden away in the habitations of the amorous" (*KKS*, Preface, 14). Because they were originally part of the informal sphere, love poems were assigned the major section of Part Two. Waka from the Bureau of Ancient Song were recited on formal occasions; their placement at the very end of Part Two may reflect the fact that they are essentially songs that employ antiquated expression. Not surprisingly, many old manuscript copies of the *Kokinshū* follow a two-booklet format. The twelfth-century Gen'ei manuscript concludes Book Ten with the words "*Kokinwakashū*, Part One."[47] The paucity of pillow words and

---

[46] A mono no na poem is a species of word game in thirty-one-syllable form. The object of the game is to have all the syllables of a given topic (necessarily short) reappear—consecutively, but possessing different meaning—in the waka. Take, for example, this poem on the topic "Kichikō no hana" ("Bellflower"):

Aki *chikō*	Soon it shall *be*
No ha *na*rinikeri	Autumn on each moor and hi*ll*:
Hatsutsuyu no	Flourishing leaves of plants,
Okeru kusaba mo	Touched by the first dews, glo*w*
Iro kawariyuku.	In colors grown ever dee*per*.

(*KKS*, 10:440)

In the romanized version, the second through eighth syllables of the waka spell the word "kichikō no hana" [and in the (inescapably free) translation, the last two letters of all lines but the third (there the first two) spell "bellflower"—Trans.]. Acrostic waka have certain features in common with tsa-ming shih, a popular genre during the Late Six Dynasties period. [Kichikō, or kikyō (Platycodon grandiflorum), is a perennial plant known in this country as a Chinese bellflower or balloon flower. Since it is one of the "seven autumn plants," the waka is appropriately concerned with autumn.—Trans.]

[47] This manuscript bears a postscript attesting that it was copied in Gen'ei 3 (1120), hence its name. Book 10 of the Sujigire manuscript *Kokinshū* is also followed by the notation "*Kokinwakashū*, Part 1" (Kyūsojin, 1960a, 152). A postscript by a latter-day reader of the Shōwagire manuscript reads, "Part 1 of this copy of the *Kokinshū* is written entirely in the hand of Lord Shunzei; of this there can be no doubt" (Kyūsojin, 1960c, 15). These notations demonstrate an awareness that the *Kokinshū* was divided into two parts.

prefaces in Part One, and the abundance of such devices in Part Two, reflects the bipartite structure of the *Kokinshū*. Proponents of the *Kokinshū*
style are not necessarily predominant in the highly informal waka of Part
Two. For this reason, traditional poetic styles survive there in good quantity and display less wittiness than in Part One. The discrepancy between
the two parts, in the number of pillow words and prefaces, can be understood only in this context.

The nature of the structural design conceived for the *Kokinshū* by Tsurayuki's circle suggests that the editors paid similar attention to smaller
points. As we have just seen, the categories of Spring, Summer, Autumn,
Winter, and Love are first seen in *Her Majesty's Kambyō Era Waka
Match*; within each category, waka topics are arranged in groups to produce development according to temporal progression. This design was
taken up and further refined in the *Kokinshū*.[48] Consider, for example, the
opening poems from Book Four, "Autumn, Part 1."

Composed on the first day of autumn.
By Fujiwara Toshiyuki

Aki kinu to	"Autumn has arrived"—
Me ni wa sayaka ni	Although not clearly visible
Mienedomo	To the human eye,
Kaze no oto ni zo	It is the sound of autumn wind
Odorokarenuru.	That startles to awareness.

(4:169)

*Composed on the first day of autumn, on accompanying
the senior courtiers on an excursion to the Kamo riverbed.*
By Tsurayuki

Kawakaze no	How very cool it is,
Suzushiku mo aru ka	The breeze blowing from the river!
Uchiyosuru	Has autumn come
Nami to tomo ni ya	Together with the little waves
Aki wa tatsu ran.	Rippling over to this shore?

(4:170)

---

[48] I have discussed, in an earlier article, the arrangement of waka in the *Kokinshū* according to the principles of progression and association (Konishi, 1958a, 99-103). Several later
studies, beginning with Matsuda Takeo's *Kokinwakashū no Kōzō ni Kansuru Kenkyū*, have
given greater accuracy to the original observations. These studies are limited, however, to the
principle of progression; scholars in Japan have yet to consider the problem of association.

Anonymous Poems on Unknown Topics

Waga seko ga	They blow the hem of
Koromo no suso o	My husband's robe inside out,
Fukikaeshi	And show its lining—
Uramezurashiki	How new and strange they seem to me,
Aki no hatsukaze.	The first gusty winds of autumn.

(4:171)

Kinō koso	It seems yesterday
Sanae torishika	We transplanted rice seedlings;
Itsu no ma ni	Now, in a moment
Inaba soyogite	The leaves of the eared plants rustle
Akikaze no fuku.	As the autumn wind blows by.

(4:172)

Akikaze no	Ever since that day
Fukinishi hi yori	The autumn wind began blowing,
Hisakata no	Not a day has passed
Ama no kawara ni	That I have not stood beside
Tatanu hi wa nashi.	The far-distant Celestial River.[49]

(4:173)

Hisakata no	Hear me, ferryman—
Ama no kawara no	You who ply the far-distant
Watashimori	Celestial River—
Kimi watarinaba	Once you've brought my lord to me,
Kaji kakushite yo.	Make sure you hide your oars!

(4:174)

Amanogawa	Could it be because
Momiji o hashi ni	Scarlet leaves might form a bridge
Wataseba ya	To span the Celestial River,

---

[49] [The speaker of this and the next three poems is the Weaver Maid—see n. 40. The seventh lunar month marked the beginning of autumn, as these poems presume. In the next poem, the celestial Weaver reasons that if the ferryman hides his oars, then his passenger, the Herdboy, will have no way to return across the river when the lovers' allotted night is over. This Tanabata legend is one of the Chinese stories that Japanese have made most their own.—Trans., Ed.]

| Tanabatatsume no | That the Weaver Maid awaits |
| Aki o shi mo matsu. | Autumn with such eagerness? |

(4:175)

Koikoite	I've yearned and yearned for him;
Au yo wa koyoi	We shall meet this very night.
Amanogawa	If only mist would rise
Kiri tachiwatari	From the Celestial River and
Akezu mo aranan.	Make it seem day does not dawn!

(4:176)

The first two poems, numbers 169 and 170, concern the first day of autumn. Its arrival is perceived only aurally in the former waka, whereas the latter captures autumn both tactilely ("cool") and visually ("waves / Rippling over to this shore"), thus conveying a deeper sense of autumn. The next waka in the sequence, number 171, also depicts the wind visually; but it clearly states, with "*Aki no* hatsukaze" ("The first gusty winds *of autumn*"), that the season is indeed autumn. Compared with the surmisals of poem 170, with its ". . . ya / . . . ran" structure, poem 171 evokes a sure sense of autumn. In poem 172 we are first taken back in time to the seedling-planting season; and our response is employed to underscore the present autumn scene of mature rice plants, their leaves rustling in the wind. Rather than follow a simple linear time flow, the sequence gains an unexpected element of retrogression as the whole progresses deeper into the autumn season.

Where poem 172 introduced temporal retrogression, poem 173 attempts spatial transposition. Unlike the Kamo riverbed, the "Celestial River" of the poem is vast—it is the Milky Way. The early autumn scene shifts from earth to the heavens. The poem is located at a temporal point, first, by the speaker's use of retrospection: the lines "Akikaze no / Fukinishi hi yori" ("*Ever since* that day / The autumn wind *began* blowing") inform us that several days have passed since the beginning of autumn. A second temporal indicator is the use of an expression to show that the speaker has waited impatiently, during these several days, for the night of her meeting with the Herdboy: this informs the reader that the poem is set at some point before the seventh day of the Seventh Month. Poem 174 gives a suggestion of the Herdboy's physical form in the word "kimi" (my lord); the day of meeting has apparently arrived, but the supposition present in the verb "watarinaba" ("Once you've brought [my lord]") reveals that their meeting has not yet occurred. The speaker's point of view shifts in poem 175. The speaker of poems 173 and 174 is the Weaver Maid. But in 175 the speaker is a human being, who looks up at a branch adorned with autumn leaves, and it seems to form a bridge spanning the Milky Way. The Herdboy conventionally crosses the Milky Way by boat, but (the speaker imagines) he could also cross on just such a bridge of autumn leaves. The leaves accent the refined beauty (en) of an imaginary world. In poem 176, the Weaver Maid reappears as speaker. At last the day of their rendezvous has come, and the Weaver Maid's wish—that their night be prolonged by just a bit—tells us that the long-awaited moment is fast approaching.

Each waka in the sequence, then, effects change through various temporal and spatial transitions, as the sequence itself progresses from early autumn to mid-autumn, and on to late autumn. I have termed this configurational principle "progression." The arrangement of waka sequences according to the principle of progression was attempted as early as *Her Majesty's Kambyō Era Waka Match*, but the precision of its progression bears no comparison to that displayed in the *Kokinshū*.

What is more, waka with subjects in common are arranged in the *Kokinshū* in sequences so as to assure progression, and further designs effectuate smooth transitions. In the group quoted above, for example, numbers 169 through 173 are all concerned with the phenomenon of wind; this strengthens the continuity between poems and creates a sequence. My quotation stops with poem 176, but poems 177 through 183 continue to deal with the Seventh Night and so form a sequence. Poem 173 echoes the "Akikaze no fuku" ("As the autumn wind blows by") of the preceding poem, 172, with its own "akikaze no / Fukinishi . . ." ("Ever since . . . / The autumn wind began blowing"); poem 173 is thus concerned both with wind and the Seventh Night, and so links two sequences. Linkage in later times was usually achieved less by common subjects than by disparate subjects having conceptual elements in common. I have termed this linkage "association." Association is a linkage in poetic atmosphere that exists despite a break in meaning: if a sequence effected by a common subject can be characterized as continuous, one effected by association might well be termed discrete-continuous. The latter attribute will be discussed further when we come to the *Shinkokinshū* period (vol. three).

This discussion of *Kokinshū* poems 169 through 176 would probably have surprised their composers. They are unlikely to have anticipated that later readers would interpret their compositions in such a fashion. Poem 177, which follows and builds on poem 176, provides good data to consider just what is going on.

Composed in the reign of Uda Tennō, when,
on the night of the seventh, His Majesty commanded that
the assembled courtiers each present a waka. The following
was composed on behalf of a certain courtier.
By Tomonori

Amanogawa	The Celestial River—
Asase shiranami	I grope and mourn among the shoals
Tadoritsutsu	In white waves unknown—
Watari hateneba	My crossing is not finished
Ake zo shinikeru.	When daybreak has arrived.

(4:177)

The forenote indicates that this waka was composed quite independently of any others and was originally unrelated to poem 176. The meaning of poem 177 is simple: the speaker, who does not know where the shallows lie in the river, makes his way through rough waves and has still not managed to cross by daybreak. When read in the context of the waka that precede it, the significance of poem 177 changes: the Herdboy has inexplicably chosen to wade through the shallows this year rather than crossing by boat as usual, or across a bridge of autumn leaves, as some human beings apparently think he might do. And because he attempts to wade across the river, he loses the chance, permitted him only once a year, to meet his beloved. Surely both he and his Weaver Maid regret this keenly.

Something here strikes one as odd, however, and the oddness becomes more apparent the more serious the Herdboy appears, as he painfully gropes his way through the shallows in an attempt to arrive at his destination within the appointed time. This oddness is not funny so much as suffused with the pathos of a man committed to reaching the woman he loves so very much. In poem 177, the composer concerns himself with the originally simple, romantic subject of the Seventh Night while also distancing himself in order to treat of a sadness that arouses human sympathies. This stance stems from a rationality that likely did not originate solely from the Yamato spirit. The dominance of a Sinified awareness is evident not only in the subject of this waka, the Seventh Night, but in its very conceptual focus.

Is it justifiable, in reading waka, to make interpretations based on meanings not conceived by the composer? Many Japanese scholars of their country's literature apparently believe that correct interpretation lies in grasping the composer's original design.[50] The interpretation offered

[50] This was long ago criticized as an "intentional fallacy" (Wimsatt, 1946, 3-18). Japanese

here clearly runs counter to this belief, although some such reading was clearly sought by the editors of the *Kokinshū*, as well as by editors of many later waka anthologies. An editor whose arrangement adds new meaning to waka may well be considered as a secondary composer. As we follow the design of the secondary composer, we discover a meaning different from that given an individual waka by its poet, the primary composer. In so doing we must seek a new way of reading. The editors of the *Kokinshū* are unlikely to have anticipated that their interpretation—or reinterpretation—would be the sole one given a poem. We know this because they included the original waka forenotes in their anthology. If, in other words, poem 177 is read to conform to its forenote, "Composed in the reign of Uda Tennō . . . on behalf of a certain courtier," the reader can recapture the meaning given it by the primary composer, Tomonori. Similarly, the "topic unknown" (dai shirazu) poems may be read individually, independent of their context in the anthology. The editors, then, recognized two methods of reading the poetry in the *Kokinshū*: as sequences, without regard to forenotes, and individually, in agreement with the forenote of the poem. This doubleness provides the new design of the *Kokinshū*. Interpretation without reference to the primary composer's intended meaning has a vital bearing on the development of renga, a point to be discussed in a later volume.

The arrangement of sequences according to the principle of progression is also found in other books of the *Kokinshū*, including those entitled "Love." The sequence evolves in an order beginning with poems on unconsummated love, moves through those on the delights of passionate love, and concludes with poems of disillusionment and bitterness. These love poems are carefully arranged within a given sequence. Book Eleven, "Love, Part 1," begins by describing the state of a lover who cannot gain access to his lady (poems 469-75); there follows the stage of a lover catching glimpses of his beloved and hearing the faint sound of her voice (476-82); the next group describes the agony of one deprived of liaisons with the subject of his love (483-541); and the concluding sequence (poems 542-51) is made up of poignant poems of yearning ordered by season, from spring through winter. Links between individual waka and between sequences are sometimes close and at other times approximate breaks: the love poetry of the *Kokinshū* does not possess so orderly a progression as do the seasonal waka. This may well be due to the fact that the compilers sought sama in the formal structures of Part One, and that, by contrast, Part Two required much less symmetry or formality.

---

scholars of their country's literature have yet to consider this question. [And Western scholars of their own literature have yet to grapple with the Asian presumption.—Ed.]

Behind the Kokinshū *Style*

The *Kokinshū* has been revered as a waka classic for over a thousand years. This knowledge makes it easy to believe that Tsurayuki's circle originally gave this anthology a form and content worthy of a classic. Yet the subjects discussed in the preceding sections all represent the most drastic poetic experiments of their time. There is a certain highhandedness in these acts, something tantamount to an impulsive decision to commence manufacturing an as yet experimental drug. The early tenth-century Japanese audience did not find in the *Kokinshū* the equilibrium and exemplary qualities we associate with the word "classic." Instead they thought it a radical venture. So innovative an experiment could not have been carried out solely by the low-ranking Tsurayuki and his colleagues. That is why I have suggested that the cloistered sovereign Uda provided substantial but inconspicuous support and impetus to the project (Konishi, 1949a, 24). Daigo Tennō was only twenty-one years old when he ordered the compilation of the *Kokinshū*. Uda, on the other hand, had exercised considerable leadership in directing *Her Majesty's Kambyō Era Waka Match*, which provided the *Kokinshū* with its prototype for waka arrangement (Takano, 1970, 332-35). Uda's interest in waka continued after he assumed cloistered status—for example, he served as the judge of the *Teiji In Waka Match*; it would thus have been natural for Uda to issue directions on compiling the royal anthology.[51] Following Uda's death in 931, circumstances seem to have altered somewhat.

It is commonly held that waka styles changed during the *Gosenshū* (951ff.) period. Certain individuals did indeed change their waka styles, but that does not mean the *Kokinshū* style pervading this period underwent alteration. Rather, what changed was the editing procedure applied, respectively, to the *Kokinshū* and the *Gosenshū* while waka itself remained unchanged in essence from the *Kokinshū* norm. The disparity between editing procedures in the two anthologies is apparent, first, in the absence of a preface to the *Gosenshū*: its editors had no great aspirations. Their principal aim, to follow the precedent set by the *Kokinshū*, accounts for the lack of editorial ambition—a lack also manifested in the title of the anthology, *The Later Collection*.

For all that, the *Gosenshū* differs from the *Kokinshū* in several respects. Waka in the *Gosenshū* do not follow a systematic arrangement. The

[51] An opposing view has the *Kokinshū* personally compiled by Daigo, with Uda taking little part (Okumura, 1954, 14-25). The theory is based on the fact that waka by Tsurayuki, Mitsune, and Tadamine, all editors of the *Kokinshū*, received little consideration at waka matches sponsored by the cloistered sovereign Uda while poets like Okikaze carried the day. There is little evidence, however, that such factions existed then. Waka by Tomonori, another of the *Kokinshū* editors, were in fact well received at waka matches associated with the cloistered sovereign Uda.

method of arranging waka according to the principle of progression is er-
ratically applied. A configurational analysis like that attempted for the
Kokinshū autumn poems cannot, regrettably, be performed successfully
with the *Gosenshū*. At best, the ordering of its waka is equivalent to that
in Part Two of the *Kokinshū*. This does not mean, however, that the *Gosenshū* rejects an orderly waka arrangement. There is a recognizable configuration based on the principle of progression. Only, it is not fully realized.[52]

The lack of full realization is evident also in the sama of individual
waka. Of course the wit that is at the core of the *Kokinshū* style also sets
the tone for the *Gosenshū*, but in the latter anthology the level of wittiness
tends to drop:

> A certain woman became a lady-in-waiting at the palace. Since she
> was a newcomer, she attracted the attention of a great many men, and
> before long she had begun a love affair with one of them. She sent this
> to her lover not long after the first of the year.

Anonymous

Itsu no ma ni	Quite suddenly
Kasumi tatsuran	Spring haze seems on the rise;
Kasugano no	On Kasuga Field
Yuki dani tokenu	The snows have yet to melt, however,
Fuyu to mishi ma ni.	And I thought winter here this while.[53]

(GSS, 1:15)

This is intended as a formal seasonal waka, and so it should ideally have
a suitable sama. It is not, however, especially witty. To be sure, one perceives a certain technique when the waka is read together with its forenote
rather than in isolation. When linked to the circumstances described in the
forenote, "Kasumi tatsu" ("Spring haze . . . on the rise") becomes a metaphor for the rumors current at court about the poet's love affair. This
technique may be more advanced than oblique expression. But if the waka
is instead read as one element in a sequence, without reference to its fore-

---

[52] The *Gosenshū* [see n. 59 below for other details] has also been seen as an anthology
arranged according to principles other than those applied in the *Kokinshū*. According to this
view, the *Gosenshū* editors attempted to arrange its waka as a waka narrative (Satō, 1970,
611). The *Kokinshū* style of arrangement, however, is emulated by every royal waka anthology from the *Shūishū* on; insofar as the *Kokinshū* configurational style serves as a criterion, then, the arrangement of waka in the *Gosenshū* is sketchily done.

[53] [The intended meaning is: People are already gossiping about something that has yet to
happen. Winter imagery is often used metaphorically for a lady's chilly behavior toward a
suitor; similarly, melting ice or snow and rising haze suggest the lady's capitulation and the
start of a love affair.—Trans.]

note, it demonstrates no techniques worth mention. Another problem is its repetition of the word "ma." As we have seen, a poem lost its round in the *Teiji In Waka Match* (913) because it uses the auxiliary "ran" twice. This is another indication of a lax attitude in waka selection.

These facts evidently reflect an editorial aim to make the *Gosenshū* supplemental to the *Kokinshū*. The *Gosenshū* has been found deficient in various ways: it includes waka already in the *Kokinshū* and tends to repeat poems in its own collection. Based on the theory that poets' names are attributed to waka in the *Gosenshū* by memos recorded during the editing process, one modern study coincides with a theory, originating with Fujiwara Kiyosuke, that the extant *Gosenshū* may be a rough draft (Katagiri, 1956, 1-15). This is no more convincing than its refutation (Satō, 1970, 440-41), since neither study establishes criteria by which to distinguish a finished text from a rough draft. Rough draft or not, the *Gosenshū* is in fact irredeemably unrealized. Its characteristics stem more likely from a desire to supplement the *Kokinshū* than from a conscious effort to display originality. The anthology was probably also influenced considerably by the nature of Murakami Tennō's (r. 946-67) role in its compilation. Apparently he did not exercise the kind of leadership displayed by Uda with the *Kokinshū*.

Unlike the waka in the *Kokinshū*, which may be read either in sequence without reference to notes, or individually in the context of the notes, the *Gosenshū* waka yield interesting techniques only in the context of their respective notes. This leads to interpretation based on the specific scenes dictated by the forenotes. A waka provided with such a scene becomes an utagatari, or waka story [discussed in the next chapter]. And an oral waka story shaped into a written composition is an utamonogatari, or waka narrative. The *Gosenshū* has been called a narrative anthology (Nishishita, 1942, 161-68), an indication of aspects it shares with the waka narrative. This interpretation is based on the fact that forenotes in the *Gosenshū* are often narrated in the third [rather than the expected first] person. Many third-person forenotes, however, also appear in tenth-century waka collections by individual poets, including the *Collected Waka of Lady Ise*, the *Ichijō Sesshō Gyoshū (Collected Waka of the Ichijō Regent)*, *Hon'in Jijū Shū (Collected Waka of Hon'in Jijū)*, and *Zōki Hōshi Shū (Collected Waka of Priest Zōki)*.[54] When material from individual collections was in-

---

[54] The "Ichijō Regent" is Fujiwara Koremasa (924-72); his waka collection is also known as the *Toyokage Shū*, Toyokage being a pseudonym used by Koremasa. Hon'in Jijū (a sobriquet; her given name is not known) was the daughter of Ariwara Muneharu (d. 898). She was well known as a waka poet and served as a lady-in-waiting at court. She was the wife of Fujiwara Tokihira (871-909), Minister of the Left, and later married Tokihira's uncle, Kunitsune (827-908). Zōki (fl. ca. 945) was a monk of the temple Enryakuji on Mt. Hiei and one of the Thirty-six Celebrated Poets. [Auth., Trans.]

cluded in the *Gosenshū*, the editors did not rewrite the original third-person narration—hence this technique is not limited to waka narratives alone. To be sure, many waka narratives are no longer extant:

> A poem was made in reply; but my text does not have it. (*Yamato Monogatari* [= YM], dan 95:277)

> These stories were circulated as monogatari. (*YM*, dan 166:335)

No longer extant waka narratives may well have provided material for the *Gosenshū* (Satō, 1970, 264-67). During this period, however, the same work might on different occasions be called a monogatari, a nikki, or a waka collection [see the next chapter]. We cannot therefore be certain that the *Gosenshū* used only waka narratives as source material. The many personal waka collections that appear in the tenth century should also be considered as potential sources: they also may employ third-person narrative techniques.

The compilation of personal waka collections in the tenth century is a notable indication of the awareness that waka and shih were literary equals. The Chinese compiled a great many personal shih collections in addition to anthologies like the *Selections of Refined Literature* and the *New Songs from the Jade Terrace* in which various poets are represented. The ninth-century *Inventory of Written Works Extant in Japan* reveals that many tens of personal shih collections had been imported. The greatest among them was of course *Po's Anthology (Po-shih Wen-chi)*, the collected poems of Po Chü-i.[55] If waka poets were to state clearly that shih and waka shared an equal status, personal waka collections were a necessity. Their rapid proliferation, in the tenth century, was a phenomenon attendant to the compilation of royal anthologies and the circumstances leading to their compilation.

I must qualify an earlier statement, that waka styles underwent no overall change between the *Kokinshū* and the *Gosenshū* periods: individual poets may well have altered their waka styles during their lifetimes. Tsurayuki's style is a case in point; a change apparently occurred in the late 920s. In 928 Tsurayuki composed the following poems on behalf of Fujiwara Saneyori (900-970), who had been asked by the royal consort Yasuko to contribute some screen waka.

Are hiki ni	Drawn along with us
Hikitsurete koso	As we pull the festal branch

---

[55] *Po-shih Wen-chi* is an alternate title for the *Po-shih Ch'ang-ch'ing Chi*. The text as it was introduced to Japan was titled simply *Wen-chi (Anthology)*, to which the Japanese added *Po-shih (Mr. Po)*. [Auth., Trans.]

Chihayaburu
Kamo no kawanami
Uchiwatarikere.

And mighty as it is,
The Kamo River sends its waves
Coursing constantly to shore.

(*TYS*, 3:244)

Hototogisu
Naku naru koe o
Sanae toru
Tema uchiokite
Aware to zo kiku.

The hototogisu—
That sound could only be its song,
And I interrupt
My gathering rice seedlings,
Listening in a rapture of delight.

(*TYS*, 3:245)

A "festal branch" (are) is a branch of the sakaki tree, decorated with little bells and colored ribbons and used in the Kamo Shrines festival. The branch was attached to ropes and borne in procession by several men who pulled the ropes, making the bells jingle: this ensured that their prayers would be answered. "As we pull the festal branch" ("Are hiki ni") introduces a pivot word, "Drawn along with us" ("Hikitsurete"), the sole technical device employed in the poem. The latter waka is equally lacking in wit.

In the Third Month of 941, Tsurayuki composed twenty-eight waka for the royal screens; two are unadorned expressions of feeling.

An Excursion on the Day of the Rat

Kaerusa wa
Kuraku naru to mo
Haru no no no
Miyuru kagiri wa
Yukan to zo omou.

Knowing full well
That I shall return in darkness,
I now wish to roam
All about the fields of spring
As long as I can see my way.

(*TYS*, 4:468)

While performing impromptu music in boats we see wisteria blooming by the lake.

Kogikaeru
Miredomo akazu
Wakarenishi
Haru no nagori no
Fujinami no hana.

Back we row again,
Never tiring of the sight:
Spring's tide may be gone,
But its reminder can be found
In the wisteria cascade's waves.

(*TYS*, 4:475)

The next two poems appear among twenty composed for the royal screens in the Second Month of 945.

A family is engaged in worshiping the gods.

Momotose no	When the Fourth Month comes,
Uzuki o inoru	We pray that our lives might
Kokoro o ba	Last a hundred years:
Kaminagara mina	Surely each and every god
Shirimaseru ran.	Knows the workings of our hearts.

(*TYS*, 4:531)

The Seventh Night

Hitotose o	An entire year
Machi wa shitsuredo	She has waited for her lover—
Tanabata no	And for the Weaver Maid
Yūgure matsu wa	How long drawn the time has been
Hisashikarikeri.	While she waits for dusk to fall.

(*TYS*, 4:534)

The expression in these poems is plain and simple, requiring no explication. The two poems given below may be the clearest manifestations of this trend; they appear in the record of a waka match held at Tsurayuki's house in 939.[56]

Itsu shika to	Much to my surprise,
Natsu ni naru rashi	Summer seems well on its way:
Utsusemi no	And the cicadas, too—
Koe mo aware ni	Their wonderfully moving voices
Nakisomen rashi.	Seem now first raised in song.

Furikurasu	Rainy and dark,
Satsuki no sora no	The sky of the Fifth Month brings
Nagame ni wa	A long vein of thought—
Ne nomi nakarete	All I do is weep on and on,
Hito zo koishiki.	So much do I yearn for her.

A strict judge might have echoed Tsurayuki's own *Tosa Diary* in objecting to these poems: "Why must he use this unpoetic language?" (*Tosa Nikki*

---

[56] The record of this match (known as *Ki no Tsurayuki Ke Utaawase; The Poetry Match at the House of Ki no Tsurayuki*) survives only in fragments. One manuscript copy fragment has fourteen waka; eight more are quoted in the *Fuboku Wakashō*.

[= *TSN*], 48). This is no accidental shift in Tsurayuki's poetry. It is the result of conscious experimentation. Tsurayuki edited the *Shinsen Waka* at the command of Daigo Tennō. He completed his task while still governor of Tosa (930-34). The anthology was intended as a selection of the best waka produced between 810 and 930; the Preface declares that these masterworks represent "both the flower and the fruit" of poetry (*Shinsen Waka*, Preface, 188). It is not always clear which were perceived as flowers and which as fruit, but the expression in the poems selected for inclusion suggests that wit was used only in moderation. Poems using relatively direct expression seem to correspond to the "fruit," and elaborately witty poems to the "flower." The *Kokinshū* was, of course, a major source for the *Shinsen Waka*; 280 waka out of the latter's total of 360 are taken from the *Kokinshū*. Seventy of the *Kokinshū* poems included in the *Shinsen Waka*, however, are principally from the quasi-*Man'yōshū* period, and all employ nonwitty expression. Eighty *Shinsen Waka* poems come from sources other than the *Kokinshū*. Eighteen of these are nonwitty poems, and four of the eighteen, moreover, are Tsurayuki's own compositions. These figures are not definitive, since distinctions between witty and nonwitty expression rely largely on personal interpretation. My own conclusion is that eighty-eight out of a total of 360 waka in the *Shinsen Waka* lack wit (Konishi, 1975, 124-25). If we postulate that Tsurayuki first adopted this editorial stance around 934, his poetic masterpiece might reasonably be dated to 936:

> Omoikane
> Imogariyukeba
>   Fuyu no yo no
> Kawakaze samumi
> Chidori naku nari.

> Unable to resist,
> I go off to be with you;
> In the winter night
> Because the river wind is cold
> The plovers cry out their pain.

> (*TYS*, 3:339)

The poets who followed Tsurayuki selected other poems as his finest. Fujiwara Kintō thought most highly of a poem in the witty *Kokinshū* style.

> Sakura chiru
> Ki no shitakaze wa
>
>   Samukarade
> Sora ni shirarenu
> Yuki zo furikeru.

> Where cherry blossoms fall,
> The breeze that blows beneath the
>   boughs
> Brings no cold at all,
> And yet there falls a kind of snow
> Quite unfamilar to the sky.

> (*SIS*, 1:64)

In Fujiwara Shunzei's opinion, Tsurayuki's masterpiece was [a poem famous for its handling of the "preface"]:

Musubu te no	As the cupped hands
Shizuku ni nigoru	Soil with their leaking drops
Yama no i no	The mountain spring,
Akade mo hito ni	So, my thirst as yet unquenched,
Wakarenuru kana.	The moment of our parting comes.

(*KKS*, 8:404)

And Fujiwara Teika's choice was this:

Hito wa isa	I cannot know
Kokoro mo shirazu	How your heart inclines at present,
Furusato wa	But in this old haunt
Hana zo mukashi no	The blossom gives off a fragrance,
Ka ni nioikeru.	The very scent of our days past.[57]

(*KKS*, 1:42)

Whatever his finest poem may be, it seems clear that his late style was simpler, less witty than the style he had earlier favored. This shift is further confirmed by the *Tosa Nikki*, written about 935. One theme of the work is frustration; and one of the principal frustrations depicted in the *Diary* is that felt when a waka does not turn out the way one would like it to do. According to the narrator of the *Diary*, waka or shih are composed when a poet can no longer keep his thoughts within the heart (*TSN*, 55). The essential nature of poetry lies in expressing one's feelings exactly as they are felt. The narrator therefore criticizes poetic approaches that toy with various techniques, not only in poems about feelings but in those depicting scenery as well. One woman in the *Diary* sees cranes in flight at Uta no Matsubara; she "looks at them with great interest, and, unable to contain herself," composes this waka:

Miwataseba	Gazing all about,
Matsu no uregoto ni	One can but believe the cranes
Sumu tsuru wa	Have been companions

[57] Shun'e expresses great admiration for "Omoikane" ("Unable to resist"), which he considers Tsurayuki's finest poem. It makes him feel chilly, he says, whenever he recites it—even in the summer (*MMS*, 90). [Teika's preference for "Hito wa isa" ("I cannot know") may owe something to its resemblance to a lovely anonymous poem—*KKS*, 3:139—that was much admired and echoed by his circle. Most of the author's original note has been transferred, with transitional additions, into the main text.—Ed.]

Chiyo no dochi to zo   Of the pine trees upon whose tops
Omou beranaru.   They have nestled through the ages.[58]

The narrator of the *Diary*, speaking for Tsurayuki, comments that "the poem cannot possibly surpass the sight itself" (*TSN*, 35-36). In 915, Tsurayuki had composed this screen waka:

Waga yado no   Cranes are nestling
Matsu no kozue ni   High atop the pines that grow
Sumu tazu wa   Along my house:
Chiyo no yuki ka to   The trees must be wondering
Omou beranari.   At this everlasting snow.

(*TYS*, 1:51)

This is certainly not a bad poem by *Kokinshū* period criteria. Some two decades later, however, Tsurayuki finds that interposing reason in a waka (because cranes and pines were attributed thousand-year lifespans, they make ideal companions) can only yield poetry far inferior to the splendor of the actual scene.

Believing that waka must have a special style to become the literary equal of the shih, Tsurayuki's circle used a sama centered on wit to build its own *Kokinshū* world. The task was carried out rather arbitrarily. One cannot but wonder how much sympathy Tsurayuki's contemporaries could summon for the kind of waka he displayed in the *Kokinshū*. The ideals put forth by Tsurayuki's circle nevertheless gained wide support within one or two decades, and the *Kokinshū* style became the touchstone for future waka. At the center of this remarkable success, Tsurayuki—by now a celebrated poet constantly besieged by orders from the powerful for screen waka—seems suddenly to have reconsidered the worth of such poetry. Was not waka, after all, that which a poet could no longer keep within the heart? When Tsurayuki expressed himself without consideration for sama, he embraced the zoku aspect of poetry and so renounced the ga world he and his colleagues had constructed. Having helped shape the ga ideal, Tsurayuki stood helplessly by as the sphere of ga expression grew to enormous proportions. He must have lacked the confidence to pit himself against it. In his old age, Tsurayuki seems to have kept his bitterness mostly to himself and continued, partly from force of habit, to mass-produce waka in the ga style. No one in the ga world would have noticed his bitterness had he expressed it. His only alternative was to disguise his bitterness in droll prose, where it would not matter if no one appreciated it. His audience would probably think his composition was a humorous

---

[58] [The translation is taken, with small changes, from Miner, 1969, 67.—Trans.]

piece, a happy misconception, because the author, in truth, wanted to laugh at his experiences. These, no doubt, were Tsurayuki's thoughts as he began to write *The Tosa Diary*, as we shall see.

The Consolidation of the Kokinshū *Style*

Despite fluctuations in individual poetic styles, the *Kokinshū* style was essentially maintained through the *Gosenshū* period.[59] The only discrepancies were in editorial methods. There was, in other words, no distinct *Gosenshū* style; the *Gosenshū* period must be seen as an episode encompassed by the *Kokinshū* period. Movements connected with various poetic circles evolved in the *Shūishū* period.[60] These movements did not break with the *Kokinshū* style, however, but further refined and purified it instead. Or, put another way, the ideals cherished by Tsurayuki's circle were realized and consolidated in the *Shūishū* (1005-1008) period. These actions were motivated by various factors, the most noteworthy perhaps being the dominance of Japanese literature by Po Chü-i's poetry.

The introduction and dominance assumed by Six Dynasties poetry was a major factor in shaping the *Kokinshū* style. Po's poetry had an extremely large audience by the ninth century; but this only meant that his poetry was mined extensively for apt lines and phrases, not that the "Po style," his most characteristic expression, had come to direct the conceptual focus of waka. By the tenth century, the Po style dominated Japanese shih, accompanied by that laxity of expression we have observed. The Po style penetrated waka expression in the *Shūishū* period, bringing about the consolidation of the *Kokinshū* style. The influence of Po's poetry on waka expression is in fact twofold. One aspect is a tendency toward plainness, represented by the works of Fujiwara Kintō; the other is a movement toward the ordinary, as exemplified by the works of Sone no Yoshitada (dates unknown).

Modern readers might not be easily convinced that Kintō best represents the *Shūishū* period. Let us consider the three of his waka that appear in the *Shūiwakashō*.[61]

---

[59] The *Gosenshū* period (936-66) is estimated to be a thirty-year period centering on the year 951, when the royal order was given to compile the anthology. This takes into account the birth year of the eldest of its five editors, Kiyowara Motosuke (908-90), and the death year of its youngest, Ōnakatomi Yoshinobu (921-91).

[60] The compilation period of the *Shūishū* is unknown. Based on the dates of the editor of the *Shūiwakashō*, Kintō (966-1041), the *Shūishū* period may be thought to extend from 985 to 1015.

[61] Kintō, who edited the *Shūiwakashō*, may have been reluctant to include more than three of his own compositions. The cloistered sovereign Kazan ordered the compilation of the *Shūiwakashō* (ten books) and the *Shūishū* (twenty books). The former anthology was probably completed first. The latter seems to have been edited by Kazan himself (Miyoshi, 1944, 229).

On passing by Arashiyama and seeing autumn leaves
falling in great profusion.

Asa madaki	The early morning
Arashi no yama no	Brings such winds to the stormy hills
Samukereba	Of Arashiyama,
Chiru momijiba o	That brocades of colored leaves
Kinu hito zo naki.	Are the clothes now worn by all.[62]

(3:131)

Topic Unknown

Shimo okanu	On this wintry night,
Sode dani sayuru	Even sleeves untouched by frost
Fuyu no yo wa	Are cold to touch:
Kamo no uwage o	My deepest sympathy goes out
Omoi koso yare.	To wild ducks in feathered coats.

(4:159)

The cherry blossoms being particularly lovely at the
Koshirakawa villa, some people came to visit.

Haru kite zo	When spring arrives,
Hito mo toikeru	People also come to visit
Yamazato wa	This remote abode:
Hana koso yado no	The cherry blossom is indeed
Aruji narikere.	Lord and master of this house!

(9:395)

There is a focus on wittiness in all three poems, a clear manifestation of
the characteristic *Kokinshū* style. Kintō compares the autumn leaves that
shower on people to their clothing, and he reasons that they are wearing
robes of leaves to protect themselves from the cold blasts from Arashiyama (lit. "Storm Hill"). Yet the wittiness of this poem is not as pronounced as that of *Kokinshū* period waka. Kintō's second poem is even
less witty: the speaker reasons that because he, with a roof over his head,
is so very cold, the wild ducks with their frosty feathers must be suffering
a great deal more. Pity for these waterbirds, sleeping on the lake surface,
is the dominant emotion; the reasoning process in the poem, concerning
the differences in temperature between the house and the outdoors, does

---

[62] [The comparison of tinted autumn leaves to brocades is so conventional that Kintō need
not explicitly mention "brocade."—Ed.]

not leave much of an impression. The last poem, a greeting to a group of flower-viewers, takes on a joking tone when the speaker concludes that the visit has been made primarily to see his cherry blossoms, not himself: here again the reasoning process is a trifling one. Light wit is one of Kintō's characteristics, as well as a hallmark of the entire *Shūishū* period.

The *Kokinshū* period had been overly aware of the equal literary merits of waka and shih and too preoccupied with the ideal of a witty sama. A century later, in the *Shūishū* period, it was no longer necessary to emphasize wit. Intellectuals served both as poet and audience; they dwelled in the subtle, polished world of ga and so felt no need for strong stimuli. They were able to find great interest in the most minute expressions of wit.

The influence of Po Chü-i's poetry must also be taken into account. Plainness is a major characteristic of Po's poetic expression. Although, as noted earlier, Po's plain style is more than just easily comprehended language, that is nevertheless how Japanese shih poets interpreted it. Japanese shih from the tenth century on therefore tended toward a mediocre kind of plain style. And since plainness was valued in shih, it very likely influenced waka, too. Shih poets, in this period, were usually waka poets as well. Compiler of the *Wakan Rōeishū (Collection of Japanese and Chinese Songs)*, Kintō is the exemplary shih and waka poet of the time. His admiration for Po's poetry is obvious: out of a total of 588 Chinese shih couplets in the *Collection*, 139 are by Po, and he broke with precedent to establish a separate heading for these couplets, titled simply "Po." Po's poetry undoubtedly contributed to the shift toward plainness in waka expression, even though we cannot determine how much of the influence was direct and how much indirect.

Kintō, however, did not devote himself exclusively to Po's poetry. Eleven of Kintō's shih appear in *Honchō Reisō (Outstanding Literature of Japan)*. They make the proper distinction between ornate expression for banquet situations and sober expression on ceremonial occasions.[63] Plainness is common to both groups, however, and difficult or ambiguous expression does not appear. The eleventh-century Japanese shih was compared earlier to a vintage wine diluted with water. This is particularly true for Kintō's shih. He became the premier shih poet of his time, not by creating his own style but by manipulating most skillfully the commonest contemporary tone. To quote a passage again, it will now be apparent that his views on waka, too, are reminiscent of a model student's seminar report.

---

[63] An example of the former is "Composed at a Banquet in Late Spring at the Tō Sanjō Residence of the Minister of the Left [Michinaga], on the Topic, 'Fallen Blossoms Dance across the Waters' " (*HR*, 1:207). An example of the latter is "Composed, at His Majesty's Command, on the Occasion of the First Lecture on *The Classic of Filial Piety*, which Was Delivered to the Eldest Prince in the Hikyōsha on a Winter's Day" (*HR*, 2:220).

A waka may in effect be deemed outstanding when it is strongly appealing, pleasing of form, and possesses something evocative in its design. A clumsy poem appears as nothing but a string of metaphors. One should compose in a simple yet confident manner. If it proves difficult to express both concept and form in a harmonious way, then it is best to concentrate only on the concept for the time being. If the concept nevertheless remains shallow, one would do well to polish the form. The waka will then take this configuration: it will sound pleasing to the ear, will be expressed tastefully and perceived as true poetry, and may employ fresh metaphors. (*Shinsen Zuinō*, 26)

This is essentially a balanced view. Po's own opinions on poetry were considerably more severe than Kintō's bland statement, and yet the only shih stance adopted in tenth- and eleventh-century Japan was an easygoing one. I do not mean to criticize such an adoption of the Po style. Although based on misinterpretation, it provided part of the impetus by which a truly medieval ga expression was consolidated.

In his *Waka Kubon (Nine Gradations of Waka)*, Kintō adapts waka criticism to the Pure Land Buddhist format of the Nine Ways to Salvation. His highest gradation in waka is given to works "possessing splendid expression and being evocative as well." Kintō quotes two poems accorded this rank (*Waka Kubon*, 32).

Haru tatsu to | "Spring has come"—
Iu bakari ni ya | The words are scarcely out and yet
Miyoshino no | In lovely Yoshino
Yama no kasumite | This morning all one seems to see
Kesa wa miyu ran. | Are hills bannered with the haze.

(*SIS*, 1:1)

Honobono to | Lightly, lightly
Akashi no ura no | In the morning mist dawn breaks
Asagiri ni | At bright Akashi,
Shimagakureyuku | And how I long for that boat
Fune o shi zo omou. | Island-hidden as it goes.

(*KKS*, 9:409)

There is little noticeable wit in the first poem [haze being a prime emblem of the whole season of spring]; it states that the advent of spring has made the Yoshino mountains hazy. "Ya," in the second line, expresses mild surprise, in this case at the earliness of the haze; the feeling thus communicated is unlike that from "ya" in its more common function of expressing doubt. This may be what Kintō found "evocative" in the poem. Taken as a whole, moreover, the poem has extremely simple expression.

The influence of Po's poetry is manifested not only in Kintō's plain style but in the quotidian nature of Yoshitada's waka. Yoshitada became quite a respected poet by the twelfth century, but during his lifetime he was criticized as "a crazy, addled fellow" ("Kyōwaku no yatsu nari"—*Fukurozōshi* [= FZS], 1:61). He was called "crazy, addled" because of the objectionable diction in this poem:

Nake ya nake	Cry out your song, cry,
Yomogi ga soma no	You crickets underneath the mugwort
Kirigirisu	Laid out in piles—
Kureyuku aki wa	For autumn darkening to its end
Ge ni zo kanashiki.	Is truly cause for sadness!

(*Sōtan Shū* [= STS], 242)

"Yomogi ga soma" (mugwort / Laid out in piles) is not a phrase suitable to waka.

There are many more such examples in Yoshitada's poetry. (Inappropriate diction is given in italics.)

Misonou no	The *mustard greens*
Nazuna no kuki mo	Growing in my garden
Tachinikeri	Are past their prime;
Kesa no asana ni	What then shall I pick
Nani o tsumamashi.	For my breakfast vegetable?

(*STS*, 84)

Misogi suru	It seems it blows—
Kamo no kawakaze	The river wind from the Kamo
Fuku rashi mo	Where they do lustration;
Suzumi ni yukan	Why not go there to cool off,
Imo o *tomonai*.	*Together with* my sweetheart?

(*STS*, 174)

Wagimoko ga	My beloved wife
Ase ni *sobotsuru*	Lies with *her night-tangled hair*
Neyorigami	*Awry* with sweat;
Natsu no *hiruma* wa	In the *daytime* of this summer
Utoshi to ya omou.	Perhaps this will *put me off*.

(*STS*, 175)

Waga mamoru
Nakate no ine mo
  Nogi wa ochite
Muramura hosaki
Idenikerashi mo.

In this *midseason*
The rice to which I give my care
Sheds its *beards*;
Here and there throughout the fields
The ears of rice seem to appear.

(*STS*, 197)

Kuyuritsutsu
Yo ni sumigama no
  Kebutaki o
Fukitsutsu *moyase*
Fuyu no yamakaze.

It keeps smouldering,
And my familiar charcoal stove
Burns so *smokily*—
You wintry mountain wind,
Clear the hut as you blow on.

(*STS*, 359)

Rui yori mo
Hitori hanarete
  Tobu kari no
Tomo ni okururu
Waga mi kanashi na.

Like a duck in flight,
And separated from its *fellows*,
To make way alone,
I too am left in sadness,
Deserted by my former friends.

(*STS*, 430)

Modern waka poets and scholars of Japanese literature might find this poetry fresh, but it was anomalous indeed to the late tenth-century waka poets. By that time they had probably come to assume that everyday Japanese vocabulary and Chinese loanwords were unbefitting the elegance of waka. To disregard this was to be a "crazy, addled fellow."

It must have required considerable determination to use everyday language in this context. How could Yoshitada have come to his decision? One factor may have been his characteristic obstinacy. That once led him to attend, without invitation, a poetry gathering, from which he was unceremoniously ejected.[64] Another, more direct source of his action may have been the knowledge that the great shih poet Po Chü-i used unadorned, commonplace language. The extent of Yoshitada's contact with Po's poetry is unknown. But not long after Yoshitada's time, *Po's Anthology* had become so well known that Sei Shōnagon could mention it in her *Makura no Sōshi (The Pillow Book)*: "For Chinese literature we have Po's

---

[64] The incident appears in "Ōkagami Uragaki" (*OK*, 412). An embellished version appears in the *Konjaku Monogatari Shū* (28:56-58). The authenticity of the event can be told from the forenote to one of Yoshitada's waka: "Composed on attending, uninvited, a gathering held by En'yū Tennō, at which I was treated terribly" (*STS*, 474).

Anthology" (*Makura no Sōshi* [= MSS], dan 211:249). We cannot easily conclude, then, that Yoshitada knew nothing of Po's poetry. Had he been unfamiliar with it, he would nevertheless have been exposed to expressions used orally by shih poets among his contemporaries and now become Japanese locutions. Such diction was not only incomprehensible as Chinese, it also incorporated a considerable amount of colloquial Japanese. Japanese shih poets thus came to employ diction that would never have been used in a proper Chinese shih. This habit extended to shih concepts, leading to the composition of shih on mundane subjects from a mundane point of view. For instance, take Ōe no Masahira's panegyric to peace in the realm:

> *Our land prospered in the Chōho and Kankō eras. I, an aged scholar, present this poem with heartfelt gratitude:*
>
> In the first years of Chōho, His Majesty chose his consorts;
> In the Kankō era they presented him with princes.
> It was I who proposed the names for these two eras,
> Hoping that the house of Ōe will continue to prosper.

(Gō Rihō Shū, 2:383)

In Chōho 2 (1000), Fujiwara Sadako was made First Consort and Fujiwara Akiko Second Consort; during the Kankō era (1004-12) two princes were born, Atsuhira (later Goichijō Tennō) and Atsuyoshi (later Gosuzaku Tennō). The content of the shih is expressed in such commonplace fashion that the piece does not seem like poetry: the Ōe family hopes to prosper because auspicious events occurred in the eras the speaker had the privilege to name.[65] Knowing that commonplace diction was widely used in shih, Yoshitada would probably have been confident enough to employ similarly humble subjects and expressions in his waka. This represents an indirect adoption of the Po style.

Yoshitada's waka are best seen as experiments in the style of the aging Tsurayuki: they are thoughts "one can no longer keep within one's heart" and are composed in "unpoetic language," heedless of the inevitable criticism. It is very difficult, however, to regard his work as a first-class realization of these possibilities. A somewhat later poet, Izumi Shikibu (b. ?976), further extended Yoshitada's orientation, and her results are strongly moving, even for modern readers. Izumi Shikibu's best work is in

---

[65] The implied meaning of the poem is as follows. Ki no Haseo proposed the name for the Engi era (901-23) and Ōe no Koretoki named the Tenryaku era (947-57), and their respective sons (Ki no Yoshimitsu and Ōe no Masamitsu) rose to cabinet rank. The speaker hopes that his house will be similarly favored as a result of his having given names to two eras.

waka that deal with the emotions; these poems express her precise feelings and have little noticeable wit. The most outstanding of her more than 1,500 extant compositions are not witty:

Love

Kurokami no	I do not even know
Midare mo shirazu	If my long dark hair is tangled.
Uchifuseba	As I lie beside you,
Mazu kakiyarishi	You, my darling, are so dear
Hito zo koishiki.	To begin by stroking it aside.

(*Izumi Shikibu Shū* [= *ISS*], 1:86)

Ruri no ji to	My beloved will think
Hito mo mitsu beshi	It a field of lapis lazuli:
Waga toko wa	He will find our bed
Namida no tama to	Sparkling with line on line
Shiki ni shikereba.	Of jeweled teardrops.

(*ISS*, 1:288)

Composed after my lover had abandoned me. I went on pilgrimage to Kibune Shrine and there saw fireflies by the sacred river.

Mono omoeba	Distressed in thought,
Sawa no hotaru mo	I take the marsh fireflies
Waga mi yori	To be my soul,
Akugareizuru	Somehow departed from my body
Tama ka to zo miru.	And flickering off in darkness.

(*ISS*, Royal Autograph manuscript:1674)

Written to someone while I was ill.

Arazaran	Soon to be no more!
Kono yo no hoka no	As a memory of this world
Omoide ni	Taken to the next,
Ima hitotabi no	I long to have you come and love me
Au koto mo ga na.	If just once more and now.

(*ISS*, Matsui manuscript:1809)

Only the second poem, "Ruri no ji to," employs a conceit, and even that is so overwhelmed by rising passion that it does not affect the reader as technique. "Ruri no ji" is a reference to the Pure Land, which is said to be paved with jewels. It is a startling concept, this comparison of a bed, evoking memories of lovemaking, to the Buddha's Pure Land. Other of her waka seem to foreshadow Saigyō's (1118-90).

Winter

Sabishisa ni	In this loneliness,
Keburi o dani mo	I feel that the smoke at least
Tataji tote	Must show some life,
Shiba orikuburu	And so I feed brushwood to the fire
Fuyu no yamazato.	In my wintry mountain village.

(*ISS*, Royal Autograph
manuscript:1571)

Others are poised and varicolored:

A screen waka for the Supernumerary Middle Counselor.
Many guests are assembled at a house where cherries
are in bloom.

Haru goto ni	Having heard the news
Hana no sakari o	That spring after spring the cherries
Oto ni kiku	Blossom better here,
Hito no kiite wa	Everyone who comes to visit
Nagaisenu nashi.	Without exception lingers on.

(*ISS*, 3:852)

Izumi Shikibu's poetry has realized Yoshitada's aims on a still higher level. Akazome Emon (fl. 976-1041), by contrast, was a woman capable of writing poetry according to Kintō's orientation, and on his level. Izumi Shikibu was known by her contemporaries for her poetic abilities, but at the time Akazome Emon was apparently considered the better poet of the two (*MSN*, 495-96). Few of her compositions, however, would greatly move the reader today.

I went to a mountain temple celebrated for its cherry blossoms
and arrived, thinking to see them in full bloom,
only to find they had already fallen. That night,
as the moon shone bright, I composed this poem.

Hana no iro wa	The tinted blossoms

Chiru o mide dani	Fell before I had the chance
Chirinikeri	To see them fall—
Nagusame ni min	My consolation will be to watch
Haru no yo no tsuki.	The moon on this spring night.

(*Akazome Emon Shū*, 20)

Judged by Kintō's criteria, her waka are expressed with the right proportions of plainness and wit. They, and not Izumi Shikibu's poems, were
therefore considered the masterworks of their day.

CHAPTER 8

Prose in Japanese

KINDS OF JAPANESE PROSE COMPOSITION

Japanese vernacular prose compositions (wabun) are prose in the broad sense of the term. They are written chiefly in pure Japanese language, with very few Chinese loanwords or colloquial expressions.[1] I am obliged to use and define this term because those conventionally employed—monogatari, nikki, and shū—are deceptively convenient, not lending themselves to systematic consideration. I shall begin by ordering these concepts and shall then proceed to examine actual facts and phenomena.

Monogatari, Nikki, and Shū

No one would question the assertion that the *Genji Monogatari (The Tale of Genji)*, *Tosa Nikki (The Tosa Diary)*, and the *Kokinshū* provide normative examples of a monogatari, a nikki, and a shū.[2] On the other hand, it is rather doubtful whether these terms accurately denote early medieval genres of prose. Depending on the variant title, certain prose compositions are called either a monogatari or a nikki, and others are called a monogatari, a nikki, or a shū. This may reflect the inability of these terms to express fully the true form of a genre. The following are some of the works with variant titles:

Ise Monogatari (Tales of Ise): Zaigo ga Monogatari (Tales of Zaigo:

---

[1] [The author's title for this long chapter is "Wabun no Hyōgen." "Wabun" designates writing mostly in the kana syllabary, particularly in hiragana, and more or less free of Chinese loanwords and Sinified Japanese. Wabun is, therefore, a kind of prose closer to waka than to that combination of the native and the Sinified that is termed wakan konkōbun, which is the basis of modern spoken and written Japanese. Wabun also implies an authorship and/or readership inclusive of, or dominated by, women. Such being the complexities, it will be referred to henceforth in the text as wabun or prose in Japanese.—Ed.]

[2] [The *Kokinshū* or, properly, the *Kokinwakashū*, was the first royally ordered poetic collection of Japanese poetry, chokusenwakashū, although it had been preceded by royally ordered collections of Chinese poetry (chokusenshishū), which were in turn preceded by the *Man'yōshū* (discussed in Volume One). From the title of the first waka collection is derived an attributive or abbreviated expression, "Kokin," used to characterize the styles or nature of poems in the collection, the age it dominated in poetry, and so forth. We shall use the Japanese names for these collections rather than *A Collection of Japanese Poetry Past and Present* for *Kokinwakashū* and drop the "waka," as is the common usage. But what is meant by "shū," "nikki," or "monogatari" in the author's radically new argument will have to emerge from his discussion.—Ed.]

"*Zaigo*" is an abbreviation for the name Ariwara Narihira), *Zaigo Chūjō no Nikki (The Diary of Zaigo Chūjō* = Captain Ariwara Narihira), *Zai Chūjō (The Ariwara Captain)*.

Heichū Monogatari (Stories of Heichū: "Heichū" is an abbreviation for the name Taira Sadafum'): *Heichū Nikki (The Nikki of . . .)*.

Tannomine Shōshō Monogatari (The Lieutenant of Tannomine): Takamitsu Shōshō Nikki (The Nikki of Lieutenant [Fujiwara] Takamitsu), Takamitsu Nikki.

Izumi Shikibu Monogatari: Izumi Shikibu Nikki, Izumi Shikibu Shū.

Takamura Monogatari: Takamura Nikki, Ono no Takamura Shū.

We would do best to set aside questions of which titles are original and which were given later and consider instead what light the fact of multiple titles sheds on the significance of the terms monogatari, nikki, and shū. Not one of the above titles was indisputably given by the author of the work; most of the compositions, if not all, were originally untitled. If the original manuscript had borne a title, variants would not likely have arisen. The variant titles listed above must therefore demonstrate how these texts were received by later audiences and transmitters.

The *Mumyō Sōshi [= MMSS] (An Untitled Book)*, written at the beginning of the thirteenth century, gives us an idea of how an early medieval audience perceived the monogatari genre. In it, monogatari are divided into "falsehoods and fabrications" and "real events."[3] The former category contains twenty-nine works (nineteen of which are nonextant), including *The Bamboo Cutter*; the latter has only the *Tales of Ise* and the *Yamato Monogatari (Tales of Yamato)*. These last two were probably considered to be monogatari because they are written in the narrative mode: a narrator's recital enables events to unfold in chronological order. But if this is the reason, why does the *Kagerō Nikki (The Gossamer Years)*, a work told in the narrative mode, have no variant title involving the term monogatari? Perhaps because *The Gossamer Years* begins by stating that many old monogatari currently available are concerned with fabrications, and that, by writing about herself instead, the narrator hopes to give freshness to her work. The subject of a nikki, then, is a kind of "real event," the life and experiences of a historical individual; in this respect nikki narrative differs from waka narrative (utamonogatari). The difference between the monogatari and the nikki is not so much one of fiction versus nonfiction; rather, the criterion is whether the narration is concerned with a single protagonist.

---

[3] "In that case, these [fictional monogatari] are fabrications and falsehoods [itsuwari soragoto]. Pray speak instead of matters that really occurred. I understand that the *Tales of Yamato* and the *Tales of Ise* treat of real events [aru koto], a wonderful thing indeed!" (MMSS, 99).

This would explain why the *Tales of Ise* was also known as *The Nikki of Captain Ariwara Narihira*,[4] whereas the *Tales of Yamato* has no alternate designation as a nikki. The protagonist of the *Ise*, known simply as "otoko" (a man), is reminiscent of Narihira, and the story is apparently concerned with him as an individual. In the *Yamato*, on the other hand, various historical characters appear in a series of episodes, and there is no single protagonist whose life and experiences are depicted throughout the work. The protagonist of each episode in the *Heichū* is also called "a man," but the "man's" characteristics are so consistent throughout the work that the reader can conclude that it is in fact concerned with a single protagonist. The work would likely have been designated a nikki even if it had lacked its concluding episode, the only one in which the protagonist has his name: Heichū.

This indicates that the difference between the monogatari and the nikki is not equivalent to that between the third- and first-person points of view. The protagonists of the *Ise* and *Heichū*, "a man," are referred to in the third person, but that is no reason why the works cannot be alternatively designated nikki. Although medieval Japanese nikki are frequently categorized as diaries in English translation, the dissimilarity between "diary" and "nikki" in its medieval sense is made apparent by the third person point of view in works like the *Takamitsu Nikki* and the *Izumi Shikibu Nikki*.[5] The point of view in nikki is not always strictly maintained. A mixed point of view, using both first- and third-person narration, appears in *The Gossamer Years* and the *Sarashina Nikki*. The reason must be that the content of a nikki need not be the author's personal experiences. This is also true for the *Tosa Nikki* [usually translated as *The Tosa Diary*], a work told in the first person but whose narrator is not its author. Izumi Shikibu, the protagonist of the *Izumi Shikibu Nikki*, is assumed to be its author because the work is a nikki. Such an approach ignores the fact that a Japanese nikki is not a "diary."[6]

Why was the *Izumi Shikibu Nikki* also called the *Izumi Shikibu Shū*?[7]

---

[4] "The Ariwara Captain wrote a fine nikki about his love affairs" (*Sagoromo Monogatari* [= *SGM*]; *NKBT*, 79 [1965], 1:55).

[5] The late thirteenth-century *Genji Monogatari Kochū* (provisional title) begins a passage with the words, "It says in the *Takamitsu Nikki*. . . ." The quotation that follows concurs with the extant text of *Tannomine Shōshō Monogatari*. Thus the title *Takamitsu Nikki* probably antedates the thirteenth century (Yoshida, 1964, 764-65). The Umezawa manuscript of the *Kohon Setsuwa Shū* has a quotation from the *Izumi Shikibu Nikki* noting that it is "written in the nikki" (*Kohon Setsuwa Shū*, 1:98-100). The title *Izumi Shikibu Nikki* therefore probably antedates the mid-twelfth century (Yoshida, 1964, 718).

[6] [The author uses the English word, "diary," to stress the degree of difference. He has in mind the differences in person, the absence of daily entries, and so forth, typical of so much nikki literature but different from natural prose diaries.—Ed.]

[7] The *Genji Monogatari Shō*, copied in 1299 (Makita Seinosuke coll.), quotes waka not found outside the *Izumi Shikibu Nikki* and gives the attribution as "It says in the *Izumi Shikibu Shū* . . ." (Yoshida, 1964, 721).

This question may be approached by examining other works that are called shū. The *Collected Waka of Lady Ise (Ise Shū)* was probably known as *Ise ga Ie no Shū (Lady Ise's Personal Waka Collection)* after the mid-tenth century. This is clearly a poetry collection. Its first fifty-one waka, however, have fairly long prose forenotes, and each poem is part of a chronological progression. If read as an independent unit, then, this section would be identical in substance and form to a waka narrative. In terms of unified progression, the *Collected Waka of Lady Ise* has, moreover, a more compact structure than the *Tales of Ise*. Some of its forenotes have a third-person, omniscient point of view (*Ise Shū*, 1, forenote):

> During the reign of Uda Tennō, a woman with parents in Yamato served in the chambers of a lady called Ōmiyasudokoro.[8] The woman had become a lady-in-waiting at her father's wish, since he loved her too much to permit her to marry a man of middling rank. Ōmiyasu-dokoro's younger brother paid ardent court to the woman and they became lovers, I know not how.[9] The woman was concerned that her father would disapprove, but he responded to the news by saying, "It must have been unavoidable. Remember, though, young men are not to be relied upon!" A few years later, her lover married a general's daughter. "Just as I had expected," thought the father on hearing this. The woman was mortified. Her former lover called on her, having come all the way from his father's house in Gojō, and tied a note to a hedge branch that had turned scarlet. The note read . . .

This style is commonly employed in both monogatari and nikki.

Another example is provided by the *Collected Waka of the Ichijō Regent*, Fujiwara Koremasa's (924-72) personal waka collection. It begins:

> Kurahashi Toyokage, recorder at the Treasury Ministry, was an insignificant minor official who, in his youth, wrote a great many love letters, and later collected accounts of the circumstances into this book. Any number of things would strike him as interesting during a romance, but he tended to forget them when pressed by official business, and later investigation would yield only trifling poems and notes. One of the women of whom he was enamored, although of the same class as he, refused to answer his letters for months. Determined to have the upper hand, Toyokage sent her this poem.

Aware to mo	She whom one would think
Iu beki hito wa	Would respond encouragingly
Omōede	Cares not at all,

---

[8] The "woman with parents in Yamato" is an indirect reference to Ise herself.
[9] The "younger brother" is an indirect reference to Fujiwara Nakahira (875-945).

Mi no itazura ni   And what have I not endured
Narinu beki kana.   As my body wastes away!

The lady finally replied, but only the one time.

Nanigoto mo   What made you hold
Omoishirazu wa   Yourself obliged to think or do
   Aru beki o   Anything about me—
Mata wa aware to   Or why should you assume
Tare ka iu beki.   I must write you that I care?

                                (*Ichijō Sesshō Gyoshū*, 1-2)

Koremasa himself compiled the text from its opening passage through the forty-first waka. No one but Koremasa—the scion of a powerful family and a man who was to attain the supreme positions of Regent and Chancelor—could have assumed the persona of the recorder Kurahashi Toyokage.[10] The *Ōkagami (The Great Mirror)* confirms Koremasa's authorship.[11] Adopting a persona is a technique that also appears in the *Tosa Nikki*, and so this style might be called characteristic of the nikki as a kind of prose literature in Japanese. Similarly, its narrative method, in which the narrator transmits recollections of events in the work by using the verbal inflection "-keri," is a characteristic of the monogatari.[12] The *Collected Waka of Hon'in Jijū* and the *Collected Waka of Priest Zōki* are other examples of shū containing elements of both the monogatari and nikki.[13]

Thus it becomes clear why the *Izumi Shikibu Nikki* is also called the *Izumi Shikibu Shū*. When a waka-prose complex, possessing certain characteristics of the monogatari or nikki, is incorporated into a waka collection, the end result is a shū. On the other hand, a desire to perceive such waka-prose complexes as no different from other sections possessing a format common to waka collections led to a view that waka sequences ac-

---

[10] A recorder in the Treasury Ministry held lower rank than the four top officeholders—the minister, vice-minister, secretary, and clerk—but it was not an especially low rank. Its modern equivalent might be an assistant section head.

[11] "This Minister was called the Ichijō Regent. He was the eldest son of Lord Kujō [Fujiwara Morosuke, 908-60], and compiled an excellent collection of his own poetry, written in the persona of Toyokage" (*OK*, 3:132).

[12] [The -keri form, with certain other inflections, indicates perfect aspect: cf. English perfect "tense." Aspect designates the degree of completion implied by the so inflected verb. The use of the perfective in monogatari roughly parallels the historical past narrative tense in English.—Ed.]

[13] The *Hon'in Jijū Shū*, *SKST*, 1:88; see also *Katsura no Miyabon Sōsho*, 9:39-46. The *Zōki Hōshi Shū*, *SKST*, 1:87. Its variant title is *Ionushi*; it was probably written between 1009 and 1011 (Abe Toshiko, 1969, 1168).

companied by prose in the monogatari or nikki style were in themselves a kind of shū. This was the basis on which works like the *Izumi Shikibu Nikki* and *Takamura Monogatari* were called the *Izumi Shikibu Shū* and the *Ono no Takamura Shū*.[14] The *Takamura Monogatari* has thirty-three waka, but its considerably longer prose sections suggest that it would be unreasonable to call it a shū. The work had been read, however, as a waka sequence accompanied by prose in the monogatari or nikki style, and it was therefore a recognized shū. This reasoning would always apply unless a waka sequence was too brief. The title *Ono no Takamura Shū* may antedate the thirteenth century, if we consider it in light of the probable century in which the title *Izumi Shikibu Shū* originated.

The significance of the terms monogatari, nikki, and shū may, then, be grasped as follows. The medieval audience did not base its use of these terms on accurate definitions; rather, each individual used his own judgment in calling a work a monogatari, a nikki, or a shū. Our modern minds might devise any number of definitions, but there is bound to be some composition that will not conform to them. If, however, the medieval audience's known and generally accepted criteria for differentiating categories were put in the form of definitions, the result might be:

1. *Monogatari.* A prose composition, written in the past tense, that is concerned with events involving either fictional or historical characters.

2. *Nikki.* A prose composition, written in the present tense, that is concerned with the life of a historical person.

3. *Shū.* A complex made up of prose in the monogatari or nikki style and a waka sequence.

The monogatari definition recognizes both fictional and historical characters, in consideration of the *Untitled Book* distinction between "fabrications" (fiction) and "real events" (nonfiction) in monogatari. The latter subcategory includes *A Tale of Flowering Fortunes (Eiga Monogatari)* and *The Great Mirror.* "Truth" and "fiction" are matters of narrative stance that do not correspond to the historical reality of the content. In the *Takamura Monogatari*, Ono no Takamura courts and marries the daughter of the Minister of the Right; on the first evening of their marriage he arrives dressed in tattered clothing to present his bride with some musty old Chinese books.[15] There is no evidence to support this as truth, and many contemporary readers probably concluded it was not. What matters

[14] The manuscript titled *Ono no Takamura Shū* is in the collection of the Royal Household Library. *Katsura no Miyabon Sōsho*, 2:37-49.

[15] *Takamura Monogatari*, 35. [In view of the author's preceding distinctions, his considered ideas—expressed by letter—should be made clear: Japanese verbs do not have tense; but "adverbs" ("mukashi"—the word consistently beginning episodes in the *Ise Monogatari*) or phrases ("Izure no ōntoki ni ka"—"In what reign was it?"—opening the *Genji Monogatari*) functioned to set the action in the past for a monogatari as distinct from the "present tense" of nikki. For further details, see n. 49, below.—Ed.]

is not the truthfulness of an event: if the narrator takes the stance that the events to be told are true, the audience must accept the monogatari as true. Tense is never mentioned in medieval sources, but it clearly has a bearing on prose works. The keynote of the monogatari is the past tense, exemplified by the verb suffix "-keri," with its connotations of transmitted recollection. Narration in the present tense is the governing principle of the nikki, although it is not an absolute condition. The *Ise Monogatari, Heichū Monogatari*, and *Takamura Monogatari* are all narrated in a mode of transmitted recollection, but variant titles label them as nikki.

Since early medieval criteria for distinguishing among monogatari, nikki, and shū were hardly stringent, it was natural that various titles for the same work would evolve in accordance with the way these criteria were applied. For certain kinds of monogatari, nikki, and shū, it is better to recognize differences of degree rather than to differentiate among them. The Japanese academic world currently divides vernacular prose (wabun) into three major categories—the monogatari, the nikki, and the zuihitsu (miscellany)—and further subdivides the monogatari into waka narrative (utamonogatari), fiction, and history. This classification system does not always facilitate a proper understanding of vernacular prose works, however, and at times it can only make us lose sight of their original character. Because the authors were aware of only vague or inconsistent criteria for the defining of genres, their works naturally have certain features that cannot be fitted into the generic mold. The correct approach, for such unclassifiable compositions, may be to try to understand them in the context of what makes them unclassifiable.

Assigning the *Izumi Shikibu Nikki* exclusively to the nikki genre because of its title makes it easy to overlook its most important property, the fact that it is a monogatari as well as a nikki. Those who consider *The Gossamer Years (Kagerō Nikki)* to be a diary, and attempt to differentiate it from the fictional *Tale of Genji*, are probably unable to understand why these two novelistic works can be subjected to some of the analysis applied to the modern novel [i.e., shōsetsu]. Furthermore, one risks considerable misunderstanding in applying the miscellany (zuihitsu) concept, nonexistent in Sei Shōnagon's day, to *The Pillow Book (Makura no Sōshi)*.[16]

---

[16] The zuihitsu genre was established in Sung China (as "sui-pi," following the brush). The first instance of the expression occurs in a work by Hung Mai (1123-1202): "I have followed the flow of my thoughts in writing. There may be some chronological mix-ups, but I have not reordered them. Thus I have called this book *Following My Brush*" (*Jung-chai Sui-pi*, 1:1). ["Zuihitsu" (meaning giving way to the lead of one's writing brush) is an untranslatable term, not so much because there are not Western counterparts as because it has such different meanings in various Japanese usages. The usual narrow current sense refers to three works: Sei Shōnagon's *Makura no Sōshi (The Pillow Book)*, Kamo no Chōmei's *Hōjōki (An Account of My Hut)*, and Yoshida Kenkō's *Tsurezuregusa (Essays in Idleness)*. But a glance at one of the standard zuihitsu compilations (jiten) will reveal hundreds and hundreds of ti-

The nature of this extraordinary work is greatly clarified if it is thought of as a nikki, in the tenth- and eleventh-century sense.

As this evidence shows, the other views summarized above, and maintained by modern Japanese scholarship, are not very useful in discussing vernacular prose written in the Early Middle Ages. My divisions are essentially the result of an attempt to organize, as relevantly as possible for modern application, genres defined by criteria that were not always clear or rational in the tenth and eleventh centuries. It is surely difficult to consent to a concept of shū as a term affixed to originally anomalous monogatari and nikki, out of a conviction that all waka-prose complexes were shū. A work in the form of a dominant waka sequence with incidental, explanatory prose might easily be regarded as a shū, but then it would not be correct to use the term "shū" in variant titles of the *Izumi Shikibu Nikki* and the *Takamura Monogatari*, where prose narration predominates.

Here it may be best to divide early medieval Japanese prose into two major categories, monogatari and nikki. Their status as narratives may be either fictional or factual, and the status is determined by the narrator's attitude or gestures. The actual truthfulness of the content pertains to a separate function.[17] Vernacular prose compositions may be subdivided into four categories: fictional monogatari, factual monogatari, fictional nikki, and factual nikki. Whether monogatari or nikki, fictional works have a single protagonist, with other characters appearing in the shadow of the protagonist. Such a character will be called a unified protagonist. In factual compositions like the *Yamato Monogatari*, the protagonist may change with each episode. Characters in such works will be called diverse protagonists. The *Yamato Monogatari* belongs to the same genre as the *Ise Monogatari* and the *Heichū Monogatari*, but its diverse-protagonist structure accounts for its not being designated a nikki in a variant title. Superior beings, ordinary beings, fantastic events, and ordinary events will be discussed in the following sections. A character whose virtue, knowledge, talents, and appearance are unattainable in reality is a "superior being," and phenomena that do not appear in the real world are called "fantastic events." Their respective opposites are signified by "ordinary beings" and "ordinary events." A waka-prose complex is a structure in which waka and prose occupy, in principle, equal proportions of a work. This is basic to the shū, but at times it also appears in monogatari and nikki. (See the accompanying diagram.)

---

tles, mostly nonliterary. In that wider sense, the word approaches in meaning the Chinese concept of a compendium of more or less classified facts.—Ed.]

[17] They do not therefore correspond to modern concepts of fiction and nonfiction. For example, the content of the *Tosa Nikki* is probably true, but creating the persona of a female narrator is a technique used in fiction. This nikki, then, is basically fictional.

CHARACTERISTICS OF EARLY MEDIEVAL NARRATIVE

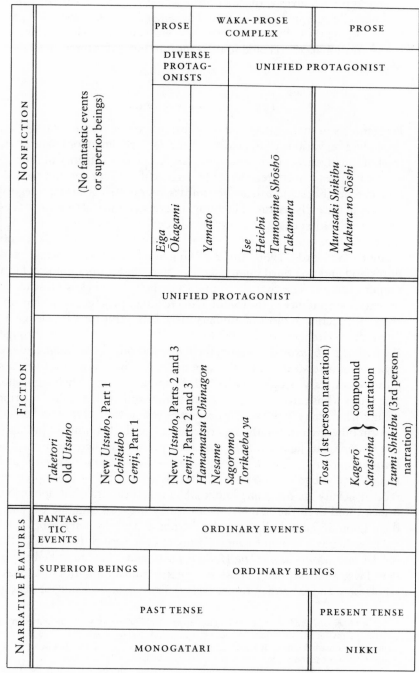

NONFICTION

PROSE | WAKA-PROSE COMPLEX | PROSE

DIVERSE PROTAG-ONISTS | UNIFIED PROTAGONIST

(No fantastic events or superior beings)

Eiga
Ōkagami

Yamato

Ise
Heichū
Tannomine Shōshō
Takamura

Murasaki Shikibu
Makura no Sōshi

FICTION

UNIFIED PROTAGONIST

Taketori
Old *Utsubo*

New *Utsubo*, Part 1
Ochikubo
Genji, Part 1

New *Utsubo*, Parts 2 and 3
Genji, Parts 2 and 3
Hamamatsu Chūnagon
Nesame
Sagoromo
Torikaeba ya

Tosa (1st person narration)

Kagerō
Sarashina } compound narration

Izumi Shikibu (3rd person narration)

NARRATIVE FEATURES

FANTAS-TIC EVENTS | ORDINARY EVENTS

SUPERIOR BEINGS | ORDINARY BEINGS

PAST TENSE | PRESENT TENSE

MONOGATARI | NIKKI

This approach gives vernacular prose genres a more logical order than the generally accepted view. It should be remembered, however, that genres, in the tenth and eleventh centuries, were understood according to vague, irrational criteria, and so there must be inevitable limits to a typology.

The Variety of Protagonists

Protagonists in monogatari and nikki belong to one of three categories, depending on various characteristic elements, including moral character, level of intelligence, talent, and appearance. The first category of protagonist surpasses a norm recognized by an actual, average society; the second matches that standard; and the third is inferior to it. The first category appears in the early narrative literature of every country. *The Epic of Gilgamesh*, the oldest extant narrative work, depicts its protagonist as handsome, brave, as big and strong as a wild bull, and unrivaled in his skill with weapons (Sandards, 1960, 18-19).[18] Gilgamesh is a special being, two-thirds god and one-third human, and so he probably does not provide a proper example. The character of Gilgamesh is nevertheless evidence of the extreme antiquity of the tradition of creating a protagonist with properties far superior to those of ordinary men. This is true for all ancient narrative, from Homer's *Iliad* and *Odyssey* and the Greek tragedies, through *Beowulf, Le Chanson de Roland,* the *Niebelungenlied,* the *Edda,* and the sagas. Characters, including the superhuman, whose attributes surpass those of ordinary people will be called superior beings. Their opposite, characters whose attributes are inferior to the norm, will be called inferior beings. Characters with average properties will be called ordinary beings.

As in other literatures, the superior being was the first kind of protagonist to appear in Japanese narrative. Kaguyahime, the heroine of the *Taketori Monogatari (The Bamboo Cutter)*—known as the "ancestor and first to appear of all monogatari" (*GM*, "Eawase," 179)—is a supremely radiant beauty, as her name implies. She is so beautiful that noblemen, princes, and even the tennō want to marry her. Kaguyahime's beauty, then, is on an entirely different level from that of ordinary people and qualifies her as a superior being. Toshikage, the hero of Part One of the old *Utsuho Monogatari (The Hollow Tree),* and Nakatada, the hero of Part Two, are described as possessing extraordinary abilities in Chinese scholarship and the zither, respectively.[19] These examples suggest that, in

---

[18] The *Gilgamesh* is a Sumerian work of unknown date. Fragments were transmitted in the Assyrian, Babylonian, Sumerian, Akkad, Hittite, and Hurri languages, and a rough reconstruction was made by piecing together these fragments. See the introduction in Sandards, 1960, 7-58, a prose translation aimed at a general audience.

[19] The sections of the "Toshikage" chapter of the *Utsuho Monogatari* that tell of Toshi-

Japanese narrative, superior beings surpass ordinary men in appearance and accomplishment, not in bravery or resourcefulness. Like Odysseus, Toshikage is shipwrecked on foreign shores and threatened with death by creatures that are half god and half beast. Toshikage, however, escapes danger not through the extraordinary ingenuity and wit of an Odysseus but instead through rescue by the Buddha. His talents as a composer of Chinese prose and poetry are of little use in confronting danger.

These prove to be reasonable features when they are considered in the context of the Early Middle Ages, the age of fūryū. The inhabitants of the fūryū world had virtually no need of certain superior traits. Having the unrivaled strength to capture and kill an enemy, or the ability to devise clever stratagems to annihilate a great army, held no attraction for them. Rather, the hero of a vernacular prose work ideally possessed superior traits appropriate to a world of poetry, music, and elegant correspondence with ladies. Nakatada, who appears in the extant old *Hollow Tree*, is also the protagonist of Part One of the new *Hollow Tree*, but despite their sharing the same identity, the latter Nakatada's personality is so different as to belong to another character.[20] Whereas Nakatada is merely a talented young zither player in the old *Hollow Tree*, the Nakatada of Part One of the new *Hollow Tree*, a continuation of the more ancient version, is superior in appearance, actions, and waka composition, as well as in music. Of all the characters in the monogatari, only Minamoto Suzushi can rival him. Yet Nakatada's superiority is not that of a fantastic superman far removed from the ordinary world; it descends, rather, to the level of an idealized image within the bounds of reality. Atemiya, the heroine of *The Hollow Tree*, displays equally superior qualities. She resembles Kaguyahime, in *The Bamboo Cutter*, in her role of an ideal beauty whose hand is desperately sought by many suitors. Atemiya's superiority, however, is closer to the human scale than Kaguyahime's. There is a difference, then, between the fantastic and the idealized when considering a character's superior nature.

The Lieutenant Michiyori, hero of the *Ochikubo Monogatari (The*

---

kage's shipwreck on strange shores (3/1/1-11/33/10) and Nakatada's instruction in the art of the zither (17/60/2-21/75/10) were written at much the same time as the *Taketori Monogatari*. I call these sections the old *Utsuho*. The extant *Utsuho* originally had "Fujiwara no Kimi" as its first chapter. At some point in the composition of the extant *Utsuho*, the plot was changed to make the old *Utsuho* character Nakatada into the protagonist; a new opening chapter, "Toshikage," was therefore added. The old *Utsuho* sections seem to have been incorporated virtually unrevised, and their style contrasts sharply with that of surrounding passages. The extant *Utsuho*, minus the old *Utsuho* sections, is here called the new *Utsuho* (Konishi, 1954b-55a; 1960).

[20] Part One of the new *Utsuho* contains the first twelve chapters, from "Toshikage" through "Okitsu Shiranami"; Part Two, the six chapters from "Kurabiraki, Pt. 1" through "Kuniyuzuri, Pt. 2"; and Part Three, the two "Rō no Ue" chapters. Each part displays marked differences in theme, structure, and style.

Story of Ochikubo)—probably a late tenth-century work—displays an idealized superiority operating within the context of the real world. His superiority is manifested in practical talents: he efficiently disposes of countless difficulties, successfully carries out a well-planned revenge, and achieves social advancement. Such superiority is not far removed from the ordinary standard. By contrast, Part One of *The Tale of Genji*, a somewhat later work, depicts far more idealized characters in its Genji and Murasaki.[21] Besides being handsome, Genji excels in everything—music, dance, waka composition, and social grace. He is fūryū personified, or, even more appropriately, something of a superman. Likewise, Murasaki is depicted as an ideal woman whom no other female character can rival. Part One of the *Genji* is faithful to the monogatari tradition in its idealization of protagonists and, in this respect alone, is written in an older style than Part One of the new *Hollow Tree* or the *Ochikubo*.

The personalities of the protagonists change dramatically in Part Two of the new *Hollow Tree*. Nakatada is no longer a superior being. He becomes very much a typical nobleman, both at home and at work in the government bureaucracy; his decisions, words, and actions inevitably elicit understanding and sympathy from a normal social perspective. Genji in Part Two of *The Tale of Genji*, and Kaoru, in Part Three, also think, feel, and act on the level of ordinary people. Genji does not of course lose the superior qualities he displays in Part One: these attributes remain and are even further refined, although it is not they but Genji's human experiences—suffering, anger, grief—that are described in Part Two. Kaoru has only one attribute appropriate to the hero of a fictional monogatari, the mysterious charisma of being born with a natural fragrance; his troubles, sorrows, and wishes do not differ from those of any normal person. The *Sagoromo Monogatari* (*The Story of Sagoromo*) and *Yowa no Nezame* (*The Tale of Nezame*) carry on the tradition of creating worlds populated by ordinary beings.

The presence of compositions with normal people as protagonists is very significant and will be discussed below. Such works, it might be noted, coexist with others that depict protagonists whose standard is beneath that of an ordinary being. A rare example is found in the *Stories of Heichū*, which has a special place in the seldom humorous corpus of Japanese literature. Nothing is known of the character of the historical personage Heichū (Taira Sadafum'), but the Heichū who appears in oral setsuwa as well as in the monogatari is always depicted as a man who does

---

[21] I follow the general view [expounded by Ikeda Kikan] that the *Genji Monogatari* is made up of three parts: Part One, the first thirty-three chapters from "Kiritsubo" through "Fuji no Uraba"; Part Two, the eight chapters from "Wakana, Pt. 1" through "Maboroshi"; and Part Three, the last thirteen chapters, from "Niou Miya" through "Yume no Ukihashi."

not quite measure up and whose actions always end in failure.[22] Heichū in the monogatari is neither foolish nor whimsical but is a sincere, ordinary man doomed to failure.

One episode will serve as a representative example. Heichū has his first rendezvous with a lady. The next evening, as he is about to set off for her house, his government superior puts Heichū in a nice fix by ordering him to go along on an unexpected business trip. Once Heichū returns, he is immediately requested to join the entourage accompanying the retired sovereign Uda on an excursion to the Ōi River. After a few days of drinking with the courtiers, he attempts to get back to his ladylove, only to find that the consort's residence where she serves as lady-in-waiting lies in an unlucky direction.[23] All he can do is send her a letter; but when he opens her reply, he finds only some locks of hair (*Heichū Monogatari*, dan 38:103-105). Having waited in vain for Heichū, the lady eventually assumes she has been thrown over and becomes a nun. Heichū is never blamed for this process. He is the hapless victim of uncontrollable circumstance, and he can do nothing to extricate himself. His misfortunes do not result from incompetency. On the contrary, Heichū tries to get himself out of his quandary: even at the Ōi River, when he is "so inebriated that for two or three days he had no knowledge of his own actions," he is always concerned with reaching his lady. He is reluctant to write her a surreptitious letter in case he might be found out and suffer ridicule from his drunken companions. The image of Heichū—worrying about making the right impression on his superiors and colleagues yet agonizing about his lover, and all the while hopelessly drunk—has many copies in modern Japan.

Neither foolish nor whimsical, Heichū simply has bad luck. Luck is actually a matter of one's abilities, however, and someone who always suffers bad luck and failure must do so because he is inferior to normal people. In this sense, Heichū is an inferior being who is very nearly an ordinary person. More obvious instances of inferior beings appear in the new *Hollow Tree*. None is a protagonist, but there are three such second-

---

[22] One Heichū story current in the mid-tenth century tells how he tries to deceive a lady into thinking he is weeping by wetting his eyelids with water from an inkstone. Heichū does not realize that the "water" is really ink and that he has blackened his face (GM, "Suetsumuhana," 268; "Wakana Jō," 5:261). [If the *Genji Monogatari* is the early exception among court monogatari for its witty, comic passages, the *Tsutsumi (Gon) Chūnagon Monogatari* is a later one. Its ten shortish stories (none of which pertains to a Tsutsumi [Acting] Middle Counselor) are witty or comic tales by a group of sophisticated people at court who may have been caricaturing contemporaries or parodying earlier writings.—Ed.]

[23] If one's destination happened to lie in the path of a directional deity called Ommyōdō on a certain day, it was thought dangerous to proceed in that direction. This was a katafutagari (unlucky direction). In such cases one spent the night in a locale lying in another direction so that one's destination the next day would lie in a lucky direction (Frank, 1958; 40-110).

ary characters: the "three eccentrics," Prince Kanzuke, Miharu Takamoto, and Shigeno Masuge.[24] They are not fools either. One, Takamoto,
is adept in practical government affairs, enjoys the trust of his sovereign,
and rises to ministerial rank (*UM*, "Fujiwara no Kimi," 43/161). This
powerful man is the butt of humor in the new *Hollow Tree* because he is
a miser. When he is stricken by a grave illness, his wife wishes to have
prayers recited for his recovery, but he forbids her to do such an unnecessary thing. He then gives his reasons.

> What a waste of money! Don't do anything for me that might in-
> volve the slightest expense. If you carry out a purification, you will
> need rice to scatter. But if you were to keep the unhulled purification
> rice and sow it instead, you would have a fine crop of rice. You would
> need five kinds of grains for an exorcism, and earth to construct an
> altar. Many plants will grow in three square inches of earth. Take the
> chinaberry: a single branch yields much fruit. It makes a fine dessert.
> Oil can be pressed from sesame seeds, and when sold brings in much
> money. Sake lees are good in making bean paste. Millet, barley, peas,
> and cowpeas are similarly useful. (*UM*, 44/165-66)

The sickness is frightened away by this speech, and Takamoto recovers.
His discussion, incidentally, is so intelligent that, if he were alive in Japan
today, he would be pressed into serving both as Agriculture Minister and
Budget Director. He was an object of laughter to contemporary readers
because they required that ordinary beings also belong to the fūryū world.
Characters who did not meet the criteria of fūryū could only be treated as
obviously inferior, less awesome beings.

For the three degrees of awesomeness of protagonists, the corresponding phenomena forming the subject matter of vernacular prose works are
fantastic events, ordinary events, and comic events. Archaic narrative in
all countries is concerned with nonrealistic phenomena and events, and
has a superior being as protagonist. In all cases the subject is fantastic
events far removed from the human world. In subsequent times, the fantastic events described tend to be special occurrences taking place in the
world of men, and at this stage the protagonist is no longer a wondrous
superman but an idealized image functioning within reality. In possessing
substandard characteristics, an inferior character is hardly likely to perform marvelous deeds far removed from reality. The subject matter corresponding to the inferior protagonist is thus limited to events in the ordinary world. If these happen to be special, they can be considered a kind
of fantastic event. Qualitatively speaking, however, an audience operating

---

[24] *Utsuho Monogatari [= UM]*, "Fujiwara no Kimi," 39/147/9-45/171/11, 47/180/3-50/
189/8, 51/195/10-52/198/7. "Matsuri no Tsukai," 108/422/9-110/431/1.

on the level of ordinary beings will think of an inferior being's actions as funny. He may behave very seriously, but since he is deficient in some respect, the more seriously he behaves, the more obvious and amusing his deficiency. These comic events are to be distinguished from fantastic events involving superior beings.

Narratives centering on fantastic events with superior beings as protagonists appear first in any country. They are followed by works in which ordinary protagonists encounter fantastic events. Although inferior beings appear relatively early in secondary or minor roles, they usually appear somewhat later as protagonists. Works centered on ordinary events and with ordinary protagonists are a much later development in any country's literature. This may be due to the extreme difficulty inherent in moving or interesting an audience by depicting a character such as might be found anywhere, especially as a protagonist encountering events such as are always encountered in daily life. Narratives bearing these qualities do not attain dominance in the West until the eighteenth-century novel. Such a work appeared in Japan in the late tenth century: *The Gossamer Years*. Of course it is hardly a work of realism, defined as I attempted to do earlier. It does, however, share some characteristics of Western realistic fiction: its subject is the everyday life of an average, ordinary person.

It should be observed that *The Gossamer Years* is concerned with noble life and not with a bourgeois, middle-class society such as that depicted in Western realistic fiction. There was no class equivalent to the bourgeois in tenth-century Japan. The audience for written works was made up entirely of the nobility, among whom the author of *The Gossamer Years* ranks herself in the middle echelon. The nikki begins:

> These times have passed, and there is one who has drifted uncertainly through them, scarcely knowing where she is. It is perhaps natural that such should be her fate. She is less handsome than most, and not remarkably gifted. Yet, as the days go by in monotonous succession, she has occasion to look at the old monogatari, and has found them masses of the rankest fabrication. Perhaps, she says to herself, even the story of her own dreary life, set down in a nikki, might be of interest; and it might also answer a question: has that life been one befitting a well-born lady? But they must all be recounted, events of long ago, events of but yesterday. She is by no means certain that she can bring them to order. (*Kagerō Nikki* [= *KN*], 1:9)[25]

The phrase, "hito ni mo aranu mi no ue" (one of lower rank than most), appears in the passage, as a contrast to "shina takaki" (a well-born lady). This situates the protagonist as a woman of middle rank. Peasants

[25] [The translation is taken, with minor changes, from Seidensticker, 1964, 33.—Trans.]

thought of the nobles as heavenly beings, but they themselves—the audience of *The Gossamer Years*—realized that a provincial governor's
daughter was of middling rank at best. In this sense the subject is middle-
class life; the author of *The Gossamer Years* shared perceptions common
to the writers of Western realistic novels.

One statement in the preface to *The Gossamer Years* is very important
indeed: the narrator, finding that the many "old monogatari" that are so
popular these days are nothing but "fabrication," decides to write of her
own experiences. As we have seen, excluding "fabrication" (soragoto)
means writing about "real events" (aru koto). This does not mean that the
author will give minute descriptions of her own experiences but that she
will write about matters considered to be natural, everyday events. The
term "nikki" leads us to think of *The Gossamer Years* as one of a kind
with the watakushishōsetsu [heavily autobiographical "I novels"] of the
Meiji and Taishō eras, yet the facts related in this nikki have never been
demonstrated to be true. If an analogy is drawn with the *Tosa Nikki, The
Gossamer Years* very likely contains a certain amount of fiction. Not that
it matters much whether the author really experienced the events related:
what is important is the ordinary nature of the subject. Marriage, the fret-
ting caused by a husband's infidelities, and a mother's sense that her sole
purpose in living is to rear her children—these commonplace matters are
the subject of *The Gossamer Years*. The author consciously omits not only
such matters as a girl born in the trunk of a bamboo, who returns to the
kingdom of the moon, or a talented young man saved by the Buddha from
death at the hands of supernatural creatures; she also rejects stories like
that of a young noble, involved in an illicit affair with his stepmother, who
becomes the victim of a plot and is forced to take holy orders, or that of
an unfortunate young lady who, with the help of her splendid lover, escapes countless dangers.

The orientation toward ordinary events is reflected in a style aimed at
making the characters in the work equally unremarkable. The protagonist
of *The Gossamer Years* describes herself as "less handsome than most,"
although the author's own looks were striking enough that she was called
"one of the three most beautiful women in Japan" (*Sompi Bummyaku
[An Anatomy of the Precious and the Base]*, 1:41). Her decision to have a
woman of ordinary looks for her heroine may have been intended to criticize the convention that protagonists are always superior beings, handsome men and beautiful women.

The idea of writing about an ordinary protagonist doing ordinary
things clearly originated with the author of *The Gossamer Years*. In the
preface the narrator states her intention to succeed in attempting a "new
contrivance" ("mezurashiki sama"), that of writing about her commonplace self. The *Tosa*, which predates *The Gossamer Years*, contains a daily

record of events in the style of a *diary* [written in English]. It is thus a different kind of work from *The Gossamer Years*, which is a nikki that could pass as a novel called *A Woman's Life*. The appearance, in the late tenth century, of *The Gossamer Years*—a work whose subject would be fitting for a realistic novel—is noteworthy in two senses. One is its external significance: it is rare in world literature for such an early work to share features with far later realistic novels. The second is internal: *The Gossamer Years* exerted considerable influence on later Japanese narrative.

The Sung period had barely begun in China in the late tenth century, and nothing characteristic of Sung literature had yet been written. A genre of narrative literature called ch'uan-ch'i had flourished earlier, during the Middle and Late T'ang periods.[26] The ch'uan-ch'i gradually took on the design of the Six Dynasties chih-kuai genre described in Volume One. The anecdotal, fantastic content of the chih-kuai, however, was narrated as fact, whereas the ch'uan-ch'i characteristically employed a few fictional techniques and added design to its structure so as to increase the interest of the story (Lu, 1924, 211). Occasionally ch'uan-ch'i, which were also typically concerned with the anecdotal and the fantastic, tell of ordinary events. One such is "The Story of Ying-ying," mentioned above. Its story is as follows.

A student named Chang lived during the Chen-yüan era (785-805). He makes a journey to P'u-chou and lodges at the house of the widow Ts'ui; he rescues her from certain difficulties. Chang meets and falls in love with the daughter of the house, Ying-ying, and, with the aid of Scarlet, the maid, arranges a rendezvous. He proposes marriage to Ying-ying, and the widow gives her approval; but Chang must immediately return to Ch'ang-an and stay there to study for the civil service examination. Ying-ying sends him affectionate letters that Chang shows to his friends. One, Yang Chü-yüan, composes a shih titled "My Lady Ts'ui"; Yüan Chen, writing from Honan, also sends Chang a long shih.[27] Chang's passion eventually cools for Ying-ying, and he marries another woman. Ying-ying also marries. About a year later, Chang comes to the Ts'ui's neighborhood on business. Introducing himself as Ying-ying's brother-in-law, he asks her husband if he might see her. He is permitted only to send her a poem. As Chang is about to leave town, Ying-ying sends her reply, suppressing her pathetic feelings. After that, all communication ceases (*TSCC*, 299-305).

"The Story of Ying-ying" was written by Yüan Chen. He creates an anonymous narrator and appears in the story himself as a character

[26] [The ch'uan-ch'i is described by C. T. Hsia as "tales of a romantic and supernatural cast"; *The Classic Chinese Novel* (New York and London: Columbia University Press, 1968), p. 131. Arthur Waley's translation of "Ying-ying Chuan," under the title "The Story of Ts'ui Ying-ying," appears in Birch, 1965, 290-99.—Trans.]

[27] Yang Chü-yüan's shih is quoted in ch. 5.

named Yüan Chen. Yang Chü-yüan passed his examination in 789 (Ceremony and Education division) and was slightly older than his friends Yüan and Po Chü-i. Not only do actual people appear in the story; the setting is also given. The widow, asked about Ying-ying's age, replies, "She was born in the Seventh Month of the year of the Rat [784] during his majesty's reign [Te-tsung, r. 780-805], and it is now the year of the Dragon [800], so she must be seventeen [Asian count]." This design is intended to give a sense of reality to the work, whose rough outlines were probably based on Yüan's own experiences.[28] The subject, moreover, concerns ordinary events, situations not uncommon in the world: a talented young man is overwhelmed by passion, but his ardor cools as he finds it necessary to advance his official career, and the girl becomes another's wife. In this respect "The Story of Ying-ying" has much in common with *The Gossamer Years*; the former might even be termed something of a *Gossamer Years* as written by a man. There are substantial differences, however, between the two works.

"The Story of Ying-ying" deals with ordinary events, but its treatment is far from ordinary. The love affair between Chang and Ying-ying is painted in the richest colors, if you will, and displays an unearthly beauty. Its unearthliness belongs to the world of the immortals, and Ying-ying is akin to the beauties who inhabit that world. Yüan Chen probably did not consciously wish to depict his heroine as resembling a female immortal; rather, it would have been conventional to follow the precedent set by "The Visit to the Immortals' Dwelling" and liken the lady in a love affair to a female immortal. The author may also have had "The Visit" in mind when he named his hero Chang. Chang composes a poem for Ying-ying called "On Meeting an Immortal." It is studded with the conventional language used to describe female immortals; hence Ying-ying is clearly treated as an immortal beauty.[29] In other words, the plot is based on ordinary events, but the tone is an extraordinary one that never appears in realistic novels. Neither the T'ang nor the Sung produced a narrative like *The Gossamer Years*, with ordinary beings for protagonists and ordinary subjects treated in a realistic tone throughout. Neither do such works exist in Korea. That is why *The Gossamer Years* is both old and new.

If, however, *The Gossamer Years* had been a single occurrence, special though it might be, it would not merit serious consideration. Yet it was followed in rapid succession by nikki that would qualify as novels by modern standards. Consider the *Sarashina Nikki*: it was written by the

---

[28] Ying-ying has been seen as modeled after a singing-girl (Liu K'ai-jung, 1947, 114). This view is not likely, however, since the basis for the conjecture is flimsy.

[29] The only women inhabiting the world of immortals are young beauties; there are no old women. Female immortals are called yü-nü. This word was typically used to express an earthly woman's beauty (Konishi, 1982b, 151).

niece of the *Gossamer* author, and its nature as literature bears the same relation to *The Gossamer Years* as niece does to aunt. The nature of nikki gradually changed, but novelistic nikki like the *Izumi Shikibu Nikki* and *Sanuki no Suke Nikki* continued to be written well into the High Middle Ages. *The Gossamer Years* is their prototype.

Its influence on monogatari is yet more important. Monogatari traditionally had superior beings for protagonists and fantastic events for their subject matter. Part One of *The Tale of Genji* provides clear evidence of this. In Parts Two and Three, however, matters change considerably. The young nobleman called the Radiant Genji is, in Part One, true to his sobriquet; he is an elegant superman, obviously superior in all respects. Genji suddenly becomes an ordinary being in Part Two, as was discussed above. This can only be explained from multiple perspectives and cannot be attributed to any one cause; and yet the existence of earlier works dealing with ordinary beings and events is an element that, at the very least, is not to be overlooked. Unlike modern Japanese, who are given to believe that the monogatari and the nikki are different genres, Heian writers and their audiences seem to have perceived the two categories simply as different narrative methods. Narratives that told of ordinary characters and events therefore elicited a rapid response from other authors.

Composition, Reception, and Transmission

The small size of the Japanese audience may account for the emergence of narratives about ordinary people and events, a kind of work rare so early in a narrative tradition. A writer who wishes to please a large, unspecific audience tends to compromise by using conventional methods and is reluctant to attempt anything radical. If, on the other hand, the audience is small, and its members are all known to an author, experiments might well succeed. The heroine of *The Gossamer Years*, for example, is called "a lady" and is spoken of in the third person, but she is in fact the author herself, known to us as The Mother of Fujiwara Michitsuna (Fujiwara Michitsuna no Haha). This fact would have been obvious to her audience, which initially consisted entirely of her intimate circle. The other characters in *The Gossamer Years* were therefore also easily identified. Audience interest in works that depict well-known people was also a factor in the popularity of watakushishōsetsu and "model" novels [those adapted from plays, and so forth, and depicting real persons] during the Meiji and Taishō eras. Narratives written for a small circle of intimates, and whose subject matter—ordinary people acting out ordinary actions—would otherwise have aroused little interest, slipped out of their confines as new works.

Paper provides the means of deducing the small size of the Heian audience. High quality paper was a luxury item in the tenth and eleventh centuries.[30] In her list of "delightful things," Sei Shōnagon mentions "acquiring Michinoku paper, or even ordinary writing paper, so long as it is of good quality" (*MSS*, dan 276:281). Another passage from *The Pillow Book* illustrates the value of paper good enough for copying books.

> There are times when the world so exasperates me that I feel I cannot go on living in it for another moment and I want to disappear for good. But then, if I happen to obtain some nice white paper, and good brushes or white-patterned poem cards, or Michinoku paper, my heart is infinitely soothed, and I decide that I can put up with things as they are a little longer. (*MSS*, dan 277:282)[31]

Sei Shōnagon wrote *The Pillow Book* because Sadako, the consort she served, gave her some bound, blank booklets (*MSS*, dan 319:331). If she had not been favored with these bound books, with their "vast quantities of paper," we would be lacking a masterpiece of vernacular prose. When paper is precious, even well-received works might not easily be copied. About twenty years after *The Pillow Book* was written, a girl who had just returned to the capital from Kazusa province set her heart on reading monogatari but had difficulty acquiring any. Her aunt then went to considerable trouble to furnish the girl with *The Tale of Genji* and some other stories, prompting the girl to write that she could not be happier if she had been made a queen (*Sarashina Nikki* [= *SSN*], 490-93). This girl was the daughter of Sugawara Takasue, a wealthy provincial governor capable of acquiring large numbers of manuscripts.

When manuscript copies are not easily obtained, the reception of monogatari and nikki can take place in only two ways. The first is by circulation of a few copies. The other is to have a lector read aloud to an audience of several people. Tamagami Takuya has shown definitively that monogatari were originally received by the latter method (Tamagami, 1950, 149-51). One famous scene from the "Azumaya" ("The Eastern Cottage") chapter in the illustrated *Genji* scrolls (Bishū Tokugawa coll.) shows a young lady, Ukifune, looking at a bound picture book while an attendant, Ukon, reads aloud from another book containing the text.[32]

---

[30] Michinaga, visiting the temple of Enryakuji, presented these gifts to the monks: "For the abbot, 10 rolls of silk and 100 quires of paper; for the bishops, 6 rolls of silk and 70 quires of paper; for the masters of discipline, 4 rolls of silk and 60 quires of paper" (*Midō Kampaku Ki* [1009], 4). On the seven nights of celebration after the birth of a prince, these gifts were received by ministers of state: "White silk, 120 rolls; cotton, 500 parcels; Shinano cloth, 500 bolts; paper, 600 quires" (ibid., 32). High-quality paper was so valued that it ranked with silk as a gift.

[31] [The translation is taken, with some revisions, from Morris, 1967, 1:217.—Trans.]

[32] The *Genji Monogatari Emaki* (Kōdansha ed., tō 53). Probably dates from 1162-84 (Ko-

This audiovisual method—looking at a scene of a story while learning aurally of the development of events—is a distant ancestor of television. The audience for a monogatari presented thus ordinarily numbered no more than ten people. It may of course be assumed that a given monogatari was read aloud any number of times to groups differing either somewhat or entirely from the original audience. We have no means of calculating the total audience, but we may estimate that, if a group unit is composed of fewer than ten people, the contemporary audience for a work would have been under one hundred.

The audience was further increased by those who were fortunate enough to obtain a copy of the work, as happened to the narrator of the *Sarashina Nikki*. This was, however, no easy matter. Another passage in the *Sarashina Nikki* describes how, with monogatari manuscripts unavailable in Kazusa, the narrator's stepmother and older sisters memorized parts of the *Genji* and other monogatari and recited them to her (*SSN*, 479). The stepmother may have heard and memorized the stories during her service at court. Not being a professional storyteller, she was not trained in transmitting a text, and her recitation probably consisted of plot summaries at best. It is questionable whether listening to such recitation constitutes *literary* reception. If reception is strictly defined as direct visual or aural reception of a text, then the audience of a monogatari at or near the time of its composition and initial circulation would not have numbered a hundred people. The audience for a nikki would have been smaller still.

The relatively small size of an audience at the time a monogatari or nikki was composed and circulated makes itself felt not so much by numbers as by the homogeneity of the small audience. The sponsor of a monogatari—the master of a powerful house, or his wife, or one of his children—formed the audience, along with any intimate attendants. The audience shared certain ideas and reactions. If a young lady and her circle of attendants were the audience for a prospective monogatari, and the writer was an attendant within this group, she would be very familiar with the kinds of monogatari the group had read or heard up to that time and with the nature of the group's response. Her story would be premised on this information. A skillful writer might even borrow characters or situations from works already familiar to her group, thereby economizing on detailed explanation. *The Tale of Genji* has a passage discussing Genji's earnestness:

> He had, however, the greatest deference toward society, and was

---

matsu Shigemi, 1971, 35-48). The *Chōshūki* (27.XI.1119) also discusses *Genji* illustrations. [Translations of *Genji* titles are from Seidensticker, 1976.—Trans.]

by nature far too serious to interest himself in flirtations and gallantry—the sort of man, one imagines, that the Lieutenant of Katano would have derided. (*GM*, "Hahakigi," 55)[33]

The Lieutenant of Katano is the eponymous hero of a non-extant monogatari, "Katano no Shōshō."[34] Since the *Genji* audience would all have known of the Lieutenant of Katano's nature and behavior, the mere mention of his name would have made the abstract "flirtations and gallantry" ("nayobika ni okashiki koto") into a clear and concrete statement. "The Lieutenant of Katano" was apparently quite popular during this time and was not necessarily known only to one group. A passage in *The Story of Ochikubo* reads,

"The Controller-Lieutenant, who is so handsome he puts all others to shame, is known in society as the Lieutenant of Katano. A certain Shōshō serves in his house, and she is my cousin." (*Ochikubo Monogatari*, 1:91)

A somewhat later passage has, "Every woman in the capital has been smitten by the Lieutenant of Katano." The Lieutenant is introduced as an adept at love-letter composition. Every recipient becomes a conquest. All ladies—not only noblemen's wives but the consort herself—enter into liaisons with this legendary lover. As a result he is censured by society and obliged to forfeit his position (*Ochikubo Monogatari*, 1:93). The Lieutenant of Katano, then, is a character in the *Ochikubo* who has been borrowed from "The Lieutenant of Katano" to play a minor role in a new monogatari. This, a radical technique for the late tenth century, was feasible only because the author of the *Ochikubo* knew that her audience group was familiar with "The Lieutenant of Katano."

The relative smallness and homogeneity of an audience group meant that an author could easily find subjects, structure, and vocabulary that appealed to the group, and that the author's choice determined the writer's popularity. The center of an audience group was the commissioner of the work—the lord of a great house, his wife, or his child—and an author was primarily concerned with the patron's reception and evaluation of the work. Much depended on the patron's wish: the "commission" may have

[33] [The translation is taken, with minor changes, from Aileen Gatten, "The Order of the Early Chapters in the *Genji Monogatari*," *Harvard Journal of Asiatic Studies* 41 (1981): 19.—Trans.]

[34] The Lieutenant of Katano is mentioned once more in the *Genji* ("Nowaki," 62). He is also mentioned in the *Makura no Sōshi* (dan 212, 292) and in "Nami no Shimeyū" (as quoted in *Kachō Yosei*). "Katano no Shōshō" was probably a brief monogatari, since it is represented in the *Fūyōshū* by only one poem (Tamagami, 1943, 123-33). There is no firm evidence, however, that the "Katano no Monogatari" quoted in the *Fūyōshū* is the same work as the "Katano no Shōshō" discussed above (Suzuki Kazuo, 1969, 215-32). [See n. 47, below, for further discussion of the *Fūyōshū*.—Trans.]

been for a monogatari whose main purpose was entertainment; or a young lady may have wished to learn about unknown aspects of married life; or a middle-aged intellectual may have wanted to contemplate human life more deeply.

In conjecturing abut the authorship of tenth- and eleventh-century monogatari, one must be extremely cautious of the logical approach whereby stylistic differences among sections of the work always indicate different authors. One could not easily write a monogatari without taking the patron's wishes into account. Paper was one problem during this period, but another great difficulty was obtaining copyists. This can be roughly conjectured from the *Murasaki Shikibu Nikki*.

> We now learn that the Consort [Akiko] is preparing to have us copy a book for the royal collection. A new day dawns, and we lose no time in attending her majesty. We select writing paper in several shades, arrange them, match each booklet of the monogatari with an appropriate amount of paper, and send them off to other quarters with notes requesting those ladies' participation. This is labor enough; but once the copying is completed, I work day and night assembling and binding the booklets. (*MSN*, 472)

The "monogatari" mentioned by Murasaki Shikibu is probably *The Tale of Genji*.[35] The passage may not concern the entire extant work, in fifty-four chapters, but it did involve a substantial amount. Akiko, Murasaki Shikibu's patron, was returning to court soon, and the copying had to be finished before then. The urgent circumstances of the task required the participation of an unusually large number of copyists. Even under normal circumstances, however, the labor and expense of copying were considerable. Long monogatari in particular could not be produced, therefore, without the support of a wealthy patron. Reasonably enough, then, a work followed its patron's orientation.

Although Murasaki Shikibu almost certainly wrote the *Genji* at Akiko's request, it did not follow her orientation alone. The *Murasaki Shikibu Nikki* demonstrates that Michinaga, Akiko's father, also took a strong interest in the *Genji*.

> I sent home for my monogatari booklets and hid them here in my room; but while I was in attendance on her majesty, his lordship stole into my room, searched it thoroughly, and presented his findings, the entire manuscript, to her ladyship the Principal Handmaid. The draft that I had revised, more or less acceptably, has quite disappeared; and the literary quality of this manuscript now in her ladyship's

---

[35] I follow Ikeda Kikan, who posits eight categories of reasons (Ikeda, 1956, 6-8). [The *Murasaki Shikibu Nikki* translation is adapted from Gatten (see n. 33), p. 8.—Trans.]

hands will, I fear, give me a reputation as a diffident writer. (*MSN*, 473)[36]

Subjects are not given in the original text, but honorific language there clearly indicates that it was Michinaga who searched Murasaki Shikibu's room and took away the draft of her monogatari. A later passage leads to the assumption that the monogatari in question is the *Genji*: "His lordship, seeing that her majesty had *The Tale of Genji* before her, begins his usual banter . . ." (*MSN*, 504).

When Michinaga, a man at the center of government affairs and with wide experience in human relationships, became a member of her audience, Murasaki Shikibu would have regarded him as the equivalent of a patron. Michinaga may not have directly sponsored the writing of the *Genji*, but he probably had Akiko act only as the nominal patron. Murasaki Shikibu would, then, have been well aware that her patrons had no interest in the kind of approach to life used to divert unmarried young ladies or to teach them proper conduct. A further possibility exists, that Murasaki Shikibu's audience also included such important intellectuals of the age as Kintō and Fujiwara Kōzei (972-1027), Michinaga's colleagues and cultural equals. Their presence would have demanded that the author create serious topics worthy of their critical standards. The nature of a work varied not only among individual writers but also with the requirements of their audience.

This approach may help to answer some longstanding questions concerning the structure of *The Hollow Tree* and the *Genji*. Part One of the new *Hollow Tree*, as noted earlier, has a superior being for its protagonist, whereas the protagonists of Part Two are ordinary beings performing actions on the ordinary plane.[37] The two parts are consequently very different in tone. The three parts of the *Genji* also differ markedly among themselves in tone and thematic nature. Such a degree of disparity within the same monogatari is due to various factors, among them the considerable weight carried by differing patrons' demands. Differences in tone need not always indicate multiple authorship. A change in the principal audience member, the patron, could produce such differences: the relatively restricted nature of the audience unit would lead to changes corresponding to the individual differences among patrons. Such a phenomenon seems very plausible indeed.

Two basic assumptions must be made before attempting to explain the differences among the individual parts of *The Hollow Tree* and the *Genji* as due to different patrons. First, a monogatari did not necessarily go into

---

[36] [The translation is adapted from Gatten (see n. 33), p. 9.–Trans.]

[37] The only exception is the opening section of "Kurabiraki, Pt. 1" (233/921/1-235/930/7), which adopts the tone of the old *Utsuho*, apparently so as to achieve continuity of plot.

circulation only after completion; and second, drafts were not always handled competently.

Modern readers find it all too easy to believe a work appears only after its completion. Such a process was probably true for short works like *The Bamboo Cutter*, or for chapter units ("maki" or "jō") in *The Hollow Tree* and the *Genji*. When transcribed in modern Japanese orthography and standard print, the *Genji* is 2,000 pages long, and *The Hollow Tree*, similarly transcribed, is approximately 1,200 pages. Neither is likely to have been circulated only upon completion. Long works were certainly circulated in sections, when the story reached an appropriate cutoff point. An author would have arrived at a convenient cutoff point when the patron changed, and the new patron issued his or her requests. The existing technique of borrowing protagonists from other monogatari for minor roles in the new story indicates that it was standard practice to request a monogatari using the characters and plot of an already popular monogatari. In a society made up of small audiences, well-received works would have been quickly passed on to other audience groups. Minister B might hear that a monogatari commissioned by young Lady A has been well received in her circle, and he will consequently request, in the name of his daughter Consort C, that the author write a new story on the same subject. If the ladies in the consort's group C were familiar with the characters and plot in the earlier story, the author would base her sequel on group C's prior knowledge, without having to summarize previous events.

The author would, then, present Consort C with a monogatari, and the audience would probably include her father Minister B and his colleagues Major Counselor D and Captain E. The theme, subject, and tone in the sequel might logically differ from the story written for young Lady A. The differences between the two, moreover, would account for the sequel's being well received by group C and its associates. When two separate works written under such circumstances are combined into one "monogatari," the modern reader senses disharmony and contradictions: the two parts, though making up one monogatari, differ greatly in tone and in other respects. Such monogatari may reasonably be taken as serial works with the second part borrowing characters and plot from the first part. The substantial differences of tone perceptible among the respective three parts of the new *Hollow Tree* and the *Genji* are of this nature and may principally reflect a difference in patrons.

Some problems, however, cannot be solved by simply invoking a change in patrons. They appear in force in Part One of the new *Hollow Tree*. The plot development in Part One is severely disordered and irrational. Matters that should be mentioned, if later passages are to be understood, are mentioned much too late, and events that occur prior to the time sequence of earlier chapters are narrated in later chapters. Ever since the Edo period, scholars have attempted to eliminate these difficulties by reordering the chapters, but the various reorderings have failed to yield a logical plot development. There are also contradictions of fact in *The Hollow Tree*. The tennō commands Suzushi to marry Atemiya (*UM*, "Fukiage," Pt. 1:142/557-58), but a later royal command is that she be married to Nakatada (*UM*, "Naishi no Kami," 189/747). Nakayori is assumed to have become a monk (*UM*, "Atemiya," 175/690), but he appears in the next chapter as a layman (*UM*, "Naishi no Kami," 211/ 836ff.). Odd textual phenomena are another factor: virtually the same content and events are repeated in "Saga no In" (84/325/5-98/381/4) and "Kiku no En" (145/571/1-158/623/1). Scholars have long debated the origin of these contradictions, illogical sequences, and repetitions, as well as the best method of emending the text to achieve a more or less intelligible plot. A definitive view has yet to emerge.[38] The key to answering these questions must lie in the assumption that the original draft of *The Hollow Tree* was lost at some point early in its history.

As we have seen, a passage in the *Murasaki Shikibu Nikki* relates that one of Murasaki Shikibu's *Genji* drafts had "quite disappeared" (this has significance even if it is not taken literally) and that she had not finished revising the text taken by Michinaga. It would have been highly unusual for someone like Michinaga to remove a manuscript forcibly. Once it had been lent through these irresistible means, however, it may never have been returned, but declared lost instead; or the person entrusted with making a clean copy may have embezzled the holograph draft as his or her perquisite; or it may have been diverted clandestinely to someone eager to possess it. An earlier passage from the nikki had related how Akiko's ladies "match each booklet of the monogatari with an appropriate amount of paper, and send them off to other quarters with notes requesting those ladies' participation." This means that several people were requested to participate in making the clean copy; some may well have been deceitful. In short, for unknown reasons Murasaki Shikibu lost possession of her *Genji* drafts. We might reasonably conclude that this also occurred with *The Hollow Tree*.

An author writing some chapters for a patron, and then requested by another to write either a sequel to that monogatari or a story connected to it, would find it necessary, if little (or none) of the original draft were at hand, to rely only on notes and memory, and inconsistencies would crop up between the new work and the earlier story.[39] They would not be no-

---

[38] The composition process of the *Utsuho* presents great problems that received scholarly attention primarily in the 1950s. See *Utsuho Monogatari Kenkyū Bunken Mokuroku* (Kansaku, 1958-66-73) and *Utsuho Monogatari Kenkyūshi Sobyō* (Washiyama, 1974, 309-12).

[39] Murasaki Shikibu seems to have kept detailed notes on the ages of her characters, their official promotions and family relations, and the time frame in which events occurred. A

ticeable if each patron read only the work personally commissioned, but if the author or an associate managed to collect all the circulated sections into a single monogatari, contradictions would necessarily appear. Scrupulous revision would correct all this; but if the author was too busy to be thorough, or did not make detailed additions where an associate had reordered the text, inconsistencies would appear: a character who is already a monk, for instance, will appear later in the story as a layman. Such phenomena would not have occurred unless the holograph draft was incompetently handled. The production of duplicates was greatly hindered by the great expense of writing paper and the considerable labor required to copy manuscripts. Thus the loss of the single holograph meant that another episode or sequel could be written only by relying on the uncertainties of the author's memory.

The *Genji* probably underwent a fairly scrupulous revision process. The traditional view, that it was written in its present order from its first chapter, "Kiritsubo" ("The Paulownia Court"), to its last, "Yume no Ukihashi" ("The Floating Bridge of Dreams"), reflects the author's scrupulous ordering and augmentation. Of course, Murasaki Shikibu fails to adjust the ages of certain characters in the course of the narrative, and doubts remain about the first three chapters of Part Three, "Niou Miya" ("His Perfumed Highness"), "Kōbai" ("The Rose Plum"), and "Takekawa" ("Bamboo River"), which fail to conform to the progression of events and contain contradictions in the ranks and offices of characters. Compared with *The Hollow Tree*, however, the *Genji* is far more conscientiously ordered as a whole. Not that this provides evidence that the extant *Genji* was written in the chapter order we now have. Lively scholarly debate continues on the question of the composition process undergone by the extant *Genji*, but no generally accepted or definitive view exists.[40] It must be acknowledged, at least, that the *Genji* appeared intermittently and in chapter groups (or in single chapters); at some point these groups or single chapters were ordered and consolidated into the present *Genji*.

The most complicated manifestation of this situation occurs in the first thirty-three chapters, Part One. Takeda Munetoshi's theory, positing that these chapters are divided into seventeen Murasaki-line chapters and sixteen Tamakazura-line chapters, concludes that the former group was writ-

---

slight lack of coordination in the progression of events is nonetheless perceptible (Inaga, 1967, 423-27). The author of the *Utsuho* probably made only rough notes.

[40] Watsuji Tetsurō first proposed that the *Genji* was not written in the order we have it today (Watsuji, 1922, 207-22). He may have been inspired by the work of Ulrich von Wilamowitz-Moenllendorff, or by Gilbert Murray's studies of Homer. Among scholars of Japanese literature, Aoyagi (Abe) Akio (Abe Akio, 1939) and Tamagami Takuya (Tamagami, 1940) have made monumental discoveries, and Kazamaki Keijirō (Kazamaki, 1950-56) has also written studies of note. Takeda Munetoshi summarizes the results of earlier works (Takeda, 1954).

278   THE EARLY MIDDLE AGES

ten first, and that the latter was divided and inserted into the corpus of the
first group in accordance with the protagonists' ages.[41] This view requires
considerable revision, but it is basically worthy of support. It is difficult to
deny that the sixteen Tamakazura-line chapters demonstrate greater accomplishment both thematically and expressively than the seventeen Murasaki-line chapters. But this does not mean that the Murasaki-line chapters are the product of a relatively early period, whereas the Tamakazura
line was written at the height of Murasaki Shikibu's creative powers; or
that once she had finished the former group, she inserted the latter, in bits
and pieces, over a period of years. What really happened may well be
along those lines, but there is not enough evidence to prove it. All we have
is internal evidence obtained from textual analysis. To link this to facts
concerning Murasaki Shikibu's mature period would require the addition
of enough evidence to support it.[42] Takeda's theory exceeds the bounds of
surmisal by internal evidence and makes inappropriate use of unproved
inference upon inference. As a result, the theories of Takeda and others
using his premises have brought about their own destruction, as far as
suppositional potential is concerned. Yet analysis does reveal a perceptible
difference in quality of expression between the Murasaki and Tamakazura lines. We need not have recourse to internal evidence to infer that this
may reflect a change in patrons. This inference becomes far sounder when
The Hollow Tree, with its marked differences in quality of expression, is
cited as supporting evidence.

The above phenomena occur in monogatari composed of chapter
units—works that might be termed multipartite long monogatari. Such
questions never arise in continuous long monogatari, with their undeviat-
ing progression throughout. Examples of the continuous long monogatari
include the *Hamamatsu Chūnagon Monogatari (The Nostalgic Counselor)*, *The Tale of Nezame*, and *Sagoromo Monogatari (The Story of Sagoromo)*. Division by chapter (Chapter 1, Chapter 2, Chapter 3) is present

[41] The chapters in the two lines, according to Takeda, are as follows. Murasaki line: (1)
"Kiritsubo," (5) "Wakamurasaki," (7) "Momiji no Ga," (8) "Hana no En," (9) "Aoi," (10)
"Sakaki," (11) "Hanachirusato," (12) "Suma," (13) "Akashi," (14) "Miotsukushi," (17)
"Eawase," (18) "Matsukaze," (19) "Usugumo," (20) "Asagao," (21) "Otome," (32) "Ume-
gae," (33) "Fuji no Uraba." Tamakazura line: (2) "Hahakigi," (3) "Utsusemi," (4) "Yūgao,"
(6) "Suetsumuhana," (15) "Yomogiu," (16) "Sekiya," (22) "Tamakazura," (23) "Hatsune,"
(24) "Kochō," (25) "Hotaru," (26) "Tokonatsu," (27) "Kakaribi," (28) "Nowaki," (29)
"Miyuki," (30) "Fujibakama," (31) "Makibashira." [I have added the numbers of the chapters involved, both to facilitate locating in the Seidensticker or Waley translation and also to
suggest the pattern of interweaving that this thesis implies. It should also be observed that all
these thirty-one chapters make up the first part of the *Genji Monogatari* in Ikeda Kikan's
widely accepted (with whatever modification or other emphasis) division of the work into
three parts: see n. 21, above.—Ed.]
[42] Useful views of the possibilities and limitations of proof by combining internal and external evidence are found in the work of Arthur Sherbo (Sherbo, 1958) and Ephim G. Fogel's
critique of Sherbo (Fogel, 1958).

in continuous long monogatari, but this is no more than a matter of convenience in producing manuscript booklets: each chapter represents the most easily handled amount of paper. Such chapter divisions need have no significance as units of narrative structure. If a series of several chapters were instead converted into Parts One and Two, the audience response would be no more than a feeling of inconvenience at holding such large books. The problem is not one of chapter titles but of producing a work either as a collection of earlier, shorter pieces or as a single long work. *A Tale of Flowering Fortunes* has chapter titles like "The Moon-Viewing Banquet," "The Middle Counselor's Quest at Kazan," and "Joyous Events."[43] Yet the narration progresses continuously; additional chapters could not be inserted into the sequence of consecutive chapters. This is, in other words, a single, long work. The difference between multipartite and continuous long monogatari is also reflected in the treatment they receive during their periods of composition—as Murasaki Shikibu's problems show so well.

One more matter to consider in connection with monogatari is the unstable nature of the author's identity. Early medieval monogatari customarily did not bear an author's name. As we saw early on, this practice reflects their status as a less than premier art. The belief that the genre was unworthy of bearing an author's name brought about a contemporary opinion that the author of a monogatari need not have a clear-cut responsibility for, or control over, work personally done. "Toshikage" in the extant *Hollow Tree*, for example, is cut through with sections from the old *Hollow Tree*. The style and the nature of its subject matter clearly demonstrate that the old *Hollow Tree*, an antecedent work, was incorporated almost verbatim into the new *Hollow Tree*. This is a literary outrage if seen in the context of modern copyright laws. There was no such context in the Heian period, of course; neither, apparently, was a monogatari perceived as a work necessarily written by one person. That is why the old *Hollow Tree*, obviously a separate work, was casually incorporated into the new *Hollow Tree* without undue protest from a contemporary audience.

The "*Genji* Shaku" ("*Genji* Commentary"; Maeda coll. manuscript) by Sesonji Koreyuki (d. 1175) is believed to date from the mid-twelfth century. It has thirteen brief quotations from a chapter called "Sakurabito" ("Cherry-blossom Girl") and appends simple commentary to each (Horibe, 1942, 157-65).[44] Observations appear in the "Commentary" after the section on "Makibashira" ("The Cypress Pillar"), with this notation

---

[43] ["Tsuki no En," "Kazan Tazunuru Chūnagon," and "Samazama no Yorokobi," the titles of the first three chapters of the *Eiga Monogatari*. The translations are from McCullough and McCullough, 1980.—Trans.]

[44] *Genji Monogatari Taisei*, 7 (Ikeda, 1956). Bibliography: 37-41. Text: 279-338.

concerning its place in the chapter order: " 'Cherry-blossom Girl': Some manuscripts have this chapter, others do not. One need not have it. It is best placed after 'Hotaru' ['Fireflies']." Koreyuki probably remarks that one need not have "Cherry-blossom Girl" in a complete copy of the *Genji* because he realizes that this chapter is not the work of Murasaki Shikibu. Prior to the mid-twelfth century, there were undoubtedly manuscript copies of the *Genji* that contained "Cherry-blossom Girl." Teika's commentary on the *Genji*, "Okuiri" ("Interlineations"), includes this remark, appended to his section on "Utsusemi" ("The Shell of the Locust"): "Some say that 'Kagayaku Hi no Miya' ['The Radiant Princess Consort'] is the second chapter of the *Genji*. No text of this chapter has ever been transmitted."[45] Certain *Genji* manuscripts evidently had a second chapter called "The Radiant Princess Consort," but none of the manuscripts Teika used in his recension contained such a chapter.[46] It, too, was probably not the work of Murasaki Shikibu but had appeared in some manuscript copies prior to the early thirteenth century. A further instance is provided by some booklet fragments copied in the mid-fourteenth century (Horibe Seiji coll.). In them, a "prince" (miya) recites this poem to a woman named Sumori (Horibe, 1942, 173).

Tsurakarishi	If I had not seen
Kokoro o mizu wa	The cruelty you meant toward me,
Tanomuru o	I would not have known
Itsuwari to shi mo	That everything I rely on
Omowazaramashi.	Has been based on a deceit.

The *Fūyōshū*, compiled in 1271, attributes this poem to Prince Niou, but it does not appear in the extant *Genji*.[47] *An Untitled Book*, written by the beginning of the thirteenth century, discusses two women, "Nakanokimi in 'Sumori' " and "Lady Sumori," in the same context as the *Genji* char-

[45] "Okuiri" is Teika's record of his interlinear comments, written while copying the *Genji* (Ikeda, 1956, 80). The translation is based on the Ōshima manuscript version (ibid., 350).

[46] "Kagayaku Hi no Miya" has heretofore been read to signify "The Shining Sun Princess." [Depending on the characters used, "hi" can mean either "sun" or "consort."— Trans.] "Hi," according to the Women's Quarters Regulations established by the Taihō Code, occupied a lesser position than kōgō [royal consort] but was superior to bunin [concubines of social status]. A royal princess who was also a consort would be called "hi no miya" (princess consort; Komatsu, 1971, 25-32).

[47] The *Fūyōshū* is a waka anthology made up exclusively of poems from Heian and early Kamakura monogatari. The monogatari represented are limited to the fictional variety; uta-monogatari and historical monogatari are not represented. [Many of the waka quoted, and the scenes described in their respective forenotes, no longer appear in the extant texts of the monogatari. The *Fūyōshū* thus provides valuable data about the early structure of such monogatari as the *Genji*, before they were given a more or less standardized form; it also gives poems from a large number of other monogatari otherwise unknown. See n. 34, above.— Trans., Ed.]

acters Niou, Kaoru, and Ukifune (*MMSS*, 40). A work from much the same period, the *Shirozōshi* (collection of the temple Shōchi In, Mt. Kōya), gives the titles of the fifty-four chapters of the *Genji* and adds these as the work of later authors: " 'Saku[ra]bito,' 'Samushiro,' 'Sumori' " (Hashimoto, 1934, 336-37). Prior to the thirteenth century, then, certain copies of the *Genji* contained a chapter called "Sumori." This fact is reinforced by the presence of characters from "Sumori" in old genealogical charts of characters in the *Genji*.[48]

These data reveal that manuscript copies of the *Genji* in the early twelfth century unquestionably contained chapters that are no longer present in the extant work. One scholar concludes from this that the twelfth century was the terminus ad quem for the compilation of these chapters, which were written by contemporaries of Murasaki Shikibu (Inaga, 1967, 485-502). There are no eleventh-century documents to provide external evidence that the chapters are contemporary with Murasaki Shikibu, nor is there sufficient cause to find the theory unworkable. Although much remains unsure, these facts at least are clear: (1) by the early twelfth century, (2) there were manuscript copies of the *Genji* with chapters no longer present in the extant work; and (3) at the time *The Hollow Tree* was written, a practice existed of an author incorporating an antecedent monogatari into a new work. These points, taken together, indicate with some certainty that from the late tenth through the early thirteenth centuries, a monogatari was thought something not necessarily the work of one author.

The transmission of monogatari was greatly influenced by the absence of guarantees that one author was responsible for a monogatari or that its text would not be altered against its author's will. Unlike shih and waka, premier arts both, monogatari are generally transmitted in manuscripts possessing extreme variants. The variants are not limited to the dimension of miscopying but often extend to changes in expression. *The Story of Sagoromo* provides the most outstanding example: it is, technically, nearly impossible to create an integrated variorum text for this work. Its large number and wide range of variants have obliged scholars of *Sagoromo* to collate the text in terms of four manuscript lines; occasionally the differences among lines strongly suggest rewriting. Transmission without regard to an individual author resulted in the widespread practice of rewriting entire monogatari. *The Tale of Nezame* and *Torikaebaya Monogatari (The Changelings)* are examples of this trend, which persisted into the High Middle Ages. The act was based on a perception that a secondary art like that of monogatari did not in effect demand a recognition of authorial

[48] *Genji Monogatari Keizu*, Shōka manuscript (Ikeda, 1956, 499-500), and *Genji Keizu Koran* (Inaga, 1967, 575-600). Both mention a "Sumori Sammi" (Sumori of the Third Rank).

responsibility and control such as was accorded the composers of shih and waka.

FICTIONAL NIKKI

The Tosa Diary (Tosa Nikki), a fictional nikki, is the oldest work of prose in Japanese with an ascertainable composition date. I therefore begin this discussion of Japanese prose genres by considering fictional nikki. Extant works are represented by *The Tosa Diary*, narrated in the first person by one of its characters; the *Izumi Shikibu Nikki*, told in the third person by an obscured narrator; and *The Gossamer Years (Kagerō Nikki)*, occupying an intermediate position with its mixture of first- and third-person narration. An examination of these narrative methods will provide the clearest grasp of the nature of fictional nikki and enable us to discover some evidence of their developmental process.

Narrated in the First Person

Nikki [usually translated as "diaries"] are readily assumed to be works written in the first person, and yet the only nikki from the tenth and eleventh centuries narrated almost exclusively from a first-person point of view is *The Tosa Diary*. The idea that "nikki" is synonymous with first-person narration must be the result of confusing the early medieval term "nikki" with the modern "diary" ["nikki," written with the same characters]. In the sphere of Chinese prose, writers recorded their experiences in a daily order from the ninth century on. Ennin's *Record of a Pilgrimage to China in Search of the Dharma* is one example of such daily records. But *The Tosa Diary* only borrows the form of a daily record; its literary nature differs greatly from that of the *Pilgrimage*. The opening words of *The Tosa Diary* reveal the presence of fictional elements in ample proportion: "It is said that diaries are kept by men, but I shall see if a woman cannot also keep one" (*TSN*, 27).[49] The narrator is definitely a fabrica-

---

[49] [Miner, trans., 1969, 59.—Trans. Since this translation and Seidensticker's of the *Kagerō Nikki* have been altered for use here, it is necessary to clarify the author's intention in holding that nikki are written, as we put it, in the present tense. By "past tense" the author refers to use of the verbal inflections -ki, -shi, and -shika. Since Japanese verbs are inflected (in these matters) for aspect rather than for tense, they refer to a degree or state of completion rather than to temporal occurrence. The reference point is, therefore, the present. See n. 15, above, on the absence of genuine tense in Japanese. The author interprets certain Heian inflections of verbs as follows:

-keri. (a) Signifying matter that has been heard or learned of; (b) signifying that things are so.

-tekeri. Signifying a strengthening of the preceding.

-tari (-te ari). Signifying continuance from a previous state to the speaker's present.

-nu. Signifying emphasis: certainly it is so.

tion. Women in the tenth century did not keep daily records, whether in Chinese or in Japanese prose; and some later passages of *The Tosa Diary* are written in a most unfeminine style, suggesting that Ki no Tsurayuki's authorship was common knowledge among contemporary readers.[50] This fictional device, apparent as such to both author and audience, may be termed the technique of persona.

The fictive speaker was a convention present as early as Hitomaro's time, as was observed in Volume One. Not that Tsurayuki copied his narrator directly from Hitomaro. The idea was probably based on the ninth-century shih convention of distance between a poet and the poetic speaker. Waka, whose development was influenced by contact with shih, also has fictive speakers: they appear particularly often in screen waka and in waka concerning the Seventh Night. Another instance of a fictive speaker in waka appears in the following poem, composed in the persona of a figure in a centerpiece (suhama) constructed for a chrysanthemum-and-waka match.

Composed on the figure of a man walking through
the chrysanthemums to arrive at an immortal's palace.
By Priest Sosei

Nurete hosu	In the little time
Yamaji no kiku no	To dry clothes wetted on the mountain path
Tsuyu no ma ni	By chrysanthemum dew,
Itsu ka chitose o	I have somehow unawares
Ware wa heniken.	Lived through a thousand years.

(*KKS*, 5:273)

The "I" of the poem is not Sosei. This technique is employed in prose with

---

With -ki, -shi, and -shika, however, the degree of perfection and of distancing from the present of the speaker/thinker is taken to be great enough to be termed "the past tense" ("kako jisei"), so to speak. In doctoring the translations, we have used present and present perfect except for those "past tense" verbs that are not clause final and therefore do not affect the author's thesis. For example, here is the close of the first lengthy unit of the *Izumi Shikibu Nikki*: ". . . kogū ni saburai*shi* kotoneri warawa nari*keri*"; this has been altered from the 1969 translation to, "it *turns* out to be that Page who *had been* in the service of the late prince," with "turns out" ("narikeri") the governing verb of the passage. See below, on *The Great Mirror* in "Monogatari Centering on Society," in the section "Factual Monogatari." —Ed.]

[50] Two waka from the *Tosa Nikki* are included in the *Gosenshū* under Tsurayuki's name (19:1356, 1364). The forenote of the former poem closely resembles that in the *Tosa Nikki*. One of the editors of the *Gosenshū* was Tsurayuki's son Tokifumi (fl. ca. 951-60). Furthermore, a personal waka collection by Egyō (fl. ca. 961-80), a friend of Tsurayuki and Tokifumi, mentions that "scenes from Tsurayuki's *Tosa no Niki* were depicted in paintings. . . ."

Tsurayuki's "I shall see if a woman cannot also keep one," and the results are impressive.

Tsurayuki appears in *The Tosa Diary* as an anonymous "passenger of honor" (funagimi). He is seen through the eyes of the narrator, one of the women in the service of the former governor of Tosa on the return with him to the capital. The protagonist, Tsurayuki's alter ego, can thus be described at an ample distance from Tsurayuki the author. Since, moreover, the story is told in the first person by the fictive narrator, a limited point of view is inevitable; this establishes an even greater distance between the passenger of honor, in *The Tosa Diary*, and its author, Tsurayuki. The narrator of this nikki can tell only those facts that she could observe; she cannot see into the hearts of other characters. And because she cannot assimilate the passenger of honor's feelings, even his most poignant emotions will be observed at a distance.

Natsume Sōseki (1867-1916) wrote *Wagahai wa Neko de Aru* (*I Am a Cat*, 1905) during a period of extreme depression in both his personal and professional lives. This is inferred from scenes he depicts later in his autobiographical novel *Michikusa* (*Grass on the Wayside*, 1915). But *I Am a Cat*, whose raw subject matter is based on experiences from this time, shows no apparent sign of the author's acute suffering. Its characters are depicted as carefree idlers whose pleasant lives are a sequence of leisurely, trivial conversations. The central figure, Mr. Kushami, is surrounded on all sides by reckless laughter and must feel constant bitterness and depression.[51] Sōseki's creative stance naturally distances the author from this bitterness, but the narration is doubtless made more effective because of a special device, to have a cat-narrator relate all the events in the work.

Tsurayuki was apparently an embittered man when he wrote *The Tosa Diary*. He was about seventy years old at his return to the capital in 935, yet he had not risen high in the government service: his highest official rank, the junior fourth, lower grade, was not reached until 945. Tsurayuki considered it his greatest honor to have been commanded by Daigo Tennō to edit the *Shinsen Wakashū*, but Daigo's death at forty-six, on the twenty-eighth day of the Ninth Month, 930—the year Tsurayuki was appointed governor of Tosa—deprived Tsurayuki of the patron for the anthology. The seemingly unfavorable reception of his new, simpler approach to waka by its arbiters in the years from about 923 to 931 was the source of another, more personal bitterness. Tsurayuki evidently experienced great disappointment in all these events, and similar worldly disappointments are the theme of *The Tosa Diary*.

[51] "Kushami" means "sneeze," but the characters with which the name is written signify a "suffering monk." "Ku" (suffering) is an essential element of human existence, according to Buddhist thought, and "shami" means a married monk. The humorous surface meaning and its more somber inner significance reflect the protagonist's complex nature.

The *Diary* has a theme and a design that give appropriate expression to that theme. Like Ennin's *Pilgrimage*, a wholly factual account, it takes the form of a daily record, but the two works differ greatly in nature. This is not merely a difference in the nature of the works, nor is it a matter of evaluation. Modern readers find Ennin's prose moving. The poignant theme of disappointment in *The Tosa Diary* is expressed mildly, humorously, and with detachment. The reader will only be moved by plumbing the depths of the work, depths that are not easily reached. Some passages in the *Diary* have been criticized as pointless jokes:

> The people present—high and low, without distinction, even the young—drink a great deal, and in the general carousing those who cannot even write a simple line are staggering crosses with their footprints. (*TSN*, 28)[52]

> We are passing the pine groves of Kurosaki: since the name means "Black Point," that is one color. The color of the pines is green. The waves upon the coast are like snow, and the shells are scarlet. Only yellow is lacking from the Five Shades. (*TSN*, 48)[53]

We must recognize, however, that this volley of silly jokes is spoken by the fictional narrator, a woman in the party of the former governor of Tosa, as distinguished from the author himself. The fictive narrator is depicted as a frivolous sort of woman who enjoys making bad jokes, but that does not mean Tsurayuki wrote *The Tosa Diary* with frivolous intent.

Tsurayuki created various characters in his task of shaping the theme of worldly frustrations and disappointments into a literary work. The narrator, with her fondness for lame jokes, is one such character, and she observes and explains events as the author has dramatized them. The author has, moreover, given her the ability to observe and explain only from a first-person, limited point of view, and so she cannot enter into the passenger of honor's inner feelings, his grief, despair, or anger. Distancing makes it possible to express the theme of frustration and disappointment on a dimension other than that of abject tears and complaints.

Expressing a poignant theme in a humorous tone would not have struck tenth-century Japanese intellectuals as ga in quality. Humor was not a principal factor in ga, either in the Early or the High Middle Ages. Because humor is part of the zoku sphere, *The Tosa Diary*, which makes much use of comic elements, might appear to be zoku literature. But that also is not

[52] ["In Japanese the point is that those illiterates who could not draw the single horizontal line for the number one are so drunk that their staggering feet draw the crossed line for ten." Miner, 1969, 60.—Trans.]

[53] [Adapted from Miner, 1969, 79.—Trans.] The Five Shades (goshiki), a Chinese concept, equates the five primary colors to the five principal directions: east = green, west = white, south = red, north = black, and center = yellow.

the case. Its theme, the frustrations and disappointments of the world, was often splendidly expressed in prose and poetry in Chinese. *The Tosa Diary* shows similar signs of care: waka appear throughout, and its prose style includes such elaborate designs as parallelism. In these respects the *Diary* is worthy of being called ga literature. Tsurayuki and his circle used the term "hikai" (indecorous or even humorous) to denote a compositional stance that was ga in some respects and zoku in others. "Indecorous Waka" (Hikai no Uta), in Book 19 of the *Kokinshū*, consists of fifty-eight waka, including the following:

Topic Unknown.
By Mitsune

Mutsugoto mo	Our words of love
Mada tsukinaku ni	Are far from being exhausted
Akenumeri	As dawn has come:
Izura wa aki no	Where then is that vaunted length
Nagashi chō yo wa.	That they give to autumn nights?

(19:1015)

Anonymous

Aki kureba	When autumn comes,
Nobe ni tawaruru	Then the fields are filled with charms
Ominaeshi	Of the ladyflowers:
Izure no hito ka	Where is the man who would see them
Tsumade miru beki.	And not desire to take them up?

(19:1017)

By Tayū

Nageki koru	My woes have reached
Yama to shi takaku	The height of those mountain tops,
Narinureba	Where sorrow-wood is cut:
Tsurazue nomi zo	Which is why, from first to last,
Mazu tsukarekeru.	I muse, my chin upon my hand.

(19:1056)

"Indecorous" waka include certain words not normally used in waka that lead the recipient to smile.[54] If indecorous waka are seen as generally ga

---

[54] "Izura wa" (1015) is a colloquialism; "tsumade" (1017) suggests giving a lady an amorous pinch; and "tsurazue" expresses a commonplace action. All therefore represent zoku

expression that includes some degree of zoku, then it follows that *The Tosa Diary* is indecorous prose. Its theme, subject matter, and syntax are in the realm of ga, but its creative stance and tone are overwhelmingly zoku. It might, indeed, be called haibun (Konishi, 1951b, 1-7). But to designate it so raises concern that these terms might be confused with the genres of haikai and haibun, established in the seventeenth century. In its stead, that new term—ga-zoku, discussed in the General Introduction to Volume One—can replace "haikai" to describe *The Tosa Diary*.

Contemporary circumstances account for the fact that for *The Tosa Diary*, the earliest work of vernacular prose, Tsurayuki chose ga-zoku as its keynote of expression. Ga literature in early tenth-century Japan was limited to prose and poetry in Chinese and to the newly enfranchised waka. The only previous, true ga variety of vernacular prose was that composed incidentally as accompaniments to waka, such as the Japanese Preface to the *Kokinshū* and the Preface to the "Waka Composed for His Majesty's Progress to the Ōi River." Tsurayuki had no choice but to attempt a ga-zoku style when he created the vernacular nikki genre. Women writers continued and gradually refined his experiment.

Narrated by Multiple Personae

The early tenth-century creation of nikki in prose was a most significant event in the history of Japanese literature. First, it marked the early appearance of narratives about ordinary people and events; second, the nikki employed the technique of point of view with considerable skill. Little is known of the content of early tenth-century fictional monogatari, but they seem to have been concerned with superior beings and fantastic events or, at their most advanced, with ordinary people encountering fantastic events. This can be deduced from a work to be discussed below, the *Sambōe*, written in 984. Its General Preface states that contemporary monogatari are either stories of personified animals and plants or love stories that "tell colorful tales about the relations between men and women." It should be noted that a narrative describing ordinary people and events—*The Tosa Diary*—had appeared some fifty years earlier. This could have resulted only from the presence of a fairly sophisticated audience. More noteworthy still, a work of this kind demonstrates an advanced accomplishment for the tenth century, chiefly in terms of its use of point of view. The earliest fiction of all countries is ordinarily narrated from an omniscient point of view, with the limited point of view appearing only at a later stage. A work like *The Tosa Diary*, moreover, with its varied characters'

---

expressions that do not reappear in later royal anthologies. ["Nageki" (sorrow, grief, or suffering) is also treated in the third poem as if its "ki" meant "tree"—a playful fancy.—Ed.]

words and actions reflecting its author's innermost thoughts, has elements
that reappear only in the eighteenth-century novel. This is not to say that
Tsurayuki had complete command of the technique of point of view. Consider this section, in which the governor's ship finally rows out of Ōmi-
nato.

> From this harbor we at last row on the open sea. It is for this final
> parting that those who follow us come to say farewell. Now as we
> row on, the people standing on the shore have grown remote, and *the
> people aboard the ship have grown out of sight of those on land.* They
> on the shore must have things they wish to say to us, and we on the
> ship have words we would like to speak to them. It is no use. (*TSN*,
> 35)[55]

The italicized lines represent a mistake by the author, who inadvertently
slips away from the limited point of view maintained in the nikki to use an
omniscient point of view. The parallel sentence structure demanded that
those on shore and those aboard ship receive balanced treatment, with the
result that the author lost track of his locus of observation. This, however,
is the only passage in the entire *Tosa Diary* to waver in its point of view—
a splendid achievement for the earliest work of Japanese narrative prose.

Its consistent point of view is particularly remarkable in light of the considerably more confused point of view in *The Gossamer Years (Kagerō
Nikki)*, written between thirty-six and forty years after *The Tosa Diary*.[56]
The opening passage of *The Gossamer Years* is narrated in the third person (*KN*, 1:9). The heroine, known in the text as "hito" (a person), is thus
expected to be a creation separate from the narrator of the nikki. Not long
into the work, however, the distinction between heroine and narrator becomes blurred. This occurs because the author maintains a limited point
of view while telling the story in the third person, with the result that the
heroine's and the narrator's loci of observation are eventually combined.
Third-person narration with a limited point of view is of course feasible.
In many modern novels, the locus of observation is given to one among
several characters, who narrates events according to a limited point of
view. Because the heroine of *The Gossamer Years* is assigned the locus of
observation, it is difficult to differentiate her from the narrator. *The Gossamer Years* is told by an obscured narrator who is easily confused with
the heroine, because the reader has no information about the narrator's
character. Not only do readers confuse the two: the author herself could
not avoid doing so.

[55] [Adapted from Miner, 1969, 67.—Trans.]
[56] Part Two was probably fair copied between XI.969 and XII.971; Part One was written
after Part Two and fair copied at much the same time; and Part Three was written around
30.XII.974 (Uemura, 1972, 128-42).

As just observed, the work begins in the third person. The text is as follows (Seidensticker trans., as adapted).

These times have passed, and there is one who has drifted uncertainly through them, scarcely knowing where she is. It is perhaps natural that such should be her fate. She is less handsome than most, and not remarkably gifted. Yet, as the days go by in monotonous succession, she has occasion to look at the old monogatari, and has found them masses of the rankest fabrication. Perhaps, she says to herself, even the story of her own dreary life, set down in a nikki, might be of interest; and it might also answer a question: has that life been one befitting a well-born lady? But they must all be recounted, events of long ago, events of but yesterday. She is by no means certain that she can bring them to order. (Seidensticker, 1964, 33)

In the Seidensticker translation this passage appears in small, italicized type, as if it should be read as an independent preface. Then the text proper begins: the narration from this point to the conclusion is in the first person.

I shall not touch upon the frivolous love notes I have received from time to time. Now the Prince is beginning to send messages. Most men would have gone through a suitable intermediary. . . . (ibid., 33)

Seidensticker's arrangement is both excellent and sensible. If the text had not been translated thus, the result would probably have been incoherent. The original text, however, does not always make clear references to person. Grammatical subjects [and topics] are infrequent in modern Japanese and were even less present in tenth-century usage, which dictated that a subject appear in a sentence only under special circumstances. *The Gossamer Years* is therefore narrated almost entirely without subjects. A literal English translation would make no sense at all, and so the translator is obliged to supplement subjects [especially by introducing pronouns without counterpart in the original]. The Seidensticker translation supplements the text in the first person. The content is not unreasonably interpreted as being narrated in the first person; this is in fact the most natural approach for a modern reader. Yet the author's intention seems to have been to narrate the story in the third person. Subjects are, as a rule, not given; but when they appear in *The Gossamer Years*, they are in the third person.

The heroine of the nikki lives with a younger sister. The sister is also married, but her husband feels ill at ease in the presence of the older sister and her husband, and so he takes away the younger sister to live elsewhere. The older sister—the heroine—is then left alone. As Seidensticker translates the relevant passage (adapted):

My sister continues to receive her husband regularly. It has not been long, however, since he has begun to find the atmosphere of the place oppressive and has taken her away to a house where, he says, he can visit her in somewhat lighter spirits. *My gloom increases.* I will not see her again, I think, and as the carriage comes to take her away I hand her a poem. . . . (ibid., 39)

The italicized sentence is in the third person in the original text: "Tomaru hito mashite kokorobososhi." But to translate that one sentence in the third person—"She who remains behind is increasingly gloomy"—would confuse the reader and fail to communicate the meaning of the sentence. The content, too, is appropriate to first-person narration. Why, then, is the Japanese text narrated in the third person?

Part One of *The Gossamer Years* is strongly characteristic of a shū [a poetic collection, particularly of love poems in this instance]. The heroine marries a youth whose rank is far above hers, and for the next fifteen years she is tormented by his infidelities: this is the subject of Part One. The waka exchanged on various occasions play a vital role in this part. Without them Part One would consist of only superficial recollections.

Nagekitsutsu	Grieving on and on—
Hitori nuru yo no	A night when one must sleep alone
Akuru ma wa	Waiting for the dawn
Ika ni hisashiki	Seems an interval that lasts forever—
Mono to ka wa shiru.	And do you know anything of this?[57]

(*KN*, 1:19)

This outstanding poem is only one example of how waka in Part One, recited in certain settings, provide the greatest interest when they are appreciated in accordance with their respective settings.

A group of waka possessing such settings is in fact a shū. Part One of *The Gossamer Years* was probably intended, to a considerable extent, as a shū, in which third-person narration is frequently found. Murakami Tennō seems to have written a nikki. Certainly a fragment is quoted in the *Saikū Nyōgo Shū (Collected Waka of the Junior Consort, a Former High Priestess).*[58]

I understand that this appears in His Majesty's nikki. One autumn

---

[57] [This poem is "easily the most famous" in the nikki. "A pun on *akuru ma*, 'the interval before dawn' and 'the interval before the door opens,' indicates to Kaneie that she knew he was there and purposely kept him out. This is rather a daring poem." Seidensticker, 1964, 170.—Trans.]

[58] The personal waka collection of Princess Yoshiko (929-85), Murakami's junior consort.

evening, when he had long been absent from the women's quarters, His Majesty happened to hear a lady [the junior consort] playing the zither very beautifully. He put on a soft white robe and hastened to her side, but the lady continued playing as if no one had come. When he asked why, she replied,

"Aki no hi no	"As the autumn day
Ayashiki hodo no	Has strangely become so early
Yūgure ni	The hour of dusk,
Ogi fuku kaze no	I mistook your sound in coming
Oto zo kikoyuru."	For wind arustle in the reeds."

I was deeply moved as I listened to her speak. (*Saikū Nyōgo Shū*, 15)

Murakami's nikki was evidently narrated in the first person.[59] This passage was recast in the third person when it appeared in the consort's shū, but one sentence remained unrevised, in the first person: "to kikitsuketa-rishi kokochi nan sechi narishi" (I was deeply moved as I listened to her speak).

It is not known which part of *The Gossamer Years* was written first, Part One or Part Two. There is no doubt, however, that Part One is a unified whole, differing somewhat from Part Two in being very much a shū in nature.[60] Part One, a collection of past events, incorporates many of the author's old waka drafts, and the style consequently resembles that of a shū. This is true in quantitative terms as well: Part One has 124 waka, compared with the fifty-five in Part Two and the eighty in Part Three. The parts also differ qualitatively. Part One contains several instances of sets of waka whose aim is to achieve interesting poetic exchange within a given situation. The waka in Part Two, on the other hand, are predominantly recited by the heroine to herself as expressions of her loneliness. In one passage, for example, her husband does not visit her but sends a messenger with a lotus pod. The heroine lies down, deeply depressed, and spends the rest of the day in a troubled mood:

. . . I do not know how far his promise is to be trusted. My desire to

---

It was compiled by a later person at some point prior to the mid-twelfth century, and the passage it quotes from Murakami's nikki is highly reliable.

[59] This can be told from the suffix "-shi," which denotes recollected experience. [See n. 49.] It is used in the sentence "to kikitsuketari*shi* kokochi nan setsu nari*shi*." These words must have been written by Murakami at some point prior to his death in 967.

[60] Part One concludes: "Indeed, as she thinks of the unsatisfying events she has recorded here, she wonders whether she has been describing anything of substance. Her nikki might rather be called a shimmering of the summer sky" (*KN*, 1:79; adapted from Seidensticker, 1964, 69). This corresponds to the introductory remarks mentioned earlier; here, there is a strong sense of a conclusion having been reached.

see it, like most of my desires, may come to nothing.[61] I murmur,
" 'Loves may bloom like the lotus and bear fruit, but I vanish from
this world, a drop of dew on the floating lotus leaf.' "
    The days go by and I feel no improvement. (*KN*, 2:85-86)[62]

Her poem, "Loves may bloom," does not appear elsewhere as a composition but merely states the heroine's own feelings in waka form. Hence
she "murmurs" it. Fourteen waka in Part Two are similarly solitary
expressions explained with such words as "omou yō," "oboyuru yō," and
"nado oboete."[63] Since these waka are expressions of the heroine's innermost feelings, the narrator is naturally assumed to be the heroine of the
work. The story, in other words, comes to be narrated in the first person.
In retreat at the temple of Hannyaji in Narutaki, the heroine listens to the
monks reciting incantations and muses,

> I had never imagined that such a thing would happen to me [wa-
> gami].[64] I had pitied such women greatly, and had even felt so supe-
> rior as to draw pictures of them, giving vent to all I wished to say.
> And now I, who had found these women so distasteful, am one of
> them. Surely some divine being has foretold it to me. As I lie wrapped
> in thought, one of my [waga] sisters enters, together with another
> person. (*KN*, 2:140)

The "person" (hito) is the heroine's aunt. Here "hito" signifies someone
other than the heroine, unlike the earlier "hito arikeri" and "tomaru
hito." It is necessary therefore that the word "waga," occurring twice in
the above passage, appear in a context that demands interpretation as a
first-person pronoun. The tenth-century usage of "waga" frequently corresponds to "his/her own" (or, as a subject, "he himself/she herself"), but
in this context it can only signify "I," "me," or "my."
    This increasingly first-person narrative stance is linked to the nature of
Part Two, which is more characteristic of a nikki than a shū. An early medieval nikki could of course be narrated either in the first or the third person, but a nikki describing one specific being would more naturally use the
first person. Part Two has little dependence on waka, relying instead on
the author's experiences for its raw material. It is therefore easily narrated

---

[61] [The heroine's husband is building a new residence, which he has promised to take her
to see when it is completed.—Trans.]

[62] [Seidensticker, 1964, 73-74. It should be emphasized that the quoted "Loves may bloom
. . ." is a poem in the original.—Trans., Ed.]

[63] *Kokka Taikan* (version edited by Matsushita Daizaburō et al., first printed in 1903;
"Nikki, Sōshi, Kashū") numbers are as follows: 190, 207, 208, 209, 210, 213, 216, 217,
218, 219, 221, 224, 235, 236.

[64] [That she would find herself escaping from a collapsing marriage by going into retreat
at a remote temple. To judge from the sentences that follow, this was a customary action for
noblewomen in the narrator's predicament.—Trans.]

in the first person. This is why the narrator gives only a brief summary of a contemporary event that "is making a great stir in society," the overthrow and banishment of Minamoto Takaakira (914-82), Minister of the Left. She explains that "Though this is a nikki in which I should set down only things that immediately concern me, the shock of the banishment has been something very close to me, and I shall be forgiven, I hope, for noting it here" (KN, 2:84).[65] This indicates that Part Two was consciously written as "a nikki in which I should set down only things that immediately concern me."

There are various kinds of nikki, including objective records of waka matches. The author of The Gossamer Years tended strongly, however, toward the concept of a nikki as a personal record—at least when she was writing Part Two. This probably resulted from the close chronological proximity of the composition period of Part Two with the events that make up its raw material. Moreover, the author's acute distress at this time made it impossible for her to maintain distance between her experiences and the events described in the work.

Part Three was probably written when the author was thirty-six years old and her son Michitsuna eighteen. She is beginning to concern herself with the boy's love affairs and marriage prospects. Appearing to achieve a certain degree of resignation and calm in Part Three, the author turns again to the shū form in writing this section. The eighty waka in Part Three are relatively few when compared with the 124 in Part One, but that is many more than in Part Two, with its fifty-five. Only five waka in Part Three, moreover, are recited by the heroine to herself.[66] The remaining seventy-five all appear in a more or less narrative setting. The conclusion of Part Three consists almost entirely of nineteen waka, exchanged between Michitsuna and a ladylove, or the narrator and her husband. This section is strongly characteristic of a shū.

The author's choice of the shū form in Part Three may have occasioned her use of third-person narration, as in the following passage:

> It is about the fifth, and he comes during the daytime, and he comes again about the tenth and again about the twentieth after *she* is abed, in dishabille. It is a strange month indeed that sees so many visits. . . . (KN, 3:204)[67]

"She" (hito) refers to the heroine, a usage similar to the earlier "she who remains behind." Such usages, however, are not so frequent in Part Three as to mark a return to third-person narration. Not long after this passage, the heroine's son Michitsuna sends a waka to his lover. She replies in kind,

---

[65] [Adapted from Seidensticker, 1964, 73.—Trans.]
[66] Kokka Taikan numbers are 255, 274, 279, 280, 281.
[67] [Adapted from Seidensticker, 1964, 141.—Trans.]

but the details of her poem are apparently unsatisfactory, since the narrator remarks, "There was a reply, but I shall not mention it" (*KN*, 3:213). The inflection "-ji" (not) in the verb "kakaji" expresses the speaker's negative intention. Thus the narrator of this scene overlaps with the heroine to produce first-person narration.[68] Part Three, then, has a mixed point of view, being narrated in both the first and the third person. This is generally true for *The Gossamer Years* as a whole. There are differences of degree, depending on which passage and part is concerned, but the narration throughout follows a mixed point of view.

This is not only a question of narrative method. The tenth-century creative awareness is also reflected here. According to this awareness, nikki, shū, and monogatari were not clearly distinguishable genres. To conceive of them as independent genres with divisible spheres of influence is to force a modern conception on the tenth century. This was still a formative period for literary prose in Japanese, and its authors progressed haltingly, with a series of trials and errors. Modern readers naturally find much that is inadequate or flawed. This is also true in terms of style. *The Gossamer Years* represents an immature stage in the history of Japanese prose. It is concerned with matters never before dealt with by that medium—human relationships and the attendant psychological complexities—but it lacks the creative force to express the subject accurately. That is why the style of *The Gossamer Years* is so difficult to understand. Another factor may lie in the fact that no extant manuscript copy of *The Gossamer Years* predates the seventeenth century, and all are replete with copyists' errors. Essentially, however, the stylistic difficulties originated with the author herself. One example has been quoted above, a passage beginning, "I had never imagined that such a thing would happen to me." This is unquestionably clear prose when read in the Seidensticker translation.[69] But the translator's splendid style masks that of the original, which is clumsy, lurching, and difficult to comprehend. The style, like the multiple-person narrative method, is an inevitable feature of the formative stage of prose in Japanese.

These elements reappear in the *Sarashina Nikki*, a somewhat later work (ca. 1060). In both works, the author's personal experiences form the raw

[68] This device, which also appears in Part Two, corresponds to the narrator's aside in fictional monogatari, discussed below. One such passage in Part Two is, "The year-end ceremonies have been of the usual sort, and I shall not stop to describe them" (*KN*, 2:122; Seidensticker, 1964, 94). In another passage, the heroine has strange dreams: "I do not know whether these dreams are good or bad, but I write them down so that those who hear of my fate will know what trust to put in dreams and signs from the Buddha" (*KN*, 2:129; Seidensticker, 1964, 98). Here again the narrator and heroine are one person.

[69] In the interests of closely approaching the style of the original, the translation given above has been used instead of the more elegant Seidensticker translation (for which see Seidensticker, 1964, 104). [Auth., Trans.]

MURASAKI SHIKIBU AND HER RELATIONS

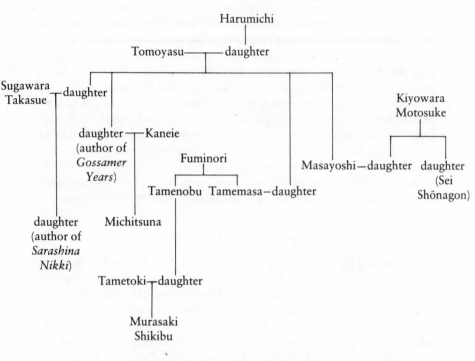

Vertical lines indicate parentage. Horizontal lines indicate marriage.
Unless specified, surnames are Fujiwara.

material for the nikki; and both, though essentially nikki, contain characteristics of the shū. The principal characters of both nikki are given fictional treatment, and their real names do not appear. For both works the narrative viewpoint should be the third person, but in fact it becomes mixed narration with the first person predominating. This is no accident: as the genealogy above shows, the author of the *Sarashina Nikki* (Sugawara Takasue's Daughter) was the niece of the author of *The Gossamer Years* (Michitsuna's Mother), and the younger writer very likely obtained a copy of her aunt's work.

It may also be noteworthy that Takasue's Daughter was related by marriage to Murasaki Shikibu and Sei Shōnagon. Murasaki Shikibu experimented boldly with the fictional monogatari, introducing ordinary beings and events into a genre that dealt in principle with either superior or ordinary beings encountering fantastic events. She would have been well aware that *The Gossamer Years*, an account of ordinary people and events, had succeeded in moving its readers. Of course Michitsuna's Mother did not expect her audience to include Sei Shōnagon and Murasaki Shikibu. In 971, the year Part One of *The Gossamer Years* is surmised to have been completed, Sei Shōnagon would have been about ten years old, and Murasaki Shikibu had probably not been born. Her audience may not have been on a par with Sei Shōnagon and Murasaki Shikibu, but it would have numbered certain female relatives and in-laws whose talent and interest in prose in Japanese would have fostered a sophisticated literary environment. It was precisely because Michitsuna's Mother expected these women to be in her audience that she wrote a nikki exclusively concerned with personal matters. Her audience knew both the author and the raw material that formed the subject of the nikki and therefore derived great enjoyment from this record of quotidian events.

Narrated in the Third Person

Narrated entirely in the third person, the *Izumi Shikibu Nikki* differs from the Japanese prose nikki hitherto discussed in its conspicuously large proportion of monogatari elements. These result from the omniscient point of view employed in the nikki. The omniscient point of view is natural to fictional monogatari but appears rarely in nikki.[70] Certain aspects of this nikki therefore entitle it to be called the *Izumi Shikibu Monogatari*. It is treated here as generally part of the nikki corpus, however, because it is cast in the present tense. I use the word "generally" in light of my view that there were no distinct boundaries between monogatari, nikki, and shū during the tenth and eleventh centuries, and that a work was assigned to a genre on the basis of differences of degree.

Scholars of Japanese literature have tended to express dissatisfaction with this "general" approach in their determination to prove whether the work is a nikki or a monogatari. Their treatment is directly linked to the question of whether the work was written by Izumi Shikibu. If the work is taken as a monogatari, then in their view she could not possibly have written it. This attitude stems from misinterpreting tenth- and eleventh-century nikki as the equivalent of modern diaries; to determine that the work is a nikki does not automatically guarantee that it was written by Izumi Shikibu. The nikki of the tenth and eleventh centuries is a work in Japanese prose about the experiences of a historical individual, but that individual is not necessarily the author of the nikki. The word "nikki," therefore, does not determine conclusively that the work in question is au-

[70] An instance occurs in the *Tosa Nikki*. One theory finds omniscient point of view in the *Kagerō Nikki*, but that is an erroneous view based on a misunderstanding of the significance of the omniscient point of view. The *Kagerō Nikki* maintains a limited point of view.

tobiographical. In fact, only one of the principal manuscript copies, the Sanjōnishi manuscript, bears the title *Izumi Shikibu Nikki*.[71]

Let us set aside the question of the authorship of the *Izumi Shikibu Nikki* and turn our attention to its writing. *The Tosa Diary* and *The Gossamer Years*, works marking the earliest stage of Japanese literary prose, have a strikingly crude, unformed style, simple narrative techniques, and events that are all observed by the narrator. If the narrator could not observe an event, it was communicated to her by another character.[72] The circulation of *The Tale of Genji*, on the other hand, influenced the style of the *Sarashina Nikki*: it is polished, with clearly structured, intelligible sentences. Its narrative techniques remain simple, however, and its events are perceived only through the narrator's eyes and ears. The *Izumi Shikibu Nikki* differs markedly in all respects, and its techniques are so polished that it cannot possibly predate the *Sarashina Nikki*. Consider, first, its opening passage.

> Day seems to follow day unnoticed as she grieves for the loss of a world of love that proved more fleeting than a dream, and it is already past the tenth of the Fourth Month as shadows gather under the trees so freshly leaved. On the earthen wall across the garden the grasses are a luxuriant green, not a sight to arrest the attention of anyone else but enough to cause her to fall into a fast reverie. Then it appears that someone is approaching through a nearby gap in the fence. As she is wondering who it might be, it turns out to be the Page who had been in the service of the late prince. (*Izumi Shikibu Nikki* [= *ISN*], 1)[73]

The reader has no idea who it is who spends her days in grief, nor is it explained why she must grieve. "The late prince" is casually mentioned, but his relationship to the grieving character is not indicated. For the contemporary audience to understand this opening passage, it would have to have substantial preparation. Unless the audience could use its familiarity with similar scenes in literature to supply, within its imagination, the surroundings in which the grieving individual finds herself, it would not respond favorably. The audience the author had in mind as she wrote her opening passage must have been quite sophisticated.

Early fictional monogatari typically begin by introducing their characters. The convention is maintained up to *The Tale of Genji* (Tamagami, 1955b, 226-28). In the *Genji*, an examination of individual chapter units

---

[71] There are three manuscript lines: the Sanjōnishi, the Ōei, and the Kangen. The Sanjōnishi "line" actually consists of a single manuscript, the Sanjōnishi manuscript (Royal Library coll.); this is the only manuscript with the title *Izumi Shikibu Nikki*.

[72] An example in the *Tosa Nikki* is the farewell banquet given for the former governor of Tosa (*TSN*, 28-29) and, in the *Kagerō Nikki*, the discussion held prior to the narrator's adoption of a foster daughter (*KN*, 3:180-81).

[73] [Adapted from Miner, 1969, 95.—Trans.]

reveals that several characters are brought into the narrative without prior introduction.

> With the new reign, the career languished, and since it was necessary to be the more discreet as higher ranks were gained, there was less to amuse. Everywhere there were complaints about aloofness.
>
> As if in punishment, one lady continued to cause pain by her standoffishness. (*GM*, "Aoi," 317)[74]

This, the opening passage of "Aoi" ("Heartvine"), presents problems to anyone unfamiliar with events in the preceding chapters. The opening is such that a reader lacking the necessary information will not discover who is complaining about what.

The bulk of fictional monogatari from the mid-eleventh century on, however, supplied their readers with numerous, mutually similar plots and characterizations that might be used satisfactorily to supplement analogous situations in other monogatari, particularly if the narrator of the monogatari in question did not provide detailed explanation. One example is the opening passage of the *Sagoromo Monogatari* (*The Story of Sagoromo* [= *SGM*], 1:29).

> The young regret the passing of spring, but still it will not linger: the twentieth of the Third Month is already past.[75] The trees before the house grow ever greener; the wisteria on the garden island comes everywhere into bloom, heedless of its reputation to "cling only to the pine," and seems to await the advent of hototogisu from the hills.[76] Round the banks of the lake, the double kerria is blooming in such profusion that the scene might well be Ide.[77]

Here, at the beginning of a long work, the narration commences without

---

[74] [Seidensticker's translation (1976, 1:158) has been doctored here to omit names and pronouns. The result is artificial, but it is closer to the original in order to substantiate—or illustrate—the author's point.—Ed.]

[75] An allusion to a couplet from a poem by Po Chü-i, "On Staying with Lu Chou-liang at the Taoist Monastery of Hua-yang Kuan in Spring" (*HKS*, 13:1932).

> Dimming the lamp, together we enjoy the midnight moon;
> Treading the blossoms, as one we regret our springtime's passing.

[Auth., Trans.]

[76] Minamoto Shigeyuki, *SIS*, 2:83.

Natsu ni koso	They have come to bloom
Sakikakarikere	Entwined about the very summer,
Fuji no hana	These wisteria flowers—
Matsu ni to nomi mo	And I had always had in mind
Omoikeru kana.	That they cling only to the pine!

[Auth., Trans. On the hototogisu, see ch. 2, n. 5.—Ed.]

[77] Ide, a few miles south of Uji in Kyoto prefecture, is famous for its kerria (yamabuki). [Auth., Trans.]

introducing the protagonists or explaining earlier events. The author of this opening passage probably assumed that the audience of the *Sagoromo* would already possess a common store of information, drawn from the many fictional monogatari then in circulation, about the typical protagonists' personalities and events generally occurring in such works.[78]

Short monogatari receive similar treatment. One good example is the beginning of "Hanazakura Oru Shōshō" ("The Lieutenant Handsome as Cherry Blossoms"; *Tsutsumi Chūnagon Monogatari; Tales of the Riverbank Counselor* [= *TCM*], 367).[79]

> He left his lady in the depths of night, misled by the full moon to think that day had dawned. She would be vexed, a pity, but he had gone too far to turn back. He made his way home, passing cottages that, at dawn, would be noisy and full of life, but where now not a sound was to be heard. In the brilliant moonlight, cherry trees were so wreathed in mist that they blended with the landscape.

This passage has much in common with the opening lines of the *Izumi Shikibu Nikki* that goes beyond the dimensions of influence and imitation. Audiences had accumulated a great deal of information about monogatari and had grown so sophisticated that meticulous explanation was considered unnecessary and even bothersome. The features shared by the opening passages of these works were based on the premise that the audience already had a general knowledge of the situation depicted. The sudden appearance of a lieutenant of the Right Guards in the *Izumi Shikibu Nikki* therefore needs no particular explanation. The mere mention that he "comes day after day with letters" for the lady informs the audience that the lieutenant is playing a role corresponding to Koremitsu's in the *Genji*. Later in the nikki, the lieutenant acts exactly in accord with such expectations by the readers.

Envisioning that her audience would be thoroughly familiar with various fictional monogatari, the author of the *Izumi Shikibu Nikki* demonstrates techniques that correspond to those used in monogatari. The climax of the nikki is the point at which the heroine, who evidently is not of very high rank, is brought by the prince, her lover, to his residence. This would probably have created a scandal in contemporary society. For that reason, the nikki audience needed to know the heroine's reasons for deciding to take such an action, or it would reject it as a clumsy mistake. The author therefore prepares the audience by creating circumstances in which an eminent personage like the prince cannot easily make indiscreet excursions. The prince's nurse, Jijū, remarks that she finds his "reckless excur-

---

[78] Yoshida Kōichi has noted the resemblance between the opening passages of the *Sagoromo Monogatari* and the *Izumi Shikibu Nikki* (Yoshida, 1957, 256-61).

[79] This point has been made by Komatsu Tomi (1980, 90).

sions most disagreeable," and, since the prince remains determined to see the lady, Jijū advises him that "it would be all right to have her here under your care" (*ISN*, 15-16).[80] The prince's amorous excursions become such a problem that they form the reason for bringing his lover into his residence. Before the nurse brings up the subject of the prince's "excursions," however, the author has the prince discuss them himself.

When he first visits the lady's house, the prince tells her, "I am not in a position to indulge in frivolous excursions" (*ISN*, 6); but the context is different from that in the prince's conversation with his nurse. He invokes his high rank and lack of future opportunities to visit her in order to persuade the lady to admit him into her bedchamber on the night of their first meeting. The prince does not seem particularly persuaded that his "frivolous excursions" are bad: he pays eight more visits to the lady's house before finally bringing her to live with him. When, at the beginning of the affair, the prince says, "I am not in a position to indulge in frivolous excursions," he is in effect concocting a pretext for his behavior at that time. But when his nurse states the same thing somewhat later in the story, it is used in a different sense—that the prince must avoid indulging in such excursions—and becomes the deciding factor for bringing the lady to the prince's residence. The author does not immediately state her primary objective but prepares for it in advance, so that when it does appear, the reader will realize that it was foreshadowed earlier. Then, at the proper moment, the author reveals her objective. Foreshadowing is known in China as "fu-pi" or "fu-hsien." Because it is employed in the structural design of an entire work, this technique is more appropriate to a long monogatari than to the usual brief nikki.

Another, similar instance occurs in the *Izumi Shikibu Nikki*. Once the heroine and the prince have had their first meeting, the prince does not revisit her for some time. He has of course been dissuaded from making "frivolous excursions," but there is another reason why he should hesitate: "His Consort is not a person given to a woman's usual intimacy with her husband, but she does regard nocturnal goings and comings with suspicion" (*ISN*, 8).[81] The prince temporarily forgoes his excursions, fearing that if he were to be out every night his powerful consort would grow suspicious, and he would find himself unavoidably enmeshed in domestic conflict. His concern is premised on the fact that his consort, while not unduly sensitive to the matter of the prince's excursions in general, would grow suspicious if they were to become frequent. Her lack of sensitivity in regard to his excursions stems from her nature: the narrator describes her as "not a person given to a woman's usual intimacy with her husband,"

[80] [Miner, 1969, 106.—Trans.]
[81] [Ibid., 100.—Trans.]

or, in other words, a woman who has grown apart from her husband. The passage focuses on whether the prince's consort will eventually notice her husband's affair with the heroine; his love relationship with his consort is of no great importance and is mentioned only for reference. It proves relevant, however, much later in the nikki. After the heroine has come to live at the prince's residence, his consort, now made fully aware of his infatuation, indignantly prepares to move back to her family house. These events create a great stir among the upper aristocracy. Ordinarily one might expect a peaceable resolution to the problem. Here, however, events progress directly toward a scandalous catastrophe, because of the longstanding discord between the prince and his consort. He strains the marriage by bringing the heroine to live with him, triggering a bitter divorce. The author is thus seen to foreshadow the divorce by mentioning, in an unrelated passage, that the prince and his consort do not share the "usual intimacy" of married couples.

The author's treatment of her characters' psychologies also suggests that she was writing for quite an advanced audience. One would expect that the *Izumi Shikibu Nikki*, narrated from an omniscient point of view, would freely portray its characters' innermost feelings. This is true up to a point, although in the most important scenes the narrator does not presume to enter into the inner workings of the characters' minds. Examples of such scenes might be the two crises that occur in the lovers' relationship. In the course of both crises, the protagonists presumably experience complex states of mind, and yet the narrator hardly exercises her special powers of omniscience to describe their shifting emotions.

The first crisis is precipitated when the prince hears a rumor that the heroine is having an affair with another man. The prince, "thinking her flighty, does not write for a long time" (*ISN*, 25). After a few days he sends a letter with this waka:

Yoshi ya yoshi	Well then, so be it—
Ima wa uramiji	Even if my little fisher's boat
Iso ni idete	Starts away from shore,
Kogihanareyuku	Leaving me by rowing on the offing,
Ama no obune o.	I shall not hate her for the loss.[82]

The prince is in essence near to breaking off the affair. The lady's reply is not very repentant.

Sode no ura ni	Truly I am she,

[82] [Ibid., 114.—Trans.] The surface meaning of the poem is, "If you've taken up with another man, I'll have to wash my hands of you."

Tada waga yaku to   The fisherwoman who has lost her boat,
    Shiotarete   Who can rely on nothing
Fune nagashitaru   But the task of producing salt
Ama to koso nare.   From the tide-soaked Bay of Sleeves.[83]

(*ISN*, 26)

This does not seem to dispel the prince's doubts completely, "and yet he cannot give her up" (*ISN*, 27). The crisis abates. "Uramiji" (I shall not hate her), in the prince's poem, is a pivot word that also signifies "I shall not see the bay" and "I shall not see behind." Added to the rhetorical pivot on a sea image, "bay," then, is another that implicitly criticizes what lies in the back of his mistress's mind: she who can show a surface love for the prince while carrying on in secret with another man must have, deep down inside, too unsavory a heart for anyone to wish to see. The lady's reply states that she burns with remorse at the evil rumors circulating about her; and that if the prince abandons her, she will be like a fisherwoman [ama] who has lost her boat, and will have to become a nun [ama].

The narrator comments that her heroine is "an imprudent creature" (*ISN*, 3). Her imprudence suggests a lively relationship with her lovers and requires little further elucidation. The heroine seems to think that she cannot always deny her imprudence and is better off communicating her present remorse and her determination to become a nun if she is thrown over. The prince then apparently has second thoughts: the idea of her becoming a nun seems to make him realize his attachment to her, and his own potential despair, like that of a fisherman who has lost his boat. Note that the characters' shifting emotions are expressed not by prose expositions or descriptions but through exchanges of poetry. The basic mode of the waka narrative (utamonogatari) is the quick resolution of events, or their final collapse, as effected by waka. Whereas events in fictional monogatari and nikki are developed and concluded in accordance with the principles inherent in the events themselves, it is a principle of the shū to rely on waka for a conclusion. The author used this technique in her nikki because she knew her audience would be quite familiar with it.

The second crisis occurs when the prince comes to visit the lady, at considerable trouble to himself, and her servant is too sleepy to open the gate, obliging the prince to go back home (*ISN*, 33-35). The heroine later writes him a long letter, interspersed with waka, that begins,

[83] ["The allegory, based on a suppressed comparison of tears and salt water, need only be mentioned; but the way in which the boat image is turned back on the Prince deserves some stress." Miner, 1969, 114n. "Shiotarete" means both "drenched by salt waves" and "sleeves wet with tears"; and "ama" can mean either "fisherwoman" or "nun." Thus the poem can also be read as, "I burn with remorse, / And the linings of my sleeves / Are drenched with tears: / Bereft of my support, / I shall become a nun."—Trans.]

The sound of the wind—it blows through branches threatening to spare no leaves—more than ever it makes one feel the true sadness of things. When a little rain seems about to scatter in drops from a sky sheeted in clouds, then one feels that the sadness is almost too great to bear.

Aki no uchi wa	During the autumn
Kuchihatenu beshi	My sleeves have moldered with my weeping;
Kotowari no	When the real drizzle
Shigure ni tare ka	Comes with the winter to bring its sadness,
Sode wa karamashi.	Who then will lend me sleeves for tears?[84]

(*ISN*, 35-37)

The prince responds with five poems. "It has been well worth her writing him" (*ISN*, 39), since the situation then ameliorates. There is no direct statement as to why the prince is satisfied with the lady's explanation, but a later reference to the incident provides a general idea:

His feelings must have been taken by the cloudy sky that night, because from then on he shows greater consideration for her and visits her with some frequency. He regards her posture intently, thinking her by no means the worldly-wise person she is made out to be. On the contrary, she looks so helpless in the world, and he feels a pang of anguish just to look upon her. (*ISN*, 42)[85]

Again, there is no psychological description. The heroine expresses her emotions in her letter: "it makes one feel the true sadness of things" (monoaware ni oboyu), "one feels that the sadness . . ." (aware ni oboete). "Sadness" (aware), in the letter, is not intended as a lament for the direction their love affair has taken; it is mentioned in reference to the wind and rain. It should also be recognized, of course, that her sadness does not merely concern the wind and rain; her feelings of sadness for herself are translated into sadness with regard to the wind and rain. The prince is moved by a different object, "the cloudy sky that night." His feelings do not manifest themselves in response to the lady's emotions, and yet her sadness is undeniably projected onto the scene of autumn leaves falling from branches in the rain. Such expression, a "fusion of scene and emotion," demands a sensitive audience.[86]

---

[84] [Miner, 1969, 121.—Trans.]
[85] [Ibid., 126.—Trans.]
[86] Descriptions ranging between nature and the characters' emotions appear in Part Two

The passage beginning, "His feelings must have been taken by the cloudy sky that night" (*ISN*, 42-45), is over thirty lines long in a revised edition of the *Nikki* and forms a single grammatical sentence reminiscent of James Joyce's long sentences in *Ulysses*. The content of the sentence shifts between thought and speech, with the narrating consciousness alternating four times between the prince and the heroine. The narrator of the nikki does not directly describe the prince's and the heroine's psychological processes. Her technique is to show the prince's view of the lady's heart and the lady's view of her lover's heart. Shifting-narrative point of view appears in nineteenth-century novels, especially around Jane Austen's time, but it is not frequently met with even in the West (Miner, 1969, 38). The linguistic characteristics of Japanese—particularly the general practice of not indicating the subject of a sentence—may partially account for the early manifestation of this technique in Japan. It may also have resulted from the author's own design: the shifting-narrative point of view takes the same form as the structure of the *Nikki* as a whole, a structure made up of alternating standpoints between the two protagonists as each observes the other.

This technique does not appear elsewhere in works from the early eleventh century, but that does not indicate that the *Izumi Shikibu Nikki* is a later work. Expressive techniques are occasionally created by chance (ibid., 38n). On the other hand, this work differs markedly from *The Gossamer Years* and the *Sarashina Nikki*. The *Izumi Shikibu Nikki* would very likely not have been written, moreover, without the presence of an audience sophisticated enough to supplement the text with what had been left unexpressed.

Fictional Monogatari

Monogatari About Superior Beings

All early narrative prose has protagonists who possess superior virtue, knowledge, talents, beauty, military prowess, or other attributes. Some of these narratives are concerned with phenomena and events that do not often occur in ordinary life, or others that are imaginary and nonrealistic—fantastic events, in other words. Let us first consider monogatari that concern extraordinary protagonists and events.

SUPERIOR BEINGS AND FANTASTIC EVENTS

Japanese archaic narrative certainly has these features. In Volume One

---

of the *Kagerō Nikki* (Itō, 1976, 234-50). These are tandem statements of nature and emotion, however, that have not yet reached the point of fusion.

of this *History*, setsuwa are divided into two groups: those dealing with deities and those dealing with the royal house. All, in differing degrees, are monogatari about superior beings and fantastic events. If we consider this point alone, that such beings and events appear in archaic narrative, little difference will be perceived between archaic narrative and early fictional monogatari. It is for this reason that stories transmitted from archaic times are thought to have been the source of early medieval fictional monogatari. Both narrative groups are thought to share common features. This is a reasonable view, since fictional monogatari contain a great many elements inherited from oral setsuwa.

One likely theory is that "mono" originally signified spirits other than the ancestral ones worshiped by an individual tribe, and that "monogatari" signified the transmission within the tribe of those alien spirits' miraculous actions; later, when men dominated mono in social life, stories (katari/-gatari) about miraculous mono gradually receded from the realm of faith, and only the unusual features of a katari, those that would attract curiosity, were sought after: the result was narrative along the lines of *The Bamboo Cutter* (*Taketori Monogatari*; Mitani, 1952, 11-17). Archaic setsuwa ought not to be considered entities separate from fictional monogatari of the Early Middle Ages. We should acknowledge a direct hereditary relationship between them, especially in terms of their subjects, superior beings and fantastic events.

All the same, obvious differences exist between archaic setsuwa and early medieval fictional monogatari. We cannot assume that the former developed naturally into the latter. One difference is that the author and the audience for a fictional monogatari were aware of the fictitiousness of its characters and events; their composition and reception were premised on their acceptance of the very fact of fictionality. In archaic setsuwa, by contrast, the audience was obliged to believe in the truthfulness of even the most unrealistic events. Common sense tells us that the story of Izanagi and Izanami giving birth to the Japanese islands is totally unbelievable. In such cases, common sense was denied, not the story: the Japanese nation exists, and so the story of the birth of the islands must be true.

The story of the old bamboo cutter, on the other hand, need not be true. Author and audience are in full agreement and understanding that the story is not true. This understanding is the basis for the audience's willingness to take the author's story as *fictionally* true. The author takes that willingness into account; it is his chief premise. Thus his story can permissibly contain unrealistic events. This, however, requires certain conventions. One convention is the equivalent of "once upon a time": this signifies that the narrated events happened long ago and have been carefully transmitted. Stories employing this convention characteristically begin in this fashion:

Once upon a time there was an old bamboo cutter. (Ima wa mukashi taketori no okina to iu mono arikeri.) (*Taketori Monogatari*)

Long ago, there was a man. (Mukashi otoko arikeri.) (*IM*)

The suffix "-keri" indicates here that the statement is a transmitted recollection of facts heard from someone. This "-keri" modifies "mukashi"
(long ago, once) in the opening formula of a story; the suffix survives in
modern Japanese nursery stories in a standard format that concludes the
equivalent of "Once upon a time" with the particles "to sa." This formula
is widely disseminated, though it takes various dialect forms according to
geographical region (Mitani, 1952, 100-108).

The formulaic narrative style is used in fictional monogatari because it
is an emblem of an awareness that what is about to be told must be accepted as fact. The emblem is manifested to the audience, who, in full
agreement that the events in the story could not happen in reality, concur
in accepting them presently as fact. This concurrence between author and
audience—the cooperation given the author by his audience—is the essential element in the formation of a work of fiction. It survives in modern
novels and plays, though differing in form and degree.

The tacit agreement between author and audience sometimes leads to a
dramatic increase in fictitiousness. As discussed in Volume One, the prototype of the first half of *The Bamboo Cutter* is an Upper Tibetan folk tale,
"Pan-chu Ku-niang" ("The Spotted-bamboo Maiden"). The heroine of
this story and its corresponding section of *The Bamboo Cutter* is a superior being, but her superiority is not excessively unrealistic. Of course, the
bamboo maiden's beauty is above the level of ordinary people's, but the
imagery used to describe her—"She was as lovely as a doe"; "The bamboo
maiden's beauty was just like a lovely flower"—gives her a sense of realistic familiarity. By contrast, Kaguyahime is described quite unrealistically: "The child possessed an unparalleled beauty so radiant that it filled
the house with light" (*Taketori Monogatari*, 10). This is probably no
more than overstatement, but the latter half of the monogatari is a fine example of fantasy: Kaguyahime reveals her true identity, that of an immortal from the kingdom of the moon, and rides her flying carriage back
home. The Tibetan story has nothing that corresponds to this: the bamboo maiden marries an ordinary man, Lang-pa, and lives happily ever
after. Kaguyahime is depicted much more unrealistically than the bamboo
maiden. Unrealistic depiction in *The Bamboo Cutter* must have been the
result of the author's expectation that his audience would pretend the
story was real while agreeing it was actually fiction, and that he could rely
on his audience to cooperate.

This readerly sophistication is very different from that of the Archaic
Age. An archaic audience would regard even an unrealistic story as true,
or would endeavor to do so, precisely because it was an oral transmission.

The two audiences regard narratives differently: the early medieval one maintains a distance between the audience and the fictional world and distinguishes fiction from reality, whereas the archaic stance has no awareness of fiction and confounds fantasy with reality.

How did the early medieval stance evolve? Possibly from influence exerted by two Chinese literary imports, the chih-kuai and ch'uan-ch'i genres. Yamanoe Okura quotes from a book called *Chih-kuai Chi*, and the "Inventory of Written Works Extant in Japan" includes the following Chinese titles:

Han Wu Nei-chuan (The Private Life of Emperor Wu of Han), 2 fascs., Ko Hung, ed.

Shen-hsien Chuan (Stories of the Immortals), 20 fascs., Ko Hung, ed.

Sou-shen Chi (Quests for Mysterious Events), 30 fascs., Kan Pao, ed.

Sou-shen Hou-chi (Further Quests for Mysterious Events), 10 fascs., T'ao Ch'ien, ed.

Hsüan-i Chi (Records of Strange Events), 10 fascs., Hou Chün-su, ed.

Ming-pao Chi (Records of Experiences in the World Beyond), 10 fascs.

Hsü Ch'i-hsieh Chi (More Records of Unusual Events), 3 fascs., Wu Chün, ed.

Han Wu Tung-ming Chi (A Record of Emperor Wu's Visit to the World Beyond), 4 fascs., Kuo Tzu-heng, ed.

Yen-shen Chi (Detailed Records of Mysterious Events), 1 fasc., Prince Hsiang-tung of Liang, ed.

Ling-i Chi (Records of Occult Events), 10 fascs.

Lieh-hsien Chuan (Stories of the Myriad Immortals), Liu Hsiang, ed.

Unlike the Japanese narratives transmitted from antiquity, these stories tell of fantastic events that took place in foreign lands. Their Japanese readers consequently felt no responsibility to perceive them as truth; it was permissible to regard them simply as unusual or interesting stories. If an audience is to find a work unusual or interesting, it must place itself in the world of the story. This stance is effected by the audience's maintaining distance between its world and events in the work. The importing of Chinese tales of the fantastic provided the impetus for creating a reading audience in Japan unlike that which had previously existed.

The titles listed above all belong to chih-kuai from the Six Dynasties period. The T'ang period saw the rise of the ch'uan-ch'i. Etymologically, "ch'uan-ch'i" means "stories of strange things," but the genre deals with various levels of strangeness. In some stories, spirits and ghosts play active roles, whereas others are concerned with unusual occurrences in the world of men; in other words, they are heightened stories.[87] Most T'ang ch'uan-

---

[87] Po Hsing-chien's "Li Wa Chuan" ("The Story of Miss Li"; *TSCC*, 3:97-108) is an example of a "strange" (ch'i) story. A young man with a brilliant future is led astray by the

ch'i tend toward realistic portrayals, but a considerable number also deal with fantastic subjects. "Ku-ching Chi" ("An Account of an Old Mirror") tells of a mirror with supernatural powers; when animal apparitions— foxes, snakes, turtles, monkeys, sharks, chickens, weasels, mice, and geck- oes—are reflected in it, they appear in their true forms and die.[88] Another, "Jen-shih Chuan" ("The Story of Mrs. Jen"), concerns a female fox who turns herself into a beautiful woman; she lives happily with a mortal man until her true identity is detected by a dog and she is mauled to death.[89] Such tales are indistinguishable in subject matter from the chih-kuai of the Six Dynasties period. There is no record of T'ang ch'uan-ch'i imported into Japan, with the exception of "The Visit to the Immortals' Dwelling." Other ch'uan-ch'i, however, probably made their way to Japan by the tenth century. We do not know whether "The Spotted-bamboo Maiden" belongs to the chih-kuai or the ch'uan-ch'i corpus, but it may have ap- peared, in some form, in Japan by the late tenth century.

The presence, at this time, of a written text of "The Spotted-bamboo Maiden" would explain why *The Bamboo Cutter* often contains diction customarily used to transpose Chinese into Japanese syntax. A Japanese trained in reading the Chinese classics would have full command of this customary, occupationally useful diction; and this diction would natu- rally appear in a monogatari written by such a person. Furthermore, as the author converted the raw material of the Chinese tale into vernacular prose, he would also have absorbed the Chinese author's attitude toward his raw material—one of conscious distancing from events in the work. Japanese readers must have quickly comprehended that the raw material in every Six Dynasties chih-kuai was narrated as a fantastic event, not part of the everyday world. The archaic idea of the truthfulness of ancient transmissions was greatly shaken by this contact with Chinese fiction.

Some T'ang ch'uan-ch'i, moreover, consciously intend to divert or en- tertain the reader with a recital of fantastic events. Shen Chi-chi, the au- thor of "The Story of Mrs. Jen," appears by name in the story, acting as the narrator; he records that the passengers on board a ship banquet dur- ing the day and tell "weird and mysterious stories" by night, and that is how the story in question emerges. This reveals an awareness of fictional monogatari.

If the transformation from setsuwa to fictional monogatari is seen as

---

charms of a singing-girl, Miss Li, and fails the provincial examinations. He is reduced to working as a professional mourner and later becomes a beggar; then Miss Li rehabilitates him and he returns to flourish in the bureaucratic world. "Ch'i" does not always signify a fantastic event. [Arthur Waley's translation of this story, under the title "The Story of Miss Li," appears in Birch, 1965, 300-13.—Trans.]

[88] *TSCC*, 1:13-24. The author is Wang Tu (Early T'ang period).

[89] *TSCC*, 1:33-42. The author, Shen Chi-chi, lived during the Middle T'ang period.

motivated by contact with Chinese fiction, then it should also be clear why *The Bamboo Cutter*, the earliest fictional monogatari, already demonstrates a fairly sophisticated design. The monogatari unfolds from the birth of its heroine, Kaguyahime, to the story of her many suitors and the difficult tasks assigned them by the adult Kaguyahime, then to her courtship by the sovereign, and it concludes with her return to the moon. Each episode is appropriately settled, and the next introduced by skillful transition. The author's design is apparent in this narrative style. Setsuwa are also the creation of an individual, and each possesses an author in the broad sense of the term. The authors of setsuwa, however, give no specific design to their creations and bear no responsibility for details of expression, with the result that setsuwa rarely attain a fixed prose form. A fictional monogatari, on the other hand, may not bear its author's name, but it would not exist if that author had not determined its literary design and been responsible for its expression. In this respect fictional monogatari differ greatly from setsuwa.

Scholars have heretofore emphasized the common lineage of setsuwa and fictional monogatari as represented by their narrative function. Little notice has been given to that great dissimilarity between the two genres that inheres in their creative functions. The dissimilarity is very great indeed. This is borne out by the content of the old *Hollow Tree (Utsuho Monogatari)*, centering on Toshikage's shipwreck and Nakatada's life in the mountains. The occurrence of several events, each developed in orderly fashion and without repetition, is a design not found in setsuwa. Another noteworthy feature of fictional monogatari is the conscious use of such stylistic techniques as parallelism. The young Nakatada, with no place to call home, meets a bear and tells it of his woes: this is indeed reminiscent of a fairy tale. And yet Nakatada addresses the bear in parallel couplets (*UM*, "Toshikage," 19/66):

takaki yama ⎱ o ⎰ orinobori ⎱ -te
fukaki tani ⎰   ⎱ makariariki ⎰

ashita ni makariidete ⎱ hodo dani ⎰ ushirometō ⎱ habereba
kurō   makarikaeru ⎰   ⎱ kanashiku ⎰

I ⎰ go up and down the high mountains,
  ⎱ walk through the deep valleys,

and when I ⎰ leave in the morning and
         ⎱ return at dusk,

I feel ⎰ uneasy and
     ⎱ saddened.

Alternating parallelism is employed here.[90] The expressive consciousness of this passage distinguishes it from setsuwa, despite the similar subject matter, superior beings and fantastic events. The passage might easily be transposed into setsuwa form by eliminating the parallelism. The hallmark of setsuwa is not its manner of saying things but its fluidity, its capacity for narrating minor events in various ways. The old *Hollow Tree* thus qualifies as a monogatari and not a setsuwa. Nevertheless, the author's obliviousness to the disharmony produced by a young man's conversing with bears and monkeys in parallel structure indicates that the techniques employed by the old *Hollow Tree* are not yet those of the mature fictional monogatari.

SUPERIOR BEINGS AND ORDINARY EVENTS

Once the author and audience are freed from the obligation to accept a story as truth, and they acknowledge that what is being told is fictitious, their release from responsibility for the veracity of a story will evolve into a tendency to relate fictitious events for purposes of diversion and entertainment. All early fictional monogatari seem to have been in the nature of diversions. The *Sambōe* was presented to Princess Takakiko in the Tenth Month of 984 by Minamoto Tamenori (d. 1011), who states in the General Preface to the work:

> Another genre is the monogatari, which serves to divert women's minds. Monogatari are more plentiful than the plants of the forest, more abundant than the grains of sand on a beach. Some have the name of a plant or tree for its title, while others use the name of a bird or a beast, a fish or an insect. All such stories give the power of speech to that which cannot speak, and discretion to that which has none. They tell only of fantastic things, and contain nothing that is factual. Stories like *The Old Lady of Iga [Iga no Tōme], The Great Lord of Tosa [Tosa no Otodo], The Fashionable Captain [Imameki no Chūjō],* and *The Nagai Chamberlain [Nagai no Jijū]* tell colorful tales about the relations between men and women. One can discover in them neither the inevitable evils nor the honesty that people truly possess. (General Preface, 5)[91]

This passage enables us to ascertain that, by the end of the tenth century:

1. Works called monogatari existed in great number.

---

[90] Complex alternation is a relatively late development in parallelism and one of the more advanced poetic techniques: see the discussion in Volume One. The presence of alternating parallelism in a boy's conversation with a bear suggests that the author may have been professionally trained in kangaku [Chinese studies] and unintentionally employs the technique here.

[91] The original text is taken from the Kanchiin manuscript.

2. Their purpose was to entertain noblewomen; they were not concerned with the realities of life.
3. Many had fantastic subjects, including personified plants, animals, and nonsentient beings.
4. Others were love stories that possessed only superficial glamor.

The passage also contains Tamenori's assertion that the most desirable
literature instructs us in the realities of life. A similar assertion later
formed the creative basis for *The Tale of Genji (Genji Monogatari)*. Tamenori, however, did not anticipate that the monogatari genre would
serve his purpose. He perceived monogatari as giddy, colorful love stories;
that is why he chose to present a collection of Buddhist setsuwa, the *Sambōe*, to the princess. About a decade earlier, Michitsuna's mother "has
had occasion to look at the old monogatari, and find them masses of the
rankest fabrication." Her decision to write a nikki may have reflected a
contemporary view that the monogatari genre was concerned with "fabrication," that is, fantasy.

There are various levels of fabrication. An exemplary variety involves
converse between men and plants or animals, as when Nakatada speaks
with a bear in the old *Hollow Tree*. But we should also keep in mind that
other monogatari "fabrications" were concerned with love affairs. A love
story, no matter how fantasized, by definition depicts events that occur
between two people; this automatically sets a limit on the degree of fantasy in the work. In such cases, the fantastic subject matter gradually
evolves into something approaching ordinary subject matter. This seems
to have been the tendency displayed by late tenth-century monogatari.
The Old Lady of Iga and the other works mentioned by Tamenori are
known only by their titles; nothing is known of their content. The hero of
another nonextant work, *Katano no Monogatari*, is a lieutenant who excels in writing love letters. One character describes him thus:

"Once you receive a love letter from the Lieutenant of Katano,
there is no escape! He is a man of extraordinary abilities—one letter
is usually enough to win a lady's heart. He has had affairs with other
men's wives, and even with His Majesty's consort! But this seems to
have brought him down in society." (*Ochikubo Monogatari*, 1:93)

Presumably each recipient of the lieutenant's love letters was captivated
by his excellent style in prose and waka, as well as by the exquisite combination of writing paper color and the object to which the letter was affixed.[92] No matter how novel the design, ingeniously contrived, elegant

[92] " 'The Lieutenant of Katano,' said the women, 'was always careful to have the flower
or the grass match the paper' " (*GM*, "Nowaki," 61-62). [Trans. by Seidensticker, 1976,
1:465.—Trans.] The color of writing paper not only had to be appropriate to the content of

letters are in effect creatures of the ordinary world and have nothing in
them that is fantastic.

The subject of the story, then, comes remarkably close to being an ordinary event. The lieutenant's conquests—a royal consort in addition to
the usual married women—are certainly not on the ordinary level. He
would probably strike modern readers as a character from a fantasy, but
the tenth-century audience, grounded in the fūryū aesthetic, would have
perceived him as a superior being. The lieutenant is quite realistic for a superior being, however, and a similarly superior character would be formidable even in a post-Meiji Restoration setting. Fictional monogatari
seem to have rapidly acquired a sense of realism by the end of the tenth
century.

We can do no more than generalize that late tenth-century fictional monogatari gradually gained in realism; only *The Story of Ochikubo (Ochikubo Monogatari)* and *The Hollow Tree* survive from this period, and the
actual state of late tenth-century prose fiction is unknown. There are
eighty-four fictional monogatari known only by title—their texts do not
survive. This number fluctuates somewhat depending on the reliability of
the data used and the method of identification. Approximately twenty-
eight of these monogatari predate the *Genji*, although it must be said that
none is of easily ascertainable date.[93]

The *Sumiyoshi Monogatari (The Story of Sumiyoshi)*, which survives in

---

a letter [i.e., bright colors for informal or love letters, darker colors for letters written in
mourning—Trans.], the color must also harmonize with the object accompanying the letter.
A letter on red paper, for instance, would be attached to a wild carnation or a small spray of
blossoming plum for delivery. Yellow paper was usually accompanied by a spray of blossoming kerria or a mandarin orange. More elaborate combinations existed as well (Konishi,
1955a, 86-88).

[93] In addition to the titles mentioned in this section—*Iga no Tōme, Tosa no Otodo, Ima-
meki no Chūjō, Nagai no Jijū, Katano no Monogatari, Hakoya no Toji,* and *Kakuremino*—
the following titles also survive: *Kamo no Monogatari (The Story of Kamo,* mentioned in
KN); *Fushimi no Okina (An Old Man of Fushimi,* mentioned in *Kannyo Ōjōgi, Advice for
Women Wishing to Enter Paradise); Miyoshino no Himegimi (A Young Lady from Fair
Yoshino,* mentioned in *Daisaiin Saki no Goshū, The First Waka Collection by the Great
High Priestess of Kamo); Toneri no Neya (The Guardsman's Bedchamber,* mentioned in
UM); *Hanazakura (Cherry Blossoms,* mentioned in *Akazome Shū, Collected Waka of Aka-
zome Emon); Mumoregi (Bogwood), Tsuki Matsu Onna (The Woman Who Waits for the
Moon to Rise), Umetsubo no Taishō (General of the Umetsubo), Dōshin Susumuru (Pious
Exhortations), Matsugae (Pine Branches), Komano no Monogatari (The Story of Komano),*
and *Monourayami no Chūjō (The Envious Captain)* (all mentioned in MSS); *Otogiki (Hearing Rumors,* mentioned in MSS, Maeda manuscript); *Kawahori no Miya (The Bat Prince,*
mentioned in MSS, Sakai manuscript); *Hitome (In the Public Eye,* mentioned in MSS, Nōin
and Maeda manuscripts); *Karamori* [a person's name], *Jōsammi (The Senior Third Rank),
Serikawa (The Seri River), Katsura Chūnagon Monogatari (The Middle Counselor of Katsura),* and *Tōgimi (Remote Lady)* (all mentioned in GM). If the old version of the *Sumiyoshi
Monogatari* is added, the total is twenty-eight titles [not all of which predate the *Genji Monogatari*—Ed.].

a version rewritten in the Kamakura or early Muromachi period, is the only one of this group whose original text can be deduced; we have only fragmentary knowledge of the content of the other works.[94] The trend in fiction was toward including fewer fantastic events, but the extent of the trend cannot be ascertained. *Hakoya no Toji*, for example, has been thought a work with many fantastic elements, including the identity of one of its main characters, a female immortal (Horibe, 1943, 23-28).[95] Another nonextant monogatari, *Kakuremino (The Magic Cloak)*, apparently told of a marvelous straw raincloak that makes its wearer invisible, so enabling its wearer to have many adventures (Matsuo, 1939, 1-19).[96] The trend toward realism in fictional monogatari did not take place simultaneously and at the same rate of speed in all works. It would be best to conclude that monogatari on fantastic subjects continued to be composed at the audience's demand, even after the majority of monogatari had been given over to ordinary subjects. Monogatari about ordinary events did, however, predominate in the late tenth century.

This can be said because the new *Hollow Tree*, which probably predates En'yū Tennō's reign (969-84), is essentially a monogatari about ordinary events. A passage in the *Dainagon Kintō Shū (Collected Waka of Fujiwara Kintō)* provides external evidence concerning the composition period of the new *Hollow Tree*.

It was during En'yū's reign, perhaps, that a discussion arose over which character in *The Hollow Tree* was the more attractive, Suzushi or Nakatada. Shinonahashi favored Suzushi, and the First Princess favored Nakatada.[97] People began taking sides, until His Majesty bade them be silent. No one could say a thing. Then His Majesty sent to tell Kintō of the matter. He responded,

Okitsu nami	Is he who dwells
Fukiage no hama ni	On Fukiage Beach where winds
Iei shite	Blow in from the sea

---

[94] Differences between the extant and ancient texts of *Sumiyoshi* can be deduced from excerpts appearing in the *Yoshinobu Shū (Collected Waka of Ōnakatomi Yoshinobu)*, variant manuscript, and the *Saishu Sukechika Shū (Collected Waka of Sukechika, Master of Ritual at the Grand Shrine of Ise*; Horibe, 1943, 39-72). The text can be further supplemented by excerpts in the *Daisaiin Saki no Goshū* (Kuwabara Hiroshi, 1967, 65-70).

[95] [Depending on one's reading of the title, *Hakoya no Toji* can be surmised to have very different content. Horibe interprets the title literally, as signifying "A Lady of Hakoya," Hakoya being a legendary dwelling of immortals. But "Hakoya" can also be taken to mean a former sovereign's palace, and "toji" a court lady.—Trans.]

[96] *Kakuremino* is mentioned in the *Sagoromo Monogatari* (Ch. 1:36, Ch. 2:192, Ch. 3:293, Ch. 4:399). Matsuo believes that *Kakuremino* predates the *Genji*.

[97] Shinonahashi is the name of an otherwise unidentified person. The *Gunsho Ruijū* edition has "Shinohashi."

Hitori suzushi to	Correct in thinking he alone
Omou beshi ya wa.	Knows what it means to feel cool?[98]

(*Dainagon Kintō Shū*, 530)

The last year of En'yū's reign was 984, the year Tamenori presented the *Sambōe* to Princess Takakiko. Tamenori does not mention either the old or the new *Hollow Tree*, probably because neither had circulated widely.[99] Tamenori was a scholar of Chinese (kangaku), and so he may certainly not have been fully informed about new monogatari: *The Old Lady of Iga, The Nagai Chamberlain,* and other works he cites as examples seem to have existed well before 984.[100] Kintō's *Collected Waka* was not compiled by the poet himself but by a family member or retainer, and there is some tentativeness in the statement, "It was during En'yū's reign, *perhaps*, that. . . ." All this suggests that the passage does not present unassailable evidence. Nevertheless, it is not unreasonable to assume that at least Part One of the new *Hollow Tree* existed prior to 984.

Suzushi and Nakatada are mentioned in connection with the beach at Fukiage, an indication that the two "Fukiage" chapters had been completed before Kintō composed his waka. We may thus conclude that Part One of the new *Hollow Tree* (up to "Okitsu Shiranami," "Whitecaps in the Offing") had been completed by this time. Part One of the new *Hollow Tree* differs completely in subject matter from the old *Hollow Tree*: the new version is essentially concerned with ordinary events. If Part One is considered in terms of smaller units, some fantastic events do surface. "Tadakoso," for example, has a wicked stepmother story; but the stepmother's motive in driving away her stepchild Tadakoso is her illicit love for him, an unusual motif not found in other monogatari about wicked stepmothers.

It almost seems as if this story is of foreign origin.[101] Several monogatari

---

[98] "Suzushi" means "cool" or "refreshing." The character Suzushi comes from a wealthy provincial family and is both handsome and talented. Kintō's poem implies that Suzushi might stand out in provincial society but that he is no match for Nakatada in the capital. [Auth., Trans.]

[99] Internal evidence suggests that 971 would be the terminus a quo for the composition of the *Utsuho* (Nakano, 1956, 31-56). The new *Utsuho*, a recent work, would have been unknown to the kangaku scholar Tamenori.

[100] It has long been known that *Imameki no Chūjō* and *Nagai no Jijū* are mentioned in Genshin's *Kannyo Ōjōgi* (fragment; Yamada, 1951, 445). The fragment is quoted in Teika's *Kokin Hichūshō* (*Secret Commentary on the Kokinshū*; 18:426).

[101] The earliest instance of the motif of a stepmother's illicit love for her stepson appears in the legend of Crown Prince Kunāla (*Divyāvadāna*). It is also found in the *Aikuō Kyō* (*Sūtra of King Aśoka*), the *Rokudo Shukkyō* (*Sūtra of Six Compilations,* fasc. 4), and the *Senjū Hyakuen Kyō* (*Sūtra of Collected Legends,* fasc. 10), as well as in the *Konjaku Monogatari Shū* (Book 4, story 4).

about wicked stepmothers existed in the late tenth century.[102] *Sumiyoshi* comes first to mind. As far as can be told from extant data, *The Story of Sumiyoshi* is concerned with ordinary events, aside from some divine favor granted the characters by the bodhisattva Kannon of Hase. The motif of a stepmother's illicit love for her stepson is considerably more unusual by comparison. On the other hand, it is one particular aspect of human relations and appears far more normal when compared with the world of the old *Hollow Tree*: there the god Amewaka makes a zither from sacred wood guarded by asuras, and the sound of the zither makes mountains crumble and buries enemy forces.

"Tadakoso" may well have been an already extant wicked stepmother story that was rewritten and incorporated into the new *Hollow Tree*. This story aside, the rest of *The Hollow Tree* is so normal, so quotidian, that it strikes the reader as a lackluster piece of fiction. "Matsuri no Tsukai" ("The Festival Messenger"), for instance, contains detailed descriptions of the Kamo festival, Suzushi's elegant banquet, a kagura performance at the Katsura mansion, and a moonviewing banquet; in addition, Atemiya's suitors begin to appear in this chapter. In quantitative terms, then, everyday events are far more dominant in the narrative. The daily events described in *The Hollow Tree* do not aid in developing the plot, nor do they serve as a backdrop heightening the protagonists' circumstances and emotions. These events have no purpose; they are merely listed. Consequently, if *The Hollow Tree* is to be considered a fictional monogatari, those sections depicting everyday events must be branded superfluous; and yet these superfluous sections are quantitatively far more plentiful than the necessary parts.

What can this mean? The sections that describe everyday events may have been written in the expectation that they would be read much like a nikki. Contemporary aristocratic society was based on Chinese culture, but it had skillfully blended it with indigenous Yamato beliefs, customs, and responses to life, and was just putting the finishing touches on a new Japanese culture. This society saw value in performing everyday actions, just as it valued nikki that described those events and the act of reading such nikki. Various natural events at court are invested with a tacit worth: Murasaki Shikibu's descriptions of the royal births at the Tsuchimikado mansion, all the ceremonies associated with them, and Ichijō Tennō's (r. 986-1011) progress to the mansion (*MSN*, 443-70); or Sei Shōnagon's descriptions of the service on the Full Canon of the Sutras, sponsored by the chancellor, Fujiwara Michitaka (953-95), and held at the Sakuzenji, and the attendance at the service of the Royal Lady Akiko (*MSS*, dan 278:284-

[102] "There are many old monogatari about wicked stepmothers" (*GM*, "Hotaru," 436).

300). The new *Hollow Tree* contains descriptions of everyday events because the author and the audience (the patron in particular) were all aware of their value.

This would explain why certain scenes in *The Hollow Tree* are not abridged. "Kasuga Mōde" ("Pilgrimage to Kasuga") contains a scene in which Minamoto Masayori and his party compose waka at the Kasuga Shrine: every waka composed by the thirty-eight people present is recorded in the text (68/263-70/271). "Kiku no En" ("The Festival of the Chrysanthemums") also lists every waka written on a set of screens depicting the twelve months and presented to the Royal Dowager (Saga Tennō's mother) on the occasion of her birthday (153/601-604). Such lists are exceedingly tedious material for a fictional monogatari, but rather a natural approach if one thinks of *The Hollow Tree* as a nikki. Part One of the new *Hollow Tree*, then, mirrors a contemporary aristocratic awareness of the value of depicting pleasurable activities. Being cut off from everyday tenth-century life, we modern readers cannot recognize the literary value of such descriptions, but the contemporary aristocracy surely thought it a delightful record of events.[103] The author seems to have lacked sufficient strength to succeed in his novel attempt to combine descriptions of ordinary events with the interest generated by plot development. The hybrid nature of *The Hollow Tree*—its fusion of nikki and monogatari characteristics—suggests that it may not have satisfied contemporary criteria either.

Compared with *The Hollow Tree*, *The Story of Ochikubo* is a fairly successful work, because it observes the techniques characteristic of a fictional monogatari. This does not include the fourth chapter, which is so poorly written that it is thought to be the work of a different author.[104] Here again the protagonist is a superior being molded to fit into an ordinary world. The *Ochikubo* is usually called a wicked stepmother story because that motif is present in the monogatari. There are relatively few passages, however, in which the heroine is persecuted by her stepmother, and more of the story is given over to the hero Michiyori's revenge. No other character in the story can rival Michiyori in resourcefulness and powers of execution, the talents that enable him to rescue the heroine from despair and danger and to chastise the stepmother. In this respect he is in-

---

[103] Events are not what moves the viewers of René Clair's film, *Sous les Toits de Paris* (1930). The Paris streets are the stars of the film; the audience is captivated by the atmosphere of Paris and the emotions of the people who live there. Unfortunately the author of the new *Utsuho* did not have access to expressive techniques worthy of René Clair.

[104] Chapter 4 of the *Ochikubo* may have been added to the first three chapters by a later author (Tsukudo Akemi, 1955, 11-25). Further evidence is necessary to support some points in this theory, but this does not alter the fact that Chapter 4 is anomalous.

deed a superior being, although his superiority is not characterized by any supernatural qualities. In other words, emphasis is placed only on a superiority functioning within the limits of daily life. Abilities similar to Michiyori's are not particularly rare in real life. Not one event in the *Ochikubo* is created or resolved by supernatural strength: all progress in accordance with the logic of the everyday world. Michiyori's actions are on the ordinary level, but the author, following an unwritten contemporary rule that a monogatari hero must be superior, felt obliged to make him so. The author's device is to make Michiyori look superior by having him associate only with characters that are mediocre or worse. Michiyori becomes a superior being by relativity, by virtue of his relations with secondary characters. His superiority would be far less striking by absolute standards, or even in the context of ordinary people.

For the most part, the *Ochikubo* is oriented toward depicting ordinary beings and events; one would therefore expect *The Tale of Genji*, a later work, to progress further in this direction. But its first group of chapters retains many elements characteristic of fantasy. The radiant Genji of these chapters is superior in all respects. Endowed with natural beauty, blessed with surpassing talents in waka composition and musical performance, and refined in his tastes, Genji is always described in terms of the highest praise. Genji dances "The Waves of the Blue Sea" at a dress rehearsal for the royal excursion to the Suzaku Palace; Tō no Chūjō, his partner in the dance, is a handsome and accomplished young aristocrat, but even he is no more than "a nondescript mountain shrub beside a blossoming cherry" when Genji is near. As Genji sings a shih couplet during the dance, his voice is so beautiful that people "believed they were listening to the Kalavinka bird of paradise" (*GM*, "Momiji no Ga," 271).[105] He is a greater lover than the Lieutenant of Katano and conducts his affairs with the utmost fūryū. Fantastic events also occur frequently in Part One, as if in correspondence to Genji's superior nature. Representative examples are the demonic possession and sudden death of Yūgao (the lady of the evening faces) and then Aoi's death, caused by the living spirit of the Rokujō lady (Rokujō no Miyasudokoro). Of course a contemporary reader would have believed such events to be possible, but they could not be called ordinary events.[106] It should also be noted that fantastic events play a vital role in these chapters, as the impetus for a new development or resolution

---

[105] [Both *Genji* quotations are from Seidensticker, 1976, 1:132.—Trans.] The Kalavinka bird dwells in Amida's (Amitābha's) paradise, where it preaches the Dharma in its exquisitely beautiful voice.

[106] "The world of Heian was heavily populated with goblins, demons, spirits and other supernatural beings" (Morris, 1964, 130).

in the plot.[107] In these respects, the opening part of the *Genji* appears to have retreated from the realism in the *Ochikubo*.

This may not be unrelated to the expectations of the audience for the first part, the patron of the work and the patron's intimate circle. The audience for a modern novel is large and unspecific, but an eleventh-century *monogatari* was written at the request of a known patron. It did not come into being simply to further literary ideals, since its author had to consider more specific circumstances. Nevertheless, not a single audience member for the first part of the *Genji* would have rated it lower than the *Ochikubo* in terms of its retreat from ordinary subjects. The marked difference between the two works is such as to render any comparison impossible. Their difference should not be seen in the dimension of characters and events taking ordinary shapes but rather in the light of accuracy in reflecting real people and society. Michiyori certainly controls and resolves situations with abilities that exist in the real world. There is not one scene in which a catastrophe is unexpectedly reversed by the action of a supernatural being or event. The problem lies in the very fact that Michiyori resolves everything by means of his own abilities. In real life, even superior people cannot always have everything go their way. The inability to have things go as we might wish—disappointment, in other words—is one true aspect of our world. Viewed from this angle, the always triumphant Michiyori appears to be a most unrealistic creation.

Genji, a superior being, paradoxically experiences frequent setbacks. His early separation from his mother may be considered beyond his control, but his illicit love for Fujitsubo, a principal plot element of the opening chapters, is certainly not satisfied. And because it is not, Genji suffers like a real human being. Genji is far more realistic than Michiyori, who never experiences suffering. Buddhism teaches that disappointment is the fabric of our world. That is not to say that Murasaki Shikibu was propounding Buddhist belief. She would naturally have been concerned with and aware of Buddhism, as were all her contemporaries, but her emphasis on disappointment cannot easily be attributed to Buddhist influence. She seems instead to have been influenced by the Chinese histories. Murasaki Shikibu notes her knowledge of the *Records of the Historian (Shih Chi)* in her nikki. Everything described in the *Records*—countries at war or at peace, on the rise or in collapse, and biographies of individuals—centers on the idea of people confronting events on the basis of their own powers and obligations. The results are frequently not what had been wished. The outlook expressed in the *Records*, namely, that life consists of disap-

---

[107] One instance is the celestial phenomena and portentous dreams that communicate the late Kiritsubo sovereign's wishes to Genji and so provide the impetus for effecting Genji's return to the capital (*GM*, "Akashi," 79).

pointments, was the impetus that made it possible, for the first time, to incorporate realism into fictional monogatari.

Monogatari About Ordinary Beings

ORDINARY BEINGS AND ORDINARY EVENTS

Genji once has occasion to criticize monogatari as "fabrications." Tamakazura disagrees: she perceives them as records of true events. Acknowledging that he may have exaggerated somewhat, Genji then embarks on a discussion of monogatari.

". . . They have set down and preserved happenings from the age of the gods to our own. The *Chronicles of Japan* and the rest are a mere fragment of the whole truth. It is your monogatari that fill in the details.

"We are not told of things that happened to specific people exactly as they happened; but the beginning is when there are good things and bad things, things that happen in this life which one never tires of seeing and hearing about, things which one cannot bear not to tell of and must pass on for all generations. If the storyteller wishes to speak well, then he chooses the good things; and if he wishes to hold the reader's attention he chooses bad things, extraordinarily bad things. Good things and bad things alike, they are things of this world and no other."[108]

Genji next explains that fabrication in monogatari serves the same purpose as the Buddhist expedients (hōben) that explicate the Dharma; and that the relation between fiction and fact is similar to that between delusion and enlightenment (*GM*, "Hotaru," 431-33).[109] It is an outstanding passage.

Murasaki Shikibu's clear exposition of the relationship between fiction and fact in prose narrative may have been inspired by the *Records of the Historian (Shih Chi)*. In the *Murasaki Shikibu Nikki*, Ichijō Tennō remarks of the author of the *Genji*, " 'She must have read the *Chronicles of Japan!* . . . She seems very learned' " (*MSN*, 500).[110] "Learned" (zae aru)

---

[108] [The translation is taken, with minor changes, from Seidensticker, 1976, 1:437.—Trans.]

[109] "Hōben" is the Sino-Japanese translation of the Sanskrit "upāya" (coming near, approach), also known as "upāya-kauśalya," "the most skillful approach." "Kauśalya" means "cleverness," or "skillfulness," and signifies approaching a man according to his own nature and talents, in order to help him understand the truth. [Hōben are, then, the Buddha's expedients—parables, accidents, even other individuals—to bring understanding of the Law or enlightenment.—Ed.]

[110] [The translation is taken, with minor changes, from Bowring, 1982, 137.—Trans. In

is a reference to Murasaki Shikibu's knowledge of Chinese studies (kan-gaku). This passage is followed by a reminiscence: when Murasaki Shi-kibu was a child and their father was teaching her older brother the *Records*, she memorized and understood the text more quickly than did her brother, much to their father's despair. Ichijō sensed that the Chinese his-tories lay behind the *Genji*; Murasaki Shikibu acknowledges that his per-ception is correct by following the passage describing his impressions with another about growing up in a family where the *Records* was taught. The nikki passages are also correlated to Genji's remark that "the *Chronicles of Japan* and the rest are a mere fragment of the whole truth." Murasaki Shikibu asserts that monogatari, like history, transmit truth about our world, and what is more, that monogatari, which are unfettered by fact, can transmit this truth more faithfully than history.

Due recognition of this point will reveal that the *Genji* and the *Records* indeed share certain properties. The latter work has a large cast of individ-ualistic characters and portrays various vicissitudes in a dynamic style. If its language were more accessible, modern readers would find the *Records* a great deal more interesting than our current popular fiction. Mu-rasaki Shikibu was strongly impressed by the *Records*, a far more varied and forceful narrative than the "colorful tales" of the tenth century. When she was requested to write a new fictional monogatari, she observed the conventions of the genre while following the example of the *Records* in attempting to depict the true aspects of her world. To succeed in her goal, she must not only describe people and events but also show their signifi-cance with respect to the realities of this world. Each section of the *Records* is followed by a short critique (tsan), in which the historian gives his opinions and makes his point concerning the facts presented in the text. This represents an advanced intellectual accomplishment. Murasaki Shi-kibu needed to express similar cogent opinions in writing about the reali-ties of life, and yet a monogatari was after all fiction, and the fictional re-quirements had to be followed. The *Genji* thus contains nothing that corresponds to the tsan: Murasaki Shikibu's critiques are instead imbed-ded in the narrative. It did not matter to her if unperceptive audiences missed her critiques. They were there for the discerning reader to find.

---

the ensuing discussion, the author speaks of the three "parts" of the *Genji*, groupings of its fifty-four chapters that are widely accepted among Japanese scholars. The long first part goes from the first through the thirty-third chapter, from "Kiritsubo" ("The Paulownia Court") to "Fuji no Uraba" ("Wisteria Leaves"); the second goes from the thirty-fourth through the forty-first chapter, from "Wakana Jō" ("New Herbs: Part One") to "Maboroshi" ("The Wizard"). The third section consists of the last thirteen chapters, forty-two through fifty-four, from "Niou Miya" ("His Perfumed Highness") through "Yume no Ukihashi" ("The Floating Bridge of Dreams"). The last ten chapters are often distinguished as Uji Jūjō (the ten Uji chapters).—Ed.]

The theme of a modern novel is a condensed version of the tsan. A theme is an author's view and criticisms of life, condensed to form the core of his work. The theme is not stated in modern fiction but instead is usually imbedded in the narrative. The audience experiences intellectual pleasure in understanding characters and events in light of the implied theme. *The Tale of Genji*, an eleventh-century work, is popular in the West as well as in Japan because its emphasis, like that of the modern novel's, is the relationship of the story to the embodied theme. Medieval Japanese audiences, however, were generally unconcerned with matters of theme. The narrator of the *Sarashina Nikki* describes how, in her girlhood, she has her first encounter with the *Genji*: she reads it exactly as we would a potboiler (*SSN*, 492-93). The patron of Part One of the *Genji* (probably the royal consort Akiko) evidently had not been liberated from the traditional response to fictional monogatari. Her wishes and requirements no doubt account for the sense of fantasy in Part One, a feeling that the story has retreated from the standard set by *The Story of Ochikubo* in its orientation toward everyday qualities.

Monogatari reception, however, was not limited to the patron and her intimate circle: outsiders could also become part of the audience. There is a scene in the *Genji* in which Genji eavesdrops on a lady-in-waiting reading a monogatari to his daughter, the Akashi girl, and this probably reflects reality ("Hotaru," 431). Men were not supposed to read fictional monogatari, but this was only a matter of appearances. In fact, they did. When Murasaki states her opinion of Atemiya, the heroine of *The Hollow Tree*, Genji is able to make his own informed response (ibid., 435). He could do this only if he was familiar with the story. It is clear from the *Murasaki Shikibu Nikki* that at least three men—Ichijō, Michinaga, and Kintō—knew what was contained in the *Genji*.[111] Anticipating that these intellectual gentlemen might join her audience, the author probably took the reasonable precaution of imbedding weighty themes in her work while knowing full well that Akiko, the patron, would have difficulty grasping them. Suppose, moreover, that someone already knowledgeable about the plot of the *Genji*, as it then existed, had requested Murasaki Shikibu to write more *Genji* chapters that would be fairly independent of the earlier narrative. If this patron had sophisticated literary tastes, Murasaki Shikibu would necessarily have prepared a text that was both thematically and technically superior to her earlier compositions. The greater proficiency displayed in the sixteen Tamakazura-line chapters, as compared with the seventeen chapters of the Murasaki line, is most logically explained if we conclude that the two groups were commissioned by different patrons.

[111] *MSN*, 470 (Kintō); ibid., 500 (Ichijō Tennō); ibid., 504 (Michinaga).

Modern readers also tend to see the mixing together of chapters centering on the main plot of the *Genji* with others centering on subplots as evidence of a loosely structured narrative. This aspect of the *Genji* would not have bothered readers familiar with the general structure of works like the *Records of the Historian*. The *Records* is made up chiefly of basic annals (pen-chi), accounts of hereditary houses (shih-chia), and biographies (lieh-chuan). The basic annals are a historical account of a kingdom or ruler and cover a long period of time. Many characters therefore appear in the basic annals; the more important ones are treated individually in separate biographies. For example, "The Basic Annals of Emperor Kao-tsu" describes the tumultuous life of the founder of the Han Dynasty, Liu Pang. It begins with his birth and boyhood and describes his conquest of Ch'in and Ch'u and, once he establishes a peaceful rule, goes on to relate his visit to P'ei, his home town, where he regales the people with banquets.[112] The annals conclude with his death shortly thereafter and the funeral ceremonies.[113] These annals are chronologically ordered. Other characters that appear in them—Hsiao Ho, Ts'ao Ts'an, Chang Liang, Ch'en P'ing—later become the subjects of biographies or accounts of hereditary houses, in which their highly individualistic activities are described. If these supplementary accounts are read together with "The Basic Annals of Emperor Kao-tsu," one will understand the entire process that led to the founding of the Han Dynasty. We may consider the seventeen Murasaki-line chapters as "The Hereditary House of Genji," accompanied by "The Biography of the Lady of the Evening Faces," "The Biography of Tamakazura," and the rest.[114] This would have been quite an acceptable reading method, at least for those familiar with the *Records*. The present *Genji* consists of the "hereditary house" chapters, arranged chronologically according to Genji's age and interspersed by the "biography" chapters.

Part One of the *Genji*, then, may very well have the properties of a Japanese *Records*. When Genji leaves the capital to live at Suma, it is not because, like Michizane and Korechika, he has been exiled. He goes willingly to escape danger. Genji's action has been thought based on the story of the Duke of Chou (Abe Akio, 1959, 652-63).[115] The duke's position is

---

[112] Michinaga alludes to this event in the last line of his shih: "May our lord graciously progress again to P'ei!" (see p. 171).

[113] ["The Basic Annals of Emperor Kao-tsu" appears in Watson, 1961, 1:77-118.— Trans.]

[114] "Basic annals" relate the deeds of an emperor or king; the "hereditary houses" tell of noblemen's deeds. Genji is eventually elevated to the status of a former sovereign; thus his story cannot easily be called "The Basic Annals of Genji."

[115] This theory appears in the *Kakaishō* but has been disregarded by the scholarly community. Abe Akio clearly demonstrates its scholastic value. Shimizu Yoshiko has partially amended Abe's thesis (Shimizu, 1966, 243-46).

threatened by groundless rumors spread by Kuan Shu and his followers, and so the duke goes to live in eastern China for two years. Inauspicious signs then appear, including a great thunderstorm that destroys the rice crop ready for harvest. King Ch'eng sees documents left behind by the duke, realizes his uncle's loyalty, and recalls him to the capital. This account appears in the *Records* ("The Hereditary House of the Duke of Chou, Ancestor of the Lu"). The great thunderstorm in the *Records* corresponds to the windstorm that precipitates Genji's return to the capital (*GM*, "Suma," "Akashi," 52-62). The inauspicious thunderstorm is also mentioned in another account of these events, "The Metal-Bound Casket" chapter of the *Shang Shu (Book of Documents)*.[116] Murasaki Shikibu is probably referring to the *Documents* as well as to the *Records*. Not coincidentally, two chapters earlier, Genji recites, "I am King Wen's son, King Wu's younger brother," when the political climate worsens after his father's death (*GM*, "Sakaki," 409).[117] Genji compares his father to King Wen and his brother Suzaku to King Wu, and so it follows that he sees himself as the Duke of Chou.

This indicates that a political theme is embedded in at least the seventeen Murasaki-line characters of Part One. The focus on politics is not that of the *Records*, in which battles decide the fate of nations. In the *Genji* the "battles" concern which family will have the chance to provide a mother for the next sovereign. The theme, however, is the same in both works: the conflicts arising over supreme political power. It would surely have been out of the question to introduce an overt political theme into a monogatari, a genre whose original purpose was to entertain women. This is why Murasaki Shikibu carefully conceals her political theme while dropping subtle hints that would be immediately taken by anyone with a basic knowledge of the Chinese classics.

The Tale of Genji begins with the words, "In a certain reign there was a lady not of the first rank whom the sovereign loved more than the rest of his many consorts and concubines" (*GM*, "Kiritsubo," 27).[118] "In a certain reign" ("Izure no ōntoki ni ka") is not merely a descendant of the traditional opening formula for a work of fiction, "Once upon a time." "In a certain reign" has a specific significance. "The Paulownia Court" strongly reflects Po Chü-i's "Song of Everlasting Sorrow," and so the opening passage of the *Genji* naturally corresponds to the first line of Po's poem: "The Han emperor, amorous, longed for a devastating beauty."[119] Specifically,

[116] [A translation of the relevant passage from the "Metal-Bound Casket" ("Chin-t'eng") appears in Watson, 1962, 35-36.—Trans.]

[117] " 'I am King Wen's son, King Wu's younger brother, and King Ch'eng's uncle. I will never be humbled in this land' " (*Shih Chi*, 33 ["Lu Chou-kung Shih-chia"]:1518).

[118] [Adapted from Seidensticker, 1976, 1:3.—Trans.]

[119] Tamagami Takuya stresses the connection these lines have to the opening lines of the *Ise Shū (Kasen Kashū* manuscript): "Izure no ōntoki ni ka ariken . . ." (Tamagami, 1955b,

Po's "Han emperor" corresponds to "In a certain reign," and "amorous, longed for a devastating beauty" corresponds to "his many consorts and concubines" ("Nyōgo kōi amata saburaitamaikeru"). "The Han emperor" in fact denotes the T'ang period emperor Hsüan-tsung; the poet avoids a direct statement by setting the poem in the Han period. "Izure no" (a certain) is a similarly equivocal expression, as is the use of "reign" for the Chinese emperor [i.e., Japanese tennō]. Thus, to be still more specific, the "Han" of Po's poem is equivalent to "a certain" in the *Genji* text, and "emperor" is equivalent to "reign" (Konishi, 1955b, 61-64). The "Song of Everlasting Sorrow," with its implied criticism of Hsüan-tsung, is the prototype for "The Paulownia Court," and so the latter work necessarily takes on political overtones.

Murasaki Shikibu tutored Akiko in the *New Ballads*, which contain some of the most politically critical of Po's poetry (*MSN*, 501). She would, therefore, have strongly sensed the criticism of Hsüan-tsung implicit in the "Song of Everlasting Sorrow," despite its classification as a poem on "heartache."[120] "The Paulownia Court" forms the preface to Part One of the *Genji*, a monogatari about royal succession as determined by blood ties and the power struggles that accompany it. This is not graphically clear to the reader, because Part One is superficially concerned with descriptions of the fūryū life. Yet Part One cannot possibly be understood without reference to its political framework. This is true only for the seventeen Murasaki-line chapters, of course: the sixteen Tamakazura-line chapters are more strongly characteristic of the fūryū-dominated monogatari.

Political subjects are rare in Japanese literature. The scarcity of political topics is, in fact, a characteristic of Japanese literature. There is, however, one more Heian work that deals with political affairs: the two "Kuniyuzuri" ("Abdication") chapters in Part Two of the new *Hollow Tree*. The tennō of the Suzaku palace decides to abdicate, so setting the scene for a momentous political battle over the nomination of the next crown prince. The two contenders are the son of the Fujitsubo consort (Atemiya), a Minamoto, and the son of the Nashitsubo consort, a Fujiwara. His Majesty eventually approves the Fujitsubo consort's son for crown prince. The struggle is impressively portrayed. The participants alternate between joy

---

221). Shimizu Yoshiko sees the interrogative "izure no" as a paradoxical reference to the Engi or Tenryaku eras (Shimizu, 1966, 10-66). [Engi, 901-23, was the second of three era names during the reign of Daigo; Tenryaku, 947-57, was the first of four era names during the reign of Murakami. There is a general presumption that the *Genji Monogatari* is set in some such idealized earlier era.—Ed.]

[120] "Heartache" (kan-shang) is one of three poetic categories Po gives in the *Po-shih Ch'ang-ch'ing Chi*. The poems on "heartache" are lyric poems on social subjects and are not necessarily sentimental poetry.

and despair, officials scurry about hoping for divine assistance in grasping political power, and the real powerholders remain behind the scenes, scheming. "The Abdication" has been highly praised for its splendid grasp of reality.[121] This grasp, however, functions almost solely on a very superficial plane. The political struggle is easily begun and is settled by means of an equally facile principle: the tennō decides for himself who shall be the new crown prince. Situations and relations between characters are meticulously prepared in the *Genji*. Its firm grasp on reality is manifested in the manner of presentation: various difficult matters gradually come to resolution within a complex of intertwining circumstances. "The Abdication" clearly suffers by comparison. Qualitative comparison has little significance in this discussion, however, since the point is that all the characters who appear in these accounts of political struggle are depicted as ordinary beings.

Nakatada and Suzushi, those normative superior beings of Part One of the new *Hollow Tree*, become ordinary beings in "The Abdication." Atemiya is depicted as if she were another Kaguyahime in Part One, but in "The Abdication" she behaves like the most ordinary of women as she struggles to have her son invested as crown prince. Atemiya hears that her side is not likely to win. She quietly ponders this as she watches her son play. What must His Majesty's stand be to give rise to such rumors? He has always been one to send frequent messages, but now no messengers come. She will become a nun if her father's worst fears come true and the Nashitsubo consort's son is made crown prince (*UM*, "Kuniyuzuri," Pt. 2: 389/1545). Atemiya's feelings are little different from those of a mother who applies to put her child in a prestigious primary school and watches in suspense as the children's names are drawn in lots.

The characters' dialogue also displays a movement toward the ordinary. A child is born to Suzushi, and Nakatada comes to the seventh-night celebration. Their conversation ranges over past and present matters and lasts for about eight pages in a modern printed edition (*UM*, "Kurabiraki," Pt. 2:288/1143-290/1151). It is wholly concerned with the small affairs of daily life, as one part of it shows:

> "There's nothing more charming than a child," said Nakatada. "I hope you're making much of it."
> "Well, it's still rather unsightly, so I've not been to see it."

---

[121] Ishimoda Tadashi was the first to praise "Kuniyuzuri" for its realistic depiction of political struggles (Ishimoda, 1943). His thesis was taken up and amplified after the war by the "historical sociologists"; they proclaimed the author's cognizance of reality in choosing a power struggle for the theme. Some even moved toward ranking the *Utsuho* above the *Genji* (Nakamura Shin'chirō, 1957, 20). Their argument, however, is basically unreasonable, in that they do not take into account the state of fictional monogatari in the late tenth century. This movement of historical sociology died a natural death, like the debate over a heroic age.

"What a dreadful thing to say! I started holding my daughter as soon as she was born."

"If only this one were a girl," said Suzushi. "None of our children outstrips the father. There's nothing to be done about a disappointing boy, but a girl can be taught the zither and receive a good upbringing, and so mingle in the best society. One of my storehouses is full of women's things."

Nakatada said, "Do let me have them. You seem to have no use for them. I'll give them to my daughter."

The reply: "Have her marry my son, and she shall have them straightaway."

"You're being unpleasant, and I'm going home. You know, I feel as if we were still boys, and yet both of us are fathers."

This is very much a world of ordinary beings and events. The theoreticians who view "The Abdication" as a bald portrayal of the realities of political infighting probably have little use for such trivial chatter. Conversations of this kind appear frequently in Part Two of the new *Hollow Tree*, reflecting the importance with which the author invested them. The audience, too, probably delighted in the freshness provided by these intimate conversations. Suzushi and Nakatada converse cleverly and intelligently, and their audience must have greatly enjoyed their skillful answers and evasions.

When such characters act like ordinary beings in the context of everyday subject matter, they can be said to act from a standpoint of realism. The word realism, however, is easily confounded with a literary trend that originated in the European novel. It is probably safer to retain my own terminology, ordinary beings and ordinary events. Monogatari about ordinary beings and events do in fact resemble realistic novels in their quotidian nature. We would do well to disregard matters of quality and note, as a literary phenomenon, that such monogatari were being written and read in late tenth-century Japan. Two short stories, "Ōsaka Koenu Gon Chūnagon" ("The Counselor Who Failed to Cross Love Slope") and "Kaiawase" ("The Shell Competition") are also extremely ordinary in their subject matter, with hardly an eventful occurrence in either.[122] The trend toward depicting ordinary beings and events in the *Genji* may reflect a growing audience interested in such subjects.

THE ACHIEVEMENT OF MURASAKI SHIKIBU

We have seen that there is a substantial difference between the "ordinariness" manifested in Part One of *The Tale of Genji* and that in Parts

---

[122] Both appear in *Tsutsumi Chūnagon Monogatari*. A shell match is a game in which two

One and Two of the new *Hollow Tree*, despite the fact that both works are concerned with ordinary events. This difference can be discerned because the *Genji* and *The Hollow Tree* can be discussed together: important shared qualities make a differential comparison feasible. It would be meaningless, on the other hand, to compare Part Two of the *Genji* with *The Hollow Tree*. No common ground exists between the two works to provide a comparative basis. From Part Two on, the *Genji* portrays a world belonging entirely to Murasaki Shikibu. Part Two is more than a continuation of Part One. Its structure is designed to transcend Part One, with the result that the earlier part gains new life and meaning when read together with Part Two. This is why the *Genji* occupies a world so much its own as to defy comparison with any other work of prose in Japanese. The uniqueness of this world is manifested in the fact that modern readers of all nationalities can effect a splendid reading of the *Genji* by employing modern methods of comprehension. Donald Keene, for one, has noted the resemblance between the *Genji* and Marcel Proust's *À la Recherche du Temps Perdu* (*Remembrance of Things Past*), particularly in regard to the element of time, and he has drawn our attention to the modernity of Murasaki Shikibu's narrative style (Keene, 1953, 75-76).

Of course, the nature of time in the *Genji* differs somewhat from that in Proust's work. If Murasaki Shikibu can be said to have a philosophical view of time, it is that embodied by Tendai Buddhism, and particularly by the sixteenth chapter of the *Lotus Sūtra*, "The Life-Span of the Thus Come One."[123] Time, as it appears in the *Genji*, is based on a concept well known to Murasaki Shikibu's contemporaries, that of karma (sukuse, lit. previous existences). This pertains to past time, before one's birth into the present life. Karma involves the acts committed in a past existence, and it is not erased by death but influences one's next life. Because acts in the present life are influenced by those committed in the past lives, past actions are in effect the sources of acts (or one's very existence) in the present life. Such sources, rooted in past time, are seen as causal from a present vantage point. The cause-and-effect relationship continues through countless rebirths [until one at last achieves enlightenment]. Proust envisions time rather differently: his past serves as a source of influence on present existence alone.

---

sides, the Left and the Right, compete in rounds to see which has the larger number of superior clamshells.

[123] [Leon Hurvitz's translation of "Tathāgata-āyuṣpramāṇa" (J. "Nyorai Juryōhon"). Hurvitz summarizes the chapter thus: ". . . the commonly accepted notions about the Buddha's life-span and teaching career have no ultimate truth, . . . the Buddha is in fact limitless in both time and space, assuming various forms in different ages and under different circumstances, but all for one and the same purpose, namely, the salvation of the beings." Hurvitz, 1976, xiv.—Trans.]

Part One of the *Genji* may have been written with a realistic theme in mind—a just royal succession, for example. Murasaki Shikibu certainly did not intend it to have a Buddhist theme like karma. Karma is the impetus of Part Two, however, and it comes to encompass Part One as well: the lives and actions of all the characters in Part One are seen to originate in acts committed in previous lives. Elements of Part One that need not be linked to karma when the work is read independently of Part Two are, when read together with it, given a new, Buddhist significance, and this new interpretation furnishes the characters of Part Three with sources of action and existence. Ultimately, the development of *The Tale of Genji* is based on Buddhist cause-and-effect relationships that span the Three Worlds of past, present, and future. Karma has long been known to be an important concept in the *Genji* (Taya, 1942, 69-82), but its meaning and importance differ depending on whether the entire work or Part One alone is considered. Genji is given the status equivalent to a former sovereign's ("Fuji no Uraba," 201), in accordance with the Korean physiognomist's prophecy: the boy Genji was not to rule, but neither was he meant to be a vassal ("Kiritsubo," 44). Murasaki Shikibu and her contemporaries believed that karma is the determining factor in such cases. But this is not necessarily the kind of karmic experience encountered in Parts Two and Three, where it seriously affects the principal characters' lives.

In Part One, the principal characters' actions are not linked to karma. The sudden death of the lady of the evening faces moves the grieving Genji to wonder, "What connection with a previous life brought this to pass?" ("Yūgao," 160). Genji concludes that "connection with a previous life" (mukashi no chigiri)—karma—has brought about the lady's death, but he does not know how to act in the face of it. Human beings do not know of their previous lives. There is no alternative but to decide on a means of dealing with a situation within the limits of human knowledge, and to act in accordance with that decision. The Genji of Part One makes decisions and acts accordingly. His public decisions and actions stand out in particular. Genji is exactly like the Duke of Chou both in realizing that a single erroneous judgment might ruin all hopes of a return to power and in escaping this dangerous situation by means of an extreme measure, voluntary exile.

Similarly, Genji asks Murasaki to take charge of the Akashi girl's upbringing so that she will have a good chance of becoming a royal consort ("Usugumo," 215). This must bring unhappiness both to the Akashi lady, who is obliged to live without her only child, and to Murasaki, who is to care for Genji's child by another woman. Genji's powers of mediation are truly extraordinary, for in the end he settles the matter amicably. Again, Genji foresees that his son Yūgiri will bear heavy government responsibilities in the future, and so he overrides the opposition mounted by Yūgiri

GENJI AND HIS RELATIONS

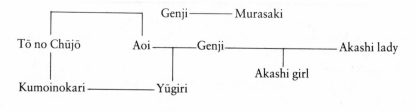

THE ROKUJŌ LADY AND HER RELATIONS

the late Crown Prince——————Rokujō lady
                        |
                  Akikonomu

Vertical lines indicate parentage. Horizontal lines indicate marriage.

and the boy's maternal relatives, insisting on enrollment in the Court School. Genji also has Yūgiri begin his government career in the lowly sixth rank ("Otome," 276-78).[124] His decisions lead to Yūgiri's becoming a trusted and popular minister of state.

Genji's political acumen is marvelous as well: ably parrying public sentiment against a succession of non-Fujiwara senior consorts, Genji raises Akikonomu to that position, apparently fulfilling the lost hopes of her ill-fated mother, the Rokujō lady. Genji's boyhood rival, Tō no Chūjō, now Palace Minister, is dissatisfied by this move, but Genji eliminates the likelihood of a power struggle by leaving all the affairs of government in Tō no Chūjō's hands ("Otome," 284). The Akashi girl later becomes a senior consort of the crown prince, Genji is elevated to the status of former sovereign, Tō no Chūjō is promoted to chancellor, and Yūgiri succeeds at last in marrying Kumoinokari, daughter of the new chancellor ("Fuji no Uraba," 189-201). Part One concludes happily for everyone.

Genji's public behavior fully manifests his wise judgment and correct actions and is paralleled by the story of his private life, a colorful and elegant woman-centered existence. This proves to be a reasonable approach

[124] It is Yūgiri's birthright to hold high rank from the start of his career. Sons of low- or middle-ranking officials customarily bettered their chances of rising in rank by attending the Court School, but such a measure was unnecessary for someone of Yūgiri's status; hence his and his maternal relatives' opposition to Genji's plan. [Auth., Trans.]

if we consider that the patrons of the *Genji* were probably women.[125] The few men in the audience must have perceived Genji as an ideal literatus who combines the pleasures of an elegant private life (which in fact has more than its share of suffering) with behavior appropriate to a superior being functioning as a public official in an actual society. Michinaga and Kintō would probably have found the theme of Part One to be the reality of life in society, as effected by Genji's decisions and actions. Or, to paraphrase the title of Mishima Yukio's novel, *Kinu to Meisatsu (Silk and Clear Insight)*, the theme might appositely be called "reality and clear insight."

Cognizant that Part One ends gloriously, the reader experiences a sudden darkening of tone on beginning Part Two. Its characters, moreover, suffer from various miseries throughout the section. Does this not strike the reader as strange? Part Two indeed depicts a world of suffering. The nucleus of Part Two may be Genji's agony in having to rear Kaoru as his own son, although Genji knows the child was born from an affair between the Third Princess, his principal wife, and Kashiwagi. It is easy for modern readers to conclude that Genji's youthful act of fathering a son by his own father's consort has brought about dreadful retribution in the latter half of his life. Yet the narrator of the *Genji* informs us that the Third Princess's pregnancy certainly is a very sad ("aware naru") karma ("sukuse"; "Wakana," Pt. 2:387). Her pregnancy, we are told, must have resulted from actions committed in a previous life that now cause suffering in the princess's present life. In other words, karma from a previous life, acts committed before either Genji or the Third Princess was born, is the cause of both illicit love affairs. The suffering that takes place in Part Two is unlike pain or suffering in the ordinary sense. Surplus energy from previous acts is carried over into one's present existence, with karmic suffering as the inevitable result. Karmic suffering, in this sense, is the theme of Part Two: more precisely, the theme is "karma and predetermined suffering."

What kind of karma brings about suffering? All the many kinds of suffering in Part Two stem from one source, which I have termed inferior lineage (Konishi, 1968, 5-8). One theory, rather strongly supported by Japanese scholars, maintains that Genji's affair with Fujitsubo results from an Oedipus complex, since he has heard that Fujitsubo is the image of his dead mother. Modern readers are free to make such interpretations. Murasaki Shikibu's unfamiliarity with Freudian analysis is no reason to reject the Oedipus theory. But it is incorrect to assert that this is the only valid interpretation. Heian aristocrats, the men in particular, wanted to marry into the high ranks. Social standing was based on blood lines, and the nobility was apparently strongly aware of eminent blood lines, superior lin-

[125] We may conclude that one was the senior consort Akiko (*MSN*, 472).

TŌ NO CHŪJŌ AND HIS RELATIONS

Minister of the Right

Tō no Chūjō ─────────────┬───────────── fourth daughter

concubine ──────┬────── Suzaku ──────┬───── junior consort

Kashiwagi ────── 2d Princess   3d Princess ────── Genji

Vertical lines indicate parentage. Horizontal lines indicate marriage.

eage. Kashiwagi is a fine example: he has always felt that he will " 'marry a princess and no one else' " ("Wakana," Pt. 1:227).[126] When the Third Princess becomes Genji's principal wife, Kashiwagi marries her older sister, the Second Princess (Ochiba) ("Wakana," Pt. 2:366). Their marriage is not a success. The reason—of which Kashiwagi himself may be unaware—is that the princess is "the daughter of a low-ranking concubine" (ibid.). Both the Second and Third Princesses are of royal blood, but the latter is the daughter of a junior consort and consequently is of superior lineage.

Although the nobility may often consciously have desired alliances with women of superior lineage, this desire would have been ordinarily concealed deeply in their minds, so the man in question remained unaware of it. The desire was particularly suppressed in cases of inferior lineage. Kashiwagi's forbidden affair stems from a complex, one probably unknown to him, about the Second Princess's mother, a concubine and therefore of more inferior lineage than her father's junior consort. Similarly, Genji's desire for Fujitsubo results from a repressed complex, at a deep level of awareness, about his inferior lineage. The opening passage of "The Paulownia Court" has great significance in this light: "In a certain reign there was a lady not of the first rank whom the sovereign loved more than the rest of his many consorts and concubines" (*GM*, "Kiritsubo," 27). The chief reason why Genji does not rule as tennō is that his mother's birth does not entitle her to occupy the higher ranks. This may well have brought an unformulated anxiety about his inferior lineage, which serves as the impetus behind his love for Fujitsubo. The significance of the lady's

---

[126] [Seidensticker, 1976, 2:544.—Trans.] The same is true for Yūgiri. He falls in love with Kumoinokari and overcomes great difficulties to marry her; but once he becomes acquainted with the Second Princess, he neglects his beloved wife to court her. He, too, seems attracted by the idea of superior lineage.

relatively lowly birth is not entirely clear to a reader beginning Part One, but on reaching the story of Kashiwagi's affair in Part Two, the reader will be aware of the impetus provided the characters by an awareness of inferior lineage.

Characters in Part Two who are born with such a karma endure predetermined sufferings, the suffering afflicting them in various forms.[127] Moreover, karmic suffering continues beyond the present existence: characters in Part Two may die, but neither karma nor suffering is extinguished with their lives. It will exist as long as the next generation lives. The characters in Part Three cannot escape. The principal characters of this section are dominated by karma from their previous lives, but their actions in past lives—the source of their present behavior—differ from those obtaining in Part Two. Niou and Kaoru both love the Eighth Prince's daughters, all of whom are, compared with their lovers, obviously of inferior lineage. This is particularly true of Ukifune, the daughter of a low-ranking lady-in-waiting to the Eighth Prince ("Yadorigi," 99). Her blood lines disqualify her as an appropriate wife for Niou, whose parents are the reigning sovereign and his senior consort, or for Kaoru, son of a royal princess and (ostensibly) a nobleman raised to the status of a former sovereign. And yet the Eighth Prince's daughters are loved by Niou and Kaoru, because both men, born with the best of blood lines, have no fixation against inferior lineage. Niou would be especially unconcerned with such matters, since he is Genji's grandson; and Genji became the lover of low-ranking women like Utsusemi, the lady of the locust shell (although his partner that night actually proves to be her stepdaughter Nokiba no Ogi), and Yūgao, the lady of the evening faces.

Kaoru suffers from thwarted desire, perhaps because he is Kashiwagi's son.[128] Lacking the ability to resolve his suffering in actual situations, he tends toward piety, seeking the goal of reality as deliverance from suffering. His piety surfaces when he meets the Eighth Prince. The prince's life has been filled with disappointment, and he hopes to find true peace not in this life but in the Buddha's realm. He leads a devout life so that his piety might be the cause leading to the desired effect of rebirth in paradise. The Eighth Prince may be the first fictional character to show the influence of the Pure Land doctrine that was gradually permeating Heian society.[129]

[127] The four basic sufferings (duhkha) in Buddhism are those of life, old age, sickness, and death. There are four more: the suffering engendered by thwarted desire [see n. 128], parting from loved ones, hatred, and the five elements of existence (form, sensation, perception, constituent impulses, and cognition). In Part Two, Genji suffers in parting from his beloved Murasaki, and from old age, and Kashiwagi suffers from thwarted desire, sickness, and death. All the principal characters of the *Genji* share in the suffering of life (Konishi, 1968, 15-16).

[128] Gufutokuku, literally an inability to gratify one's desires—one of the eight sufferings of Buddhism [see n. 127]. [Auth., Trans.]

[129] Which is to say, the Pure Land (Jōdo) thought inherent in Tendai belief (Abe Akio, 1959, 517-46). The Pure Land school of Buddhism was not founded by Hōnen until 1175.

Kaoru's first attraction is to the prince, and his thoughts turn to the daughters only at a later stage. Yet Kaoru's piety seems uncertain, ceaselessly drifting. It is Niou's behavior that set his piety adrift, affecting the Eighth Prince's daughters as well as Kaoru. Ukifune, the youngest, tries to drown herself because she cannot decide between Niou and Kaoru. This produces a great uproar but settles nothing. Ukifune's life is saved, and she is driven to become a nun. But she is a nun in name only. Her heart remains occupied with worldly concerns, her future relations with Kaoru are left unclear, and everything is shrouded in mist. The characters in Part Three wander lost in the midst of endless change. If Part Two is a world of suffering, Part Three is one of illusion. Illusion signifies uncertainty as to the truth, an aspect of avidyā (J. mumyō), spiritual blindness. The theme of Part Three is "piety and spiritual blindness."

The three themes of the *Genji*—reality and clear insight, karma and predetermined suffering, piety and spiritual blindness—are not simply contiguous elements. When the *Genji* consisted of only Part One, its theme was reality and clear insight. When Part Two appeared, the theme of Part One was enveloped by Part Two and was dissolved to form an element in creating the theme of Part Two, karma and predetermined suffering. This is the theme of Part Two, but it is also a comprehensive theme held in common with Part One. The completion of Part Three led to its theme, piety and spiritual blindness, enveloping the earlier themes, which become elements of a theme for the entire *Tale of Genji*. Their relationship is outlined below.[130] The *Genji* as a whole can be explained in the light of the theme of piety and spiritual blindness, but when only the first two parts are considered, the theme of karma and predetermined suffering obtains. The

Reality and Clear Insight	} Part One		
Karma and Predetermined Suffering		} Part Two	} Part Three
Piety and Spiritual Blindness			

[130] Motoori Norinaga asserts that the *Genji* should be read in terms of deep human emotion (mono no aware) rather than from a Buddhist standpoint. This was an outstanding view in its day and is generally accepted even now. It cannot be seen, however, as the only valid interpretation. My reading is based on Kamakura period theories, which I have recast in modern terms. I believe that a perceptive stance more proximate to that taken in Murasaki Shikibu's time is likely to yield a more accurate reading.

theme of reality and clear insight regains its effectiveness when Part One is read on its own.

What methods did Murasaki Shikibu employ to express these themes? Her use of waka technique is immediately noticeable. One such technique is the use, in narrative prose sections, of expression resembling pillow words and prefaces; but this is a trivial matter.[131] We would do better to address the question of why Murasaki Shikibu dared to experiment with poetic expression. In the famous discussion of monogatari in "Fireflies," Murasaki Shikibu has Genji say, " 'But the beginning is when there are . . . things that happen in this life which one never tires of seeing and hearing about, things which one cannot bear not to tell of and must pass on for all generations' " (GM, "Hotaru," 432). This narrative passage is reminiscent of a passage from the Japanese Preface to the Kokinshū: "Because human beings possess interests of so many kinds, it is in poetry that they give expression to the meditations of their hearts in terms of the sights appearing before their eyes and the sounds coming to their ears" (KKS, Preface, 9).[132] Motoori Norinaga (1730-1801) may have been influenced by this resemblance when he wrote,

> Murasaki Shikibu profoundly understood deep emotion [mono no aware]. She wrote . . . about the profound meaning of varied circumstances in this world, and the hearts and actions of both good people and bad, as grounded in the sights appearing before her eyes, the sounds coming to her ears, and the experiences she shared. All the deep emotions of our world are contained in this monogatari. (Tama no Ogushi, 2:214)

Therefore, Norinaga asserts, "This monogatari expresses in various ways all the feelings people are likely to experience, and evokes deep emotion" (ibid., 203).

This excellent opinion has long been upheld by scholars of Japanese literature. To be sure, Norinaga's attempt to solve all the problems of the Genji by means of his ideas, and his refusal to consider any interpretation based on Confucian or Buddhist perspectives, are indicative of his occasional lapses into excessive logicality. Nevertheless Norinaga pinpoints Murasaki Shikibu's intent, to acknowledge that monogatari are of equal worth with waka. Of course, Murasaki Shikibu did not expect that the fictional monogatari, up to her time a mere diversion, would gain immediate recognition as a premier art equivalent to waka. One of her characters

---

[131] Because the Genji is a prose work, its narration naturally follows the plot development. When the narrator arrives at an important place in the story, however, plot progression ceases, to be replaced by an emotional lyricism (Ramirez-Christensen, 1982, 21-61). This is an important point.

[132] [Miner, 1968, 18.—Trans.]

speaks for her when he says, " 'The *Chronicles of Japan* and the rest are a mere fragment of the whole truth.' " That is her only comment on the subject. If, however, we assume that Murasaki Shikibu wrote with an awareness of the premier arts, then her use of expression resembling pillow words and prefaces is, despite their insignificant bearing on monogatari, noteworthy as indicating the presence of such an awareness.

One more valuable indication of Murasaki Shikibu's awareness of equality between waka and monogatari is her use of literary authorities (junkyo). These authorities have been a source of debate since the *Shimyōshō* and the *Kakaishō* were compiled, but the meaning of the term is not always clear.[133] Shimizu Yoshiko has made a thorough study of the various kinds of *Genji* authorities and has systematized their usage. She concludes that the most frequent usage of an authority occurs when a given character or event in the *Genji* conforms to historical fact: that fact is invoked as an authority or source. But there are also instances of echoed poems [hikiuta, extant waka quoted either in part or entirely and incorporated into the *Genji* text] serving as authorities, as in the *Genchū Saihishō*.[134] The *Kōan Genji Rongi*, moreover, has instances of other monogatari, alluded to in the *Genji* text, being cited as authorities (Shimizu, 1966, 74-136).[135] Such instances demand a reconsideration of the sense in which "authority" is used. The *Kakaishō*, for example, notes that "the time period depicted in the *Genji* seems to have the reigns of Daigo, Suzaku, and Murakami for its authority" (*Kakaishō*, 1:186). Yamada Yoshio's research on music in the *Genji* supports this. The significance of the statement, however, is best interpreted as a question of setting: Murasaki Shikibu intended the *Genji* as a historical novel rather than one with a contemporary setting (Yamada, 1934, 438-50). More important, characters and events in the *Genji* correspond to others outside the work, with the result that the story is made more interesting. The nature of this effect resembles that of allusive variation (honkadori) in waka.

Norinaga states that "authorities exist only in the author's mind, and later readers cannot be sure that their conjectures will be correct." Those

---

[133] The *Shimyōshō* is a *Genji* commentary compiled by Sojaku (dates unknown) between 1289 and 1294. It is based on the Kawachi recension of the *Genji*, which was edited and revised by Minamoto Mitsuyuki (1163-1244) and his son Chikayuki (fl. ca. 1200-25), both governors of Kawachi. The *Kakaishō*, another *Genji* commentary, was compiled in 1363 by Yotsutsuji Yoshinari at the command of Ashikaga Yoshiakira. It refers to both the Kawachi and Aobyōshi recensions and amalgamates various Kamakura period theories.

[134] Compiled before 1364. Gyōa (dates unknown), Chikayuki's grandson, here revises theories put forth by successive generations of his family. [For hikiuta, as for other literary instances of authority, the usage is tantamount to allusion: but since history is also involved with yet other kinds of authority, the term is broad and ambiguous, as the author mentions.—Ed.]

[135] The *Kōan Genji Rongi* was completed in 1279. It is cast in the form of Buddhist dialogues and discusses various aspects of the *Genji* in sixteen sections.

authorities were of little consequence to him, and he mentions them only because they have long been the object of scholarly attention (*Tama no Ogushi*, 1:178-79). His interpretation equates authorities, in effect, with later ideas of models in modern novels, as in Sōseki's modeling his school principal, Slydog, in *Bottchan* on Kanō Jigorō, President of the Tokyo Higher Normal School. If this is all that is involved in the *Genji*, Norinaga is correct in asserting the futility of assigning models to characters and events in the *Genji*, since we have no way of knowing the author's actual intention. Authorities, however, more likely signify the author's attempts to portray realistic people and events for her audience. In its turn, the audience took pleasure in this detached style, in which fictional characters and events might be matched with actual individuals and occurrences. One passage in the *Genji* notes of worthless women, "Are not the parents who reared them equally worthless?" (*GM*, "Yūgiri," 143). A waka by Saigyō (written under his name in religion, En'i, with "Saigyō" being a pen name-like religious name) was apparently cited by one old commentary as the authority for this sentence. But it is criticized as "probably an unsatisfactory authority" in the *Genchū Saihishō*, because the poem postdates the *Genji* ("Yūgiri," 582-83). The fact that echoed poems are treated as one kind of authority indicates that an authority produces much the same detached interest in relation to its text that a waka does in combination with the poem that is the source of its allusion. In that case, they do not exist in the author's mind but are instead the precedents the audience is expected to think of in the act of reading. In terms of literary works, the *Odyssey* is an authority for James Joyce's *Ulysses*.

The monogatari was not made into a premier art equal to waka simply by introducing waka techniques. The monogatari has its own techniques, which needed refinement if monogatari expression was to rise to the level of waka. One such refined technique is the sōshiji, or narratorial intrusion. The term itself is first used in the fifteenth century, but the technique appears frequently in the *Genji* as well as in other monogatari. With intrusion, the narrator of, say, the *Genji*, briefly makes her presence known and offers explanations or opinions from a first-person perspective. Consider, for example, the passage from "Suma" in which Genji, about to leave for Suma, writes to his various ladies.

> He did write to certain people who should know of the event. *I have no doubt that there were many fine passages in the letters with which he saddened the lives of his many ladies, but, grief-stricken myself, I did not listen as carefully as I might have.* (*GM*, "Suma," 13).[136]

The italicized area represents the narratorial intrusion. The Western technique of authorial intrusion corresponds to it and frequently appears in

[136] [Seidensticker, 1976, 1:220.—Trans.]

modern Japanese fiction.[137] In the *Genji*, the calculated effect of the narrator's intrusion is much like that of a zoom lens: its use extends or shortens the psychological distance between the audience and circumstances and characters in the work. Murasaki Shikibu's experiment is surprisingly original for the eleventh century.

Her experimentation is noticeable above all in the multilayered narration of the *Genji*. The narrator who speaks to the audience from within the *Genji* will be termed the primary narrator. In this setting, the primary narrator has not directly witnessed the events from the story: she has been told them by another, a secondary narrator.

> Though no one has asked me to do so, I should like to describe the surprise of the assistant viceroy's wife at this turn of events, and Jijū's pleasure and guilt. But it would be a bother and my head is aching; and perhaps something will someday remind me to continue the story. This is what I heard. (*GM*, "Yomogiu," 160)[138]

The narratorial intrusion ends with the words "to zo" ("this is what I heard"), an indication that the story has been told to the primary narrator by someone else. "This is what I heard" is spoken by the primary narrator, and the secondary narrator speaks the rest of the passage, from "Though no one has asked me to do so" through "to continue the story." Secondary narration is performed by more than one person.

> The story I am about to tell was heard at second-hand from certain obscure *women* discharged from Genji's family after his death. They found employment in Higekuro's house, where they lived into old age, and there volunteered this story. It may not seem entirely in keeping with the story told by Murasaki's *women*; but those at Higekuro's house say that there are numerous inaccuracies in the accounts we have had of Genji's descendants, and distrust Murasaki's women, who they say were so old that they had become forgetful. I would not presume to say which story is right. (*GM*, "Takekawa," 251)[139]

The primary narrator has gathered and recorded accounts by several secondary narrators, the "obscure women" (warugotachi, noblewomen of

[137] Shima Ryōtarō's novels, for instance, often have sections, corresponding to narrator's statements, that occupy over half a chapter; sometimes an entire chapter consists of the narrator's statement. [Sōshiji is variously taken as authorial or narratorial intrusion. In poststructuralist critical talk, it might be "the voice of the text." For junkyo, the postulation of historical reference makes "intertextuality" inadequate, just as philological "sources" is inadequate from another point of view.—Ed.]

[138] [Taken, with minor changes, from Seidensticker, 1976, 1:302.—Trans.]

[139] [Adapted from Seidensticker, 1976, 2:751.—Trans.] The narrator introduces this statement because the chapter is concerned with characters who are connected to Higekuro and his family and who have no direct connection to Genji and Murasaki.

relatively low origin) of the text.[140] The ladies are clearly fictional narrators; the setting of primary and secondary narrators establishes considerable distance between the readers and the characters and events of the *Genji*. When a secondary narrator does not appear, the reading audience draws proportionately closer to the characters and events. At times the audience is even unaware of the primary narrator's existence, and at such times it directly experiences situations described in the work and feels as if it is entering into the characters' innermost hearts. Then a narrator's statement will suddenly appear: "What a fainthearted fellow!"[141] The audience is thereupon pulled back to a scene in which the primary narrator is speaking. The technique of varying an audience's proximity to situations and characters in the *Genji* is somewhat reminiscent of the manipulation of a cinema lens, which shows an audience a close-up of a scene and then recedes from it.

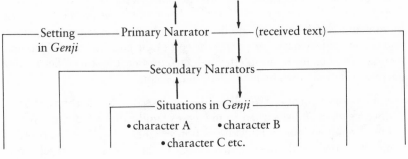

READING OR HEARING AUDIENCE

Setting in *Genji* — Primary Narrator — (received text)

Secondary Narrators

Situations in *Genji*

• character A   • character B
• character C etc.

Such techniques are extremely effective in portraying the psychologies of the characters. Immediately after a character's thoughts or feelings have been described, the narratorial intrusion is introduced. Because early medieval fictional monogatari are without exception told from an omniscient point of view, they run the risk of appearing shallow and monotonous by

---

[140] This was first suggested by Tamagami Takuya (Tamagami, 1955a, 247-65). He has been criticized for confusing literary analysis with a discussion of the composition process (Nakano, 1964, 94-113). If Tamagami's theory is corrected so that it clearly distinguishes between author and narrator, it remains applicable. The pattern described above represents my revision of aspects of Tamagami's theory.

[141] Genji, in retreat at the Urin'in, suddenly thinks of becoming a monk; but he then remembers Murasaki, and his concern for her overwhelms his pious feelings. The primary narrator injects her impression of Genji into the text with quoted comment on his lack of resolve. [The author's comment that at times we are "even unaware of the primary narrator's existence" touches on very complex matters familiar to all who have read the Japanese but difficult to convey in terms exciting general consent. Noguchi Takehiko of Kobe University has remarked, for example, that in Heian and other Japanese narrative, there may be not only first- and third-person narrative but also personless (muninshō) narrative.—Ed.]

comparison with modern psychological novels. These unwelcome characteristics can sometimes be modified by employing the technique of a
narratorial intrusion. In "Suetsumuhana" ("The Safflower"), Genji
spends his first night with the safflower princess but must wait until dawn
to see her face for the first time:

> Though his face was politely averted, Genji contrived to look obli-
> quely at her. He was hoping that a really good look might show her
> to be less than irredeemable.
>   *That was not very kind or very realistic of him.* (GM, "Suetsumu-
> hana," 256-57)[142]

Genji's thoughts are told by an omniscient narrator, and the result is a
sense of excessive directness. Once the audience is exposed to the primary
narrator's criticism of Genji's incorrigible ways, though, it is pulled back
from an intimate view of Genji's mind to the narrator's point of view. This
provides a perspective from which to observe Genji's character more or
less objectively and avoids overly direct narration.

Murasaki Shikibu is not only adept in her use of the narratorial technique. She also seems to have mastered the technique of achieving the
proper distance in psychological portrayal. Consider, for example, the
scene from "Yūgiri" ("Evening Mist") in which Yūgiri pursues the Second
Princess into a large closet and has his first glimpse of her face.

> It was dark inside, but the morning light somehow came seeping in,
> dimly revealing her form. He pulled away the quilts and smoothed
> her tangled hair. She was very graceful, delicate, and ladylike. (GM,
> "Yūgiri," 162)[143]

Formally speaking, the last sentence is the narrator's comment. It may in
effect be seen, however, as Yūgiri's own feelings. We know this from an
earlier passage, in the second "Wakana" chapter ("New Herbs: Part
Two"), in which the narrator notifies the reader that the princess is not a
great beauty: ". . . although she was quite attractive compared to the general run of women" ("Wakana," Pt. 2:366). When the same narrator pro-
nounces the princess "very graceful, delicate, and ladylike" in "Evening
Mist," she is not voicing her own opinion but narrating Yūgiri's observations and impressions of the princess at this moment. If Yūgiri's feelings
had been entered into and explained—"He found her very graceful, delicate, and ladylike"—the result would be excessively direct and explicit
narration. The purpose of this sentence is to link the audience's consciousness to the primary narrator's viewpoint; the technique also effectively
transmits Yūgiri's emotions.

[142] [Seidensticker, 1976, 1:124.—Trans.] Heian noblewomen were not seen by adult men
other than their father and husband or lover (Morris, 1964, 211).
[143] [Adapted from Seidensticker, 1976, 2:708.—Trans.]

Explicating a character's emotions from the narrator's position is a technique frequently found in fictional monogatari written from an omniscient point of view. Murasaki Shikibu attempts a new technique in touching on a character's emotions while maintaining some distance from the individual. This signals a movement toward a yet more complex technique, that of suggesting the characters' innermost thoughts rather than stating them outright. This is reminiscent of novels written from a limited point of view, including the later works of Henry James. When, in "New Herbs, Part One," Genji is asked by his brother, the abdicated Suzaku, if he will marry the Third Princess, he agrees with little demurral ("Wakana," Pt. 1:237). Up to then, Genji has shown no great interest in the girl, and the reasons and motives underlying his decision are not explained. The Third Princess's marriage is the major event of Part Two. An omniscient narrator would be at liberty to describe Genji's emotions at length, as he arrives at his decision. Murasaki Shikibu does not allow her narrator this freedom, instead choosing to hint at Genji's motives in a speech made by a minor character, a certain middle controller. He hears from his sister, the Third Princess's nurse, of Suzaku's intent to marry the girl to Genji; the controller observes that as long as Murasaki is alive, things will be difficult for the princess. He adds,

> "Yet I have heard him say, without making a great point of it, that his life has been too well favored in this degenerate age, and that it would be greedy and arrogant of him to want more; but that he himself and others too have thought that in his relations with women he has not been completely successful. I think he truly feels this way." ("Wakana," Pt. 1:222)[144]

The precise nature of Genji's lack of success with women is left unstated. But the controller, noting that none of Genji's ladies is of the highest birth, thinks the Third Princess would make "the most suitable wife" for Genji. Of course, this is only the controller's interpretation of Genji's speech. The audience naturally feels confused about the extent to which it can rely on a minor character's opinion. On the other hand, facts supporting the controller's interpretation appear somewhat earlier in the chapter:

> "It would seem that Genji still has the old acquisitive instincts and that he is always on the alert for ladies of really good pedigree. I am told that he still thinks of the former high priestess of Kamo and sometimes gets off a letter to her." ("Wakana," Pt. 1:220)[145]

[144] [Adapted from ibid., 542.—Trans.]
[145] Ibid., 541.—Trans.]

This, too, is only an opinion spoken by one of the Third Princess's nurses. There is no other mention in the text of Genji's conscious longing for an alliance with a woman of superior lineage. The abdicated Suzaku, who has solicited the nurse's opinion, comments that his only worry is Genji's well-known weakness for women. He does not touch on Genji's desire for "ladies of really good pedigree," but neither does he deny it.

Absorbing all these remarks, the reader is given to believe that Genji's desire to marry the Third Princess stems from a desire—whether he is aware of it or not—for a lady of superior lineage. Henry James excels in the technique of casting light on the hidden recesses of a protagonist's heart by portrayal through the eyes of secondary or minor characters. Such characters serve as "reflectors," or "centers of consciousness" (Booth, 1961, 151-53). Although the controller and his sister, the Third Princess's nurse, do not necessarily have an identical function, there are similarities in Murasaki Shikibu's use of minor characters to reflect a protagonist's own thoughts (Konishi, 1971a).

Full psychological portrayal first appears with Part Two of the *Genji*. A work that does not employ the narrator to explain the characters' thoughts, but that instead has the reader follow carefully placed clues that will eventually lead to their discovery, presents a text made comprehensible only through repeated, careful reading to oneself. Such comprehension is impossible through hearing, in which a lector reads the text to an audience. I do not mean to deny that Part Two was probably aurally received. Aural reception would have been quite acceptable to those interested only in enjoying the plot development. Yet the kind of reception Murasaki Shikibu seems to have anticipated most as a writer would have been possible only through reading by oneself. This would also have been true for Part Three, especially as concerns its use of symbolism.

As we have seen, the theme of Part One is reality and clear insight, that of Part Two is karma and predetermined suffering, and that of Part Three is piety and spiritual blindness. Spiritual blindness, an inability to understand the truth, is linked to the imagery of darkness. Avidyā, the Sanskrit term for "spiritual blindness," can be literally translated as "inability to see." This explains the opening sentence of Part Three: "The radiant Genji was dead, and there was no one to take his place from among his many descendants" (*GM*, "Niou Miya," 219). Genji, the protagonist of Parts One and Two, is a being whose superiority is manifested by the sobriquet "radiant" (hikaru). No one can rival him. Of course, it is only in Part One that he appears as an idealized, superior being. In Part Two the radiant hero experiences a series of disappointments, and although his superiority still illumines the heavens, it begins to take on sunset colors. Nonetheless, it continues to be radiant.

The characters in Part Three, by contrast, experience only disappoint-

ment. Nothing goes as they expect; they are plagued by unwelcome results. There is no radiance here. Part Three is a world of darkness. Thus it
is no accident that the male protagonists of Part Three are called "Niou"
(Perfume) and "Kaoru" (Scent). Contemporary readers of the *Genji* knew
that even in the dark one could appreciate fragrance; this was thought especially true for plum blossoms, as one famous waka attests.

Haru no yo no   On the spring night
Yami wa ayanashi   The darkness fails in its ends:
    Mume no hana   For the flowering plum
Iro koso miene   May have its colors kept from us,
Ka ya wa kakururu.   But its fragrance cannot be concealed!

(KKS, 1:41)

This is why both Niou and Kaoru are frequently associated with plum
blossoms. There are too many instances to enumerate, but a few might be
mentioned: Kōbai sees "a rose plum in full bloom" ("Kōbai," 241) and is
reminded of Niou.[146] When Kaoru's natural fragrance is first described,
an image is evoked of "his sleeves brushing a spray of plum blossoms"
("Niou Miya," 226).[147] There is also a scene in which Niou and Kaoru
play the thirteen-stringed zither and chat, as "the scent of plum blossoms"
drifts in ("Sawarabi," 13). It is perhaps reasonable that the more energetic
Niou is associated with the rose plum and Kaoru with the white.

When Murasaki Shikibu wrote Parts One and Two, she probably did
not envision them as symbolizing a world of light. A tradition, dating back
to the Ancient Age, dictated that a superior being be described in luminous
terms; hence Genji's epithet. Before her death in "Minori" ("The Rites"),
Murasaki bequeaths her rose plum and cherry trees at the Nijō Palace to
Niou, as a remembrance of her ("Minori," 180). This is the origin of
Niou's association with rose plum blossoms, but it is not an underpinning
for Part Three. As soon as Part Three was completed, however, all these
elements came to possess symbolic significance. Genji's epithet no longer
denotes the radiance of the ancient hero and heroine whose "dazzling
countenances illumined their villages."[148] It has been transformed into the
glory of worldly success, behind which is darkness, the Buddhist symbol
of spiritual blindness. The relationships among the three parts have been
given above, and now we can add their symbols.

Other thematic aspects of Part Three cannot be satisfactorily symbol-

---

[146] [Ibid., 746.—Trans.]
[147] [Adapted from ibid., 739.—Trans.]
[148] This is a description of Samuta no Iratsuko and Aze no Iratsume. The text appears in
Hitachi Fudoki (72).

Reality and
Clear Insight: } Part One
Daylight   }   }
                                                 }
Karma and   } Part Two: Light }
Predetermined   } Part Three: Darkness
Suffering: }
Sunset   }   }

Piety and
Spiritual   }
Blindness

ized by the imagery of darkness. Piety, the search for truth in the midst of spiritual blindness, cannot be summed up by the image of darkness alone. Two more images may serve to symbolize, respectively, piety and spiritual blindness: mountains and the river. Most of the action in Part Three takes place at Uji, an evocative landscape of mountains and river. The Uji mountains represent piety to characters in the *Genji*. The mountains are mentioned in "Hashihime" ("The Lady at the Bridge") in connection with the profoundly pious Eighth Prince, who can find serenity only at a mountain monastery: "There happened to be in those Uji mountains an abbot, a most saintly man" (*GM*, "Hashihime," 304).[149] The prince considers his temple "a quiet place" ("Shiigamoto," 350), since his secular residence is near the Uji River with its constant sound of coursing water. "The roar of the fish weirs was more than a man could bear, said the Eighth Prince as he set off for the abbot's mountain monastery, there to spend a week in retreat" (*GM*, "Hashihime," 310).[150] The sound of rushing water signifies more than physical noise: it frequently appears in connection with spiritual suffering. Whenever the characters of Part Three are lost in grief, the sound of the river comes inevitably to their ears. The coursing river is compared, moreover, to the evanescent world:

> Strange, battered little boats, piled high with brush and wattles, made their way up and down the river, each boatman pursuing his own sad, small livelihood at the uncertain mercy of the waters. "It is the same with all of us," thought Kaoru. . . . "Am I to boast that I am safe from the flood, calm and secure in a jewelled mansion?" (*GM*, "Hashihime," 322)[151]

---

[149] [Seidensticker, 1976, 2:780.—Trans.]
[150] [Adapted from ibid., 783.—Trans.]
[151] [Ibid., 790.—Trans.]

344 THE EARLY MIDDLE AGES

The conceit may be partially due to a waka convention, in which the "u" of "Uji" is used homophonically to signify "misery." It might also have originated from the Buddhist convention of employing river and sea imagery as metaphors for the world of love-torments.[152]

Perhaps the most outstanding metaphorical use of river and sea imagery to suggest the world of men, replete with wordly attachments and suffering, appears in a chapter of the Lotus Sūtra, "The Former Affairs of the King Fine Adornment."[153] One of the king's sons says that " 'A Buddha is as hard to encounter . . . as it would be for a one-eyed tortoise to encounter a hole in a floating piece of wood.' "[154] The tortoise and the piece of wood are metaphors for all living things, who have little likelihood of coming to know the truth, and the sea on which they drift represents the human world. This metaphor evokes the epithet "ukifune" (floating boat) accorded to one of the heroines of Part Three. She is never actually called Ukifune in the Genji. Readers probably drew her "name" from a poem and the chapter title derived from it, "Ukifune" ("A Boat upon the Waters").

<table>
<tr><td>Tachibana no</td><td>Leaves of the orange tree</td></tr>
<tr><td>Kojima wa iro mo</td><td>On Little Orange Island</td></tr>
<tr><td>Kawaraji o</td><td>Hold fast in color</td></tr>
<tr><td>Kono ukifune zo</td><td>But this boat drifting on the waters</td></tr>
<tr><td>Yukue shirarenu.</td><td>Does not know her destination.</td></tr>
</table>

(GM, "Ukifune," 237)

It is of little importance that the character is not named Ukifune in the text. What is significant is that the readers who gave her the appellation fixed on the image of a boat floating on the river as fitting to the heroine's life. In that boat loose in the current, Ukifune, who is already Kaoru's mistress, crosses the Uji River by boat with Niou and spends the night with him there in a cottage. During their river crossing, she recites her waka about the little isle with its orange trees. She is indeed a small boat drifting on the river of love, this woman torn between Kaoru and Niou and carried off by the course of events. The title of the final chapter of the Genji, "Yume no Ukihashi" ("The Floating Bridge of Dreams," may also be considered boat imagery. A "floating bridge" (ukihashi) is a pontoon bridge:

[152] Expressions like "river of love" and "sea of love" appear in Buddhist scripture. Compassion is the sublime Buddhist virtue, whereas love is accorded little importance. Hatred is inevitably the reverse side of love, and love is by definition accompanied by attachment.

[153] [Hurvitz so translates the title of the twenty-seventh chapter, "Śubha-vyūha-rāja," or J. "Myōshōgon'ō Honjihon."—Trans., Ed.]

[154] [Hurvitz, 1976, 327-28.—Trans.]

the hulls of small boats are lashed together and planks put on top of them to provide a temporary crossing. If the ropes that hold the boats break, each craft will drift off, its destination unknown. Part Three must be symbolized by the image of a boat adrift on a river that flows between darkening mountains.

The world of Part Three is symbolized by four images: the mountains for piety, the river for spiritual blindness, the boat for those drifting between piety and spiritual blindness, and growing darkness as a comprehensive image.[155] Strictly speaking, this imagery applies only to the Uji chapters, the ten chapters from "The Lady at the Bridge" through "The Floating Bridge of Dreams." It does not appear in the three preceding chapters, "His Perfumed Highness," "The Rose Plum," and "Bamboo River." It is only when these three chapters are considered together with the Uji chapters that this imagery has meaning for the former group.

The Uji chapters abound in imagery. In addition to the repeated images of mountain, river, and boat that are linked to the themes of Part Three, there is also symbolic significance in images appearing infrequently, or even once. Some examples are mist, winter rain, and the bridge. I call them symbols, which leads one to conceive of them in terms of modern Western symbolism; this might precipitate some misunderstanding. The difference between the imagery of the Uji chapters and modern symbolism is that, in the former case, there is no strict relationship between the image and its corresponding tenor, no fixed relation between signifier and signified. My proposal that the river symbolizes spiritual blindness is intended to deepen the significance of Part Three, but its function as a signifier is not limited to this signification; and a different one might well provide a more profound meaning. Murasaki Shikibu would not mind which signification is chosen, and a reader is free to determine its nature providing some kind of meaning is grasped from within the *Genji*.

I approach the imagery of the Uji chapters in this fashion because of the peculiar nature of Buddhist figural imagery. The kind of imagery found in the Uji chapters does not appear in Chinese *shih* or in other Chinese works. Murasaki Shikibu's only point of reference was the Buddhist scriptures. Buddhist imagery can be interpreted in various ways, however, depending on the ability of the person receiving instruction. In the introductory chapter of the *Lotus Sūtra*, for example, Śākya emits light from the tuft of white hair between his eyebrows, and illuminates eighteen thousand worlds to the east.[156] This light is the central image of the entire sutra, but there is no definitive interpretation of its significance. One of the

---

[155] The year before my article on imagery in the *Genji* was published (Konishi, 1965), Ivan Morris pointed out that the river is the central image of the Uji chapters (Morris, 1964, 271-72).

[156] [The relevant passage is found in Hurvitz, 1976, 4.—Trans.]

346 THE EARLY MIDDLE AGES

many interpretations made over the centuries is highly plausible.[157] But other interpretations, including those just occurring to oneself, are correct if they deepen one's own religious experience. Murasaki Shikibu applies this to literature: she presents us with only an outline within her work so as to force us to discover meanings beyond those given in the text. It can be interpreted in accordance with the individual reader's abilities, and so is seen to have multiple correct interpretations. What I have attempted here is only one relatively accurate interpretation.

Murasaki Shikibu's achievement first takes shape along the lines of the *Records of the Historian* and is then gradually influenced by the *Lotus Sūtra*. This sets the *Genji* apart from all other contemporary monogatari and nikki.

ORDINARY BEINGS AND FANTASTIC EVENTS

After *The Tale of Genji*, the fictional world changes. Only a masterpiece among monogatari can attract an audience by telling of ordinary beings and events. Less confident authors understandably tended to write about ordinary beings and fantastic events, and fictional monogatari became more fantastic from the middle of the eleventh century. This was due less to a revival of tenth-century tastes or the search for novelty than to an orientation toward fantastic content, an attraction common to any period. Parts Two and Three of *The Tale of Genji* were extraordinary for their time; and yet, in the centuries immediately following the composition of the *Genji*, the orientation toward fantasy came under criticism, an indication of how the Japanese literary consciousness had been raised by the *Genji*. *An Untitled Book* criticizes more than ten monogatari, all probably written in the latter half of the eleventh century, for lacking plausibility. It notes of the *Hamamatsu Chūnagon Monogatari* (*The Nostalgic Counselor*), for example: "It makes little distinction between China and Japan, muddling them together most *implausibly* [makotoshikarazu]" (*MMSS*, 78).[158]

The plot of *The Nostalgic Counselor* commences with the hero of the tale, a middle counselor (chūnagon), learning in a dream that his deceased father has been reborn as an imperial prince in China. The middle coun-

---

[157] This is the traditional Tendai reading that the ray of light emitted from between the Buddha's eyebrows symbolizes the eternal, omnipresent logos. [Auth., Trans.]

[158] [Our translation of the title, *The Nostalgic Counselor*, has been worked out with the author. Both the title and the poem by the counselor in the first extant chapter allude to a poem by Yamanoe Okura (660-ca. 733); *Man'yōshū*, 1:163. While in China on a T'ang Embassy, Okura longs for home, where he imagines "Mitsu no hamamatsu" (the pines on the beach of Naniwa) yearning for his return from China. *Mitsu no Hamamatsu* is in fact the title used by Fujiwara Teika (1162-1241) and, many think, the original title.—Trans., Ed.]

selor then travels to China and meets the Kauyau Empress.[159] Rebirth is certainly an implausible event for most modern readers.[160] *An Untitled Book* does not, however, find it an unnatural element. On the contrary, the design of the monogatari is pronounced "splendid" (medetashi); but the story is faulted for the overly complicated relations among the cast of characters, which includes both Chinese and Japanese. The Kauyau Empress's parents, for instance, are a prince, the Chinese ambassador to Japan, and a Japanese lady, the daughter of Prince Kōzuke. The empress's younger half-sister, a Japanese, lives in Yoshino. Mishima Yukio based his tetralogy, *Hōjō no Umi (The Sea of Fertility)* on *The Nostalgic Counselor*, and his central motif is also rebirth.[161] Mishima's story takes place in areas as exotic as Burma, but his narrative is so meticulously set that the reader senses no artificiality whatsoever. The overly easy way in which characters come into relation and the blatant fictitiousness of *The Nostalgic Counselor* on the other hand are obvious deficiencies. These are the "implausible" features criticized by *An Untitled Book*.

A modern critical approach might find that *The Nostalgic Counselor* makes no thematic use of its interesting motif of rebirth. Mishima's tetralogy is concerned with the origins of human existence. His theme is the grand paradox of rebirth: it is caused by karma, which human beings are powerless to alter, and yet karma can be stopped, not by superhuman strength but by an ordinary person's small, almost meaningless actions.[162] *An Untitled Book* is more concerned with the treatment of events in fictional monogatari than with matters of theme. When the hero of *The Story of Sagoromo*, a general, becomes tennō at the end of the story, *An Untitled Book* labels this a "shocking, *implausible* series of events" (*MMSS*, 62). Its implausibility lies in the fact, known to every contemporary reader, that the son of a royal family member who has been made a

---

[159] The extant *Hamamatsu Chūnagon Monogatari* lacks its opening chapter, but the plot of the missing portion is known from various sources. Matsuo Satoshi made the first detailed study on this subject (Matsuo, 1939, 176-212). The empress is known by what is probably a fictitious place name, Kauyau, which, like most Chinese names, is written in kana in the original. Chinese characters have since been assigned the names, usually with no way of judging applicability. For the empress, "Kauyau" has been assigned characters read in Chinese as "Hoyang," corresponding to an area of Honan province. If the author did in fact intend "Hoyang" by "Kauyau," it shows her limitations in Chinese history, since an empress's sobriquet never included the name of her home district. [Auth., Trans.]

[160] Suzuki Hiromichi has pointed out unnatural and unrealistic elements in eleventh- and twelfth-century fictional monogatari (Suzuki Hiromichi, 1968, 28-41).

[161] Matsuo Satoshi was a professor at the Gakushūin School when he wrote his study of *Hamamatsu* (see n. 159). It made an impression on one of his students, Hiraoka Kimitake (Mishima Yukio), who was inspired by it to write *Hōjō no Umi*. Matsuo gave Hiraoka the pen name Mishima Yukio.

[162] Further details will appear in the fifth volume of this work.

commoner cannot succeed to the throne.[163] In other words, it is quite acceptable to attempt various fictional events in one's story, but those incompatible with the real social system are best excluded. The conviction that fictional monogatari must not contain matters contrary to common knowledge probably dates from the eleventh century.

An Untitled Book also lists, under the rubric of "unpalatable matters," the god Amewaka's descent from heaven upon hearing Sagoromo's splendid flute playing, and the god's attempt to lure Sagoromo to heaven (*Sagoromo Monogatari* [=SGM], 1:45-47), as well as the manifestation of the bodhisattva Fugen at the temple of Konakawadera (SGM, 2:209-10; MMSS, 61-62). Here unrealistic elements are noted. The motif of the descent of a heavenly being seems to have been quite popular: *The Tale of Nezame* (*Yowa no Nezame* [= YN], 1:46-49) and the late twelfth-century *Ariake no Wakare* (*Parting at Dawn; Ariake no Wakare*, 3:295-98) also employ this design. *An Untitled Book* criticizes the matter of Nezame's resuscitation from death, although the author of the remark does not make clear whether the grounds of her criticism are that the event is possible but unnatural, or completely unrealistic. Because the resuscitation episode does not survive in the extant *Nezame*, we have no precise knowledge of what exactly happened.[164] Komatsu Tomi has found that Nezame apparently dies and is then brought back to life by some secret art (Sekine-Komatsu, 1960, 63-65). To be sure, the *Book* excuses the resuscitation itself as "an event determined by karma from past lives and therefore beyond criticism." The object of opprobrium is Nezame's attitude: heedless of this

---

[163] [Not all tennō's sons remained princes. It was decided, when the boy was quite young, whether he had sufficient backing from maternal relatives to receive princely rank and become a candidate for the position of crown prince, or whether the boy should be withdrawn from competition by reducing him to commoner status. Those in the latter category usually took the family name Minamoto and were eligible to hold any court rank and office available to the aristocracy; but they and their sons were barred from becoming tennō. Genji (whose very name means "Minamoto Clan") is the normative example of a tennō's son who becomes a Minamoto. His putative son Kaoru, like the Sagoromo General, is a tennō's grandson who—according to the rules of Heian society—cannot become tennō himself.—Trans.]

[164] *Yowa no Nezame* survives in five chapters. There are missing chapters between the present Chapters 2 and 3, and following the present Chapter 5. The content of the missing chapters can be surmised from various sources: the Nakamura manuscript of *Yowa no Nezame Monogatari* (a condensed version of the original, written in the High Middle Ages), along with quotations from the original *Nezame* that appear in the *Shūi Hyakuban Utaawase* and the *Fūyōshū*. The resuscitation scene, however, does not appear in the Nakamura manuscript. [The title of the work is variously given. The author gives it as *Yowa no Nezame (Monogatari)*, writing "Yowa" with the character for "Yoru." The work is also called *Yoru no Nezame* or *Nezame*. For a full translation, see the unpublished thesis by Kenneth Richard, "Developments in Late Heian Prose Fiction: *The Tale of Nezame*" (University of Washington, 1973). There is also a published partial version, Carol Hochstedler, *The Tale of Nezame: Part Three of Yowa no Nezame Monogatari*, East Asia Papers 22 (Ithaca, N.Y.: Cornell University, 1979). This seems to correspond to the extant Chapters 3 through 5, with summaries of earlier chapters and conjectures about nonextant parts.—Ed., Trans.]

inauspicious occurrence, she returns nonchalantly to her old life. This is found to be "terribly improper" (*MMSS*, 73). *Asaji ga Tsuyu (Dew in the Neglected Garden)*, an early thirteenth-century work, also concerns itself with a resuscitation to life. The topic seems not to have struck readers as particularly unrealistic.

We can perceive a common thread running throughout the criticism of *An Untitled Book* toward fictional monogatari written in the latter half of the eleventh century. Rebirth, the descent of heavenly beings, and the resuscitation of the dead are not especially unrealistic subjects to the author of the *Book*. A work is criticized, however, when its characters behave unnaturally, in a manner contrary to common social expectations. Or, seen from another perspective, things that are fantastic when measured by twentieth-century standards were not particularly fantastic in the late eleventh through the early thirteenth centuries. We might well note that the frequent appearance of such phenomena in works from this period signifies that they were demanded by contemporary audiences. A basic plot line, keeping to generally accepted social norms, was maintained throughout a work, with extraordinary events appearing only in strategic places. This, I believe, reflects a demand for interesting plots to which many authors acceded.

The first half of the eleventh century marked the developmental stage for fictional monogatari, and audiences had not yet matured sufficiently to appreciate well-made plots. The characters encountered in Part Two of *The Tale of Genji* bear the continuous relationships necessary to a long monogatari, and they may have awakened readers to the concept of plot interest and to a demand for a certain order or consolidation in the development of a story. Order in a story meant not only good sequential correspondence but also the creation of excitement, at some point in the work, so as to avoid monotony. Events removed from the everyday world were probably employed as sources of such excitement.

Plot emphasis manifested itself in two ways in the latter half of the eleventh century. The first was in the continuous long monogatari, a good example of which is *The Story of Sagoromo*. *The Nostalgic Counselor* and *The Tale of Nezame* survive only in large fragments and so, unfortunately, cannot provide firm evidence of being continuous long monogatari. The *Sagoromo*, however, is acknowledged as a fully formed example of a continuous long monogatari. Compared with the *Genji*, which retains much that is characteristic of the multipartite long monogatari, the *Sagoromo* is well endowed with plot development, foreshadowing, and correspondences. It indeed represents the continuous long monogatari, as well as the mature period of the fictional monogatari. These statements relate to the formal aspects of the *Sagoromo*, as differentiated from an evaluation of its content.

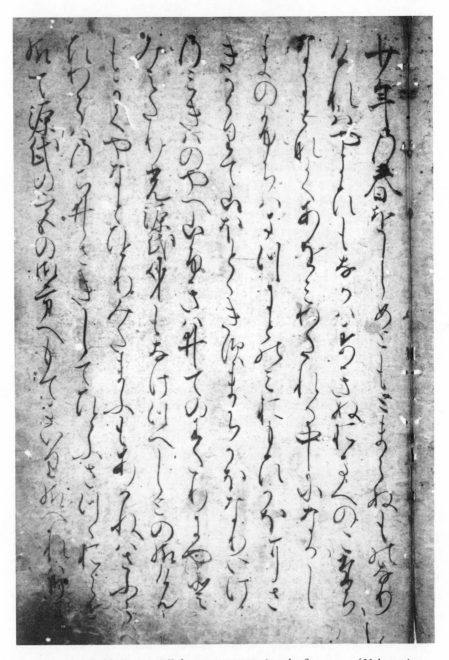

5. *Sagoromo Monogatari*, Fukagawa manuscript, the first page of Volume 1, now in the possession of Professor Yoshida Kōichi, Tōyō University. Copied in the 13th century

The continuous long monogatari, with its emphasis on plot treatment, was the mainstream for fictional monogatari until at least the twelfth century. Even the *Nezame*, which has been called a psychological novel, has its critical focus in its plot and subject matter, whereas its psychological depictions are significant only in their volume. The extant text has sixteen passages of psychological description in Chapters 1 and 2, and about eighty in Chapters 3, 4, and 5 (Nagai, 1960, 17). Some of these passages are quite lengthy, as much as thirty-three lines long in the revised printed edition (*YN*, 5:325-27).[165] But a large proportion of psychological description does not always mean the work in question is a psychological novel. Part Two of the *Genji* is qualitatively closer to the twentieth-century psychological novel. By modern criteria, the best creations in the *Nezame* are the character of the old regent, a secondary figure, and the passages concerning Nezame's affection for him. The old regent is unparalleled in monogatari for his magnanimity and forbearance: he marries Nezame full knowing that she already has a fine young lover (Naidaijin) and is pregnant by him; and the regent is so besotted by his beautiful young wife that he forgets all about his own children. He is reminiscent of a character from a modern novel (Nakamura Shin'ichirō, 1957, 44-45).

I am attracted still more by Nezame's changing emotions toward her husband. At first she dislikes him and treats him coldly, but gradually she comes to love him. After the regent's death, Nezame is unable to feel the same attachment for Naidaijin that she did in the past. This is an astonishing conception, when compared with the sort of stories in which a beautiful girl is married to a splendid youth, and they live happily ever after. Nezame's married life with the regent, however, is described in a nonextant section of the text and has been reconstructed from other sources. The psychological descriptions in *Nezame* are concerned with events other than the heroine's marriage. We must conclude, then, that the plot design gave rise to the unique world of Nezame and her elderly husband.

Plot emphasis manifests itself in another way in short monogatari. Tamagami Takuya's theory, that fictional monogatari antedating *The Hollow Tree* were as a rule short, may well be irrefutable (Tamagami, 1943, 110-17). None survives. But as we have seen, all are thought to have been essentially fantasies. Although stories dealing with love affairs would have tended strongly toward realistic content, substantial emphasis on fantastic elements was probably necessary to satisfy audiences. Once exposed to the advanced literary techniques of the *Genji*, however, such au-

---

[165] Another passage is thirty lines long (*YN*, 3:328-29). *Nezame* is also characterized by its lengthy dialogues. Naidaijin's declaration to the Lay Priest (Nezame's father) of his love for Nezame is fifty-four lines long (*YN*, 5:340-43). Long narrated passages are typical of *Nezame* and happen to take the form of characters' thoughts occasionally. This is not sufficient reason to call *Nezame* a psychological novel.

diences were unlikely to remain so little sophisticated as to enjoy only fantastic stories. The authors of short monogatari had these readers in mind when they employed a new technique: they dealt with ordinary subject matter but created a design that aimed for an intellectual or emotional effect through the use of structural techniques.

One example is the surprise ending to "The Lieutenant Handsome as Cherry Blossoms," which probably dates from the latter half of the eleventh century.[166] The lieutenant, the hero of the story, has designs on a young lady intended to become a royal lady-in-waiting. He forces his way into her room and succeeds in bundling the lady, "prostrate and very small," into a carriage. But his captive turns out to be the lady's grandmother, a nun, who had taken the lady's place out of anxiety for her (TCM, 367-71). The basic plot takes a form familiar to readers of the Genji, who would recognize its similarity to the scene in which Genji abducts the young Murasaki. The characters and scenes would be equally formulaic when paired with this kind of subject matter. A little under ninety-two percent of the entire text has a formulaic air, but the few lines that make up the ending are very effective indeed. The surprise ending, O. Henry's specialty, is a technique demanding a tight, carefully planned structure so that the ending will have the maximum effect. Hence the story should contain only necessary elements. But roughly ninety-two percent of "The Lieutenant Handsome as Cherry Blossoms" is a selective description of the hero's life—his absorption in fūryū pursuits—that seems to have no function in creating the impact of the surprise ending. Scholars of Japanese literature have defended the story by stating that the medieval Japanese short monogatari is unlike the modern Western short story and should therefore not have to conform to the criteria of the latter. This is not a useful defense. The short monogatari and the Western short story share similar technical properties, and so there is no reason why the two genres must be treated differently. They differ only in the relative tightness of their structure, a probable reflection of differences between the tastes of their audiences.[167]

[166] Contained in Tsutsumi Chūnagon Monogatari, a collection of ten short monogatari. Its date of compilation and the origin of the title are unknown. One of the stories, "Yoshinashigoto," appears to date from no earlier than the late fourteenth century (Suzuki Kazuo, 1980, 305-307). The composition date of "Hanasakura Oru Shōshō" is similarly unclear, but it shares stylistic, grammatical, and compositional features with "Ōsaka Koenu Gon Chūnagon" (1055) that suggest it dates from roughly the same period. [The heroes of monogatari commonly start off with the rank of shōshō (lieutenant), or middle counselor (chūnagon). In the case of Hamamatsu, the hero remains a middle counselor to the end. The author has suggested elsewhere that that strange fact and other details probably are to be explained by the author's lack of familiarity with the court, being of the lower noble class of provincial governors (zuryō).—Ed.]

[167] If we compare readers of modern Western novels and Japanese novels written after the

Within one's own group at least, late tenth-century monogatari audiences seem to have shared information or knowledge about already extant monogatari. When the hero of "The Lieutenant of Katano" was borrowed to play a secondary role in *The Story of Ochikubo*, the premise of the action was that the audience shared common information or knowledge about the Lieutenant of Katano. A marked increase in monogatari in the late eleventh century was accompanied by the appearance of audiences who were thoroughly familiar with these monogatari. Within their individual groups, each possessed a rich store of shared information about how a given character acts in a given scene of a certain monogatari. Monogatari writers were usually members of an audience group; and since group membership was limited, an author would be well aware what information or knowledge her fellow members had about various monogatari. Because monogatari were written on the premise of prior group knowledge, the information a group held in reserve might well be omitted in a new story. An author might, for example, begin a story by writing about how a man, mistaking the bright moon for daybreak, leaves his lady's house in the middle of the night (*TCM*, 367). The author need not detail how the man came to frequent the lady's house, or what the lady's circumstances are, because the audience is expected to substitute appropriate scenes from already familiar monogatari.

This expectation may have been based on the fact that contemporary fictional monogatari generally had a similar import. An audience group consisted of people whose upbringing and culture were homogeneous. They lived in a closed society devoid of strong movements, and so repetition probably evoked a sense of security in them and was considered worthy writing. For the same reason, recurrent diction and themes are found in contemporary waka.

To put matters somewhat differently, the fictional monogatari had formed a ga world equivalent to that of waka. Previously, monogatari had been evaluated as works that "give the power of speech to that which cannot speak" and that "tell only of fantastic things." This was due to their tendency to depict implausible events. Fictional monogatari certainly belonged to the zoku world at this point, when there was as yet no conscious value attached to repetition in monogatari of statements of similar import. Writers working in the latter half of the eleventh century, however, had the towering achievements of the *Genji* before their eyes. They reproduced characters and situations having much in common with the *Genji* and sensed the value present in their repetition. These works are generally per-

---

late nineteenth century with readers of eleventh-century fictional monogatari, the difference will be seen to lie in the degree of value each allots to tight structure.

ceived as imitative of the *Genji*, but it would be better to recognize here an approach to monogatari composition similar to the technique of allusive variation in waka.[168] As an awareness of ga transformed monogatari, its subject matter moved toward ordinary events while unusual elements corresponding to fabulous events continued to be sought. The result, we may conclude, was the surprise ending, a structural manifestation of import.

A growing awareness of ga aspects in monogatari, similar to those in waka, was present in the late eleventh century, as may be ascertained from the monogatari match held in 1055 at the house of the Kamo High Priestess of Rokujō (*Goshūishū*, 15:876, forenote). Following the form established by waka matches, twenty ladies presented their own newly composed fictional monogatari (*EM*, 37:471). The competing poems in one recorded waka match are all drawn from the monogatari presented on this occasion (*Ruiju Utaawase Maki*, "Hommon Hen," 131-33). From this we know that "The Counselor Who Failed to Cross Love Slope," the first story in the *Tsutsumi Chūnagon Monogatari (Tales of the River-bank Counselor)*, first appeared at this monogatari match, and that its author was a lady named Koshikibu (Horibe, 1939, 255-66).[169] The use of a waka-match format for monogatari indicates not only that monogatari were perceived as equal to waka, but also that the audience regarded monogatari as equivalent to waka in assumptions. "The Counselor Who Failed to Cross Love Slope" consists entirely of descriptions of the aristocratic fūryū life. Needless to say, there are no fantastic events, nor is there so much as a trace of a technique like the surprise ending. In this sense, "Love Slope" is a typical, ga short monogatari. Where, then, is the interest in such a work? My interpretation is that the interest stems from participation.[170] In 1051, about four years before "Love Slope" was written, Goreizei Tennō (r. 1045-68) held a sweet flag root match.[171] The 1055

[168] In allusive variation (honkadori), a poet incorporates into his own work the motifs, diction, or imagery of an extant outstanding waka and anticipates arousing complex interest through the superpositioning of his waka on the original one.

[169] Unknown points remain, including whether the monogatari match occurred independently of or concurrently with the waka match; whether there were twenty or eighteen competing authors; and whether the match or matches took place on the third day of the Fifth Month, on the fifth of that month, or whether more than one day was required.

[170] Creating a special effect by having as subject matter situations in which author and readers are or have been involved.

[171] [The first half of "The Counselor Who Failed to Cross Love Slope" is concerned with just such a match at the royal palace. The Heian aristocracy was fond of matches of all kinds: for example, fans, shells, flowers, pictures, and bird and cricket songs, as well as the more ordinary waka and shih matches. Sweet flag matches tended to be held in the Fifth Month, during the Sweet Flag Festival (Tango no Sechi). The roots (properly, rhizomes), like iris rhizomes, are shallow and grow horizontally in the ground, and they can reach impressive sizes. The object of the Festival is summarized by McCullough and McCullough, 1980 (1:412): "The Sweet-Flag Festival . . . represented an effort to ward off the diseases that tended to

monogatari match, moreover, took place at the beginning of the Fifth Month, during the sweet flag season (Suzuki Kazuo, 1953-54, 287). The subject matter selected for "Love Slope" dealt with a recent event familiar to members of the audience. Such an event, when made part of a fictional monogatari, has a special effect on readers. This technique came to be called "atekomi" [working out good prospects] in kabuki.

People took special pleasure in composing and exchanging waka about situations in which only they had directly participated (or were participating). Much of the interest in informal waka relies on the participatory element. Although this was common enough in waka, fictional monogatari had traditionally been narrated on a fairy-tale basis. Incorporating one's actual experience into an unlikely story probably gave it, unlike waka, a certain strangeness. Naturally the strangeness was not on the level of that produced by fantastic subject matter, nor did it have the excitement of a surprise-ending structure. Nonetheless, such stories must have made a considerable impact in the ga world, where audiences valued the equilibrium presented by already existing expression and responded sensitively to the smallest nuance of fresh expression. The composition and reception of monogatari in a ga setting provides one more basis for my view that the latter half of the eleventh century marks the mature period of fictional monogatari. As noted earlier in regard to *Sagoromo*, the "mature period" does not necessarily signify the high point for monogatari in terms of their literary value.

FACTUAL MONOGATARI

Most prose works composed in Japanese during the tenth and eleventh centuries have characteristics embracing the monogatari, the nikki, and the shū. Assigning them to one or another category involves assessment of preponderant qualities. Not infrequently, the most outstanding aspect of a work provides the basis for determining its tentative classification. One clearly discernible group consists of monogatari narrating fact rather than fiction. There are two kinds of monogatari within this group: those resembling shū, in which waka forms the core of the work; and those having properties in common with nikki, in which narration of events is central. The former will be called "monogatari centering on waka" (utagoto no monogatari) and the latter, "monogatari centering on society" (yogoto no monogatari).

---

strike with the onset of hot weather. It embraced a variety of ceremonies and customs, most of them involving the aromatic leaves and roots of the sweet flag . . . to which the Chinese and Japanese, like the medieval Europeans, ascribed medicinal properties."—Trans.]

Centering on Waka

In the sense used here, "factual" indicates an authorial attitude or claim. The author purports to narrate facts, but the content of the work is not limited to events that actually happened. The *Tales of Ise* is one example. Most of its episodes adopt a narrative style that begins with the words, "Once there was a man" ("Mukashi otoko arikeri"), but the anonymous "man" (otoko) is not the only character in the work. Sixteen historical figures, including Ki no Aritsune (815-77), appear twenty-two times in the *Ise*, a reflection of the narrator's factual claim.[172] A manifestation of the influence exerted by this is the fact that the "man" recites waka found in the royal anthologies under the name of Ariwara Narihira. For this reason, the figure of the "man" was taken as designating Narihira, and a variant title arose for the *Ise, Zaigo Chūjō no Nikki (The Nikki of the Ariwara Captain)*, and *An Untitled Book* included the work under the category of "real events." For all that, no reader was likely to have believed the factuality of an episode in which demons gobble up a woman in a single bite (*IM, dan* 6:114). Such a story requires only that its narrator seriously proclaim it as true. The audience need not actually believe the story as long as it is willing to listen attentively, temporarily suspending disbelief. Even so, there seem to have been some skeptical readers, because a postscript was later appended to the story about the demons, indicating that they were in fact two older brothers of the Nijō Consort, Fujiwara Mototsune (836-91) and Kunitsune (827-908; ibid., 114-15). This is part of the framework of the story, a confirmation that some such event did occur.

One might also recognize the presence of stories that were other than fictional in aim, that were factual monogatari whose raw material was an actual event. The enormous difficulty of proving how much is indeed true in such works, however, renders it rather pointless to classify factual monogatari according to the criterion of actual occurrence. Factual monogatari are more effectively divided by form. One category represents what might be called a waka-prose complex, a linkage of waka and prose so organic that the waka cannot be removed without the prose section losing its meaning. In a second category, development occurs solely through the order and logic of the prose sections. An occasional waka may appear in such works, but it will have only secondary importance to the narrative.

---

[172] The sixteen figures are Ki no Aritsune (dan 16, 38, 82), Minamoto Itaru (39), Junna Tennō (39), Takaiko (39), Prince Kayō (43), the Nijō Consort (5, 76, 95), Fujiwara Tsuneyuki (77, 78), Takakiko (77, 78), Prince Koretaka (82, 83), Montoku Tennō (77), the Cloistered Prince of Yamashina (78), Fujiwara Yoshichika (101), Ariwara Yukihira (101), Fujiwara Toshiyuki (107), Kōkō Tennō (114), and the Horikawa Minister (97). Historical figures also appear in postscripts to certain episodes. These postscripts are probably later accretions.

One work that falls between the two categories is *Tannomine Shōshō Mo-nogatari (The Lieutenant of Tannomine)*, a chronologically ordered description of events set in motion by Fujiwara Takamitsu's (b. 939) sudden decision to become a monk. The chronological structure of *The Lieutenant of Tannomine*, together with its concordance with historical fact, clearly mark it as a kind of work different from the *Tales of Ise*. On the other hand, the *Tannomine* is a rather short piece, containing eighty-one waka (two of which are chōka, long poems). This waka group can stand alone as an object of reading, a property differentiating it from the later *Eiga Monogatari (A Tale of Flowering Fortunes)* and *Ōkagami (The Great Mirror)*. The prose parts of the *Tannomine* may be omitted, and still its waka corpus will offer its own interest so long as the reader is informed of the setting for each waka. This is a characteristic of the shū, and is a feature common to both the *Tales of Ise* and *The Lieutenant of Tannomine*. In this respect the two works can be seen as a single kind. One of the variant titles of the *Tannomine* is the *Takamitsu Nikki*. The work does have some properties of a nikki, inasmuch as it relates a specific person's circumstances. But the verbal suffix "-keri," indicating transmitted recollection, is employed in the prose sections, and the story is told in the "past tense." We should, therefore, accord greater weight to its monogatari properties.

There are obvious differences between the *Ise* and the *Tannomine*. The former retains some signs of oral composition and transmission, whereas the latter is a literary composition in conception and execution. Masuda Katsumi's important theory posits that the *Ise*, regularly termed an uta-monogatari (waka narrative), was not a literary creation transmitted in writing but evolved through utagatari—short, orally transmitted stories connected with specific waka composed by members of the aristocracy. These stories were written down and eventually compiled into the longer waka narrative (Masuda Katsumi, 1953, 15-22).

Ever since the Ancient Age, there had been transmissions of anecdotes linked to given waka or to the origin of that waka (a matter treated in Volume One). This practice, carried on into the Middle Ages, yielded oral waka stories.[173] It is natural that oral narration would result in frequent variant transmission, and that frequent, substantial variants in episodes within a waka narrative would seldom occur in a genre composed and transmitted in writing. Frequent variants and fluidity of content are aspects shared with the setsuwa, and certain kinds of oral waka stories might well be called waka setsuwa. This is not to say that the waka nar-

---

[173] One example of usage of "utagatari" will suffice. "I remember that while I was ill someone told me an odd utagatari about a place called Kainuma Pond. I said I would try to compose a waka about it" (*Murasaki Shikibu Shū*, 88, forenote).

rative is simply a collection of waka setsuwa. Certain waka narratives have specific, recognizable properties.[174]

Let us consider those episodes [dan] of the *Tales of Ise* in which the anonymous "man" acts as protagonist. There is no interconnection or interrelationship among the events described in these episodes, and yet the man displays an identifiable nature throughout. He is associated solely with the amorous, courtly life and has no connection with the world of power and fame. "Concluding that he was a useless fellow," the man journeys to the East Country (*IM*, dan 9:116-17), but his only major activity on the trip is reciting waka. His actions are performed to affirm that his reason for being lies in amorousness and courtly ways. Feng-liu/fūryū originally became a worthy principle for the literati's life because it complemented orthodox Chinese morality. Having shed its orthodox Chinese aspects, fūryū created a unique world ɔf amorousness and courtly acts, and fūryū itself underwent a considerable transformation. This is discerned in matters of tone. The feng-liu that delights Po Chü-i is cheerful and accommodating, a contented quality, whereas the anonymous "man's" amorous and courtly acts are often linked to disappointing circumstances. The man does not have his way in the world of power and fame, and he also encounters frequent disappointments in his many journeys through the world of love. In one case, a woman whom the man loves deeply avoids his ardent pursuit by hiding where he cannot reach her. The man lies on the bare floor of her former room, now stripped of its doors and sliding panels, and longs for the past. The moon sets. He recites this waka and goes home at dawn in tears (*IM*, dan 4:112-13):

Tsuki ya aranu	This is not that moon!
Haru ya mukashi no	Nor is this spring the spring that was
Haru naranu	In those days bygone!
Wagami hitotsu wa	My being the single thing
Moto no mi ni shite.	Remaining as it ever was . . .[175]

This episode is noteworthy as an excellent example of disappointed am-

[174] Utamonogatari, waka setsuwa, and utagatari are closely related terms, but their individual properties must be kept in mind. Definitions follow. (1) Utamonogatari (waka *narrative*): a *literary* creation, transmitted in writing, of a story or collection of stories, each of which focuses on a single waka as the climax of the story. (2) Waka setsuwa: a *story*, transmitted either orally or in writing, whose subject matter concerns one or more waka. The story is not shaped so as to focus on the waka, and there is no carefully planned style, unlike that of the waka narrative. (3) Utagatari (oral waka *story*): an *orally* transmitted story, usually short, about events linked to one or more waka. One or more waka stories can provide the raw material for a waka *narrative*. [Auth., Trans. The author later gives examples of these kinds.—Ed.]

[175] [Perhaps the most famous, and certainly one of the most difficult to translate, of waka, this poem also appears as *KKS* 15:747.—Ed.]

orousness treated as worthy by its context. Love, which we may think delightful, is here seen in its classically true, grievous form. The idea of disappointed love as the truest form of love survives into the High Middle Ages (*Tsurezuregusa*, dan 3:89). Critics of linked poetry also perceived that love should be sung of in this vein: "Deep in love, he longs to see her; but she remains beyond reach and his suit fails to prosper as body and soul seem to fade away" (*Ubuginu*, 175). The *Ise* episode is the source of such expression: it demonstrates the shift from assigning worth to a fūryū of contentment to valuing disappointed amorousness.

Implicitness—a preference for sorrow over joy, stillness over motion, and the feminine over the masculine—is an important characteristic of Japanese literature, a point discussed in the General Introduction in the first volume of this *History*. An awareness of the value of implicitness probably arose during the period when the Narihira figure within oral waka stories—the epitome of disappointed amorousness—took shape as a character. The actual Ariwara Narihira followed a relatively smooth course both in official life and in his social affairs, with no special evidence of despair or disappointment. These elements were shaped for the Narihira of oral waka stories, out of a conscious effort to acknowledge the worthiness of disappointed love. The anonymous man in the *Ise* therefore never feels contentment. The myth of Narihira was an oral transmission created within aristocratic society and is to be distinguished from popular setsuwa.[176] Some scholars of Japanese literature with ethnological interests have seen the man's journey to the East Country as a crude example of the motif of the nobleman wandering through strange lands, but this approach immoderately magnifies the role of setsuwa motifs.[177]

The extant text of the *Tales of Ise* is undoubtedly based on such oral waka stories, but it hardly appears to be a written compilation that has been orally transmitted. The present text contains many literary elements. This can be concluded from the unified tone of the extant *Ise* text, which is present in all manuscripts. I once wrote that the special nature of the *Ise* lies in its "pristine passion" (Konishi, 1953c, 42). One example is. the "well-curb" (izutsu) episode. A boy and a girl, who have long played together by a well, grow up and become attracted to each other. They eventually marry, but the man's affections soon shift to another woman. His wife does not resent his inconstancy, she only yearns to have him back.

---

[176] In this case "myth" is used as a critical term and signifies the relating of unreliable facts in a manner that strikes the audience as reliable. This also applies to the myth of Heichū, discussed later in this section.

[177] The motif of the wandering noble (first discerned by Origuchi Shinobu) has a circular structure: a man who does not obey the logic of his community is driven from there and exiled, but his crime is redeemed by the hardships encountered in his wanderings, and he eventually returns to the community (Araki, 1982). Not all stories of wandering nobles conform to this motif.

Moved by her steadfastness, the man returns (*IM*, dan 23:126-27). He is
moved by the purity of her love, which first blossomed in childhood and
remained throughout adulthood. The purity of love is an element common both to episodes with a Narihira character as protagonist and to
others in which the hero is a historical figure. Modern readers are also
struck by such purity.[178]

Simple recording and compilation would not likely yield a unified tone.
The present text of the *Ise* underwent a complex process of composition.
At its earliest stage, it probably consisted of fewer than twenty episodes,
all concerning Narihira's waka (Katagiri, 1968, 286). At some point prior
to the compilation of the *Gosenshū*, the corpus apparently grew to approximately forty episodes, or about one-third of the present text (ibid.,
261-90). We do not know what relationship exists, in terms of composition, between the extant *Ise* text and the earlier versions, but in the process
some individual or individuals must have consolidated and revised episodes.

The somewhat later *Stories of Heichū* has a more pronounced unity in
tone throughout. Again, an anonymous "man" is the hero of the monogatari. He is described in each episode as having the same personality traits,
leading to a strongly received impression that the "man" of the episodes
is one and the same character. When the name "Heichū" appears in the
final episode, the reader concludes that the "man" of the earlier episodes
must have been Heichū all along. Yet the "man" in the *Heichū* is of a very
different nature from the "man" in the *Tales of Ise*. The difference is that
Heichū's love affairs end up as comic failures. He does strive very seriously to succeed at love, but his efforts always result in failure. He would
seem to be an inferior inhabitant of the amorous world, since he constantly loses at love, and yet he amounts to more than a humorous figure.
The seriousness with which he goes about his failures gives him a sense of
humanity that moves the reader, whose position is that of the ordinary
beings in monogatari. The man even has about him a certain pathos, some
features that cannot be laughed at. Yet his world may be termed a comic
one, as suggested earlier. Heichū is every bit as disappointed in his amours
as the "man" in the *Tales of Ise*, but he is presented in an entirely different
tone. There are few consistently comic works in Japanese literature, and
so Heichū is an exceptionally noteworthy character.

[178] While yet young Mishima Yukio wrote: "One feels a sense of awe in reading a classic
like the *Ise Monogatari*. Certainly a [modern] Japanese would want to write something like
it. It is marvelous and compelling enough to be taboo to modern writers, who must protect
their nerves. If the *Ise* were the only Japanese classic, all our writers would hang themselves.
. . . So many of life's crises are depicted in that monogatari. How terrifying that they are presented in such an offhanded way!" (Mishima, 1942, 40). The nature of the seventeen-year-
old Mishima's sensations differs from my own. Indisputably, however, the *Ise Monogatari*
has an indescribable charm.

The character of Heichū was probably shaped by the compiler of the
Heichū rather than taking on its own form as oral waka stories evolved.
The consistent, unified tone is one indication of the compiler's influence;
another is the farcical—as opposed to comic—nature of the Heichū myth
that was transmitted orally in contemporary aristocratic society. A cari-
caturized Heichū episode—in which the man, wishing to look properly
tearful, unknowingly splashes his face with ink instead of water—was current before the *Genji* was written and was widely transmitted in setsuwa
from the twelfth century on, because the usual Heichū image was farcical.[179] Yet that story of the inkstained Heichū that must have been the
source of later versions does not appear in the *Stories of Heichū*. The non-
farcical, comic Heichū of the monogatari was probably created by a specific author in the course of integrating composition.

The *Yamato Monogatari (Tales of Yamato)* has neither a single protagonist nor a definite tone. It might also be noted that the waka that are the
foci of many of the episodes are treated in a way different from those in
the *Tales of Ise* and the *Stories of Heichū*. This is seen very clearly when
the same story appears in both the *Ise* and the *Tales of Yamato*. Consider
the "well-curb" story mentioned earlier. In the *Ise* version, the boy and
girl who played by the well marry later, and when the husband's affections
shift to another woman, the wife expresses no resentment. But the husband, suspecting that his wife must have a lover, hides in the garden of the
house. The woman assumes her husband has gone off to see his new lover
in Kawachi and recites,

Kaze fukeba	As the wind blows,
Okitsu shiranami	In the offing the whitecaps rise
Tatsutayama	Like Tatsuta Mountain;
Yowa ni ya kimi ga	Are you now crossing its peak
Hitori koyu ran.	All alone this midnight?

The man "felt boundless love for her and went no more to Kawachi." So
the *Ise* version. In the *Yamato* version, the following events are presented
as occurring after the poem.

The woman lay down, weeping, and put a metal basin filled with
water against her breast. The man watched in amazement. What
might she be doing? The water began to boil, whereupon she threw it
away, and again filled the basin with cold water. The man, seeing this,
was filled with love. He ran up to the house and said, "How grieved
you must be to do such a thing!" He took her in his arms, and they

[179] The story appears, for example, in *Konjaku Monogatari Shū* (30:212-15), *Kohon Setsuwa Shū* (story 19, 1:56-59), and *Uji Shūi Monogatari* (3:147-50).

lay together. Thereafter he strayed no more, but remained always at her side. (*YM*, dan 149:320-21)

In the *Tales of Ise*, the man is moved by the waka and returns to his first love. In other words, the waka resolves the complexities of the plot. The *Yamato* story has the same plot, but the man is not immediately motivated by the waka to return to the woman he has known from childhood. His decision is made only after he witnesses a fantastic event: a basin filled with cold water boils when the emotionally feverish woman puts it to her breast. Her poem is not the direct impetus behind the resolution of events.

The genre others have termed utamonogatari (waka narrative) has been said to possess a characteristic form: a waka marks the climactic point in the plot development and provides the impetus by which problems in the story are either resolved smoothly or end in catastrophe (Suzuki Kazuo, 1953-54, 117). According to this definition, episode 149 of the *Tales of Yamato*, whose climactic point is a fabulous event rather than a waka, cannot be called a waka narrative. Compared with its parallel "well-curb" episode in the *Tales of Ise* (dan 23), the *Yamato* version has more expository elements. This is due to the author's wish to shape a climax marked not by a waka but by facts related in the prose story, which must unavoidably emphasize the exposition of those facts. This episode and others like it are best seen not as waka narratives but rather as waka setsuwa, works whose subject matter is an oral account having to do with a waka.

Of course, Suzuki Kazuo's definition does not always enable us to distinguish between waka narratives and waka setsuwa. The difference between the two remains, in the end, a question of degree, a matter of how far the expository elements predominate. Consider episode 38 of the *Stories of Heichū*, for instance, in which a misunderstanding results in the hero's beloved becoming a nun. This story also appears in the *Tales of Yamato* (dan 103) and the *Tales of Times Now Past* (30:story 2). In the *Heichū* version, the climactic point is the scene where the hero receives a waka from the woman that informs him she has become a nun. The other two versions have the same content but include detailed narration about the transition of events. Consequently, in those versions the woman's poem (which one might expect to be the focus of the story) is made inconspicuous by the many expository passages. A work having this much exposition may be termed a waka setsuwa. Other *Yamato* stories, like "Ikutagawa" ("The Ikuta River"; *YM*, dan 147) and "Ashikari" ("The Reed Cutter"; *YM*, dan 148) are setsuwa pure and simple. They were probably included in the *Yamato* only because they happen to have waka in their texts.

Utagatari, oral waka stories, are the source of both the waka narrative (in Suzuki's sense) and the waka setsuwa, and they represent oral transmissions within aristocratic society. Unlike folklore, oral waka stories were not always transmitted from times long past. When Taira Kanemori (d. 990) was serving as provisional governor of Echizen, there was a grandson of Seiwa Tennō (r. 858-76) living in Kurozuka. [The literal meaning of the place name is "black burial mound."] Kanemori sent a waka to the man's daughter, asking for her hand in marriage:

Michinoku no	Is the hearsay true,
Adachi ga hara no	That a wraith is hidden
Kurozuka ni	In Black Burial Mound,
Oni komoreri to	There in the Field of Adachi
Kiku wa makoto ka.	In the land of Michinoku?

The parents refused his suit on the grounds that the girl was too young. After Kanemori returned to the capital, the woman married another man, and Kanemori suffered great loss of face (YM, dan 58:257-58). She had taken Kanemori's jest seriously, interpreting "wraith" as implying that she was a demon.[180] Angered at Kanemori's apparent rudeness, she sought to spite him by rushing into marriage with another man. What is noteworthy about this story is its date of composition. The prototype text of the extant Yamato, probably compiled in 951, seems to differ little from the text we have today (Abe Toshiko, 1954, 18-30). If this is the case, the oral waka story that was the source of this episode evolved during Kanemori's youth and was immediately incorporated into the ancestor of the present Yamato text.

The fact that an oral waka story was incorporated into writing as soon as it appeared can only indicate that such stories flourished in contemporary aristocratic society. The compilers' aim, to appreciate waka within a narrative "field," surely transformed the poems in the familiar reality of readers' lives.[181] In the main, their aim was not to make existing prose traditions into means of information but rather to present waka within a vivid narrative field. Ever since the Ancient Age, recorded traditions have presented a background for waka, in the form of forenotes and afternotes. The "miscellaneous waka, accompanied by stories" of the Man'yōshū (16:3786-889), provide one such instance. This practice, however, is not always identical to the act of appreciating waka within a narrative field.

[180] "Oni" is usually translated "demon," but it apparently had another, milder meaning in the Heian period, signifying a supernatural being who is not easily seen. Kanemori seeks to court the girl wittily, by implying that he has heard of a maiden living in Kurozuka, treasured by her parents and kept from prying eyes. His poem backfires because "oni" has an ambivalent meaning: the girl thinks Kanemori is insinuating that she is a demon haunting the "Black Burial Mound." [Auth., Trans.]

[181] "Field" here refers to the context presumed and employed for interpretation by the author and reader. The term is analogous to the "field" of "electric field" and "gravitational field."

Oral waka stories have been shown to differ in style from the forenotes in waka collections, and so waka stories very likely did not evolve from amplified forenotes (Sakakura, 1953, 12-17). They represent in effect the lively, practical behavior of contemporary aristocratic society. Oral waka stories may have used certain of the miscellaneous *Man'yōshū* waka-story complexes or information in their forenotes and afternotes as material, but the narrative nature of the oral stories differs from that of the *Man'yōshū* contexts.

The creation of an active "field" for waka, in which they could be appreciated in settings other than their original ones, is a phenomenon dating from the *Kokinshū* period. Progression in a collected series of poems is one such field: the changing seasons, for example, or the course of a love affair. The field can act on the waka to create a new meaning heretofore absent in the individual poem, as has been shown. On the other hand, these were fields concerned with natural change [as in a sequence compiled in a royal anthology], differing fundamentally from the narrative field of a plot. The writing and reading of waka in a narrative field developed in the tenth century. We might note that, with the compilation of the *Tales of Yamato* in the mid-tenth century, the fictional elements of plots increased. One manifestation of this is the increased proportion of waka setsuwa episodes over waka narratives in the *Yamato*. The middle of the tenth century was also the time when a great many monogatari were written "that tell only of fantastic things." Waka setsuwa probably arose from the same expressive awareness that gave rise to the fictional monogatari. But waka setsuwa were not treated as fiction. They might strike an audience as a bit strange sometimes, but their truthfulness remained outwardly unchallenged. This way of reading continued beyond the twelfth century. Several waka setsuwa appear in works on poetics by Minamoto Shunrai (1055?-1129?) and Fujiwara Kiyosuke (1104-77), discussed in the third volume of this *History*. The authors did not record them at random but because they felt that a waka could not be properly appreciated unless its circumstances of creation were known. Scholarship, in those days, was the transmission of such information to posterity. The *Tales of Yamato* should therefore be acknowledged as a factual monogatari.

Centering on Society

When we encounter an author or narrator clearly seeking to relate factual matters, we accept the view: the work is a factual monogatari. Its "factual" nature does not demand that all the content be true. The Japanese prose works known as "historical [rekishi] monogatari" may contain much that is true to fact, but there is no guarantee that their narratives are historically accurate throughout. A modern reader thus anticipates little of the factual rigor generally suggested by the word "historical." This is why I call these works "monogatari centering on society." In so doing, I shall seek to solve the problem of historicity and literariness in the "historical monogatari."

The first monogatari to center on society was the *Eiga Monogatari (A Tale of Flowering Fortunes)*. It differs greatly in one sense from monogatari centering on waka, although all are members of the factual monogatari genre: *A Tale of Flowering Fortunes* uses factual nikki for its principal sources, at least for the thirty chapters of its "main section."[182] This has been ascertained from the text of the eighth chapter, "Hatsuhana" ("First Flower"), a part of which is based on the *Murasaki Shikibu Nikki*. Excepting some additions and omissions, this section—beginning with the words, "As autumn begins to make its appearance" (8:259) and concluding with "The poem embossed in reed-script on the box was probably in reply" (8:276)—is drawn almost verbatim from the *Murasaki Shikibu Nikki*. A comparison of a passage from the two texts shows the resemblance:

["First Flower" version:]

I worry about having to recite a poem if I am asked to drink. Murasaki murmurs some lines to herself in preparation:

Mezurashiki	Wonderful it is,
Hikari sashisou	Shining with its copious light—
Sakazuki wa	The wine-bright moon—
Mochinagara koso	It will hold forever full
Chiyo wa megurame.	As a thousand ages pass.

Since the Shijō Major Counselor [Kintō] is seated near the blinds, she is even more concerned about her voice and bearing than about the quality of her poem. (*EM*, 8:265)[183]

[*Murasaki Shikibu Nikki* version:]

Waka are composed. We murmur poems to ourselves, preparing them in case we are asked to drink. Mine is:

---

[182] The *Eiga Monogatari* is made up of forty chapters, of which the first thirty and the last ten differ in certain essential ways. The first group is generally called the "main section" (seihen) and the second group the "sequel" (zokuhen). Stylistic differences suggest that they are not the work of a single writer (Yamanaka, 1952, 146-56). The main section was probably written between 1029 and 1033, and the sequel between 1092 and 1107 (Matsumura, 1956, 275 and 599).

[183] [Adapted from McCullough and McCullough, 1980, 1:279.—Trans. I have changed the translations here and in the next quotation from the earlier translations to give some sense of the word play: "Sakazuki" means "sake cup," but its "-zuki" (tsuki) means moon; "Mochinagara" means "even as it is full" or "even as it is held" (referring to the sake cup), but its "Mochi-" represents the "full" moon.—Ed.]

Mezurashiki	Wonderful it is,
Hikari sashisou	Shining with its copious light—
Sakazuki wa	The wine-bright moon—
Mochinagara koso	It will hold forever full
Chiyo wa megurame.	As a thousand ages pass.

We whisper our concerns to one another: "If it falls to me to offer the cup to the Shijō Major Counselor [Kintō], of course I shall worry about the quality of my poem, not to mention how I'll declaim it properly!" But other matters arise and, perhaps because the hour is late, the gentlemen retire without selecting any of us. (*MSN*, 457-58)

The author of *Flowering Fortunes* employs various devices to convert the *Nikki* passage, which is of course written in the first person, into third-person narration. She supplies the subject "Murasaki," and she simplifies the text somewhat. Because the *Murasaki Shikibu Nikki* survives, we know how its text was rewritten for *Flowering Fortunes*. Now non-extant nikki were also mined for source material. This can be surmised from the fact that waka and prose passages not present in the *Murasaki Shikibu Nikki* appear in sections based on that nikki. One view has it that the *Nikki* is incomplete and that the *Flowering Fortunes* passages are quotations from lost sections, but this is probably incorrect. The thirty main chapters of *Flowering Fortunes* are several tens of times longer than the extant *Murasaki Shikibu Nikki*. Unless the compiler of *Flowering Fortunes* made use of nikki by people other than Murasaki Shikibu, she would not have been able to assemble such a large volume of material (Yamanaka, 1958, 162-64).

One source of data for the compiler were nikki thought to have been written by nuns. The sixteen chapters from "Utagai" ("Doubts," ch. 15) through "Tsuru no Hayashi" ("Crane Grove," ch. 30) contain much literary narrative and contrast with the fourteen preceding chapters, which are of a more marked historical nature. Five of the "literary" chapters—"Doubts," "Ongaku" ("Music," ch. 17), "Tama no Utena" ("The Mansion of Jade," ch. 18), "Tori no Mai" ("Dance of the Birds," ch. 22), and "Crane Grove"—differ particularly in import from the rest of *Flowering Fortunes*. Their central subject is Fujiwara Michinaga's Pure Land view of Buddhism, and in each chapter a nun or nuns appear in important scenes. The five chapters are therefore thought to be based on nikki kept by the nuns who appear as characters in these scenes (Matsumura, 1956, 291-94). The hypothesis is well founded, since Murasaki Shikibu tends to appear in those sections based on her nikki. Consider, moreover, this passage from "Doubts," describing the dedication of the Buddha Hall at the temple of Jōmyōji in Kohata.

The petition that day was recited by Ōe no Masahira, senior clerk in the Ministry of Ceremonial. It is a lengthy document, but I record only its gist. Earlier, I asked to see the draft, and found much difficult language there, as well as several places where I did not understand the kana. That is why I cannot transcribe it all. (15:452-53)[184]

In a fictional monogatari this passage would correspond to the narratorial intrusion. The narrator is presented as a woman with a weak grasp of Chinese prose and of the katakana syllabary used to supply a Japanese reading. This is a pretense: a somewhat later passage contains such splendid Japanese translations of Buddhist petitions and other prose in Chinese (15:457) that they are acknowledged early examples of the mixed prose style. Because most laywomen would have had difficulty transposing Chinese prose into Japanese, these sections are probably drawn from nikki written by nuns, women with considerable knowledge of Buddhist scripture.

The words "I cannot transcribe it all" in the passage above indicate written transmission. It is unusual, however, for a nun's nikki to have entries copied from another work. Most such nikki seem to have recorded oral statements. A passage concerning the dedication of the Hōjōji temple bears this out.

Many people will feel called upon to write of the amazing and overwhelming events of that exemplary day; and those fortunate enough to have seen and heard everything close at hand will undoubtedly to able to memorize and record the proceedings especially well. It is embarrassing to think of all the mistakes that must have crept into this account, which was taken down from the varying oral reminiscences of a group of ignorant nuns. (*EM*, 17:74)[185]

Various kinds of nikki were principal source material for *Flowering Fortunes*, but there were probably other sources as well. There is, for example, a waka sequence about the change to summer clothes in the Third Month of 1019 (15:445) that may be drawn from a personal waka collection.

Next, let us consider the nature of *A Tale of Flowering Fortunes*. Our presumptions will be, first, that its principal sources are factual nikki, and

[184] The text of the petition was of course written in Chinese, but to aid in its recitation—carried out in a Sinified form of Japanese—one of the two syllabaries, katakana, was used to supplement the Chinese text. The narrator declares that she, like most literate women of her time, is unaccustomed to reading katakana, and that its use in an ecclesiastical document makes it doubly difficult. Hence she records only the "gist" of the petition. [Auth., Trans.]

[185] [The translation is taken, with slight changes, from McCullough and McCullough, 1980, 2:559.—Trans.]

second, that—to exaggerate somewhat—it is a virtual compendium of Heian Japanese prose nikki. The historical and literary aspects of *Flowering Fortunes* have been frequently discussed, and several scholars have debated whether it is in fact history or literature. But the dichotomy is a delusion stemming from the use of "historical monogatari," a term coined around 1905, and the dichotomy results from assuming that *Flowering Fortunes* has historicity, in the modern sense of the word.[186] Certainly one of its aspects is that of a Japanese prose history. The main section is intentionally begun with the reign of Uda Tennō (r. 887-97) so as to pick up just after the last of the six Histories (Rikkokushi; the *Nihon Sandai Jitsuroku [Annals of Three Reigns in Japan]*), that is, with the reign of Kōkō Tennō (r. 884-87). The author is consciously writing a historical work through the first seven chapters, but from "First Flower" on, she concentrates on describing Michinaga's heyday. The result might be titled *The Story of Michinaga (Midō Kampaku Monogatari)*. The main section, consequently, ends with Michinaga's death in 1028. If *Flowering Fortunes* had been presented like one of the official histories, it would have been continued past Michinaga's death to record the eight remaining years of Goichijō Tennō's (r. 1016-36) reign. It makes no sense to break off the narrative after Michinaga's death, in mid-reign. The first seven chapters become a mere preface to the twenty-three-chapter corpus of *The Story of Michinaga*, and the main section as a whole inevitably forfeits its nature as Japanese history. Its very title is an elegant expression for Michinaga's successes, his "flowering fortunes."

If *Flowering Fortunes* is to be seen as history, what of the fact that it has no "historian's eye"? Important historical events are its subject matter, but the author hardly ever attempts to understand and evaluate their meaning. In many cases, the author narrates only surface phenomena and makes no attempt to investigate the truth behind an event (Kawakita, 1961, 41-55). It has also been noted that the author, although aware of the truth, sometimes distorts her material. Michinaga, for example, clearly combined intrigue with overt pressure to make Sanjō Tennō (r. 1011-16) abdicate. *Flowering Fortunes*, however, states that Sanjō abdicated because he was suffering from demonic possession and because he felt a strong sense of impermanence after the palace compound burned down (Kawakita, 1972, 153-74). Similar instances appear in several other places in the work. This approach differs from the "fiction" of fictional monogatari. *Flowering Fortunes* cannot be considered literature simply

---

[186] "Rekishi [historical] monogatari" appears to have been first used in its modern sense in *Nihon Bungakushi*, published in 1905 by Hayashi Moritarō (Matsumoto, 1979, 295). The term had been used earlier by Kurokawa Mayori (1829-1906; Matsumura, 1967, 145-52). Kurokawa, however, defined "rekishi monogatari" as including works like the *Heike Monogatari*; hence its meaning differs from that of the term as it has been used since.

because it has many fictional elements. Fiction, within a fictional monogatari, is the invention of things that do not happen in the real world. Its audience enjoys the fiction, knowing full well that it is fabrication. Of course
truth can be expressed by fiction in a way not found in history books. But
in such cases, too, the facts narrated in a fictional monogatari must be
such as never occurred in the real world. *Flowering Fortunes*, however, is
narrated as a record of events that actually happened, and so the fictitious
elements in its narrative differ in nature from fictiveness as an ingredient
in literary writings.

Fabrications presented as facts can only be construed as misrepresen-
tations by historians. Yet *Flowering Fortunes* is not in fact telling history,
and so it presents no especial grounds for being criticized as misrepresen-
tation. It shares certain characteristics with yogatari, entertaining anecdotes about society.[187] These permit a certain amount of fabrication in the
narrative if it will give the story greater interest. This is the sense in which
I conceived the genre of "monogatari centering on society." In "Hikage no
Kazura" ("Cord Pendants," ch. 10), ladies-in-waiting are shown talking
about Sanjō's children.

"No recent sovereign has had as many children as Sanjō."

"Well, the late Murakami Tennō had quite a large family, and I am
told that their ladies-in-waiting were dressed beautifully both day
and night."

"I have heard that the princes kept court ladies vying with one another in fine dress during Uda's reign, too."

"Not to mention Yōzei's sons with their elegant, amorous ways.
Once one of them [Prince Motoyoshi] sent the same poem to several
ladies of his acquaintance:

Ku ya ku ya to	There is this pain and that—
Matsu yūgure to	This of the dusk when you await him,
Ima wa tote	That of the next dawn,
Kaeru ashita to	When he says goodbye and leaves;
Izure masareru.	Which of these is worse to you?

"The prince's favorite reply came from a lady called Hon'in Jijū:

| Yūgure wa | In the evening |

[187] One instance of a yogatari will suffice: "The marriage was private, but it became an
interesting topic of conversation, revealed in confidence from one person to another and finally whispered abroad as an unusual *yogatari*" (*GM*, "Makibashira," 118-19). [The marriage is Tamakazura's to Higekuro. It arouses particular interest because of Tamakazura's
odd situation: Genji, her ostensible father, is in love with her, but marries her off to Higekuro
with no apparent remorse. "Yogatari" might be described as anecdotes or gossip about
members of one's society.—Trans. It is to be observed that here, and whenever possible, the
author uses and seeks to define the terminology of the age being treated.—Ed.]

Tanomu kokoro ni   I find that my trusting heart
  Nagusametsu   Gives me some comfort,
Kaeru ashita wa   But when at dawn he takes his leave
Kenu beki mono o.   I feel myself about to die."

The ladies interspersed their anecdotes about the past with observations about Sanjō's sons. (10:321-22)[188]

Prince Motoyoshi (890-943) was famed as an amorous man; his waka exchange with Hon'in Jijū appears in almost identical form in a collection of
setsuwa, *Kohon Setsuwa Shū* (1, story 35:101-13; Matsumura, 1956,
522-23). The story about Prince Motoyoshi contains two waka, and so
qualifies as an oral waka story. The anecdotes about Uda's and Murakami's sons, however, are told in a more concrete way, and are thus examples of yogatari, entertaining stories about society. The latter group does
not of course form the basis of *Flowering Fortunes*, which more likely depended on factual nikki for its principal material. Yet factual nikki, like
factual monogatari, are not simply recorded facts but records of *interesting* facts that were written down and read precisely because of their interest. It is in this respect that they share common ground with the yogatari,
and in this sense that *Flowering Fortunes* is a monogatari centering on society. This does not necessarily deny a historicity in *Flowering Fortunes*.
Its subject, the reigns of historical tennō, is clear evidence of historical
awareness. But history is only its framework, used as the "sekai" (world)
is used in Edo period kabuki.[189] *A Tale of Flowering Fortunes* is a collection of social anecdotes that makes use of the "world" of history.

The *Ōkagami (The Great Mirror)* is also called a historical monogatari,
and like *Flowering Fortunes*, it is a monogatari centering on society.
Whereas *Flowering Fortunes* follows a chronological format, *The Great
Mirror* takes the form of annals and biography, and so adopts a somewhat
more positive procedure as historical writing. Essentially, however, the
two works do not differ. Annals and biography are the two principal
structural elements of Chinese history; the basic annals tell of emperors
and kings, and the biographies describe commoners and literati who are
not noblemen. All serious Chinese histories take this form, beginning with

[188] [Adapted from McCullough and McCullough, 1980, 1:330. For Hon'in Jijū, see Chapter 7, note 54.—Trans. The poems have been retranslated.—Ed.]

[189] A "sekai" was a fictional world (its events, characters' names, etc.) suggested by famous old monogatari, which provided the framework for a plot. For example, the subject of
the kabuki play *Sukeroku Yukari no Edozakura* (first performed in 1761) is an event that
took place in the Yoshiwara licensed quarter during the Edo period, but the hero Sukeroku
appears as Soga no Gorō, a thirteenth-century figure. The play makes use of the "*Soga*
world" suggested by the *Soga Monogatari*. Other kabuki "worlds" include the "*Taiheiki*
world" and the "*Sumidagawa* world." Further details appear in the fourth volume of this
History.

the *Shih Chi* (*Records of the Historian*). Modeled as it is on the annals-and-biography form, *The Great Mirror* shows a strong awareness of the Chinese histories. Yotsugi's assertion to his audience that "you should think, as you listen to me, that you are hearing the *Chronicles of Japan*" (*OK*, 1:60) stresses the historical, factual aspect of the narrative.[190] Again, however, this is only a view of narrative process: history is the framework adopted for the monogatari to indicate that it is not fictional. Yet that does not mean that history is indeed the subject. Let us suppose that *The Great Mirror* is history in the manner of the *Records of the Historian*. How, then, are we to explain the fact that the "basic annals" of *The Great Mirror*—"the history of the generations of tennō"—occupy less than seven percent of the total text? Another notable feature of *The Great Mirror* is its exceptionally large proportion of passages relating to Michinaga. This is reflected in the introductory section of the work, which contains this passage:

"I have only one thing of importance on my mind," Yotsugi goes on, "and that is to describe Lord Michinaga's unprecedented successes to all of you here, clergy and laity of both sexes. It is a complicated subject, so I shall have to discuss a fair number of tennō and their senior consorts, ministers of state, and senior nobles first. Then when I reach Michinaga himself, the most fortunate of all, you will understand just how everything came to pass in our world." (*OK*, 1:39)[191]

In other words, *The Great Mirror* is yet another *Story of Michinaga* that seeks to relate "how everything came to pass in our world" by depicting his life. In this respect *The Great Mirror* is no different from *A Tale of Flowering Fortunes*.

The Great Mirror has also been found to depart from historical fact at several points in its narrative, and this has led to the view that the work contains fictional elements characteristic of literature (Hosaka, 1979, 119-34). These elements, like those in *Flowering Fortunes*, are not identical to the basic element of fictional monogatari, and yet they are certainly not directed toward historicity. Of course I do not mean to deny the presence of fictional elements in *The Great Mirror*, since it is more fictitious than *Flowering Fortunes* in one respect. This "respect" is the narrative setting of *The Great Mirror*. The work is set at the Urin'in, a Buddhist temple on the outskirts of the capital. The narrator, who has come there to hear the yearly enlightenment sermon, encounters Ōyake Yotsugi, aged

---

[190] [The translation is taken from McCullough, 1980, 86.—Trans.] In this passage, *Nihongi* (*Chronicles of Japan*) signifies an official history and does not necessarily refer only to the *Nihon Shoki*.

[191] [Adapted from McCullough, 1980, 68.—Trans.]

190, and Natsuyama Shigeki, aged 180. While they wait for the preacher to arrive the narrator, Shigeki and his aged second wife, and a young attendant from a noble household listen to Yotsugi tell of the past, and Shigeki and the others make occasional comments. It is not unusual to have a fictitious speaker: other examples appear in Yamanoe Okura's "Dialogue on Poverty" (*MYS*, 5:892-93) and Kūkai's *Indications of the Goals of the Three Teachings*, and in the fu, cast in the dramatic mode, that inspired these works, beginning with Ssu-ma Hsiang-ju's "Master Imaginary" and "The Imperial Park."

The question is less one of what inspired the author of *The Great Mirror* to use a fictitious speaker than one of the degree to which *The Great Mirror* is fictionalized by such a narrator. Ōyake Yotsugi ("Record of the Royal Succession") and Natsuyama Shigeki ("Dense Forest in the Summer Mountains") are of course fictitious names that share the properties of names like Master Tortoise-Hair and young Lord Leech's-Tusk. Yotsugi's and Shigeki's ages—190 and 180, respectively—are also deliberately unrealistic.

With its strongly fictitious basic narrative setting, *The Great Mirror* is richer than *Flowering Fortunes* in literary features. Or, to restate matters more correctly, what is richly literary is not the strongly fictitious properties themselves but the effect of temporal distancing based on a fictional setting. Yotsugi, for example, relates Sugawara Michizane's exile to Dazaifu in what is essentially the present tense, giving the reader a sense of immediacy. But his speech occasionally includes two verbal suffixes, "-keri" and "-ki," that denote, respectively, transmitted and experienced recollection: "Kono ōnkodomo o onaji kata ni tsukawasazari*keri*" (*OK*, 2:72; *I have heard* that [Michizane's] other sons were not sent to the same general area [as Michizane]), or "Kono shi ito kashikoku hitobito kanji-mōsare*ki*" (*OK*, 2:74; His shih *was* the object of great admiration). The suffixes lead the reader to perceive that a past event is being related. But then Yotsugi praises one of Michizane's waka—" 'That is a clever poem. He must mean that the moon and sun, at least, will bear witness to the purity of his heart' " (*OK*, 2:73)—and the reader is transported from the ninth century to the year 1025, the historical setting for *The Great Mirror*.[192] The narrator continues with a description that further alerts the reader of the setting, the enlightenment sermon at the Urin'in.

Not only is Yotsugi acquainted with political matters of great moment, but he reels off Japanese and Chinese poems in so fluent and impressive a manner that the spectators are fascinated. Stimulated by the awareness that even people of superior understanding have edged

[192] [Ibid., 98.—Trans.]

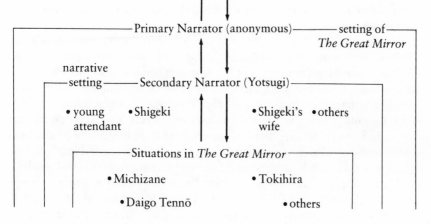

very close to watch and listen, he is spinning out his story like someone unravelling a skein. It is a rare sight! (*OK*, 2:73)[193]

Yotsugi's speech, "That is a clever poem . . . ," corresponds to narratorial
intrusion in a fictional monogatari, and the passage quoted immediately
above corresponds to description.

Thus the setting of *The Great Mirror* utilizes fictional monogatari techniques. This becomes very clear when *The Great Mirror* is compared with
the earlier figure for narrative process in *The Tale of Genji*. Of course,
the *Genji* uses an omniscient point of view, whereas Yotsugi, the secondary narrator of *The Great Mirror*, tells his story in terms of what he
has seen and heard, presenting the work from a limited point of view.
The author must make use of extreme fabrication—the matter of Yotsugi's great age—in order to employ a limited point of view. In this respect
its limited point of view differs from that in the modern novel. What
should be noted here, however, is that *The Great Mirror* uses newer narrative techniques than the *Genji*. Its limited point of view enables the
reader to sense the immediacy of situations in the work and then to return
to the "present," the year 1025, through Yotsugi's narratorial intrusions,
so that Michizane's circumstances can be contemplated from a distance.
When the anonymous primary narrator then remarks on the setting, the
enlightenment sermon at the Urin'in, we readers are made aware that it,
too, is fictional, so being transported back to our own time, a real year

---

[193] [Adapted from ibid.—Trans.]

much later than 1025.[194] But when Yotsugi resumes his story, the reader reenters the ninth century. The effect of moving back and forth in time is made all the more impressive by a limited point of view cast in the dramatic mode.

The Great Mirror adopts the form of a history book, but it only pretends to be a work of history. It is, in fact, a more literary work than *A Tale of Flowering Fortunes*, not because it has more fictitious elements, but because these elements are used as fictional techniques. Those who would emphasize the historicity of *The Great Mirror* might respond to my view by noting that the work contains some severe historical criticisms. Mekada Sakuo's detailed thesis deserves particular notice. He points out the abundance of strikingly severe criticisms, both direct and implied, toward actions taken by sovereigns, the royal family, and powerful nobles, and concludes that this critical stance is shared by every Chinese history since the *Records of the Historian* (Mekada, 1979, 922-44). We require further investigation to determine whether the criticism offered in *The Great Mirror* is of the same nature as that found in the Chinese histories. Chinese history is concerned with events: it records their origins, processes, effects, and repercussions, and uses these data to elucidate, from a Confucian perspective, the correct actions a government should take. Individual conduct is also criticized from the same perspective. But criticism in *The Great Mirror* is different. Not only does it pass over in silence events that a real history would be obliged to criticize, but the criticism it does offer lacks a sufficient grasp of origins and effects and is seldom based on political principles (Matsumoto, 1969, 90-99). We must not be too hasty in declaring that *The Great Mirror* and the Chinese histories have a common critical procedure.

I would prefer to see as the hallmark of *The Great Mirror* not a lack of critical judgments but rather a concentration of criticism in several loci. This is not a matter of the amount of criticism but one of its nature, whether, in other words, it is criticism worthy of a history. Criticism must of course have criteria. The criterion operating in the Chinese histories is Confucian morality, the unidimensional basis on which all events and actions are judged. Judgments in *The Great Mirror* are, on the other hand, made according to multidimensional criteria. This is manifested by the nature of justice (dōri) in the work: this basis of judgment is not always unidimensional. "Dōri" is used a total of ten times in *The Great Mirror*; its antonym, "hidō" (injustice), is used three times; and "rihi" (justice and injustice) is used once. In all cases, the approval of members of society

[194] Various theories have been proposed for the composition date of the Ōkagami, but none offers decisive evidence. The terminus a quo has been put as early as 1041, and the terminus ad quem as late as 1151 (Hosaka, 1979, 2-13). We have no choice but to conclude that the Ōkagami was written at some point between these two years.

present at the time of an event indicates its "justness." Prince Atsuakira (994-1051), for example, was eminently qualified to become crown prince, and so his elevation was greeted with approval by society, which pronounced it "a just choice" (OK, 2:100). The qualifications befitting a crown prince were determined by universally acknowledged custom within contemporary aristocratic society, not based on fixed, unidimensional principles.

One example of "injustice" is the story of Prince Tamehira (952-1010), who was expected to become crown prince. His consort was Minamoto Takaakira's daughter, however, and the Fujiwara disliked the idea of linking the royal succession to the Minamoto clan. The Fujiwara forced Tamehira's younger brother (the later En'yū Tennō) to accept the position instead. Yotsugi criticizes this as "unjust" (OK, 3:119). Again, Confucian political mores are not the governing criteria behind Yotsugi's conclusion. The event is deemed unjust because it goes against the social consensus. One more example: Fujiwara Kōzei held the sixth rank when he was appointed a head chamberlain. Ichijō Tennō was concerned about the propriety of a junior courtier occupying this important post. The unusual event came about, however, because the outgoing head chamberlain, Minamoto Toshikata (960-1027), strongly recommended Kōzei. Precedent existed whereby an outgoing head chamberlain recommended a successor, "so it was only just that Kōzei won the post. It used to be customary to appoint a new head chamberlain on his predecessor's recommendation" (OK, 3:140).[195] Once again, this is not a matter of impartial social justice but a private standard of "justice." Sometimes a more specific, local justice was applied, although it represented no acknowledged precedent for society at large. The temple of Yamashinadera, an independent body in terms of its religious administration, took positions that would be "unjust" under ordinary circumstances but were accepted by society as "Yamashina justice": "Yamashinadera is an awesome and holy temple. Even the worst injustice is condoned, if the temple is involved; people simply dismiss it as 'Yamashina justice' " (OK, 5:235).[196] Every criticism in The Great Mirror diverges from the goal of the Chinese histories, which seek to achieve social justice by applying unified principles.

It was commonplace during the twelfth century to criticize a given event or act according to notions of generally accepted, precedented "justice." The practice is not limited to The Great Mirror. On the other hand, The Great Mirror devotes more of its text to critical remarks than does A Tale of Flowering Fortunes, and it is here that The Great Mirror displays its twelfth-century character. Setsuwa from this period often contain similar

[195] [Adapted from McCullough, 1980, 144.—Trans.]
[196] [Ibid., 205.—Trans.]

criticisms. They appear in large number in the oral stories that are the raw material of the secular tales in the *Konjaku Monogatari Shū* (*Tales of Times Now Past*) and share certain characteristics.

> Now think: the stepmother was terribly stupid. If she had reared the child as if he were her own, he would not have gone astray, but would have been a dutiful son. Thus her wrongheadedness ruined her in this life and the next. So the tale's been told, and so it's been handed down. (26:427)[197]

> Therefore one should never stop at an unfamiliar place. And it is even more rash to spend the night there! So the tale's been told, and so it's been handed down. (27:486)

> Therefore in all matters, even those one finds agreeable, pause to think things through, and clarify any dubious points, where an unfamiliar person is concerned. So the tale's been told, and so it's been handed down. (29:169)

It is typical of *Tales of Times Now Past* to append such remarks to certain setsuwa. They contain implied criticism of people in the story for acting as they have. Because the stories are concerned with popular, secular events, the appended criticism differs in purport from that directed toward political events and actions. Yet in both *Tales of Times Now Past* and *The Great Mirror*, the "justice" on which the authors' criticism is based consists simply of generally accepted, precedented matters.

Anything diverging from such "justice" receives unfavorable treatment from those who have heard the story:

> How people who heard this must have detested him—and how they must have laughed! So the tale's been told, and so it's been handed down. (28:71)[198]

> The countrypeople were said to revile Lord Michimune. So the tale's been told, and so it's been handed down. (31:286)

Similarly, those who are properly "just" are praised:

> This is a splendid example of a warrior's alertness and resourcefulness. So the tale's been told, and so it's been handed down. (25:394)

---

[197] [In this and the following *Konjaku* passages, I use Marian Ury's translations of the formulas, "Kore o omou ni" ("Now think") and "to namu kataritsutaetaru to ya" ("So the tale's been told, and so it's been handed down"). The former is frequently used to signal the beginning of the narrator's criticism or moral of the story, and the latter formula is almost always employed to conclude a tale. Marian Ury, *Tales of Times Now Past* (Berkeley and Los Angeles: University of California Press, 1979).—Trans.]

[198] [The translation is from Ury, 1979, 182. The protagonist is a provincial governor whose greed blinds him to danger.—Trans.]

This became known in society, and he was praised for his fine deed. So the tale's been told, and so it's been handed down. (28:75)

It may have been common practice in the twelfth century for the audience of such stories to conclude the recitation by expressing opinions, be they positive, negative, or sympathetic. In that case the formalistic appending of such remarks to the end of stories in *Tales of Times Now Past* may reflect the true shape of yogatari.

If we conclude that *The Great Mirror* used oral anecdotes current in twelfth-century aristocratic society for much of its raw material, we should be able to understand why it has a large proportion of criticisms. There has been spirited discussion of the fact that *The Great Mirror* contains stories also found in *Tales of Times Now Past*, in the *Gōdanshō (Excerpts from the Conversations of Ōe no Masafusa)*, and in the *Shunrai Zuinō (Shunrai's Poetic Essentials*; Matsumoto, 1969, 152-222).[199] The purpose of the debate is to posit a year of composition for *The Great Mirror*, but the very complex transmission relationship among setsuwa renders it generally impossible to prove that story A is based on story B. *Tales of Times Now Past* and the rest are useless as data for determining a year of composition, but they obviously share certain setsuwa with *The Great Mirror*. The fact that *The Great Mirror* contains these setsuwa (leaving aside questions of order or the adoption process) means that it also incorporated the appended didactic comments characteristic of the oral anecdotes on which written setsuwa were based. The result is that certain works share a basis for social criticism. In this sense, *The Great Mirror* is also a monogatari centering on society.

FACTUAL NIKKI

A Tale of Flowering Fortunes, a monogatari essentially presented as history, used material from the *Murasaki Shikibu Nikki* at a time when the latter work retained much of its original form. This means that the *Nikki* was acknowledged, as early as the middle of the eleventh century, to be nonfiction. I shall call such works factual nikki. The term may be deceptive: factual nikki are not guaranteed to relate everything according to fact. It is very possible that another source used by *Flowering Fortunes*,

---

[199] [The translation of the last two titles are from McCullough, 1980, 13. McCullough describes *Gōdanshō* as "a work in six chapters, consisting of stories told by an eleventh-century scholar, Ōe no Masafusa (1041-1111), to someone who probably recorded them between 1104 and 1108. [It] contains legends, stories about official ceremonies and other court affairs, tales centering on poetry, on famous musical instruments, on Emperors [= tennō] and other prominent members of the aristocracy . . ." (ibid.). *Shunrai Zuinō (Shumpi Shō)*, compiled by the poet Minamoto Shunrai (Toshiyori; 1055?-1129?), is described as a record of "gossipy bits about men of letters" (ibid.).—Trans.]

the various nikki kept by nuns, contained "mistakes" (higagoto), things at variance with the truth. We may assume, however, that the mistakes stemmed from memory lapses or other sources beyond the authors' control, and that the foundation was fact.

This is confirmed by the labeling of factual records as "nikki." A written record of the proceedings of a waka match was called a nikki, for example. The content and style of such records are strikingly like certain passages in the *Murasaki Shikibu Nikki* and the *Makura no Sōshi (The Pillow Book)*. Let us compare passages from the *Nikki* and *The Pillow Book* with an excerpt from a nikki appended to the records of the *Dairi Utaawase (Royal Waka Match*, also known as the *Tentoku Waka Match)*, which was held on the thirtieth of the Third Month, 960.[200]

[Tentoku Waka Match]

Four page-girls carry in the centerpiece [suhama]. They are wearing blue under lined willow-green garments that perfectly match their hair in length. The embroidered centerpiece cover is dyed a deeper blue around the hem. The centerpiece rests on a cushion of pale blue gauze. The upper parts of the centerpiece are made of dark aloeswood wrapped in gold wire, and the lower parts of light aloeswood wrapped in silver wire. The poems, written on fine paper, are presented as follows. Waka on blossoms are tied to silver- or gold-blossoming branches, depending on their content.[201] Poems on burning love are placed in the brazier of a miniature cormorant boat. Those on late spring are piled in the boat. Poems on the warbler are held in miniature warblers' beaks. (*TTU*, 94)

[Murasaki Shikibu Nikki]

When they have finished serving, the women go out and sit down by the blinds. Everything sparkles in the lamplight, and some women in particular stand out. Lady Ōshikibu—wife of the Governor of Michinoku and His Excellency's [Michinaga's] envoy, you know— has a beautiful train and jacket, both embroidered with the little pines of Mount Oshio. Taifu no Myōbu has left her jacket as it was, but her train has a striking wave pattern painted on it in silver, not overly conspicuous but most pleasing to the eye. Ben no Naishi has a

---

[200] As recorded in *UAS (Nihon Koten Taikei*, 74).

[201] [Waka on cherry blossoms, for instance, would be tied to an artificial branch with silver blossoms, since the pale pink cherry blossom is better reproduced by silver than gold. Similarly, waka on kerria flowers, bright yellow in hue, would be tied to a branch with gold blossoms.—Trans.]

train painted with a very unusual design, a crane standing in a silver seascape. (457)[202]

[The Pillow Book]

Two page-girls and four maids come from the consort's residence, through the Sen'yōden and the Jōganden, apparently bringing water for their lady's morning toilette.[203] Half a dozen ladies-in-waiting are seated toward our end of the gallery with the Chinese roof. The consort's party finds it crowded, and so half of them return after delivering the water. It is presented to the consort by the page-girls, who look very pretty and smart in pale pink formal aprons with long trains, worn over robes of spring green and plum. Shōshō, the daughter of Sukemasa, Director of the Royal Stables of the Right, and Lady Saishō, daughter of the Kitano consultant, are in attendance near the consort, with their court jackets of patterned silk slipped from their shoulders. (dan 104:161)

Each setting is different: a waka match, the celebrations after a royal birth, and the reception of the crown prince's consort.[204] They are identical, however, in that all portray participants in a formal event, dressed in the finest and showiest clothes, delighting in a ceremony carried out in luxurious surroundings. This was an important part of aristocratic life. The daily records kept by men in Chinese contain equally detailed descriptions of formal ceremonies, in such quantity as to cause an initial bewilderment and eventual boredom in modern readers. The attention to detail springs from necessity: unfamiliarity with precedent in connection with a given event—how people dressed, what accessories they carried, the furnishings used, the participants' roles—would mean ignorance of the appropriate behavior to display when it came time for the writers or their descendants to attend a similar event. Adherence to precedent became fixed in aristocratic society from the tenth century on, as did the spirit of ga, delight in discovering a subtle freshness within a precedented framework. Keeping detailed records of formal events was therefore a necessary, important duty for the aristocracy (especially its upper reaches).

---

[202] [Adapted from Bowring, 1982, 67.—Trans.]

[203] [The "consort" is Fujiwara Motoko, recently married to the crown prince, Okisada (later Sanjō Tennō). She has just paid her first visit to her older sister Sadako, senior consort of Ichijō Tennō, since the former's marriage. Motoko has spent the night at Sadako's palace residence, the Tōkaden, and now water and toiletries are being brought from her own residence, the Kiritsubo. The two buildings are separated by two others, the Sen'yōden and the Jōganden, through which Motoko's servants must pass to reach Sadako's residence. All four buildings have interconnecting galleries (rō).—Trans.]

[204] See Chapter 7 for a description of a formal waka match.

Daily records in Chinese were family treasures bequeathed to future generations. The kana nikki on royal waka matches, on the other hand, record the proceedings of a formal event in Japanese prose.[205] The passages quoted above from the *Murasaki Shikibu Nikki* and *The Pillow Book* are of much the same nature.

The kana nikki describing waka matches were records limited to a single event, unlike such daily records as the *Midō Kampaku Ki* and the *Shōyūki*.[206] Similarly, the passages from the *Murasaki Shikibu Nikki* and *The Pillow Book* are excerpted not from daily records but from autonomous accounts, respectively, of the events surrounding the birth of Prince Atsuhira (999?-1050) and the ceremonies that took place when Fujiwara Michitaka's second daughter Motoko (891?-1002) became consort to the crown prince. In this respect they are identical to the kana nikki describing waka matches. They are quite unlike these nikki, however, in their authors' tendency to intersperse descriptions of formal events with their own private thoughts. This is particularly marked in the *Murasaki Shikibu Nikki* and makes both works different in nature from simple records. This is what I meant by labeling them "of much the same nature" as the kana nikki.

Prevailing opinion has found the formal sections of the *Murasaki Shikibu Nikki* to be a celebration of splendid events, written at the request of the author's royal mistress and her powerful family. But this does not explain the personal reflections scattered throughout the text. Waka composed by Murasaki Shikibu in connection with the same events and included in her waka collection, the *Murasaki Shikibu Shū*, are far more characteristic of the formal paean (Kōchiyama, 1980, 150-53). It was probably a contemporary practice for a lady-in-waiting proficient at writing prose to be asked by a great family to record one of its memorable events. It is another matter whether the *Murasaki Shikibu Nikki* was written under such circumstances. The passages recording the prince's birth (*MSN*, 445-60) certainly adopt a congratulatory, laudatory stance toward the great event, but Murasaki Shikibu praises and congratulates from an individual, private perspective rather than as a public representative of the family's and retainers' collective response. *A Tale of Flowering Fortunes* omits passages in the *Nikki* told from a private perspective and limits itself to parts having a public significance.

---

[205] Waka matches are also described in nikki written in Chinese. I use the phrase "kana nikki" to distinguish nikki in Japanese from those written in Chinese.

[206] [*Midō Kampaku Ki* (*Records of the Regent Who Constructed the Hōshōji Temple*) is the daily record kept by Fujiwara Michinaga. It seems to have consisted of 30 fascicles originally, of which 14 survive, all in Michinaga's hand. The *Shōyūki*, the daily record of Fujiwara Sanesuke, is in 61 fascicles and covers a period from 982 to 1030; its full and proper title is *Ono no Miya Udaijin no Nikki* (*Record of the Minister of the Right Who Lived in the Ono Palace*). Both, of course, are written in Chinese.—Trans.]

Murasaki Shikibu's faithful descriptions of grand aristocratic occasions probably offer nothing of interest to a modern reader. The evocations of nature Murasaki Shikibu wrote as backdrops for the grand events are bound to impress us much more. Everyone who favorably evaluates the *Murasaki Shikibu Nikki* quotes, as if by prearrangement, its opening passage, a description of nature.

> As autumn deepens, the Tsuchimikado mansion becomes indescribably beautiful. The trees by the lake and the grasses by the stream are a blaze of color that intensifies in the evening glow and makes the voices in ceaseless sutra recitation sound all the more impressive. A cool breeze gently stirs, and throughout the night the endless murmur of the stream blends with the sonorous chanting. (*MSN*, 443)[207]

Certainly this passage makes a splendid backdrop, setting off the grandeur and beauty of the ceremonies.

Natural description is employed to similar striking effect as a backdrop for human affairs any number of times in *The Tale of Genji*. One example is the famous scene from "Sakaki" ("The Sacred Tree") where Genji makes his way through the autumnal fields of Sagano to visit the Rokujō lady. The scene has great symbolic effect, evoking associations between Genji's parting from a lady past her prime and the autumn wind blowing through a reed plain filled with fading flowers; and between their love affair—now the stuff of memories—and faint strains of elegant music. This excellent technique probably originated with Murasaki Shikibu. But it remains a technique, with no more than an auxiliary role in the work itself. In the *Nikki*, Murasaki Shikibu endeavors to write about grand events, the glory of Heian aristocratic society. Her contemporary audience would have been chiefly interested in the fact that their life was the subject of the work. Modern readers, cut off from a direct sense of Heian life, are perhaps inevitably bored by Murasaki Shikibu's descriptions of grand events. Similarly, those unfamiliar with Paris cannot share an ordinary Frenchman's deep emotions when viewing the film, *Sous les Toits de Paris*.

Murasaki Shikibu and the audience for her nikki were not the only people interested in descriptions of splendid events. Their contemporaries evidently shared that interest. It was noted earlier that descriptions of events in *The Hollow Tree* may share certain features with nikki. This must reflect contemporary readers' interest in those occurrences. *The Hollow Tree* has been regarded as the inspiration and model for Murasaki Shikibu's choice of formal events as the subject for her nikki (Kōchiyama, 1980, 164-81). Certainly Murasaki Shikibu, and Sei Shōnagon as well,

---

[207] [Taken, with slight changes, from Bowring, 1982, 43.—Trans.]

were familiar with *The Hollow Tree,* and so one cannot assert that they did not have it in mind when they wrote about formal events. But this is to perceive these two gifted women as the kind of people who cannot write without models for inspiration. *The Hollow Tree* need not be their sole source, either, since formal events were also apparently described in now nonextant nikki. To determine a dependent relationship on the single basis of similarity between accounts is odd reasoning. Formal events were always conducted according to the same procedures, and anomalies were not permitted. Therefore all records of a given kind of event are written in the same way, as is indicated by the general resemblance among kana nikki recording waka matches. We would do better to note that such descriptions had an acknowledged literary value than to debate questions of dependent relationships. These accounts are not of a kind with more modern realism, and yet the fact that tenth- and eleventh-century audiences were moved by works whose only content concerns ordinary people doing ordinary things may demonstrate the presence of literary realism in some form.

The *Murasaki Shikibu Nikki* records more than grand formal events: it also includes a section known as "the letters."[208] It contains critiques of well-known ladies-in-waiting, among them Izumi Shikibu, Akazome Emon, and Sei Shōnagon, and differs entirely from the sections depicting events. One view, current since the late nineteenth century, is that the "letters" are a later contamination.[209] This theory has elicited both support and refutation over the last ninety years, and a settlement has yet to be reached.

I have doubts about the very idea of a contaminated text. "Contamination" signifies, after all, that a text has been entered into a larger corpus, where it does not belong. Arguments both for and against the theory that the "letters" are a contaminating element are based on the idea that the *Nikki* was written and submitted according to a plan and made public in a coherent form. Thus sections diverging from this process are perceived as contaminations; or, conversely, if a section is perceived to be compatible with the process, it is found not to be a contaminating element. But were Japanese prose nikki written, submitted, and circulated in this fashion during the eleventh century?

Japanese prose nikki concerned with a given event would naturally be

[208] *MSN,* 486(l.13)-502(l.16). The "letters" section differs from the rest of the *Nikki* text in the frequent appearance of the auxiliary verb "haberi," used in conversation and letters. There is no connection in content between the "letters" and surrounding *Nikki* passages. Richard Bowring calls the "letters" Part B and suggests that the lack of coordination between Part B on the one hand and Parts A, C, and D on the other may indicate an incomplete text (Bowring, 1982, 20-21).
[209] Advocated by Nakane Kōtei and Kimura Kakū, among others, no later than 1899 (*MSN,* "Kaisetsu," 407).

arranged around that event, as illustrated by the kana nikki concerned with waka matches. This marks them as fundamentally different from the daily records kept in Chinese, which span a period of several years. Further, if a nikki on a given event were written at the behest of the author's patron, it would probably be submitted in the form of a clean copy, using beautiful writing paper. In other cases, a writer might have anticipated probable public circulation of a work at some point, and so decided to write down as much as possible in what we might call private drafts. Because paper was a precious commodity, a private draft would probably be written on coarse paper and frequently left in a fairly disorganized state. If the author were lucky enough to be asked to produce the work during her lifetime, it could be ordered and revised, and a clean copy made and submitted to the patron. And when the opportunity to make a clean copy did not come during the author's lifetime, a descendant or other interested relative might decide to take on the task in order to make the text accessible for later generations.[210] In such cases, however, lost sections could not be recovered, and the only alternative would be to assemble the remaining parts and copy them down.

We may most reasonably conclude that the extant *Murasaki Shikibu Nikki* consists of the author's private drafts, which were later assembled and recopied.[211] This is not conjecture. The extant texts of personal waka collections reveal striking instances of what can only be several private drafts pieced together and copied down as one work.[212] The difficulty at the time in distinguishing between shū and nikki (described earlier) suggests that the nikki genre followed a composition process similar to that of the personal waka collection.

Sei Shōnagon's *Pillow Book* followed much the same composition process. It is generally held to belong to the zuihitsu (miscellany) genre and is relegated to a separate category from the *Murasaki Shikibu Nikki*, identified by its title as a *nikki*. Yet in Sei Shōnagon's time, and on into the High Middle Ages, no one thought of *The Pillow Book* as a miscellany.[213]

[210] The author might do this herself in some cases. The editing and copying processes would, however, remain much the same in either case.

[211] Five of the seventeen "nikki poems" appended to the Katsura no Miya manuscript *Murasaki Shikibu Shū* (Royal Library Coll.; *Katsura Murasaki Shū*, 78-81) do not appear in the extant *Murasaki Shikibu Nikki*. This suggests that other private drafts, not used for the extant *Nikki*, once existed. To the best of my knowledge, Ishimura Shōji has done the most outstanding work on this subject (Ishimura, 1955, 12-24). His conclusions are generally supported in scholarly circles (Bowring, 1982, 263-64).

[212] As we have seen, the opening passage of the *Ise Shū*, for example, differs in nature from the rest of the text and gives clear evidence that unrelated private drafts were joined together to make the extant text.

[213] Evidently the first work to call the *Makura no Sōshi* a zuihitsu (miscellany) was a historical survey of the Japanese classics, *Kunitsufumi Yoyo no Ato* (1777), by Ban Kōkei (Nakamura Yukihiko, 1982, 169). The concept of zuihitsu (Ch. sui-pi, "following the brush")

If we could ask eleventh-century readers what *The Pillow Book* might be, they would no doubt reply, "A nikki, of course!" The lists that are the hallmark of *The Pillow Book* are not present in the *Murasaki Shikibu Nikki*, and so the two works are certainly not identical in nature. Both, however, belong to the nikki genre. They have much in common, particularly in terms of their composition processes.

The following passage appears in a postscript to *The Pillow Book* (Sangan manuscript line):[214]

> I wrote these notes at home, when I had a good deal of time on my hands and thought no one would notice what I was doing. Everything that I have seen and felt is included. Since it contains certain slips of the tongue that might give offense to other people, I was careful to keep my book hidden. But now it has become public, which is the last thing I wished. (*MSS*, dan 319:331)[215]

The author seems overly modest in declaring that no one was likely to notice what she was doing. This should probably not be taken at face value, although Sei Shōnagon may indeed not have intended to circulate her book in public. In other words, *The Pillow Book* is an amalgam of private drafts, written at various times and assembled by the author. Of course, she used high-quality writing paper, quite unsuited to private drafts. This paper had originally been intended to serve as booklets on which to copy a waka collection or a monogatari. It was given to Sei Shōnagon's mistress, the senior consort Sadako (976-1000), by the palace minister, Fujiwara Korechika, the consort's brother. Sadako in turn gave the paper to Sei Shōnagon. We may be sure that the author, with her love of stationery, delighted in having "very nearly an endless supply of paper" for her writing.[216] Her private drafts were found and taken away by Minamoto Tsunefusa (969-1023), who returned them considerably later, having presumably copied them in the interval. *The Pillow Book* states that this is the

---

originated in China around the twelfth century [and has been subject to differing definition in Japan over the years; even today compilations of zuihitsu—zuihitsu jiten—vary widely.—Ed.]

[214] Some have thought that the postscript is not the work of Sei Shōnagon; it is reasonable, however, to see it as her own work (Hayashi Kazuhiko, 1964, 574-82). The *Makura no Sōshi* survives in two very different forms. In the first, represented by the Sangan ("3-fascicle") and Nōin manuscript lines, sections of the work follow no set arrangement. In the second category, represented by the Maeda manuscript (the oldest extant manuscript of the work) and the Sakai manuscript line, related sections are grouped together. The former group is generally thought the original form of the text, although Ikeda Kikan maintains that the latter, categorized form originated with Sei Shōnagon. [Auth. Trans. Readers should be aware that the text used by Morris is not that used by the author, although Morris's "Finding List" makes cross-reference feasible.—Ed.]

[215] [Adapted from Morris, 1967, 1:267.—Trans.]

[216] For example: *MSS*, dan 31 (p. 72), dan 276 (p. 281), and dan 277 (p. 282).

first time the book was circulated in public (*MSS*, dan 319:332). The post-script provides valuable data on the composition, reception, and trans-mission of eleventh-century Japanese prose nikki.

Now, this postscript was written after Sei Shōnagon's private drafts were returned, so it would not have been part of the text circulated by Tsunefusa. In other words, the text that was first circulated is not identical to the extant text, which contains the postscript. Evidently their dissimi-larity was not limited to the presence or absence of the postscript but was manifested in several other areas as well. We cannot easily assume that Sei Shōnagon, having had her book restored to her, added only the postscript and then put the book away. Variants, substantial both in quantity and quality, exist among the major manuscript lines of the extant *Pillow Book* text: the Sangan manuscript line, the Nōin manuscript line, the Maeda manuscript, and the Sakai manuscript line.[217] These variants must stem from later additions and revisions, some of which were very likely made by Sei Shōnagon herself. The variants displayed between the Sangan and Nōin manuscript lines, in particular, may stem chiefly from the author's own augmentation and revision.[218] She would certainly have revised the text returned by Tsunefusa, pasting new paper over passages to be rewrit-ten, and writing in the margins and between the lines. In this respect the circumstances of the composition of *The Pillow Book* differ from those of the *Murasaki Shikibu Nikki*, since the latter was apparently copied as a single work only after a later person had pieced together fragments of Mu-rasaki Shikibu's private drafts.

Sei Shōnagon composed certain kinds of episodes just as they came to her (drawing on her royal stock of paper), whereas others could not have been written without reference to fairly detailed memoranda. Her episode on the Dedication of the Complete Scripture at the Sakuzenji Temple, for example (*MSS*, dan 278:284-300), is of a workmanship to rival the de-tailed descriptions of the events surrounding the birth of Prince Atsuhira in the *Murasaki Shikibu Nikki*. Sei Shōnagon must have kept detailed notes of the event, since her memory alone would probably not have en-abled her to write at such length. The memoranda were apparently not so detailed as to equal public records in accuracy, because errors appear: the Dedication is recorded to have taken place on the twenty-first of the Sec-ond Month in *The Pillow Book*, for example.[219] Nevertheless, she prob-ably wrote down all the important points about the progression of events.

---

[217] The manuscript line divisions, which remain standard, were first made by Ikeda Kikan (Ikeda, 1932, 2-16).

[218] Tanaka Jūtarō, among others, has argued persuasively along these lines (Tanaka, 1960, 297).

[219] *Honchō Seiki* (13:179), *Nihon Kiryaku* (Kōhen, 9:177), and *Fusō Ryakuki* (27:261) all record the event as occurring on the twentieth of the Second Month.

Several episodes in *The Pillow Book* describe formal occurrences, in addition to episode 104, quoted in part above: others include episodes 35 (pp. 76-81), 78 (pp. 112-13), 94 (pp. 144-45), and 142 (pp. 196-99). All would have been based on similar memoranda. Individual accounts, based on memoranda and kept hidden and uncirculated, correspond to private drafts.

These drafts were not concerned only with formal events. A large proportion dealt with the subject of routine life in service at the palace. They were kept hidden, as Sei Shōnagon writes, because some included passages that might offend people. These parts of *The Pillow Book* correspond to Murasaki Shikibu's critiques of court ladies in the "letters" section of her nikki. One is:

> That Sei Shōnagon, what a remarkably self-satisfied person! She acts so learned, and litters her writings with Chinese characters, but if you examine them closely, they leave a great deal to be desired. (*MSN*, 496)[220]

This is the kind of "slip of the tongue that might give offense to other people." Murasaki Shikibu probably kept her "letters" well hidden from the public. Sei Shōnagon edited her own private drafts, whereas Murasaki Shikibu's were assembled and recopied by a later person. This difference notwithstanding, both are private documents that were made public. This process is common both to *The Pillow Book* and the *Murasaki Shikibu Nikki*. If the latter work were to contain, in addition to the "letters," a few more informal accounts of daily life as a royal lady-in-waiting, its nature would not be easily distinguished from that of *The Pillow Book*.

The many episodes devoted to lists of things and places in *The Pillow Book* seem to furnish the greatest reason why it has been said to belong to a genre different from that of the *Murasaki Shikibu Nikki*.

> Markets. Tatsu Market, Sato Market, and Tsubai Market. I particularly wonder if it is Tsubai's connection with Kannon that always draws the Hase pilgrims to stop there, of all the markets in Yamato. Ofusa Market, Shikama Market, Asuka Market. (*MSS*, dan 14:57)

> Peaks. Mock Laurel Peak, Amida's Peak, and Iyataka Peak. (*MSS*, dan 15:57)[221]

---

[220] [Adapted from Bowring, 1982, 131.—Trans.] Murasaki Shikibu's report is true: Sei Shōnagon's seemingly unrivaled erudition in Chinese literature was largely drawn from the *Wakan Rōeishū* and the *Meng-ch'iu*, a T'ang children's textbook of mnemonic verse and assembled facts. Her knowledge probably did not come from any other original Chinese sources.

[221] The interest in these peaks derives from their names. Mock Laurel ("Yuzuruha": modern "yuzuriha") is a tall evergreen tree with large, laurel-like leaves (hence the scientific name Daphnephyllum macropodum) that Sei Shōnagon describes elsewhere as "having abundant,

Plains. Mika Plain, Ashita Plain, and Sono Plain. (*MSS*, dan 16:57)[222]

Things that make one's heart beat faster. To keep a sparrow chick. To pass a place where babies are playing. To burn fine incense and relax in solitude. To notice that one's elegant Chinese mirror has become a little cloudy. To see a gentleman stop his carriage before one's gate and instruct his attendants to ask permission to enter.

To wash one's hair, make one's toilette, and put on scented robes; even if not a soul sees one, these preparations still produce an inner excitement. Nighttime, when one is expecting a visitor. Suddenly one is startled by the sound of raindrops, and the wind blowing against the shutters. (*MSS*, dan 29:72)[223]

The Pillow Book contains both simple lists of things and other instances in which the author adds explanations or responses. Clearly, her basic stance toward both is to seek interest in lists of related items. This is of a different nature from descriptions of formal events, and so a work containing such lists would seem out of place in the nikki genre. It seems so, however, because we tend to confuse the Heian nikki with the modern diary. In the tenth and eleventh centuries, "nikki" meant a work about anything encountered in one's life, be it a formal event or assorted informal matters. It is not in the least inappropriate to regard the entire *Pillow Book* as a nikki.

Though *The Pillow Book* belongs to the nikki genre, its lists are certainly of a nature different from the rest of the text. Undeniably, the uniqueness of *The Pillow Book* is found in the lists, and so the question of their origin has naturally attracted scholarly atttention. One noteworthy theory, advocated since the Edo period, is that Li Shang-yin's *Tsa-tsuan (Miscellany)* provided the model.[224] There are indeed points of resemblance.

Shameful things, unfit to be seen: a bad-mannered bride; a pregnant nun; a wrestler with a swollen face; a rich man suddenly ruined; an unmarried girl giving rise to gossip; getting drunk while in deep mourning. (3:495)

Unbearable things: a fat fellow in the summer; coming home to a

---

glossy leaves and bright red, gaudy bracts. It is a bit bizarre but pretty" (dan 40, p. 89). "Iyataka" means "ever higher," a name that, like "Amida's Peak," must have struck the author as particularly fitting for a mountain peak. [Auth., Trans.]

[222] All three place names appear frequently in waka, hence their interest. [Auth., Trans.]
[223] [Adapted from Morris, 1967, 1:31.—Trans.]
[224] The theory is apparently first mentioned in Yamaoka Matsuaki's (1712-80) *Ruiju Meibutsu Kō*, book 266 (5:689).

nagging wife; having a cursed miser for a boss; vulgar co-workers; a long journey in blistering heat; a lengthy session with a coarse man; getting rained on in a boat; a tumbledown house in dirty, damp surroundings; a governor who likes to meddle. (22:508)

Mere resemblance, however, is not sufficient evidence of influence. Before we conclude that Sei Shōnagon based her work on Li's *Miscellany*, it must first be ascertained whether the text was then present in Japan. Not only is there no evidence that it was; its attribution to Li Shang-yin is also dubious. The similarities between the two works are no more than an interesting comparative research topic (Mekada, 1975, 24). Another theory posits that Sei Shōnagon was influenced by *Totsura* (*Ten Equestrians*; Kawaguchi, 1951-59, 715-21).[225] It, too, is a series of lists, much like those in *The Pillow Book*. For example:

Dreary things: a moonlit night in the Twelfth Month; a fan in the Twelfth Month; smartweed syrup in the Twelfth Month; an old woman's makeup; a drunken woman; an old cucumber; a drunken monk dancing.[226]

Again, there is no evidence that the *Ten Equestrians* existed in the early eleventh century, and so its influence on *The Pillow Book* cannot be demonstrated (Hayashi Kazuhiko, 1964, 98-135). Similar lists frequently appear in imayō (new style) songs:

Waka anthologies good for recitation are—
Gosenshū,
Kokinshū,
Shūishō,
Shinsenshū,
Kingyokushū,
The Collection of Japanese and Chinese Songs,
The Six-Book Anthology, and
The Two Waka Matches in Fifteen Rounds.

(RH, 1:14)[227]

Interesting places in Ōmi, mentioned in waka anthologies—
Oiso,
Todoroki,

[225] The Totsura celebration was held at the Kamo, Iwashimizu, and Hachiman Shrines. Ten men, each in formal dance costumes, mounted a horse and rode about a course. Spectacle, not racing, was the point. The author of *Totsura* likens his array of miscellaneous items to this celebration. The composition date of *Totsura* is unknown. [Auth., Trans.]
[226] *Kakaishō,* 9:205.
[227] *Kingyokushū* (1 fasc.) was compiled by Fujiwara Kintō. He also compiled the first *Waka Match in 15 Rounds*; the compiler of the second *Match* is unknown. [Auth., Trans.]

Gamō Plain,
The Pond of Fuse,
The Aki Bridge, oh,
Lake Yoga at Ikago and
The lakeshore of Shiga,
The Buddha Hall Shiragi built, and
The Hall of Golden Columns.

(RH, 2:325)[228]

Such lists may be taken as a hallmark of imayō song. Imayō in irregular form are known to be ancient, as we have seen, and some of them were being sung in the eleventh century.[229] We may thus conclude that lists of related objects already existed as a form in Sei Shōnagon's time. There is no need to invoke Chinese influence.

It is nevertheless true that the lists in *The Pillow Book* greatly resemble Li's *Miscellany* and the *Ten Equestrians*, which provide very interesting comparative data. We must note carefully that Sei Shōnagon apparently wrote with a specific audience in mind. Modern readers cannot understand why a list of mountain peaks is interesting, and yet the Heian audience, which shared the same education as the author, would have immediately understood why those names in particular are mentioned. Her imagined audience would read "Mika Plain, Ashita Plain, and Sono Plain" and instantly remember waka in which these names figure. Then, drawing on interest inspired by the waka, they would understand why these plains are singled out. In other words, Sei Shōnagon adopts an affective-expressive stance, built on the premise that homogeneous reception will occur without the need for explanation or comment. No such audience exists now, and so these passages have quite lost their interest. To be sure, Sei Shōnagon envisioned an audience that delighted in having shared responses skillfully indicated, but that did not provide all the interest. To be very interesting, the work must also contain fresh elements, previously unknown to the audience. The best such elements were extremely subtle. An audience that perceived great interest in the subtlest degree of freshness—the sphere of ga, in other words—were precisely the people for whom Sei Shōnagon wrote.

---

[228] "Shiragi" is a reference to Shiragi Saburō Yoshimitsu (d. 1127). The "Hall of Golden Columns" is one of the sanctuaries at the temple of Ishiyamadera, whose columns were originally covered with gold leaf. [Auth., Trans.]

[229] "Imayō are sung in a long, drawn-out way, to strange music," notes the *Makura no Sōshi* (dan 280:301), showing that imayō were sung in Sei Shōnagon's time. The *Murasaki Shikibu Nikki* also has a passage, "They sang 'Waterplant on the Lake' " (503-504), a probable reference to the song beginning "First you made me trust you, then you went and jilted me" (*RH*, 2:339). Another imayō from the *Ryōjin Hishō* appears in the *Sagoromo Monogatari* (3:235): "A weasel plays the flute and a monkey joins in" (2:392). This is supporting evidence that irregular-form imayō date from at least the beginning of the eleventh century.

A subtle degree of freshness need not mean an unvarying quantity. Indeed, if it did, the audience's response would diminish. Sei Shōnagon occasionally increases the degree of freshness, as in this episode.

> A palm-leaf carriage should move slowly, or else it loses its dignity. A wickerwork carriage, on the other hand, should go fast. Hardly has one seen it pass a gate when it is out of sight, and all that remains is the attendants who run after it. At such moments I enjoy wondering who the passengers may be. But, if a wickerwork carriage moves slowly, one has plenty of time to observe it, and that becomes very dull. (*MSS*, dan 32:73)[230]

The palm-leaf (birōge) carriage was used by aristocrats. The carriage was faced with woven fountain-palm leaves, and it was pulled by oxen, as was the wickerwork (ajiro) carriage. The outer body of the latter was faced with narrow strips of bamboo woven in diagonal patterns. It was a somewhat less imposing type of carriage than the palm-leaf, and eminent people used it for excursions and on other informal occasions. Sei Shōnagon was probably the first to perceive the connection between the formality of a carriage and its proper speed, and her contemporary audience would have derived great interest from her ingenious transformation of static visual shape into an equivalent of speed. We modern readers learn about palm-leaf and wickerwork carriages only as objects of information. This enables us to conjecture to the degree shown here, but we cannot really know what they were like. Those who did had frequent contact with such vehicles. Despite our limitations, however, we will find this episode considerably more expressive than those on mountain peaks and plains.

By comparison, the excerpts quoted earlier from Li Shang-yin's *Miscellany* and from the *Ten Equestrians*, also compendiums of lists, all elicit a sympathetic response from modern readers. They belong to a cultural sphere different from Sei Shōnagon's—she does not concern herself with what she would perceive as inhabitants of the zoku sphere. The lists in the *Miscellany* and the *Ten Equestrians* were evidently intended for a fairly uneducated audience. Instead of straining to find signs of Chinese influence without adequate evidence, we would perform a far more important task in comparing the lists in *The Pillow Book* with the *Miscellany* and the *Ten Equestrians* and, through qualitative comparison, discover how Sei Shōnagon's work differs. Of course this is not to say that *The Pillow Book* is devoid of episodes that might elicit a modern reader's sympathy. Precisely because there are many such episodes, *The Pillow Book* continues to be read in the twentieth century. One can easily sympathize with the content of these passages, for instance:

[230] [Taken, with minor changes, from Morris, 1967,1:32-33.—Trans.]

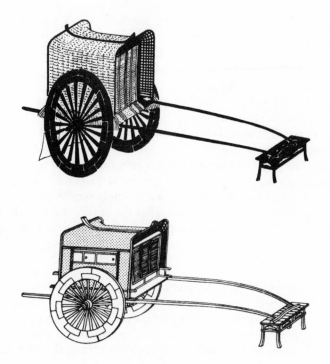

6. *Birōge* and *ajiro* carriages

Things that lose by being painted. Pinks, iris, cherry blossoms. Men or women who are praised in monogatari as being beautiful. (*MSS*, dan 116:170)

Extremely frightening things. Thunder at night. When a thief enters the house next door. If he breaks into one's own house, one is too terrified to feel anything. A fire in a nearby house is also frightening. (*MSS*, dan 264:274)[231]

This, however, is a shallow level of response. *The Pillow Book* could not be called a great work if that was its affective extent.

The famous opening episode of *The Pillow Book* combines lists with observation:

In spring it is the dawn that is most beautiful. As the sky gradually lightens, the mountain rim grows a little brighter, and wisps of purplish cloud trail in the sky.

[231] [Adapted from ibid., 124 and 212.—Trans.]

In summer the nights. Not only when the moon shines, but on dark nights too, as clusters of fireflies flit to and fro. Even one or two, glimmering faintly as they fly, make a charming sight. And when it rains, how beautiful it is!

In autumn the evenings, when the sunset light makes the mountain rim seem very close. Crows, hurrying back to their nests in threes and fours, twos and threes, are also moving. When the sun has set, one's heart is touched quite beyond description by the sound of the wind and the hum of the insects.

In winter the early mornings. It is beautiful indeed when snow is falling, but splendid too when the ground is white with frost; or even when there is no snow or frost, but it is simply very cold and one hurries to make a charcoal fire and carries the brazier through the corridor, how well this fits the season's mood! But as noon approaches and the cold wears off, the brazier fire soon becomes a pile of white ashes, a disagreeable thing. (*MSS,* dan 1:43-44)[232]

This episode evokes a very different quality of response from that evoked by episodes 116 ("Things that lose by being painted") and 264 ("Extremely frightening things"). The content of the opening episode is based on typical contemporary responses, and premised on a shared understanding between author and audience that a certain situation is appropriate to a given setting.

By the middle of the tenth century, waka had achieved a shared understanding about the appropriate subjects for a given situation. Doubtless this shared understanding existed outside the sphere of waka when appropriate situations were being considered. But Sei Shōnagon relies on more than an understanding shared with her audience: she expresses her own feelings to the full within the boundaries of the typical. Now, her sense of self differed from the personal feelings of a modern individual. Sei Shōnagon's self-expression consisted of choosing, from a store of responses shared with her audience, the most befitting aspect of the setting that was to be her subject. The "most befitting" aspect of an object, based on a shared understanding, is called "hon'i" in waka. Hon'i was not yet an established concept in Sei Shōnagon's time, but the ideas on which it was to be based did exist (see the third volume of this *History*). "Hon'i" corresponds to the modern "honshitsu" (essence). Although it is unlikely that Sei Shōnagon's creative outlook had advanced to the point of seeking out the essence of her subjects, her observations in the opening passage to *The Pillow Book* are nevertheless oriented toward it. That is what evokes a re-

---

[232] [Adapted from ibid., 1.—Trans. The particular identifications here of a given time of day with a season were to endure in poetry and other writing for centuries.—Ed.]

sponse from modern readers, because essence cannot be restricted to time or setting.

The Pillow Book has another major characteristic in addition to its lists: its miscellaneous form. Its various kinds of episodes are arranged not according to any perceptible plan but appear in what can only be called a jumbled order. This is the case for the Sangan and Nōin manuscript lines but does not apply to the Maeda manuscript, in which episodes of similar nature have been grouped together. Moreover, Ikeda Kikan has maintained that the latter, categorized form preserves the original shape of *The Pillow Book*, and that the miscellaneous form is a later development (Ikeda, 1938, 75-102). The formal discrepancy between the two manuscript groups, together with Ikeda's influential opinion, suggests that there remain several problems in positing the miscellaneous form as an important characteristic of *The Pillow Book*. But Ikeda offers no explanation of how the various miscellaneous-form manuscripts evolved from the original categorized form; his theory should be regarded as still within the realm of hypothesis (Kishigami, 1970, 347). Similarly, refutations of Ikeda's theory do not have sufficient data to prove that the miscellaneous form is original to *The Pillow Book*, and so they, too, remain hypotheses. If we examine these various conclusions according to scholarly rules of evidence, the correct answers to the question of the original form given *The Pillow Book* is that there is no solution at present, with the data we now have. It might nevertheless be emphasized that the miscellaneous-form manuscripts are clearly the more interesting.

Even if the categorized version of *The Pillow Book* had become fairly well known to readers, rather than remaining in the Maeda family library, people still would probably not have liked it so much as to vie in copying it, or to put it into print. Only the miscellaneous form of *The Pillow Book* received wide circulation, a fact that surely reflects the interest inherent in this form. There is a definite impression, underlying all refutations of Ikeda's theory, that the miscellaneous form is the more interesting. Various deductions have even been put forward to confirm and strengthen this impression. Brevity is one of the hallmarks of Japanese literature, and the Japanese fondness for brevity over the centuries may well be called a national orientation (see the General Introduction, in the first volume of this *History*). I greatly respect this orientation. Up to now, the author's position has been given undue attention, with the result that only the original form of a text, or something approximating it, could yield the correct reading of that text. I fully acknowledge the importance of an original textual form, but I also accord the same degree of importance to the circulated version of a text, accepted and sustained by society for centuries. We would do well to reflect on our tendency to underrate the audience's preferred textual form as compared with the form created by the author.

The popular preference for brevity made the miscellaneous-form *Pillow Book* the circulated version. Brevity is most conspicuous when the reader of a series of unconnected episodes does not know what is coming next. When, on the other hand, episodes of a similar nature are grouped together, the reader senses the connections among them, and brevity tends to be lessened. This is true not only for the lists but also for episodes in which Sei Shōnagon tells of private experiences during her service at the palace. If these were rewritten in chronological order, one likely result would be a text something like *The Gossamer Years*—allowing of course for the difference between home and palace life. Paradoxically, random arrangement strengthens the impression of interest in each episode and accounts for the longstanding popularity of *The Pillow Book* in comparison with the chronically neglected *Gossamer Years*. *The Pillow Book* reaps the maximum effect from short passages. It is no match for *The Tale of Genji* in literary standing, but *The Pillow Book* is much more Japanese in nature than is the *Genji*.

CHAPTER 9

The Zenith of Song

Song [kayō] is not mentioned as a genre in the Early Middle Ages, not because songs did not exist, but because there were few worthy of mention as literary phenomena. Various monogatari and nikki record the aristocratic preference for saibara and fuzoku songs, but their lyrics date from the Ancient Age and are thus inappropriate for treatment as medieval literature. Rōei, the singing of waka and shih, also flourished during this period. But their lyrics were drawn from already extant shih and waka that were not conceived originally for song. There remains Buddhist song [bukkyō kayō], including wasan, hymns sung in Japanese. Although Buddhist song was performed in the Early Middle Ages, its significance for Japanese literary history is easier grasped if it is also considered in the context of the High Middle Ages. In other words, the subject of this chapter will serve as a bridge between the Early and the High Middle Ages.

THE JAPANESE SECULAR AND THE
BUDDHIST HYMN TRADITIONS

Saibara, fuzoku, and rōei were sung at aristocratic banquets in the tenth and eleventh centuries, but many other kinds of song undoubtedly existed among the common people and the provinces. Three sailors' songs, for example, appear in the *Tosa Nikki* (TSN, 36 and 43):

> In the spring fields, I cry aloud in pain—
> The young plumegrass has cut, has cut my hands;
> I manage at last to pluck some shoots,
> And shall I take them to my parents?
> Will my mother-in-law make them a meal?
> I'll go home regardless!

> Haru no no ni te zo ne o ba naku
> Wakasusuki ni
> Te o kirukiru tsundaru na o
> Oya ya maboruran
> Shūtome ya kūran
> Kaera ya.

> I wish I had caught the boy I met last night—

I'd squeeze my money out of him!
He told me a lie,
He bought some things on promise,
But he doesn't bring the money,
He doesn't even come.

Yombe no unai mogana
Zeni kowan
Soragoto shite
Oginoriwaza o shite
Zeni mo motekozu
Onore dani kozu.

Always I look back toward my native place,
To where my parents are,
And I long to come home![1]

Nao koso kuni no kata wa miyararure
Waga chichi haha ari to shi omoeba
Kaera ya.

Fragments of popular songs also appear in *The Pillow Book* (MSS, dan 87:127), but not enough data survive from this period to give us an accurate picture of contemporary popular or provincial song. Songs survive in good quantity from the late twelfth century on, however, and form a basis from which to surmise the general condition of song in the tenth and eleventh centuries.

Most of the data are contained in *Ryōjin Hishō* (*The Secret Store of Marvelous Song*), a collection of imayō songs compiled by the cloistered tennō Goshirakawa (1127-92).[2] Imayō, or modern songs, are of various kinds, all evolving after the furuyō, or old-fashioned songs: kagura, saibara, and fuzoku songs (but not rōei). Seven kinds of imayō survive with lyrics: the nagauta, the koyanagi, the imayō proper (or tada no imayō), the hōmonga, the kamiuta quatrain, the kamiuta couplet, and the kurotoriko. Other kinds are known only by name: the sararin, the kataoroshi, the sōga, the hatsuzumi, the ashigara, the ichiko, the furukawa, the furu-

---

[1] Dialect vocabulary is barely present, and the grammar of the third song in particular is no different from that used in the capital during this period. Tsurayuki may have unconsciously given it more sophisticated language, in transcribing the song from memory (Konishi, 1951b, 134). [The translations are taken, with slight changes, from Miner, 1969, 68 and 75.—Trans.]

[2] ["Ryōjin" literally means "dust on the roofbeams" and alludes to two ancient Chinese singers, Yü Kung and Han E, whose voices were so beautiful that when they sang, the very dust on the rafters was moved to dance. Thus "ryōjin" is an elegant expression for "marvelous singing" or "marvelous song."—Trans.]

koyanagi, the mononoyō, and the tauta. The imayō proper subcategory was apparently considered the most characteristic of the various kinds of imayō songs. The term refers to a quatrain with lines of equal, fixed meter that were sung to a particularly "modern" melody (Konishi, 1941, 84-92).[3] To avoid confusion between this particular form and the larger song category, I shall distinguish between them thus: songs in quatrain form with lines in an equal, fixed meter and sung in a new melodic style will be called imayō proper, and the various other kinds of "modern" songs listed above will be termed imayō in the general sense.

The kamiuta quatrain is one imayō in the general sense of the word. "Quatrain" ("shiku") indicates a standard rather than a set form: kamiuta quatrains were not always four lines long. Songs sharing melodies and rhythm with kamiuta were probably treated as kamiuta quatrains, regardless of their number of lines. Consider these kamiuta quatrains—none in four lines—from *The Secret Store of Marvelous Song*.

First you made me trust you, then you went and jilted me—
I hope you turn into a triple-horned demon,
So everyone will keep away from you!
I hope you turn into a waterfield bird, and frost and snow and hail fall
    on you,
So your feet will get very, very cold!
Oh, turn into a floating waterplant on the lake,
And drift here, then drift there,
Move around and wander about!

Ware o tanomete konu otoko
Tsuno mitsu oitaru oni ni nare
Sate hito ni utomare yo
Shimo yuki arare furu mizuta no tori to nare
Sate ashi tsumetakare
Ike no ukikusa to narinekashi
Tō yuri kō yuri
Yurare arike.

(2:339)

Right underneath a big rose bush,
A weasel plays the flute and a monkey joins in.
Locusts enthusiastically beat time,

---

[3] The hōmonga is another example of an imayō (in the general sense) in quatrain form and having lines in fixed meter. Since hōmonga share this form with imayō proper, the difference between them must lie in their respective melodic styles. Hōmonga music probably retained much of the solemnity characteristic of Buddhist hymns, whereas imayō proper had gayer melodies.

And as for the crickets, why,
They are quite skilled, quite skilled on the little gong.

Ubarakogi no shita ni koso
Itachi ga fue fuki saru kanade
Inago maromede hyōshi tsuku
Sate kirigirisu wa
Shōgo no shōgo no yoki jōzu.

(2:392)

Dance, dance, Mr. Snail!
If you won't I shall leave you
For the little horse, for the little ox to tread under his hoof,
To trample to bits.
So perform your dance,
And if you do it handsomely
I will carry you to play at a garden of flowers.[4]

Mae mae katatsuburi
Mawanu mono naraba
Uma no ko ya ushi no ko ni kuesaseten
Fumiwaraseten
Makoto ni utsukushiku
Mautaraba
Hana no sono made asobasen.

(2:408)

These are evidently folk or children's songs whose lyrics were cast in a ka-miuta arrangement.

The irregular kamiuta "quatrains" may preserve an ancient form, whereas true kamiuta quatrains belong to a later stage. Examples of the latter group are:

> At Sumiyoshi, at the four great shrines,
> Are a multitude of goddesses, pretty things all.
> When I ask one who her boyfriend is,
> She says he's a playboy from Matsugasaki.[5]

[4] ["Dance, dance, Mr. Snail!" is a translation by Arthur Waley (revised by me in the last three lines—Ed.) in "Some Poems from the Ryōjin Hishō," *Journal of the Royal Asiatic Society* (April 1921). The author found the translation (see also notes 9 and 10) in the 1923 edition of Ryōjin Hishō, ed. Sasaki Nobutsuna, pp. 193-99. We have been unable to verify either source.—Trans., Ed.]

[5] The "goddesses," of course, are of the earthly variety. They worked as shrine attendants while doubling as prostitutes.

Sumiyoshi yosho no omae ni wa
Kao yoki nyotai zo owashimasu
Otoko wa tare zo to tazunureba
Matsugasaki naru sukiotoko.

(2:273)

Are we born for lives of easy pleasure?
Are we on this earth to flirt and sport?
When I hear children's playful voices,
My whole body shakes with remorse.[6]

Asobi o sen to ya umareken
Tawabure sen to ya umareken
Asobu kodomo no koe kikeba
Waga mi sae koso yurugarure.

(2:359)

Head lice frolic on my skull,
They fill the hollow of my nape with bites;
Through the comb's teeth they descend
Upon a box-lid, and there expire.

Kōbe ni asobu wa kashirajirami
Onaji no kubo o zo kimete kū
Kushi no ha yori amakudaru
Ogoke no futa nite mei owaru.

(2:410)

Such songs very likely evolved when the originally irregular-form kamiuta took on the quatrain form of the Buddhist hymn (shōmyō) tradition.

The above examples follow an 8-5 meter with occasional fluctuations (8-6 / 8-5), and the following quatrains are in a 7-5 meter (or very nearly so, in the case of the first) throughout.

I stop to rest in the shade of the pines,
And cup my hands in spring water running down the crags;
Doing so, I cease longing for my fan's cool breeze,
Convinced that this year there is no summer!

Matsu no kokage ni tachiyorite
Iwa moru mizu o musubu ma ni
Ōgi no kaze mo wasurarete

[6] The speaker is a courtesan, reflecting on her life.

Natsu naki toshi to zo omoinuru.

(2:433)

Around the cool shores of the lake,
We have not the slightest glimpse of summer.
The breeze blowing through the tall pines
Has told us, "It is autumn."

Ike no suzushiki migiwa ni wa
Natsu no kage koso nakarikere
Kodakaki matsu o fuku kaze no
Koe mo aki to zo kikoenuru.

(2:434)

These belong to the newest stage. The elegant vocabulary of the two songs suggests aristocratic composers and audience.[7]

Thus far, quotations from *The Secret Store of Marvelous Song* have been kamiuta quatrains. The lyrics of the last two songs (433 and 434) are identical in expression to the lyrics of imayō proper. In both cases, diction and subject stem from the sphere of waka. Consider one of the "Two Hundred and Sixty-five Imayō" in *Marvelous Song*:

Favorite poetry topics, early spring:
Mount Yoshino with its trailing mists,
Windflowers, warblers, and Lady Sao,[8]
Wild geese northbound, heedless of the blossoms.

[7] Number 433 consolidates and adapts two waka:

Matsukage no	Shaded by the pines,
Iwai no mizu o	I cup my hands to drink spring water
Musubiagete	Running through the crags,
Natsu naki toshi to	And find myself considering
Omoikeru kana.	"This year there is no summer."

(*SIS*, 2:131)

and

Musubu te ni	With my hands cupped,
Ōgi no kaze mo	I cease to long for the cool breeze
Wasurarete	Stirred by my fan,
Oboro no shimizu	For I have been refreshed by
Suzushikarikeri.	The spring waters of Oboro.

(*Rokujō Shurishū*, 214)

[The Oboro springs, located at Ohara in the northern outskirts of the capital, were well known as a subject for waka.—Trans.] The composer of the song was probably a nobleman. Number 434 appears in *Yuishimbō Shū* (36), with the fourth line reading "Koe mo aki to zo kikoyu naru." It is very likely the work of Jakunen (dates unknown), a poet active in the late twelfth century and well represented in the *Shinkokinshū*.

[8] [Lady Sao (Saohime) is the goddess of spring.—Trans.]

Haru no hajime no utamakura
Kasumi tanabiku Yoshinoyama
Uguisu Saohime okinagusa
Hana o misutete kaeru kari.

(1:13)

The difference between a kamiuta quatrain and an imayō proper is, then, apparently more a matter of melody and rhythm than text. On the other hand, the texts of imayō proper have a much higher incidence of fixed meter and adherence to the quatrain form. Book One of the extant *Marvelous Song* survives in fragments, and only ten imayō proper survive out of 265 originally included. Generalizations are therefore difficult to make. All imayō proper appearing in later sources nevertheless display a tendency toward a fixed form, as in this song from *The Tale of the Heike* (5:340):

> Before me lies our former capital,
> Fallen into ruin, become reed plains.
> The moonlight shines unblemished,
> And the autumn wind alone chills me to the core.

> Furuki miyako o kite mireba
> Asaji ga hara to zo arenikeru
> Tsuki no hikari wa kuma nakute
> Akikaze nomi zo mi ni wa shimu.

Imayō proper are therefore considered to have developed at a later stage than the kamiuta quatrain.

Much the same holds for the kamiuta couplet form. To begin with, many songs in the "Kamiuta Couplet" section of *Marvelous Song* are in fact more than two lines long. For example:

> Listen to me, waves, talk about it, beach, look at me, pines!
> If a breeze comes blowing, one that pleases me,
> I'll gladly be tempted to drift to another shore.

> Nami mo kike koiso mo katare matsu mo miyo
> Ware o ware to iu kata no kaze fuitaraba
> Izure no ura e mo nabikinan.

(2:457)

> Rain is falling down,
> And you insist that I leave:
> I have nothing with me,

No broad-brimmed hat, no raincape to keep off the damp,
And oh, accursed people of this village, who refuse
To lodge me for a night!

Ame wa furu
Ine to wa notabu
Kasa wa nashi
Mino to te mo motaranu mi ni
Yuyushikarikeru sato no hito kana
Yado kasazu.

(2:467)

Other songs in this group show obvious signs of adherence to a couplet form. Some examples of this transitional stage are the following:

But yesterday I came from the East, and brought no bride with me;
I pray you, take this purple cloak I wear, and give me your daughter in
   return![9]

Azuma yori kinō kitareba me mo motazu
Kono kitaru kon no kariao ni musume kaetabe.

(2:473)

To what shall I liken you? To a pine growing on a crag of Tortoise
   Mountain—
Oh, the long-lived tortoises, dwelling by the shore.

Waga kimi o nani ni yosoen ura ni sumu Kameyama no
Iwakado ni oitaru matsu ni yosoen.

(2:479)

As the kamiuta couplet becomes further fixed, it develops the same metric form as the tanka:

Like the rattan whip that the chief ranger wears fastened to his waist,
Would that I were pressed to the body of one who loved me.[10]

Yamaosa ga koshi ni saitaru tsuzurabuchi
Omowan hito no koshi ni sasasen.

(2:483)

In the dusk, I stroll along the beach, and you mistake me
   for a fisherman,

[9] [Adapted from Waley; see n. 4, above.—Trans., Ed.]
[10] [Adapted from Waley; see n. 4 above—Trans., Ed.]

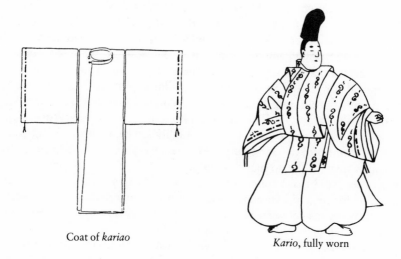

Coat of *kariao*   *Kario*, fully worn

7. *Kariao* (originally a hunting undercloak), part of ordinary dress
for a Heian nobleman

You beg me for part of my catch—me, a man who's
    never fished!

Yūgure ni hama yuku maro o ama ka tote
Io kou nushi ka tsuri mo senu mi o.

(2:557)

The content of these two songs seems to derive from folk song. Eventually,
the kamiuta couplet developed expression worthy of waka, and occasionally waka were sung as kamiuta couplets. Two examples follow.

Though the winter come, scarlet oak leaves, do not fall!
Never fall, oh, never fall, so I might see your color hold.

Fuyu ku tomo hahaso no momiji na chiriso yo
Chiri so na chiri so iro kaede min.

(2:454)

Long is the journey through the fields of Ikuno, across Ōe Mountain,
And so I've never set foot in Ama no Hashidate.

Ōeyama Ikuno no michi no tōkereba
Mada fumi mo mizu Ama no Hashidate.

(2:489)

The second was composed by Koshikibu no Naishi (*Kin'yōshū*, 9:586).[11]
Another section in *Marvelous Song*, titled "Jinja Uta" (Shrine Songs), has
a very high incidence of kamiuta couplets adapted from existing waka.

Two major points emerge from this evidence. First, there is a gradual
evolution from songs with irregular meter and form to songs with fixed
meter and form. And next there is a similar evolution from expression
reminiscent of folk song (and, at times, children's song) toward expression
in the aristocratic style. The change is quite noticeable. It is almost irrational, for example, to have both the highly irregular-form "Ware o tanomete konu otoko" (First you made me trust you . . . , 2:339) and the
elegantly metric "Ike no suzushiki migiwa ni wa" (Around the cool shores
of the lake; 2:434) as kamiuta quatrains. Could two songs possessing such
different forms and expression have been grouped together as kamiuta
quatrains because of some property common to this song category? Both
songs probably shared a melody and rhythm. But why were a common
melody and rhythm present? I believe that these shared elements may have
resulted from various kinds of folk song and provincial shrine songs coming to the attention of the nobility, who arranged the songs to accord with
their tastes (Konishi, 1941, 147-53).

Each of the various kinds of folk song and shrine songs would have had
its own characteristic melody and rhythm. But after the nobility altered
the melodies and rhythms to their tastes, several song varieties would have
evolved with completely new melodies and rhythms—although vestiges of
the original songs remained. The many subdivisions of imayō—ashigara,
ichiko, furukawa, tauta—must indicate the wide variety of original melodies. They were grouped together as imayō in the general sense because
their new, polished style gave a sense of freshness when compared with the
traditional kagura, saibara, and fuzoku songs. "Imayō" does not denote,
therefore, a specific textual form or expression; it signifies the freshness,
the novelty of the songs. It follows that once a song style like the kamiuta
quatrain took shape, any song sung in that style was called a kamiuta
quatrain, regardless of its textual form and expression. This hypothesis efficiently explains why there are so many irregular-form songs among the
kamiuta quatrain corpus, and why it contains songs reminiscent of both
folk song and waka.

[11] Koshikibu's work—which originated as a waka—contains a pun on "fumi mo mizu."
The surface meaning is "I've never set foot in," but the words can also mean "I've not had
a letter [from someone]." The forenote to this waka in the *Kin'yōshū* explains the matter.
Koshikibu was the daughter of the famous Izumi Shikibu, then living in Tango province with
her husband, Fujiwara Yasumasa, governor of the province. Still in the capital, Koshikibu
was invited to participate in a waka match. So gifted was she that gossipers said her mother
composed her poem. When Fujiwara Sadayori teased Koshikibu about this, Koshikibu replied with the waka quoted. Ikuno and Ōeyama, both in Tango, lie on the road to Ama no
Hashidate, where the governor's seat was located. [Auth., Trans.]

How, then, did the various kinds of folk song and provincial shrine songs develop into new, sophisticated song? Here we must consider the intermediary function performed by asobi (waterfront prostitutes) and kugutsu (itinerant performers). Asobi plied their trade at river or seaside port areas, and their ostensible art was song performance. Ōe no Masafusa records their way of life in his "Yūjoki" ("An Account of Courtesans").[12] We know that the asobi sang imayō from a letter in Fujiwara Akihira's "Izumo Correspondence," in which he invites his friends to divert themselves with the prostitutes of Eguchi.[13] Akihira's information came from direct experience. He writes, "The asobi board a couple of boats floating among the reeds, and sing imayō songs. It is great fun." Contemporary noblemen apparently took part openly in such amusements and provided the circumstances through which imayō evolved into a sophisticated song style.[14]

Kugutsu are the subject of another of Masafusa's works, "Kugutsuki" ("An Account of the Kugutsu").[15] Masafusa describes the kugutsu as nomads, something highly unusual in Japan. The men hunted and worked as puppeteers and jugglers. The women were generally prostitutes, but their ostensible skills lay in "imayō, furukawayō, ashigara, kataoroshi, saibara, kurotoriko, tauta, kamiuta, saouta, tsujiuta, mago, fuzoku, shushi, and betsuhōshi," according to Masafusa.[16] Asobi worked the waterfront while the kugutsu roamed the countryside, but both groups used their singing talents to come into contact with aristocrats.[17] It was very likely in such settings that folk and shrine songs began to evolve into appropriately sophisticated banquet songs. Goshirakawa, reflecting on his own training in the art of imayō, states:

There were indeed few people with whom I did *not* sing. I sang of

[12] *Chōya Gunsai*, 3:66-67.

[13] *Unshū Shōsoku* (3, pt. 2):539.

[14] *Chōshūki*, the diary of Minamoto Morotoki, has this entry for 3.IX.1119: "We left the ladies-in-waiting in their boat at the pier, and went off to the house of an asobi [gap in the text]. From there the governor of Iyo [Fujiwara Nagazane] and the rest took their women to Kosai's house. We sang songs till midnight, and returned to our lodgings as dawn approached. The consultant [Minamoto Moroyori] asked for Yuya, the governor of Iyo had Kinzu, and the captain [Minamoto Akimasa] took his pleasure with Kosai. I have never had much liking for that sort of thing, and so I went to bed alone" (1:160-61). Note that Morotoki is careful to record the names of his fellow courtiers' partners for the night.

[15] *Chōya Gunsai*, 3:67, as collated with the *Gunsho Ruijū* printed edition (new rev. ed., 135:467).

[16] Shushi are not songs but a different art altogether (Nose, 1938, 137-51). Nothing is known of betsuhōshi.

[17] The *Roppyakuban Utaawase (Waka Match in 600 Rounds)* has a section, "Asobime ni Yosuru Koi" ("On Making Love to Asobi"; 1141-52), that deals exclusively with waterfront scenes. The next section, "Kugutsu ni Yosuru Koi" ("On Making Love to Kugutsu"; 1153-64), is by contrast concerned only with dry land. This is a clear demarcation of the two groups' spheres of influence.

course with the courtiers, both senior and junior, as well as with men
and women of the capital, subordinates and servants from various
places, asobi from Eguchi and Kanzaki, and kugutsu from the provinces. Naturally, some were skilled singers, but others were simply familiar with imayō. (*RH*, "Kudenshū," 10:97-98)

Not only noblemen, then, but even the cloistered sovereign readily associated with asobi and kugutsu.[18]
    We see that various kinds of folk and provincial shrine songs became
sophisticated city songs through the medium of asobi and kugutsu. This
phenomenon represents the transformation of originally zoku songs into
song worthy of the ga sphere. Such an event is termed "low-born, upward
moving" in the General Introduction to the first volume of this *History*.
These songs became ga, but ga of a far lower degree than that accorded
the truly ga arts of shih, waka, and calligraphy. Goshirakawa nevertheless
compiled the twenty books of *The Secret Store of Marvelous Song* out of
a concern that the proper performance methods for imayō might otherwise remain untransmitted. His action would not have been taken unless
imayō, in the general sense, was an acknowledged ga form. It was vital to
the ga world that artistic standards be maintained and transmitted to posterity. A zoku creation, imayō in that general sense, ascended to the sphere
of ga. That did not signal the extinction of zoku song. The various kinds
of folk and provincial shrine songs on which imayō (in the general sense)
were based lived on in the zoku world beyond the thirteenth century. As
late as 1872, songs that appear in *The Secret Store of Marvelous Song*
were performed at Onshi kagura held at Ise.[19] Those songs that ascended
to the sphere of ga, affected by an endless search for freshness, underwent
dramatic change and occasionally fell into decline. Some vanished altogether. But the songs on which they were based—down in the depths of
the zoku world—generally retained their original form throughout the
centuries.

---

[18] Uda Tennō (867-931) also summoned asobi to his villa at Torikai (*YM*, dan 146:310-
11). Apparently this was not an act deserving censure.
[19] Fujita Tokutarō first revealed this fact to the scholarly world (Fujita, 1930, 137-44).
Onshi kagura was performed at Ise during the period when the Grand Shrine sanctuaries
were restricted to the royal family. Commoners wishing to pray at Ise stayed with shrine officials called Onshi, whose houses provided both lodging and a place of worship. There were
approximately twenty to thirty Onshi at any given time up to 1872, when the office was
abolished. Kagura were performed at the houses to invite the gods to hear the pilgrims' prayers, and some of the songs sung at these performances survive in manuscripts. Some of this
number have been found to appear in the *Ryōjin Hishō*, which means that the songs were
transmitted from the twelfth century down to the end of the nineteenth. Because the kagura
performed at the Onshi houses in Ise differed dramatically from court kagura, they were
called Onshi kagura. Omodaka Hisataka, the great *Man'yōshū* scholar, belonged to an Onshi family in Ise, and Onshi kagura were performed in his grandfather's time. [Auth., Trans.]

Toward Song in Seven-Five Prosody

We have seen how various kinds of folk song and provincial shrine songs came, through the medium of the asobi and kugutsu, to acquire a sophisticated, polished form and to evolve into imayō in the general sense of the word. Song texts were refined along with their melodies. What was the contemporary model for the transformation from irregular into regular meter and form? Waka was clearly the model for songs in couplet form. By the twelfth century, waka had achieved a fixed 5-7-5 metric form for its kami no ku, or first three lines, and a 7-7 meter for its shimo no ku, the last two lines. We may conclude without difficulty that this configuration is reflected in the couplet song form. The quatrain form, on the other hand, was evidently influenced by the Buddhist hymn (shōmyō) tradition.

The Buddhist hymn corpus includes several kinds of songs and chants, among which the Japanese hymn (wasan) occupies the most important position in the history of song in Japan.[20] Wasan are hymns sung in Japanese, so distinguishing them from those in Sanskrit (bonsan) or in Chinese (kansan). The Japanese hymn is a song of praise for the Buddha, bodhisattvas, founders of religious orders, or their doctrine. The hōmonga, one kind of imayō in the general sense, were originally single stanzas from Japanese hymns. The kamiuta quatrain probably evolved from a merging of kamiuta with the hōmonga, a quatrain form in regular meter. The kamiuta quatrain given below is a good illustration of this process. It appears in *The Secret Store of Marvelous Song*.

> The Great T'ien-t'ai Master was a teacher of teachers;
> His eyebrows made two lines arched on his forehead.[21]
> He came into the world to preach the Holy Law,
> And was very close indeed to being a buddha himself!

> Tendai Daishi wa nōke no su
> Mayu wa hachiji ni oiwakare
> Nori no tsukai ni yo ni idete
> Hotōdo hotoke ni chikakariki.

$$(2:296)$$

---

[20] "Shōmyō," a translation of the Sanskrit "śabdavidyā," signifies a knowledge of language and, by extension, the recitation of passages from the sutras. It eventually came to refer to songs and chants performed at Buddhist ceremonies. Besides wasan, other examples of Japanese shōmyō are the kyōge and the kunkada.

[21] [More literally, "His eyebrows form a Chinese figure eight." The character for "eight" is written with two diagonal lines resembling a gable in growing farther apart below, but without meeting at the top. Thick eyebrows so arched were the Chinese emblem of an eminent man. The "great T'ien-t'ai Master" is Chih-i: see n. 24.—Trans., Ed.]

This song was excerpted from "Tendai Daishi Wasan" ("Hymn to the Great T'ien-t'ai Master") and later consolidated in quatrain form.[22] The following hōmonga also appears in *Marvelous Song*.

> The Master went to visit each in turn—
> The ancient dwelling of Po Tao-yu,
> The historic site of Prince Chin—
> Exactly as it had been revealed in his dream.[23]
>
> Haku Dōyū ga furuki muro
> Ōji Shin ga moto no ato
> Ichi ichi ni megurite mitamō ni
> Mukashi no yume ni koto narazu.
>
>   (2:224)

Since the former song, "The Great T'ien-t'ai Master was a teacher of teachers," was originally part of a Japanese hymn, we may reasonably conclude that it, too, was first sung as a hōmonga.

The hōmonga and the kamiuta quatrain are generally differentiated on the basis of content: the hōmonga texts are heavily imbued with Buddhist thought, whereas kamiuta are not. Nevertheless questions remain that can only be answered by hypothesizing a further difference, in melodic form. The Buddhist content of hōmonga suggests that their melodic form was firmly in the Buddhist hymn tradition. They eventually came to be sung for entertainment, and their music was apparently transposed to kamiuta melodies. Because no musical scores survive from this period, we can only conjecture about melodies. One process, however, must be recognized: single stanzas from Japanese hymns were sung first as hōmonga and were later transposed into kamiuta quatrains. "The Great T'ien-t'ai Master" provides the only evidence that hōmonga were transposed into kamiuta quatrain music. This is nevertheless sufficient basis to propose that the quatrain form was brought to the kamiuta from hōmonga.

With very few exceptions, hōmonga are in a quatrain form, one bequeathed them by the Japanese hymn. Even the longer Japanese shih and songs do not have stanzas. Indeed, the absence of stanzas is a hallmark of traditional Japanese shih and song. The Japanese hymn is the sole exception, and as a rule each of its stanzas consists of a quatrain. The quatrain

---

[22] The hymn is attributed, without evidence, to the famous Genshin (942-1017). Its composition date is similarly vague (Takeishi, 1969, 4-10).

[23] Another portion of the wasan corpus includes the T'ien-t'ai Master's dream, in which a bodhisattva prophesies that the Master will meet these men. Po Tao-yu was a legendary fourth century monk, and Prince Chin was the son of King Ling of the Chou dynasty (r. 571-44 B.C.) and a flute virtuoso. Legends say that both became immortals, the prince riding to heaven astride a crane.

form displayed by the hōmonga and the kamiuta quatrain are based on the Japanese hymn structure. In fact, however, this structure did not originate with the Japanese hymn but was inherited from Chinese hymns. The Chinese hymn corpus—containing songs of praise to the Buddha, the bodhisattvas, founders of religious orders, and their doctrines, sung in Chinese—typically has four lines for each stanza of its hymns. The "Hymn to the Great T'ien-t'ai Master," mentioned above, is based on Yen Chen-ch'ing's (710-85) "In Praise of Master Chih-i" (Tsukudo Reikan, 1931, 219).[24] In Yen's poem, four consecutive lines have the same end-rhyme, the next four have another end-rhyme, and so on to form a pattern. This is clearly a four-line stanza form that varies its end-rhymes in a way uncommon to Chinese shih. Yen's source, I believe, lay in Sanskrit hymns, sung in praise of the Buddha, the bodhisattvas, and Buddhist doctrine.

The śloka is the exemplary poetic form in Indian song and verse-prose. It is made up of two-line units, and each line consists of two eight-syllable phrases. In phrase units, then, the śloka consists of four phrases with a total of thirty-two syllables.[25] The śloka form appears in works as early as the *Rāmāyaṇa* and the *Mahābhārata*.[26] Yet the Indian people still seem to feel a very great closeness to this form, despite its antiquity.[27] Aware of the Indian love for śloka, Chinese intellectuals followed suit by casting their hymns in four-phrase stanza units. Chinese hymns later became the model for Japanese hymns, and so the same form was retained. The hymn structure, four-phrase units with interconnected meaning, would have facili-

---

[24] More commonly known by the title "Tendai Daishi Gasan." It appears, with a commentary compiled by Enchin (814-91), in *Dai Nihon Bukkyō Zensho*, 72. Chih-i (538-97) is the founder of T'ien-t'ai (Tendai) Buddhism.

[25] Meter in Indian poetry and verse-prose is formed by configurations of long and short syllables. If we represent a long syllable by a dash (—), and a short syllable by an asterisk (*), one line of a śloka would look like this:

$$* \_ \_ * * \_ \_ \_ \quad \_ \_ \_ \_ * * \_ \_ * *$$

Besides the śloka, there is the triṣṭubh form, consisting of two lines with a total of twenty-two or twenty-four syllables (each line has two phrases with eleven or twelve syllables); and the āryā, consisting of two lines with eight phrases each. In the latter form, long syllables are not fixed: each line has seven phrases with four short syllables plus one phrase of a single syllable. The śloka is the most easily understood Sanskrit poetic form for Indians: an Indian who is familiar with Sanskrit can apparently compose śloka poetry extemporaneously without difficulty (Winternitz, 1908, vol. 1, 424A).

[26] The original *Rāmāyaṇa* dates from the third century B.C., and the extant text was probably completed by the second century A.D. (ibid., 439-40). The *Mahābhārata* may date from either the fourth century B.C. or the fourth century A.D. (ibid., 403). Both works are principally written in the śloka form.

[27] I once attempted a partial translation of the *Divyāvadāna*, together with Ms. Malati Shendige. Much of the text was extremely difficult because its vocabulary and grammar were unrelated to Sanskrit or Prākrit. But when a king or some other eminent character spoke in the narrative, the text would be in śloka, written in elegant Sanskrit. Whenever we came to such passages, Ms. Shendige would exclaim, "Oh, beautiful! It's śloka," and, beating time with her finger, she would recite the lines most pleasantly.

tated the reception of a four-phrase unit in isolation. This probably provided the impetus behind the creation of the hōmonga.

We can readily understand that the quatrain, originally a foreign poetic form, enjoyed little popularity in Japan because it was not indigenous to Yamato. Imayō (in the general sense) reached its zenith at the end of the twelfth century. A formal imayō match, held from the first day of the Ninth Month, 1174, through the evening of the fifteenth, may have marked the pinnacle of its fortunes.[28] Bunkibō Ryūen (dates unknown), looking back on this time, wrote that "during Goshirakawa's reign, there were still many splendid musicians."[29] Even at its height, however, signs of decay were appearing in imayō. Goshirakawa's motive for compiling *The Secret Store of Marvelous Song* suggests this.

> I had hoped to pass on my knowledge, gained from many years of diligent practice, to someone who would perpetuate my school of imayō. People study imayō, but, much to my regret, I have no students to carry on my orthodox school. (*RH*, "Kudenshū," 10:107)

Goshirakawa wrote this in 1179.[30] The passage might easily be interpreted to mean that the last quarter of the twelfth century was a period of decline for imayō, but this was not the case. For Goshirakawa, the true imayō tradition had been transmitted from the late eleventh century, when his teacher, the asobi Otomae, had learned how to sing all the various imayō (in the general sense). He laments the fact that imayō has now reached the point where the orthodox singing method is no longer being transmitted. But imayō itself was flourishing. Otomae transmitted imayō (in the general sense) in its formative and developing periods, when an imayō song retained its basic melody—its shape as folk or provincial shrine song—under its modern style of presentation. The imayō match of 1174, however, was an aristocratic event, and that meant that contemporary imayō was developing a textual and musical shape designed to appeal to elite tastes.

By the thirteenth century, the various kinds of imayō—the koyanagi, the kataoroshi, the kurotoriko, the ashigara, the ichiko, the furukawa—were hardly ever sung, and the word "imayō" signified only imayō proper. It was during this time that imayō proper reached their zenith. Imayō were of course widely sung, but a further indication of the aristocratic fondness for this song form was the practice of composing Japanese poems in 7-5

---

[28] *Hyakurenshō*, 8:90. See "Sōan Imayō Awase" (Shimma, 1947, 33-46).

[29] *Bunkidan*, Kikutei manuscript, 1:6 recto.

[30] According to internal evidence in *Ryōjin Hishō*, "Kudenshū," 10 (Konishi, 1941, 39-40). Another opinion dates the document to 1180-85 (Shida, 1958, 412-16).

prosody and quatrain form under the name of "imayō."[31] But its rise into aristocratic society and it evolution into a fixed form meant that imayō, whose essence [songs in modern style] was constant innovation, was condemned to stagnate. It entered into rapid decline after the middle of the thirteenth century. The zenith of imayō was all too brief, compared with the millennium and more that waka has flourished, and imayō never became a mainstream art. We might most reasonably conclude that the short, superficial career of imayō resulted from the foreign origin of the quatrain form, which did not suit the Japanese temperament.

Why, despite the foreign origin of the quatrain form, did imayō (especially imayō proper) enjoy its brief period of success? I believe that it was due to the attractions of its 7-5 prosody. In the first volume of this *History*, I stated that the prosody of five and seven syllables provides the most natural form for the Japanese, a discussion based on Kanda Hideo's (1937) research. Song and waka have clearly evolved, since the Archaic Age, from irregular syllabic meter toward a regular prosody in five and seven syllables. The elements of syllabic meter could only have been fixed at five and seven because those syllabic groups provided to Japanese what seemed the most natural meter. But five- and seven-syllable lines had always been connected in a 5-7 order, never in 7-5. A chōka, or long poem, took the form expressed in the formula n $(5 + 7)$ $+$ 7. Given the traditional preference for 5-7 over 7-5 prosody, how did the latter form come into existence?

The generally accepted explanation up to now has been that 7-5 prosody evolved from Japanese hymns. I do not have sufficient evidence to refute this view, although it is not unassailable. The many Japanese hymns composed in the tenth and eleventh centuries—Sengan's (dates unknown) "Gokurakukoku Mida Wasan" ("Hymn to Amitābha in the Land of Paradise"), Genshin's "Gokuraku Rokuji San" ("Hymn on Paradise, Sung at the Six Monastic Offices") and "Hymn to the Great T'ien-t'ai Master," and Chinkai's (dates unknown) "Bodaishin San" ("Hymn on the Search for Supreme Enlightenment")—have led scholars to assume that the quatrain form and 7-5 prosody obviously originated in the Japanese hymn. The problems before us, however, are not so easily solved. The authorship of these hymns is in question: the attributions to Sengan, Genshin, Chinkai, and others are late and unsubstantiated. On the other hand, *Marvelous Song* has two works, a hōmonga ("The Master went to visit each in turn"; 2:224) and a kamiuta quatrain ("The Great T'ien-t'ai Master was a teacher of teachers"; 2:296), that are clearly based on the "Hymn to the Great T'ien-t'ai Master." Since the hymn cannot possibly be based on the

---

[31] Four imayō in *Shūgyokushū* (Jingū Bunko manuscript) and fifty in *Yuishimbō Shū* were probably received as a form of literature.

hōmonga and the kamiuta quatrain, we must conclude that the "Hymn to the Great T'ien-t'ai Master" must have predated the other two songs. Thus we may properly find the origin of the quatrain form in the Japanese hymn; but this does not mean that we can draw a similar conclusion about 7-5 prosody.

The imayō presents one problem. Imayō proper are usually defined as songs in 7-5 prosody and quatrain form, but this definition is based on concepts formed prior to the 1911 discovery of a manuscript copy of *Marvelous Song* that contradicts the traditional view in certain respects. A study of syllabic prosody in imayō proper and in hōmonga and kamiuta quatrains with a similar structure reveals that 8-5 is a more frequently used prosody than 7-5. This is a mathematical fact, although its interpretation elicits opposing views.[32] Rather than question which view is correct, we should remember that the only extant manuscript of *Marvelous Song* is an early nineteenth-century copy with many errors and omissions, and that the manuscript accordingly provides uncertain data on which to base a strict statistical study centering on the presence or absence of a single syllable.

There is a similar problem with the Japanese hymn. Nearly all extant manuscript copies and early printed editions of Japanese hymns date from the mid-eighteenth through the nineteenth centuries, and so they provide unreliable data in demonstrating that eleventh- and twelfth-century hymns had a 7-5 prosody. If we agree that the quatrain form was taken from the Japanese hymn, we can also conclude that it provided imayō in the general sense with 7-5 or 8-5 prosody. But we cannot state that imayō drew only 7-5 prosody from the Japanese hymn. This is why I employ the term "regular prosody," which, if seen to comprehend both 7-5 and 8-5 prosody, enables us to acknowledge that regular prosody originated with the Japanese hymn.

Now, regardless of its prosodic count, the fixed syllables of Japanese hymn and imayō alike are greater in the first half (seven or eight syllables) than in the second half (five syllables), and so run counter to the 5-7 pattern in existence since the Archaic Age. What brought about this counter-movement? One likely agent is the influence exerted by Chinese prosodic patterns. The kind of shih that were written in Japan invariably consisted of either five- or seven-character lines. In either case the structure is broken down into a 3:2 or 4:3 ratio, with the first half of the line having more syllables than the second. This is borne out by both the meaning and the tonal patterns of the line. The Japanese intellectuals who, from the eighth century on, encountered five- and seven-character-line shih grew accus-

---

[32] Takagi Ichinosuke, Shida Engi, and Fujita Tokutarō have discussed this subject. I, too, have stated an opinion (Konishi, 1938, 33-43).

tomed at some point to prosodic patterns with more syllables in the first half of a line than in the second, and they came to think these patterns worthy. The Chinese hymn may have been a chief agent in introducing this metric structure to Japanese composers of shih and song. Some Chinese hymns consist of four-character lines, but most of those introduced into Japan had lines of five or seven characters. Composers of Japanese hymns probably used these as models, and so they experimented with 7-5 or 8-5 prosody. I do not believe that the fixed 5-7 syllabics of waka are patterned after the five- and seven-character lines of Chinese shih. Classical Chinese, with its four tones, often has syllables of differing lengths, unlike the regular syllabic value of Japanese.[33] The Chinese and Japanese lines are the same formally, since the number of syllables, five or seven, is identical in both cases. In syllabic value, however, five or seven Chinese syllables are definitely not the equivalent, respectively, of five or seven Japanese syllables.[34] Nevertheless, we have no other apparent reason but the influence of Chinese poetry to explain how the indigenous Japanese 5-7 prosodic pattern was reversed for song into 8-5 or 7-5 prosody.

A seven-character shih line breaks down into 4-3 meter, but this is often further divided into a 2-2-3 ratio. If converted into a Japanese prosodic pattern, this ratio might become 4-4-5, a subdivision of 8-5 meter. Thus 8-5 prosody in imayō (in the general sense) represents a fixed form rather than a deviation from 7-5 prosody or a hypermetric prosody. After the thirteenth century, 7-5 prosody clearly triumphed over 8-5 prosody to become a basic metric form. Both the sōga (or enkyoku) and nō libretti are organized in rhythms based on 7-5 prosody.[35] In the history of Japanese song, the Middle Ages established these song forms together with the 7-5 prosody itself. The 8-5 prosody fell into disuse because, as was noted earlier, the most natural measure for Japanese is that in seven and five syllables. The 7-5 prosody continued to thrive long after the rapid decline of the foreign quatrain form, an indication that a prosody of five and seven syllable lines or units arose from elements peculiar to the Japanese language.

[33] ["In Classical Chinese, there are four tones: 'p'ing' or 'level,' 'shang' or 'rising,' 'ch'ü' or 'falling,' and 'ju' or 'entering.' For metrical purposes, the first tone is regarded as Level, while the other three tones are regarded as Deflected (tse). These tones differ from each other not only in pitch but in length and movement. The first tone is relatively long and keeps to the same pitch; the other three are relatively short and, as their respective names indicate, move upward or downward in pitch, or stop suddenly." James J.-Y. Liu, 1962,21.—Trans.]

[34] The value of one spoken Chinese syllable in the rising tone, for example, corresponds to three syllables spoken in Japanese.

[35] This will be discussed in Volume Three of this History.

CHRONOLOGICAL TABLE

Christian Era		Japan	China	Korea	China, Korea, P'o-hai
A.D.	751	*Kaifūsō*, preface composed.	T'ang	Silla	
	752	Ōuta first appear in document.			
	755	Fujiwara Kadonomaro born.			Civil war by An Lu-shan begins.
	756	Fujiwara Sonohito born.			Emperor Hsüan-tsung flees to Shu.
	757	Draft of semmyō first appears.			Wang Ch'ang-ling dies?
	759	The last dated waka in the *Man'yōshū*.			
	762				Li Po dies.
	766	Abe no Nakamaro dies in China.			
	768				Han Yü born.
	770	Sugawara Kiyokimi born?			
	772	*Kakyō Hyōshiki* is written.			Po Chü-i born.
	773				Liu Tsung-yüan born.
	774	Kūkai born. Fujiwara Fuyutsugu born. Asano Katori born.			Chang Chih-ho composes a tz'u, "The Fisherman's Song."
	778	The fourteenth enbassy to T'ang dynasty returns.			
	779				Yüan Chen born.
	781	Kammu Tennō accedes to the throne. Before this year the Bureau of Ancient Song is established.			"Jen-shih Chuan" is written.
	785	Ōtomo Yakamochi dies. Yoshimine Yasuyo born. Shigeno Sadanushi born. Between this year and 823 *Nihon Ryōiki* is compiled.			Chang Hsiao-piao born. Yen Chen-ch'ing dies.
	786	Saga Tennō born.			

Christian Era	Japan	China	Korea	China, Korea, P'o-hai
A.D. 789	Kuwahara Haraaka born.	T'ang	Silla	Yang Chü-yüan passes the examination for chin-shih.
790				Wei Ying-mu dies? Shen Chi-chi dies.
792	Prince Abo born. Prince Nakano born.			
794	Ennin born.			
797	*Rōko Shiiki* written. *Sangō Shiiki* written.			
798	Kammu Tennō has a waka party at Kitano Shrine.			
800	Shinzei born. Prince Kadono born.			Han Yü composes "A Preface to the Farewell Poem for Meng Tung-yeh." Po Chü-i passes the official examination.
802	Ono no Takamura born.			
803	Waka of encouragement composed at the farewell party for the sixteenth embassy to T'ang Dynasty.			Tu Mu born.
804	The sixteenth embassy leaves for T'ang with Saichō and Kūkai aboard.			"Ying-ying Chuan" is written.
805	Fujiwara Sekio born.			Hui-kuo dies. Po Chü-i composes "Ch'ang-hen Ko."
807	Princess Uchiko born. Fujiwara Sadatoshi born. *Kogo Shūi* compiled.			
810	Minamoto Makoto born.			
812	Minamoto Tokiwa born.			Li Shang-yin born. Wen T'ing-yün born.
814	*Ryōun Shinshū* is compiled. Wang Hsiao-lien, ambassador from P'o-hai, visits Japan. Enchin born.			Meng Chiao born.
815	Minamoto Sadamu born.			

Christian Era		Japan	China	Korea	China, Korea, P'o-hai
A.D.	818	*Bunka Shūreishū* compiled. Fujiwara Kadonomaro dies. Fujiwara Kunihito dies.	T'ang	Silla	
	819				Liu Tsung-yüan dies.
	820				Li Shan-fu born.
	822	Saichō dies.			Po Chü-i is appointed to the governorship of Hangchow.
	823	"Five Mixed-Meter Songs on Fishing" composed.			*Yüan-shih Ch'ang-ch'ing Chi* is compiled.
	824				Han Yü dies. Po Chü-i resigns from the governorship of Hangchow. *Po-shih Ch'ang-ch'ing Chi* in 50 volumes is compiled.
	825	Kuwahara Haraaka dies. Ariwara Narihira born.			
	826	Fujiwara Fuyutsugu dies.			Po Hsing-chien dies.
	827	*Keikokushū* compiled.			
	828	Fujiwara Tsuguhiko dies. Shimada Tadaomi born. About this time kana is used in the notes for *Konkōmyō Saishō-ō Kyō (Suvarna-prabhāsa Sūtra)* now at Saidaiji temple.			
	830	Yoshimine Yasuyo dies.			
	831				Yüan Chen dies.
	833	*Ryō no Gige* is compiled.			
	834	Minamoto Tokiwa dies. Miyako Yoshika born.			
	835	Kūkai dies.			
	838	The seventeenth embassy leaves for the T'ang, with Ennin aboard. Ono no Takamura exiled. Anthologies of Yüan Chen and Po Chü-i are brought to Japan.			
	839	The seventeenth embassy to the T'ang returns.			

Christian Era	Japan	China	Korea	China, Korea, P'o-hai
A.D. 843	Asano Katori dies.	T'ang	Silla	Chia Tao dies.
844				Egaku copies *Po-shih Ch'ang-ch'ing Chi* while staying in T'ang. Han Wu born.
845	Sugawara Michizane born. Ki no Haseo born.			
846				Po Chü-i dies.
847	Princess Uchiko dies. Miyoshi Kiyoyuki born.			
849	Higher monks of Kōfukuji temple dedicate waka of congratulation for the long life of the tennō.			
850	Semmyō of conferment for Tatsuta Shrine and Hirose Shrine are composed.			
852	Ono no Takamura dies. Shigeno Sadanushi dies.			Tu Mu dies.
855	Prince Michino dies. Michizane's earliest Chinese poem is composed.			
857				Ch'oe Ch'i-wŏn of Silla born.
858				Li Shang-yin dies.
859	Princess Hiroi dies.			
860	Shinzei dies. Fujiwara Sadatoshi dies.			
863	Minamoto Sadamu dies.			
864	Ennin dies.			
867	Prince Nakano dies. Uda Tennō born. Kana is used in the census register documents of Sanuki province.			
868	Minamoto Makoto dies.			Ch'oe Ch'i-wŏn of Silla is sent to T'ang to study.
870				Wen T'ing-yün dies?
874				Ch'oe Ch'i-wŏn passes the official court examination.

Christian Era		Japan	China	Korea	China, Korea, P'o-hai
A.D.	875	Fujiwara Tadahira born.	T'ang	Silla	
	879	Miyako no Yoshika dies.			
	880	Ariwara Narihira dies.			
	881				Ch'oe Ch'i-wŏn composes "A Manifesto to Huang Ch'ao" for T'ang general.
	882	P'o-hai envoy visits Japan; exchanges Chinese poems.			
	885	Michizane composes "Preface to 'In Spring, Beauties Quite Lack Energy.'" During this year and 887 *Zai Mimbukyō Ke Utaawase* compiled.			Ch'oe Ch'i-wŏn returns to Silla.
	886	Fujiwara Korehira born.			
	888	Ōe no Koretoki born. *Dairi Kikuawase* is compiled.			In Silla *Samdaemok* compiled.
	889	Between this year and 898 *Kambyō no Ōntoki Kisainomiya Utaawase* compiled. Around this year *Nihonkoku Genzaisho Mokuroku* compiled.			
	891	Shimada Tadaomi dies. Enchin dies.			
	893	Before Ninth Month of this year *Koresada no Miko Ke no Utaawase* is compiled.			
	896	Before Sixth Month of this year *Suzakuin Ominaeshiawase* is compiled.			
	898	Between this year and 901 *Ki no Shishō Kyokusuien Waka* is compiled.			
	900	Michizane offers his personal anthology of Chinese poems to Daigo Tennō.			Ts'ui Tao-jung dies.
	903	Michizane dies.			
	905	Daigo Tennō orders compilation of *Kokinshū*.			

Christian Era	Japan	China	Korea	China, Korea, P'o-hai
A.D. 908	Kiyohara Motosuke born.	Later Liang	Silla	Su-k'ung T'u dies.
911	Minamoto Shitagō born.			
912	Ki no Haseo dies.			
913	*Teijiin Utaawase* compiled.			
914	Prince Kaneakira born. Around this year *Kokinshū* is compiled.			
918	Miyoshi Kiyoyuki dies.			
921	Ōnakatomi Yoshinobu born.			
923	Taira Sadafum' dies.			Han Wu dies.
924	Fujiwara Koremasa born.	Later T'ang		
926				P'o-hai destroyed.
930	Ki no Tsurayuki appointed to governorship of Tosa province. Daigo dies.			
931	Uda dies.			
935	Civil War of Taira Masakado begins. Ki no Tsurayuki returns to Capital. Around this year *Tosa Nikki* is written.		Koryŏ	
939	*Ki no Tsurayuki Ke Utaawase* is compiled.	Later Chin		
940	Civil War of Taira Masakado quelled. Minamoto Hideakira dies.			*Hua-chien Chi* is compiled.
942	Genshin born.			
945	Fujiwara Nakahira dies. Tsurayuki appointed to Lower Junior Fourth Rank.			
946	Fujiwara Korehira dies.			

Christian Era	Japan	China	Korea	China, Korea, P'o-hai
A.D. 951	Murakami Tennō orders compilation of *Gosenshū*. Inferred date of compilation of the original text of *Yamato Monogatari*.	Later Chou	Koryŏ	
952	Ōe no Masahira born.			
957	Fujiwara Sanesuke born.			
		Sung (Northern)		
960	*Tentoku Utaawase* compiled.			
963	Ōe no Koretoki dies.			
966	Fujiwara Michinaga born. Fujiwara Kintō born.			
969	Between this year and 971, Parts 1 and 2 of *Kagerō Nikki* probably composed.			
972	Fujiwara Koremasa dies. Fujiwara Kōzei born.			
974	The third part of *Kagerō Nikki* inferred to be written after this year.			
983	Minamoto Shitagō dies.			*T'ai-p'ing Yü-lan* is compiled.
984	Fujiwara Korechika born. *Sambōe* compiled.			
985	Sone no Yoshitada forces his way into a court poetry party held by En'yū.			
986	An account of this year seen in *Makura no Sōshi* (*The Pillow Book*).			*Wen-yüan Ying-hua* is compiled.
987	Prince Kaneakira dies.			
989	Fujiwara Akihira born.			Mang Chung-yen born.
990	Kiyohara Motosuke dies. Taira Kanemori dies.			
994	An account of dedication for Shakuzenji temple held in the Second Month of this year is seen in *Makura no Sōshi*.			

Christian Era	Japan	China	Korea	China, Korea, P'o-hai
A.D. 995	Mother of Michitsuna dies?	Sung (Northern)	Koryŏ	
996	Fujiwara Korechika is demoted.			Li Fang dies.
997	Yoshishige Yasutane dies.			
1000	The last datable account in *Makura no Sōshi*.			
1008	Prince Atsuhira born. By this year some portion of *Genji Monogatari* is written.			Sung edition of *Kuang-yün* is published.
1010	Fujiwara Korechika dies.			
1011	Minamoto Tamenori dies.			
1012	Ōe no Masahira dies.			
1017	Genshin dies.			
1020	Account of *Sarashina Nikki* begins with this year.			
1025	The dated account of the *Ōkagami* ends with this year.			
1029	The first part of the *Eiga Monogatari* is inferred to be written between this year and 1033.			
1041	Fujiwara Kintō dies.			
1044	Approximate inferred date of compilation of *Hokke Kenki*.			
1046	Fujiwara Sanesuke dies.			
1055	A waka contest on newly written monogatari held at Kamo Priestess's mansion at Rokujō. *Ōsaka Koenu Gon Chūnagon* written.			
1056	Fujiwara Mototoshi born.			
1060	Daughter of Sugawara Takasue still alive this year at the age of 53.			*Hsin T'ang-shu* is compiled.
1062	*Mutsu Waki* contains accounts up to this year.			

Christian Era	Japan	China	Korea	China, Korea, P'o-hai
A.D. 1066	Fujiwara Akihira dies.	Sung (Northern)	Koryŏ	Su Hsün dies. *Tzü-chih T'ung-chien* compiled.
1071	*San Tendai Godaisan Ki* written.			
1072				Ou-yang Hsiu dies.
1078	Shirakawa Tennō orders compilation of *Goshūishū*.			
1086	*Goshūishū* compiled.			Ssu-ma Kuang dies. Wang An-shih dies.
1092	The last part of *Eiga Monogatari* inferred to be written between this year and 1107.			
1011				Su Shih dies.
1104	Fujiwara Kiyosuke born.			
1111	Ōe no Masafusa dies.			
1114	Fujiwara Shunzei born.			Koryŏ imports Sung court song, "Ta-ch'eng Lo."
1119	An account of illustrations of *Genji Monogatari* seen in *Chōshū Ki*.			
1120	Gen'ei text of *Kokinshū* copied.			Yejong of Koryŏ composes "Tojangga" ("Elegy for Two Generals").
1127	Goshirakawa Tennō born.	Sung (Southern)		
1142	Fujiwara Mototoshi dies.			
1145				In Koryŏ *Samguk Sagi* compiled.
1153	Kamo no Chōmei born?			
1162	Fujiwara Teika born.			
1174	Contest of imayō songs held by Goshirakawa.			
1175	Jōdo sect of Buddhism becomes independently established.			
1177	Fujiwara Kiyosuke dies.			*Ssu-shu Chi-chu* written.

Christian Era		Japan	China	Korea	China, Korea, P'o-hai
A.D.	1179	The 10th volume of *Ryōjin Hishō Kudenshū* is inferred to be written.	Sung (Northern)	Koryŏ	
	1191				In Koryŏ *Samhansa Kuiham* compiled.
	1192	Goshirakawa dies.			
	1200				Chu Hsi dies.
	1204	Fujiwara Shunzei dies.			
	1205	*Shinkokinshū* compiled.			
	1212	*Hōjōki* written.			
	1216	Kamo no Chōmei dies.			
	1241	Fujiwara Teika dies.			Yi Kyu-bo of Koryŏ dies.

SELECT BIBLIOGRAPHY

Three sections follow. The first includes editions and collections referred to in the main text of this volume. The second includes Japanese studies, and the third non-Japanese studies. Unless otherwise specified, the place of publication is Tokyo.

A title preceded by an asterisk designates a work that, in the text, is cited by part rather than by page.

The citation under an author's name of, for example, "1951b" without a preceding "1951a" implies the existence of another work published in 1951 that is cited as "1951a" in another volume of this *History*. (Separate bibliographies and indexes are not being supplied to each volume of the Japanese version.)

Certain large series editions are cited under "Editions," although actual citations are keyed to individual works within the series.

A. Editions

Akazome Emon Shū. Akazome Emon; SKST, 2:13. See SKST.

Ariake no Wakare. Ariake no Wakare no Kenkyū (Ōfūsha, 1969). Edited by Ōtsuki Osamu.

Asaji ga Tsuyu. Asaji ga Tsuyu Kenkyū (Ōfūsha, 1974). Edited by Ōtsuki Osamu.

BSS = *Bunka Shūreishū*. See *Bunka Shūreishū*.

**Bunka Shūreishū [BSS]*. Bunka Shūreishū; NKBT, 69 (1964). Edited by Kojima Noriyuki.

Bunkidan. Bunkidan (Kyoto: Kichō Tosho Eihon Kankōkai, 1935). Reproduction of Kikutei manuscript, with an introduction by Suzuka Sanshichi.

Chiang Li-ling Chi. Chiang Li-ling Chi; HLPMC, 5. See HLPMC.

Chien-wen-ti Chi. Liang Chien-wen-ti Chi; HLPMC, 5. See HLPMC.

Chikuba Kyōginshū. Chikuba Kyōginshū, Biblia, no. 43 (Tenri: Tenri Library, 1969).

Chisha Daishi Gasan. Chisha Daishi Gazōsan Chū; Dai Nihon Bukkyō Zensho, 72 (Suzuki Gakujitsu Zaidan, 1972).

Chōshūki. Chōshūki; Shiryō Taisei, 6-7 (Naigai Shoseki, 1934). Edited by Yano Tarō.

Chōya Gunsai. Chōya Gunsai; SZKT, 29a (1938).

Chuang Tzu. Chuang Tzu; Hsin-pien Chu-tzu Chi-ch'eng, 3 (Taipei: Shih-chieh Shu-chü, 1978).

Ch'üan T'ang-shih [CTS]. Ch'üan T'ang-shih (Peking: Chung-hua Shu-chü, 1960).

Ch'üan T'ang-wen [CTW]. Ching-ting Ch'üan T'ang-wen (Taipei: Ch'i-wen Ch'u-pan-she, 1961).

Chung-kuo Wen-hsüeh P'i-p'ing Tsü-liao Hui-pien (Taipei: Ch'en-wen Ch'u-pan-she, 1978-79). Edited by Ts'eng Yung-i et al. 11 vols.

CTS = *Ch'üan T'ang-shih*. See *Ch'üan T'ang-shih*.

CTW = *Ch'üan T'ang-wen*. See *Ch'üan T'ang-wen*.

**Dainagon Kintō Shū*. See Kintō Shū.

Dai Nihon Bukkyō Zensho. Dai Nihon Bukkyō Zensho (Bussho Kankōkai, 1912-22). 100 vols. Reproduced by Meicho Fukyūkai, 1980-1983.

Dairi Kikuawase. Dairi Kikuawase; HCUT, 1. See HCUT.

Denshi Kashū. Denshi Kashū; SGRJ, 6 (1931). Edited by Hanami Sakumi.

Eiga Monogatari [EM]. Eiga Monogatari; NKBT, 75-76 (1964-65). Edited by Matsumura Hiroshi and Yamanaka Yutaka.

Eika no Taigai. See *Karon Shū.*

*Ekyō Shū. Ekyō Shū: Kōhon to Kenkyū (Ōfūsha, 1978). Edited by Kumamoto Morio.

EM = Eiga Monogatari. See *Eiga Monogatari.*

Fukurozōshi [FZS]. Fukurozōshi Chūshaku (Hanawa Shobō, 1974-76). Edited by Ozawa Masao, Gotō Shigeo, Shimazu Tadao, and Higuchi Yoshimaro. 2 vols.

Fusō Ryakuki. Fusō Ryakuki; SZKT, 12 (1932).

Fūyōshū. Zōtei Kōhon Fūyō Wakashū (Kyoto: Yūzan Bunko, 1970). Edited by Nakano Shōji and Fujii Takashi.

*Fuzoku(uta) [FZ]. See *Kodai Kayō Shū.*

FZ = Fuzokuuta. See *Kodai Kayō Shū.*

FZS = Fukurozōshi. See *Fukurozōshi.*

GDSE = Gyokudai Shin'ei. See *Gyokudai Shin'ei.*

Genji Monogatari [GM]. Genji Monogatari; NKBT, 14-18 (1958-63). Edited by Yamagishi Tokuhei.

Genji Monogatari Emaki. Genji Monogatari Emaki (Kōdansha, 1971). Reproduction of the original scrolls.

Genji Monogatari Kōza (Yūseidō, 1971-73). Edited by Yamagishi Tokuhei. 9 vols.

Genji Monogatari Taisei. Genji Monogatari Taisei (Chūō Kōronsha, 1953-56). Edited by Ikeda Kikan. 8 vols.

Genzai Shomoku. See *Nihonkoku Genzaisho Mokuroku.*

GM = Genji Monogatari. See *Genji Monogatari.*

Gōdanshō (rufubon, well-circulated version). *Gōdanshō; SGRJ,* 21 (1930). Edited by Matsumoto Hikojirō.

Gōke Shidai. Shintei Zōho Kojitsu Sōsho, 2 (Meiji Tosho and Yoshikawa Kōbunkan, 1953).

Gō Rihō Shū. Gō Rihō Shū; SGRJ, 6 (1931). Edited by Hanami Katsumi.

*Gosenshū [GSS]. Gosen Wakashū Sōsakuin (Ōsaka Joshi Daigaku, 1965). Edited by Katagiri Yōichi et al.

*Goshūishū. Daisenjibon Goshūi Wakashū (Ōfūsha, 1971). Edited by Fujimoto Kazue.

GSS = Gosenshū. See *Gosenshū.*

Gyokudai Shin'ei [GDSE]. Gyokudai Shin'ei [= Yü-t'ai Hsin-yung]; KST, 1. See *KST.*

Hachidaishū Shō. Hachidaishū Shō; Hachidaishū Zenchū, 1-2 (Yūseidō, 1960). Edited by Yamagishi Tokuhei.

Haku Kōzan Shishū [HKS]. Haku Kōzan Shishū [= Po Hsiang-shan Shih-chi (PSC)]; KST, 2. See *KST.*

Hamamatsu Chūnagon Monogatari. Hamamatsu Chūnagon Monogatari; NKBT, 77 (1964). Edited by Matsuo Satoshi.

Hanazono Tennō Shinki. Hanazono Tennō Shinki; Shiryō Taisei, Zokuhen, 33-34 (Naigai Shoseki, 1938). Edited by Yano Tarō.

HCUT = Heianchō Utaawase Taisei. Heianchō Utaawase Taisei (published by the editor, 1957-69; reprinted by Dōhōsha, Kyoto, 1979). Edited by Hagitani Boku. 10 vols.

Heichū Monogatari. Heichū Monogatari Sōsakuin (Hatsune Shobō, 1968). Edited by Soda Fumio.

Heike Monogatari. Heike Monogatari; NKBT, 32-33 (1959-60). Edited by Takagi Ichinosuke, Ozawa Masao, Atsumi Kaoru, and Kindaichi Haruhiko.

Hitachi Fudoki. Fudoki; NKBT, 2 (1958). Edited by Akimoto Yoshirō.

HKS = *Haku Kōzan Shishū.* See *Haku Kōzan Shishū.*

HLPMC = *Han-Wei Liu-ch'ao Po-san Ming-chia Chi. Han-Wei Liu-ch'ao Po-san Ming-chia Chi* (Kyoto: Chūbun Shuppansha, 1976). 6 vols. Reproduction of original Chinese version.

HM = *Honchō Monzui.* See *Honchō Monzui.*

Ho Chi-shih Chi. Ho Chi-shih Chi; HLPMC, 6. See HLPMC.

Hokke Kenki. Hokke Kenki; Nihon Shisō Taikei, 7 (Iwanami Shoten, 1974). Edited by Inoue Mitsusada and Ōsone Shōsuke.

Honchō Monzui [HM]. Honchō Monzui; SZKT, 30 (1938).

Honchō Mudaishi. Honchō Mudaishi; SGRJ, 6 (1931). Edited by Hanami Sakumi.

Honchō Reisō [HR]. Honchō Reisō; SGRJ, 6 (1931). Edited by Hanami Sakumi.

Honchō Seiki. Honchō Seiki; SZKT, 9 (1933).

Honchō Shojaku Mokuroku. Honchō Shojaku Mokuroku; SGRJ, 21 (1930). Edited by Matsumoto Hikojirō.

Hon'in Jijū Shū. Hon'in Jijū; SKST, 1:88. See SKST.

Hou Han Shu. Hou Han Shu (Peking: Chung-hua Shu-chü, 1965). 12 vols.

Houn Sŏngsaeng Happu. Houn Sŏngsaeng Happu (Seoul: Hoesangsa, 1967).

HR = *Honchō Reisō.* See *Honchō Reisō.*

Hsiao Ching. Hsiao Ching; SCC, 8. See SCC.

Hsieh Hsüan-ch'eng Chi. Hsieh Hsüan-ch'eng Chi Chiao-chu (Taipei: Taiwan Chung-hua Shu-chü, 1969). Edited by Hung Shun-lung.

Hsüeh Ssu-li Chi. Hsüeh Ssu-li Chi; HLPMC, 6. See HLPMC.

Hyakurenshō. Hyakurenshō; SZKT, 11 (1929).

Ichijō Sesshō Gyoshū. Koremasa; SKST, 1:87. See SKST.

IM = *Ise Monogatari.* See *Ise Monogatari.*

Ise Monogatari [IM]. Ise Monogatari; NKBT, 9 (1957). Edited by Ōtsu Yūichi and Tsukijima Hiroshi.

Ise Shū. Ise; SKST, 1:50. See SKST.

ISN = *Izumi Shikibu Nikki.* See *Izumi Shikibu Nikki.*

ISS = *Izumi Shikibu Shū.* See *Izumi Shikibu Shū.*

Izumi Shikibu Nikki [ISN]. Izumi Shikibu Nikki Sōsakuin (Musashino Shoin, 1959). Edited by Tsukahara Tetsuo and Maeda Kingo.

Izumi Shikibu Shū [ISS]. Izumi Shikibu Kashū; Iwanami Bunko (Iwanami Shoten, 1956). Edited by Shimizu Fumio.

Jikaku Daishi Zaitō Sōshinroku. Jikaku Daishi Zaitō Sōshinroku; TSDK, 55. See TSDK.

Jimmu Zenki. Nihon Shoki, 3. See *Nihon Shoki.*

Jūjūshin Ron. Kūkai; Nihon Shisō Taikei, 5 (Iwanami Shoten, 1975). Edited by Kawasaki Tsuneyuki.

Jung-chai Sui-pi. Jung-chai Sui-pi Wu-chi (Shanghai: Shang-wu Ying-shu-kuan, 1935).

Kagaku Taikei. See NKGT.

Kagerō Nikki [KN]. Kagerō Nikki Sōsakuin (Kazama Shobō, 1963; rev. ed., 1981). Edited by Saeki Umetomo and Imuda Tsunehisa. 1981 edition used.

*Kagura(uta) [KR]. See *Kodai Kayō Shū.*

Kakaishō. Shimyōshō, Kakaishō (Kadokawa Shoten, 1968). Edited by Ishida Jōji.

*Kambyō no Ōntoki Kisai no Miya Utaawase. Kōtaibunin Hanshi Nyoō Utaa-
    wase; HCUT, 1. See HCUT.
*Kanke Bunsō [KB]. Kanke Bunsō; NKBT, 72 (1966). Edited by Kawaguchi
    Hisao.
Kanke Kōshū [KKKS]. Kanke Kōshū; NKBT, 72 (1966). Edited by Kawaguchi
    Hisao.
Karon Shū. Karon Shū; NKBT, 65 (1961). Edited by Hisamatsu Sen'ichi.
Katsura Murasaki Shū. Murasaki Shikibu Shū; Katsura no Miyabon Sōsho, 9
    (Tenri: Yōtokusha, 1954). Compiled and edited by the Library Division,
    Royal Household Agency of Japan.
Katsura no Miyabon Sōsho. See Katsura Murasaki Shū.
KB = Kanke Bunsō. See Kanke Bunsō.
Keikokushū [KK]. Keikokushū; SGRJ, 6 (1931). Edited by Hanami Sakumi.
Kewŏn P'ilgyŏng. Kewŏn P'ilgyŏng; Houn Sŏnsaeng Happu (Seoul: Hoesangsa,
    1967).
Kinkafu [KKF]. See Kodai Kayō Shū.
Ki no Shishō Kyokusuien Waka [KSKW]. "Ki no Shishō Kyokusuien Waka ni
    Tsuite," Nihon Kagaku no Genryū. See Yamada, 1948.
*Kintō Shū. Kintō; SKST, 2:12. See SKST.
*Kin'yōshū. Kin'yō Wakashū Sōsakuin (Osaka: Seibundō, 1976). Edited by Ma-
    suda Shigeo et al.
Kisai no Miya Inshi Ke Utaawase. Kisai no Miya Inshi Utaawase; HCUT, 1. See
    HCUT.
KK = Keikokushū. See Keikokushū.
KKF = Kinkafu. See Kodai Kayō Shū.
KKKS = Kanke Kōshū. See Kanke Kōshū.
KKS = Kokinshū. See Kokinshū.
KN = Kagerō Nikki. See Kagerō Nikki.
Kodai Kayō Shū. Kodai Kayō Shū; NKBT, 3 (1957). Edited by Konishi Jin'ichi.
Kō Fuhō Den. Himitsu Mandara Kyō Fuhō Den; Kōbō Daishi Zenshū, 1 (Kōya:
    Mikkyō Bunka Kenkyūjo, Kōyasan Daigaku, 1965).
Kogo Shūi. Kogo Shūi, Takahashi Ujibumi (Gendai Shichōsha, 1976). Edited by
    Yasuda Naomichi and Akimoto Yoshinori.
Kohon Setsuwa Shū. Kohon Setsuwa Shū Sōsakuin (Kazama Shobō, 1969). Edited
    by Yamauchi Yōichirō.
*Kokinshū [KKS]. Kokinwakashū; Iwanami Bunko (Iwanami Shoten, 1981). Ed-
    ited by Saeki Umetomo.
Kokin (Waka) Rokujō. Kokin Waka Rokujō; Toshoryō Sōkan (Tenri: Yōtokusha,
    1967-69). Edited by the Library Division, Royal Household Agency of Japan.
    2 vols.
Konjaku Monogatari Shū. Konjaku Monogatari Shū; NKBT, 22-26 (1959-63).
    Edited by Yamada Yoshio, Yamada Tadao, Yamada Hideo, and Yamada To-
    shio.
Koresada no Miko Ke Utaawase. Koresada no Miko Utaawase; HCUT, 1. See
    HCUT.
Kōya Zappitsu Shū. Kōya Zappitsu Shū; ZGRJ, 12a. See ZGRJ.
KR = Kagurauta. See Kodai Kayō Shū.
KSKW = Ki no Shishō Kyokusuien Waka. See Ki no Shishō Kyokusuien Waka.
KST = Kanshi Taikan. Kanshi Taikan (Seki Shoin, 1936-39; rpt. Ōtori Shuppan,
    1974). Edited by Saku Setsu. 5 vols.

Kuang-yün. Hu-chu Chiao-cheng Sung-pen Kuang-yin (Taipei: Lien-kuan Ch'u-pan-she, 1975). Edited by Yü Nai-yung.

Kyōgen, Torahiro Manuscript. Nō, Kyōgen; Iwanami Bunko (Iwanami Shoten, 1942-45). Edited by Sasano Ken. 3 vols.

Liang Chien-wen-ti Chi. See *Chien-wen-ti Chi.*

Liang Yüan-ti Chi. See *Yüan-ti Chi.*

Li Chi. Li Chi; SCC, 5. See *SCC.*

Lieh-hsien Chuan. Lieh-hsien Chuan; Ts'ung-shu Chi-ch'eng, 326. See *Ts'ung-shu Chi-ch'eng.*

Ling-chai Yüeh-hua. Ling-chai Yüeh-hua; Ts'ung-shu Chi-ch'eng, 481. See *Ts'ung-shu Chi-ch'eng.*

Li T'ai-po Shih-chi. See *Rishi.*

Makura no Sōshi [MSS]. Makura no Sōshi; NKBT, 19 (1958). Edited by Ikegami Shinji.

*Man'yōshū [MYS]. Man'yōshū, Yakubunhen (Hanawa Shobō, 1972). Edited by Satake Akihiro, Kinoshita Masatoshi, and Kojima Noriyuki.

Meigō Ōrai. See *Unshū Shōsoku.*

Midō Kampaku Ki. Midō Kampaku Ki; Dai Nihon Kokiroku (Iwanami Shoten, 1952-54). Edited by the Data Editing Office, Tokyo University. 3 vols.

Mitsune Shū. Mitsune Shū; SKST, 1:29. See *SKST.*

MMS = Mumyōshō. See *Karon Shū.*

MMSS = Mumyō Sōshi. See *Mumyō Sōshi.*

Montoku Jitsuroku. Montoku Jitsuroku; SZKT, 3 (1934).

MSN = Murasaki Shikibu Nikki. See *Murasaki Shikibu Nikki.*

MSS = Makura no Sōshi. See *Makura no Sōshi.*

Mumyōshō [MMS]. See *Karon Shū.*

Mumyō Sōshi [MMSS]. Mumyō Sōshi; SNKS (1976). Edited by Kuwabara Hiroshi. See *SNKS.*

Murasaki Shikibu Nikki [MSN]. Murasaki Shikibu Nikki; NKBT, 19 (1958). Edited by Ikeda Kikan and Akiyama Ken.

Murasaki Shikibu Shū. Murasaki Shikibu Shū; SKST, 1:154. See *SKST.*

MYS = Man'yōshū. See *Man'yōshū.*

Nakamurabon Yowa no Nezame. Yowa no Nezame Monogatari (Koten Bunko, 1954-55). Edited by Kaneko Takeo. 2 vols.

NGJK = Nittō Guhō Junrei Kōki. See *Nittō Guhō Junrei Kōki.*

NGK = Nihon Goki. See *Nihon Goki.*

Nihon Goki [NGK]. Nihon Goki; SZKT, 3 (1934).

Nihongi Kyōen Waka. Nihongi Kyōen Waka; ZGRJ, 15a. See *ZGRJ.*

Nihon Kiryaku [NKR]. Nihon Kiryaku; SZKT, 10-11 (1929).

Nihonkoku Genzaisho Mokuroku. Nihonkoku Genzaisho Mokuroku (Koten Hozonkai, 1925). Reproduction of the 14th-century manuscript.

Nihon Ōjō Gokuraku Ki. Ōjōden; Nihon Shisō Taikei, 7 (Iwanami Shoten, 1974). Edited by Inoue Mitsusada and Ōsone Shōsuke.

Nihon Ryōiki [NRK]. Nihon Ryōiki; NKBT, 70 (1967). Edited by Endō Yoshimoto.

Nihon Shoki. Nihon Shoki; SZKT, 1 (Yoshikawa Kōbunkan, 1951). Edited by Kuroita Katsumi.

Nittō Guhō Junrei Kōki [NGJK]. Nittō Guhō Junrei Kōki; Dai Nihon Bukkyō Zensho, 72 (Suzuki Gakujitsu Zaidan, 1972).

Nittō Shingu Shōgyō Mokuroku. Nittō Shingu Shōgyō Mokuroku; TSDK, 55. See *TSDK.*

NKBT = *Nihon Koten Bungaku Taikei* (Iwanami Shoten, 1957-67). Edited by Takagi Ichinosuke et al. 100 vols. See the headnote to this bibliography.

NKGT = *Nihon Kagaku Taikei*. *Nihon Kagaku Taikei* (Bummeisha and Kazama Shobō, 1940-81). Edited by Sasaki Nobutsuna, Kyūsojin Hitaku, and Higuchi Yoshimaro. 15 vols.

NKR = *Nihon Kiryaku*. See *Nihon Kiryaku*.

Nomori no Kagami. *Nomori no Kagami; NKGT*, 4. See *NKGT*.

NRK = *Nihon Ryōiki*. See *Nihon Ryōiki*.

Ō I. *Ō Yūjō Shū [= Wang Yu-ch'eng Chi]*. *Ō Yūjō Shū; KST*, 2. See *KST*.

Ochikubo Monogatari. *Ochikubo Monogatari; NKBT*, 13 (1957). Edited by Matsuo Satoshi.

OCS = *Ōe no Chisato Shū*. See *Ōe no Chisato Shū*.

Ōe no Chisato Shū [OCS]. "Ōe no Chisato Shū," *Heian Jidai Bungaku to Hakushi Monjū: Kudai Waka, Senzai Kaku Kenkyūhen*. See Kaneko, 1943.

Ōjō Yōshū. Genshin; *Nihon Shisō Taikei*, 6 (Iwanami Shoten, 1970). Edited by Ishida Mizumaro.

OK = *Ōkagami*. See *Ōkagami*.

Ōkagami [OK]. *Ōkagami; NKBT*, 21 (1960). Edited by Matsumura Hiroshi.

Pan Lan-t'ai Chi. *Pan Lan-t'ai Chi; HLPMC*, 1. See *HLPMC*.

Pen-shi Shih. *Pen-shi Shih; Tzeng-pu Chin-tai Pi-shu*, 7 (Kyoto: Chūbun Shuppansha, 1980). Reproduction of original Chinese version.

Po Hsiang-shan Shih-chi [PSC]. See *Haku Kōzan Shishū*.

Po-shih Ch'ang-ch'ing Chi. *Po-shih Ch'ang-ch'ing Chi* (Peking: Wen-hsüeh Kuchi K'an-hsing-she, 1955). Reproduction of Sung publication.

PSC = *Po Hsiang-shan Shih-chi*. See *Haku Kōzan Shishū*.

Rengaron Shū. *Rengaron Shū; NKBT*, 66 (1961). Edited by Kidō Saizō.

RH = *Ryōjin Hishō*. See *Ryōjin Hishō*.

Rishi. *Ri Taihaku Shishū [= Li T'ai-po Shih-chi]; KST*, 1. See *KST*.

RK = *Ruiju Kokushi*. See *Ruiju Kokushi*.

Rōko Shiiki. "Rōko Shiiki, Sangō Shiiki Ichiranhyō," *Sangō Shiiki*. See *Sangō Shiiki*.

Roppyakuban Utaawase. *Shinkō Roppyakuban Utaawase* (Yūseidō, 1976). Edited by Konishi Jin'ichi.

Ruiju Kokushi [RK]. *Ruiju Kokushi; SZKT*, 5-6 (1933).

Ruiju Meibutsu Kō. *Ruiju Meibutsu Kō* (Kondō Keizō, 1904; rpt. Rekishi Toshosha, 1974).

Ruiju Utaawase Maki. *Sanshū Ruiju Utaawase to Sono Kenkyū* (Bijitsu Shoin, 1945). Edited by Horibe Seiji.

RUSS = *Ryōun Shinshū*. See *Ryōun Shinshū*.

*Ryōjin Hishō [RH]. *Ryōjin Hishō; Iwanami Bunko* (Iwanami Shoten, 1933; rev. ed., 1957). Edited by Sasaki Nobutsuna. 1957 edition used.

Ryō no Gige. *Ryō no Gige; SZKT*, 22 (1939).

Ryōun Shinshū [RUSS]. *Ryōun Shinshū; SGRJ*, 6 (1931). Edited by Hanami Sakumi.

Sagoromo Monogatari [SGM]. *Sagoromo Monogatari; NKBT*, 79 (1965). Edited by Mitani Eiichi and Sekine Yoshiko.

*Saibara [SBR]. See *Kodai Kayō Shū*.

*Saikū Nyōgo Shū. *Saikū Nyōgo; SKST*, 1:96. See *SKST*.

Sambōe. *Shohon Taishō Sambōe Shūsei* (Kasama Shoin, 1980). Edited by Koizumi Hiroshi and Takahashi Nobuyuki.

Samguk Sagi. Samguk Sagi (Seoul: Chikazawa Shoten, 1928). Edited by Imanishi Ryū. Rev. ed. by Suematsu Yasukazu, 1941 (rpt. of 1941 ed.; Kokusho Kankōkai, 1971). 1971 edition used.

Samhansi Kugam. Samhansi Kugam (Seoul: Iu Chulp'ansa, 1980). Reproduction of 1556 publication.

Sandai Jitsuroku [SJ]. Sandai Jitsuroku; SZKT, 4 (1934).

Sangō Shiiki [SGSK]. Sangō Shiiki; NKBT, 71 (1965). Edited by Watanabe Shōkō and Miyasaka Yūshō.

Sarashina Nikki [SSN]. Sarashina Nikki; NKBT, 20 (1951). Edited by Nishishita Kyōichi.

Sasamegoto. See *Rengaron Shū.*

SBR = Saibara. See *Kodai Kayō Shū.*

SCC = Shih-san Ching Chü-shu. Shih-san Ching Chü-shu (Taipei: I-wen Yin-shukuan, 1976).

Seireishū [SRS]. Seireishū; NKBT, 71 (1965). Edited by Watanabe Shōkō and Miyasaka Yūshō.

Seireishū Shiki. Seireishū Shiki; Shingonshū Zensho (Kōya: Shingonshū Zensho Kankōkai, 1936).

*Senzaishū. Senzaiwakashū (Kasama Shoin, 1969). Edited by Kubota Jun and Matsuno Yōichi.

SGM = Sagoromo Monogatari. See *Sagoromo Monogatari.*

SGRJ = Shinkō Gunsho Ruijū. See the headnote to this bibliography.

SGSK = Sangō Shiiki. See *Sangō Shiiki.*

Shasekishū. Shasekishū; NKBT, 85 (1966). Edited by Watanabe Tsunaya.

Shih Chi. Shih Chi (Peking: Chung-hua Shu-chü, 1959).

Shih Ching. Shih Ching; SCC, 2. See *SCC.*

Shih-chou Chi. Hai-nei Shih-chou Chi; Lung-wei Pi-shu, 1 (Taipei: Hsin-hsing Shu-chü, 1972).

Shin Sarugaku Ki. Shin Sarugaku Ki; SGRJ, 6 (1931). Edited by Hanami Sakumi.

Shinsen Man'yōshū. 1. *Shinsen Man'yōshū to Kenkyū* (Toyohashi: Mikan Kokubun Shiryō Kankōkai, 1958). 2. *Shinsen Man'yōshū: Heian Wakasō* (Fukuoka: Nishi Nihon Kokugo Kokubun Gakkai, 1962). Edited by Noguchi Motohiro. 3. *Shinsen Man'yōshū: Kyōto Daigaku Kokugo Kokubun Shiryō Sōsho* (Kyoto: Rinsen Shoten, 1979). Edited by Asami Tōru.

*Shinsen Waka(shū). "Kōchū *Shinsen Wakashū,*" *Kokinshū Igo ni Okeru Tsurayuki* (Ōfūsha, 1980). Edited by Kikuchi Yasuhiko.

Shinsen Zuinō. See *Karon Shū.*

Shoku Nihongi [SNG]. Shoku Nihongi; SZKT, 2 (1935).

Shoku Nihon Goki [SNGK]. Shoku Nihon Goki; SZKT, 3 (1934).

Shōmon Ki. Shōmon Ki (Gendai Shichōsha, 1975). Edited by Hayashi Rikurō.

Shōyūki [SYK]. Shōyūki; Dai Nihon Kokiroku (Iwanami Shoten, 1959-82). Edited by the Data Editing Office, Tokyo University. 10 vols.

Shūgyokushū. Kōhon Shūgyokushū (Yoshikawa Kōbunkan, 1971). Edited by Taga Sōshun.

Shūishō. Shūishō, Kōhon to Kenkyū (Kyoto: Daigakudō Shoten, 1977). Edited by Katagiri Yōichi et al.

Shūishū [SIS]. Shūishū no Kenkyū (Kyoto: Daigakudō Shoten, 1970-76). Edited by Katagiri Yōichi. 2 vols.

Shumpi Shō. Shunrai Zuinō; NKGT, 1. See *NKGT.*

SIS = Shūishū. See *Shūishū.*

SJ = Sandai Jitsuroku. See *Sandai Jitsuroku*.

SKST = Shikashū Taisei. *Shikashū Taisei* (Meiji Shoin, 1973-76). Edited by Wakashi Kenkyūkai. 8 vols.

SNG = Shoku Nihongi. See *Shoku Nihongi*.

SNGK = Shoku Nihon Goki. See *Shoku Nihon Goki*.

SNKS = Shinchō Nihon Koten Shūsei. *Shinchō Nihon Koten Shūsei* (Shinchōsha, 1976—). 100+ vols.

Sompi Bummyaku. *Sompi Bummyaku*; SZKT, 4 vols. (1957-64).

Sōtan Shū [STS]. *Sone no Yoshitada Shū no Kohon Sōsakuin* (Kasama Shoin, 1973). Edited by Kansaku Kōichi.

SRS = Seireishū. See *Seireishū*.

SSN = Sarashina Nikki. See *Sarashina Nikki*.

STS = Sōtan Shū. See *Sōtan Shū*.

Sui Shu. *Sui Shu* (Peking: Chung-hua Shu-chü, 1973).

Sui Yang-ti Chi. See *Yang-ti Chi*.

Suzakuin Ominaeshiawase. *Suzakuin Ominaeshiawase*; HCUT, 1. See *HCUT*.

SYK = Shōyūki. See *Shōyūki*.

SZKT = Shintei Zōho Kokushi Taikei (Yoshikawa Kōbunkan, 1929-66). Edited by Kuroita Katsumi et al. 66 vols. See the headnote to this bibliography.

Taedong Sisŏn. *Taedong Sisŏn* (Seoul: Cho Lyong-sŭng, 1978).

Takamitsu Nikki. See *Tannomine Shōshō Monogatari*.

Takamura Monogatari. *Takamura Monogatari*; NKBT, 77 (1964). Edited by Endō Yoshimoto.

Taketori Monogatari. *Taketori Monogatari*; SNKS (1979). Edited by Noguchi Motohiro. See *SNKS*.

Tama no Ogushi. *Genji Monogatari Tama no Ogushi*; *Motoori Norinaga Zenshū*, 4 (Chikuma Shobō, 1967). Edited by Ōno Susumu.

Tannomine Shōshō Monogatari. *Tannomine Shōshō Monogatari: Hommon oyobi Sōsakuin* (Kasama Shoin, 1972). Edited by Kokubo Takaaki.

T'ang-Sung Ch'uan-ch'i Chi [TSCC]. *T'ang-Sung Ch'uan-ch'i Chi* (Peking: Wenhsüeh Ku-chi K'an-hsing-she, 1956); rpt. in *Lu Hsün Ch'üan-chi*, 10 (Peking: Jen-min Wen-hsüeh Ch'u-pan-she, 1973). 1973 edition used.

T'ang-Sung Pa-chia-wen. *Teihon Tō-Sō Hakkabun Tokuhon* (Taimeidō, 1932). Edited by Ikeda Roshū. 2 vols.

T'ao Peng-tzu Chi. *T'ao Peng-tzu Chi*; HLPMC, 3. See *HLPMC*.

T'ao Yüan-ming Shih-chi. See *Tōshi*.

TCM = Tsutsumi Chūnagon Monogatari. See *Tsutsumi Chūnagon Monogatari*.

Teiji In Utaawase [TJI]. See *Utaawase Shū*.

Tendai Daishi Wasan. *Nihon Kayō Shūsei*, 4 (Tōkyōdō, 1960). Edited by Takano Tatsuyuki.

Tentoku Utaawase [TTU]. See *Utaawase Shū*.

TJI = Teiji In Utaawase. See *Utaawase Shū*.

To Shōryō Shishū [TSS]. *To Shōryō Shishū [= Tu Shao-ling Shih-chi]*; KST, 2. See *KST*.

Tōdaiji Yōroku. *Tōdaiji Yōroku* (Osaka: Zenkoku Shobō, 1944). Edited by Tsutsui Eishun. (Reproduced by Kokusho Kankōkai, 1971.)

Torahirobon Kyōgen Shū. See *Kyōgen, Torahiro Manuscript*.

Tosa Nikki [TSN]. *Tosa Nikki*; NKBT, 20 (1957). Edited by Suzuki Tomotarō.

Tōshi = Tō Emmei Shishū. *Tō Emmei Shishū [= T'ao Yüan-ming Shih-chi]*; KST, 1. See *KST*.

Toshi Bunshū. Toshi Bunshū; SGRJ, 6 (Naigai Shoseki, 1931). Edited by Hanami Sakumi.

Tsa-tsuan. "Kōhon *Gisan Zassan* to Tsūshaku," *Makura no Sōshi Ron*. See Mekada, 1975.

TSCC = T'ang-Sung Ch'uan-ch'i Chi. See *T'ang-Sung Ch'uan-ch'i Chi*.

TSDK = Taishō Shinshū Daizōkyō. Taishō Shinshū Daizōkyō (Taishō Issaikyō Kankōkai, 1924-34). Edited by Takakusu Junjirō et al. 100 vols.

TSN = Tosa Nikki. See *Tosa Nikki*.

TSS = To Shōryō Shishū. See *To Shōryō Shishū*.

Ts'ung-shu Chi-ch'eng. Ts'ung-shu Chi-ch'eng (Shanghai: Shang-wu Yin-shu-kuan, 1935-37). Edited by Wang Yüng-wu et al. 516 vols.

Tsurayuki Shū [TYS]. Ki no Tsurayuki Zenkashū Sōsakuin (Kyoto: Daigakudō Shoten, 1968). Edited by Katagiri Yōichi et al.

Tsurezuregusa. Tsurezuregusa; Nihon Koten Zensho (Asahi Shimbunsha, 1947). Edited by Tachibana Jun'ichi.

Tsutsumi Chūnagon Monogatari [TCM]. Tsutsumi Chūnagon Monogatari; NKBT, 13 (1957). Edited by Teramoto Naohiko.

TTU = Tentoku Utaawase. See *Utaawase Shū*.

Tu Shao-ling Shih-chi. See *To Shōryō Shishū*.

TYS = Tsurayuki Shū. See *Tsurayuki Shū*.

UAS = Utaawase Shū. See *Utaawase Shū*.

Ubuginu. Kaishū Ubuginu; Renga Hōshiki Kōyō (Iwanami Shoten, 1936). Edited by Yamada Yoshio and Hoshika Muneichi.

Uji Shūi Monogatari. Uji Shūi Monogatari; NKBT, 27 (1960). Edited by Watanabe Tsunaya and Nishio Kōichi.

UM = Utsuho Monogatari. See *Utsuho Monogatari*.

Unshū Shōsoku. Unshū Shōsoku; SGRJ, 6 (1931). Edited by Hanami Sakumi.

Utaawase Shū [UAS]. Utaawase Shū; NKBT, 74 (1965). Edited by Hagitani Boku and Taniyama Shigeru.

Utsuho Monogatari [UM]. Utsuho Monogatari, Hommon to Sakuin (Kasama Shoin, 1973). Edited by the *Utsuho Monogatari* Kenkyūkai.

Waka Kubon. See *Karon Shū*.

Wakan Rōeishū [WRS]. Kōi Wakan Rōeishū (Kyoto: Daigakudō Shoten, 1981). Edited by Horibe Seiji. Supplement edited by Katagiri Yōichi.

Wakatei Jusshu. Wakatei Jusshu; NKGT, 1. See *NKGT*.

Wang Yu-ch'eng Chi. See *Ō I*.

Wen Hsüan [WH]. Wen Hsüan (Hong Kong: Shang-wu Yin-shu-kuan Fen-kuan, 1936).

WH = Wen Hsüan. See *Wen Hsüan*.

WRS = Wakan Rōeishū. See *Wakan Rōeishū*.

Yamato Monogatari [YM]. Yamato Monogatari; NKBT, 9 (1957). Edited by Abe Toshiko and Imai Gen'e.

Yang-ti Chi. Sui Yang-ti Chi; HLPMC, 6. See *HLPMC*.

YC = Yü K'ai-fu Chi. See *Yü K'ai-fu Chi*.

Ying-ying Chuan. See *T'ang-Sung Ch'uan-ch'i Chi*.

YM = Yamato Monogatari. See *Yamato Monogatari*.

YN = Yowa no Nezame. See *Yowa no Nezame*.

Yowa no Nezame [YN]. Yoru no Nezame; NKBT, 78 (1964). Edited by Sakakura Atsuyoshi.

Yüan-ti Chi. Liang Yüan-ti Chi; HLPMC, 5. See *HLPMC*.

Yüeh-fu Shih-chi. Yüeh-fu Shih-chi (Peking: Chung-hua Shu-chü, 1979).

Yu Hsien-k'u. See *Yüsenkutsu.*

**Yuishimbō Shū. Yuishimbō Shū; SKST*, 3:8. See *SKST.*

Yü K'ai-fu Chi [YC]. Yü K'ai-fu Chi; HLPMC, 6. See *HLPMC.*

Yü-p'ien. Yü-p'ien; Tse-ts'un-t'ang Wu-chung (Shanghai: P'ei-ying-kuan, 1888).

Yüsenkutsu [= Yu Hsien-k'u]. Kan'yaku Yüsenkutsu (Tsuka Shobō, 1948). Edited by Ogaeri Yoshio.

Yü-t'ai Hsin-yung. See *Gyokudai Shin'ei.*

Zeami Shū. Zeami; Nihon Shisō Taikei, 24 (Iwanami Shoten, 1971). Edited by Omote Akira.

Zentō Shiitsu. See *Ch'üan T'ang-shih.*

ZGRJ = Zoku Gunsho Ruijū. Zoku Gunsho Ruijū (Zoku Gunsho Ruijū Kansei-kai, 1902-28). 70 vols.

Zōki Hōshi Shū. Ionushi, Hommon oyobi Sakuin (Hakuteisha, 1971). Edited by Masubuchi Katsuichi.

B. STUDIES PUBLISHED IN JAPANESE

ABE Akio
  1939   "*Genji Monogatari* Shippitsu no Junjo," *Kokugo to Kokubungaku* 16, nos. 8-9 (1939).
  1959   *Genji Monogatari Josetsu* (Tokyo Daigaku Shuppankai, 1959).

ABE Toshiko
  1954   *Kōhon Yamato Monogatari to Sono Kenkyū* (Sanseidō, 1954; revised and supplemented in 1970). 1970 edition used.
  1969   *Utamonogatari to Sono Shūhen* (Kazama Shobō, 1969).

AOKI Masaru
  1935a   "Shina no Shizenkan," *Iwanami Kōza Tōyō Shisō* (Iwanami Shoten, 1935). Retitled "Shinajin no Shizenkan" and republished in *Shina Bungaku Geijitsu Kō* (Kyoto: Kōbundō, 1942). Republished in *Aoki Masaru Zenshū*, vol. 2 (Shunjūsha, 1970). 1970 edition used.

ARAKI Hiroyuki
  1982   "Kishu Ryūridan no Kōzō," a paper read at the seminar on "Japanese Literary Theory and Practice," at the Woodrow Wilson Center for International Studies, Washington, D.C., April 1982.

ASANO Kenji
  1953   "Kyō Murasakino Imamiya Chinkasaika ni Tsuite," *Yamagata Daigaku Kiyō: Jimbun Kagaku* 2, no. 2 (1953).

FUJII Kiyoshi
  1966   *Man'yōshū Ikoku Fūbutsushi* (Bunri Shoin, 1966).

FUJITA Tokutarō
  1930   "*Kinkafu* oyobi Kehi Kitamikado no Kagurauta ni Tsuite," *Kokoro no Hana* 34, nos. 1-5 (1930); republished in *Kodai Kayō no Kenkyū* (Kinseidō, 1934). 1934 edition used.

FUKUI Kyūzō
  1948   *Inu Tsukuba Shū: Kenkyū to Kōhon* (Chikuma Shobō, 1948).

HANABUSA Hideki
  1960   *Hakushi Monjū no Hihanteki Kenkyū* (Kyoto: Ibundō, 1960).
  1971   *Haku Kyoi Kenkyū* (Sekai Shisōsha, 1971).

HASHIMOTO Shinkichi
  1934   "*Renchūshō* no Ichi Ihon, Shirozōshi ni Tsuite," *Kokugo to Kokubun-*

gaku 11, no. 5 (1934). Republished in *Denki, Tenseki Kenkyū: Hashimoto Shinkichi Hakushi Chosakushū*, vol. 12 (Iwanami Shoten, 1972). 1972 edition used.

HAYASHI Kazuhiko
1964   *Makura no Sōshi no Kenkyū* (Yūbun Shoin, 1964).

HAYASHI Kenzō
1959   "Saibara ni Okeru Hyōshi to Kashi no Rizumu ni Tsuite," *Nara Gakugei Daigaku Kiyō* 8, no. 1 (1959).
1960   "*Hakuga Tekifu Kō*," *Nara Gakugei Daigaku Kiyō* 9, no. 1 (1960).

HAYASHIYA Tatsusaburō
1960   *Chūsei Geinōshi no Kenkyū: Kodai kara no Keishō to Sōzō* (Iwanami Shoten, 1960).

HAZAMA Tetsurō
1962   "Mibu no Tadamine Sen *Wakatei Jusshu* o Utagau," *Kashiigata*, no. 8 (1962).

HIROKAWA Yōichi
1975   *Heshiodosu Kenkyū Josetsu: Girisha Shisō no Seitan* (Miraisha, 1975).

HORIBE Seiji
1942   "*Sakurabito, Samushiro, Sumori Kō*," *Kokugo Kokubun* 12, no. 3 (1942). Republished in *Chūko Nihon Bungaku no Kenkyū: Shiryō to Jisshō* (Kyōiku Tosho, 1943). 1943 edition used.
1943   "San'itsu Ko Monogatari Zakki: *Hakoya no Toji Monogatari* to *Komano no Monogatari*." Original monograph not available; *Chūko Nihon Bungaku no Kenkyū* used.

HOSAKA Hiroshi
1979   *Ōkagami Kenkyū Josetsu* (Kōdansha, 1979).

IKEDA Kikan
1932   "*Makura no Sōshi* no Keitai ni Kansuru Ichikōsatsu," *Iwanami Kōza Nihon Bungaku* (Iwanami Shoten, 1932).
1938   "*Makura no Sōshi* no Genkei to Sono Seiritsu Nendai," *Kokugo* 3, no. 3 (1938).
1956   *Genji Monogatari Taisei: Kenkyūhen, Shiryōhen* (Chūō Kōronsha, 1956).

INAGA Keiji
1967   *Genji Monogatari no Kenkyū* (Kazama Shoin, 1967).

ISHIGAMI Gen'ichirō
1979   "Nitobe Inazō," *Kokusai Kōryū* 5, no. 4 (1979).

ISHIMODA Tadashi
1943   "*Utsuho Monogatari* ni Tsuite no Oboegaki," *Rekishigaku Kenkyū*, nos. 115-116 (1943).

ISHIMURA Shōji
1955-56   "*Murasaki Shikibu Nikki* no Genkei to Genson Keitai," *Kokugo* 4, nos. 1 and 4 (1955-56).

ITŌ Hiroshi
1976   *Kagerō Nikki Kenkyū Josetsu* (Kazama Shoin, 1976).

KANDA Hideo
1937   "Onsūritsu no Kaku o Nasu Sosū Keiretsu no Sonzai ni Tsuite," *Kokugo to Kokubungaku* 14, no. 2 (1937).

KANDA Kiichirō
1965-67   *Nihon ni Okeru Chūgoku Bungaku: Nihon Tenshi Shiwa* (Jigensha, 1965 and 1967). 2 vols.

KANEKO Hikojirō
1942 "*Hōjōki* to Shina Bungaku to no Kankei ni Tsuite no Kenkyū: Shū to Shite Haku Rakuten Shibun to no Kankei," *Teikoku Gakushiin Kiyō* 1, no. 1 (1942).
1943 *Heian Jidai Bungaku to Hakushi Monjū: Kudai Waka, Senzai Kaku Kenkyūhen* (Baifūkan, 1943; revised in 1955; reprinted by Geirinsha in 1977). 1955 edition used.

KANSAKU Kōichi
1958-66-73 "*Utsuho Monogatari* Kenkyū Bunken Mokuroku." See *UMKK* [this section], 1958-66-73.

KASUGA Masaji
1936 "Wakan no Konkō," *Kokugo Kokubun* 6, no. 10 (1936). Republished in *Kokunten no Kenkyū* (Kazama Shobō, 1964). 1964 edition used.
1943 *Saidaiji-bon Konkōmyō Saishōōkyō Koten no Kokugogaku-teki Kenkyū* (Fukuoka: Shidō Bunko, 1943). 2 vols. Reproduced in 1 vol. by Benseisha, 1969.

KATAGIRI Yōichi
1956 "Gosen Wakashū no Honsei," *Kokugo Kokubun* 25, no. 2 (1956).
1968-69 *Ise Monogatari no Kenkyū* (Meiji Shoin, 1968-69). 2 vols.

KATAYAMA Tetsu
1956 *Taishū Shijin Haku Rakuten: Iwanami Shinsho*, no. 261 (Iwanami Shoten, 1956).

KATŌ Seishin
1935 *Kōbō Daishi Sangō Shiiki: Iwanami Bunko* (Iwanami Shoten, 1935).

KAWAGUCHI Hisao
1951-59 *Heianchō Nihon Kambungakushi no Kenkyū* (Meiji Shoin, 1951-59). 2 vols. Revised in 1964, 1 vol. 1964 edition used.

KAWAKITA Noboru
1961 "Eiga Monogatari no Tokushoku to Shudai no Nigensei," *Gengo to Bungei* 3, no. 3 (1961). Republished in *Eiga Monogatari Kenkyū* (Ōfūsha, 1968). 1968 edition used.
1972 "*Eiga Monogatari* no Kyokō to Sono Tokushitsu: Maki 12, 'Tama no Muragiku' o Rei to Shite," *Chūko Bungaku*, no. 9 (1972). Republished in *Eiga Monogatari Ronkō* (Ōfūsha, 1973). 1973 edition used.

KAZAMAKI Keijirō
1950-56 "Genji Monogatari no Seiritsu ni Kansuru Shiron" (7 articles published from 1950 to 1956 in different periodicals); collected in *Nihon Bungakushi no Kenkyū*, vol. 2 (Kadokawa Shoten, 1961); republished in *Kazamaki Keijirō Zenshū*, vol. 4 (Ōfūsha, 1969). 1969 edition used.

KIM Sa-yŏp
1973 *Chōsen Bungakushi* (Kanazawa Bunko, 1973).

KISHIBE Shigeo
1960-61 *Tōdai Ongaku no Rekishiteki Kenkyū: Gakuseihen* (Tokyo Daigaku Shuppankai, 1960-61).

KISHIGAMI Shinji
1970 *Makura no Sōshi Kenkyū* (Ōhara Shinseisha, 1970).

KŌCHIYAMA Kiyohiko
1980 *Murasaki Shikibu Shū, Murasaki Shikibu Nikki no Kenkyū* (Ōfūsha, 1980).

KOJIMA Noriyuki
1951 "Kodai Kayō," *Nihon Bungaku Kōza*, no. 1 (Kawade Shobō, 1951).

1962-64-65   *Jōdai Nihon Bungaku to Chūgoku Bungaku* (Hanawa Shobō, 1962-64-65). 3 vols.
1968-73-79   *Kokufū Ankoku Jidai no Bungaku* (Hanawa Shobō, 1968-73-79). Not yet completed.

KOMATSU Shigemi
1971   "*Genji Monogatari Emaki* no Seisaku Nendai: Kotobagaki no Tachiba kara." An introduction to the reproduction of *Genji Monogatari Emaki* (Kōdansha, 1971).

KOMATSU Tomi
1971   "Hinomiya Kō," *Atomi Gakuen Tanki Daigaku Kiyō*, nos. 7-8 (1971).
1980   *Izumi Shikibu Nikki Zenyakuchū*, *Gakujitsu Bunko*, vol. 1 (Kōdansha, 1980).

KONISHI Jin'ichi
1938   "Imayō no Keishiki," *Kokugo* 3, no. 4 (1938).
1941   *Ryōjin Hishō Kō* (Sanseidō, 1941).
1948-51a-53d   *Bunkyō Hifuron Kō*, 3 vols. (Vol. 1: Oyashima Shuppan, 1948. Vol. 2: Kōdansha, 1951. Vol. 3: Kōdansha, 1953).
1949a   *Kokin Wakashū: Shinchū Kokubungaku Sōsho* (Kōdansha, 1949).
1951b   *Tosa Nikki Hyōkai* (Yūseidō, 1951).
1953b   "Chūsei ni Okeru Hyōgensha to Kyōjusha," *Bungaku* 21, no. 5 (1953).
1953c   "Yōembi: Bantōshi to no Kōsho," *Kokugo Kokubun* 22, no. 7 (1953).
1954a   "Toshikage no Maki Shiken," *Kokugo Kokubun* 23, no. 1 (1954).
1954b-55a   "*Utsuho Monogatari* no Kōsei to Seiritsu Katei," *Nihon Gakushiin Kiyō* 12, no. 3, and 13, no. 1 (1954-55). Republished in *Heianchō Monogatari, II: Nihon Bungaku Kenkyū Shiryō Sōsho* (Yūseidō, 1974). 1974 edition used.
1955b   "Izure no Ōntoki ni ka," *Kokugo to Kokubungaku* 32, no. 3 (1955).
1956   "Michi no Keisei to Kairitsuteki Sekai," *Kokugakuin Zasshi* 57, no. 5 (1956).
1960   "Furu *Utsuho* to Ima *Utsuho*," *Gengo to Bungei* 2, no. 4 (1960).
1961   *Nōgakuron Kenkyū* (Hanawa Shobō, 1961).
1962b   "Nō no Keisei to Tenkai," *Nō Kyōgen Meisakushū; Koten Nihon Bungaku Zenshū*, vol. 20 (Chikuma Shobō, 1962).
1965   "*Genji Monogatari* no Imagery," *Kaishaku to Kanshō* 30, no. 7 (1965).
1968   "Ku no Sekai no Hitotachi: *Genji Monogatari* Dainibu no Jimbutsuzō," *Gengo to Bungei* 10, no. 6 (1968).
1971a   "*Genji Monogatari* no Shinri Byōsha," *Genji Monogatari Kōza*, no. 7 (Yūseidō, 1971).
1973   "Kūkai no Shibun," *Kokugo to Kokubungaku* 50, no. 10 (1973).
1975   "Tsurayuki Bannen no Kafū," *Bungaku* 43, no. 8 (1975).
1978   "Jo to Makurakotoba no Setsu," *Jōdai Bungaku Kōkyū* (Hanawa Shobō, 1978).
1982b   "Fūryū to Miyabi," *Kokubungaku* 27, no. 14 (1982).
1983b   "Kūkai no Bunshō Hyōgen." In *Bukkyō to Bunka*, ed. Department of Buddhism, Kōyasan University (Kyoto: Dōhōsha, 1983).

KOYAMA Shin'ichi
1928   "Daiei no Hattatsu," *Kokugo to Kokubungaku* 5, nos. 5-6 (1928).

KUWABARA Hiroshi
1967   *Chūsei Monogatari Kenkyū: Sumiyoshi Monogatari Ronkō* (Nigensha, 1967).

KUWABARA Takeo
1946 "Daini Geijitsu: Gendai Haiku ni Tsuite," *Sekai*, no. 11 (1946).

KYŪSOJIN Hitaku
1960a,b,c-61 *Kokin Wakashū Seiritsuron* (Kazama Shobō, 1960-61). 4 vols.

MASUDA Katsumi
1953 "Utagatari no Sekai," *Kikan Kokubun*, no. 4 (1953).

MASUDA Kiyohide
1975 *Gafu no Rekishiteki Kenkyū* (Sōbunsha, 1975).

MATSUDA Takeo
1965 *Kokinshū no Kōzō ni Kansuru Kenkyū* (Kazama Shobō, 1965).

MATSUMOTO Haruhisa
1969 *Ōkagami no Kōsei* (Ōfūsha, 1969).
1979 *Ōkagami no Shudai to Kōsō* (Kasama Shoin, 1979).

MATSUMURA Hiroshi
1956-60-67 *Eiga Monogatari no Kenkyū*, 3 vols. (Vol. 1: Tōkō Shoin, 1956. Vol. 2: Tōkō Shoin, 1960. Vol. 3: Ōfūsha, 1967).

MATSUO Satoshi
1939 "*Kakuremino no Monogatari*," *Bungei Bunka* 2, nos. 3-4 (1939). Republished in *Heian Jidai Monogatari no Kenkyū* (Tōkō Shobō, 1955). 1955 edition used.

MEKADA Sakuo
1975 *Makura no Sōshi Ron* (Kasama Shoin, 1975).
1979 *Ōkagami Ron: Kambungei Sakkaken ni Okeru Seiji Hihan no Keifu* (Kasama Shoin, 1979).

MISHIMA Yukio
1942 "*Ise Monogatari* no Koto," *Bungei Bunka* 5, no. 11 (1942).

MITANI Eiichi
1952 *Monogatari Bungakushiron* (Yūseidō, 1952).

MIURA Sukeyuki
1975 "Kichirikichiri Kō," *Seijō Bungei*, no. 75 (1975).

MIYOSHI Eiji
1944 *Kōhon Shūishō to Sono Kenkyū* (Sanseidō, 1944).

MOROHASHI Tetsuji
1955-60 *Dai Kanwa Jiten* (Taishūkan, 1955-60). 13 vols.

MURAKAMI Tetsumi
1980 *Kakyo no Hanashi: Shiken Seido to Bunjin Kanryō* (Kōdansha, 1980).

MURASE Toshio
1971 *Kokinshū no Kiban to Shūhen* (Ōfūsha, 1971).

NAGAI Kazuko
1960 "*Nezame* no Kōzō," *Heian Bungaku Kenkyū*, no. 25 (1960). Republished in *Nezame Monogatari no Kenkyū* (Kasama Shoin, 1968). 1968 edition used.

NAKAMURA Shin'ichirō
1957 *Ōchō no Bungaku: Shinchō Sōsho* (Shinchōsha, 1957). Republished as *Ōchō Bungaku Ron: Shinchō Bunko* (Shinchōsha, 1971). 1971 edition used.

NAKAMURA Yukihiko
1982 *Kinseiteki Hyōgen: Nakamura Yukihiko Chojutsushū*, vol. 2 (Chūō Kōronsha, 1982).

NAKANO Kōichi
1956 "*Utsuho Monogatari* no Seiritsu Nendai," *Kokubungaku Kenkyū*, no.

14 (1956); republished in *Monogatari Bungaku Ronkō* (Kyōiku Shuppan Center, 1971). 1971 edition used.

1964   "*Genji Monogatari* no Sōshiji to Monogatari Ondoku Ron," *Gakujitsu Kenkyū*, no. 13 (1964); republished in *Monogatari Bungaku Ronkō* (Kyōiku Shuppan Center, 1971). 1971 edition used.

NISHISHITA Kyōichi
1942   *Nihon Bungakushi*, vol. 4 (Sanseidō, 1942).

NOSE Asaji
1938   *Nōgaku Genryū Kō* (Iwanami Shoten, 1938).

OGAWA Tamaki
1958   *Tōshi Gaisetsu: Chūgoku Shijin Senshū*, supplementary volume (Iwanami Shoten, 1958).

OGI Mitsuo
1977   *Nihon Kodai Ongaku Shiron* (Yoshikawa Kōbunkan, 1977).

OKADA Masayuki
1929b   *Nihon Kambungakushi* (Kyōritsusha, 1929). Revised edition by Yamagishi Tokuhei and Nagasawa Kikuya (Yoshikawa Kōbunkan, 1954). 1954 edition used.

OKUMURA Tsuneya
1954   "*Kokinshū* no Seiritsu: Uda Tennō to Daigo Tennō," *Kokugo Kokubun* 23, no. 5 (1954).
1971   *Kokinshū, Gosenshū no Shomondai* (Kazama Shobō, 1971).

OKUNO Jun'ichi
1975   *Ise Jingū Shinkan Renga no Kenkyū* (Nihon Gakujitsu Shinkōkai, 1975).

ŌNISHI Yoshinori
1943   *Man'yōshū no Shizenkanjō* (Iwanami Shoten, 1934).
1948   *Shizen Kanjō no Ruikei* (Kaname Shobō, 1948).

OZAWA Masao
1961   *Kokinshū no Sekai* (Hanawa Shobō, 1961). Revised in 1976. 1976 edition used.
1963   "*Sakumon Daitai* no Kisoteki Kenkyū," *Setsurin*, no. 11 (1963).

SAEKI Arikiyo
1978   *Saigo no Ken Tō Shi: Gendai Shinsho*, no. 520 (Kōdansha, 1978).

SAKAKURA Atsuyoshi
1953   "Utamonogatari no Bunshō: 'Nan' no Kakarimusubi o Megutte," *Kokugo Kokubun* 22, no. 6 (1953).

SATŌ Takaaki
1970   *Gosen Wakashū no Kenkyū* (Nihon Gakujitsu Shinkōkai, 1970).

SEKINE-KOMATSU (SEKINE Yoshiko and KOMATSU Tomi)
1960   *Nezame Monogatari Zenshaku* (Gakutōsha, 1960). 2 vols. Enlarged and revised in 1972. 1972 edition used.

SHIDA Engi
1958   *Nihon Kayōkenshi* (Shibundō, 1958).

SHIMADA Ryōji
1969   "Kokinshū no Makurakotoba," *Jimbun Gakubu Kiyō*, no. 3 (1969). Republished in *Kokin Wakashū: Nihon Bungaku Kenkyū Shiryō Sōsho* (Yūseidō, 1976). 1976 edition used.

SHIMIZU Yoshiko
1966   *Genji Monogatari Ron* (Hanawa Shobō, 1966).
1976   "Byōbuuta Seisaku ni Tsuite no Kōsatsu," *Kokubungaku*, no. 53

(1976). Republished in *Genji Monogatari no Buntai to Hōhō* (Tokyo Daigaku Shuppankai, 1980). 1980 edition used.

SHIMMA Shin'ichi
1947   *Kayōshi no Kenkyū: Imayō Kō* (Shibundō, 1947).

SHIMODE Sekiyo
1975   *Dōkyō to Nihonjin, Gendai Shinsho*, no. 411 (Kōdansha, 1975).

SUGANO Hiroyuki
1978   "Michizane ni Okeru Wakashūteki Hyōgen ni Tsuite no Ichikōsatsu," *Wakayama Daigaku Kyōiku Gakubu Kiyō: Jimbun Kagaku*, no. 27 (1978).

SUZUKI Hiromichi
1968   *Heian Makki Monogatari Ron* (Hanawa Shobō, 1968).

SUZUKI Kazuo
1953-54   "*Haizumi, Kono Tsuide* o Megutte: Utamonogatari Keiretsu ni Tatsu Tsukurimonogatari ni Tsuite," *Kokugo* 2, no. 1, and 3, no. 2 (1953-54). Republished in *Tsutsumi Chūnagon Monogatari Josetsu* (Ōfūsha, 1980). 1980 edition used.
1969   "*Katano no Shōshō* o Megutte," *Gengo to Bungei* 11, no. 3 (1969). Republished in *Tsutsumi Chūnagon Monogatari Josetsu* (Ōfūsha, 1980). 1980 edition used.
1980   "*Tsutsumi Chūnagon Monogatari* Oboegaki," in *Tsutsumi Chūnagon Monogatari Josetsu* (Ōfūsha, 1980).

SUZUKI Torao
1936   *Fushi Taiyō* (Fuzambō, 1936).

TAKANO Taira
1970   *Shinsen Man'yōshū ni Kansuru Kisoteki Kenkyū* (Kazama Shobō, 1970).

TAKEDA Munetoshi
1954   *Genji Monogatari no Kenkyū* (Iwanami Shoten, 1954).

TAKEISHI Akio
1969   *Bukkyō Kayō no Kenkyū* (Ōfūsha, 1969).

TAMAGAMI Takuya
1940   "*Gengo* Seiritsukō: Kakuhitsu to Kahitsu to ni Tsuite no Ichikasetsu," *Kokugo Kokubun* 10, no. 4 (1940).
1943   "Mukashi Monogatari no Kōsei," *Kokugo Kokubun* 13, nos. 6, 8, 9 (1943). Republished in *Genji Monogatari Kenkyū: Genji Monogatari Hyōshaku*, Supplement 1 (Kadokawa Shoten, 1966). 1966 edition used.
1950   "Monogatari Ondokuron Josetsu: *Genji Monogatari* no Honsei, 1," *Kokugo Kokubun* 19, no. 3 (1950). Republished in *Genji Monogatari Kenkyū: Genji Monogatari Hyōshaku*, Supplement 1 (Kadokawa Shoten, 1966). 1966 edition used.
1953   "Byōbue to Uta to Monogatari to," *Kokugo Kokubun* 22, no. 1 (1953). Republished in *Genji Monogatari Kenkyū: Genji Monogatari Hyōshaku*, Supplement 1 (Kadokawa Shoten, 1966). 1966 edition used.
1955a   "*Genji Monogatari* no Dokusha," *Joshidai Kokubun*, no. 7 (1955). Republished in *Genji Monogatari Kenkyū: Genji Monogatari Hyōshaku*, Supplement 1 (Kadokawa Shoten, 1966). 1966 edition used.
1955b   " 'Kiritsubo' no Maki to 'Chōgonka' to Ise no Go," *Kokugo Kokubun*

24, no. 4 (1955). Republished in *Genji Monogatari Kenkyū: Genji Monogatari Hyōshaku*, Supplement 1 (Kadokawa Shoten, 1966). 1966 edition used.

TANAKA Jūtarō
1960   *Makura no Sōshi Hommon no Kenkyū* (Hatsune Shobō, 1960).

TAYA Raishun
1942   "Hikaru Genji no Sukuse," *Kokugo Kokubun* 12, no. 2 (1942). Republished in *Genji Monogatari no Shisō* (Kyoto: Hōzōkan, 1952). 1952 edition used.

TŌDŌ-KOBAYASHI (TŌDŌ Akiyasu and KOBAYASHI Hiroshi)
1971   *Onchū Inkyō Kōhon* (Mokujisha, 1971).

TOYOTA Minoru
1944   "Chūban Tōshi no Nikeikō," *Tōhō Gakuhō* 19, no. 1 (1944). Republished in *Tōshi Kenkyū* (Tenri: Yōtokusha, 1948). 1948 edition used.

TSUGITA Jun
1938   "Jōko no Shokubutsu Sūhai to Bungaku to no Kankei," *Kokugo to Kokubungaku* 15, no. 3 (1938).

TSUKISHIMA Hiroshi
1981   *Kana: Nihongo no Sekai*, vol. 5 (Chūō Kōronsha, 1981).

TSUKUDO Akemi
1955   "*Ochikubo Monogatari* no Seiritsu Katei," *Nihon Bungaku*, no. 5 (1955). Republished in *Heianchō Monogatari, 3: Nihon Bungaku Kenkyū Shiryō Sōsho* (Yūseidō, 1979). 1979 edition used.

TSUKUDO Reikan
1931   "Bukkyō Bungaku Kenkyū: Toku ni Hōgi no Bungaku ni Tsuite," *Iwanami Kōza: Nihon Bungaku* (Iwanami Shoten, 1931). Republished in *Tsukudo Reikan Chosakushū*, vol. 3 (Serika Shobō, 1976). 1976 edition used.

UEMURA Etsuko
1972   *Kagerō Nikki no Kenkyū* (Meiji Shoin, 1972).

UMENO Kimiko
1979   *En to Sono Shūhen: Heian Bungaku no Biteki Goi no Kenkyū* (Kasama Shoin, 1979).

UMKK (*Utsuho Monogatari* Kenkyūkai)
1958   *Utsuho Monogatari Shinron* (Koten Bunko, 1958).
1966   *Utsuho Monogatari Shinkō* (Koten Bunko, 1966).
1973   *Utsuho Monogatari Ronshū* (Koten Bunko, 1973).

USUDA Jingorō
1938   "Saibara no Seiritsu ni Kansuru Ichimen," *Kokubungaku Ronkyū*, no. 7 (1938).

WASHIYAMA Shigeo
1974   "*Utsuho Monogatari* Kenkyūshi Sobyō," *Heianchō Monogatari, 2: Nihon Bungaku Kenkyū Shiryō Sōsho* (Yūseidō, 1974).

WATSUJI Tetsurō
1922   "*Genji Monogatari* ni Tsuite," *Shisō*, no. 19 (1922). Republished in *Watsuji Tetsurō Zenshū*, vol. 4 (Iwanami Shoten, 1962). 1962 edition used.

YAMADA Yoshio
1934   *Genji Monogatari no Ongaku* (Hōbunkan, 1934).
1937   *Renga Gaisetsu* (Iwanami Shoten, 1937).
1948   "*Ki no Shishō Kyokusuien Waka* ni Tsuite," *Kokugo Kokubun* 17, no.

2 (1948). Republished in *Nihon Kagaku no Genryū* (Nihon Shoin, 1952). 1952 edition used.

1951   *Sambōe Ryakuchū* (Hōbunkan, 1951).

YAMAGISHI Tokuhei
1935   "Chūko Kambungakushi," *Kokugo Kokubungaku Kōza*, no. 16 (1935). Republished in *Nihon Kambungaku Kenkyū* (Yūseidō, 1972). 1972 edition used.

YAMANAKA Yutaka
1952   "*Eiga Monogatari* no Rekishisei to Monogatarisei," *Nihon Rekishi*, no. 48 (1952). Republished in *Rekishi Monogatari Seiritsu Josetsu* (Tokyo Daigaku Shuppankai, 1962). 1962 edition used.

1958   "*Eiga Monogatari* no Seiritsu Junjo ni Tsuite," *Nihon Gakushiin Kiyō* 16, no. 2 (1958). Republished in *Rekishi Monogatari Seiritsu Josetsu* (Tokyo Daigaku Shuppankai, 1962). 1962 edition used.

YAMANOI Motokiyo
1966   *Saibara Yakufu* (Iwanami Shoten, 1966).

YOSHIDA Kōichi
1957   "*Sagoromo Monogatari* Bōtō no Ichi-kōsatsu," *Bungaku Ronsō*, no. 9 (1957). Republished in *Izumi Shikibu Kenkyū*, vol. 1 (Koten Bunko, 1964).

1964-67   *Izumi Shikibu Kenkyū* (Koten Bunko, 1964-67). 2 vols.

YOSHIKAWA Kōjirō
1949   *Chūgoku Sambun Ron* (Kyoto: Kōbundō, 1949). Republished in *Yoshikawa Kōjirō Zenshū*, vol. 2 (Chikuma Shobō, 1973). 1973 edition used.

1974   *Chūgoku Bungakushi* (Iwanami Shoten, 1974).

YOSHIZAWA Yoshinori
1923   "*Man'yōshū* yori *Kokinshū* e," *Rekishi to Chiri* 11, no. 1 (1923). Republished in *Kokugo Kokubun no Kenkyū* (Iwanami Shoten, 1927). 1927 edition used.

C. STUDIES NOT PUBLISHED IN JAPANESE

BIRCH, Cyril
1965   *Anthology of Chinese Literature* (New York: Grove Press, 1965).

BOOTH, Wayne C.
1961   *The Rhetoric of Fiction* (Chicago and London: University of Chicago Press, 1961).

BOWRING, Richard
1982   *Murasaki Shikibu: Her Diary and Poetic Memoirs* (Princeton: Princeton University Press, 1982).

BROWER-MINER (BROWER, Robert H. and Earl MINER)
1961   *Japanese Court Poetry* (Stanford: Stanford University Press, 1961).

FOGEL, Ephim G.
1958   "Salmons in Both, or Some Caveats for Canonical Scholars." In *Evidence for Authorship: Essays on Problems of Attribution*, ed. David V. Erdman and Ephim G. Fogel (Ithaca, N.Y.: Cornell University Press, 1958).

FRANK, Bernard
1958   "Katami et katatagae: Etude sur les interdits de direction à l'époque

Heian," *Bulletin de la Maison Franco-Japonaise*, n.s. 5, nos. 2-4 (1958).

HAKEDA, Yoshito S.
1972 *Kūkai: Major Works* (New York: Columbia University Press, 1972).

HURVITZ, Leon
1976 *The Scripture of the Lotus Blossom of the Fine Dharma* (New York: Columbia University Press, 1976).

KEENE, Donald
1953 *Japanese Literature* (London: John Murray, 1953).

KONISHI Jin'ichi
1949b "*Kokinshūteki* Hyōgen no Seiritsu," *Nihon Gakushiin Kiyō* 7, no. 3 (1949). Translated by Helen C. McCullough as "The Genesis of the *Kokinshū* Style," *Harvard Journal of Asiatic Studies* 38, no. 1 (1978).
1958a "Association and Progression: Principles of Integration in Anthologies and Sequences of Japanese Court Poetry," tr. Robert H. Brower and Earl Miner, *Harvard Journal of Asiatic Studies* 21 (December 1958).
1962a "*Fūryū*: An Ideal of Japanese Esthetic Life," tr. Earl Miner, *Orient/West* 7, no. 7 (1962). Republished in *The Japanese Image*, ed. Maurice Schneps and Alvin D. Coox (Tokyo and Philadelphia: Orient/West, Inc., 1965). 1965 edition used.

KŪKAI   See Hakeda, Yoshito S.

LIU, James J.-Y.
1962 *The Art of Chinese Poetry* (Chicago: University of Chicago Press, 1962).

LIU Kai-jung
1947 *T'ang-tai Hsiao-shuo Yen-chiu* (Shanghai: Shang-wu Yin-shu-kuan, 1747). Revised in 1955. 1955 edition used.

LIU Ling-sheng
1936 *Chung-kuo P'ien-wen Shih* (Shanghai: Shang-wu Yin-shu-kuan, 1936).

LO Ken-tse
1931 *Yüeh-fu Wen-hsüeh-shih* (Peking: Wen-hua Hsüeh-she, 1931).

LU Hsün
1924 *Chung-kuo Hsiao-shuo Shih-lüeh*, 4th printing (Peking: Pei-hsin Shu-chü, 1927). Republished in *Lu Hsün Ch'üan-chi*, vol. 9 (Peking: Jen-min Wen-hsüeh Ch'u-pan-she, 1973). 1973 edition used.

McCULLOUGH, Helen Craig
1980 *Ōkagami: The Great Mirror* (Princeton: Princeton University Press, 1980).

McCULLOUGH-McCULLOUGH (McCULLOUGH, William H. and Helen Craig McCULLOUGH)
1980 *A Tale of Flowering Fortunes: Annals of Japanese Aristocratic Life in the Heian Period* (Stanford: Stanford University Press, 1980). 2 vols.

McCUNE, Shannon
1975 *The Ryukyu Islands* (Harrisburg and Stackpole: Newton Abbot and David & Charles, 1975).

MINER, Earl
1958 *The Japanese Tradition in British and American Literature* (Princeton: Princeton University Press, 1958).
1968 *An Introduction to Japanese Court Poetry* (Stanford: Stanford University Press, 1968).

1969   *Japanese Poetic Diaries* (Berkeley and Los Angeles: University of California Press, 1969).

MORRIS, Ivan
1964   *The World of the Shining Prince: Court Life in Ancient Japan* (London: Oxford University Press, 1964).
1967   *The Pillow Book of Sei Shōnagon*, 2 vols. (New York: Columbia University Press, 1967).

RAMIREZ-CHRISTENSEN, Esperanza
1982   "The Operation of the Lyrical Mode in the *Genji Monogatari*." In *Ukifune: Love in The Tale of Genji*, ed. Andrew Pekarik (New York: Columbia University Press, 1982).

REISCHAUER, Edwin O.
1955   [Ennin's] *Diary: The Record of a Pilgrimage to China in Search of the Law* (New York: Ronald Press, 1955).

SANDARDS, N. K.
1960   *The Epic of Gilgamesh* (Penguin Classics, 1960).

SANSOM, George
1958   *A History of Japan to 1334* (Stanford: Stanford University Press, 1958).

SEIDENSTICKER, E. G.
1964   *The Gossamer Years: The Diary of a Noblewoman of Heian Japan* (Tokyo and Rutland, Vt.: Charles E. Tuttle, 1964).
1976   *The Tale of Genji*. 2 vols. (New York: Alfred A. Kopf, 1976).

SHERBO, Arthur
1958   "The Use and Abuse of Internal Evidence." In *Evidence for Authorship: Essays on Problems of Attribution*, ed. David V. Erdman and Ephim G. Fogel (Ithaca, N.Y.: Cornell University Press, 1958).

WALEY, Arthur
1949   *The Life and Times of Po Chü-i* (London: Allen & Unwin, 1949).

WATSON, Burton
1961   *Records of the Grand Historian of China*. 2 vols. (New York: Columbia University Press, 1961).
1962   *Early Chinese Literature* (New York: Columbia University Press, 1962).

WIMSATT, W. K., Jr.
1946   "The Intentional Fallacy," *Sewanee Review* 54 (Summer 1946); republished in W. K. Wimsatt, Jr., *The Verbal Icon: Studies in the Meaning of Poetry* (Lexington: University of Kentucky Press, 1954); issued in paperback by the same press in 1967. 1967 edition used.

WIMSATT-BROOKS (WIMSATT, William K., Jr., and Cleanth BROOKS)
1957   *Literary Criticism: A Short History* (New York: Alfred A. Knopf, 1957).

WINTERNITZ, Moriz
1908-20   *Geschichte der indischen Literatur* (Leipzig: C. F. Amelang, 1908-20). 3 vols. (Republished Stuttgart: K. F. Koehler Verlag, 1968.) 1968 edition used.

INDEX

Attribution of authorship follows the ideas of our author, as do spellings (i.e., pro-nunciations) of titles, and so forth. Sovereigns are entered by royal name followed by "Tennō" and priests by their best known name in religion, without a title, both as in most Japanese dictionaries. Regal wives of sovereigns and of crown princes are designated "Consort." Some titles are entered in romanized versions of the Japanese (or Chinese or Korean) and some in English translation, depending on which seems more useful to readers of this book. Whatever inconsistencies are in-volved, numerous cross-references are supplied and matter is added in parenthe-ses. The Contents and Chronological Table should also be consulted.

This book has been composed and printed by
Princeton University Press
Designed by Jan Lilly
Typography: Linotron Sabon and Zapf Chancery
Paper: Warren's 1854

Library of Congress Cataloging-in-Publication Data
(Revised for vol. 2)

Konishi, Jin'ichi, 1915-
A history of Japanese literature.

Includes bibliographies and indexes.
Contents: v. 1. The archaic and ancient ages—
v. 2. The early middle ages.
1. Japanese literature—History and criticism—
Collected works.   I. Miner, Earl Roy.   II. Title.
PL717.K6213 1984   895.6'09   83-43082
ISBN 0-691-06592-6 (v. 1 : alk. paper)
ISBN 0-691-10146-9 (v. 1 : pbk.)